Early Black Baseball
in Minnesota

Early Black Baseball in Minnesota

The St. Paul Gophers, Minneapolis Keystones and Other Barnstorming Teams of the Deadball Era

TODD PETERSON

McFarland & Company, Inc., Publishers
Jefferson, North Carolina, and London

LIBRARY OF CONGRESS CATALOGUING-IN-PUBLICATION DATA

Peterson, Todd, 1963–
Early Black baseball in Minnesota : the St. Paul Gophers,
Minneapolis Keystones and other barnstorming teams
of the deadball era / Todd Peterson.
p.   cm.
Includes bibliographical references and index.

ISBN 978-0-7864-3816-7
softcover : 50# alkaline paper ∞

1. African American baseball players—Minnesota—History.
2. St. Paul Gophers (Baseball team) 3. Minneapolis Keystones (Baseball team)
4. Baseball teams—Minnesota—History. 5. Baseball—Minnesota—History.
6. Baseball—United States—History. I. Title.
GV863.M6P5   2010   796.35709776—dc22   2010023625

British Library cataloguing data are available

©2010 Todd Peterson. All rights reserved

*No part of this book may be reproduced or transmitted in any form
or by any means, electronic or mechanical, including photocopying
or recording, or by any information storage and retrieval system,
without permission in writing from the publisher.*

On the cover: Team photograph of the 1908 St. Paul Gophers in mid-season
(courtesy of Fred Buckland); (background) map of Minnesota (J.H. Young)

Manufactured in the United States of America

*McFarland & Company, Inc., Publishers
Box 611, Jefferson, North Carolina 28640
www.mcfarlandpub.com*

Table of Contents

Preface — 1

ONE • Fowler to Williams to Ball (1873–1899) — 5
TWO • The Whole Show (1900–1906) — 14
THREE • Fast Team in the City (1907) — 31
FOUR • The Road Leads Somewhere — 49
FIVE • Cutting a Wide Swath (January–June 1908) — 64
SIX • Saints, Sinners, and Keystones (July–December 1908) — 79
SEVEN • Can You Hear the Noise? (1909) — 99
EIGHT • The Boys Are Back in Town (1910) — 120
NINE • Not So Fast (January–June 1911) — 145
TEN • On the Way Home (July 1911–1912) — 160
ELEVEN • By Any Other Name (1913–1948) — 177
TWELVE • After Many a Summer — 203

Appendix I. Game Chronologies and Team Statistics — 223
Appendix II. Player Register — 253
Appendix III. Rosters of Minnesota Black Teams 1876–1945 — 265
Chapter Notes — 271
Bibliography — 291
Index — 297

By the gate he stopped me and asked "where are you riding to sir?"
I answered, "Away from here, away from here, always away from here.
Only by doing so can I reach my destination."
— Franz Kafka, *My Destination*

Preface

One of the most exciting baseball games ever played in the state of Minnesota took place on a sweltering July afternoon in 1909 at a tiny stadium in downtown St. Paul. The combatants that day were two African American teams, the Leland Giants of Chicago, black baseball's premier club, and the upstart St. Paul Gophers. When Eugene Milliner, the Gophers' quicksilver left fielder, approached home plate to lead off the bottom of the eighth inning, his team trailed the Giants 2–0 in the fifth and deciding game of a grueling and bitterly fought series "to determine the colored championship of the world." On the mound was Leland's outstanding left-hander, Pat Dougherty, who had surrendered only one run to the locals in 17 previous innings that week, and on this day had yielded no hits at all.

Less than thirty minutes later the game had passed into history, where it remains as the high-water mark of Minnesota black baseball. However, the Leland-Gophers finale was only one of several memorable Midwestern showdowns contested for over 75 years by many outstanding athletes, cruelly barred from Organized Baseball because of the color of their skin.

1909 St. Paul Gophers (pre-season). Back Row (Left to right): William McMurray (3B), George "Rat" Johnson (C), Bobby Marshall (1B), Phil Reid (Owner), Julius London (P), William Binga (RF), Felix Wallace (2B). Front Row (Left to right): Archie Pate (P), Eugene Milliner (LF), Dick Garrison (P, in street clothes), Sherman Barton (CF), Arthur McDougall (SS). (Transcendental Graphics)

In fact, although they never placed a franchise in any of the major Negro Leagues, the Twin Cities area was once home to *two* black teams of major league caliber. During the early years of the 20th century the Gophers and their bitter cross-town rivals, the Minneapolis Keystones, dominated the diamonds of the North taking on and defeating all comers. There were significant Minnesota blackball clubs before and after these two squads, and African American superstars such as George Wilson and John Donaldson built their legends high on its prairie ball fields. No local player or outfit captured the local and national imagination the way the Gophers and Keystones did, though.

One indication of the popularity of the two clubs lies in their photographic record. Images of the Gophers in particular remain in high demand, and a 1908 postcard of the team was recently auctioned off for around one thousand dollars. During their heyday, publicity shots of individual Gophers appeared in mainstream newspapers all over the Northwest — an honor usually reserved for only the elite white players of the time. Impossibly rare, many of these photographs are reproduced in these pages for the first time in over a century. Although some of the pictures have faded a little or are a bit ragged around the edges, they testify to the magic and uniqueness inherent in the Gophers and Keystones. This book is the story of these teams, the men who played on them, and the tremendous impact they made all those summers ago.

Acknowledgments

For better or worse I have always been a Minnesota Twins fan. I came of age when the team's best players, Rod Carew, Larry Hisle, and Lyman Bostock, happened to be African Americans. My love for these great players and all things baseball eventually led to my discovery of Robert Peterson's *Only the Ball Was White*, at the old Minneapolis Downtown Public Library. Drawn in by its plaintive cover and intriguing title, I was enraptured by the book and the whole new world it introduced. Like all good histories, Peterson's sparked a desire to discover more about the subject, as did John Holway's *Voices from the Great Negro Leagues*.

My deepest appreciation goes out to Moorhead State University professor Steve Hoffbeck, who patiently edited an early draft of this volume and steered me the right way on many of the photo identifications. His own account of Minnesota blackball, *Swinging for the Fences*, was a goldmine of information, as were the many other articles he has produced on the subject. Fellow Twins fan and researcher extraordinaire Pete Gorton provided invaluable information and assistance to this project. If John Donaldson doesn't end up in the Baseball Hall of Fame where he rightfully belongs, it won't be for lack of effort on Pete's part. (Please check out the Donaldson Network at http://johndonaldson.bravehost.com/.)

Twin City archivist Fred Buckland's prior work on the Gophers raised their profile in the public consciousness and led to their recognition by the Minnesota Twins among others. Fred was kind enough to let me use the remarkable image of the 1908 team that graces the cover of this book. Ron and Kathy Ebert gave permission to reproduce their 1907 photo of Daddy Reid's squad and contributed some intriguing background information about Ron's great-grandfather, Johnny Davis.

Among those who filled in other important pieces of the story are Gary Ashwill, via his exceptional Agate Type website; Joe Niese, who fleshed out George Wilson's time in Wisconsin; and boxing authority Kevin Smith, who set me straight on the pugilistic career of Topeka Jack Johnson. Dr. Jeremy Krock led an informative tour of Burr Oak Cemetery and uncovered a few skeletons in Bill Gatewood's family closet. Mike Johnson did a lot of leg work on my behalf in Michigan sorting out the Page Fence Giants saga. Richard Ratcliff sent along some great photos of John Merida's Spiceland, Indiana days.

I am beholden as well to Stew Thornley and the Halsey Hall chapter in Minnesota for initiating me into all things SABR. Special kudos go out to Halsey Hall member Kyle McNary, who offered early encouragement; Rod Nelson, who guided me through SABR's Yoseloff Grant process; and Jim Charlton, who put up with my incessant revisions of the resulting article, published in *The Baseball Research Journal*. For their help in securing many of the photos for this book I need to acknowledge Pat Kelly at the National Baseball of Fame Library in Cooperstown; Sheila Morris at the Waseca County Historical Society; John Decker at the Stearns History Museum; Brent Peterson of the Washington County Historical Society; James A. Davis and Gene Baker from the State Historical Society of North Dakota; and Mark Rucker of Transcendental Graphics.

I am indebted to the terrific personnel at the Minnesota Historical Society for their time and patience. Brendan Henehan's black newspaper index at the MHS was a particularly useful resource. Many fine archivists and librarians at the State Historical Society of Wisconsin, the State Historical Society of Iowa, the South Dakota State Historical Society, the State Historical Society of Missouri, and the Library of Congress were nice enough not to toss me out on my ear after an endless stream of questions and requests. This account is all the stronger because of the employees at the Abraham Lincoln Presidential Library in Springfield, Illinois (sorry about the microfilm!), the Reference and Access Services departments of the Kansas City, Missouri, Public Library, and the Indiana State Library in Indianapolis.

I would be remiss not to mention my friends from the SABR Negro Leagues Committee for their continued help and support: Dr. Leslie Heaphy, Geri and Trey Strecker, and five-tool historian Larry Lester.

My blessings and best wishes go out to the wonderful students and staff at Divine Mercy Catholic School in Faribault, Minnesota, and Nativity Parish School in Leawood, Kansas. To the Peterson and McCarthy families I extend my eternal love and gratitude. Without my wife, Ellen, I would still be writing notes for this project on index cards. Or on rocks. Lastly, to name-check one of my favorite bands, I have truly been guided by voices of those mostly anonymous newspaper writers without whose contemporary reporting this book would not have been possible. I do regret however, that they did not publish a few more box scores!

Chapter One

Fowler to Williams to Ball
(1873–1899)

Not even the abomination of slavery could prevent black men and women from playing baseball. African Americans took up the national pastime while imprisoned in the South during the 18th century, with the first organized black teams emerging just prior to the Civil War.[1]

Unfortunately, after the great conflict, black ball players discovered that their newly won freedom did not extend to the baseball diamond. In December 1867 the country's first major baseball organization, the National Association of Base Ball Players, openly banned "any club which may be composed of one or more colored persons." The Association's rationale would be repeated *ad nauseam* many times in many places over the next 80 years: "If colored clubs were admitted there would be in all probability some division of feeling, whereas by excluding them no injury could result to anyone."[2]

In the state of Minnesota, however, black and white ball players were able to compete with and against each other. In 1873, Prince Honeycutt, a 31-year-old African American barber from Tennessee, helped form the Fergus Falls North Stars ball club in western Minnesota. On the Fourth of July in 1875, Honeycutt led the Fergus Falls nine to a 23–21 victory over their rivals, the Perham Norwesters, by swatting six hits and scoring three times.[3]

The first notable contest between two Minnesota black teams took place on an "exceedingly warm" day in late August 1876, when the Unions of Minneapolis defeated the Blue Stars of St. Paul, 37–28. After the game, Dick Jackson of the Unions outran a black man from St. Paul named Liverpool in a 100-yard footrace "upon which some little money was put up." Three weeks later the Blue Stars gained their revenge when they routed the Unions, 23–0. The Minneapolis club withdrew after the third inning and claimed after the game that the St. Paul nine had unfairly used three professionals from Chicago. There would be no third match between the two handsomely uniformed squads. For the time being at least, "colored baseball ardor" in the Twin Cities had cooled, although the rivalry between the two cities hasn't abated to this day.[4]

This was not the first time nor would it be the last that a Minnesota team imported a black player from Chicago. The previous September, W.W. Fisher, a pitcher and infielder with the Chicago Uniques, helped the Winona Clippers outlast the St. Paul Red Caps, 24–22, for the state championship in St. Paul. A month later, the Red Caps prevailed 8–7 in a rematch in Winona for a $100 purse and presumably, a considerable amount of money in side bets. Many of those in attendance noticed that Fisher had let a couple of ground balls get by him at second and the general feeling was that the contest had been "manipulated in the interest of a lot of gamblers." Three nights later, Fisher, previously lauded in Winona as "a master of the game in all the fine points," snuck out of town leaving behind a sworn affidavit confessing that a "certain party" had induced him to throw the game for $250.[5]

In February 1876, a few months after Fisher hightailed it out of southeastern Minnesota, the National League was formed in New York City. Although more sophisticated than the organizations that preceded it, the new circuit nevertheless established a "gentlemen's agreement" amongst its clubs that excluded black ball players. Not all leagues or cities would follow suit; as many as seventy African Americans played organized professional baseball in the last quarter of the nineteenth century. In 1884 two brothers, Fleetwood and Weldy Walker, played for the Toledo Blue Stockings in the then major league American Association and that same summer a team in Stillwater hired the first black man ever to play Organized Baseball in Minnesota. He was a small, wiry, mustachioed pitcher named John Fowler, who was known as "Bud" because that was what he called everyone else.[6]

Bud Fowler was born John W. Jackson in Fort Plains, New York, in 1858, and grew up learning to play the game in nearby Cooperstown, where he claimed to have played on Abner Doubleday's legendary first diamond. Jackson first attracted attention in April 1878 when he out-dueled forty-game winner Tommy Bond and the Boston Red Stockings, 2–1, in an exhibition game. Pitching for a "picked nine" of Chelsea, Massachusetts, amateurs, the 20-year-old set the National League champs down on three hits. Jackson used less than 80 pitches and allowed only four base runners after the first inning. That May, the young pitcher broke the initial color line in professional baseball when he tossed a two-hitter for the Lynn, Massachusetts, Live Oaks of the International Association.[7]

Having adopted the name of Fowler, "Bud" continued playing for the next 26 years, from flyspeck towns to the high minor leagues and all points in between. In all, he donned the uniforms of at least 45 teams in 22 states and Canada. Fowler began his career as a pitcher and a catcher, but after hurting "his arm five different times," he became an infielder who "never wore a glove, taking everything that came his way with the bare hands." As a second baseman he "was considered the equal of any man who ever covered the position" in addition to being "a fairly good sticker and an excellent base runner." During his career the *Sporting Life* would call Fowler "one of the best general players in the country," while admitting that "if he had a white face he would 'be' playing with the best of them."[8]

In the early 1884 Fowler was signed by attorney Charles Gregory to play for Stillwater, a river town located 20 miles northeast of St. Paul. Most of Gregory's club would be drawn from Chicago and parts farther east. Stillwater, with a population of 15,000, was the smallest city in the 12-team Northwestern League and could not compete with fellow circuit members Minneapolis and St. Paul for the best local players.[9]

Fowler broke into the lineup for Stillwater on May 3, catching and playing center field in a 12–8 loss at Peoria, Illinois, going two for five with a triple. He pitched for the first time four days later and gave up the tie-breaking run in the ninth as the team dropped a 3–2 decision to Quincy, Illinois. The *Quincy Whig* enthused:

> The playing of Fowler, the colored pitcher of the Stillwaters, was one of the features of yesterday's game. After capturing two long flies in the left field, he was placed in the box at the commencement of the seventh inning and did some excellent pitching. His base throwing was also quick and accurate.

The *Stillwater Daily Sun* was less impressed: "[Fowler] throws a straight but very swift ball, but the Quincys found no difficulty in hitting him."[10]

Although six of their players would go on to play in the major leagues, the Stillwaters were by all accounts a terrible team that didn't pitch or field particularly well. It didn't help any that numerous difficulties and delays encountered in overhauling their home field forced the club to play their initial 26 games on the road. Fowler was on the mound for Stillwater's first victory after 15 defeats, a 7–5 thumping of Fort Wayne, Indiana, on May 26. This pleased some fans of the team so much they gave him a ten-dollar bonus and a new suit of clothes.[11]

Fowler's play would be the lone bright spot of the Stillwater season. Numerous problems, including three changes in field managers, constant player turnover, lackluster attendance, and a six-game losing streak during which they were outscored 59 to 12, resulted in the team disbanding on August 4, $7,500 in the hole.[12]

Despite pitching with a sore arm for much of the summer, Fowler managed a 7–8 won-loss record for a team that won only 22 games out of 63. He was a success at the plate as well, finishing with a .302 batting average and leading the league in hits with 57. Fowler was in particularly fine form in late June and early July, when he went 16-for-31 at the plate and led the Stillwaters to two extra-inning victories in Minneapolis. He also lost his bonus along the way, being fined ten dollars for an errant throw that let in two runs. There is no mention as to whether or not he got to keep his new suit.[13]

By 1887 the doors that had been briefly open to African Americans in Organized Baseball were beginning to slam shut. During that season Fowler's teammates on the Binghamton, New York, nine of the International League refused to take the field for a game unless he was removed from it. The Binghamton management fined the mutineers $60 each, but on July 7 Fowler, batting .350 at the time with 23 stolen bases, was released. One week later the International League board of directors voted to approve "no more contracts with colored men" when those teams without black players narrowly outpolled those who did. The sad truth of the matter was that many if not most white professional baseball players were opposed to integration, and they violently demonstrated this on the ball field by throwing at black players and treating them as open game on the base paths. While with Binghamton, Fowler was forced to strap wooden guards over his lower legs in order to protect himself against players sliding into second base trying to spike him.[14]

Although they couldn't play in the International League anymore, black ball players continued to make some noise in Minnesota. At an August 1, 1887, picnic in the Twin Cities suburb of Excelsior, the St. Paul Quicksteps defeated the Minneapolis Brown Stockings "for the championship of the Northwest." The Quicksteps, composed mostly of African American waiters from the Hotel Ryan and the Minnesota Club, were managed by William Carter and captained by second baseman Charles Lett, a former player with the Lake View House nine of Cleveland, Ohio. Two weeks after the Excelsior picnic, the team easily handled a club from Fort Snelling, 11–5, behind pitcher James Duke.[15]

On the morning of August 28 the Quicksteps boarded a train at the Union Depot and traveled 30 miles to the southwest to take on the Shakopee Reserves. Duke was unable to pitch due to a sore arm and the Reserves fell upon his replacement for eight runs in the fourth inning en route to a 23–4 victory. Still smarting over the 16–6 defeat that the Lyndale club of the Twin Cities had administered to the locals a week before, the *Shakopee Scott County Argus* remarked that "the gentlemen from St. Paul were an orderly and decent team, their excellent deportment forming quite a contrast with their white brethren of Minneapolis.... There was no loud talking and profane language to mar the pleasures of the national game."[16]

This subtly patronizing commentary about the Quicksteps' behavior was one that would be repeated by Minnesota newspapers for many decades to come. Good manners were frequently described as some sort of an accomplishment for black clubs, while any sort of contrary behavior, such as "kicking" (questioning) about umpire's calls was almost always vilified. The Quicksteps started a local precedent of their own, later echoed by black teams such as the St. Paul Gophers, by avowing that they had been "handsomely treated" by their Shakopee hosts.[17]

Despite the Quicksteps' limited success, the black community in the Twin Cities was not yet large enough to support a professional team. The 1880 U.S. Census recorded only 476 African Americans living in the Minneapolis area while but 491 resided in and around St. Paul. Even though the black population in Minneapolis had risen to almost 900 by June 1888 when the Little Diamond club challenged "any colored club in Minnesota to play them," it is unlikely they found many takers.[18]

With their opportunities in Organized Baseball dwindling, black professionals responded by forming their own full-time salaried teams, the most notable being the Cuban Giants who started playing on Long Island in the fall of 1885. The Giants, made up from the cream of the crop of New York and Philadelphia area players, originally passed themselves off as foreign born in order to secure bookings. Few were fooled, but the high quality of the Giants play led to the formation of many other black squads (who were almost always named "Giants," a name soon synonymous for "black team").[19]

Two years later the Chicago Unions were organized, like the Quicksteps 350 miles to the northwest, as an amateur team that only played on weekends. The Unions, led by businessman/ first baseman William Peters and attorney/outfielder Frank Leland, went undefeated in their first season as they quickly became the premier black club of the West. The squad evolved into a full-time professional operation in 1890, playing town teams throughout Illinois, Indiana, Michigan and Wisconsin during the week, before returning to Chicago on Sundays for lucrative games with leading semi-pro clubs.[20]

It was here, on the diamonds of South Chicago, that the seeds of Minnesota blackball began to take root. During their first 12 years of existence, the Unions won over 80 percent of their games while establishing the template that many black barnstorming clubs would follow. Several future Gophers honed their skills with the club, including pitchers William Horn, Tommy Means, Clarence Lytle, and outfielder Willis Jones, the Unions captain, who was described as the "pride of the team."[21]

The Unions' dominance would eventually be challenged by a club from Adrian, Michigan, a small town 60 miles southwest of Detroit. In the summer of 1894 the indomitable Bud Fowler and a young slugger named Grant "Home Run" Johnson concocted the idea of organizing a baseball team that would travel the Midwest by train and give parades before every game they played. This was old hat for Fowler. He created one of the very first black traveling teams in 1887, after Binghamton cut him loose, and had often resorted to barnstorming whenever he couldn't find work in organized ball. That fall, aided by two white businessmen, Len Hoch and Rolla Taylor, Fowler formed the Page Fence Giants with the backing of the Page Fence Woven Wire and Monarch Wheel Bicycle Companies. According to Giants outfielder John "Pat" Patterson, Fowler "had this team in his noodle for six years before anyone ever knew it. He is a great schemer."[22]

During 1895 the Giants barnstormed through Ohio, Indiana, Michigan, and Illinois in a private railroad car that also served as their sleeping quarters. Nattily attired in black and maroon uniforms and red firemen's caps, the club would bicycle into each town they visited to stir up interest before taking on and usually defeating the hometown nine. Fowler recruited some of the best players in Blackball for his team and most of the Giants had attended college—a rarity in the 19th century for any team, black or white. Many players who got their start with the Page Fence Giants would soon go on to make their mark in Minnesota baseball, including third baseman William Binga, outfielder Sherman Barton, and catcher George "Rat" Johnson.[23]

In late April, the 37-year-old Fowler led his new charges into Minnesota to take on the Minneapolis and St. Paul Western League entries. It was reported that members of a "local colored club" and a brass band would meet the Giants private car (where they lived like "island princes") at the Minneapolis Depot and a parade through the city streets would follow. A black organization, The Minneapolis Social and Literary club, was to throw the team a ball at Exposition Hall with "dancing until 4 o'clock A.M., interspersed with a cake walk of the genuine kind."[24]

The games themselves were something of a cakewalk as the Minneapolis Millers pounded out four victories over the neophyte Giants, 17–1, 17–5, 25–2, and 18–7. The Michigan club was no more competitive with the St. Paul Saints, dropping a pair of games by scores of 15–2 and 9–2. The Western League nines blasted out 96 hits, of which 44 went for extra bases including eight home runs. While the Giants pitchers gave up 29 walks and hit seven batters, only 48 of the 93 runs they allowed were earned as the team committed 40 errors behind them. Before the final scheduled contest with the Millers was mercifully called off due to poor weather, the bicyclists had led for a total of one inning in the six games that were played.[25]

In 1895, the Western League was the second leading circuit in the land, only a small step below the National League. Facing many former and future major leaguers, 19-year-old southpaw George Wilson bore the brunt of the Millers and Apostles attack, as he started and lost four of the games. Chief among Wilson's tormentors was Miller first baseman and captain Perry "Moose" Werden, who went 12-for-21 with three doubles, four homers, while scoring 12 runs. Playing in tiny Athletic Park, the Millers averaged *ten* runs a game that year as Werden slugged 37 of his Organized Baseball record 45 round-trippers there.[26]

The lone Giants highlight was pitcher and outfielder Billy Holland's inside-the-park home run during the first game in St. Paul. On the initial pitch of the eighth inning Holland "got a full body swing at the sphere and sent it spinning out to left field. It was a terrific hit. At no time was the ball more than 15 feet above the diamond and it passed about three feet above Ollie Smith's head." The fleet-of-foot Holland easily beat the relay home and "cut" the Saints lead to 12–1.[27]

The Giants recovered from their drubbing in the Twin Cities sufficiently enough to amass a record of 118–36–2 (.762) and, more significantly, turn a profit. Bud Fowler, with his light "fading amidst the galaxy of stars," jumped ship in July after losing control over the team's personnel decisions, to join first the Adrian and later the Lansing entry in the Michigan State League.[28]

In 1896 the Page Fence Giants, behind Holland and a more seasoned George Wilson, won 82 of their first 100 games and in September defeated the Cuban X-Giants 11 games to six for the "colored championship." In early May the Michigan squad returned to Minnesota and convincingly swept a three-game set from the Winona ball club. During the series, Giants third baseman Bill Binga began his four decades long assault on Minnesota pitching by knocking three balls over the Winona fences, good for two doubles, a home run, and five runs batted in. Wilson set down the Winonas 17–2 in the series finale, and added two hits to his own cause. Appearing before an overflow Sunday crowd of 1,100, "Wilson, the best left handed pitcher in the world occupied the box for the Giants and seemed to puzzle the Winona boys."[29]

The Giants were back in Winona in July 1897 and clobbered the home team three more times, including a 17–0 four hit shutout by Wilson, "the heavy man of the cast." Winona finally beat the Giants on the Fourth of July, 21–8, behind the "splendid and effective" pitching of former St. Louis Brown great Charlie Comiskey. The Giants lost only a handful of games in 1897, but apparent financial difficulties caused the team to relocate to Chicago midway through the following season. At the conclusion of the 1898 campaign the Michigan aggregation threw in the towel, although as Giants first baseman George Taylor recalled, "the management told us the year we were broken up that the past season had been unsuccessful, but we had been playing to comparatively good crowds and the players had no thoughts of disbanding." Under the aegis of the Columbia Social Club and local mover and shaker Alvin Garrett, the team was reorganized as the Chicago Columbia Giants in 1899, securing a field near the intersection of Thirty-Ninth Street and Wentworth Avenue, only a few blocks from the Union's home grounds.[30]

Besides being "the finest and best equipped colored team that was ever in the business," the Columbia's strong financial backing allowed them to raid the Chicago Unions roster. One of the Giants first moves was to sign ace left-hander Bert Jones away from the Unions—or so they thought. The *Chicago Tribune* reported that "Jones, it is claimed signed a regular contract, and received $100 advance money, which by the way is more than a National League star receives these days." Soon after this, Unions boss William Peters offered Jones even more money to rejoin *his* club, much to the chagrin of Columbia Giants manager John "Pat" Patterson who threatened to sue. The *Tribune* sardonically noted:

> There is an intense rivalry between the two colored teams. They have not scheduled any games against each other. Should such contests be arranged they doubtless would be fiercely fought if razors did not take the place of bats before the game was finished.[31]

The Unions ducked the Columbia Giants as long as they could, and battled eastern clubs such as the Cuban X-Giants instead. In September 1899 public pressure finally forced a meeting between the two longtime antagonists. Behind the pitching of George Wilson, the Columbia Giants swept a best-of-five series from the Unions and won "a big bunch of money."[32]

Frank Leland would have the last laugh. When baseball magnate Charlie Comiskey moved his St. Paul franchise to Chicago in 1900, he purchased and decided to expand South Side Park, effectively evicting both the Unions and the Columbia Giants from their home grounds in the process. While both teams were looking for places to play, Leland, with the aid of Comiskey, found a new field two miles away at the corner of Seventy-Ninth and Wentworth. In July 1901 he filed papers creating a *new* club, the Chicago Union Giants, effectively freezing out his former partner William Peters, as well as Alvin Garrett and his Columbia Giants.[33]

Although the Twin City African American community of this time was relatively small and had no team the equal of the Chicago Unions or Columbia Giants, it did produce a couple of promising young players. William Frank Williams, the first in a long line of black Minnesota sluggers, was born in St. Paul in 1877 and first gained notice as a baseball and basketball star at the city's Mechanic Arts High School. Before graduating in 1897, he set the state high school shot put record with a heave of 43 feet, 11 inches; the 182-pound youngster also found time to man left end on the football team for three years.[34]

In 1894, the 16-year-old Williams reportedly began his professional baseball career with the Spaldings of St. Paul. Playing for the leading semi-pro team in the city, Billy, as he was familiarly known, rapidly became one of the area's top amateur players. In a photograph of the Hamm's Exports baseball club that ran in the April 14, 1898, edition of the *St. Paul Pioneer Press*, Williams was prominently featured in the center of the back row and was listed as the team's right fielder. That Sunday at Lexington Park, with then Western League and future American League president Ban Johnson on hand, Williams went three-for-five at the plate with a double and a run scored in the Export's 13–3 loss to the St. Paul Saints. But Billy Williams never played for any one team very long. During that summer of 1898 alone, the "local favorite" spent time at first base and the outfield for the St. Paul Capitols, New Brighton Packers and the Shakopee Browns. Williams was invariably good for at least a couple of hits and chased down pop flies "like the wind."[35]

Billy Williams, the first of the great Minnesota black sluggers. (*Minneapolis Tribune*, August 7, 1910; Minnesota State Historical Society, St. Paul)

In September 1900 the big first baseman was in the lineup for the southeastern Minnesota river town of Red Wing when they dropped a 7–6 heartbreaker to the visiting Chicago Unions. Williams singled and scored a run despite being pitched around by the Unions Will Horn. The Unions were impressed enough to offer the hard hitting and slick fielding Williams a contract for the following year. He opted instead to keep his job as assistant athletic director at the St. Paul Y.M.C.A and to continue to offer his services on weekends to any team in the state that could afford him.[36]

While Billy Williams was tearing it up with his "phenomenal batting," a fellow graduate of the St. Paul sandlots was making a name for himself on the mound. Walter Ball, perhaps the best pitcher ever to come out of the Saintly City, was born in Detroit around 1881. When he was eight years old, Ball's family settled in St. Paul where his father John found work as a barber and porter. Local newspaper accounts first mention the young pitcher in the summer of 1896 and by the following year he had emerged as one of the city's top amateurs.[37]

Ball began the 1897 season pitching with the New Homes club before joining the Funk's Exports in time for the *St. Paul Pioneer Press* sponsored 17-and-under championship. The tourney did not begin well for Ball or the Exports. On August 9 the team dropped their opening game at Lexington Park to the Laurels, 14–4. The next day, Ball gave up the winning run in the bottom of the tenth to the Young Cyclones after the Exports had tied the game with four runs in the top of the ninth. Ball struck out eight and doubled twice, but he quit the team after the game, alleging they had "[weakened] in their support because he was a colored man." The *St. Paul Dispatch* reported that Ball was thinking of joining another club. Making Ball sound like he had stepped out of a minstrel show, the *Dispatch*'s account (later refuted by the *Pioneer Press*) has the pitcher avowing: "...I doan join no silk stockin' outfit. I'se going to a club that will be in de push at de end of de tournament."[38]

When the tourney resumed in mid-September, Ball was on the mound for the Young Cyclones. He came back to haunt Funk's Exports by whipping them twice on successive Sundays, 16-8 and 13-7, striking out 27 batters to lead the Cyclones to the championship.[39]

From the accounts that can be pieced together, Ball went 13-2 in 1897. The following year, he began to support himself by pitching for a number of St. Paul semi-pro clubs. Ball, at this point a work in progress with "terrific speed, good control and all the curves," struck out 20 Merriam Park Crescent batters in an 11-6 late-April win by the L.G. Hoffman Caterpillars. A month later, he fanned 14 and allowed only two hits while leading the Bostons to a 7-2 victory over the Horeja Brothers outfit before 1,000 fans at Lexington.[40]

During the season of 1899 Ball began to pitch for teams outside of the Twin City area. That summer he also got even for the *St. Paul Dispatch* misquoting him by leading the Pioneer Press club to a 12-8 victory over the Dispatch nine, going four-for-four with a homer and two triples. In late August it was reported that the 19-year-old pitcher was trying to form an all-black team to barnstorm through Minnesota, Iowa, Illinois, and Wisconsin. No evidence has been found to indicate whether Ball succeeded in getting his squad out of town, but it has been suggested that he played on a South Dakota club around this time with the well-traveled Bud Fowler.[41]

If their paths did cross on the Dakota prairie it marked a true changing of the guard. Walter Ball was in the early stages of a 25-year career, while Fowler's teammates had just forced his release from the Findlay, Ohio, team he had played on for several seasons. Stricken with pernicious anemia and often down on his luck, the tenacious second baseman continued to play and promote black baseball right up until his death in 1913 at the age of 54. "He has had all kinds of chances to make money and still he hasn't a cent," John Patterson said of the man they called "the colored player's

Twin City product Walter Ball pitched for the St. Paul Gophers in 1907 and for the Minneapolis Keystones in 1908. (***Minneapolis Tribune,*** June 15, 1908; Minnesota State Historical Society, St. Paul)

champion." Fowler, who hit .308 and stole 190 bases over ten minor league seasons, once reflected that "my skin is against me. If I had not been quite so black, I might have caught on as a Spaniard or something of that kind. The race prejudice is so strong that my black skin barred me."[42]

Walter Ball spent the next couple of years pitching for a number of clubs in North Dakota. In 1900, the light-complexioned Ball posted a record of 11–2–1 and led Grand Forks to the state championship, but the following April his teammates drew the color line and forced him off the team. As the *Grand Forks Daily Plain Dealer* lamented, "There is nothing under the sun against Ball excepting his color."[43]

Chapter Two

The Whole Show (1900–1906)

As the 19th century drew to a close, the awful specter of Jim Crow was on the rise in the United States. The 1896 Supreme Court ruling *Plessy vs. Ferguson* legalized the operation of separate though allegedly equal transportation facilities for whites and blacks, thus opening the door for the widespread segregation of schools, restaurants, hotels, drinking fountains, and baseball teams.[1]

In 1899 Bill Galloway became the last acknowledged African American to play Organized Baseball (a few light-skinned black players would later be successful in passing themselves off as white) for 47 years when he spent 20 games roaming the outfield for Woodstock, Ontario, in the Canadian League. A little further to the south in Minnesota, African Americans were still allowed to join white, albeit amateur or semi-professional, teams. Around the turn of the 20th century several Chicago Unions and Columbia Giants drifted north to play, lured by small town nines willing to pay big money for their services.[2]

The migration of the black Chicago ball players coincided with the golden age of independent baseball. Cities all over the Midwest were fielding clubs in hopes of achieving some sort of baseball immortality, or at least bragging rights over the other villages in their section. The enlistment of black professionals provided many town teams with just the edge they were looking for.

Prior to the beginning of the 1900 season one such outfit, the Waseca Blues, of southern Minnesota, employed the services of Ed "Doggie" Woods, a veteran left-handed pitcher for the Chicago Unions. Woods first attracted the attention of the locals in June 1899 when he hung a 13–4 defeat on the Blues while pitching for the Winona Picketts. It was the first loss of the year for Waseca and one of only four they would suffer that season. The *Waseca Radical* reported that "Mr. Wood, the Winona pitcher who is a Negro, had all the Waseca team on his stuff and not until the fourth inning where we able to get a score." Woods struck out 13 in the effort and batted cleanup as well, knocking out four hits including a double.[3]

"Doggie" made his debut for Waseca on May 13, 1900, against neighboring Elysian and struck out eight batters on his way to a 16–4 victory. Woods also went three-for-five at the plate with a home run and two stolen bases. He scored three runs, one on a passed ball, and was called out for cutting second base. Blackball, as we know it, had come to Minnesota.[4]

The Waseca squad, under the direction of businessmen William Armstrong, Roscoe Ward, and Lewis Sterling, soon transformed themselves from a town team that played only on Sundays into a full-time independent nine that took on the best clubs in Minnesota, Iowa, Wisconsin, and South Dakota. In August they ditched the Blues moniker and became the Waseca EACO Millers, donning the dark green, orange and black striped jerseys of the Everett and Aughenbaugh milling company.[5]

The uniforms weren't the only things changing color. In early July Bob Footes, Wood's

1900 Waseca, Minnesota, EACO's. Catcher Bob Footes is standing at far left and infielder Robert Joyner is standing third from left in the back row. Pitcher Ed "Doggie" Woods is seated at far right in the front row. (Photograph courtesy of the Waseca County Historical Society, Waseca, MN)

catcher with the Chicago Unions, signed on, giving Waseca one of the first of the all-black batteries that would proliferate the Upper Midwest for the next 50 years. Less than two weeks later, longtime Union shortstop Bill Joyner arrived in town, bringing with him a knack for comedy and a "foghorn voice [that could] be heard clear out of Cook County."[6]

Woods was the early anchor of the club, winning 12 out of 17 decisions, and was "undoubtedly the hardest hitter on the team and [did] much toward winning many a game he has played in by his timely hitting." According to the *Waseca Journal*, the bewhiskered Footes was "a perfect base thrower and a hard hitter," while the 32-year-old Joyner was a valuable addition on and off the diamond: "He has made himself very popular with the fans by his funny coaching. He has the credit of not striking out in a single game in this city this season and but four times away from home."[7]

The Waseca management was not done improving their team. Following a couple of losses to archrival Albert Lea, Minnesota, in early September, the Millers snatched two key players off the disintegrating Columbia Giants roster. Sad-eyed Billy Holland was a clever finesse pitcher of major league quality who was once described as being "funnier than an end man in a minstrel show," an "end man" being that particular performer who sits at the far side of the stage and banters with the straight man. He was also something of a vagabond, prone to jumping from team to team in search of a better opportunity. The maverick left-hander from Alabama came to prominence with the Chicago Unions in 1894 and had twice raised the ire of Frank Leland by deserting the club first for the Page Fence Giants and then the Chicago Columbia Giants.[8]

While with the Page Fence Giants, Holland had first made the acquaintance of George Wilson, a son of former slaves who was to become "the king of all colored pitchers in the world." After his poor showing in Minnesota in April 1895, Wilson had joined the Adrian, Michigan, entry in the Michigan State League, winning 29 games against only four losses, while also playing in the outfield and hitting .327.[9]

Wilson was a mercurial fastball pitcher who threw both overhand and submarine style, and was an "earnest student of the science of curves and drops," according to the *Adrian Daily Times and Expositor*. The Palmyra, Michigan, native tossed several no-hitters in his career and was also a powerful slugger who regularly batted cleanup on the white and black teams he played for, a rarity for a pitcher even in those pre–Ruthian days. Wilson was tall, sinewy, and his long, lean arms could "fire the ball over the pan like a streak of lubricated lightning." He also possessed an enormous self-confidence and a flair for the dramatic. At the plate for the Page Fence Giants during an 1896 game in Sheboygan, Wisconsin, Wilson found himself down in the count two strikes to lefty curve-baller Bill Wolf. A clamor arose from the grandstand in anticipation of a strikeout. Big George turned to the assembly, took off his cap, and reportedly announced, "Say, white folks, I ain't half out yet." Wilson proceeded to knock the next pitch out of the park.[10]

In Holland and Wilson, the EACO's, representing a town of less than 10,000 people, now had two of the best baseball players in the country. This must have been a great culture shock for all concerned. Wilson and his teammates were probably the only African Americans to be found in most of the towns they visited that summer. Between 1880 and 1910 the number of black citizens listed as residing in Waseca County held steady at five.[11]

With Holland and Wilson leading the way, Waseca won 18 of their final 22 games, including three decisive victories over Albert Lea. Wilson also pitched the team to two wins over the tough Lennon and Gibbon club of St. Paul, during which the big southpaw struck out 34 batters. Waseca claimed the state amateur championship on the strength of its 40–15–2 record (.719), and nearly broke even financially. But the EACO's were only getting started. Wilson, Holland and Footes were all retained for the 1901 season, with Wilson commanding $105 and expenses out of an $800 monthly payroll. Waseca boasted a lineup that featured many former and future minor leaguers including Sam Foster at first base and his younger brother Will in center field. Wilson anchored a formidable pitching staff that also consisted of Holland and former Albert Lea ace Charles McCleary, a noted area hurler who was later a frequent opponent of the Gophers and Minneapolis Keystones.[12]

Beginning on April 21 with a 22–6 thrashing of nearby Mankato, the EACO's proceeded to win 22 of their first 25 games. After a 10–1 victory in May during which Wilson struck out 15 more Lennon and Gibbons batters, the *St. Paul Pioneer Press* marveled:

> Wilson, the colored twirler for the Waseca team, seems to be stronger this season than ever before. He dished them right over the pan every time but his assortment was so puzzling that the locals could not find them at all. Usually he announced to the batter that he would fan out as he was coming to the plate and only in remote instances did he fail to make good.[13]

In mid–June Minneapolis of the reformed Western League failed to show up for a scheduled game in Waseca, leaving over 2,500 disappointed fans literally waiting at the station. The Millers management claimed that they were reluctant to be involved in "a gambling game," but in all probability they didn't see the up side in playing and possibly losing to a small town team.[14]

Injuries to key players proved to be the biggest obstacle the EACO's would face that year. In June, Footes was struck in the head by a pitched ball while batting against Albert Lea and was knocked unconscious for seven minutes. He returned to the game and played seven more innings until he again fell to the ground and was forced to retire for the day. He was brought back to Waseca that night still dazed and unable to recognize anyone. Footes was back catching soon after, although injuries to his fingers put him on the shelf on two separate occasions.[15]

Billy Holland had a particularly difficult summer. On June 30 he collapsed after doubling against the Nebraska Indians due to a reported attack of "heart failure" and had to be removed from the game. Three weeks later Holland crumpled to the ground after pitching six innings in a reportedly 118 degree heat at Britt, Iowa, and did not regain consciousness for 30 minutes. The beleaguered Holland was under the weather for several days thereafter, but he did not miss a turn when it was his time to pitch. Two years later in a game with Fort Dodge, Iowa, Holland was seized with what was described as an epileptic fit and remained unconscious for over two hours.[16]

Injuries aside, the EACO's dominated the Upper Midwest, taking season series from all the leading independent nines in Minnesota, Iowa, and South Dakota. The two clubs that gave Waseca the most trouble were the Algona Brownies and the Flandreau Indians, a Native American boarding school team from South Dakota, with whom the EACO's split eight and 16 games, respectively.[17]

The Algona team, operated by banker Edward Murtagh, had featured African Americans on their roster since as far back as 1898. Taking a cue from Waseca, who had beaten them two out of three times the previous year, the north central Iowa squad hired five black players for 1901 including Waseca defector "Doggie" Woods and first baseman and future Gopher Haywood "Kissing Bug" Rose.[18]

In late July Waseca scored three runs in their final at-bats to edge Algona, 5–4, for the championship of a baseball tournament in Garner, Iowa. Ironically, the game was officiated by Adrian "Cap" Anson, the former player-manager for the National League's Chicago White Stockings. Anson, once the most popular athlete in America and a virulent racist, had been instrumental in driving African Americans out of Organized Baseball. In 1883 he had attempted to cancel a game against Toledo unless Fleetwood Walker was pulled from the lineup, allegedly screaming "Get that nigger off the field." On this day, however, the Marshalltown, Iowa, native "...made a good umpire. His decisions were impartial, and while not better than ordinary umpires make, they came with authority and the players did not kick." Anson was later quoted as saying that Billy Holland was fastest fielder in the county, and that he would give $10,000 for Wilson, "if someone would only whitewash him."[19]

On August 11 Waseca journeyed to Lexington Park in St. Paul to take on Litchfield for the state independent championship. The Litchfield nine, while not a full-time salaried team, had been good enough to shut out the St. Paul Saints of the Western League, 4–0, a month before. Taking no chances, the EACO's strengthened their roster for the occasion by adding longtime Chicago Union third baseman Harry Hyde. Not to be outdone, Litchfield enlisted the services of black slugger Billy Williams, who had keyed their big win over the Saints by going three-for-four with a double, a stolen base, and a run scored.[20]

The contest was highly anticipated. According to the account the next day in the *St.*

1901 Waseca, Minnesota, EACO's. Pitcher George Wilson is standing at far left in the back row. Catcher Bob Footes is seated second from right in the front row and pitcher Billy Holland is seated next to him at far right. Pitcher Charles McCleary, a frequent opponent of both the Gophers and Keystones, is standing second from right. (Photograph courtesy of the Waseca County Historical Society, Waseca, MN)

Paul Pioneer Press, 9,270 fans, the largest crowd to witness a game in the Twin Cities in years:

> ... began pouring into the grounds by two o'clock and half an hour before the game was called every seat was filled. The aisles in the grandstand were preempted by late arrivals, and others stood in the rear of the stand and sweltered. When the crush became too great, the gates leading to the grounds were thrown open and the eager spectators swarmed out over the field. Every car leading to the park was packed with people and many of the spectators could not reach the grounds until after the game had been called. When umpire McCarthy called the play the audience completely circled the diamond and the space in front of the stand was packed.

Much to his everlasting regret, the manager of Lexington Park rejected a 40 percent share of the paid admissions and rented out the grounds for a flat $40 fee, because he didn't think the game would draw enough people to pay for ushers. In fact the gate receipts came to $2,500 and the unfortunate manager was fined $30 by the park owners for leasing the field to outside teams.[21]

Both "ringers," Hyde and Williams, made their presence felt almost immediately. In the bottom of the second Hyde singled and stole home, which combined with two walks and two Litchfield errors gave Waseca an early 2–0 lead. Williams drove two men home in the top of the third with a triple off of Wilson to tie the score, but Wilson promptly untied it in the bottom of the inning with a home run. Litchfield fell apart in the fourth when their ace Cox allowed three singles, hit a batter, and watched errors by his shortstop and second baseman keep a five-run Waseca inning alive. Wilson then slammed the door, finishing with a 9–2 victory in which he struck out nine and scattered eight safeties. He also knocked out two hits on his own behalf to go along with a stolen base. Holland in left, added two hits to the Waseca attack including a double, and also pilfered a base, while third baseman Hyde stole *two* bases, singled twice and scored three runs.[22]

During the next week Waseca followed their state title win with three more convincing victories over Litchfield in southern Minnesota and swept a baseball tournament in Lake Benton, Iowa. The EACO's earned a $250 purse by clobbering a Willmar, Minnesota, club (substituting for a dazed and demoralized Litchfield), 11–0, when McCleary threw a no-hitter, and dismantling Flandreau, 18–7, when Wilson did not.[23]

Waseca completed their remarkable season with a series of games with the Kansas City and St. Paul teams of the Western League. The EACO's could do little with the Saints who routed them twice in St. Paul, but on September 19 in Waseca they defeated Kansas City, 6–1. Wilson held the league champions to five safe drives while his teammates found Kansas City ace Wilbert Otto "Bill" Wolfe (not to be confused with Sheboygan hurler Bill *Wolf* or William Wolfe, a pitcher for the Norfolk Skippers; Bill Wolfe was *the* name to have if you were a pitcher around the turn of the 20th century) for 11 safeties. The Blues rebounded by taking two close games with the EACO's, edging them, 4–2, in ten innings at St. Cloud and nipping them, 6–4, at Owatonna. Waseca finished at 53–31 (.630) and was a reported $3000 to the good in early September. Wilson wound up the year at 18–8, Holland got 11 wins out of his sore arm against only three losses, and McCleary went a respectable 15–10.[24]

Hyde and Footes rejoined the Union Giants in 1902 leaving Wilson and Holland as Waseca's only black players when they began the season on May 11 with a 6–2 victory over the Minneapolis ZZ's (The Toozes). By this time the EACO's previous successes had made them a marked team. After the team dropped a 5–4 decision in Fort Dodge, Iowa, when many calls didn't go their way, the *Waseca Journal-Radical* groused, "During the past three seasons ... the umpire has been brought up to give decision[s] against Waseca and in order to receive their money they are compelled to play against such odds." The fact that Fort Dodge fans had laid a considerable sum of money on their team before the game made many of the umpire's decisions seem even more suspicious.[25]

While the EACO's were still winning a clear majority of their games, the competition was catching up with them. Algona now fielded a nearly all African American squad. Much like Waseca had two years previously, the Brownies benefited from an infusion of several black Chicago players including outfielder Sherman Barton and pitchers Bert Jones and Will Horn, future Gophers all.

The two teams battled it out all summer with the Brownies gaining a decisive if narrow edge by taking 10 out of 16 games, including six in a row in late June. On Sunday June 23, a horde 5,100 strong filled Lexington Park in St. Paul to watch Algona beat Waseca, 9–6, in a sloppy error-filled contest in which 19 men were left on base and all 15 runs were unearned. The *St. Paul Pioneer Press* opined the next day: "The Waseca team is not the one which made such a good record here in former years. Many of the old men are on the team, but the club, as a whole, is not putting up the game it did a year or two ago."[26]

On the Fourth of July, the EACO's, behind the six-hit pitching of Wilson, bounced back to defeat Algona, 6–1, for a $500 purse before a huge holiday crowd of 6,000 in Marshall, Minnesota. Two weeks later in Mason City, Iowa, Waseca captured the "championship games" of Minnesota and Iowa when Wilson shut down Albert Lea, 6–0, and Webster City, 2–1, on consecutive days, allowing only four hits in the process.[27]

The EACO's travels that summer also took them into central Minnesota for a series of games with the St. Cloud, Brainerd, and Aitkin teams of that region. While not of the same caliber as Waseca or Algona, the St. Cloud nine emerged as a local power in 1902, thanks to the pitching of their 22-year-old black ace, Walter Ball.

During the spring of 1902, Ball had signed with a semi-pro nine in Duluth only to finally land with a similar club in St. Cloud when protests against Sunday baseball caused the Duluth team to disband. By the time Waseca arrived in the Granite City in mid–July, the young hurler had fashioned a record of 8–3 facing a wide array of competition including Anoka High School, St. John's University, and Grand Forks of the Northern League. Relying mostly on his fastball, Ball had struck out 101 batters in 82 innings of work, while allowing on average only three runs per game.[28]

The handsome right-hander had also evolved into an all-around player who played center field and batted fourth for St. Cloud on the rare occasions when he did not pitch.

1902 St. Cloud, Minnesota, baseball team. Pitcher Walter Ball is seated at far left in the front row. (Stearns History Museum, St. Cloud, MN)

In 39 games that summer, Ball hit .307 with 24 extra base hits including five triples, and his fielding was "phenomenally good."[29]

Inexplicably, Ball was missing from the St. Cloud lineup on July 12 when Waseca shut out the Saints, 7–0. Without him St. Cloud could only muster four lonely singles against Wilson, "by far the fastest pitcher who has ever played on the local grounds," who struck out 13 and drove in four runs with a homer and a double.[30]

Ball was on the mound the next afternoon when the Saints mounted a rousing comeback and defeated "the champions of three states," 8–5, before an enthusiastic Sunday congregation. The EACO's roughed Ball for three runs in the first and two in the second on eight hits, and only a couple of base running miscues prevented them from scoring more. Ball would steady the rest of the way and permitted only two hits while striking out four and walking none. He reached on an error in the bottom of the second and keyed a two-run inning that ignited the St. Cloud rally. The Saints added another in the fifth with a single and a double, and when Waseca starter Joe Koukalik walked Ball to put men at first and second, Wilson came in from right field to replace him. The big man was not as dominant as the day before and two singles, a walk, and an error later St. Cloud had a 6–5 lead. Right fielder John "Alf" Dominick, a University of Minnesota grad and a semi-pro star for many years, threw Sam Foster out at the plate in the top of the eighth, and Ball iced the game with a two-run triple in the bottom of the inning. Waseca did "enough kicking to last until the end of the season," but Wilson later admitted that Ball's dagger was the best swing off of him in years.[31]

Waseca came back to St. Cloud three weeks later to settle the score. This time it was to be Ball versus Holland but, as usual, it was Wilson who made all the difference. In the first he touched Ball for a triple to center and jogged home when the relay throw was juggled by the second baseman. After St. Cloud tied the game in the bottom of the fifth, Wilson beat out an infield single to lead off the sixth and later scored on a double. St. Cloud tied the game again in their half of the eighth, but Waseca came right back with two runs in the top of the ninth to the dismay of the large Friday multitude. Diggins, the St. Cloud first baseman, sent a long drive to left in the bottom of the inning, but the flamboyant Wilson chased it down near the fence and "reached over and touched the fence with the ball, just to show Diggins how near he came to pacing the stations." Holland struck out 11 and walked none en route to a 4–2 victory over an uncharacteristically ineffective Ball, who issued three free passes and gave up seven hits.[32]

St. Cloud would go on to finish their season with a 29–12 (.707) record and Ball wound up at 17–7 with a remarkable 217 strikeouts in 207 innings pitched. A frequent opponent of Ball and the Saints that summer was his contemporary from St. Paul, Billy Williams. On August 2, Ball struck out Williams twice and held him hitless in five at-bats when the Saints beat the Lennon and Gibbons club, 6–2, but the big slugger went 2-for-4 a day later and scored the decisive run in the L&G's 6–4 victory.[33]

On August 17 Williams was enlisted to play right field with St. Cloud for a big game in Stillwater. Pitching before a Sunday crowd of over 2,000, Ball struck out nine and allowed only seven hits, but two outfield errors, including one by Williams, gave the Stillwater starter Ford the only run he needed to record a two-hit shutout. Ball got one of those safeties, but Williams "was unable to hit the ball, something remarkable for him." The next year Williams left St. Paul to help the Chippewa Falls team win the championship of Wisconsin, before returning home to take a job as a secretary and assistant to Governor-elect John A. Johnson. Williams would stay in this post as executive aide for the next 52 years, although his ball playing activities were limited to a few weeks each summer.[34]

Walter Ball also left Minnesota in 1903, but except for a few instances, he never came back. The St. Cloud management, with an eye towards joining Organized Baseball's Northern League, informed Ball in early March of that year that they were drawing the color line and would no longer require his services. Shortly after this Frank Leland wrote to Ball asking him to join the Union Giants and the right-hander departed for the Windy City. He would spend the next four years establishing his name in blackball, shuttling between Leland's clubs in Chicago and eastern teams such as the Cuban X-Giants and the Brooklyn Royal Giants.[35]

Billy Holland's duel with Ball was also the highlight of a late-season surge by the EACO's, which went largely unnoticed in Waseca. After a mid-June series with Algona, the team, due to public apathy, and/or a desire to get out of town, spent much of the remainder of the season on the road. The final two home games of the season were played in late August when the EACO's beat Fort Dodge, 4–3 and 6–4, during the Waseca Street Carnival. The next spring, a small note appeared in the *Waseca Journal Radical*, relating the sad news that "Waseca is not to have a ball team this season. Nearly all the players of our popular nine that won so much fame the past few seasons have signed for the summer elsewhere." Without Wilson and his teammates, Waseca soon disappeared from the baseball map. The town would return to the spotlight 76 years later, but unlike the glorious heyday of the EACO's, the occasion proved to be one of the lowest points in the annals of Minnesota baseball.[36]

With the demise of the EACO's the Algona Brownies had a clear run of the field in 1903. Waseca's Billy Holland and several other stars, including catcher George "Rat" Johnson, outfielder Willis Jones, and 20-year-old pitching phenom Johnny Davis were added to Algona's now entirely black roster. Johnson, Jones, and Davis would later spend significant time with the St. Paul Gophers. In fact, when it was all said and done, nine Brownies would also wear the Gophers uniform.[37]

That summer Algona roared through Iowa, Illinois, South Dakota, and southern Minnesota on their way to an 88–15–2 (.847) record. Along the way, the Brownies beat Frank Leland's Chicago Union Giants 11 times in 15 games to nab the western blackball title. In mid-September Algona traveled to St. Paul for a dramatic showdown series with the Winnipeg Maroons, champions of the Northern League.[38]

The first game was scheduled for Saturday, September 19, at the new Downtown Park. Fifteen hundred fans, including several hundred from Algona, witnessed a sideshow pitching match-up between the "very tall and slim" Will Horn of the Brownies and Frank "Demon" Shaw of Winnipeg, who at five feet tall and 125 pounds was the smallest pitcher in Organized Baseball. The main feature in Winnipeg's 8–6 win was the play of their captain and second baseman William Kelley, who collected two of the ten Maroon hits, including a double. Kelley, the brother of Saints manager Mike Kelley, was hit by a pitch and came around to score during the five-run fifth inning Winnipeg rally that decided the game. Horn probably nailed Kelley on purpose; William Annis, the previous hitter had just homered and Shaw had knocked down three Brownie batters.[39]

The next afternoon at Lexington Park nearly 2,500 watched Winnipeg jump off to 1–0 lead in bottom of the first when Kelley doubled again, driving in Annis, who had been hit with a pitch. This was the only run Billy Holland would allow, however. The crafty left-hander scattered six hits and struck out 14 Maroon batters, while his teammates scored single runs in the third, fifth, sixth, and seventh on their way to a 4–1 win. Holland's opposite, Perry Sessions, allowed nine hits, walked six, and uncorked two wild pitches. The St. Paul Saints hurler also hit Willis Jones with a pitch, but as his command was so poor it is hard to tell if he meant to or not.[40]

When William Kelley approached the plate in the bottom of the eighth his team was three runs down. According to the account in the *Pioneer Press* the next day, Kelley tried to dodge a "high and wild" curveball by Holland but was hit full force on the left side of his head, above the ear (an eyewitness account in the *Manitoba Free Press* claimed Kelley froze as the pitch approached). Kelley crumpled to the ground unconscious and was taken over to the Winnipeg bench were he was revived by cold water. After a physician who was summoned from the grandstand found that Kelley had almost no pulse, he was immediately rushed by police ambulance to St. Joseph's Hospital. The Winnipeg captain slipped in and out of consciousness for the next several hours and was reported to be on death's door, but by the following night his condition had improved considerably.[41]

Billy Holland was arrested shortly after the game was over, but he was released after an investigation ruled that the beaning had been accidental. The incident surely *looked* suspicious. There were two out when Kelley was hit, Algona had a comfortable lead, and Holland was a control pitcher.

While Kelley was recuperating in St. Paul, Algona and Winnipeg barnstormed through southern Minnesota and Iowa, with the Brownies beating the Maroons four straight times during the course of a week. At Mason City, Algona pulled out a 9–8 win on a ninth inning pinch-hit home run by George Wilson, who had just joined the team after one of the greatest individual seasons in the history of Minnesota baseball.[42]

When Waseca decided not to field a team in 1903, Wilson and Billy Holland enlisted to pitch with a semi-pro club in Duluth called the Fashions. When the Fashions merged with another Duluth team and joined the segregated Northern League, Holland hooked up with Algona and Wilson signed with St. Cloud for the princely sum of $100 a month. Wilson's arrival on the Granite City team's roster was preceded by former EACO infielders Sam Foster and Bill Minor, who recruited their former teammate after St. Cloud decided not to enter the Northern League after all.[43]

In the season opener on May 15 against the Winnipeg Maroons, Wilson struck out 13 batters but he "weakened perceptibly" in the seventh inning and lost, 3–2. The large host present seemed "to be well pleased with his twirling," and Wilson's good-natured "sallies of wit and humor won the enemies over to his camp." Wilson had lost none of his élan. A local paper noted that "in a fit of sauciness he would paw the earth with his pedal extremities and dance a little jig of indifference."[44]

Wilson bounced back a couple of days later and beat the future Northern League champs, 12–3, rationing out six hits and striking out nine more Winnipeg batters. The big port-sider would eventually win 21 of the 29 games he threw for St. Cloud and the few other area teams he was loaned out to. Despite pitching with a sore arm for much of the summer, Wilson struck out a reported 251 batters in 227 innings while allowing only 1.59 runs per game on average. He fanned ten or more batters in a game ten times while also tossing 11 shutouts, six two-hitters, three one-hitters, and a June 3 no-hitter against the Pillsbury club of Minneapolis.[45]

From May 24 to June 13, Wilson was pretty much untouchable. He hurled five consecutive shutouts, struck out 59 batters and allowed only eight hits in the five games. After Wilson silenced the La Crosse, Wisconsin, team, 9–0, on June 21, the *La Crosse Press* ventured the opinion that although 17 other men participated in the contest, "Wilson was the

1903 St. Cloud, Minnesota, baseball team. Pitcher George Wilson is seated in the middle of the front row. His longtime teammate Sam Foster is at far right in the back row. (Stearns History Museum, St. Cloud, MN)

whole show and the other young men who flitted around in uniform were merely used to fill in. They were supernumaries [sic]." The paper also suggested that only prejudice was keeping Wilson, "one of the best players in the country," out of the majors. If he couldn't play in the big leagues, Wilson could at least make some good money; he placed several bets on himself "giving the odds required by the La Crosse sports."[46]

Alternating between center field and first base on the days he didn't pitch, Wilson paced the St. Cloud attack by batting .395 with ten triples, five home runs, and 41 runs scored in the 41 games records have been uncovered for. The Granite City nine would finish with a 46–11–1 (.801) record and lay claim to the state semi-pro championship. The season was also a success financially as many fans throughout the area came out to see Big George pitch. After manning the initial sack in a 10–0 St. Cloud rout of neighboring Sauk Center:

> The spectators and local players requested that Mr. Wilson throw an extra inning as an exhibition. The colored boy turned on the steam and to the batsmen the ball looked like a meatless peanut with the shell off. Each man up hamered [sic] the ozone.[47]

As the summer waned, the team embarked on a three-week tour of western Minnesota and North Dakota, with an outfit from Glencoe, fronted by former EACO Ed "Doggie" Woods. St. Cloud won 10 of the 16 games played in a series marred by inclement weather and the poor health of Wilson and Woods, who left an August 10 game in Wheaton, Minnesota, suffering "from heart failure of the real variety." "Doggie" was considered to be "very sick" and likely to be out of action for some time.[48]

Back in St. Cloud the citizenry was growing impatient with the club's prolonged absence, with the general belief that the "team should play a few more games at home, where the money for their support was secured in the first place." This sentiment underscored the dilemma facing semi-pro nines like Waseca and St. Cloud. Because the local fan base was so small they had to barnstorm to make money, thus alienating and ultimately killing their fan base.[49]

After appeasing the hometown cranks by blasting White Bear, 20–0, on Labor Day, St. Cloud closed their season by once again traveling down to Stillwater. Wilson was back in top form, striking out ten batters while allowing only two hits, but *eight* St. Cloud errors enabled their river city nemesis to post a 4–1 victory. Joe "Ace" Stewart of the St. Paul Saints pitched for Stillwater who also "played [Henry] Martin in the umpire's position and he earned his salary." St. Cloud manager John Pattison complained:

> The home plate had a nail in the centre [sic] of it — when Wilson pitched — and if the ball did not pass over the nail it was no strike. It was the rottenest judging of balls and strikes I have seen in many a moon."

Wilson also had to contend with a Stillwater assembly who made "one or two allusions ... on account of his color." This was to be George Wilson's last game for St. Cloud, and the end to the Granite City team's successful run. The *Fargo Forum* announced that Wilson would pitch for Bismarck the following season, but the great left-hander signed with the strong semi-pro nine of Chippewa Falls, Wisconsin, instead.[50]

Wilson's departure from St. Cloud and Eddie Murtagh's decision to fold the Algona Brownies provided a tremendous opportunity for the up and coming Renville ball club. Using a combination of homegrown talent and a few hired players, the southwestern Minnesota town's 1903 squad had been so successful that the local management decided to upgrade the operation. Their first move was to bring back that baseball gypsy, Ed "Doggie" Woods, who had pitched a few ball games for the Renville nine that summer before moving on to Glencoe. When the word came out in early winter that some of the Algona Brownies might play in Mason City, Iowa, team manager Henry Stabeck, "by a clever maneuver," swooped and signed three of them for the Renville All-Stars: first baseman Bert Wakefield, infielder George Richardson, and the estimable Billy Holland. Algona's center fielder, Harry Moore, was also recruited but when he opted to go with the Cuban X-Giants, Brownie pitcher and outfielder Bert Jones was added in his place.[51]

Stabeck was a 29-year-old banker and president of the Renville Athletic Association, a group of men who were "anxious to secure the best that can be had at any cost." He boasted to the *Minneapolis Tribune* that the well-heeled farm town would field "the fastest aggregation in the state ... which will make the league teams look small in comparison at the end of the season, should games be arranged." Stabeck's ambition was far larger than the Minnesota River valley town he represented. With a populace of just over 1,200 people (a little more than 100 years later the population has soared to just over 1,300), Renville made Waseca look positively cosmopolitan. The town didn't install its first gas streetlights until 1903, and Renville wasn't incorporated until 1906.[52]

The two Berts, Jones and Wakefield, had each played three seasons of Organized Baseball in the Kansas State League before moving on to the Chicago Unions and then Algona.

By the time he arrived in Renville, the 26-year-old Jones had established himself as "a hard throwing southpaw with a reputation for being a character."[53]

The season opened on April 30 in Renville before a large crowd in town for a free auction. Holland struck out nine in a 6–2 victory over of a team from Fort Snelling, while Jones set down the "soldier boys" 16–2 the following day in Glencoe. The gray and maroon clad All-Stars made their Twin Cities debut on May 8, dropping a 5–4 ten-inning decision to the Minneapolis Javas club before several thousand cranks at Bryn Mawr Park. Renville had to contend with several "rank decisions" by the umpires and the large Minneapolis throng who swarmed along the baselines and milled about the field disrupting the game. In the bottom of the tenth inning with two down and a runner on second, Holland induced Javas second baseman Billy Hoke to lift a lazy pop fly near first base. Wakefield was about to make the catch, but a few crowd members grabbed him "and shoved him back until the base runner was home."[54]

Although slowed by a number of rainouts, Renville won 23 of their first 28 ball games, including two defeats of the Javas, and a 4–1 victory over Fargo of the Northern League.

1904 Renville, Minnesota, All-Stars. Pitcher Ed "Doggie" Woods is standing at far left in the back row. Fellow twirler Bert Jones is standing second from left and first baseman Bert Wakefield is standing next to Jones. Second baseman George Richardson is sitting in the middle row, second from right and pitcher Billy Holland is seated in the front row at the far right. Team owner Henry Stabeck is seated in the middle of the photograph and All-Stars third baseman and future Gophers opponent Pat Finnegan is seated next to Holland. (*Renville Star Farmer*, June 3, 1904; Minnesota State Historical Society, St. Paul)

Fargo's manager, ex–Millers slugger Perry Werden, had been reluctant to schedule Renville because he didn't think they were good enough, and some of his players made many "highly humorous remarks about farmers and rubes" before Holland went out and shut them down.[55]

Shortly after the season began it became evident that Ed Woods was not the pitcher he once was, and former minor leaguer Pat Finnegan was signed to take his place in the rotation. After several errors by Woods cost the team a victory against Delano, he lost his job in the outfield and the *Redwood Falls Gazette* pointedly remarked that "he is a good player — on the bench." A few weeks later "Doggie" left Renville to twirl for a team in Grey Eagle, Minnesota. Soon after his arrival, a club from Sauk Center pounded his new squad, 10–0, and it was suggested that while Woods, the man who had started the exodus of black players into the Upper Midwest, was once "a pretty hard proposition to run up against ... the boys had no difficulty in making connections with his curves."[56]

Much of Renville's schedule consisted of a series of contests with the two other top semi-pro teams in the area. From May 29 to July 9, a club from Webster, South Dakota, led by college stars Homer Hillebrand of Princeton (a future Pittsburgh Pirate) and Ed Rogers of Minnesota, beat Stabeck's outfit in eight out of 15 games thanks to some reckless base running on Renville's part. The Minnesota team would come back to even the series with a 9–5 victory at Ortonville on August 6, as the *Renville Record* crowed, "There is no joy in Webster, Hillerbrand has been knockt [sic] out."[57]

On July 10, Renville began another 16-game set, this time with the powerful Chippewa Falls, Wisconsin, Gotzians featuring George Wilson and his old pal Sam Foster. The two teams split the first ten games of a series notable for several duels between Billy Holland and the temperamental Wilson. In a game at Renville on July 13, the home team scored four runs in the bottom of first that:

> ... so enraged Wilson that after kicking over a decision, of the umpire he left the field in disgust and started up town. It looked for a time as though the game would come to a sudden termination but after awhile he was induced to return after sending someone after him.

When Renville scored three more in the eighth to lengthen their lead to 7–4, Wilson again made "a kick over a decision that didn't suit him, and after that he made no further effort to play, but merely tossed the ball over the plate much to the disgust of the crowd."[58]

Wilson was ready to play a month later when the two teams met at Lexington Park to decide the "Minnesota and Wisconsin championship." Pitching before a Sunday gathering of 2,200, Big George "had the Renville players at his mercy throughout the game," allowing only two hits and striking out 17 batters in a 10–2 Chippewa Falls rout. Billy Holland "evidently had an off day" for Renville, giving up 12 hits, including two home runs, two doubles, and a triple. Over the course of the next week, the shoe company nine beat the All-Stars four more times in Chippewa Falls before Renville finally stopped the bleeding with a 2–1 victory in 11 innings.[59]

The All-Stars salvaged some pride by sweeping a five-game set from the Menomonie, Wisconsin, team to close the year with a 55–26–1 (.676) record. The season was regarded as a success on the field as well as for the free advertising it had given the town. Thanks to the four ex–Brownies, Renville out-hit and out-fielded every team they encountered "with the possible exception of Chippewa Falls."[60]

Holland and Jones anchored a staff that had limited their opponents to a .177 batting average. Despite pitching in tough luck much of the time, Jones won several games through his use of "bewildering curves" and a "tantalizing slow ball" that nearly broke the backs of many opposing batters. When he wasn't making "pretty running catches" in center field, Holland was tossing "gilt edged ball" thanks to his "marvelous control" and assortment of "benders" and "twisters."[61]

Both Wakefield and Richardson fielded well for Renville, but they didn't hit much. Holland and Jones led the All-Stars attack, as both scored over one run per game on average and nearly half of their hits went for extra bases. Jones led the team in batting with a .310 average and triples with ten. Holland stole bases "most shamelessly," and his daring base running had infields "tied up in bow knots ... trying to get him located."[62]

The Renville management was determined "to go one better" in 1905, by hiring a traveling manager and stocking the team with "none but the very best base ball timber." When the All-Stars defeated the Lund Land team from Minneapolis, 5–4, in the home opener on April 27, only Jones, Finnegan, and back-up catcher Frank Kurke remained from the previous year's squad. Billy Holland was said to be "on the string," but he opted to return to Chicago and join the newly organized Leland Giants.[63]

The team was considerably strengthened in early May when George "Rat" (short for Rastus) Johnson, "the great colored catcher," arrived from Philadelphia, bearing a familiar pedigree. Born in 1876 in Bellaire, Ohio, Johnson began playing on local semi-pro teams when he was only 13 years old, and broke into professional blackball in 1896 with the Page Fence Giants. After stints with the Chicago Columbia Giants and the Algona Brownies, Johnson ventured east to catch for the Philadelphia Giants. The dapper catcher batted .352 for the Giants during their 1904 playoff with the Cuban X-Giants, literally betting his underwear on the series, which "fortunately for Johnson" the Phillies won.[64]

Renville opened the season on a tear, with their only loss in their initial 24 ball games being a 4–3 defeat at Chippewa Falls on May 17, when Johnson fumbled a throw home in the bottom of the ninth and two runs scored. Undeterred, the team went on to take four straight from their Wisconsin rivals, which pleased the Renville sports to no end. The only difficulty remaining for the All-Stars was in finding suitable competition. On May 28, a poor display put on by the Northern Pacific nine during a 14–0 Renville thrashing prompted a large Sunday congregation to leave "the ground in absolute disgust." Stabeck canceled the rest of the three-game series and sent the St. Paul team home "by the first train." A subsequent intra-squad game proved to be more entertaining, as the "Johnsonites" edged the "Jonesites," 3–2, on a bases-loaded walk-off hit by Johnson. While the contest had been fiercely contested, "Johnson made considerable fun with his continuous flow of hot air and everyone left the ground feeling that they had spent their time and money well."[65]

In late June Stabeck's crew won five out of six games in Chippewa Falls (with the sixth contest ending in a 5–5 tie) causing a shake up in the Gotzians ranks. George Wilson, not being able to beat Renville, decided to join them. The *Eau Claire Leader* wrote that his defection forced the Chippewa Falls club to carry on like a production of "Hamlet with Hamlet left out."[66]

With Big George pitching and playing left field, the All-Stars went on a successful tour of the Dakotas, only dropping a July 17 game at Carrington, North Dakota, 8–5, that was "given" to the home team by the umpire. A week later in Iowa, the team began a series of games with the tough semi-pro nine of Hawarden. Playing for side-bets of $100 a contest, the two teams split a pair of 2–1 decisions before Wilson and Johnson took over. With a $100 purse again on the line, the domineering southpaw took to the mound determined "to show the Hawarden lads a few things about baseball." Despite the best efforts of another biased umpire, Wilson "reaped a harvest of sixteen fan-outs," and hit a solo home run in Renville's 4–2 victory. Johnson homered twice, with his second blast bringing Wilson home with him.[67]

The All-Stars closed their season on September 2 by demolishing Hawarden, 20–0, giving them 12 wins in 16 tries with the fast Iowa bunch. Renville had "cleaned up all the independent teams of Wisconsin, Iowa, North and South Dakota and Minnesota," while dropping only 11 out of 75 games they played. Supported by a hard-hitting lineup that "butchered" most of the pitchers they ran up against, the All-Stars staff threw an amazing 23 shutouts. Wilson tossed at least six of those during his two-month tenure, and the eccentric Jones, who was said to own a fox that followed behind him as a mascot, lost but one game all year.[68]

In October, Johnson and Wilson made their way to Chicago where they helped Frank Leland's *old* team, the Union Giants, battle his *new* team, the Leland Giants, to a draw in a bitterly contested series. "Rat" Johnson rejoined the Philadelphia Giants in 1906, while Bert Jones and three other Renville players helped the Brookings, South Dakota, Reds become the Northwest's preeminent club.[69]

Wilson returned to Wisconsin to twirl for a team in Sheboygan. One hundred years later, it would not be hyperbole to suggest that he remains the best pitcher ever to don the uniform of a Minnesota team. Longtime Chicago player and pundit David Wyatt avowed,

1905 Chicago Union Giants. From left to right: Alex Irwin (SS), Willis Jones (LF), Fred Roberts (2B), Haywood Rose (C), Tom Washington (C), Harry Hyde (3B), Clarence Lytle (P), George Hopkins (CF), "Topeka" Jack Johnson (1B), George Taylor (1B). Every man pictured here, with the exception of Washington, played for the Gophers, Keystones, or both. (Chicago History Museum, SDN-003080)

"With the possible exception of Walter Johnson and Grover Cleveland Alexander, old leaguers will tell you that they never gazed upon a more perfect pitching machine than Wilson."[70]

George Wilson was indeed the whole show. When he and the rest of the Renville All-Stars went their separate ways in September of 1905, the days of the small town barnstorming team had come to an end in Minnesota. A new era was about to begin.

Chapter Three

Fast Team in the City (1907)

In 1907 a black man with a mitt and a modicum of talent could make good money playing baseball. Blackball had undergone an unprecedented expansion in the early 20th century with dozens of semi-pro and professional teams springing up all over the map. By the start of the 1906 season there were top-flight black nines operating in such diverse places as Baltimore, Birmingham, Indianapolis, St. Louis, Paducah, Topeka, and San Antonio to name but a few.

The managers of the very best black squads soon discovered that on-the-field success invariably led to off-the-field headaches, such as rising salaries and player raids by rival clubs. The three-time blackball champion Philadelphia Giants went 108–31–6 (.765) in 1906 but still finished in the red. In November the Giants owner, Walter "Slick" Schlichter, reduced the team's per diem to 15 cents, moved payday to the end of the month and demanded that the players pay for their own uniforms. These penny-pinching moves were the last straw for pitcher Andrew "Rube" Foster, black baseball's best and most widely known player, and the rest of the Giants, who thought they were getting a raw deal as it was. Foster gathered his teammates together and suggested that they strike out on their own, reasoning that, "if they were going to starve, the best policy would be to starve trying to better themselves."[1]

They found a place to "starve" in Chicago. Like their Philadelphia counterparts, the Leland Giants were mowing down their opposition, winning 112 out of 122 games in 1905, but they were also losing an alarming amount of money. Despite their gaudy record, the team was commanding less than 40 percent of the gate, and they had lost several important weekend games in the autumn of 1906 to rival semi-pro clubs. Frank Leland needed a star attraction and he got one by luring Foster, who had broken in with the Union Giants in 1902, back to Chicago by giving him a raise and making him the player-manager of the club. When Rube insisted on bringing seven premier eastern players, including four fellow Philadelphia Giants, along with him, Leland released his entire team.[2]

Among those being shown the door was St. Paul's own Walter Ball who had returned to Leland's employ in late July, after starting the season with the Quaker Giants of New York. Ball's biggest sin seemed to have been dropping a hard-luck 2–0 contest to the Chicago Spaldings in mid–September, despite giving up only one hit. Ball and his teammates were now out of work, but as the saying goes, when one door is closed, a window is opened. Climbing through this particular open window was Phil "Daddy" Reid, a nearly perfectly rotund black man replete with a handle bar mustache and bow tie.[3]

Phillip Edward Reid was born June 10, 1854, in Frankfort in the slave state of Kentucky. Reid began his career as a waiter for the railroads and by 1878 was working on the *Clarendon*, the first hotel rail car running between St. Louis to New York. Reid eventually left the railroad service, "where he was known throughout the country by the traveling public," and by the spring of 1880 he was waiting tables in a Minneapolis hotel. Around 1888 Reid began tending bar for John H. Cunningham at the Eureka Saloon, located at 384 Minnesota Avenue in downtown St. Paul. Reid served drinks for Cunningham for several years before going into business with childhood friend John J. Hirschfield.[4]

Hirschfield had been born in Iowa in 1858, but spent his formative years in St. Louis. Like Reid, he moved to St. Paul in the late 1880's and sometime in 1901 the two opened a "popular and successful" saloon at 40 East Third Street (now Kellogg Boulevard) in downtown St. Paul. Hirschfield and Reid were both loyal members of a fraternal organization, the Gopher Lodge of the Improved Benevolent and Protective Order of Elks, and Reid was also a prominent Freemason and a Knight of Pythias. Photographs of Reid from this time reveal a confident and heavyset man, frequently wearing a three-piece suit and bowler hat. This "prince of good fellows" was considered to be "one of the most influential and wealthy Negroes of the northwest" and was renowned for being "of a cheerful disposition, always willing to do an act of kindness."[5]

From all accounts Reid was fairly ambitious and a true "sport" who was interested in all things pleasurable: gambling, cigars, good clothes, fast times and faster money. The big fellow counted Rube Foster and heavyweight champ Jack Johnson, perhaps the two most prominent black athletes in the country, among his friends. Like many other black entrepreneurs of the day, he evidently decided that owning a baseball team would give him as well as his establishment the prestige he desired. Reid and Hirschfield were also astute businessmen. The relative financial successes of the Waseca, St. Cloud, and Renville ball clubs had proven that Minnesotans would pay to see black athletes play.

Phil "Daddy" Reid, owner of the St. Paul Gophers 1907–1910. (*St. Paul Appeal*, October 26, 1912; Minnesota State Historical Society, St. Paul)

In the spring of 1905, one D. Saunders organized a team called the St. Paul Giants out of Reid and Hirschfield's place. The Giants were allegedly made up of the "best colored talent" in the West and their local debut was scheduled for Sunday June 11 against the powerful Renville All-Stars. The *St. Paul Daily News* reported that Billy Williams, the Giants captain, had run the team through their first practice two nights before the game, and that George Wilson was scheduled to pitch for them.[6]

In fact, the two black stars involvement was all a hoax. It was a common practice of the time to advertise the appearances of well-known players to drum up attendance, and the 600 fans who showed up at Lexington Park were unwitting "victims of a large joke." Wilson and Williams "were conspicuous by their absence," and it took Renville only an hour and ten minutes to dispose of a collection of "diminutive colored bellboys and bootblacks" by the score of 13–0.[7]

The *Pioneer Press* griped that the Giants "made very little pretense of playing ball" and "were content at disporting themselves after the manner of circus clowns and acrobats." The shortness of the game was said to be its most redeeming feature. The Giants management had planned to play a series of Sunday games with the best teams in the region, but their poor showing against Renville more than likely put an end to any future activity.[8]

In early 1907 Reid and Hirschfield announced the formation of "a real colored baseball team" called the St. Paul Gophers. The nature of Reid's relationship with the St. Paul Giants is unclear, but he was no doubt anxious to lend a degree of legitimacy to his newest enterprise. To that end hometown hero Walter Ball was hired to organize a "professional baseball team," composed solely of ball players with "a national reputation," not "an amateur affair confined to local players." Like Reid, the pitcher was a former railroad man, having spent a few off-seasons working as a porter in North Dakota. By mid–February Ball was firing off letters to presidents of teams in the Wisconsin League requesting games for the fledgling club.[9]

Ball convinced his former Leland Giants infielders George Taylor, Fred Roberts, Albert Toney, Dangerfield Talbert, and catcher Andrew Campbell to join the new venture. He also persuaded the entire Chicago Union Giants outfield of Willis Jones, Sherman Barton, and Jesse Schaeffer to sign on, and nabbed the Union Giants ace, Clarence Lytle, for good measure.[10]

1907 St. Paul Gophers (pre-season). Back Row (Left to right): Jesse Schaeffer (C), Dangerfield Talbert (3B), Sherman Barton (CF), George Taylor (1B), Willis Jones (LF). Front Row (Left to right): Albert Toney (SS), Clarence Lytle (P), Walter Ball (P), Fred Roberts (2B), Andrew Campbell (C). (*St. Paul Dispatch*, May 18, 1907; Minnesota State Historical Society, St. Paul)

All ten of the original Gophers were Chicago baseball veterans who had competed with and against each other for years. An early publicity photo shows the team, resplendent in white caps, confidently positioned around a smiling Walter Ball, with the initials STPG emblazoned across the left side of their presumably navy blue shirts.[11]

The club, as was to be its custom, got ready for the season by training in and around Chicago. Their first game was slated for April 7 against once and future White Sox manager Jimmy Callahan's Logan Squares, featuring the New York Giant's star center fielder "Turkey" Mike Donlin. Callahan had left the Sox a year earlier in order to launch the Chicago City League, an outlaw organization of the area's top semi-pro teams; the league played its games on Sunday mornings, with moonlighting major leaguers often participating under assumed names. In any event, the contest never came off due to heavy rains in the area. The following weekend the team scheduled a couple of games with the South Bend, Indiana, squad of the Central League, but these too were cancelled due to some "December" weather "forcing itself on the baseball season."[12]

On Sunday, April 21, the Gophers finally made their debut against the Riverviews, a member of the Lake Shore League, which was a slightly lesser version of the City League. The game, played before a large assembly, was the lid opener for the brand new Riverview Park, on the north side of Chicago. Playing third base for the Gophers was former Leland and Union Giant James Smith, replacing Talbert who was back on the Leland payroll.[13]

The Gophers took an early 1–0 lead in the second inning and increased it to 4–1 by the end of the sixth, on the strength of a double by Taylor and two singles apiece by Barton and Roberts, when the roof fell in. The Riverviews scored four in the top of the seventh (at this point in time the home team could choose to bat first or last), aided by a controversial umpiring decision made at second base with the bases loaded. The Riverviews tacked on a run in the ninth, and held on for a 6–4 victory that was "marred by continuous kicking by the visitors." Ball struck out eight batters, but was decidedly not sharp, walking seven and giving up nine hits in the loss. Former major leaguer Fred "Crazy" Schmidt pitched rather deliberately for the Riverviews and also gave up nine hits, although he walked only two. The *Chicago American* remarked that 41-year-old left-hander "may be crazy and do a whole lot of foolish things on a ball field, but the whole team of St. Paul Gophers apparently is composed of Schmidt's of a darker color."[14]

The Riverview game proved to be the only contest Albert Toney ever played for the Gophers before Frank "Bunch" Davis of the Union Giants replaced him at short. Andrew Campbell departed as well and the catching duties fell, as was the custom of the day, to Schaeffer, the most inexperienced player on the squad. By the time the Gophers left Chicago to play the Wisconsin League team in Green Bay later that week, two more former Leland Giants, pitchers Will Horn and Thomas Means, had been added to give the squad more depth.[15]

To keep expenses down and profits up, black teams such as the Gophers were usually 11-man units consisting of a catcher, four infielders, two outfielders, and three pitchers. On the days they didn't start, one of the pitchers would play right field while another would umpire and count the gate to make sure the club wasn't being shortchanged. If a player had to leave a game due to ejection or injury, the third pitcher would have to fill in. There was no injured reserve; if a player became seriously hurt he was out of a job.

The entire organization was a stripped-down affair. Reid was referred to as the Gophers president and manager, which essentially meant he was the owner. In an article that ran in the *St. Paul Appeal* in August 1907, Hirschfield was described as the club's treasurer. It remains unclear if this really was an indication that he was the team's financial backer or that he was just the paymaster and bookkeeper. As the captain of the ball club, Ball was the equivalent of the modern day manager, being in charge of the team on the field, responsible for setting the lineup and deciding game strategy.[16]

The original Gophers were "composed of the fastest colored players in America," with "fast" meaning excellent in the parlance of the day. Jesse Schaeffer, "the youngest African American catcher," was a fire hydrant of a man, with a build not unlike future Minnesota Twins great Kirby Puckett. At the plate he was a powerful slugger and in the field he was a "terror to base stealers." First baseman George Taylor had played close to 20 years of professional baseball, starting with a stint in 1889 with Aspen in the Colorado State League. The Michigan native had once been a great hitter who batted .350 in 1895 with the Page Fence Giants. In six games against the Millers and Saints that spring, Taylor hit .318 with a homer and four stolen bases. The Gophers possessed a "brilliant" fielder in Frank Davis at shortstop, a player short in stature, but considered by many to be the star of the team. Fred "Pop" Roberts, the pride of Danville, Illinois, was a "clever" fielder and batter at second base and Spanish-American War veteran Jimmy Smith rounded out the infield at third.[17]

The outfield was anchored by 32-year-old Sherman "Bucky" Barton, a hard-hitting center fielder from Illinois, who had a cannon-like arm. The *Indianapolis Freeman* once noted that "when it comes to fielding and retiring runners, Bucky Barton of the St. Paul Gophers ranks with the big leaguers. They all fear him." In 1898 the flame-throwing Barton tossed a three-hitter for the Page Fence Giants during a 9–1 triumph over Chatham, Ontario, and their future Hall of Fame pitcher, Rube Waddell. While manning center for the Cuban X-Giants in 1906, Barton tagged Rube Foster for three hits including a double during a playoff game.

The Gophers left fielder was little Willis Jones, a fleet-of-foot base runner and left fielder, "brim full of ginger," known for keeping "the spectators in good humor with his antics." If a ball game were lacking in entertainment value, Jones would give "vocal exhibitions which cheered the fans amazingly." Carter Wilson, a later teammate of Jones on the Union Giants, remembered that the Cincinnati native was a "great clown":

> Sometimes he might go out to his position in the outfield with a newspaper and cut a little hole through and pretend he was reading it. And if a ball was hit to him and the game was lopsided in our favor, he wouldn't run after the ball. The centerfielder would have to go and get it.[18]

The Gophers pitching staff relied more on brains and personality than brawn. Tommy Means, "the funniest coacher in the business," was an effective if fragile starter adept at keeping "the crowds in good humor all the time." The lanky 12-year veteran hurler Will Horn was jokingly said to be so tall that if he just fell towards first base after hitting a ball he would be safe. In July 1904 while pitching for the Philadelphia Giants, Horn struck out 12 and set the Oxford, Pennsylvania, team down without a hit. Clarence Lytle was a clever, reliable twirler and a "crack spitball artist." Not a power pitcher by any means, the "Dude" was "a cute one, and what he can't do with his arm he can do with his head." While twirling for the Union Giants in 1906, Lytle shut out a powerful Brooklyn Royal Giants squad featuring Home Run Johnson, Billy Holland, and Andrew Payne on one hit. The 27-year-old Lytle was also something of a ladies man and following his return to Chicago after the season, his mail courier was reportedly "overburdened."[19]

With Davis at short and Barton in center the club was strong up the middle defensively, especially when the slick-fielding Lytle was on the mound. The few fly balls the pitching staff allowed were invariably caught by fielders who seemed to "travel as fast as the ball." After a 5–4 victory over Decorah, Iowa, in mid–September, the local paper mourned, "The Gopher outfielders covered territory like ice yachts in a gale and time and time again long dives that looked like a three bagger ended in a dusky mitt."[20]

The club's journey to Green Bay, where they were billed as the Chicago Colored Gophers, proved unfruitful as all three scheduled match-ups were again washed away by bad weather. Walter Ball took advantage of the postponements by zipping back to the Windy City that weekend to pitch the Union Giants over the Artesians, 11–4, before catching up with the squad for a series in Eau Claire, Wisconsin.[21]

In Eau Claire, the Gophers gave the young bush league hopefuls a baptism under fire while capturing the first two wins in franchise history. On May Day, the two teams were tied at two in the sixth inning when Taylor singled with one out and Barton doubled him to third. Roberts then laid down a perfect squeeze bunt and when Eau Claire third baseman George O'Leary threw on to first to retire him, Barton raced all the way home from second to score the final run in the 4–2 Gophers victory.[22]

The sixth inning proved fateful the next day as well, when Willis Jones walked and Schaeffer snapped a 1–1 deadlock by launching a drive that traveled so far to the rear of the park that he, "in spite of his corpulence, made a circuit of the bases before it was fielded." Schaeffer also doubled two runners home in the seventh and Walter Ball made the 6–1 lead stand up, striking out eight and pitching well in the clutch.[23]

Upon the club's subsequent return to St. Paul, Ball hired a Native American named Johnson to shore up the catching position, but as it turned out neither player would remain a Gopher for very long. A Saturday contest at the Downtown Park with the Lund Lands was snowed out and when the Minneapolis semi-pros failed to show for a Monday make-up game, a quick phone call brought the Calumet, Michigan, team of the Northern League across the river to play instead.[24]

Len Schroeder, the Calumet starter, helped his own cause by belting a three-run homer and the Michigan lads edged the Gophers, 5–4, in a hard-fought battle called after seven innings because of darkness. Ball allowed nine hits, and the Gophers committed three errors behind him, including one by Smith in the sixth that let in the go-ahead run.[25]

The loss to Calumet would be the only game the Gophers would play for almost two weeks. Because news of the team's existence had been met with incredulity as well as a lack of enthusiasm by the Twin Cities public, the club had difficulty booking games. To make matters worse, the spring of 1907 was the coldest on record in more than 50 years and the future, for "both the managers and players, looked very shady," indeed.[26]

Into the breach stepped Irving L. Williams, a waiter at Reid's place, who assumed the role of the club's secretary, responsible for scheduling, arranging transportation, and garnering publicity. Thanks to Williams' acumen and Reid's "determination to succeed at all costs," the Gophers soon had requests from over 25 cities for Sunday games and invitations to play in Chicago and Kansas City. In what may have been a pre-arranged move, Walter Ball returned to Chicago in mid–May to join the Leland Giants and his crony, James Smith, became the Gophers captain.[27]

Williams got the ball rolling by matching the Gophers against the best semi-pro clubs in the Twin Cities and the Sunday League, an organization of nearby town teams. On Saturday, May 18, the Gophers played their first game in Minneapolis, edging the Lund Lands, 10–9, in a ragged contest before only 200 souls at Nicollet Park. The next afternoon the new club took on the Austin-Western outfit of the Sunday League before a racially-mixed

1907 St. Paul Gophers (early season). Back Row (Left to right): Clarence Lytle (P), Fred Roberts (2B), Sherman Barton (CF), Will Horn (P), Jesse Schaeffer (C), George Taylor (1B). Front Row (Left to right): Willis Jones (LF), James Smith (3B), Frank Davis (SS), Thomas Means (P). (*Chaska Valley Herald*, August 1, 1907; Minnesota State Historical Society, St. Paul)

gathering of over 750 who braved unseasonably cold weather at Lexington Park to witness the contest.[28]

Johnson was no longer the catcher, and the new man behind the plate was Bobby Marshall, perhaps the finest athlete Minneapolis ever produced. Robert Wells Marshall was born in Milwaukee in 1880, but he grew up in the Twin Cities, leading Minneapolis Central High School to three state football championships and two state baseball titles. Marshall matriculated to the University of Minnesota where he won seven letters for football, baseball, *and* track from 1903 to 1907. With Marshall lining up at end on both offense and defense, the Minnesota eleven went 27–2 from 1904 to 1906, while outscoring the opposition 1,283 to 63. In November 1906, Bobby burst onto the national scene when he kicked a 39-yard field goal in the rain and mud of Marshall Field to beat the defending national champion Chicago Maroons, clinching a share of the Big Nine (now Big Ten) crown for the visiting Gophers. The *Chicago Tribune* applauded Marshall for his "magnificent playing," noting that he was the only man who stood between Minnesota and defeat. Marshall studied law at the university, while supporting himself and his family as a janitor, but sports was where his interest lay. He became the first-ever black pro hockey player in the United States in 1905, and broke into semi-pro baseball with the Lund Lands in 1906.[29]

On this day, however, a few rookie jitters on Marshall's part helped the Austin-Westerns take a 1–0 lead in the third inning. The collegian's troubles started when Wallace, Austin's shortstop, reached on a fielder's choice. He promptly pilfered second and advanced to third when Marshall's peg down to second sailed into center field. A few moments later Wallace scored when one of Dude Lytle's tosses got past Marshall.[30]

Wallace soon returned the favor when his error put Taylor on board at first to lead off the next inning. The grizzled veteran stole second and advanced to third when Austin's catcher Carroll threw down to first after dropping Barton's third strike. Pop Roberts then followed with a squeeze bunt and Taylor scored the equalizer by beating third baseman Dell's tardy throw home.[31]

It was a fait accompli that when a Gopher reached base he was going to try to steal, and Roberts soon lit out for second. He scampered to third when the catcher's throw down to second was mishandled. Roberts then got a little *too* aggressive and the Austins had him picked off, but Dell could not handle the throw and the cagey vet raced home with the go ahead run. After Bunch Davis popped out, Marshall dumped a Texas leaguer into right for the Gophers first and only hit of the inning. No doubt anxious to atone for his catching miscues, the local favorite stole second and scored the third run of the inning when the unfortunate Dell threw Lytle's grounder into the bleachers.[32]

The "Dude" allowed only four singles while cruising to a 3–1 victory, backed by the infield play of Smith and Davis who "possessed wings that no major leaguer would be ashamed to own." The Gophers struck out nine times and managed only six hits off of the Austin-Westerns pitcher Sullivan, but they stole five bases and forced the Sunday Leaguers into six errors. Speed kills and the Gophers running game that summer put a tremendous amount of pressure on their opponents, who had rarely seen anything like it. Scribes all over the region were quick to bemoan the numerous bonehead plays the Gophers caused their local favorites to commit.[33]

The *Pioneer Press* complained that the light-hitting Gophers "played a fairly good game, but they are not nearly as strong as any of the other colored organizations that have been seen here." The St. Paul paper was also less than kind to Marshall, stating that "Bobby's forte is evidently football. He catches fairly well but cannot throw or bat." It had been advertised that Marshall would be the Gopher's new catcher, but he instead rejoined the University of Minnesota squad and helped them win the 1907 Big Nine title. Along with a few college teammates, he then ventured out West and spent part of the summer manning third base for a team in Lamoure, North Dakota.[34]

Playing a steady diet of Twin City semi-pro and town teams in southern Minnesota and western Wisconsin, the Gophers won 37 of their first 40 ball games. They didn't lose their third game of the season until a June 2 rematch with the Austin-Westerns at Lexington Park. The contest, played before a good-sized Sunday gathering of 1,200, was the first Gopher start for ex–Union Giant Johnny Davis, a "star pitcher" reputed to be of major league quality. The slightly built, 26-year-old Kentuckian was described as a "clever cross fire artist" known for possessing a "very tantalizing slow curve and fine control of a change of pace delivery." Batters who faced him said that his pitches "seemed to come from third base and all corners." When the occasion warranted, Davis could also mix in an overpowering fast ball "which showed top speed."[35]

The Gophers could only parlay seven stolen bases and seven Austin-Western errors into two runs, being stymied by University of St. Thomas standout Fred "Lefty" Miller, who gave up but three hits and stuck out seven. The Gophers loaded the bases in the eighth when Schaeffer doubled and Barton and Roberts walked, but Miller, who later pitched in the Northwestern and Pacific Coast Leagues, preserved the 2–2 tie by striking out Bunch Davis. The St. Paul semi-pros pushed the winning run across the plate in the bottom of the ninth, on a pinch-hit single by Dell, a Bunch Davis throwing error, and a squeeze bunt by Meehan, the Austin catcher.³⁶

In mid–June the team journeyed north of the Twin Cities for the first time, easily defeating clubs in Fergus Falls, Crookston, and Fargo, North Dakota, before veering back across the state to play the Hibbing Colts, a team that would prove to be its fiercest rival. Hibbing was a booming mining community of about 8,000 located on the Iron Range in northeastern Minnesota. The large iron ore mines in Hibbing and the neighboring towns of Chisholm, Eveleth, and Virginia, provided much of the raw material for the nation's burgeoning industries and their ball clubs were a huge source of community entertainment and pride. Municipal Judge Thomas Brady spared little expense in financing and outfitting Hibbing's crack team, all of whom had played organized ball.³⁷

On Sunday June 23, over 3,000 fans from all over the Iron Range crammed into Hibbing's ballpark to witness a classic pitching duel. For 13 innings neither Johnny Davis nor Hibbing's Dwight Booth allowed a run and only once could each team get a base runner as far as third base. Saying that he could not go on much longer, Booth wanted to quit after the 11th, but Manager Brady convinced him to pitch on. In the top of the 14th the southpaw finally weakened and "the Gophers made a lucky hit that was not properly taken care of and the runs began to fall over home plate." Davis set Hibbing down in the bottom of the inning to secure a 4–0 win that was the talk of the area for many years to come. Certainly Dwight Booth, who on that day "had everything that any pitcher ever had," never forgot it. His arm had suffered terrible damage and although he remained a key player on the Colts roster for two more decades, his pitching days were mostly over.³⁸

The Gophers had expected to find a "regular back country club," but, after the first game, Reid instructed his charges to bear down all the time. After a Monday rain out, Will Horn's three-run blast over the right-field fence keyed Dude Lytle's 7–3 win on Tuesday. The following afternoon, the Colts new twirler, Dartmouth alum John Glaze, delighted another large weekday crowd by giving up only three "measly little hits" and Hibbing used the five Horn dispensed to pile up a 5–1 victory.³⁹

Returning to the Twin Cities, the club broke in a new second baseman while squashing the Minneapolis Toozes, 8–1 and 6–2, over the weekend. Jimmy Smith had left the squad before they arrived in Hibbing to rejoin the Union Giants and George Taylor succeeded him as the third Gopher captain in as many months. The well traveled Taylor was reported to know more about black ballplayers than anyone in the country and closely monitored the progress "of every man with even a slight reputation." Pop Roberts took Smith's spot at third base, making room at second for Sammy Ransom, said to be "the greatest prep colored athlete" of the day.⁴⁰

Born on the Fourth of July in 1883, Samuel L. Ransom had won fame at Chicago's Hyde Park High School, playing in the backfield of their nationally renowned 1902 and 1903 football squads with the legendary Walter Eckersall. Ransom became the first African American to captain the Hyde Park eleven and was later named to their all-time team. According to Eckersall, the 5'9", 154-pound Ransom was quick, agile, "hard as nails, and a fairly fast runner." Eckersall also recalled that "the slogan of all Hyde Park's opponents was 'get the negro'" and that "no matter how hard opposing players tried to disable Ransom, the harder he played." Ransom manned a forward spot on the prep school's basketball team as well spearheading their national championship track and baseball squads. In April 1903 he pitched Hyde Park to an 8–3 exhibition win over Johnny Davis and the Union Giants. The young scholar worked his way through school as a night bell boy in the Del Prado Hotel, before moving on to Beloit College in Wisconsin where he became "one of the three great colored players" in early 20th century collegiate football. As it transpired, Ransom was only with the Gophers for two months, but he would remain in St. Paul for most of the next 63 years.[41]

On a trip through the southeastern part of the state, the Gophers put together an impressive string of victories that included three shutouts in a row. The final whitewashing occurred on July 2, when Johnny Davis tossed a 1–0 no-hitter against the La Crosse team of the Wisconsin State League. Willis Jones drove the first pitch of the game by former Pittsburgh Pirate 30-game winner "Pink" Hawley far into right field for a double and was bunted over to third by Ransom. Schaeffer then singled between first and second, scoring Jones with the only run that Davis, who allowed only two balls to be hit out of the infield, would need. The La Crosse papers were more interested in the humorous banter of the "darkies ... who uttered almost everything in the dictionary and some that must have been invented to suit the occasion." Three days later the shutout string was broken during a 14–1 Gophers victory over Rushford, Minnesota. In the bottom of the second inning a local batter named Casey slammed one of Dude Lytle's pitches off of a tree located in "extreme" right field. When the ball hit the ground none of the Gopher outfielders could find it and Casey came all the way around to score.[42]

In mid–July the Gophers embarked on a three-week tour of western Minnesota and South Dakota without Will Horn, who had left for Chicago to join the Union Giants. The club played 22 contests on their western swing and won them all, pushing their winning streak to over 30 games in a row. In one three-game stretch the Gophers outscored the Britton and Aberdeen teams 72–20. They were only seriously challenged a couple of times, edging Wessington Springs, 5–4, and Webster, 8–6, both in ten innings. The team finagled a run in the Wessington Springs game when the umpire they supplied conveniently forgot that a throw to the plate on a bases-loaded squeeze bunt was a force out and called the Gophers runner safe.[43]

Along the way the Gophers acquired a mascot, a coyote named Jim who was put on display at the Log Cabin Buffet. The *St. Paul Dispatch* recounted a faintly racist tale wherein Phil Reid had captured the animal while hunting small game with Vessey, the manager of the Wessington Springs Cowboys. Vessey had seen a coyote sneak into a pile of rocks on the side of a hill, but mischievously told Reid that he had spotted a jackrabbit instead. Vessey then had Reid stand waiting, rifle in hand, on one side of the den, while he was vigorously fanning smoke into the other side. The Gophers manager was soon startled by a snarl and he "turned around just as the mother coyote shot out of the den, bumped into his legs and he sat down—flat on one of the little coyotes that had followed its mother from the smoke-filled den." The *Wessington Springs True Republican* reported that Reid had, in actuality, bought the coyote from the local team.[44]

The Gophers returned from out West in early August and put its streak on the line against the best of the Minnesota town teams. Stillwater almost put an end to their marvelous run on Sunday August 4, but Mother Nature intervened. As the game began, a light drizzle was falling and the rain intensified throughout, until it became a downpour in the last of the seventh inning and the two teams were unable to continue. An overflow legion of 2,000 fans that had filled the grandstand and stood ten rows deep in front of the bleachers, implored umpire "Honest" Andy Thompson to resume the 2–2 contest, but the rain persisted and after 20 minutes the game was called. Stillwater reached Lytle for five singles, but some sharp fielding by the "Dude" and four great catches by Barton in center minimized

1907 St. Paul Gophers (mid-season). Back Row (Left to right): Sam Ransom (2B), John Davis (P), George Taylor (1B), Fred Roberts (3B). Front Row (Left to right): Sherman Barton (CF), Willis Jones (LF), Clarence Lytle (P), Phil Reid (Owner), Frank Davis (SS), Jesse Schaeffer (C), Thomas Means (P). (Courtesy of Roger and Kathleen Ebert)

the damage. The Gophers were handcuffed by Fred Blanchard, a big lanky hurler from St. Paul, who struck out six and allowed only one hit, a double by Ransom in the fifth that gave the professionals a brief 2–1 lead. Phil Reid and his coyote were on hand to take in the proceedings, as were some 200 black men and women from the Twin Cities, who had traveled to Stillwater via four special streetcars that Irving Williams had arranged for.[45]

A couple of days later, the Chaska club took their shot during a baseball tournament in Lester Prairie. Playing before another gathering of over 2,000 people, the Gophers captured a $150 purse by "outclassing" the White Diamonds, 9–3. Most of the damage was done in the second inning, when the Gophers scored five times aided by six White Diamond errors. Billy Williams played first base and captained the Chaska nine, but Johnny Davis deliberately gave him little to hit. After the game Bunch Davis finished third in a foot race around the bases, clocking in at 15 and ⅕ seconds. It was such a "beastly hot" day that during the race Davis became overheated and nearly died, according to a local paper.[46]

The Gophers beat the Rochester Stars a couple of times, including a 12–0 no-hitter by Lytle, before venturing north to take on Hibbing and a few other Iron Range teams. The team's 36th straight win came on Saturday, August 10, when they nipped Brady's Colts, 4–3. The club fell behind 3–0 after two innings, but two throwing errors by Hibbing starter John Glaze combined with doubles by Schaeffer and Bunch Davis gave the Gophers the game. Hibbing again jumped out to an early lead the following day when Dwight Booth drove one of Johnny Davis's first-inning offerings high over the park's tall board fence. The Gophers tied it up in the second when Barton reached on an error and scored on a double by Bunch Davis. Over 1,200 enthusiastic loyalists watched as Hibbing added a run in the fourth on a single by their right fielder Jimmy Fagan and another in the fifth on a home run by center fielder Bobby Geiselman. The red-hot Frank Davis pulled the Gophers back within one with a eighth inning homer but Geiselman singled and scored in the bottom of the inning, and future St. Louis Brown Jack Gilligan retired the Gophers in order in the ninth for a 4–2 Hibbing win — the first loss for the Gophers since the Colts beat them 5–1 way back on June 26.[47]

The Gophers split a couple of more contests with Hibbing and then won all five of the games they played in Chisholm, Eveleth, and Virginia. When the team came back from the range their record stood at an astounding 74–5–1, and they had become an attractive candidate for county fairs and baseball tournaments. At one such tourney in Watertown, Minnesota, the Gophers rallied from a 5–1 deficit to nip the host Stars 6–5 in ten innings and capture the $150 prize money. Watertown was aided considerably by the imported battery of Toozes southpaw Alf Dominick, who fanned ten while holding the Gophers hitless for seven innings, and ex–Brookings, South Dakota, catcher "Bat" Johnson who had three timely hits and threw out five would-be Gopher base stealers. Schaeffer keyed the comeback with two late safeties, including a home run.[48]

The Gophers journeyed back to western Minnesota for a couple of wild and wooly games with the hard-hitting Alexandria nine. The local squad, a thorn in the Gopher's side for years to come, featured University of Minnesota standouts Helon Leach and Al Dretchko, who batted .470 and .406, respectively, that summer. Dretchko would hit .340 in 1910 for Edmonton in the Western Canada League. Alexandria also had on their roster two ball players from St. Louis, who sat out the series because they "refused to play the national game with a colored team."[49]

On Friday, August 28, the home club aided by a "high wind" that carried fly balls "far into the field" collected 20 safe drives including four home runs and three triples and pounded the Gophers, 22–15. The visitors collected 18 hits of their own, but they were hampered when Jones sprained his ankle chasing a fly ball in left and when another one of their number had to retire after being struck in the head by a throw down to second. The Gophers bounced back a day later, lashing out 21 more hits, including 17 in the first four innings, as Lytle cruised to a six-hit, 13–3 decision.[50]

In early September the Hibbing Colts battled the Gophers for a $500 side bet (nearly $12,000 in today's currency) during four well-attended games in the Twin Cities. Unfortunately for Reid's wallet, injuries had begun to take a toll on his club. In addition to Jones' ankle, Lytle and Davis were wearing down from the strain of pitching every other day because Tommy Means was either missing his regular turn or couldn't finish the games he started. To make matters worse, Ransom was in and out of the lineup with a broken shoulder and the club had to use local sandlot players to fill out the roster.[51]

At the Downtown Park on Saturday, the Gophers could only muster a single and double by Schaeffer off of Jack Gilligan, who struck out seven batters in the 4–3 Hibbing victory. Down 3–0 at Lexington the next afternoon, Johnny Davis helped his own cause with a fifth-inning single. The crafty pitcher scored on a double by Bunch Davis, who in turn came around on a base hit by Schaeffer. The following inning, the Gophers began bunting the ball repeatedly in rapid succession, and by the time the Hibbing infielders had stopped kicking the ball around, six runs were in and an 8–3 verdict was secured.[52]

THREE • *Fast Team in the City (1907)* 43

The series and the wager went the Rangers way on Monday when Gilligan struck out another six batters and scattered five singles while blanking the home team, 5–0. The Colts light-hitting second sacker, Charlie Calligan, scored three of his club's runs, once after Lytle hit him with a pitch. The Gophers, who had not been shut out all season, were blanked on successive days when another future St. Louis Brown, Dode Criss, no-hit them in the finale on Tuesday, 4–0. The big Mississippian, who had been loaned out for the game by the Saints on the sly, fanned 13 Gophers and "took great delight in mowing down the colored cracks."[53]

The banged-up Gopher squad stumbled into western Wisconsin and right smack into a brouhaha in Hudson. The trouble began when the second Gopher batter of the game was called out after a close play at second. The base runner, along with other members of the club, angrily charged at umpire Rob Roe, at which point the Hudson team joined the melee. Concerned that "a mix-up might take place," Hudson Chief of Police John O'Keefe took to the playing field and "one of the Gophers who became particularly abusive was collared by the policeman and marched off the grounds." Some of the Gophers left the park immediately, while others stayed and tried to work out an amicable solution. Ultimately, the game was called off and the fans were given their money back. The locals "were much disgusted at the proceedings" and, not surprisingly, the Gophers never played Hudson again.[54]

Means started the next day in nearby Osceola, but he had to leave in the third inning with an injury and the club down 3–2. Lytle came in and held the Bethanias down without a hit as his teammates, led by Schaeffer's three safeties, rallied to tie the game in the sixth. In the last of the ninth, however, the Dude walked two batters and Osceola's first baseman,

1907 St. Paul Gophers (mid-season). Back Row (Left to right): Jesse Schaeffer (C), Sam Ransom (2B), Irving Williams (Secretary), Sherman Barton (CF), Frank Davis (SS). Middle Row (Left to right): Willis Jones (LF), George Taylor (1B), Phil Reid (Owner), John Hirschfield (Treasurer), John Davis (P), Thomas Means (P). Front Row (Left to right): Fred Roberts (3B), Clarence Lytle (P). (*St. Paul Appeal*, August 31, 1907; Minnesota State Historical Society, St. Paul)

Garfield Downend, slashed a game-winning single. Lytle's difficulty in locating the strike zone was exacerbated by the man behind the plate, Stillwater's Henry Martin, never the most impartial of umpires. Over 2,000 people from all over the St. Croix River valley witnessed "this fine game of baseball," while a crowd of only 400 showed up to watch the Saints beat the Milwaukee Brewers a few miles away in St. Paul.[55]

As the season wound down, the Gophers success led to the increased frustration of their opponents. After a play at third base during a game in Chaska on September 8, Pop Roberts was assaulted by a White Diamond base runner named Graves, and a "free for all was narrowly averted." Roberts had the last laugh, doubling home Bunch Davis with the decisive run in the 5–4 Gopher win. Johnny Davis struck out 15 for the Gophers, while Billy Williams, the "Professor of Applied Swatology," ripped two "sky scraping fouls over the right field fence" and a "grass cutting" RBI single for Chaska. Jesse Schaeffer launched another home run, but he also allowed *eight* stolen bases.[56]

Shortly thereafter, Roberts moved back to second because Ransom could no longer continue and the Gophers tabbed Willie McMurray, yet another Chicago Union Giant, to play third. McMurray, a 25-year-old graduate of the St. Louis sandlots, was a versatile, hard-working player with an ability to lead. He was also a jovial sort, known for joshing with fans "and being ever ready with repartee."[57]

With McMurray on board, the Gophers took off on another successful rampage through southern Minnesota. Reid made back the money he had lost to Hibbing when the team captured a $500 purse by topping the Red Wing Furriers, 5–0, during the Zumbrota Street Fair. Johnny Davis gave up only four hits while Sunday Leaguer and future St. Louis Brown Fred "Hack" Spencer was roughed up for 12 safeties, including yet another Schaeffer home run. The team earned another $200 a day later at the Fillmore County Fair in Preston, Minnesota, when they managed only four hits off of Adolph Eiken but still beat the strong rural nine from Harmony, 5–3. The hurler from nearby Caledonia struck out ten Gopher batters for the second time that year, but his teammates couldn't do much against Davis, who relieved Means once again in the seventh and shut the country boys down.[58]

In early September it was announced that the Gophers had scheduled a series with the St. Paul Saints. Although they had finished dead last in the American Association with a dismal 58–96 (.376) record, the Leaguers were fairly confident they could take "a little easy money" from the Gopher supporters. To supplement their squad, the Saints added three Minneapolis Millers and a few homegrown Minnesotans from other minor league teams. The squad that lined up against the Gophers included eight former major leaguers including Alphonso "Lefty" Davis, who had played that season for the Cincinnati Reds, Lew Drill, who went on to become a gangster-fighting U.S. District Attorney for Minnesota, and George "Peaches" Graham, who may have been the small-time hustler Billy Maharg (Graham spelled backwards) who helped fix the 1919 World Series. Also among the Saints number was future Yankee super scout "Vinegar" Bill Essick, who would later sign Hall of Famers Tony Lazzeri, Lefty Gomez, and Joe DiMaggio.[59]

The first game was dominated by the two starting pitchers, Lytle and the Saints Frank "Rube" Farris, as well as by a strong southwestern breeze, "from over the corner where Louis Liverpool mops his head." This was possibly the same Liverpool who had lost a footrace to a Minneapolis Union player over 30 years before. Louis was now a rather large fixture, literally and figuratively, at the Downtown Park, whose job it was to make sure that spectators didn't abscond with the balls that were hit over the fences.[60]

The strong wind helped the Gophers take an early lead in the top of the fourth. Pop

Roberts led off the inning by lifting a Farris pitch high in the air near third base. Peaches Graham settled under the pop fly, but the September gale got hold of the ball and pushed it back towards the plate with Graham in pursuit. The ball plummeted to the earth only a few feet from home and by the time Farris picked it up, Roberts was diving head first into second. Schaeffer was up next and he drove a pitch over the right-field wall for a ground rule double and the first run of the series.

Though the Saints kept putting men on base and had runners on both first and second many times, they couldn't get anyone to third. Lytle kept smearing "field paste" on the ball, which made it seem "dead" when the Saints hit it. With one out in the bottom of the eighth, Lew Drill singled to left and Graham came up with a base hit over second. Lytle escaped again by popping Bill Essick out to first and retiring E.J. Rodebaugh on a flare to short. The game ended shortly thereafter with the Gophers on the front end of the 1–0 score.

Farris whiffed 13 Gopher batters, allowed only five hits, and issued only one free pass. The Saints had no trouble hitting Lytle's deliveries, but they couldn't get many balls out of the infield, and they ended up with five lonely singles. "That the color championship is a popular one," *the Pioneer Press* noted the following day, "was proved by the large outpouring of gallants and beauts, all arrayed in colors suitable for the momentous occasion. And when it was all over, there was a general wringing of mits and collecting of bets, while in the evening a cloud of joy, several feet thick, hung darkly over Third Street."[61]

The two teams took their act out to South St. Paul on Sunday the 22, and the American Association team evened the series with a 6–3 win. Saints second baseman Jack "Skeeter" Dunleavy smacked the first pitch of the game by Johnny Davis for a home run, and Northern Leaguer Ted Corbett, who had umpired the first game of the series, knocked a two-run homer in the third for a 3–0 Saints lead. The Gophers came back with a three-run, two-out rally in the sixth, but the Leaguers got the three tallies back in the top of the seventh when they bunched a few hits around an error. South St. Paul twirler Ed Heimkes kept the Gophers at bay until the sixth, when a muff at first by local semi-pro Jimmy O'Malley opened the floodgates. Corbett, who had won nine games for the 1903 pennant-winning Saints, came in relief of Heimkes and shut the Gophers down the rest of the way.[62]

The stage was now set for a Monday rubber match back at the Downtown Park, and Reid, taking no chances, brought Rube Foster all the way from Chicago to take the hill for the Gophers. Foster and the revamped Leland Giants had set the Windy City on its ear in 1907 by capturing the City League title and winning a huge series from the Mike Donlin All-Stars. Rube had three one-hitters to his credit that summer, and a week earlier he had no-hit the strong South Chicago team led by ex-major leaguers Jake Stahl and Homer Hillebrand.[63]

Foster had also gained a lot of weight, which did not go unnoticed by the St. Paul scribes who estimated his girth at about "308 pounds" and mused that "when Rube is through as a pitcher he can make a comfortable living moving houses and pianos. He looked as big as a fully matured hippopotamus." Foster proved to be "the biggest man on the field in more ways than one," as he allowed only five hits and struck out ten Saints batters. The big man from Texas pitched well enough to shut out the Leaguers, but the Gophers usually fine fielding was not in evidence as they and the Saints spent the day tossing the ball wildly all over the lot.[64]

The teams combined to commit seven errors in a tumultuous third inning. Willis Jones began the Gophers' half of the frame by reaching on an error by Phil Geier at short. McMurray then put down a sacrifice and when Gene Ford dropped the throw to first, Jones scored. Bunch Davis followed by sacrificing McMurray along, who later tallied the Gophers second run of the game on an errant throw by the Saints starter Ed Rodebaugh. Ford doubled to start the Saints third and he advanced to third when Rodebaugh was retired at first. Foster got Skeeter Dunleavy to hit a grounder to short, but Davis threw it against the grandstand and the Saints were on the board. Lefty Davis coaxed a walk from Foster and he and Dunleavy then pulled off a double steal. When Schaeffer's peg to second was off the mark, Dunleavy scored and Davis raced to third. Lefty recorded the go-ahead run a few moments later when Roberts committed the third Gopher throwing error of the inning, on a "wild heave to first." Thanks to a little luck, the Gophers were soon on top again. With two out in the top of the fourth and Taylor on first, Barton hit a fly that passed through a small hole in the left-field netting, good for a home run, according to the vagaries of the stadium's ground rules.[65]

The Downtown Park was known as the "pillbox" for good reason. Built on a small St. Paul city block and surrounded by a high fence topped by a 20-foot wire screen, the wooden structure had virtually no foul territory with the grandstand and bleachers being located less than seven yards from the field of play. Because the outfield dimensions were only 280 feet down the left-field line and no more than 210 feet to right, foul pops and triples were almost unheard of. Right fielders played with their backs against the fence only a few feet behind the second baseman, and often threw runners out at first after would-be singles to right. At the Downtown Park, shortstops seldom covered second, and the second basemen had very little to do. Balls hit over the right- and left-field fences were ground rule doubles, with only pitches knocked over a limited area in center field being counted as home runs. Barton's drive evidently circumvented the rules by going *through* the screen.[66]

The Gophers added an insurance run in the seventh when Jones again reached on an error at first, and scored on a double by Bunch Davis. Trailing 5–3 in the bottom of the ninth, the Saints had one last rally in them. Bill Essick reached after one man was gone on an error by McMurray at second. Foster proceeded to walk pinch-hitter Jimmy O' Malley. After Rodebaugh flew out, Dunleavy singled to load the bases.[67]

Rube had recently written in Sol White's *Baseball Guide* that a pitcher with men on base should "not worry. Try to appear jolly and unconcerned. I have smiled often with the bases full with two strikes and three balls on the batter. This seems to unnerve them." Smiling or not, Foster got Lefty Davis to hit a "easy one" to the mound and the "championship of the state" belonged to the Gophers.[68]

A fourth game between the two teams was played the following afternoon, but it disintegrated into something of a farce before umpire "Perry Werden got mad and went home." Playing in frigid conditions before less than 100 people, neither team seemed to be trying very hard; the contest, replete with errors, passed balls, and wild pitches, ended in a 4–4 eight inning tie. Joining in on the fun was the Downtown Park's groundskeeper, Bill Le Claire, who managed a sacrifice and scored a run for the Saints.[69]

The Gophers closed their season on a sour note by losing five of their final games. One day after the Saints series, Reid's club returned to western Wisconsin for a rematch with Osceola before a huge swarm at the Polk County Fair. Thanks to the stellar work of backstop "Bat" Johnson and southpaw hurler Andy "Peaches" Nelson, who briefly appeared in the majors the following year with the Chicago White Sox, the Bethanias bested the Gophers for the second time in a month. Osceola's 5–0 triumph proved, if only to the local *Osceola Sun,* "how much better they are than the Gophers."[70]

The team spent the last weekend of the regular season in Minneapolis, taking on the

Faribault Flecks, the champs of the Sunday League. On Saturday September 28 at Nicollet Park, the Flecks clobbered the Gophers, 10–3, roughing up Johnny Davis for 15 hits, with most of these coming in their decisive six-run third inning. Fred Spencer had the Gophers' number this time, scattering eight hits and striking out eight batters.[71]

The next day, Faribault's second baseman Tousignant went three-for-four against Lytle and drove in all the Sunday Leaguer's runs in their 4–2 victory at the Minnehaha Driving Park. With two on and none out in the Gopher ninth, Charles McCleary, the former Waseca EACO pitcher, struck out Bunch Davis and induced Roberts to hit into a 4–6–3 game-ending double play.[72]

Although he had imported Rube Foster only a week earlier, Phil Reid was nevertheless indignant that Faribault had stocked their lineup with ringers, including several Toozes, and Peaches Graham, who caught the second game. The many Gopher backers were also at a loss, especially those who had been "offering any sort of money on their diamond heroes."[73]

In early October a makeshift Gophers squad played a couple of games back in Chicago. The team probably should have heeded Dave Wyatt's warning about what the local clubs would do to them if they came back to town with "swelled heads." A lineup consisting of Taylor, Roberts, Lytle, Barton, Johnny Davis plus a few lesser Chicago lights, including Harry Hyde and catcher Dick 'Noisy' Wallace, were pummeled, 10–4, by the Union Giants before being edged, 2–0, by the Felix Colts. The Giants were led by future Minneapolis Keystones "Topeka" Jack Johnson, who doubled and scored twice, and Charles Jessup, who stuck out five batters. The Colts game marked the first appearance in a Gopher uniform for hitting machine William Binga, who had recently been released by the Philadelphia Giants due to "rheumatism."[74]

Despite their poor finish, the season had been a resounding success, on and off the field. The club had turned a profit, played to huge crowds, and had traveled to places where no black team had gone before. Not counting the post-season contests in Chicago, the Gophers won a reported 92 games, lost only 15 and tied 2, good for a remarkable .880 winning percentage.[75]

Although the statistical information for the season is incomplete, it is a safe assumption that Lytle and Johnny Davis both won close to 30 games, and were responsible for most of the Gophers 25 shutouts. While not as prolific, Tommy Means allowed only 2.64 runs per game on average and didn't lose a decision all year. Offensively, Jesse Schaeffer led the team with a .320 batting average and a slugging percentage of .513, while everybody stole a lot of bases.[76]

Pundits all over the country were singing the Gophers' praises. Sol White claimed that the team, along with the Leland Giants, "had thrown the West in a fervor of enthusiasm that bids fair to culminate in the formation of a National League of Colored Baseball Teams." Hibbing's local paper called the club "a gentlemanly lot of young men," and noted how the Gophers were "a living example of what the colored man can and will do if given an opportunity." The *St. Paul Dispatch* rhapsodized that: "the Gophers have been a great advertisement to the city of St. Paul this season":

The St. Paul team is a wonder and would beat many of the American Association teams. They play with perfect system, winning by inside baseball. They never seem to get rattled. It is a high salaried aggregation and every player is a star, most of whom would be playing in the big leagues but for their color. An American League player who saw them play two games declares that their team play is equal to that of any team in America.[77]

Similarly, the Gophers had been impressed with Minnesota. George Taylor told the *Indianapolis Freeman* that "the Northwest is not only a good country for baseball, but good for any colored man that wants to work." Apparently, St. Paul wasn't quite far enough north for Willis Jones. After the season ended it was reported that the diminutive outfielder had packed his bags and moved to Montreal.[78]

Chapter Four

The Road Leads Somewhere

Although barred from Organized Baseball, the St. Paul Gophers pursued their living with a freedom ironically similar to that of the current major league ball player. Unlike the reserve clause-bound big leaguers of their day, the Gophers enjoyed total free agency, with the ability to improve their lot at a moment's notice. Hall of Fame shortstop John Henry "Pop" Lloyd summed up the financial attitudes of black ball players succinctly when he recalled, "Wherever the money was, that's where I was."[1]

And the money wasn't bad. According to Sol White the average black baseballist in 1906 made $466 for a five-and-a-half month season, roughly $85 a month. By comparison, most American workers of the era took home about $13 a week after laboring nearly 60 hours for a whopping 22 cents an hour. No Gopher ever earned as much as a mechanical engineer, who made about $5,000 in 1907, but playing ball beat teaching school, as teacher's salaries at that time came out to about $325 per year. It should be remembered too that the cost of living was cheaper 100 years ago; $1 back then bought as much as $22 does today. In 1907 a first class stamp cost two cents, sugar went for a nickel a pound, and for two dimes you could buy a pound of bacon. Arthur Hardy, who pitched during this era for the Topeka and Leland Giants, recalled that a good meal cost a quarter and a nice hotel room twice that amount.[2]

Despite operating in an era of great player mobility, the Gophers were a relatively stable franchise, with roster moves usually being the decision of the management and not the athlete. Even Gophers players who had short tenures with the club tended to stick around for at least 60 days, meaning that contracts were most likely of an eight-week duration that were either rolled over or terminated at the end of the second month.

The lack of substantial player jumping throughout most of the team's existence would also indicate that the front office had little trouble meeting payroll, and that they paid well. Little financial information about the Gophers has surfaced, but their salaries probably ranged from between $75 and $100 a month ($9,500 to $13,000 in the current economy). Prior to the 1909 season, former Gophers captain Jimmy Smith boasted that he would once again head up the club and that "the old three figures looks pretty good." Smith wasn't in a Gophers uniform when the season began, but "Rat" Johnson was, reportedly carrying a contract for that same "three figures." A century later, Yankee slugger Alex Rodriguez, who would not have been allowed to play in the majors in 1907, signed a contract guaranteeing him at least *eight* figures a year.[3]

Sol White also noted that minor leaguers (who were all white) made $571 on average during the 1906 season, over $100 more than black players, and that major leaguers (also all white) earned about $2,000 per man. While the disparity in pay between the two races was especially galling to White, it also reflected the fact that Organized Baseball generated bigger gates and more revenue than blackball. The patrons of the era had to plunk down a quarter to watch the Gophers play, with a grandstand seat (if there were any) going for 35 cents. If they didn't sneak in first, children under the age of 15 were usually admitted for a dime or 15 cents. As a point of contrast, general admission to a major league game during the deadball era cost around 50 cents, the grandstand 75 cents, and box seats went for a dollar and a half.[4]

The Gophers were able to keep their overhead low because their transportation and lodging expenses where often paid for by the cities they visited. For the most part, the officers of teams throughout the Upper Midwest were more than willing to meet the club's demands. Occasionally, though, a town would find the Gophers price too steep. The *Bemidji Daily Pioneer* reported in 1907 that:

> Walter Ball, the manager of the famous colored "Gopher" team of St. Paul, wrote here for a game next Sunday, but as the colored players wanted the Earth with a good sized picket fence around it, Manager Otto did not feel justified in signing a contract for their appearance here.

Two years later, the Gophers' terms were apparently more amenable to the good folks of Bemidji and they brought the club in for a couple of "splendid" ball games that were witnessed by "several hundred fans."[5]

The Gophers were generous and business savvy enough to keep their customers satisfied. When one of their games during the 1909 Fillmore County Fair was washed out by rain, the club charged the Fair organizers "no railroad fare at all and only one day's board, although they were here two days." The *Preston Times* complimented the Gophers, albeit backhandedly, by commenting, "People of our own race could not act "whiter" than this and needless to say the Fair management appreciates this."[6]

Not that the small town gentry were above trying to put one over on a black ball club. Before a contest with the Gophers in 1908 the management of the Red Wing, Minnesota, team tried to keep the substantial grandstand receipts for themselves, claiming they had not been included in the original contract. Only after the St. Paul squad refused to take the field was the dispute "easily settled." Likewise, after an overflow throng of about 3,500 people showed up for a 1909

George "Rat" Johnson, catcher extraordinaire and a three-figure salary recipient. (***Pine Island Record***, May 21, 1908; **Minnesota State Historical Society, St. Paul**)

game in Cogswell, North Dakota, the Gophers "demanded an additional bonus of $75" before they would play.[7]

Under Reid, the Gophers would forego a straight guarantee for their appearances in favor of a risky winner-take-all (or most) strategy; the St. Paul squad would receive 60 percent of the gate receipts if they won, or 40 percent if they lost. And as The *Lake Crystal Union* pointed out after a 1908 victory by the Gophers over their local club, "They always receive the 60 percent. They take care of this fact."[8]

A group of professional black ball players losing to a small town team was not only embarrassing, it was also very bad for business. In June 1909 the Long Prairie nine of central Minnesota took the first of a two-game set from the Gophers, bringing "a sharp reprimand from the manager and also one from the owner of the club which came over the telephone from St. Paul. The visitors knew it was up to them to do business or some one was going to lose a job."[9]

That the Gophers operated out of Minnesota was no coincidence. By the time the team set up shop in 1907, the state was emerging as one of the most progressive and quirkiest places in the country. Admitted to the Union in 1858, the "Land of Sky Blue Waters" was one of the first states to institute an income tax and to invest heavily in public education. Many late 19th and early 20th century Minnesota leaders were also reformers. Ignatius Donnelly, "Honest John" Lind, and John A. Johnson helped improve the economic status of farmers and common laborers by regulating the local railroads, milling companies, and insurance agencies. During this time the state also instituted a minimum wage for woman and children, established workers compensation insurance, and increased the amount it spent in caring for the mentally ill.[10]

Less progressive was Minnesota's attitudes towards indigenous peoples and famous criminals. One day after Christmas in 1862, 38 Santee Sioux were hung *en masse* at Fort Snelling in St. Paul as result of their participation in an armed uprising that summer. If President Abraham Lincoln had not intervened, 270 more of the Dakota would have also been put to death. Still, as one exuberant spectator exulted, the event proved to be "America's greatest mass execution."[11]

On September 7, 1876, the Jesse James–Cole Younger gang attempted to rob the First National Bank of Northfield, Minnesota, located 40 miles south of the Twin Cities. Accustomed to their fellow Missourians who had cheered on and abetted their illegal activities, the outlaws were horrified when the populace of Northfield not only shot back at them, but also organized a 2,000-strong posse that pursued them for several weeks. Frank and Jesse James eluded capture, but three of their fellow gang members were killed and the three Younger brothers were imprisoned in the Stillwater Penitentiary.[12]

The Gophers found themselves strangers in this strange land. Almost all of the state's nearly two million inhabitants were white and of Northern European ancestry. In 1907 there were only about 4,000 African Americans in Minnesota, of which around 1,500 lived in Minneapolis and slightly more than 2,200 called St. Paul home.[13]

African Americans had moved to Minnesota for the same reasons that everybody else did — the promise of employment, land, and a better way of life. As a Minneapolis black newspaper boasted in 1899, "There is not another city in the Union where white people are so friendly disposed toward African Americans." In reality, Twin City blacks faced major obstacles such as job discrimination, school segregation, and indifference by the much larger white populace.[14]

Twin City African Americans were mostly poor and working class. The men were generally employed as porters, cooks, waiters, and janitors by the local hotels, restaurants, and railroads. The women usually found work as domestic servants or laundresses. Because their pay scale was so low, only 45 percent of the black males and 58 percent of the black females in St. Paul could afford to get married in 1910.[15]

In 1900 almost 86 percent of the African Americans in St. Paul held the titles to their own homes, which was the highest percentage for any city in the entire United States. By 1910, though, St. Paul blacks possessed the deeds to only 28.7 percent of the properties they lived in, which was only slightly better than across the river in Minneapolis where only about 24.7 percent of the black residential units were self-owned.[16]

Confronted with such a minuscule and financially strapped black population, the Gopher brain trust quickly realized that they would need the patronage of fans of all colors for the team to succeed. In the spring of 1908 a letter by St. Paul lawyer William T. Francis was published in the *St. Paul Appeal*, the leading African American newspaper of the Twin Cities. The future United States minister to Liberia began his missive by extolling the virtues and achievements of the club while enthusing about its prospects during the upcoming season. Francis encouraged the public to turn out in large numbers whenever the Gophers were in town and closed his note by admonishing the behavior of some of the team's rowdier fans:

> The team should be encouraged by your presence and applause, but I desire to suggest to the rooters that they be extremely careful not to be offensive to the opposing players, and particularly to other attendants because by so doing you will injure the attendance and affect the financial interests by driving away regular patrons of the game. This criticism was made against the Gophers' games last season and let us see to it that it does not work an injury this season. Remember, that their financial success depends upon a large white attendance and we should not become so intoxicated with the success of our team that we will offend and discourage that attendance. Unnecessary boisterousness and loud bets should be dispensed with and each one should be assiduous in promoting good feeling in the audience. Don't be too quick in criticizing the decisions of the umpire, or in resenting some passing remark in the crowd. The team can play good enough ball to overcome those things. We can help most by always being good natured and respectful.[17]

Even though they turned out in droves to see the Gophers play ball, the attitudes of white Minnesotans towards African Americans were mostly ambivalent and sometimes downright hostile. In 1899 Governor John Lind enacted the Minnesota civil rights law which ostensibly prevented the color line from being drawn in such public places as restaurants, hotels, bars, and theaters. However, during the Black Elks convention in August 1908, the Hotel and Restaurant Keepers Association of St. Paul offered to foot the bill for the rental of the meeting's auditorium if the delegates would avoid their establishments. The Elks agreed to stay instead at the homes of local black residents and "a few of the less prominent hotels and restaurants." The following spring a brick was thrown through a black dentist's window in the Crocus Hill neighborhood of St. Paul in an attempt to drive him out of the area.[18]

In spite of such incidents, many of the nation's leading African Americans resided in the Twin Cities. In addition to William Francis who served as a presidential elector in 1920, the list of prominent black Minnesotans included journalist John Q. Adams, who transformed the *St. Paul Appeal* into one of the leading black newspapers in the country, and civil rights activist Frederick McGhee, who was instrumental in the creation of both the Niagara Movement and the National Association for the Advancement of Colored People

(NAACP). The Gophers were a point of pride for this burgeoning black professional class, and, according to Francis, were "one of the important Afro American enterprises of our city."[19]

The African Americans of St. Paul were justifiably proud of their team, but they were too few in number and too light in the pocketbook to warrant more than a handful of home games each year. As a result, the Gophers were compelled to barnstorm in order to make their money. After playing a few exhibitions with area minor league teams, the club would usually open their campaigns with a couple of weekend games in St. Paul. The team then took to the road for most of the summer, returning only for important series with local or national semi-pro squads.

Due to the inclement spring weather in the Upper Midwest, a typical Gophers season wouldn't really get going until early May, with games with clubs in western Wisconsin and southern Minnesota. The team would then venture west to the Dakotas and work their way back to St. Paul in July after trips to the Iron Range and northern Wisconsin. By the time August rolled around, the Gophers would head south for Iowa before returning to Minnesota for the county fair circuit and a late September contest in St. Paul to close the year out.

Because working people were most likely to attend a ball game on the weekends, the Gophers carefully scheduled the more lucrative Saturday and Sunday contests in the Twin Cities or large-sized towns like Fargo, North Dakota, or Stillwater, Minnesota. The team would also make their way to a relatively bigger burg on holidays, especially the Fourth of July, as witnessed in 1908 and 1909 when the Gophers played to "unusually large" crowds in Hibbing.[20]

Before each season began Irving Williams would write to prospective nines and place advertisements in the *St. Paul Pioneer Press* and the *Minneapolis Tribune* requesting that teams interested in scheduling the Gophers should "contact Secretary Williams at 40 East Third Street, St. Paul. T-3682-J." Williams would likewise contact managers of the minor league teams in Minnesota and Wisconsin to set up a few pre-season games for the club.[21]

Once on the road the Gophers would correspond with clubs in the general vicinity of where they were headed to fill out their schedule; open dates meant lost revenue and were to be avoided at all cost. When the Gophers were venturing back from South Dakota in July 1907, Irving Williams dashed a note off to the manager of the team in Edgerton, Minnesota, whom the Gophers had played on their way west:

> Mr. Meacham: I received yours today also a letter from Mr. Reid who states that your team is the best that he has met on his present trip and one of the best he has met this season. We are arranging a return home your way and will let you know in a day or two what date we will give you. Respectfully yours, Irving Williams.

Once the season started, the only off days the team had were the odd Monday or two, when attendance was bound to be light, or if a game was postponed by rain.[22]

The Gophers not only had a game if not two every day, but they usually played in a different city daily. From late April through August 1908 alone, the team journeyed over 5,000 miles to more than 70 towns in Minnesota, Michigan, Wisconsin, Iowa, and the Dakotas. Unlike the Negro Leaguers of the '20s and '30s who crisscrossed the country in buses and touring cars, the Gophers traveled exclusively and sometimes unpleasantly by train — the lack of air conditioned rail cars made for some miserably hot trips during July and August.[23]

The team often rode the rails with the very fans that came to see them play. After a September 1908 game at the Garden City Fair, the Gophers found themselves on a train "crowded to overflowing" with fairgoers, most of whom couldn't even stand, but had to just "hang on." A writer from the *Lake Crystal Union* complained that:

> One of the darkey ball players, on boarding the train at Garden City, sat his grip down in a seat and was standing in the middle of the car 10 feet away from it. A couple of ladies were trying to get a seat and they saw this one, so removed the grip and sat down. The black rascal yelled out, "that's my seat, get out of thar."

The less-than-enlightened reporter also griped that "if such an occurrence had taken place in the south the darkey would have been fired bodily off the train which he deserved."[24]

Because some of the distances between the cities they played in were quite long, the Gophers were obliged to leave a few games early and hustle to make their connection to the next scheduled town. The passenger cars the team road in were also at risk of being sidetracked in favor of freight trains which had the right of way. In August 1910, a wreck on the main railway line between Chippewa Falls and Spooner, Wisconsin, caused the club to miss a Saturday date with the Hayward, Wisconsin, nine. Fortunately, the two teams were able to make up the game as part of a doubleheader the following day.[25]

The willingness of the towns the Gophers visited to pick up their expenses helped keep them in business. By 1908 it cost about two cents per passenger per mile to travel by train, not counting the charges for meals or sleeping berths, which was a substantial cost for a major league club, let alone a barnstorming unit such as the Gophers. The team also depended on the decency of the towns where they played when looking for places to stay, since there wasn't always room, or tolerance, at the inn. Upon arriving in Rochester, Minnesota, one night in September 1907, the Gophers discovered that every hotel in town was "full." The team had to endure the humiliation of spending the night in the city jail, because, as one local paper put it, "that is one place of entertainment that never draws the color line."[26]

Not only was locating suitable lodging hard, but keeping the schedule full was also difficult. The competition for the small town dollar was fierce, with the Gophers vying for bookings with black clubs such as the Chicago Union Giants as well as other Midwest barnstormers such as Guy Green's Nebraska Indians, the Hopkins Brothers nine of Des Moines, Iowa, and various Bloomer Girl outfits. To keep the requests for games coming in, the Gophers had to be both great ball players *and* good entertainers.[27]

In his *Official Baseball Guide*, Sol White pointed out that while "the funny man in colored baseball is becoming extinct," most fans still went to games with black ball players hoping to be amused. According to contemporary accounts, the Gophers were a collection of "bright, mouthy fellows" whose "grotesque capers" and "droll remarks and witty sayings" kept their audiences "in a continuous uproar." The Gophers *modus operandi* was to grab an early lead over the home team, before switching gears and devoting their energies to "comedy stunts while waiting for the locals to come up within hailing distance on the score board."[28]

As a typical game unfolded, the Gophers would speak in a "rag time" style, sing "snatches of songs," hop about "like a chicken on a griddle," and spring "the usual end man gags." A large part of the team's act was trash talking their opponents. A nervous Lindstrom, Minnesota, nine discovered in 1908 that "the continued joshing of the Gophers was not of the nerve steadying variety." Former major leaguer Pink Hawley, pitching for the La Crosse Champs the previous summer, found the "funny things" the Gophers first base coach vocalized in his direction "particularly exasperating."[29]

Initially, Willis Jones was the Gophers player primarily responsible for injecting a dose of comedy when "the grandstand was not getting much baseball entertainment." After Jones left the club, Willie McMurray inherited the role of making "fine sport with the spectators" and keeping the Gopher's opponents "in a stew" with his "incessant talk." Since many of the team's games were one-sided affairs, the comedy routines ensured, in the words of a Fairmont, Minnesota, paper, "that a good many people stayed until the last dog was hung."[30]

The Gophers played during the height of the deadball era, so named because the baseballs used were a heavier, less tightly wound proposition than today's more easily driven spheres. These balls were rarely removed from play and if the pitchers weren't spitting on them, they were scuffing them and applying all sorts of substances to make the old horsehide swoop and dive away from the hitter. In this low scoring period, sacrifice bunts, stolen bases, and the hit-and-run were the order of the day. Most hitters choked up on the heavy, thick bats then in vogue with a split grip and they were more defensive at the plate, chopping down at pitches or slapping them, in the words of Baltimore Oriole great "Wee" Willie Keeler, "where they ain't."[31]

This was a fluid, fast paced brand of baseball with no stoppages for commercials or sausage races. The rhythm and quality of play were considered almost as important as the result. Most Gopher games lasted slightly less than two hours, although in 1909 they disposed of New Richland, Minnesota, in just 55 minutes. A year earlier, the Gophers and the Hibbing Colts were able to score a total of ten runs in a slugfest that took only one hour and 22 minutes to play.[32]

The advent of night baseball was still several years away. Most Gophers games were afternoon affairs that began at 3:00 P.M. During late June and early July the club would schedule some 6:00 evening contests in western Minnesota and North Dakota, where the longer days and higher latitudes would allow them to squeeze in a few after-supper innings.[33]

Along with their good humor and exciting style of play, the Gophers also brought a big league touch of class to the ball park. They quickly gained a reputation throughout the region as "a gentlemanly lot of fellows" who "govern themselves, both on and off the diamond in a manner deserving of respect." The *Ashland Daily Press* marveled that "a better behaved team, white or colored never visited Ashland."[34]

Although their manners and ball playing abilities were highly admired, newspapers throughout the Northwest commonly illustrated the Gophers appearances with cartoons that portrayed them as grinning caricatures with coal black skin, bug eyes and grotesquely thick lips. Midwestern scribes routinely referred to the Gophers as "coons," "darkies," "chocolate drops," and "niggers." The players on the club were also classified in print at various times as "dusky sons of Ham," "brunettes," and "colored monkeys."[35]

Not content to demean the Gophers with derogatory images or by name calling, the newspapermen would also infuse their game reports with ridiculous dialects that the Gophers supposedly used. The *Alexandria Post News* alleged that a Gopher player approached the Alexandria bench during a 1907 game shouting, "Look here, Id want to see the size of dem bats. Dey looks awful big and powerful to me." When the black club dropped a couple of games in Chisholm, Minnesota, the local paper crowed, "Mammy's baby din lost all de bacon." The *Chisago County Free Press* chose to recap the 1909 game between the Gophers and the Lindstrom, Minnesota, team this way:

> An, lo and behold sah, our boys done got licked ba dose jolly niggahs, and aftah de big game was clear thru, sah, dem niggahs had some fine old juicy watermelon on de Lindstrom folks. Oh lordy way up in de sky, how dose niggahs did toss det er ball around.[36]

Chasing victories and stereotypes. A cartoon printed in the *St. Paul Dispatch* prior to a Gophers-Minneapolis Toozes game. (*St. Paul Dispatch*, May 8, 1907; Minnesota State Historical Society, St. Paul)

Occasionally, racist feelings would spill into the grandstand or onto the playing field. A 1908 game in Viroqua, Wisconsin, turned ugly when "someone on the sidelines made a remark in rooting that injured the feelings of the visitors, and from that time they hardly conducted themselves as gentlemen." During the latter stages of their 4–3 victory, the Gopher batters struck out on purpose and "seemed to be mad all the time." One of Viroqua's papers believed that "it would be better in the future for the management to pass up organizations of this kind, if the unpleasantness of Sunday is to be repeated."[37]

A year later in Hankinson, North Dakota, a club was hurled at one of the Gophers from the third base bleachers by a "stranger" who was "roundly hissed at." In 1910, members of the Minot, North Dakota, Magicians made some derogatory comments during a 10–6 victory over the St. Paul nine. To add injury to insult, three Gophers were hit by pitches thrown by "Doc" Spillane, the Minot starter. According to a local reporter:

> The race question entered into things yesterday to an unfortunate degree. However, the attendance is paying to see the game and not to hear the individual opinions of the players on a subject that is so much mooted. The Gophers are to be congratulated on their forbearance. It stamps the man.[38]

The Gophers preferred not to get mad, but to get really even. The team responded to the Magicians' slurs by easily winning the four remaining games in the series, and the Gophers pitchers knocked down *four* Minot batters.[39]

Another occupational hazard for a black traveling team was biased umpiring. As Daddy Reid put it, "Most every place we play we have to stack up against ten men, the players and the umpire—and we rather expect it." Reid wasn't just crying in his beer. The *Zumbrota News* reported that during a 1907 game with Red Wing, Minnesota, an umpire named Kolbe twice "called two Gopher runners who were safe by a mile, out." Inconsistent strike zones and bad calls were the norm, forcing Gophers hitters to swing at nearly everything, "even wild pitches."[40]

Not surprisingly, Alexandria and Hibbing, the two most successful Minnesota town teams of the era, were among the biggest culprits when it came to "home cooking." The Gophers wouldn't play Alexandria in 1908 because the umpiring in that city "usually favors the home team" and the following spring the club dropped a contest in Hibbing after some "decidedly lumpy" calls that went against them. The St. Paul nine ran into a Hibbing signal caller in 1911 who had apparently worked "in a guessing factory one summer" and whose "raw" calls were so bad that only the visitors "gentlemanly" nature prevented a fight from breaking out.[41]

When the Gophers suspected they were going to get a really raw deal they would insist on a two-man umpiring crew—one hometown and one Gopher ump to maintain balance. If the Gophers weren't happy with the local arbiter's performance they would use their pull to have him replaced, as they did to poor Joe Maloney of Sheldon, Iowa, in 1908. If the calls were particularly bad the club would leave the field and threaten to quit if the decisions didn't improve. Most of the time, however, the Gophers refrained from wrangling and kicking about bad calls.[42]

The small town ball parks the Gophers played in also left something to be desired, and the bucolic nature of these fields lent a comic although sometimes dangerous touch to their games. While going after a fly ball during a 1907 contest with the Gophers, Red Wing right fielder George Thompson cut the palm of his hand on a barbed wire fence and had to leave the game. Earlier that summer, a Sioux Falls, South Dakota, right fielder had slipped in an outfield covered with quack grass and reeds while chasing a Gopher drive. Three Gopher runs scored on the play and the ball was not found for 20 minutes.[43]

Phil Reid's club was ready to play ball, no matter what the conditions. A team from Lake Crystal, Minnesota, traversed to nearby Mankato for a 1908 game with the Gophers even though "the diamond was more like a stock yard than anything seen outside of a cattle pen." There was "mud and water everywhere" and "not one inch of dry ground was visible to put your foot upon." The Gophers won handily and the Lake Crystal management had to shell out four bucks to repair the field. Conversely, a club from Sherburn, Minnesota, ducked out of a September 1909 match with the Gophers because the grounds they were to play on were wet and the grass was three feet high in the outfield — there would be no lost balls for the Sherburn lads.[44]

For their home games in St. Paul, the Gophers rented out the tiny Downtown Park, which was nestled snugly between Robert, Minnesota, 12th, and 13th streets in the shadow of the new State Capitol building. Due to the "pillbox's" intimate dimensions, home plate was situated so close to the stands that it was not visible to many spectators. The fans' view was also obstructed by the protective wire screen that covered the grandstand and bleachers, but did not protect umpires and visiting players from the clearly audible taunts of hecklers The field itself had no drainage system to speak of and quickly became a quagmire when it rained.[45]

Protests from a nearby church prevented usage of the Downtown Park on the Sabbath. Because of the Sunday ban and the fact that the small stadium could only hold a few thousand patrons, the Gophers played several contests at the more spacious Lexington Park. Located about one mile west of downtown St. Paul, Lexington was a pitcher's paradise compared to the pillbox, with the stadium's nearest outfield fence (until it was renovated in 1909) being a remote 570 feet from home plate. The Gophers also played a few times at Premo Park on St. Paul's west side.[46]

Before there was a Metrodome. The Downtown Park, St. Paul, MN, 1909. (*St. Paul Pioneer Press*, April 23, 1909; Minnesota State Historical Society, St. Paul)

When the Gophers ventured down river to Minneapolis, their games usually took place at storied Nicollet Park, the home of the American Association's Millers. Nicollet, which could be found a short distance south of the city's downtown core, was notable mainly for a cozy 279-foot right field porch and its proximity to a confluence of local street car lines. The Gophers also played some of their Mill City contests within the confines of the Minnehaha Driving Park, a horse racing track in southeastern Minneapolis.[47]

During their heyday, the Gophers received fairly good coverage from the five daily newspapers in the Twin Cities: The *St. Paul Pioneer Press*, *St. Paul Dispatch*, *St. Paul Daily News*, *Minneapolis Tribune*, and the *Minneapolis Journal*. All five papers carried photographs, information and game reports about the team, with the *Pioneer Press*, *Dispatch*, and *Tribune* being the most consistent. Two young Minneapolis sportswriters were especially helpful allies. Frank E. Force and I.J. Hentschell, both of the *Minneapolis Tribune*, gave a lot of ink to the Gophers and also organized and umpired many of their games.[48]

The major African American paper in town, John Q. Adams' *St. Paul Appeal*, also did its best to promote the team, but it didn't have the resources or column inches to write about the squad with much depth. Coverage of the Gophers activities improved drastically in the spring of 1910, when a second black weekly, the *Twin City Star*, began publication. Founded by Phil Hale and Charles Smith, members of the local Colored Waiters Union, the *Star* ran items on the Gophers in nearly every issue, with occasional analysis of the team and their games. It surely didn't hurt that Irving Williams, the secretary of the Gophers, was also a trustee of the paper.[49]

Unfortunately, the rural newspapers around the Midwest didn't always share the *Star's* enthusiasm or grasp the true significance of the Gophers visits. Many times if a small town team played well against the Gophers or even won, the entire play-by-play of the contest would be published in the local rag along with the box score and a game commentary. Losses by the hometown team, though, were mentioned briefly in passing if at all. After the Gophers demolished the P.V. Lands team of Redwood Falls, Minnesota, in 1909, the *Redwood Reveille* noted, "We could find no one willing to furnish a write up of Wednesday's game with the Colored Gophers." The paper rationalized the defeat by musing that "it was a hard jolt such as we all get occasionally when we get out of our class."[50]

Before the advent of radio and television, the small town papers were *the* vehicle in which a traveling ball club like the Gophers could publicize their games. A couple of times each season, Reid and Williams would assemble the club for a team portrait and would then forward these photos to the newspapers in the towns in which they were headed to play. The photos would usually run a week or two before the upcoming contest, with a little blurb about the squad and the relevant date, time, and price of admission. Handbills and posters were also nailed up in advance of the team's arrival and it is possible that the Gopher management tried to generate a little publicity and extra income by selling postcards of the team when they hit town.[51]

In the spring of 1908, individual shots of Gopher players in various states of action, such as winding up or catching a ball, were photographed at the Downtown Park. These same portraits would continue to be published in the region's papers for many years to come, even after the players pictured had left the squad. Thus the 1908 images of Gopher players Haywood Rose and Willis Jones were printed in a 1910 issue of the *Waconia Patriot*, with captions identifying them as Armstrong and McDougall, two then members of the team. In April 1910 the Collins company of St. Paul took some studio photographs of individual players, but only a small handful of these surfaced in the local press.[52]

Along with the mismatched photographs there was some confusion as to the moniker the team was advertised under. Daddy Reid probably named his ball club after the Gopher lodge of the Black Elks to which he belonged. The use of a small burrowing rodent as a symbol for Minnesota dates back to a 1857 political cartoon that depicted nine gophers bearing the visages of local railroad tycoons. During 1907 the team was often referred to as simply the St. Paul Gophers, and the player's shirts and caps bore the "STPG" logo. Perhaps to avoid confusion with the University of Minnesota's teams that were also named the Gophers, the club's management and the mainstream press began calling the squad the "Colored Gophers," and it was under this appellation that they were most commonly known.[53]

Of more pressing concern to the Gophers than their name was the strong opposition provided by amateur teams in towns like Faribault and Albert Lea, Minnesota — places that would continue to field excellent baseball clubs throughout much of the next century. The team also took on many salaried outfits in cities such as Virginia, Minnesota, Charles City, Iowa, and Devils Lake, North Dakota, that were as good if not better than the independent league clubs of the present day. In the same class with the Charles City's of the world were Twin City semi-pro nines like Sam Coughlin's Austin-Westerns or Henry Martin's H.P. Conrads whom the St. Paul club battled on a regular basis. Many of the teams the Gophers encountered employed players who had spent time at some level of professional baseball.[54]

It was not unusual for amateur and semi-pro teams to hire a ringer or two or three to strengthen their squad before taking on the Gophers. The tradition of importing quality players to ambush a superior opponent is as old as baseball itself, but it didn't always work against the Gophers. Mazeppa, Minnesota, brought a ringer to face the St. Paul club in 1907, but "he did not play well" and the home team was crushed, 28–0. Other Gopher opponents such as Wycoff and Winnebago, Minnesota, were also let down by hired guns, who financially drove them "still deeper in the local mine," but generally "did not do as well as the home men."[55]

Pitching is the great equalizer in baseball and those twirlers who had any kind of success against the Gophers, like former Waseca lefty Charles McCleary or ex–White Sox and Millers ace Roy Patterson, were brought in numerous times to face the club. The cost to a small town team could be steep, though, as a good semi-pro pitcher of the time could command up to $20 (about $400 nowadays) for a big game.[56]

Willis Jones was the Gophers left fielder and chief comedian from 1907–1908. In 1908, the fleet-of-foot base runner stole 48 bases before the first of August. (*Alexandria Post News*, June 10, 1909; Minnesota State Historical Society, St. Paul)

Ringers aside, the Gophers usually had the game won before they even took the field. Facing off against the Gophers in 1907, the Crookston aggregation developed "a bad case of stage fright" it was reported after their 13–1 loss, "and some have not recovered yet." Nervous Gopher opponents were prone to making errors, throwing wild pitches, giving up a boat load of walks, fighting amongst themselves, and swinging wildly at any pitch thrown to them. After the St. Paul club thumped the Waconia, Minnesota, nine 14–6 in 1910, the local paper bemoaned "the balloon trip by 'our boys' who promptly went into the air at the call of 'play ball.'" The Gophers scored three runs in the second inning without the benefit of a hit "and when they got on the bases went around like a wheel, and so fast you could hardly see the spokes, making the local boys dizzy. They cannot be run down between the bases, or tagged at the bag any more than a lot of cats."[57]

Although their players may not have looked forward to seeing the Gophers arrive in town, the managers of the small town teams certainly did. A ball club was a costly enterprise and a visit by a squad such as the Gophers pulled many teams out of the red ink and into the black. During the Gophers' era, it took about $600 to get a small town team off the ground, the seed money being raised mostly through subscriptions from the local citizenry and fundraisers such as dances. Once the season got under way the majority of team's cash overlay was spent on salaries, but there was also a myriad of other expenses including advertising, long distance telephone charges, building materials for the grandstands, lodging, transportation, uniforms, umpire fees, and the cost of bats and balls.[58]

The large crowds the Gophers attracted translated into big gate receipts, even though the usually vanquished local clubs only received 40 percent of the cut. The small town moguls weren't going to get rich, but they could at least keep their hometown team afloat for another glorious summer or two. In 1908, Gophers' adversary Charles City, Iowa, reported a profit of $45.90 and the town team in Red Wing claimed to have $581.27 in the bank at season's end. On the other hand the Gophers played the Hibbing Colts 14 times in 1909, but that didn't prevent Judge Brady's club from losing over $1,000.[59]

When the game was over and they were counting up their winner's share of the receipts, the ever gracious Gophers usually made a point of complimenting their opponents. In the summer of 1907 alone, Phil Reid told the respective managers of the Caledonia, Edgerton, Wessington Springs, Hibbing, Rochester, and Harmony nines that *their* club was "the hardest battling team they had run across this season."[60]

Reid's team had to walk the fine line of keeping their ball games fun and competitive, while making sure that they always came out on top. In fact there is some evidence that the Gophers followed a distinct formula. Canadian author John Craig spent a summer before the Second World War playing first base on former Gopher Chappie Johnson's barnstorming All-Stars. In his autobiographical novel *Chappie And Me*, Craig recounts how Johnson instructed his team to beat the clubs they played by exactly *two* runs:

> That was the margin Chappie liked best. He was dead set against running up the score because "rubbin' it in gets people's blood angry." On the other hand, one-run leads made him uneasy. "Never can tell in this game," he said. "Now say we got one run on them, and they comin' up in the ninth. 'Spose they puts a runner on some way. Then 'spose somebody gets lucky 'n hits one out. It can happen. Ain't just that we lose, but maybe other teams start thinkin' they can beat us. And then it ain't so nice any more."

With Johnson at the helm in 1908, the Gophers won eight games by the two-run advantage he preferred and 11 times they triumphed by three runs. After a close decision over Albert Lea it was reported "that the Gophers kept two runs ahead at all times." It must have been a nerve-wracking year for the great catcher, though, as the team was involved in at least 21 one-run contests, eight of which they lost.[61]

To avoid embarrassing a small town team, the Gophers were known to let up a little on the throttle once the game was in hand to avoid scoring more runs. When the St. Paul squad demolished the Aberdeen White Stars, 17–3, in 1907, the feeling was that they could have won 50–0 "if they so chose." In the eighth inning, Sherman Barton grew so bored with the proceedings that he doubled to center with a one-handed swing. Following one Gophers game in Grand Forks, North Dakota, it was noted, "After making enough scores to keep the victory safe, they did not attempt to run the bases, unless some member of the team became ambitious and wanted a little exercise." If they were feeling especially magnanimous, the Gopher pitchers would also let their opponents score a run or two. After a 1910 Gophers thrashing of their local heroes, a paper in Fairmont, Minnesota, claimed, "When they allow an ordinary team to score at all it is purely an act of Christian charity."[62]

It was this penchant for mercy and their amazing skill that won the team fans all over the Upper Midwest. The scribes in Red Wing were amazed in 1907 when 90 percent of the locals on hand pulled for the Gophers in their game with the home town Furriers: "One would naturally suppose that these fans would prefer to see their own race win, but they swarmed around the negroes like bees, cheering them on to victory." A similar scene occurred a few years later in Hibbing when a large Sunday crowd "found that there was not opportunity enough to root for the home team, it rooted for the visitors. It just had to root for somebody, you know."[63]

Prior to the country's entry into the First World War, baseball provided a welcome diversion for small town America. The game was often the only athletic activity and entertainment around. A

Sherman Barton was the Gophers center fielder from 1907 through 1910. According to the *Indianapolis Freeman*, "When it comes to fielding and retiring runners, Bucky Barton of the St. Paul Gophers ranks with the big leaguers." (*Redwood Falls Gazette*, September 15, 1909; Minnesota State Historical Society, St. Paul)

town's baseball team was a symbol of community pride, a means of demonstrating a city's quality, and a vessel through which people might cope with the alienation of rural life.[64]

The Gophers provided a unique experience when they came to town. Prior to a 1908 game in Renville, the local paper exhorted everybody in the area to "come and have a good time once in your life" while reminding them to "just reflect how long you will watch the growing daisies upside down after you are dead." The year before the Gophers had played a Fourth of July game in Caledonia, Minnesota, to over 3,000 enthusiastic fans:

> Early in the morning the teams began to roll into town from the surrounding country bringing in the farmers and their families. The morning passenger train from the west brought about 500 people from Spring Grove and other towns on the Preston branch. People were packed like sardines in the cars while others rode on top of the coaches and even on the coal in the tender.[65]

If the Gophers were in a city for a weekday game, it not uncommon for children to be let out early from school in order to watch them play or for the local businesses to close for the duration of the contest. Upon their arrival the club might be serenaded by that great American tradition, the marching band. After the Gophers disembarked in Langford, South Dakota, for a game in 1907, "the band boys and the ball teams formed in line at the opera house and marched to the ball park, followed by one of the largest crowds that ever assembled on the local grounds." The Gophers and the Langford nine eventually got down to business, but not until "every seat in the grandstand" was occupied and "a long string of carriages lined both sides of the diamond."[66]

The enormity of the Gophers' talents and the unfairness of their plight were not lost on the places they visited. Over and over again it was remarked that they were "some of the best ball players in the United States, players who but for their color would be in the big leagues." Not that the Gophers needed to be reminded of this fact.[67]

Chapter Five

Cutting a Wide Swath
(January–June 1908)

Because 1907 had been one of the most lucrative blackball seasons ever, many wheeler-dealers were eager to form a league to cash in on the situation. A few organizational meetings were held involving owners and managers from Cleveland, Cincinnati, Detroit, Kansas City, St. Louis, Pittsburgh, Chicago and Louisville, but scheduling conflicts and lack of financing ultimately doomed the circuit before it began. As the average distance between St. Paul and the proposed towns was over 500 miles, the Gophers were not included in any of the league talk.[1]

Back in the Saintly City, Reid and Hirschfield focused their intentions on building the best ball club that money could buy — a concept that would be lost on the vast majority of subsequent Minnesota team owners. Irving Williams was dispatched to Chicago in early 1908 to sign players for the upcoming campaign, and upon his return to the Twin Cities in March he boasted he had assembled a team that would "cut a wide swath."[2]

Dude Lytle, Bunch Davis, Will McMurray, Willis Jones, and Sherman Barton all returned from the previous year's squad, but aging veterans such as George Taylor and Pop Roberts had been axed. New to the team were three of the most significant players and leaders in blackball history: catcher George "Rat" Johnson, pitcher "Big" Bill Gatewood, and second baseman Felix Wallace.[3]

Since leaving the Renville All-Stars following their 1905 championship, Rat Johnson had played a couple of seasons out east with the Philadelphia Giants and Brooklyn Royal Giants, as well as two winter ball campaigns with Havana of the Cuban league. The 13-year blackball vet, whom Hall of Fame Cubs manager Frank Chance once called the greatest catcher in America, was renowned for his throws down to second that were so fast and so accurate "as to discourage all attempts to steal." The new Gophers captain was an innovator who caught with one hand long before it was fashionable, and, according to onetime teammate Fred Langford, later traversed the country teaching players how to line the inside of their catchers' mitts with goose feathers. The dignified yet flamboyant backstop would psych out opponents by telling them what pitches were coming and was known to kneel in silent prayer at home plate before batting.[4]

"Chappie," as he later became known, dressed in the latest styles off the field, including spats and a walking cane, unencumbered by his baggage, which was carried by a personal valet. He was also camera shy or perhaps superstitious. In almost every known photograph of the legendary catcher, he never looks directly into the camera, preferring to stare off into the distance. More importantly, the 32-year-old Johnson was probably the first black coach in Organized Baseball history, spending several spring trainings around this time tutoring fledgling pitchers for the Boston Nationals, St. Paul Saints, and other "big teams." While out east, the Rat was said to have taught the rudiments of pitching to a young Rube Waddell.[5]

FIVE • *Cutting a Wide Swath (January–June 1908)* 65

1908 St. Paul Gophers (early season). Back Row (Left to right): George "Rat" Johnson (C), Howard Petway (P), Phil Reid (Owner), John Hirschfield (Treasurer), Sherman Barton (CF), Haywood Rose (1B). Middle Row (Left to right): Frank Davis (SS), William McMurray (3B), Irving Williams (Secretary), Clarence Lytle (P), Bill Gatewood (P). Front Row (Left to right): Willis Jones (LF), Team Mascot, Felix Wallace (2B). (*Red Wing Daily Republican*, June 26, 1908; Minnesota State Historical Society, St. Paul)

In sharp contrast to the measured, composed Johnson was his new batterymate: a volatile, hard living 26-year-old from San Antonio named William Gatewood. After paying his dues in the Texas Colored League, the 6'7", 240-pound flame-thrower had crashed into the big time with the Leland Giants in 1906. Playing in Florida that winter, he helped a team of blackball players cum waiters from the Royal Poinciana and Breaker's hotels defeat a squad of white major leaguers representing the Palm Beach and Miami resorts. With the score knotted at one in the last of the ninth of the seventh and final game, the strong-hitting Gatewood singled home the winning run and was carried off the field by a throng of "frenzied" supporters.[6]

Gatewood had a sub-par year pitching for Leland in 1907 and it was cryptically noted that "he is a good man when in condition." Being "out of condition" was an euphemism for drunkenness and carousing in the vernacular of the early 20th century sporting press. Big Bill was known to drink an entire bottle of corn whiskey before games in which he was scheduled to pitch. After watching Gatewood do this many times without any seeming ill effects, an astounded rookie once asked the pitcher about his odd habit. "This is only water," the novice was told. "The people think it's liquor, and they are amazed I can still pitch. It's all for show."[7]

Show or not, controversy would shadow Gatewood throughout his lifetime. The big right-hander possessed a nasty temper and a well deserved reputation for throwing at batters. Both attributes were on display during a game in June 1921 when the well traveled veteran took the mound for the Detroit Stars against August Molina's Cuban Stars. Apparently upset over an argument he had with a teammate just before the contest, Gatewood threw his first pitch right at the leadoff man's head, and proceeded to drive the Cubans "all over the lot as they ducked his dusters." As the game developed the Cuban players soon began protesting that Big Bill's pitches were doing "funny things." After two balls were found to possess nicks, Gatewood was searched by the umpire and more than a half dozen bottle caps were discovered in the pitcher's hip pocket. Remarkably, the unrepentant twirler stayed in the game and commenced a pattern of forcing the Cubans off the plate early in the count before breaking over a "couple of curves" to finish them off. When it was all said and done, Gatewood had struck out ten batters en route to a 4–0 victory and the first no-hitter in Negro League history.[8]

As a Gopher, however, Gatewood was still trying to establish himself as a big-time pitcher. He had traveled to Cuba during the fall of 1907 as a member of a Philadelphia Giants squad that included Johnny Davis, but he lost all three games he started and went hitless in 21 at-bats. Gatewood opened 1908 with the Leland Giants, but after pitching ineffectually in their opener against the Logan Squares and committing a costly error in a 4–1 loss to the Spaldings, he found himself in Daddy Reid's employ.[9]

The young hurler arrived in the Gophers camp with "an easy motion that brings out wonderful speed — His spitter is a marvel; he has control and curves that break like the gustful winds of March." When he was hitting on all cylinders, the *St. Paul Dispatch* marveled, "No pitcher around these parts can touch him.... The way he mixes up the slow ones and fast ones, the drops and the dope balls, the corner cutters and the breaks is a revelation." Said to possess a fastball as good as the Cubs' Ed Ruelbach or any other "pitcher who wears a toe plate," Gatewood could throw the sphere so hard that "even his catcher didn't see much of it, except the jar of his arms when the ball hit his mitt."[10]

Another teammate of Gatewood's in Cuba, infielder extraordinaire Felix Wallace, also came north with the 1908 Gophers. Born in Owensboro, Kentucky, in 1882, the one-time tobacco steamer began his baseball career with the Paducah, Kentucky, Nationals in 1903 before moving on to the New York–based Cuban Giants in 1906 for a couple of seasons. Wallace had no equal during the first two decades of the century at shortstop *or* second base. Possessing tremendous range, he was very fleet of foot, a clever base runner, and a steady, clutch hitter to boot. According to a report in the *St. Paul Dispatch*, "Wallace at second could not be improved upon and reminds one of Miller Huggins, in that he makes most of his throws to first with that quick short arm motion while standing in almost any position." While in Cuba Hall of Famer John Henry Lloyd was moved over to second to make way for Wallace at short, where his "splendid" defensive plays drew ovations from the Havana fans.[11]

The Gophers vacant first base position was filled by 35-year-old Haywood "Kissing Bug" Rose, a longtime player for the Chicago Unions, Union Giants, and Leland Giants, who was said to be "head and shoulders" better than the departed George Taylor. Rose's colorful nickname was possibly based on his ability to "eat 'em up at first" — kissing bugs are a rather nasty species of insect that transforms "from being flat as a wafer to a globular form" while feeding on vertebrate blood.[12]

The new first sacker was said to be "worth the price of admission all by himself" and was "one of the best coaches in the business, and an equally good "jollier." Rose knew that discretion was sometimes the better part of valor. While playing for the Algona Brownies in 1901, he let an easy pop-up fall to the ground during a game in Chamberlain, South Dakota, after an irate cowboy shouted, "Drop it, nigger, or else." Kissing Bug was also a fine catcher with a strong arm who was once compared favorably to Cubs' great Johnny Kling.[13]

Left-hander Howard Petway, the Gophers' other new pitcher, hailed, like Rose, from Nashville, Tennessee. The older brother of catching great Bruce Petway, the "clever little southpaw" had been part of the Leland Giant rotation along with Bill Gatewood in 1906. The 24-year-old Petway threw sidearm and was said to possess a good changeup and "mudball."[14]

Haywood "Kissing Bug" Rose "ate em up" at first for the Gophers in 1908. (*Waconia Patriot*, August 12, 1910; Minnesota State Historical Society, St. Paul)

Johnny Davis had followed up his stellar 1907 season with the Gophers by pitching well for the Philadelphia Giants in Cuba that fall, winning seven games while posting a minuscule 0.68 ERA. Five of his victories came over Cuban Hall of Famers Luis Padron, Jose Munoz (twice), and Emilio Palomino. Both Davis and Felix Wallace played a Cuban league game for Fe in January 1908, before hopping on the S.S. *Proteus* en route to New Orleans. Curiously, Davis and Jesse Schaeffer were absent from the Gophers camp when the team began training, although they soon resurfaced on the roster of the Galesville Grays of western Wisconsin. It is unclear whether the pair was released by the Gophers or if they defected on their own, but it proved to be a costly move for Schaeffer who never again had a season like he did in 1907.[15]

The two professionals took their new assignment seriously ("Both are hard workers in practice. They don't loaf") but this didn't prevent Davis from getting off to a slow start in which he lost his first four decisions. The Grays didn't always give the little right-hander the best support in the field, which deteriorated further when Schaeffer and his .320 batting average left the club in mid–July. Davis rallied to finish the season with a 10–6–1 record while giving up, according to surviving accounts, about 3.66 runs per game. As it turned out, both Davis and Schaeffer would cross the Gophers' path before the summer was over.[16]

The Gophers went into training in Chicago during the middle of April, in preparation for a series of games with clubs from the Wisconsin–Illinois League. After an April 26 game against the semi-pro Alamos in Chicago didn't come off, the team opened their season three days later at wintry Riverview Park with an 8–3 thumping of Duluth of the Northern League. Petway allowed only four hits and struck out six to pick up the win while Barton collected two safeties including a double.[17]

The club had the tables turned on them the following afternoon at Rockford, Illinois, when the Wisconsin–Illinois Leaguers set them down, 7–1, on another cold and raw day.

The Gophers jumped off to an early 1–0 lead, but Rockford employed the sacrifice bunt to great effect against Gatewood and won going away. The *Rockford Daily Register Gazette* condescendingly noted that the Gophers were "exceedingly merry" at the outset of the contest but that:

> The gleeful gab was replaced by clam-like silence and they showed all the characteristics of the race. The way they quit when the white folks got ahead would have furnished a nice sermon for Booker Washington could he have viewed it.[18]

Haywood Rose was injured during the Rockford game and was replaced in the lineup by Willie Green, "a former St. Louis boy" who had been listed on the Gophers pre-season roster. With Green in-tow the Gophers ventured to Madison, Wisconsin, to take on the minor leaguers there. The St. Paul club fell behind 5–1 and 5–0 in their two games with the Colts, but they rallied for a 5–5, 14-inning tie in the first contest and won the second 8–7. Gatewood relieved in both games and hit a two-run homer to key the comeback in the first tussle.[19]

The Gophers concluded the minor league portion of their schedule by dropping two games to the Oshkosh, Wisconsin, Indians by 8–5 and 6–1 scores. The shortstop for the Indians was 18-year-old Henry "Heinie" Groh, just beginning a storied baseball career in which he played in five World Series and hit .292 over 16 major league seasons. The man who became famous for his milk bottle bat singled three times off of Bill Gatewood in his professional debut, "and still the big fellow smiled." The Gophers were less pleased with the "lively banter" of Joe Graggion, the Oshkosh second baseman, and "every move he made was commented on by the Gophers with exaggerated applause or wholehearted criticism."[20]

The Gophers found the going a little easier the next couple of weeks as they toyed with a series of town teams in western Wisconsin and southern Minnesota. The club started the tour on May 11 with a 10–0 five-inning thrashing of Grand Rapids, Wisconsin (present day Wisconsin Rapids), in which "they ran the bases until they were tired" which in turn "made the crowd tired." A couple of days down the line Bill Gatewood registered the squad's third shutout in a row when they downed Johnny Davis, Jesse Schaeffer and their Galesville compatriots, 6–0. A week later the Gophers defeated the Dodge Center, Minnesota, nine, 9–4, but the story of this game was the performance of Lynch, the local catcher. In the first inning a foul tip broke a small bone in the unfortunate receiver's throwing hand and he lost a nail on the same appendage in the second, but he nevertheless caught all nine frames.[21]

Willie Green was gone and "Kissing Bug" Rose still out of the lineup when Reid's club arrived back in St. Paul in late May. Even more distressing to the Gopher management was the fact that they were no longer the only game in town — a new African American club called the Minneapolis Keystones was on the prowl and looking to steal the Gophers' thunder.

Although they are collectively known as the Twin Cities, the denizens of Minneapolis and St. Paul have conducted a spirited rivalry for much of their more than 150-year existences. Minneapolis, "the first city of the West," progressive and Protestant, has historically been a town primarily interested in profit and industry, be it lumber, flour or technology. St. Paul, "the last city of the East," working class and Catholic, is the seat of the state capitol and has defined itself over the years through its diverse neighborhoods and by being all things "not Minneapolis." Minneapolis was a planned municipality, while a future governor of Minnesota would claim that the maze-like streets of St. Paul were laid out by drunken

Irish workmen. The main fact to know about the two cities, a 1930s *Fortune* magazine article asserted, was that "they hate each other." It was only natural that after the Gophers were organized in St. Paul, a black team from across the river would rise up to challenge them.[22]

The new club was the brainchild of a young flamboyant African American saloon owner called "Kidd" Mitchell. Born in Little Rock, Arkansas, around 1880, Edward Franklin Mitchell soon headed north as did many other ambitious black southerners of his time and somewhere along the way was taken under the wing of Chicago politician and blackball bigwig, Major Robert R. Jackson. By 1906 Mitchell was running the Keystone Hotel and Buffet, located at 1313 Washington Avenue in downtown Minneapolis, where one could get a drink as well as "rooms and meals by the day, week, or month — Special rates for theatrical people."[23]

Like Phil Reid, Mitchell was a proud member of the fraternal groups, the Black Elks and most notably, the Knights of Pythias, where he ascended to the uniformed rank of Colonel. But the "Kidd" was flashier than his St. Paul counterpart and possessed a great deal of personal jewelry or "bling" long before it became fashionable. The *Indianapolis Freeman* marveled: "Say! Didn't Kidd Mitchell wear some few diamonds! He is certainly worth talking about."[24]

The "diamond bedecked manager" was quick tempered, tight-fisted, and litigious. Under his direction the Keystones would cancel dates or refuse to play if the financial terms were not to their liking and on at least two instances the Kidd instigated lawsuits over alleged breach of contract. In 1908 Mitchell and his Keystones began a melee in Superior, Wisconsin, when they exhibited "a few guns in attempts to awe their opponents." A year later the Kidd pulled a firearm during an altercation in Waterville, Minnesota.[25]

The Colonel had a knack for irritating almost everyone he came into contact with. Tobe Smith, who owned the Kansas City, Kansas, Giants, once accused Mitchell of making misleading statements about him that were "wholly devoid of everything which would enable its readers to know anything ... concerning our misunderstanding." Mitchell's prickly attitude was a revelation to the white mainstream, although it was not always appreciated. The final contest of the Keystones three-game set in Breckenridge, Minnesota, was cancelled in 1908 when Mitchell refused to honor the free passes given to local newspapermen in exchange for advertising the series. After he was informed by the Breckenridge management that the passes would be recognized or the Keystones would not be paid, Mitchell instructed his

Edward "Kidd" Mitchell, owner of the Minneapolis Keystones 1907–1911. (*Indianapolis Freeman*, April 16, 1910; Wisconsin Historical Society, Madison)

team to pack up their gear and leave. The offended (and offending) scribes remarked that "the Keystone manager was as insulting as only a presumptuous nigger can be."[26]

The Keystones had their origins in a semi-professional nine who played a handful of weekend contests in 1907. Only two reports of the Keystones games from that summer have surfaced. In early June the club was crushed by a team from Hopkins, Minnesota, 25–3, and two months later the squad received a 14–0 pasting from Monticello; Minnesota. The Keystones had to leave after the seventh inning of the Monticello game to catch a train home — "a place," the local paper mused, "they never should have left." It was also hoped that "they will never come here again." The most notable player on the fledgling team was former Minneapolis Central High standout Charley Myrick, who had been a member of the ill-fated St. Paul Giants in 1905, and was the son of ex–Minneapolis Unions player Abe Myrick.[27]

In late March 1908 Kidd Mitchell decided to "get into the game with a will" and form a professional black club that would be "faster and stronger than the Colored Gophers." With the help of Secretary Eddie Davis and rumored "big financial backing," seven "first class players" were inked to Keystone contracts within two weeks of the team's conception.[28]

Charley Myrick and ex–Gopher Sam Ransom were listed as early members of the club but they weren't on the roster when the Keystones started playing ball games. The eventual Keystones lineup did feature four players who had donned the Gopher uniform in 1907: catcher Andrew Campbell, second baseman Fred "Pop" Roberts, outfielder Dick "Noisy" Wallace, and utility man Bobby Marshall.

The signing of hometown hero Marshall was both a public relations coup for the new team and an acquisition of a rare talent. Long before Bo Jackson came along, Bobby Marshall *knew* sports. After playing semi-pro baseball in North Dakota during the summer months of 1907, the intrepid Marshall led the Minneapolis Deans to the independent football championship of Minnesota that fall. During the winter the "Idol of the Gridiron, the Star of the Diamond, the Pet of the Lady Fans" skated with the Struck Eagles hockey team and also found time to open his own law office in the Metropolitan Life Building in downtown Minneapolis.[29]

Mitchell also followed the Gophers lead by signing several ex–Chicago Union Giants

A portrait of future Keystone George Hopkins in 1890. Proclaimed by Sol White to be "the star of the West," Hopkins began his career as a dominating pitcher and regularly struck out 12 to 15 men a game. (*Indianapolis Freeman*, September 13, 1890; Library of Congress, Washington, D.C.)

FIVE • *Cutting a Wide Swath (January–June 1908)* 71

including shortstop Alex Irwin, infielder "Topeka" Jack Johnson, and 50-year-old center fielder George Hopkins. The mustachioed Hopkins had emerged on the big time blackball scene way back in the 1880s with the New Orleans Pinchbacks. Originally a dominating pitcher whom regularly struck out 12 to 15 men a game, he was proclaimed by Sol White to be "the star of the West." After 1894 the strong hitting Hopkins made the transition to second base and then the outfield for teams such as the Chicago Unions, Page Fence Giants, and Algona Brownies.[30]

Alex "Happy" Irwin was described as "one of the best infielders ever seen in the Northwest independent ranks," and "the talk of every town" the team played in. Once in a Union Giants game against the Jenkins Brothers team from Kansas City, Irwin grabbed a ball kicked his way by second baseman Fred Roberts, stepped on second, and made the relay to first to complete a double play. The original captain of the Keystones was also an accomplished musician and was said to be even smaller than the 5'6", 138-pound Andy Oyler of the Minneapolis Millers. Truly a tiny dancer, the "whirlwind shortstop" from Evanston, Illinois, announced at one point that he was opening a dancing academy in Minneapolis.[31]

In sharp contrast to the diminutive Irwin was the 6'1", 190-pound "Topeka" Jack Johnson, a former sparring partner of soon-to-be heavyweight champion Jack Johnson. "Topeka" Jack "played ball in a big league style" and was once called "the best negro batter in the world." His "swift" fielding was "above criticism" and he reportedly covered as much ground as anyone.[32]

In a boxing career that lasted into the late 1920s, "Topeka" Jack took on many of the leading fighters of the era including Hall of Famers Johnson, Joe Jeannette, and Sam Langford, the "Boston Tar Baby," whom he battled to a ten-round draw in 1921. One night in April 1906 Johnson defeated Texas brawler Jim McCormick in a nine-round prize fight and the following afternoon he lead his Topeka Giants to a 6–4 victory over Iola of the Kansas State League. "Topeka" Jack did not exhibit any ill effects from his match save for "a little stiffness in his throwing wing," caused perhaps by McCormick who had fouled him "by biting a big mouthful" out of his shoulder. In the ring Johnson always fought "a particularly clean game," while displaying "speed and the powers of assimilation."[33]

Also on board for the Minneapolis nine were two athletes with Minnesota connections: 39-year-old third baseman William Binga, late of the Philadelphia Giants, had made several appearances in the state with the Page Fence Giants, and former Leland Giant Eugene "Cherry" Barton was the younger brother of the Gophers' Sherman Barton. The 28-year-old left fielder soon earned a reputation as "the heavy hitter for the Keystones," and became a fan favorite for making "all kinds of crazy catches."[34]

Bill Binga was a seasoned vet of nearly twenty blackball campaigns, and a truly professional batsman who was racking up multiple hit games well into his forties. In the field "he worked like a big leaguer," and although limited in range, he never forgot an opposing batter or how and where he liked to hit. During one two-game stretch in July 1908 he cleanly handled 18 chances while at third.[35]

Initially, Mitchell and Davis "experienced some trouble in landing the right kind of pitchers," but in mid–April they inked hurlers Charles Jessup and Graham (first name unknown) who had both toiled for the Union Giants in 1907. A potentially bigger signing occurred two days later when local legend Walter Ball "attached his signature to a Keystone contract." Ball was coming off a stint in the Cuban winter league with the Fe club after a strong season split between the Leland Giants and Chicago Union Giants. His "phenomenal catch" in right field had carried the day for the Lelands in the sixth and deciding game of their hugely popular series with Mike Donlin's All-Stars. Ball was now considered "one of the best colored twirlers in America," with a style of "bluff pitching" that demoralized his opponents. From the mound he would threaten to hit the enemy batters before "sending the spheres down one, two, three, swift as comets."[36]

Charles Jessup was a hard throwing 27-year-old from Kentucky whose unlimited, lightning-like speed soon "made him feared throughout the section," and made batters "almost helpless." Although "inclined to be wild" at times, the "tall, rangy" right-hander was able to pull himself out of several jams due to his "clever fielding."[37]

When the Keystones made their debut on Sunday April 19 it was Graham, "the plucky right hander" who was on the mound facing the strong semi-pro Lund Lands squad. Over 2,000 fans swarmed into the Minnehaha Driving Park to watch Graham and career minor leaguer Len Schroeder take a 1–1 duel into extra innings. Neither pitcher was razor sharp with Graham allowing nine hits and Schroeder walking seven batters and hitting one. William Binga collected two of the Keystones five hits and scored their first ever run on a fourth inning single by Noisy Wallace. With two down and the bases loaded with Lunds in the bottom of the ninth, Binga made a "hair raising" one-handed stop of a ball and made a perfect throw to first to retire the side In the bottom of the 11th, with two on and none out, Binga speared a "terrific" drive by Schroeder down the third base line to again save the day. Unfortunately, the next man up, Lund center fielder Spike Anderson, beat out a bunt and Graham then walked the winning run home.[38]

The following Sunday Walter Ball took the hill against Schroeder and the Lunds before another good crowd of 1,500 at Minnehaha. Although he "used nothing but a perfectly straight ball during the entire game," Ball skunked the semi-pros, 5–0, striking out nine and allowing only four hits. Binga scored three of the Keystone runs and collected more two hits in a contest played on a muddy, "miserable field." A week later the Keystones traveled up river and shut out the Stillwater team, 5–0, behind Charles Jessup. St. Paul Saints prospect Andrew Stephenson took the loss despite striking out 12 batters, including Bobby Marshall three times.[39]

While Eddie Davis, who had been "showered with offers," was busy arranging a schedule with the top clubs in the Midwest, the Keystones spent the rest of early May practicing daily and "perfecting signals and general team work." The club eventually embarked on a three-week tour on May 17, traveling through southeastern Minnesota, western Wisconsin and the Iron Range. The Minneapolis nine went an impressive 13–2–1 on their initial soiree, but "rain played havoc with the gate receipts" by washing out several games and the club limped home "with a bad financial balance."[40]

One of the most intriguing games on the trip occurred in Galesville, Wisconsin, where Johnny Davis and Walter Ball hooked up in a dogfight that ended in a 2–2 tie after 11 innings had been played. Ball allowed but four hits and struck out six, while Davis punched out five Keystones and was tagged for five safeties. The first three Galesville batters of the game all hit safely, loading the bases for Jesse Schaeffer who then launched a deep fly to center. The ball was caught by a Keystones outfielder at the edge of a creek bank, but for some reason the Galesville runner on third played it halfway and did not score on the play. Ball escaped the jam by striking out the next two batters. The Grays scored in the second, the Keystones tied it in the third and both teams tallied in the 10th inning before the game was called so the Keystones could catch their train.[41]

The tour ended two weeks later after a wild June 5 contest in Superior, Wisconsin. The local nine took a 5–2 lead after three innings and knocked Graham out of the box in

FIVE • Cutting a Wide Swath (January–June 1908) 73

the fourth, before the Keystones combined ten base hits, two hit batsman, and five Superior errors to pull out a 8–5 victory. Binga, Hopkins, and Eugene Barton each collected two hits, including a double apiece. Walter Ball came on in relief of Graham and struck out six Superior batters during his five scoreless innings to get the win. The game's atmosphere was "kept somewhat agitated" when both teams repeatedly questioned the umpire's decisions, leading to widespread "hooting" by the large and "decidedly active crowd" that seemingly included the "entire colored population of Superior." Many of the patrons on hand rushed the field in the eighth inning after a controversial call by a Keystone umpire. The Minneapolis club responded by brandishing some guns, but fortunately for Mitchell's charges "a riot was quelled without difficulty."[42]

Shortly after the Keystones arrived back in Minneapolis, Walter Ball "severed his connection" with the team for reasons he "refused to give out when questioned." Frank Leland reportedly facilitated Ball's release, but the talented pitcher might have just grown tired of the club's shenanigans. Adopting the tone set by Kidd Mitchell, the Minneapolis Keystones, perhaps more than any other team of their era, anticipated the athlete of the 21st century: independent, defiant, and proud to a fault—"Ready to down anything that crosses bats with them."[43]

The Keystones preferred to use intimidation in resolving their conflicts. Small town umpires were a frequent target of the team's "abusive language," and more than one arbiter threatened to quit a game because of their "beefing" and "senseless kicking."[44]

Unlike the Gophers who were only asking for a fair shake, the Keystones were looking for umpires that they could push around. During one game with Redwood Falls, Minnesota, *five* different umpires were trotted out before the professionals could find two they could live with. Even when they got their way the Keystones weren't always satisfied. Following a 1909 loss to Long Prairie, Minnesota, a paper noted, "The visitors did a good deal of kicking but were hardly in a position to say much as both umpires were of their own selection and Jessup was one of their players."[45]

Mitchell's team would often gather "up their paraphernalia" and threaten to leave the premises unless they got their way. In July 1908 the Keystones departed the playing field in Manchester, Iowa, shortly after Binga struck out leading off the game, charging that the local pitcher had delivered the ball from in front of the proscribed pitching box. After a half-hour conversation with the "mahogany hued hot air dispenser" Jack Johnson, the Manchester management relented and the balls-and-strikes ump was replaced. Three days later, however, the West Union, Iowa, club stood their ground and claimed a 9–0 forfeit win when "the Keystones packed their bats and went away mad" after a call at the plate went against them.[46]

The Minneapolis club's bullying tactics extended to the pitching mound, where their hurlers were not above using a fastball to the ribs to make a point. The Keystone pitchers knocked down at least 18 enemy batters in 1908 and 27 more in 1909. Because many of their statistics have been lost in the mists of time, those numbers are undoubtedly much higher. By comparison, the 1907 Gopher pitching staff hit only three batters.

Mitchell's squad was also physically imposing. With a roster that included a professional boxer and football player, the Keystones were "a big burly" bunch that were "much heavier" than most of the teams they ran across. The pundits in Galesville, Wisconsin, evinced that "the Keystones are as fast as the Gophers and they are a heap bigger."[47]

If verbal or physical intimidation didn't work, the Keystones found outright cheating would. On occasion, the Keystones were accused of practicing "dirty ball" and their "crooked tricks and rowdy ways ... earned the just displeasure of both crowd and umpire."[48]

As arbiters, the Keystone players would frequently make calls that went in their teammates' favor. In the early stages of a 1908 contest in Chippewa Falls, Wisconsin, Bobby Marshall coaxed a free pass and advanced to third when umpire George Hopkins ruled that Binga's foul drive over third base was a base hit. Marshall then stole home while Campeau, the Chippewa Falls catcher, "was monkeying around the pitchers box" as the Keystones grabbed a 6–2 victory. The following summer the club was trailing 11–10 in the eighth inning of a game in Rochester, Minnesota, when a Keystone batter who had grounded out to the pitcher crashed into the Rochester first baseman, causing him to drop the ball. Even though the first sacker had held on to the ball "for an appreciable time" the unidentified bruiser was called safe by the Keystone arbiter and subsequently came all the way around to tie the game, which the Minneapolis squad won with another run in the ninth.[49]

Interestingly, Eugene Barton was at the center of many of the Keystones escapades. In July 1909 he was called out after attempting to bat out of turn with the bases loaded during a game in Redwood Falls. A month later in Long Prairie "Cherry" (nicknamed after the street on which he grew up in Normal, Illinois) tried to score from third without tagging up on a fly ball by Hopkins, but his "bluff would not work, however, as the umpire had seen that he had not returned to the bag." Barton "put up quite a roar but it availed nothing and the side was out."[50]

That the Keystones were "a remarkable bunch of fine players" made up "entirely of stars" was undisputed, and it was acknowledged "that they could meet the teams of the American Association on equal terms." Unfortunately, their on-the-field behavior "invited a lot of criticism from the fans" in the section and earned them a reputation as an "aggregation of conceit." Eventually this would cost them.[51]

The new-look Gophers made their first Twin City appearance on May 23 with a Saturday game with the Lund Lands at Nicollet Park. A good crowd of 2,000 was on hand as Bill Gatewood made an auspicious debut. The big pitcher held the Lunds hitless for the first six innings and allowed only three safeties all day while striking out nine in a 6–0 Gopher whitewash. The Lunds borrowed Minneapolis Millers southpaw Charles Biersdorfer for the contest, but the St. Paul club found him for seven hits, stole six bases and scored twice on squeeze plays. Gatewood also got the Gophers on the board in the first inning, driving in Bunch Davis with a two-out triple to center that was one of the longest drives seen at Nicollet "for many a day." The dangerous Billy Williams played first base for the Lunds, but he went hitless in four at bats.[52]

Sam Ransom filled in at first base for the Gophers during the Lunds contest, but "Kissing Bug" Rose was finally back in the lineup the following Saturday when the club met the revamped Austin-Westerns at the Downtown Park. The Gophers had taken a short but successful dip through southern Minnesota after a second Lund game was rained out and came back to St. Paul with a sparkling record of 20–3–1.[53]

The Austin-Western squad included center fielder Benny Meyers who hit .271 for the St. Paul Saints that year, Saints catcher Joe Laughlin, and the inevitable Billy Williams at first, who was back for yet another crack at the Gophers. Over 900 cranks braved cold, wet weather to watch Gatewood oppose Austin starter Tom O' Neil in a wild and wooly game which inspired such rooting that "has seldom been heard in a ball park."[54]

The Gophers snatched an early lead in the first inning, when Frank Davis singled and scored after Laughlin overthrew third base trying to nab him stealing. Willis Jones doubled home Willie McMurray for the second Gopher run in the fourth, but the Austins came back with a vengeance an inning later thanks to some sloppy Gopher fielding. Benny Meyer led off with a double, pilfered third, and scored when McMurray let Johnson's throw down to third get away from him. Laughlin then grounded to short with what should have been the third out of the inning, but Bunch Davis threw the ball under the grandstand and the Austin receiver circled the bases to tie the game.[55]

More misplays by the Gophers let the St. Paul semi-pros forge ahead in the seventh. Laughlin grounded out to second to start the inning, but "Kissing Bug" Rose couldn't handle Felix Wallace's throw and he wound up on second base. Moments later the Gophers had Laughlin picked off third base, but Wallace's throw to back to the bag got away from McMurray and the fortunate backstop scored when it rolled all the way to the fence. The Gophers' deficit grew to two in the eighth, when Benny Meyers walked and scored on a triple by Austin third sacker McNamara.[56]

In the bottom of the eighth the Gophers loaded the bases, but Laughlin picked Davis off of third, saving a run when O'Neil promptly gave a free pass to Barton to load them up again. McMurray and Jones followed with run producing singles, but Meyers threw Sherman Barton out at the plate to keep the game knotted at four apiece. Joe Laughlin scored his third run of the game for the Austins in the top of the ninth when he reached on another error by Davis and eventually scored on a squeeze bunt by the second baseman Greaves.[57]

The first two batters in the Gophers ninth went out, and the Austins only needed to retire Frank Davis to win the game. Instead O'Neil, who had already walked nine batters, hit him with a pitch. Davis stole second base and went to third when Laughlin again made an overthrow trying to gun him down. Felix Wallace, the next man up, hit a drive over third base that the *St. Paul Pioneer Press* later conceded "was undoubtedly fair" but the umpire ruled it foul and disallowed Davis' tying run. The Gophers refused to continue the contest and the Austins claimed a tainted 9–0 forfeit win.[58]

The two St. Paul teams were involved in another tight game the next afternoon at Lexington. Howard Petway hooked up in a duel with Dell of the Austins before 1,200 hardy fans who showed up "despite the somewhat chilly atmosphere and ... numerous other attractions."[59]

In the first inning, the Austins scored on a slashing, bases-loaded single by Benny Meyers, but Petway got Joe Laughlin to ground into a double play to get out of the jam. The Gophers quickly tied the game with a little of their customary élan. Davis walked to lead off the Gopher first and Wallace singled him over to

Frank "Bunch" Davis, the Gophers shortstop in 1907 and 1908, was a "brilliant" fielder who was considered by many to be the star of the team. (*St. Paul Dispatch*, August 23, 1908; Minnesota State Historical Society, St. Paul)

third. Wallace eventually reached second and drew a throw trying to double him off after Bill Gatewood popped a squeeze bunt up to the pitcher Dell. Davis now broke for home, but the throw to catch him at the plate was in plenty of time and Laughlin chased the nimble shortstop back to third. Seeing that Dell had failed to cover the plate, Davis reversed course and raced past Laughlin to score.[60]

The Gophers went up, 2–1, in the seventh after Barton doubled to lead off the frame and scored one out later when Jones, trying to get out of the way of a pitch, "shoved his bat against the sphere" and placed it safely between first and second. Neither team scored the rest of the way. The Austins had several chances to tie or win the game but Reid's outfit turned two more twin killings behind Petway and Rat Johnson threw out a couple of would-be base stealers.[61]

In early June the Gophers set out for a two-week trip through southeastern Minnesota and western Wisconsin. The club won every game, including at least five by shutout, and were only really tested a couple of times on their trek. In a June 3 contest with Hastings, Minnesota, the Gophers overcame an early 3–0 deficit and scored all their runs in the final four innings of an 8–6 victory. The following day at New Richland, Minnesota, Charles McCleary stymied the Gophers on three hits and held them scoreless through nine innings. The locals could only manage three safeties off of Bill Gatewood, however, and the game went to extra innings. In the 10th the Gophers combined three singles, a double, and two New Richland errors, including one by McCleary, and emerged with a 5–0 win.[62]

On June 7, the Gophers made it back to Stillwater, Minnesota, where, like the year before, the game was played in a steady drizzle that turned into rain halfway through. This time umpire Andrew Thompson wore a rain coat throughout the contest, and the two teams finished all nine frames. The Gophers broke open a tight game by scoring eight runs in the fifth inning, on the strength of two singles, two doubles, a hit batsman, and *nine* Stillwater errors, including two passed balls. The St. Paul club also stole home three times during their at-bat and shut out the home side, 11–0. Bill Gatewood struck out ten Stillwater batters, but he also walked seven of them. Two months later, Gatewood and Thompson would have further trouble with balls and strikes in Stillwater.[63]

The Gophers returned to the Twin Cities on June 14 for a game at Minnehaha with the pesky Lund Lands. A Sunday afternoon assembly numbering 2,000 watched minor league twirler Ed Kellar pitch the game of his life. The former Northern Leaguer didn't allow a base hit through the first six innings and picked off a couple of Gopher batters who reached base via a walk. Felix Wallace finally broke up the no-hitter with a single in the seventh, one of only four safeties that Kellar would gave up on the day. Bill Gatewood was nearly as good, striking out ten more batters while also allowing but four safe drives. Sadly for Big Bill, three of those base hits came in the Lund half of the sixth.[64]

Griffin, a left fielder from the University of St. Thomas, led off the inning by beating out an infield roller to short, and one out later West, the Lunds shortstop, singled to left. By means of "daring base running" young Griffin then drew a throw from Rat Johnson which sailed over second and both base runners moved up a base. Minor leaguer Spike Anderson followed with a perfect squeeze bunt and Griffin beat the throw to the plate with his "lightning work."[65]

The game ended with a bang in the bottom of the ninth. The Gophers placed runners on second and third with only one out as Gatewood, "the Gophers heaviest hitter," came up with a chance to win his own game. Big Bill hit a smash to West at short, "who scooped it up in great style" and threw home to the Lunds catcher Sam Kinkle, who tagged out the

Gophers lead runner. In the meantime Frank Davis, who seemingly threw caution to the wind while on the base paths, had rushed past third on the play and was now caught in a rundown which concluded the Lunds 1–0 triumph.[66]

Both the Gophers and the Lunds had scheduled games for the following week with the Cuban Stars. When several injuries suffered by the Cubans in Chicago caused the squad to cancel their Twin Cities dates and return to New York for reinforcements, Phil Reid and Lund's manager Sam Coughlin decided to pit their clubs against each other for a couple of mid-week games in St. Paul.[67]

A large crowd came out to the Downtown Park on Tuesday to watch Brady, Coughlin's newest recruit, pitch against Clarence Lytle. The Dude had won every game he had pitched that year, including seven by shutout. Lytle started slowly against the Lunds however, walking first two men he faced and giving up a couple of two-run doubles. Third baseman Will McMurray complicated matters with a pair of throwing errors, and the Gophers found themselves down six runs after only four and a half innings had been played. Waking out of their collective coma, Reid's club rallied against the Wisconsin Leaguer Brady and pulled to within 7–4 in the bottom of the fifth on the strength of two Rat Johnson doubles. With two on and nobody out, the St. Paul club looked poised to steal the game back, but Ed Kellar came on in relief of Brady and again saved the day. The newly discovered Gopher killer yielded a mere two safeties the rest of the way and the Lunds prevailed 7–5.[68]

Bill Gatewood was the story the following afternoon at the Downtown Park. The big right-hander permitted but three hits, and but one Lunds base runner reached third base in a 3–0 Gopher beatdown. Facing Brady for the second straight day, Bunch Davis doubled and scored twice to lead the professional's seven-hit attack. Gatewood helped his cause with a successful squeeze bunt and Sherman Barton drove in the other two runs as the Gophers evened the season series at two wins apiece.[69]

Following their games with the Lunds, the Gophers immediately left St. Paul on another arduous trek, a 26-day excursion that

Howard Petway with the Gophers in the spring of 1908, before he was sidelined by an arm injury. (*Breckenridge Wilkin County Gazette*, June 19, 1908; Minnesota State Historical Society, St. Paul)

would take them first to western Minnesota and then the Iron Range. The tour kicked off on June 18 in Long Prairie where the Gophers won a pair of 3–1 decisions before crowds "that were pretty small for the nature of the attraction."[70]

Howard Petway started the second game in Long Prairie, "but he was nervous" and walked the first two batters before Rat Johnson pulled him and put Bunch Davis into pitch in his stead. Eight days earlier, the lefty had been removed from a game in Hayward, Wisconsin, and he had not appeared in any of the games against the Lunds. In late–July it was reported that Petway was "laid up with a sore arm" and he never suited up for the Gophers again.[71]

The Gophers slashed through western Minnesota winning every game they played without much opposition. The tour was not without its features. In Long Prairie, Sherman Barton suffered the ignominy of the hidden ball trick when Bungo, the local first baseman, tucked the ball under his arm pit and tagged the Gopher center fielder when he took too "frisky" a lead off the initial sack. A day later the squad beat Staples, Minnesota, 4–1, finally besting Ed Kellar, who was unable to down the black professionals for a third straight time.[72]

Prior to leaving for the Iron Range, the St. Paul club journeyed 45 miles down the Mississippi River for a June 28 match with Red Wing. A Sunday host of 2,000, including a "large number" of Gopher supporters, braved a light rain to watch Reid's boys cruise to a 5–0 win. Fred Spencer took the mound again for Red Wing, but the Gophers knocked the future major leaguer around for nine hits including three each by Wallace and Barton, both of whom also doubled.[73]

Dude Lytle twirled for the Gophers and the wily one gave up only two scratch hits and struck out seven batters with a "change of pace delivery." Lytle's fielders provided great support behind him by snaring six line drives, three of which were apparently headed for extra bases. Interestingly, an item had been printed a week before the game claiming that Lytle had "been sick much of the time this year, and his arm isn't as good as it was." Unfortunately for the Dude, the strain on his arm was going to get a lot worse before it got better.[74]

Chapter Six

Saints, Sinners, and Keystones (July–December 1908)

As the summer of 1908 wore on, the sporting public began clamoring for a playoff between the Gophers and the Keystones. On July 19 the *Minneapolis Tribune* carried an item announcing that the two black clubs would meet in a three-game series in late August. A week later Kidd Mitchell wrote to the *Tribune* pleading ignorance of the proposed series, although he claimed that he had tried to schedule games with the Gophers, "but that for some reason the St. Paul colored nine refused to listen to any definite terms or arrangements." The Colonel openly begged for a crack at the Gophers, boasting that his Keystones were the stronger outfit.[1]

The August 2 edition of the *Tribune* published a pointed response by Phil Reid to Mitchell's broadside:

> I wish to state that the Keystones have been offered two series with our team, the first proposed series being on July 17, 18 and 19. A second series was tendered for Aug. 27, 28, 29 and 30. Both of these proposed series were dodged by the Keystone management. They, however, try by the use of your valuable column to mislead the public into believing that for an 'unexplained reason' we failed to meet them. If the Keystone club believes that their nine is superior to the Colored Gopher aggregation we are willing to meet them in a series of three or five games at any date they wish to name except Sept. 17 and 18 and prior to Sept. 30.[2]

Reid also announced that the Gophers management was willing to place a side-bet on the result of the series for any amount that the Keystones could cover. The *Tribune* enthused that "a series between the two would draw big crowds and would be well worth witnessing," but the two sides still couldn't come to terms. Instead, both clubs scheduled games with the Birmingham Giants for the last week of August, when the National Black Elk convention would be in town.[3]

Even with the defection of Walter Ball to the Leland Giants in early June, the Keystones had been on a roll. On the eve of Ball's departure, the Flour City squad clouted 22 safeties and tallied 29 times during a pair of wild slugfests with the Lund Lands. On June 6 at Nicollet Park the Keystones raced out to a huge lead by scoring four times in the third inning against minor leaguer Frank Speiser. The Lunds came way back and tied it in the seventh by clubbing Charles Jessup for six hits and six runs in the seventh. The semi-pros added another run in the eighth on the strength of a walk and two singles and held on for an 8–7 win.[4]

Jessup struck out seven Lunds, but he also gave up 13 safeties, including three doubles, walked three and hit a batter. Andrew Campbell led a 14-hit Keystones onslaught with a double and two singles. Walter Ball played right field and went hitless in four at-bats in his Keystone finale before Noisy Wallace pinch-hit for him in the ninth.[5]

The two clubs moved out to Minnehaha the following afternoon for a Sunday match played "on a diamond heavy with mud." Despite the sloppy track, the Keystones sprinted to another big advantage on the strength of eight hits, six free passes, two passed balls, one wild pitch and six Lund errors. The professionals were up 12–1 after seven-and-a-half innings, but Coughlin's group fell on Graham for seven safe drives, two walks, and seven runs to pull within four. The Lunds narrowed the gap to 12–10 in the ninth on the strength of a double by minor league catcher Jerry Ronesch, before Jessup came on to get the last two outs of the ball game. Fred Roberts rapped out two hits, scored three times, and made the play of the game in the sixth when, after stretching flat on the ground to retrieve a hard hit grounder, he threw the ball from behind his back to retire the batter at first.[6]

As the Keystones made their initial forays into southern Minnesota, the Dakotas, and Iowa during June and early July, Bobby Marshall assumed Ball's place in the rotation and won eight out of nine starts. Marshall's "benders were a complete puzzle" to many batters in the region and he allowed about 3.29 runs a game on average. The club wheeled off 12 wins in a row before Hastings, Minnesota, stopped them, 3–1, on June 30. The Keystones showed up for the game two hours late, only to find that most of the spectators had left the grounds; because of the delayed start, the contest was called on account of darkness after seven innings.[7]

In late June the Keystones suffered another potential blow to their lineup, when Andrew Campbell, their husky, hard-hitting catcher, left to play for and captain the Long Prairie, Minnesota, nine. Dick "Noisy" Wallace replaced Campbell behind the plate, and although he wasn't as powerful a slugger, opposing teams had "a very poor chance of base pilfering" against him. A couple of weeks later, the erratic Graham was replaced during the squad's Iowa trip by pitcher W.J. Freeman, a 6'6", 225-pound "giant in stature" who had previously twirled for "leading semi-pro clubs" in Omaha, Kansas City, Chicago, as well as Anaconda and Butte, Montana.[8]

The Keystones plowed through southern Minnesota and Iowa winning 20 games against only one loss, a 5–2 defeat on July 6 in Osage, Iowa, where the local squad had "but little difficulty" in hitting Marshall. The Keystones didn't help their young pitcher by being "purposely careless and over confident in their fielding work."[9]

On July 12 the Minneapolis club and the team from Oelwein, Iowa, played "three hours and thirty-one minutes of the greatest game of base ball ever pulled off in northeastern Iowa." On the bump for Oelwein was Joe Hovlick, a 23-year-old local spitballer who later made it to the majors with Washington and the White Sox. He also won 24 games in 1914 while pitching for Milwaukee in the American Association.[10]

Oelwein got off to a fast start when their catcher Tommy Anderson "mashed" Charles Jessup's first pitch of the game to left for a double. Minor league third baseman Roy Glockner doubled Anderson home and later scored on a single by the Oelwein left fielder, Monahl. The Keystones got a run back in the third when Bobby Marshall beat out an infield hit, stole second, and scored when one of Hovlick's spitters hit the front end of home plate and bounced over the grandstand.[11]

In the top of the fourth, Alex Irwin likewise reached first, swiped second, and scored the equalizer when *another* of Hovlick's wet ones struck home plate, this time bounding over the grandstand into North Frederick Street. The *Oelwein Register* later lamented, "Did anyone ever hear of such a happening in base ball?" Oelwein scored again in the sixth thanks to two singles and an error by Fred Roberts. Undaunted, Roberts rapped out a base hit and scored for the Keystones as the game headed into extra innings. The home team had many chances to score the winning run, amassing 11 hits off Charles Jessup to go along with seven

Keystone errors, but the unyielding speed-baller struck out 11 and stranded 14 Oelwein batters. Joe Hovlick whiffed 17 Keystones, surrendered only two safe drives through the first 16 innings, and received an ovation from the appreciative Oelwein loyalists that was supposedly greater than the one Presidential candidate William Jennings Bryan received at Denver the week before.[12]

Finally in the top of the 17th inning Noisy Wallace singled and Jessup sacrificed him to second. William Binga drove in Wallace with an infield hit to short and later scored when Oelwein second baseman Russell dropped a high fly ball off the bat of George Hopkins. This two-out muff was Russell's fifth error of the day and helped the Minneapolis club pull out a 5–3 marathon win.[13]

The following day, Hovlick yielded only four hits and held the Keystones scoreless for *eight* more innings at West Union, Iowa, before the professionals tromped off the field after the locals scored a pair of disputed runs. A few days later in Decorah, Iowa, the Keystones were up big in the eighth inning when, according to the *Decorah Republican*, Kidd Mitchell ordered all of his infielders and outfielders to the bench. While Charles Jessup remained on the mound, the rest of the Keystones "took part in a watermelon feast, while the pitcher fanned all the men up to bat in the last two innings." The *Decorah Journal* reported that the home team actually scored a "gift" run in the ninth against Jessup, but that the Keystones antics in the inning "reminded one of a minstrel show."[14]

The Gophers pulled into Duluth, Minnesota, on July 1 to begin a series of 12 games in 12 days with the leading teams of the Iron Range. First up was a two-game set against Hibbing at Duluth's Athletic Park that was witnessed by every black man in Duluth or nearby Superior "who had or could beg, borrow, or steal the two-bits admission." The Gopher supporters were said to have enjoyed themselves immensely and "the coin flowed freely" as they bet on everything from wild throws to home runs.[15]

Minor leaguer William Gilchrist scattered six Gopher drives and pitched out of two jams as Hibbing took the opener, 4–2. Bill Gatewood allowed only three hits, but he was undone by Haywood Rose who committed three errors in the first four frames before switching positions with catcher Rat Johnson. To make matters worse, Will McMurray badly sprained his ankle in the fifth inning and had to be examined by a doctor. McMurray finished the contest, but he would miss the next ten games. His place was taken by a light-hitting player named Harry Boone who was installed at second base while Felix Wallace moved to third.[16]

Hibbing took a 6–2 lead a day later against Dude Lytle, "who didn't have very much," but the Gophers came back with a four-run seventh to tie it against Colt southpaw George "Slow Ball" Freeman. Gilchrist came on to retire all six Gopher batters he faced, and an error by Boone enabled the Colts to push a run across in the ninth for a 7–6 decision. The two teams left for Hibbing the following morning to continue the series.[17]

With McMurray hurt and Howard Petway out of commission, Bill Gatewood and Dude Lytle were now forced to pitch every other day. The overmatched Boone was moved to right field, which meant that the weary pitchers would also have to alternate at second base. The pair certainly didn't display any fatigue during the first game in Hibbing, as Lytle homered against Colts starter Couture, another one-time minor leaguer, and Gatewood gave up only six hits in a 4–1 Gopher win.[18]

While the combined attendance for the first three games in the series had been less than 1,400, nearly 2,500 "enthusiastic rooters" turned out on the Fourth of July holiday to take in "one of the most spectacular games that has ever been seen" in the Iron Range town. The Gophers had apparently taken their measure of Gilchrist as Rat Johnson banged a two-run home run in the top of the first inning that was quickly followed by a solo blast from Bill Gatewood. Unfortunately, in the bottom of the inning, Dude Lytle passed two batters and gave all three runs back before Johnson brought Gatewood in to relieve him.[19]

The Gophers recovered to take leads of 5–3 and 6–5 on the strength of a third-inning home run by Lytle and three doubles by Willis Jones. Gatewood couldn't stand success either and relinquished both leads, with Hibbing knotting the game at six in the sixth inning on a squeeze play. With one down and the game still tied in the last of the ninth, Gatewood hit right fielder Frank Kleffman with a pitch. Colts shortstop Charlie Calligan forced Kleffman at second, and it looked as though the game would go into extra innings. Gilchrist had other ideas and smashed his third hit and second double of the day to the fence—Calligan just beat the throw home and the Colts walked off with another 7–6 triumph.[20]

The following afternoon 1,700 rangers watched as the Gophers jumped out to a 3–1 lead against future major leaguer Jack Gilligan, propelled by two more base hits and a stolen base by Willis Jones. Hibbing collected only six safeties off Dude Lytle, but he was wild again, and the Colts tied the game at three with two runs in the bottom of the fifth. In a disastrous sixth inning Lytle walked three locals, hit one, and allowed four runs as Hibbing annexed the Sunday contest, 7–4. An exhausted Lytle issued eight free passes in all and hit first baseman Dwight Booth twice with pitches, probably because Booth had stolen home for the second time in two days.[21]

Clarence "Dude" Lytle twirled for the Gophers in 1907, 1908, and 1911. In 1908 the crafty spitballer threw at least 303 innings, and won 27 games, including 11 shutouts, against only six defeats. He also pitched for the Keystones in 1910. (*Red Wing Daily Republican*, September 12, 1908; Minnesota State Historical Society, St. Paul)

The beat-down continued on Monday when Bill Gatewood squared off against former Milwaukee Brewer pitcher Leo Sage, the fifth different hurler Judge Brady had trotted out in the series. This time it was Hibbing's turn to surrender an early lead as the Gophers, lifted by another home run by Gatewood, scratched back from a 4–1 third-inning deficit to tie the game at four in the sixth. In the bottom of the seventh Sage put Hibbing back on top with a two-run double, and he shut down the Gophers the final two frames to ice a 6–4 Colt win.[22]

The Gophers limped out

of Hibbing and headed 28 miles eastward to take on another strong semi-pro club in Eveleth, Minnesota. In the first game on July 7, the Gophers, "stealing everything they saw on the bases," thumped out 13 hits and forced nine errors as Dude Lytle cruised to a much needed 15–3 victory. Eveleth turned the tables on the St. Paul club the following afternoon, roughing up for 14 hits including two doubles and two triples in a 9–6 win.[23]

Back in Hibbing on Thursday, the Colts jumped out to a 3–0 lead off Lytle after four innings. Jack Gilligan threw four perfect innings to open the game before Sherman Barton singled leading off the top of the fifth. Bill Gatewood followed with a single, and Willis Jones doubled both runners home. Rat Johnson hit a three-run homer in the sixth inning and Barton scored Wallace and Johnson with a triple down the third-base foul line in the eighth. Dwight Booth homered to lead off the bottom of the eighth, cutting the Gopher lead to 7–4 and the Colts proceeded to load the bases before Lytle induced Calligan to bounce into a double play. Hibbing also put their first two batters on in the ninth, but the Dude got out of the jam with only one run coming across as the Gophers got a little payback with an essential 7–5 triumph.[24]

The Gophers concluded their desultory range trip with three games against an all-salaried team in Virginia, Minnesota. Earlier that season Virginia had lured former major league pitcher Oscar Graham away from the Minneapolis Millers by paying him a whopping $350 a month. The hefty price tag was probably worth it as Virginia would ultimately take the season series from their bitter rivals in Hibbing, 13 games to 10.[25]

Big Bill Gatewood, perhaps rejuvenated by a three-run Gopher first, allowed only two hits on July 10 and shut out Graham's club, 4–0. Lytle scattered five hits the next afternoon and Virginia made nine errors in a 4–1 Gopher win; the only Virginia run came home when a fly ball sailed over Barton's head.[26]

In the Sunday closer, 1,200 fans watched as Gatewood "twirled a beautiful game," striking out six batters and again giving up only two hits. A listless Gophers club committed five errors behind the big pitcher, however, as Oscar Graham shut them out, 4–0. Taking a cue from Hibbing who had found success against the Gophers by working the bunting game, Virginia successfully sacrificed five times and stole four bases.[27]

One of Rat Johnson's throws down to second trying to nab a Virginia base stealer hit the home plate umpire "in the backside," and "the suddenness with which he straightened up created the loudest laugh during the game." Their wasn't much laughter in the Gopher camp. During the game, the tensions of the long road trip finally surfaced when according to a Virginia paper, "a couple of the colored men started a 'scrap' over some of their rank plays, and it required the combined efforts of all the other players to get them apart."[28]

It was a crippled Gopher club that reappeared in the Twin Cities for a pair of mid–July contests with the Austin-Westerns, sandwiched around a rematch with the Hastings nine. Will McMurray had returned to the lineup for the finale in Virginia, but Sherman Barton was now said to be "on the injured list" although he didn't miss any games. To fortify the squad, Jesse Schaeffer was hired away from Galesville, Wisconsin. It was also reported that Johnny Davis would rejoin the team, but it didn't come to pass.[29]

On July 14 the Gophers and the Austin-Westerns crossed bats in front of 1,600 cranks at the Downtown Park in the first of two games "arranged by special request" for a Shriner convention that was in town. The Austins converted four hits, a stolen base, an error by Bunch Davis, and a wild pitch by Clarence Lytle into a 4–0 lead in the second inning. The semi-pros were leading 5–1 in the eighth when the Gophers finally got to Austin starter Fred Spencer; four singles, two errors, one double later they tied the score at five. The game was still knotted at five in the bottom of the ninth when Bill Gatewood, who had replaced Lytle in the eighth, fanned the first two batters before Billy Williams reached on an error at third base by Jesse Schaeffer. Bernstein, the Austins second sacker, followed with a long double, scoring Williams and sending Gatewood to a 6–5 hard-luck loss.[30]

The misery continued for Reid's club a day later at Hastings when the home team cracked a couple home runs, and drove Lytle from the box in the sixth inning on their way to a 7–4 upset win. Baasen of the locals only gave up six hits and struck out six Gopher batters. Bunch Davis came in to relieve Lytle, but he couldn't prevent the St. Paul club's ninth loss in their last 14 games.[31]

Another good sized gathering of 1,100 was on hand at the Downtown Park for a Friday matchup between Bill Gatewood and Cy Pietz, a 6'4" hurler from Enderlin, North Dakota, who allegedly had "as much smoke as a switch engine." Gatewood reportedly "went into the box a sick man" but it was Pietz who left it that way.[32]

The Austins dashed off to a 2–0 lead in the first, but the Gophers came back with two in the bottom half and tacked on single runs in the next three frames for a 5–2 lead. Pietz only gave up two base hits through the first five innings, but he walked four, and a pieced together Austins lineup was guilty of six errors. Following the fifth inning, the big fellow from North Dakota fell victim to a "sun-stroke" and had to be carried off the field. According to the *St. Paul Dispatch* his life was "barely saved by prompt medical attention."[33]

A couple of days later, the *Minneapolis Journal* picked up the story and wrote that Pietz's fainting spell had been caused by contaminated drinking water and that Sam Coughlin, the "associate advisor" of the Austins was "out looking for gore":

> It was a hot day and the tall pitcher went often to the water tank, complaining that the city water was not like the alkali springs of his native sod. In the sixth inning the tall twirler from the high grass fainted and Sam hurried to his assistance. The man was down and every time he breathed he blew bubbles. Sam smelled of his breath and hiked for the water tank. Floating on the top of the ice water was a cake of a famous brand of soap, guaranteed to float and be 99 percent pure soap. It was floating but also dissolving and impregnating the drinking water with its soapy superiority.[34]

The *Journal* ran a cartoon with their account showing Coughlin pricking the bubbles coming from the mouth of a stricken Pietz while a Gopher player laughed uproariously in the background. Coughlin was quoted as saying, "I don't know who put that cake av soap in the water tank, but I have me suspicions. If I find 'em to be correct there is going to be a series of first-class Egyptian funerals from some av' thim St. Paul Zion Baptist churches." The Gophers iced their 7–4 win with a couple of runs in the seventh "on the best exhibition of the hit and run ever seen on the grounds." Gatewood struck out six and survived six more Gopher errors, including three by a substitute third baseman named Williams.[35]

The Gophers had no sooner caught their breath when they were sent out on the road again, this time for a 34-day odyssey through southern Minnesota, South Dakota, northern Iowa, and eastern Wisconsin. Even with their recent bad run, the Gophers record at midseason was a healthy 58–10–1 (.847). As July came to an end, Bill Gatewood had only lost four of the 41 games he had pitched while Willis Jones' stolen base total stood at 48 and Felix Wallace was working on an errorless streak of 17 games.[36]

Jesse Schaeffer was in right field for the St. Paul club when they downed Charles McCleary and Faribault, 7–5, on July 19 but he then headed out west to join up with the Keystones. With only nine players left on the roster, the mysterious Williams (possibly sec-

Soaping the drinking water. A cartoon from the *Minneapolis Journal* following a Gophers-Austin-Westerns game. (*Minneapolis Journal*, July 19, 1908; Minnesota State Historical Society, St. Paul)

retary Irving Williams) filled in until the club signed pitcher Nathan Knight, a former teammate of Willie McMurray from the St. Louis Giants, in late July.[37]

The tour began on July 20 when Lytle and the Gophers downed Renville, 4–3, before a large multitude. Renville imported Bert Jones from Bryant, South Dakota, to man third base and he played an outstanding game for his former club. With Knight in tow the Gophers mowed through the southern half of the region, losing only three out of 32 games. Madison, South Dakota, beat them 4–3 in 12 innings on July 30 when spitballer Fred Norton struck out 12 Gophers and worked out of several bases loaded jams. Cresco, Iowa, turned the trick on August 12 when right fielder Teddy Mellang "won immortal fame" by clouting a two-run double off Dude Lytle for a 3–1 victory. Five days later the Spring Grove, Minnesota, Indians stopped the Gophers cold, 4–1. Future minor league pitcher John Wolford struck out six of Reid's men and gave up but four hits to get the win.[38]

The club veered east near the end of their month-long marathon. On August 14, a host of nearly 4,000 saw the Gophers outclass the barnstorming National Indians of Lawrence, Kansas, 6–1, at the homecoming celebration in Fennimore, Wisconsin. Five days later Bill Gatewood broke up a tight game with the Rochester Stars by launching a three-run home run into the Zumbro River to punctuate the Gophers 8–6 victory. The trip concluded on August 21 with the St. Paul nine downing Waseca, 3–2. The Gophers edged Charles McCleary once again, although the old EACO hurler struck out eight and was only reached for three base knocks.[39]

The Gophers returned to St. Paul with only nine players left on their roster. Nathan Knight beat ex–Saints hurler Roy Waldren and Winnebago, Minnesota, 12–3, on August 7, but when he left the squad shortly thereafter, the club was again reduced to a two-man rotation of Lytle and Gatewood, although one of the position players would occasionally take a turn in the box.[40]

The Keystones were also having trouble finding reliable starting pitching. Having established themselves as a big draw, the Minneapolis squad made their way back to the Twin Cities in early August for a three-game set with the Lund Lands. Collectively, the club was batting at a .290 clip and had stolen 60 bases while racking up a record of 56–8–2 (.863). The team got an added boost in late July when Jesse Schaeffer was lured away from the Gophers to assume the catching duties. The one fly in the ointment was new pitcher W.J. Freeman, who "proved to be an easy proposition" for most of the clubs he faced.[41]

On July 26, Mitchell's club raced to a 3–1 lead in Albert Lea before the Grays knocked Freeman out of the box with three runs in the fifth inning. Hired gun Roy Waldren surrendered 11 hits but he also whiffed 14 Keystones and tied the game at five with a two-out base hit in the sixth. The score was still 5–5 in the bottom of the tenth when Big Roy lined one of Charles Jessup's deliveries to the creek in left field, driving the winning run home and sending 700 local fans into a frenzy. Five days later Freeman yielded five runs in the ninth inning of an 8–3 Keystones loss to the Breckenridge–Wahpeton Island Park outfit; less than a month after his arrival, the big pitcher was gone.[42]

Prior to Freeman's departure Kidd Mitchell signed pitcher and second baseman William Dewberry, a former Union and Leland Giant, who had a recent decision over the fading Cuban Giants to his credit. Soon after Dewberry's arrival, the Colonel inked Charles "Slick" Jackson, a "clever youngster" who was said to be "a steady hurler as ever twirled a ball." A newspaper in Red Wing, Minnesota, would characterize the lanky right-hander as "the choicest chocolate drop of the bon-bon box" who was "invincible with men on base" and that batters "could not get around him with a silver tweezer."[43]

On Sunday August 2, the Keystones hammered the Lunds, 12–4, at the Minnehaha Driving Park, rapping seven hits off ex–Millers pitcher Ralph Cadwallader in four-and-a-third innings. Charles Jessup struck out ten Lund batters and won his 30th game of the season against only five losses and a tie. William Dewberry made his first start for the Keystones the following day at the Downtown Park in St. Paul as the two Minneapolis squads opted to finish their season series on a "neutral site." The 33-year-old Georgian whiffed seven, but the semi-pros reached him for nine hits in a 9–1 Lund rout. Charles Jackson had a more auspicious debut the next afternoon at Lexington. The Lunds hit him hard, but the Keystones gave "Slick" an early lead and he held it for a 6–4 victory that annexed the city title for Mitchell's outfit.[44]

In early August the Keystones invaded northern Wisconsin and found the going rougher than they might have expected. The Merrill, Wisconsin, management reportedly offered a watermelon for every triple and a spring chicken for every home run the Keystones could hit against their strong semi-pro nine. They were able to keep most of their produce as Merrill thrashed the Keystones, 11–5, on August 8 and ex-minor leaguer Percy Koons shut them out, 2–0, before a big Sunday crowd of 1,500 the next day. Merrill knocked Jackson around for 18 hits in the first contest, while his teammates struck out nine times against the Merrill twirler, Bies.[45]

The Keystones recovered to go 7–3 on their Wisconsin excursion, with their only other loss being a 7–5 defeat on August 14 to Cumberland, Wisconsin. The following afternoon, Mitchell's squad trounced the New Prague, Minnesota, Seals, 10–2, and then headed south to Faribault for a Sunday match with the Flecks. Charles McCleary hadn't had much success with the Gophers in 1908, but he was masterful against the Keystones. The "Fleck wonder" struck out nine Keystones while hurling a 2–0 no-hitter. The southpaw gave up one walk and hit a batter. The closest the Minneapolis club came to a base hit was a ninth-inning line drive by Bill Binga that landed a foot foul. Charles Jessup was the hard luck loser, striking out seven batters, and giving up only five hits. The only runs in the game came in the first on a two-run homer by Faribault third baseman and ex-minor leaguer Claude Lamb.[46]

Kidd Mitchell was not the kind of owner to stand pat. Shortly after the Faribault game Noisy Wallace, one of the team's leading hitters, and their top base stealer Pop Roberts were released for being "out of condition." Andrew Campbell came back from Long Prairie to catch, Jesse Schaeffer took Roberts spot at second base, and the club registered five shutout wins in nine days over Twin City area teams. On August 18 the Keystones revisited Monticello, Minnesota, having been laughed out of town the year before and whitewashed the Giants, 6–0.[47]

After the Gophers had wrapped up their long southern junket they played a couple of games in and around the Twin City area. On August 22 the club took advantage of eight errors by the local club and easily downed Lindstrom, 8–3. The Gophers, along with about 100 black supporters from St. Paul, then ventured out to Stillwater for a Sunday engagement. Another big swarm numbering 1,000 gathered to watch Bill Gatewood and former minor leaguer Fred Blanchard duel. The Stillwater grandstand was packed, the bleachers were filled to overflowing, and the outfield was ringed by "throngs of men and boys" who sat twenty rows deep in some places. And then all hell broke loose.[48]

In the bottom of the fourth inning, Gatewood became irate when umpire "Honest" Andy Thompson ruled that one of his deliveries to Stillwater first baseman Art Lyman had missed the strike zone. "What's that?" Gatewood reportedly asked. "A ball" replied Thompson. At that point, Gatewood who "had all along been acting in an insulting way to the local players" took off his glove and violently threw it at Thompson, hitting him in the shoulder, or the face, depending on which account you believe. The umpire fell back in surprise and the cap came off his head. Seconds later, hundreds of men from the bleachers and grandstand angrily stormed the field "with threats of vengeance and violence."[49]

Big Bill's timing couldn't have been worse. Just nine days earlier seven people had been killed, dozens injured, and more than 70 homes and businesses destroyed during a horrific race riot in Springfield, Illinois. At the climax of the rioting, an 84-year-old black man named William Donnegan, whose only transgression seemed to have been his 32-year marriage to a white woman, had his throat cut by a mob, who then hung him from a tree near his home. At least 88 other African Americans were also lynched in the United States in 1908, as racial tensions were high throughout the country.[50]

As the angry horde menacingly advanced towards Gatewood with shouts of "put him out" Thompson held up his hands in the air, "as a token to refrain from violence," and two "husky" uniformed policemen with drawn clubs rushed to the mound to protect the Gopher twirler. Simultaneously, Stillwater mayor J.G. Armson, along with several "muscularly" leading citizens of the city, waded into the fray to keep the mob from getting further out of hand. Very helpful as well were the actions of "a dozen colored men from St. Paul" who helped calm the locals by condemning Gatewood's behavior as they mingled in the crowd.[51]

After Gatewood had been cordoned off, a few of his teammates promptly "started the trouble afresh" by insisting that the burly pitcher continue playing; "it required careful

1908 St. Paul Gophers (mid-season). Back Row (L-R): Haywood Rose (1B), George "Rat" Johnson (C), Clarence Lytle (P), Phil Reid (Owner, seated), Bill Gatewood (P), Sherman Barton (CF), William McMurray (3B). Front Row (L-R): Frank Davis (SS), Felix Wallace (2B), Willis Jones (LF). (Courtesy of Fred Buckland)

management to prevent a riot starting the second time." Eventually Gatewood was tossed from the game by Thompson over the protests of the Gophers, who only had nine players and argued that Big William should be allowed to play another position. Ralph Nelson, the Stillwater starting second baseman who had been benched earlier in the contest because of poor play, was loaned to the St. Paul club so that the game could continue. "That big bully Gatewood," who the *Stillwater Daily Gazette* claimed had "been offensive in his attitudes to players and spectators before," was escorted from the grounds by the police for his own safety and thrown into jail in downtown Stillwater.[52]

What made Gatewood's outburst more amazing was the fact that the Gophers were leading 7–1 at the time of the incident. When the game eventually resumed, Dude Lytle replaced Gatewood on the slab as the Gophers, in a rare display of pique, demolished the hapless Stillwater club, 22–2. The Gophers roughed up four Stillwater pitchers for 14 hits, stole 11 bases, and frightened the hometown team into committing 14 errors.[53]

The *Daily Gazette* correctly predicted that "there will probably be no more teams of colored base ball players in Stillwater." The next morning Gatewood "got his punishment, according to law" and the team blew town never to return. The incident proved to be financially costly. Because of the Stillwater row, the Gophers missed their game in River Falls, Wisconsin, later that day, disappointing a large assembly who came out to see them.[54]

When the Gophers slunk back to St. Paul to prepare for a home series with the Hibbing Colts and Birmingham Giants, more bad news awaited them. The Alabama club had just lost a playoff for the championship of the South to the San Antonio Black Bronchos. Unable or unwilling to make the more than 1,200-mile trek from Texas to the Twin Cities, C.I. Taylor's Giants failed to show up and neglected to let anybody know they weren't coming.[55]

The Giants no-show left the Gophers and Keystones management scrambling to fill the now-vacated dates that were slated to be the featured attraction of that week's Black Elks convention. With their backs against the wall, the two clubs finally relented to play each other. On Monday, August 24, Edward Dickinson, the secretary of the Minneapolis Baseball Association, "secured the signatures of both teams" for a game at the Minnehaha Driving Park that upcoming Sunday. The Gophers and Keystones also decided to squeeze in a contest on Thursday in St. Paul, as a prelude to their match-up in Minneapolis.[56]

Before taking on the Keystones, the Gophers kicked off one of their longest homestands ever with a Wednesday game against Hibbing, the "independent champs of the Northwest." The Colts had recently strengthened their club by adding Dick Brookins, a fleet-footed third baseman who had hit .307 in 1907 for Houghton, Michigan, in the Northern Copper County League. Brookins was a light-skinned African American who passed himself off as a Native American and made the rosters of several minor league teams of the era, including the 1908 Indianapolis Indians of the American Association. Inevitably, when suspicions were raised about his heritage, Brookins would be released by the professional clubs and he would come back to play for Hibbing. As the *Duluth News Tribune* stolidly noted, "If he is an Indian he has a perfect right to play league baseball. If he is a negro he will be forever barred from taking part in games played under the supervision of the National association."[57]

The Gophers first game with Brady's Colts was played "before practically empty stands" after an early afternoon rain dissuaded many fans from venturing out to Lexington Park. Both Hibbing's Leo Sage and Bill Gatewood pitched well, but the big man was let down by two costly errors and the rangers escaped with a 6–3 decision. The loss dropped the Gophers record to 68–16–1 (.805). When the Keystones headed over to St. Paul the next afternoon, their season's tally stood at 74–10–2 (.872).[58]

Although their August 27 contest would be the initial meeting between the two clubs, the individual Gophers and Keystones had played with and/or against each other countless times. Edward Dickinson had promised the two nines would "fight to the death" and there was certainly little love lost between their respective backstops. In August 1903 Rat Johnson, then with the Algona Brownies, tried to score from second on a base hit to left field in a game against the Chicago Union Giants. Andrew Campbell, catching for the Giants, got the ball well in advance of Johnson's arrival and tagged Rat "good and plenty" in the "short ribs." The two catchers then "rolled together on the ground" before a dazed Johnson rushed at Campbell and landed a left and right to his head. A Union Giant jumped into the melee swinging a bat wildly, as an ensuing brawl between the teams had to be broken up by a police detail.[59]

Even with the last minute nature of the contest, over 1,800 fans turned out at the Downtown Park to watch the first-ever game in the Twin Cities between two black professional teams. Considering the abilities of the combatants involved, it is no stretch to say that it was also the first game in Minnesota between two major league clubs. The advance dope on the series was that "the Keystones are not the finished players the Colored Gophers are in the fielding line, but excel their colored brethren with the stick."[60]

In any event, the Gophers took the opening game of the series, 6–2, with the "very consistent" Gatewood gaining the upper hand over Jessup, who was hit "at opportune times." The Gophers pounded out nine hits with Wallace, Barton, Lytle, and Rose each collecting two. McMurray went hitless, but he scored twice as the Keystones committed four errors behind Jessup, who walked three and uncorked a wild pitch for good measure.[61]

A little luck and another curious Downtown Park ground rule also worked in the Gophers' favor. During the game a Keystone batter propelled a high drive that cleared the right-field fence by about four feet. As the ball descended it started to curve and although it passed over the fence in fair territory, it landed "about two feet to the right of the white board that marks the foul line." The next day a writer from the *St. Paul*

William McMurray was a catcher and utility man for the Gophers from 1907 through 1909. The graduate of the St. Louis sandlots was a versatile, hard working player with an ability to lead. (*Alexandria Post News*, June 10, 1909; Minnesota State Historical Society, St. Paul)

Dispatch answered a curious fan's query that in Downtown Park, "a ball going over the fence is fair or foul, not as it goes over, but where it disappears from view."[62]

Desperate for pitching, Phil Reid placed another call to Chicago and brought back his old pal Rube Foster to pitch the Friday afternoon game against Hibbing. So far that season Rube had lost only three games in 20-plus starts, and had guided the Leland Giants to the championship of the Chicago City League.[63]

Foster didn't disappoint Reid or any of the 1,600 in attendance at Downtown Park when he shut down Hibbing, 5–0, without allowing a single base hit. Facing a lineup featuring mostly ex-minor leaguers, the big man walked only two batters, hit one, "and never displayed signs of weakening for a single instant." The only other Colt base runner reached on an error when Gopher third baseman Will McMurray misplayed a bunt attempt. McMurray made up for his bobble in the third inning when he singled, pilfered second, and came home with the first run of the game on a double by Rat Johnson. The erstwhile third sacker would later double, steal a base, and score another run in the Gophers' four-run sixth that salted the game away. The Gophers pounded 12 safeties off of Jack Gilligan, with Haywood Rose leading the way with three, including a double. The St. Paul club also stole six bases and pulled off two double plays to preserve Foster's no-no.[64]

The day after Foster's gem the Gophers clubbed 12 more hits off William Gilchrist and cruised to an 8–2 victory behind the four-hit pitching of Dude Lytle. The only blemish on Lytle's record was a freak two-run home run by Dwight Booth that found yet another hole in the netting near Downtown Park's right-field foul pole. The two teams went their separate ways on Sunday, as Hibbing traveled to Faribault to take on the Flecks, and a weary Gopher squad crossed over to Minneapolis to meet the comparatively well-rested Keystones.[65]

The cancelled Birmingham dates had worked in the Mill City club's favor as they had two days off while the Gophers were busy tangling with Hibbing. A huge throng of 4,000 spectators, which included visitors to the Minnesota State Fair, Black Elk conventioneers, and 1,000 Gopher supporters from St. Paul, filled the Minnehaha Driving Park to take in the team's second meeting—the largest attendance for an independent ball game in the twin towns in several years. Perhaps unaccustomed to pitching before such large numbers, Keystones starter Charles Jackson hit two batters, passed two more, and committed an error, but he didn't allow a hit through the first six innings. The Gophers took advantage of Jackson's wildness when Bunch Davis maneuvered his way around the bases to give the St. Paul club a 1–0 lead in the first; a great catch by Dude Lytle in right kept Mitchell's team off the scoreboard in the bottom of the inning.[66]

The Keystones tied the game in the second, but the Gophers came back and put their first two batters of the third inning aboard when the pivotal play of the game occurred. Alex Irwin made a "spectacular stab" of a line drive and threw to Bobby Marshall at first to double up a straying Gopher base runner. The Keystones scored three times in the bottom of the inning and proceeded to trounce St. Paul club, 9–2. Eugene Barton blasted a home run to the left-field fence, Jack Johnson tripled twice, while Irwin chipped in with a double and "brilliant plays at critical times." Bobby Marshall pulled off an unassisted double play, collected two hits, stole a base and scored twice. Slick Jackson lost his no-hitter when Bunch Davis singled and scored again in the seventh, but he permitted only two more safe drives and finished with four strikeouts.[67]

The Gophers aided the Keystones cause by making six errors, including two each by McMurray and Gatewood. Big Bill, "who had been a puzzle to nearly all the teams that he had pitched against," was shelled for 12 base hits, walked four, and hit a batter. Rat Johnson had a bad day as well, going 0–4 with an error, while the aggressive Keystones stole four bases off him. A glum Phil Reid remarked that it was the poorest game that the Gophers had played all season.[68]

With a win apiece, the two clubs took their leave of each other — three weeks would pass before they would meet again to settle up. The reenergized Keystones set sail on a return visit to Iowa and Wisconsin. Their trip started well with a 2–0 victory over Cresco, Iowa, on September 1. Charles Jessup fanned six, gave up only three hits, and preserved his win by snaring a eighth-inning line drive to double up the ubiquitous Teddy Mellang off third base. The Keystones also took on a couple of black teams. On September 4 they conquered the Des Moines Invincibles, 15–4, and "but for courtesy could have shut out the locals." A couple of days later the Keystones journeyed a few miles south of Des Moines to take on the Buxton, Iowa, Wonders. Buxton, a coal mining town with a predominantly black population, had been founded in 1895 by the Consolidation Coal Company of Chicago. Sponsored by the local YMCA, the Wonders played and defeated many of the leading black nines of the time, although the results of their games with the Keystones remain unknown.[69]

When the Keystones came north out of Iowa they were waxed in back-to-back games in St. Peter, Minnesota, and Medford, Wisconsin. On September 12, the White Sox of St. Peter pounded William Dewberry for 11 hits, including two doubles and a triple, and loaded the bases off him with nobody out in the sixth inning of a 4–4 contest. Charles Jessup relieved Dewberry and promptly surrendered a bases-clearing triple to Lyle Pettijohn, a future baseball and football star for the University of Minnesota. Eighteen-year-old St. Peter native Harry Hughes, who later pitched in the Pacific Coast League, came on in the bottom of the sixth and gave up only one hit from then on to save the 10–4 White Sox victory.[70]

Robert Worman, another future minor league hurler, beat the Keystones, 3–1, the following afternoon at Medford, Wisconsin. Worman scattered eight hits and struck out ten of the professionals including two in the ninth inning. Jacobson, the Medford catcher, threw out all five base runners who tried to steal second on him. Mitchell's club bounced back to pound Medford, 8–1, and then finished out their Wisconsin sortie by thrashing Menomonie, 11–3 and 17–0.[71]

Following their trouncing by the Keystones at Minnehaha Park, the Gophers returned to St. Paul and split the final two games with Hibbing before a only a handful of spectators. More lucrative for the team's ledger was their 14–7 victory in a tournament on September 4 over the host Watertown Stars. The win netted the club a $125 prize and the privilege of being serenaded all day by the Watertown Silver Cornet Band.[72]

Next up for the Gophers was a novelty match of sorts at the Downtown Park versus the Prairie Island Indian nine, representing the Mdewakanton Dakota reservation near Red Wing. The "redskins," as they were unfortunately called, came into the game with a record of 41–4 and featured on their roster several former Carlisle, Pipestone, and Nebraska Indian players.[73]

The Prairie Island club hung with the professionals for awhile, although they reportedly were "dead on the bases, could not field," and only mustered three hits against surprise Gopher starter Rat Johnson. Johnson struck out eight Indian batters, but he also walked eight and hit two of them. The game was tied 3–3 when the Gophers broke it open by scoring two runs in the sixth and eight more in the seventh en route to a 13–5 thumping. The St. Paul club collected 12 hits off Prairie Island starter Weldon, including seven in the decisive seventh inning, but they also committed seven errors as, according to the *St. Paul Dispatch*, the game disintegrated into:

> one of the most farcical exhibitions of the national game that has been offered the St. Paul baseball fans for a long time. It was a combination of a team that couldn't, and a team that didn't want to play and the result emptied the grandstand before the ninth inning was finished.[74]

The club took off the following day for a two-week tour of southern Minnesota. That Sunday, September 6, the Gophers scored eight runs in the fifth inning against Charles McCleary and waltzed to a 10–2 decision over Faribault. A couple of days later the St. Paul squad downed Albert Lea, 8–6, at the Martin County Fair in Fairmont, Minnesota. The game was played in a high wind (that prevented a scheduled balloon ascension) before an overflow congregation where several spectators were hit by foul balls, including one woman who was struck in the neck but "walked away unassisted."[75]

The Blue Earth County Fair in Garden City, Minnesota, was next on the agenda and Reid's nine turned back the Austin-Westerns, 9–6 and 5–4, to garner a $350 purse put up by the fair association. More good news came later that week as the Gophers overworked pitching staff was finally reinforced when Will Horn reappeared after a year's absence to start a big Sunday contest in Red Wing.[76]

Back in September 1900, Horn had beaten Red Wing while pitching for the Chicago Unions. The river city nine had to wait eight years before they got another shot at the veteran twirler, but they made the most of their opportunity. Red Wing battered Horn for seven hits and five runs in the first three innings before he eventually settled down. The professionals were handcuffed by early by Red Wing starter Mueller, a former Baltimore Oriole, but Rat Johnson homered over the center-field fence in the seventh inning to pull the Gophers to within 5–3. Felix Wallace singled with out in the ninth to bring Johnson to the plate again, but he hit into a double play to end the game.[77]

The Gophers and the St. Paul Saints hooked up again in mid–September for two games in the southern Minnesota town of Winnebago, followed by a grand finale at

George "Rat" Johnson, who played for the Gophers between 1908 and 1909, was once called the greatest catcher in America by Hall of Fame manager Frank Chance. (***Luverne Rock County Herald**,* July 17, 1908; Minnesota State Historical Society, St. Paul)

the Downtown Park. The Saints had stumbled to another last-place finish in the American Association cellar with a 48–105 record (.313), despite leading the circuit with a .272 batting average that was ten points higher than any other team in the loop. Their pitching wasn't very good and the team committed 438 errors during the 153-game season. Once again the Saints added a few ringers to their lineup and trotted out nine former or future major leaguers to face the Gophers including two promising youngsters: Southpaw Charley "Sea Lion" Hall, who would win 15 games for the 1912 World Champion Red Sox, and John Tortes "Chief" Meyers, who was the starting catcher on four National League pennant winners.[78]

Over 1,000 Winnebago-area fans turned out Tuesday, September 15 (reportedly a great crowd for a primary election day), to watch the Saints out-slug the Gophers, 8–7, in the opener. Neither Saints starter Hank Gehring nor the Gophers Bill Gatewood was particularly sharp and the game was a see-saw affair. The Gophers took leads of 2-1, 3-2, 6-5, and 7-6 before the Saints tied it in the eighth and finally won it in the tenth. Fred Cook, the Saints right fielder, banged out four hits including a triple. Phil Geier also tripled and Lefty Davis launched a home run for the leaguers. Gatewood and Bunch Davis both tripled and Willie McMurray homered for the Gophers, but it wasn't enough.[79]

The next afternoon, 1,500 locals witnessed a well played game full of "ginger and snap." The Gophers scored two quick runs in the first against Charley Hall, but he steadied thereafter and wouldn't give them a look in. Facing Gatewood who was pitching on no days rest, the Saints scored three times in the fourth and twice more in the eighth for a 5–2 win.[80]

Before travelling back to St. Paul for their last contest with the Saints, Reid's club scurried 115 miles eastward to Preston, Minnesota, to make an appearance at the Fillmore County Fair. First up for the Gophers was a Thursday game with a strong team from Harmony whom they had disposed of 9–4 back in mid–May. Over 6,000 fair-goers, one of the largest gatherings in Gophers history, watched Dude Lytle face off against Dennis Hastings, a pitcher for the La Crosse Pinks of Wisconsin-Illinois League.[81]

Early stage fright by the amateurs led to "several errors and fumbles" that helped the Gophers establish a 6–0 lead by the middle of the second inning. Harmony scored twice in the bottom of the second, however, and "playing like fiends" they narrowed the gap to 7–6 after six innings before things got *really* interesting. In an extraordinary piece of gamesmanship, Harmony brought in none other than Johnny Davis to face his former employer in the seventh. The Gophers countered by having Bill Gatewood replace Lytle in the bottom of the frame. Davis held his old mates to a solitary base hit until Harmony managed to send the game into extra innings by scoring a run in the last of the ninth. Davis shut the Gophers out again in the top of the tenth, and in the lower half, with "the excitement tremendous, everything in an uproar," a Harmony batter tripled and "scored soon after for the white race." A day later at the fair the Gophers took out their frustrations on another Native American aggregation, this time from Black River Falls, Wisconsin, and battered them, 17–2. The win was the club's first in a week and allowed them to escape Preston with a much needed $250 purse.[82]

Many fans showed up at the Downtown Park on Saturday expecting to watch Rube Foster and the Gophers take on the St. Paul Saints. Foster did not appear as advertised, sorely disappointing the more than 1,200 people on hand, none more than Bill Gatewood, who had to pitch for the fourth time in five days.

The game began on a promising note for the Gophers when Felix Wallace led off the first with a double off of Hank Gehring. Rat Johnson followed with a liner that Fred Cook caught in right field; Cook's throw to second arrived before Wallace could scramble back, effectively ending the rally. Red Geier doubled to start the Saints half of the frame, and after a one-out walk to Jack Dunleavy, John Meyers singled Geier home for the first run of the day. Third sacker Lee Quillen's long fly to right plated Dunleavy before second baseman Pete O'Brien reached on an error, Charley Hall singled and Gehring doubled for a 5–0 Saint lead. The leaguers scored three more runs in the fourth and added another in the eighth, pounding out 12 hits in a 9–2 shellacking of the Gophers. A weary Gatewood did not field his position very well and it was remarked that he "lost his heart when not supported by his teammates." The listless Gophers committed six errors, including three by Kissing Bug Rose, and "they did not seem to be putting up their best article of ball." Wallace collected three of his team's nine safeties, including two doubles, but the Gophers couldn't hit when it mattered, and John Meyers threw them out every time they tried to steal second. Incredibly, the woeful Saints had swept the Gophers and, perhaps mindful of their good fortune, never scheduled them again.[83]

Reid's club had little time to lick their wounds, as their turf war with the Keystones resumed the following afternoon. Not wishing to compete with a season-ending Saints and Millers doubleheader, the two clubs had waited until September 20 before reconvening for another Sunday showdown at Minnehaha Park. Edward Dickinson played matchmaker again, offering up a percentage of the gate receipts and a cash prize for the winner. The teams agreed to wrap up their series with a game on the 21st at the Downtown Park to be followed the next day with a contest at Nicollet Park in Minneapolis. Bragging rights and big money were at stake — Phil Reid and Kidd Mitchell had a $500 wager riding on the outcome and there were many smaller side bets placed between the supporters of the two teams.[84]

Lytle was pegged by the Gophers to start the crucial third game of the series while Charles Jackson got the ball again for the Keystones. Both starters were in "great form" and had it not been for critical errors by both sides, "the teams might be playing yet." Slick gave up only five Gopher hits, while the Dude permitted only six Keystones to reach safely, and both twirlers struck out four of the opposition.[85]

Each pitcher also hit two batters, which when combined with seven Keystone errors, three Gopher miscues and a Lytle wild pitch "were big factors in the score-getting." Reid's club grabbed an early lead with a run in the first, but the Keystones tied in the second and went ahead 2–1 in the fourth. The Gophers scored in the sixth to knot the game at two, but the Minneapolis nine "drove another run around" and took the lead again in the seventh.[86]

The Keystones' advantage was short-lived as errors by Jack Johnson and Alex Irwin (his third of the contest) helped the Gophers to tie the game at 3–3 in top of the eighth. Later that inning the St. Paul nine had the bases loaded and made a bid to blow the game wide open. Felix Wallace met one of Jackson's deliveries with a "vicious smash," but Johnson made amends for his earlier miscue by spearing the drive near second, thus retiring the side.[87]

After the Keystones failed to score in their half of the eighth, Slick Jackson set the Gophers down with a "blank" in the top of the ninth. Facing the lower part of the Keystone order in the bottom of the inning, Lytle got Irwin out, before Jackson reached on the second error of the day by Frank Davis. Bill Binga was the next man up and he "drove out a terrific fly to the tall grass," far beyond the Gopher outfielders, which scored Jackson with the winning run in a Keystones 4–3 victory. Binga stopped at third with a triple, "but he could have undoubtedly have completed the circuit had it been necessary."[88]

The Gophers had now lost six of their last seven ball games and had arrived at a critical juncture in their brief existence. A series loss to the upstart Keystones following on the heels of their defeat by the Saints would make choice bookings and large paydays that much harder to come by. Unless the Gophers took a "big brace" and quickly won some games they would soon be "down among the weak independent teams." Looking to wrap up the series, the Keystones trotted out William Dewberry to pitch the next day at the Downtown Park, while the Gophers countered with old Will Horn.[89]

The Keystones jumped on Horn for single runs in the first and second innings and looked poised for the kill in the third when they loaded the bases with nobody out. The Gophers brain trust decided to roll the dice and bring in an overworked Bill Gatewood to relieve old Will. Big Bill was now pitching in his fifth game in seven days, but he got out of the jam with no further damage done, and from then on the Keystones could only manage a measly run in the fifth. In the bottom of the fourth the Gophers "drove Duberry from the slab" and scored six times before Charles Jessup came on to get the Keystones out of the inning. Jessup pitched well the rest of the way, aided by a great catch by Hopkins off the center-field fence, but the cat was out of the bag as Gatewood and the Gophers prevailed, 6–3. The St. Paul club out hit their Mill City rivals ten to six and both teams were sloppy in the field again, committing three errors apiece.[90]

The deciding game at Nicollet Park was a pitching rematch of the contest two days earlier, as Dude Lytle again got the call for the Gophers while Charles Jackson went for his third straight victory over Reid's outfit. This time around the Gophers used a combination of hits and errors to score four times in the first on their way to a 6–0 victory and "the colored championship of the Northwest." Lytle scattered nine safeties while applying a "coat of kalsomine" to the Minneapolis nine and the Gophers played perfect ball behind him. Jackson gave up seven hits, but the Keystones stumbled all over themselves, committing three more errors.[91]

The revived Gophers finished out the week by appearing at two more county gatherings. On September 23, the St. Paul club beat the Wright County All-Stars at the fair in Howard Lake, 6–1. In the eighth inning an unnamed Gopher (probably Haywood Rose) was hit on the back of the head by a ball thrown by the Wright County pitcher while heading into third base and had to be assisted off the field. For whatever reason, Rose didn't return to the lineup the rest of the year and Tommy Means was added to fill out the squad.[92]

The Shakopee Rock Springs fell to Gophers, 10–1, a day later at the Scott County Fair and the St. Paul club headed eastward to take on the Osceola Bethanias. On September 26 at Amery, Wisconsin, Clarence Lytle outdueled Len Schroeder in a five-inning, rain-shortened contest won by the Gophers, 5–0. For the rematch the following day the soft drink company nine brought in Minneapolis Millers ace Roy Patterson to face Bill Gatewood.[93]

The 32-year-old Patterson had posted a mark of 21–13 for the Millers in 1908, and would go on to win over 20 games for the Mill City club three more times before his career ended in 1919. In 1901, the "Boy Wonder" threw the first pitch in American League history, on his way to a 20-win season for the Chicago White Sox. Pitching before "a record breaking crowd" in St. Croix Falls, Wisconsin, the spitballing right-hander struck out seven Gophers while scattering nine hits and took a 4–1 lead into the ninth inning. Johnson, Barton, and McMurray all singled to start the frame, but Patterson easily retired the next three batters to nail down a 4–2 victory.[94]

The Bethanias only managed six singles off Gatewood, but they bunched them together with three Gophers errors and four free passes. Big Bill struck out seven, but he probably didn't get many breaks from umpire Henry Martin, the manager of the Stillwater nine. The rarely neutral Martin was quoted as saying that "Roy twirled a beautiful gem" and that "it was a pleasure to umpire behind him."[95]

Meanwhile, a mutiny was brewing in Minneapolis. Kidd Mitchell had positioned the Keystones to take on an all-star team of area major and minor leaguers at Minnehaha on September 27, but cold weather caused the postponement of the game until the following Sunday. Topeka Jack Johnson had other ideas and scheduled an 11-game barnstorming series with the Gophers to kick off later that week in southern Minnesota. Mitchell got wind of the tour and fired off a letter to the *Minneapolis Tribune*:

"Topeka" Jack Johnson was an infielder for the Minneapolis Keystones in 1908, and also found time to box a round or two. (*Minneapolis Tribune*, June 28, 1908; Minnesota State Historical Society, St. Paul)

> It has been advertised that the St. Paul Colored Gophers and the Minneapolis Colored Keystones were to play a series of games this week in the towns of Rochester, Winona, and La Crosse. I wish to have it made plain that the Keystone team has disbanded and the only game left on its schedule is the contest booked for Minnehaha Park next Sunday against the picked team of Twin City professional players. The game is to be played between the Minneapolis Keystone team and the above said professionals. I have not given sanction to any body of colored players to use my name for a barnstorming tour and if such a thing is being done it is the work of fakers and imposters.[96]

Faker or not, Jack Johnson was the Keystones starting shortstop when the team took on the all-stars on October 4, but Will Binga, Jesse Schaeffer, and Eugene Barton were AWOL and Mitchell's club was crushed, 11–0. Charles Jackson was knocked around for ten hits by an all-star lineup that boasted four former major leaguers, including Frank Jude, the great Ojibwe footballer and pole-vaulter. A Minnehaha Park crowd of 1,000 watched Hank Gehring allow a rag tag Keystone squad, supplemented by a couple of sandlot players, a mere two hits while striking out eight.[97]

Even with losses in their last three games, the Flour City team ended their inaugural season with a mark of 88–19–2 (.816), "one of the best records ever attained by a professional team in the Northwest." The 1908 Keystones had been an intriguing blend of minstrel show, ball club, and train wreck that had delighted area fans with "their quaint talk and witticisms." They were fast on the bases as well as with the one liner. When the umpires in Eau Claire, Wisconsin, announced a local battery of Olive and Derouin, one of the Keystones had evoked "great roars of laughter" by remarking, "What! Olives in Durham?"

Although the proposed barnstorming tour never came off, Topeka Jack Johnson still had some unfinished business left in Hibbing. In late September the big infielder signed on for a proposed 15-round match to be held there against Walter Whitehead, an eccentric black boxer from Duluth. Sometime during the Keystones' previous stay on the range, Johnson and Whitehead had entered into a "friendly sparring match" at a local club "just for the fun of it." After a couple of light rounds, the two fighters began getting rough, laying over "some stiff wallops" with the result that Whitehead "just escaped with his life." When the two got together for real on October 29, Topeka Jack, who outweighed his opponent by ten pounds, had the better of it for the first eight frames before Whitehead started pouring it on. In the early part of the 11th, Whitehead "floored Johnson with a swing to the jaw," and when the Keystones leader got on his feet after a count of nine, the Zenith City pugilist quickly knocked him down again, ending the "fastest glove contest seen on the range in years."[98]

The Gophers wrapped up their campaign with two games in La Crosse against an aggregation consisting mostly of players from the town's minor league squad. Binga, Schaeffer, and Cherry Barton resurfaced in a patched up Gopher lineup along with holdovers Gatewood, Rat Johnson, Jones, Horn and Means. Because the Gophers were still short a player, Botts, a La Crosse groundskeeper, was enlisted to man right field.[99]

Botts singled and a swiped a base in the first game on October 3 as the Gophers, "who had a joke to spring on every play," scored seven runs in the second inning against Jack Wolford, and held on for a 7–6 victory behind Bill Gatewood. A big Sunday crowd showed up the next afternoon as La Crosse reversed the outcome on the St. Paul nine by a 4–1 score. La Crosse minor leaguer Ross Jones got the decision over Willis Jones, who was hit hard, but kept the score down by "pitching well in the pinches."[100]

Despite being hampered by injuries that reduced the team to a two-man rotation of Lytle and Gatewood for much of the summer, the Gophers won more than 95 games in 1908 with only 28 losses and a tie. Clarence Lytle hurled over 303 innings and won at least 27 contests, including 11 shutouts, against only six defeats. Bill Gatewood pitched well over 350 innings by years end and probably won close to 50 ball games. Felix Wallace had a breakout season by playing "sensationally" in the field while posting a batting average around .325. Phil Reid blamed the injuries along with a tougher schedule as the reasons behind the Gophers failure to equal their record of the year before, but on the whole the magnate "was satisfied with the work of the boys" and believed them to be "the equal if not superior of any semi-pro club in the Northwest." With the Keystones vanquished and the Upper Midwest in their hip pocket, the St. Paul Gophers were ready to take on the world.[101]

Chapter Seven

Can You Hear the Noise? (1909)

By the time the 1909 season rolled around, the Gophers management had evolved into a two-man operation. Although he maintained co-ownership with Phil Reid in their establishment at 40 East Third Street, Treasurer John Hirschfield was no longer mentioned in conjunction with the club or appeared in any subsequent photographs of the team.[1]

In early April, Reid and Secretary Irving Williams announced that according to a new club policy their players "above all ... must be gentlemen." The pair's early signees included Felix Wallace, Sherman Barton, Will McMurray, and Rat Johnson from the 1908 club, as well as Minneapolis Keystones third baseman Bill Binga who was added to bring "zest and strength" to the infield. Bruce Petway, Robert Gilkerson, and Frank Duncan were among the other prominent black players mentioned as potential Gophers, but they weren't around when the season started.[2]

Phil Reid was determined to field his strongest squad ever. With this in mind the rotund entrepreneur embarked with his friend Rube Foster and the Leland Giants on their landmark spring training junket throughout the South, ostensibly searching for players for his club. On April 6 the Giants took off from Chicago on a 4,465-mile tour that would take them to Memphis, Birmingham, and several cities in Texas. The Giants made their journey in a private railcar to avoid "complications" with Jim Crow laws that prevented whites and blacks from traveling together. This railway apartheid didn't prevent the Lelands from winning all 16 games on their trek or Daddy Reid from having "the finest time of his life."[3]

The Gophers owner proved to be an astute judge of talent and was able to convince a quartet of top-notch ball players to venture north to play in St. Paul. With a little more luck (or cash) the Twin Cities magnate might have assembled one of the greatest blackball lineups ever. It was originally reported that Reid had secured future Hall of Famers Ben Taylor and "Cyclone" Joe Williams, but when the ink had dried it was two other Taylor brothers, Jim and John, that had been enlisted instead along with infielder Arthur McDougall and pitcher Julius London. Williams and the Taylor brothers grabbed Reid's attention while playing for the Birmingham Giants during a two-game set in mid–April against the Lelands. Joe Williams lost a 3–0 duel to Bill Gatewood, while "Steel Arm" Johnny Taylor dropped a tough, 4–2, game to Rube Foster and Walter Ball. The *Indianapolis Freeman* noted that Jim Taylor's play at third base during the series was said to be "good enough for any team."[4]

The Taylors elected to remain in Birmingham with their manager/older brother C.I. for the time being, but both McDougall and London ventured north to join the Gophers. "Artie" McDougall was a former teammate of Felix Wallace's from the Paducah, Kentucky, Nationals and had also played with Will McMurray on the 1906 St. Louis Giants. The diminutive yet sure hitting shortstop possessed "an arm like a mule's hind leg" and was coming off a season spent shuffling between the New Orleans Black Pelicans, Memphis Union Giants, and San Antonio Black Bronchos of the Texas Colored League.[5]

McDougall was likewise acquainted with Julius London, a 26-year-old twirler from

Texas, who had been a teammate of the little infielder on the 1908 Memphis Union Giants. Supposedly London, like Chicago Cubs great Mordecai Brown, only had three digits on his pitching hand, although the exact nature of his disability was never revealed. Daddy Reid nicked "the three fingered wonder" off the roster of the Houston Black Buffaloes and he soon established himself as the "big hurler of Gophers" who was "all to the merry when danger threatened."[6]

London was only the latest addition to what was an entirely new pitching staff for the St. Paul nine. Both Bill Gatewood and Dude Lytle had taken their tired arms back to Chicago for the '09 campaign, which was just as well as they didn't exactly embody the new team policy of gentlemanliness. Assuming their place in the Gophers rotation were Archie Pate, a young submarine spitballer late of Chicago Union Giants, and Pittsburgh native Richard "Buster" Garrison, who despite being only about five feet high had "speed and curves to burn." The *Freeman* once classified Garrison as a "midget" and a Wisconsin wag noted that "when he crouches forward to make his delivery he looks like a dwarf."[7]

Phil Reid didn't get back to St. Paul until Sunday May 2, so the Gophers' third season was put on hold until the following weekend when they began a three-game series in La Crosse. Just before the team left for Wisconsin the management made yet another major signing by luring slugging first baseman Bobby Marshall away from the Keystones camp.[8]

During his short tenure with the Kidd Mitchell's club, Marshall had developed into a good base stealer with some pop in his bat, and he had a long reach at first — Bobby, it was said, "has arms like the sweep of a windmill and nothing anywhere near first base gets away from him." Michigan pro footballer Vic Turosky, who competed against Marshall in the 1920's, recalled a play where the 6'1", 180-pounder picked him up by an ankle, flung him into the air, and slammed him on his head. Turosky marveled, "That's when I knew what real power was."[9]

The La Crosse nine was winding down its exhibition schedule while the newly assembled Gophers hadn't played a game when the two squads opened their series on Saturday, May 8. Not surprisingly, the Minnesota-Wisconsin Leaguers jumped off to a 7–0 lead after two innings on the strength of six hits, two Gopher errors, and two hit batsman by Dick Garrison. La Crosse starter Jack Wolford walked five Gopher batters, but he also struck out five and scattered six safe drives to pick up an easy 8–3 win.[10]

A good-sized gathering turned out on Sunday to watch a slugfest in which the two starters, Allen of La Crosse and Archie Pate, "were hit hard and often." The game was a see-saw affair in which the Gophers outhit the Outcasts 16 to 12, but also committed seven errors and "did not make the most of their opportunities." The St. Paul club fell behind, 6–3, after four innings, before roaring back to tie the game, 9–9, in the sixth thanks to three hits apiece from Rat Johnson and Artie McDougall. Pate proceeded to give up a run-scoring triple to La Crosse center fielder Ed Kline in the seventh, and the leaguers held on for a 10–9 decision. Future St. Louis Terrier Charles "Doc" Watson relieved Allen in the sixth and blanked Reid's nine during the last three frames, while "shambling" La Crosse catcher Gus Fogel "delighted the fans" by throwing three would-be Gopher base stealers out at second.[11]

Pitching before only a "few spectators" Julius London put forth a solid performance for the Gophers on Monday afternoon, scattering nine hits and giving up only four scores. Outcasts starter Alvin Lett was even better, however, and didn't allow an enemy runner past second until the ninth inning, when the Gophers plated their only two runs in a disappointing 4–2 loss. The professionals rapped out eight safeties, but they also were victimized by four stolen bases and one La Crosse run scored when no Gopher bothered to cover third on a pickoff attempt by Rat Johnson. Suitably humbled, the Saintly City squad caught the 5 P.M. train back to the Twin Cities with their proverbial tail between their legs.[12]

Part of the Gophers' problem in Wisconsin was the fact that they had played the entire series without a proper right fielder and a pitcher was forced to man the corner spot. The club also appeared to be slow on the base paths. Both of these deficiencies were addressed with the arrival in St. Paul of Eugene "Gabbie" Milliner, perhaps the fastest man in all of baseball, and "a fiend to hit." Dave Wyatt reckoned that "the speed marvel" had Ty Cobb and Tris Speaker "tied to a post" when it came to running to first. The 30-year-old Arkansas native had played for several top blackball teams including the Brooklyn Royal Giants and was renowned for slamming vicious drives that rocketed down the third base line "like a shot."[13]

On May 17 the Gophers registered their first win of the season after Julius London whitewashed the locals, 6–0, at the Grand Norwegian Celebration in Kenyon, Minnesota. Later that week the club essayed north to the Iron Range to begin a big five-game set with the Hibbing Colts. Upon on their arrival at Hibbing's Union Depot on the morning of May 20, the "dusky warriors of the diamond" were welcomed by Colts captain Bobby Geiselman. Unfortunately, a local umpire named Lyman was unable to extend the courtesy when the first contest began a few hours later.[14]

The game started promisingly enough for the Gophers when Eugene Milliner launched a second-inning pitch by Hibbing pitcher Leo Sage over the fence and into the city's new hotel, giving the visitors a 1–0 lead. Umpire Lyman then began to make his presence felt and one of his rank decisions gave Hibbing two gift runs; according to one local paper, "the Gophers were defeated right from the start and should have been given an even break." Neither Archie Pate nor reliever Julius London were able to overcome the biased arbiter, two errors by McDougall, or a general lack of stuff as the Colts pounded out 14 hits on their way to a 11–2 triumph.[15]

The Gophers jumped off to a 4–1 lead after two innings had been played the following day, thanks in part to a couple of doubles by Sherman Barton and three Hibbing errors. "Dad" Williams, the Colts starter, didn't allow the St. Paul squad a look in for the next seven innings, and helped his own cause with three hits including two doubles as Hibbing knotted the game at four in the bottom of the fifth. Williams and the Gophers "Buster" Garrison carried their duel into the top of the 10th when Rat Johnson sent a "pretty drive" over the fence for a homer that was the difference in a 5–4 Gopher win.[16]

The Saturday game was described as the "worst drubbing Hibbing ever got" as the Gophers waxed the home team, 17–2, lashing out 17 safeties against two Colts pitchers including Leo Sage's brother George. Archie Pate scattered six hits to record the win for Daddy Reid's club, but he was overshadowed by Willie McMurray who homered and scored four times. Every Gopher hit safely at least once, led by Barton who rapped out four hits. Hibbing returned the favor on Sunday afternoon, roughing up London for 21 hits, good for 33 total bases as they crushed the Gophers, 16–6. Former minor leaguer Red Carroll mashed two of the Colts' four home runs and Dwight Booth doubled three times for the rangers. The Gophers reached Dad Williams for ten hits of their own, and McMurray cracked another home run but to no avail.[17]

McMurray doubled to extend his extra-base string on Monday, and the Gophers laced 13 more hits to capture the series finale, 8–2. Garrison gave up seven hits to Judge Brady's "pets," but the Colts failed to take advantage of several scoring opportunities. The Iron

Rangers were impressed but not awed by the victors. The *Hibbing Tribune* reflected that the 1909 Gophers were "the best hitters, base runners and fielders that have ever come to Hibbing" but that their pitching staff was weak and "far from equal of last year."[18]

On their way back to the Twin Cities the Gophers escaped an unheralded squad from Moose Lake, Minnesota, by a 12–10 count in a contest "that was distinguished by a monotony of poor playing all around." The Gophers made their first Downtown Park appearance of the season on May 27 when Julius London tossed a two-hit, 11–0, shutout against the H.P. Conrads. The St. Paul squad amassed ten more hits and knocked former Saints hurler John Bartos out of the box with a seven-run fourth inning. The Gophers beat the Conrads again the following afternoon despite being held to four hits by Pacific Coast League hurler Phil Dellar and then headed 50 miles south to Faribault for two games with the always pesky Flecks.[19]

Rat Johnson did not accompany the club, instead leaving the Gophers to manage and catch for the Long Prairie, Minnesota, nine. The move had been announced before the season began while the "Rat" was still coaching for the St. Paul Saints in Little Rock, Arkansas, and was perhaps motivated by Johnson losing his role as Gophers captain to Felix Wallace. The Gophers management was said to be "not at all pleased" at losing their great backstop, and the lesser fielding Will McMurray now took Johnson's place behind the plate.[20]

Johnson's defection also meant that their right fielder would again be an extra pitcher as Eugene Milliner was shifted over to left during the Faribault series to fill the spot vacated by McMurray. Archie Pate, the Gophers starter for the first Faribault game, was familiar with the semi-pros having stymied them 3–2 in ten innings on May 16 while moonlighting for the Hudson-Collins team of western Wisconsin. The Flecks were likewise familiar with Pate and they bunched two singles, a double, and a home run by first baseman Eddie Kehoe to grab a 4–2 lead in the bottom of the fourth.[21]

Faribault starter Claude Lamb proved to be no puzzle for the Gophers, who touched him for 13 hits including a pair of doubles by Felix Wallace, as they stormed back to take 7–4 lead in the top of the

Second baseman Felix Wallace batted over .320 for the Gophers in 1908. In October 1909 the great infielder collected a couple of hits off of Three Finger Brown during the Leland Giants-Chicago Cubs series. (*Redwood Reveille,* September 17, 1909; Minnesota State Historical Society, St. Paul)

eighth inning. The Flecks scored four times in the bottom of the frame for a 8–7 advantage and only some "fast fielding" by the St. Paul nine kept the score down. The Gophers tied it at eight in the top of the ninth, but Kehoe singled off Pate to open the hometown half of the inning, and, after a double by Flecks left fielder Mahling, scored the winning run on a base hit by second baseman Malloy. Pate gave up 14 hits in all, including a triple and another double to Mahling, in addition to walking four batters.[22]

Fifteen hundred loyalists packed into Doyle's Park on May 31 to see if their hometown heroes could make it two in a row over the Gophers. The Decoration Day assembly completely filled the Faribault grounds and their buggies ringed the outfield. Charles McCleary was on the bump for the Flecks but the Gophers battered their longtime nemesis for three runs on 12 hits, and only great support by the Flecks fielders kept the Gophers to scoring more. Faribault could only muster three hits against London, but they all came in the same inning and allowed the Flecks to knot the game at three.[23]

The score was still tied in the top of the eighth when Arthur McDougall smacked a drive that struck the top of a buggy parked in left field and bounded over the fence. The Gophers claimed that McDougall's clout was a home run (his second of the game and fourth hit overall), but the Flecks countered that the ground rules clearly stated that any ball hit into the crowd was a ground-rule double. After McDougall refused to return to second base "in the proper amount of time" umpire McCarthy forfeited the game to Faribault; Reid then took his team off the grounds, claiming they were "getting the worse end of the deal."[24]

The great McCleary was back in form three days later when he set down the Gophers on only five hits in a contest at nearby New Richland. London was equally effective, giving up only three lonely singles as the New Richland club failed to advance a single runner past first. Sherman Barton doubled to left field with two outs in the fourth inning and Milliner promptly singled him home with the only run of the game.[25]

After their brief dip through Southern Minny, the Gophers returned to St. Paul for another weekend clash with the H.P. Conrads. On Saturday the semi-pros routed Archie Pate early to grab a 4–2 win at the Downtown Park, but London and the Gophers prevailed, 11–8, in a wild Sunday shootout. The Conrads out hit the Gophers, 10–8, but they also committed six errors on a Premo Park field that was "rough and made fast fielding impossible." Bill Binga picked up three of the Gophers hits, slightly offsetting a two home run performance by Conrads first baseman Lefty Dehmer.[26]

The setback to the Conrads was only a minor blip in another great run by the Gophers. Not counting the disputed Decoration Day game in Faribault, the St. Paul nine won their 11th game in 13 tries when they blitzed the Sherburn, Minnesota, club, 9–0, on June 10. The club received an extra boost with the arrival that week of two more players that Phil Reid had signed during his southern excursion. Twenty-four-year-old Jim Taylor took over at third base, moving Binga to right field, while his older sibling Johnny inherited the struggling Pate's turn in the rotation.[27]

The second eldest of four legendary baseball-playing brothers, clean living, hard working, John Boyce Taylor was given the sobriquet "Steel Arm" in 1898 by a white reporter from the *Charlotte Observer,* who witnessed his blazing fastball mow down the Shaw University nine. Possessing a good assortment of curves to complement his heater, Taylor averaged between 30 and 40 starts a season during his six years with the Birmingham Giants, while losing fewer than 40 games in that span. During a July 1908 game in San Antonio, with the bases loaded and nobody out in the last of the ninth, Steel Arm Johnny struck out the side to win a 2–0 duel against "Cyclone" Joe Williams. Two days later Taylor edged Williams and the Black Bronchos, 1–0, on a two-hitter. Steel Arm Johnny had already won 9 out of 12 games for Birmingham in 1909 before joining up with the Gophers.[28]

Jim Taylor carried a big bat, both literally and statistically, hitting no lower than .290, with a high of .340 in 1907, during five seasons with the Birmingham Giants. His fielding average at third base was "exceptionally high," and on the base paths he was "inclined to create the impression of dogginess, but he is quicker than chain lightning in a pinch." Long-time blackball pitcher and executive Dizzy Dismukes would later rate Taylor as the greatest black third baseman of all-time.[29]

The Taylors broke in with the Gophers during a two-game Downtown Park series with the Hibbing Colts. The *St. Paul Daily News* reported that Judge Brady's club arrived in the Twin Cities ready to bet on themselves "with their pockets bulging with coin." The weekend began unprofitably for the Iron Rangers as the Gophers captured the opener on Friday, June 11, 9–8.[30]

Little Dick Garrison took the ball for Reid's boys on Saturday and he continued his mastery over the Colts by scattering four hits over 11 innings. Garrison's opposite number, George Sage, gave up only six safeties in a hard-fought contest played on another muddy field. Hibbing grabbed a one-run lead on four separate occasions, and each time the Gophers came back to tie it, including in the bottom of both the ninth and tenth innings. The Colts did not score in the top of 11th and in the lower half of the frame, McMurray walked, Milliner sacrificed him to second, and Binga singled him home with the game-winner.[31]

The Taylor brothers had no sooner hit town than the Gophers departed on the longest road trip in their history, a 38-games-in-34-days slog through the Dakotas, Wisconsin, Michigan and northern Minnesota. Johnny Taylor won his first 14 decisions for the club, sparking the team to a 30–7–1 mark during their five-week sojourn.[32]

Julius London got the tour off to a good start by downing Bert Jones and Renville, 8–1, on June 13, as the club proceeded to win eight out of their first nine games on the trip's western leg. The Hankinson, North Dakota, club "skinned" the Gophers, 4–2, on June 18, behind local hurler George Rennix, who struck out eight and scattered five hits thanks to a spitball that "was a complete enigma to the colored bat wielders." A day later the team grabbed a $100 purse by downing the Groton, South Dakota, outfit, 4–2, before about 3,000 people at the Old Settlers Day celebration in Cogswell, North Dakota.[33]

The Gophers then made their way back to Alexandria, Minnesota, for a tough three-game series where "a single score meant much." In the first game of a twilight doubleheader on June 22, London got local masher Helon Leach to pop out with two on and two down in the last of the ninth to preserve a 1–1 tie. Alex took the nightcap, 2–1, when a "beautiful hit" by Chrissie Raiter off Buster Garrison drove home the winning run in the ninth frame. The next afternoon, the Gophers pounded Al "Lefty" Dretchko and future minor league twirler Louis Tretter for 12 hits and John Taylor made it stand up for a 7–2 victory.[34]

Next up was a two-game showdown with nearby Long Prairie and renegade catcher Rat Johnson. A legion of fans from "the country and towns down the line" piled into the home grounds on June 25 to watch area hurler Cal Wilson take on the Gophers' Dick Garrison. Long Prairie knocked the tiny twirler out of the game with a four-run third inning and although Johnny Taylor struck out eight men in relief, the damage had already been done. Wilson allowed eight hits, but he also struck out seven Gopher batters, including two instances when there were two out and a runner on third base. Rat Johnson's "coaching and handling of the batters" were also mentioned as big factors in Long Prairie's 4–0 upset; one account estimated that Johnson was "about one half the team."[35]

A local paper gleefully reported that the St. Paul nine was severely chastised by their management after being shut out for the first time all season. The Gophers were said to have been "considerably surprised at the unexpected strength of the locals" and lost "their heads several times" during the contest. Suitably embarrassed, the professionals exploded for 17 hits the next day and erased Long Prairie, 7–0. Sherman Barton rapped out two singles and two doubles while Eugene Milliner counted a home run among his three safeties. London gave up only two hits and struck out six more local batters to record the win.[36]

After easily sweeping a pair of two-game series in Bemidji and Grand Rapids, Minnesota, the Gophers invaded the Iron Range in early July for eight contests in Hibbing and neighboring Eveleth. However, unlike their disastrous range trip of the summer before, the Gophers managed to hold their own in another wild set of games.[37]

In the July 1 opener, a ball hit by William Binga off of Leo Sage in the eighth inning took an "unlucky bounce" along the left-field fence, and gave the Gophers the deciding two runs in a 5–3 thriller. One day later Dwight Booth's ninth inning smash to the center-field fence against Julius London plated the winning run all the way from first in a 3–2 walk-off Hibbing victory.[38]

Booth followed up his three-hit game with a double and a home run the following afternoon against Dick Garrison. The Colts racked up 14 hits in all against the "stubby" pitcher and scored six runs in the first two innings on their way to an easy 8–4 win. Johnny Taylor restored some semblance of order for the Gophers the next day when he beat the Colts, 5–1, striking out seven batters and giving up only five hits, three of which were of the "scratch" variety. Will McMurray went four-for-four and Milliner added three safeties of his own in a 14-hit Gopher barrage.[39]

Because the Fourth of July holiday had fallen on a Sunday, the town of Hibbing celebrated Independence Day on Monday the 5th instead. The local fans that "filled the baseball park to overflowing" looked on delightedly as the Colts annexed the first game of a doubleheader, 3–2, on the strength of late homers by Dick Brookins and Bobby Geiselman.[40]

After Hibbing won the second game, 8–0, the players on both teams and the huge holiday crowd struck around for a series of field day events. Members of the Hibbing High School, Oliver, and Militia Company ball teams competed in such activities as the shot put, running broad jump, pole vault, and hop-skip-and-jump. In the "100 yard special," the Gophers Eugene Milliner out ran Bobby Marshall and a local athlete named McCleod in a time of 10 and $4/5$ seconds.[41]

On July 6 the two rivals took their show over to Eveleth where the versatile Felix Wallace doled out only five hits and held "Hibbing at his mercy" in an 8–1 Gophers victory. Sherman Barton backed up Wallace with several "hard catches" and won a $5 prize offered by the Miners National Bank by propelling a home run over the left-field fence.[42]

But Wallace was only getting warmed up. Inserting himself into the lineup as a catcher against Eveleth the day after his pitching masterpiece, the Gophers captain singled twice, in addition to doubling, tripling, and hitting a home run. Wallace's cycle helped the St. Paul team carry a 10–10 tie into the 11th inning when the Gophers fell on Long, the Eveleth starter, for seven runs as the hurler's "anchor rope was chopped and the sky rider went up." Johnny Taylor relieved Garrison after a seven-run Eveleth fourth and picked up the 17–10 win before 1,200 locals.[43]

The Gophers were operating like a well-oiled machine by the time they wrapped up their successful marathon with eight wins against outfits in northern Wisconsin and Michigan's Upper Peninsula. After Johnny Taylor's 9–0 shutout of the hometown squad on July 11, the *Ashland Daily Press* recounted how Gophers catcher Will "McMurray returned the ball to the box as fast as it was delivered and Taylor would shake his glove as if it was coming too fast."[44]

Moon, "the big southpaw" of the Bessemer, Michigan, club, almost took the machine apart when he took a 2–0 no-hitter into the ninth inning against the Gophers on July 13. What made the port-sider's effort more astounding was that in the sixth inning one of the fingers on his pitching hand was injured so badly that it had swollen to twice its natural size. With one out in the top of the ninth, Bobby Marshall reached on an error by the Bessemer second baseman, and moved up a base on a wild pitch by Moon. The gutsy hurler, whose hand was now so sore that he could barely grip the ball, inched one out away from semi-immortality by retiring the next batter before Felix Wallace singled to break up the no-hitter, the shut-out and possibly Moon's heart. To make matters worse, the second sacker made another error on the play that allowed Wallace to score and tie the game at two. Will McMurray singled and later scored in the tenth frame, sending the Gophers to a 3–2 victory and rendering Moon's great effort for naught.[45]

The only blight on the Gophers' tour was the poor pitching of Dick Garrison, who dropped five of the seven games the team lost and was ineffective in several other contests. When the team came back from Wisconsin, Garrison was released in favor of prodigal hurler Johnny Davis. The slender twirler returned to the club in a July 17 game against Mankato, Minnesota, and was a trifle wild before settling down to fan six in the Gophers 7–1 win.[46]

The next afternoon Eugene Milliner dropped a third-inning fly ball hit by Charles McCleary, sparking a rally that gave Mankato a 3–1 lead. The Gophers loaded the bases in the first on McCleary, twice had runners on second and third in the same inning, but could only muster one run off their frequent foe. The Gophers also got a man to third base in the ninth, but Jim Taylor flied out to center to end the contest. The 3–1 defeat to the southern Minnesota squad was the Gophers' first loss in 15 games.[47]

With the addition of Johnny Davis, Phil Reid believed he now had "the classiest bunch of twirlers found anywhere outside of Chicago." All three pitchers were on display in Alexandria when the Gophers pulled into town on July 20 for another anticipated three-game series. The St. Paul club won the opener, 6–5, by pushing four runs across in the fifth against Louis Tretter on three hits, one of which went *underneath* the outfield canvas for a home run. London was torched for five runs on eight hits, before Davis came on in the eighth inning and pitched two scoreless frames. Johnny Taylor was the whole story of the second game as he gave up only four base knocks in an 8–2 Gophers conquest.[48]

The final contest pitted Johnny Davis against Al "Lefty" Dretchko, who had briefly pitched for the St. Paul Saints that spring. Davis was good, allowing one run on only two safe drives, but the ex–University of Minnesota southpaw was better, shutting out the Gophers on four safeties. Chrissie Raiter's "sensational" work at second base was also a feature of the game and he scored the only Alexandria run in the second inning on a Gophers' error.[49]

Even with the loss to Dretchko, the Gophers had pretty much wrapped up the "championship of the west" by winning the season series from the semi-pro powerhouses in Alexandria and Hibbing. Reid's nine now readied themselves for another battle for supremacy with their "dusky rivals from the down river town," the Keystones.[50]

The Keystones camp had been badly stung by the defections of first Bill Binga and then Bobby Marshall to the Gophers. Kidd Mitchell managed to save a little face by coaxing left fielder Willis Jones, shortstop Frank Davis, and first baseman Haywood Rose of the 1908 Gophers to throw in with his Mill City squad. Most of the previous year's team also opted to re-up with the Colonel, namely Andrew Campbell, Charles Jessup, Charles Jackson, Jesse Schaeffer, Eugene Barton, and the ageless George Hopkins.[51]

Mitchell was looking to add a "crack Philadelphia shortstop" (most likely John Henry Lloyd) and announced he had signed future blackball great Frank Wickware to pitch for his club. Unfortunately neither of these great players ever appeared in a Keystones uniform as ex–Philadelphia Giant catcher Willie Green (another former Gopher) and Milroy McCune, a 25-year-old third baseman from Texas, were added instead. The mid–May acquisition of Robert Sandford, a hurler for the Leland Giants and many eastern teams, completed the roster of what Mitchell crowed was "the greatest aggregation of colored players ever assembled in the Northwest."[52]

A cold April in the Twin Cities prevented the Keystones from practicing outdoors, so the club went inside to work out at local gyms. A makeshift version of the team fell 10–4 to Minneapolis South High School in a practice game on April 20, but the regular season didn't get under way until May 16 when the Keystones pulled into Merrill, Wisconsin, to take on the local nine for a couple of games. Naturally for Kidd Mitchell's club, the weekend began with a bit of controversy.[53]

Willis Jones left the Gophers in 1909 to play for the rival Minneapolis Keystones. (*Minneapolis Tribune*, June 13, 1909; Minnesota State Historical Society, St. Paul)

The afternoon started innocently enough when the ball teams, led by a marching band, paraded into the home grounds where almost 1,000 fans had filled the grandstands and all the space on the side lines. Charles Jessup maintained a 3–0 lead into the bottom of the eighth inning when Merrill infielder William Summerville singled and reached second on a passed ball. Jessup retired the next two batters before Merrill left fielder Brennan doubled Summerville home. The throw back from the outfield apparently went into the crowd, but Keystone backstop Andrew Campbell claimed he had caught the ball on a bounce and tagged Brennan out at third. Even though it was only the bottom of the eighth inning the Keystones left the field and forfeited the game to the home team.[54]

Charles Jackson gave up a bases-loaded single in the bottom of the 10th the next day and Merrill copped the second game legitimately, 2–1. Three days later in Ellsworth, Wisconsin, the Keystones committed six errors behind Robert Sandford, who was knocked out of the box in the fifth inning of a 6–4 loss. Mitchell's lads left Wisconsin with not much to show for their efforts, and a need to get things turned around in a hurry.[55]

Kidd Mitchell had surprised many local observers by securing several potentially lucrative weekend dates at Nicollet Park while the Millers were on the road. In the May 22 home opener with the Faribault Flecks, Charles Jessup struck out 12 batters and surrendered but one hit to a Faribault lineup that included ex–Brooklyn Dodger Eddie Wheeler. Fleck starter "Lefty" Marsh was sharp as well, fanning ten Keystones and holding the professionals hitless until George Hopkins singled Frank Davis home in the sixth with the first and only run of the game.[56]

Davis had gotten on base by getting hit by a pitch. The following afternoon, Keystones captain Willis Jones reached in the bottom of the 11th in a scoreless game when Faribault pitcher Claude Lamb hit *him* with a pitch. Davis then took a strike before socking the next ball thrown to him all the way to the center-field fence for a game-ending triple. Charles Jackson struck out 12 more Flecks and retired the last 12 batters to face him to get the win.[57]

A trip to the Iron Range in late May was marred by "very unfavorable weather conditions" and three games with Hibbing were played "mostly in the mud." The Keystones clubbed the Colts, 8–3 and 7–5, to capture the first two contests before the rangers rocked Jessup for four runs in the eighth inning of the third game to salvage a 7–5 win. The Keystones left town without playing the other two games that had been scheduled, as poor weather and lost dates would continue to plague the club for the rest of the season.[58]

After beating Rice Lake, Wisconsin, 6–3, and laying waste to a club from nearby Barron, 21–3, the Keystones returned to Nicollet Park for a pair of games with Judge Brady's Colts. On June 5, Charles Jessup and Hibbing's Leo Sage took a 1–1 duel into the ninth inning. Although the Keystones had rapped out ten hits off Sage and had placed their leadoff man aboard in each of the first five frames, they didn't score until George Hopkins raced home on a wild pitch in the sixth. Jesse Schaeffer started the bottom of the ninth by reaching first after striking out on a wild pitch by Sage. Schaeffer took second on a passed ball by Hibbing catcher Red Carroll, advanced to third on a infield out, and scored the game winner on yet *another* wild pitch.[59]

The game the next day was again played under muddy conditions, but Hibbing's George Sage threw no wild pitches. In fact, the career minor leaguer faced only the minimum number of batters during the first six innings of the contest and permitted only two hits overall. Jackson started for the Keystones, but he was "hit opportunely" and gave way to Jessup after six innings with his club down, 2–0. George Hopkins evened the game with a two-run single in the bottom of the seventh, and the contest was still tied when Jessup walked Bobby Geiselman with two down in the top of the ninth. The Hibbing captain proceeded to steal second base and sloshed all the way home to score when Dick Brookins beat out an infield hit. Sage easily retired the Keystones in their half of the inning to finish off a 3–2 win before a surprisingly big crowd, considering the conditions.[60]

The weather was again a factor the following weekend when the Merrill, Wisconsin, nine was booked at Nicollet. The game on Saturday was postponed and the Sunday contest was played in a rain which kept the attendance down. The Keystones edged the Badger club and ex–Northern Leaguer Ted Smith, 3–1, in an "uninteresting game" that was a financial disaster for all involved. Mitchell's club left town a few days later, looking for dryer climes during a month long trip through southern Minnesota, Iowa, and South Dakota.[61]

The other constant in the Keystones' history besides bad weather was their inability to find a consistent third starting pitcher. Robert Sandford left the team in early June and, shortly thereafter, Mitchell announced the signing of speed-baller William Dismukes who had reportedly gone 12–0 in 1908. "Dizzy" Dismukes later became an ace for the Indianapolis ABC's as well as a manager and club officer for many blackball teams during the course of a remarkable 47-year career, but the 19-year-old from Birmingham, Alabama, didn't pitch well for the Keystones and was released after only a couple of weeks.[62]

Dismukes was replaced in the rotation by yet another Gopher retread. Following his loss to the Conrads in early June, Archie Pate was let go by Daddy Reid's club, having allowed almost six-and-a-half runs per game on average. The 22-year-old spitballer landed a spot pitching for a team in Janesville, Minnesota, where he attracted the attention of the Keystones management by striking out nine batters and allowing only two hits in a hard luck, 1–0, 14-inning loss to New Richland on June 20.[63]

Kidd Mitchell got the Keystones' tour off to a raucous start in Waterville, Minnesota, on June 22, by drawing a gun on a mulatto man named Emil Kletschka, Sr. Perhaps not coincidentally, Emil Kletschka, Jr., had been hit by a pitch while going three-for-three with a double in Waterville's 8–4 loss to the Minneapolis outfit and the Colonel was required to post bond before leaving town. A few weeks later, Eugene Barton led off a game in Waukon, Iowa, by sticking his tongue out at pitcher "Peanuts" Fuelling and making other faces until the hometown hurler finally nailed him with a "in-shoot on the head"— Fuelling would plunk Barton again with a pitch during the Keystones 4–2 victory.[64]

Controversy of a different sort occurred in Cresco, Iowa, where the Keystones swept the locals, 3–2 and 6–3, in late June. Burke, the Cresco catcher, was accused by a local paper of intentionally giving his pitcher a wrong signal, thereby causing the bases-loaded balk that decided the first game. In the second contest, the Keystones scored three times in the ninth inning to break a 3–3 tie, thanks again to Burke who after dropping a third strike, suspiciously held on to the ball after recovering it instead of throwing the batter out. Burke was released after the game and there were "few mourners" in Cresco.[65]

The club's weather woes continued during their trek. At Oelwein, Iowa, on July 5, Charles Jackson, "the smiling pitcher," had a no-hitter going through seven innings before rain began pouring down in torrents bringing an unsatisfactory end to a scoreless tie. The Keystones' summer of mud continued in Red Wing a week later when only 300 locals showed up for a Sunday game because of threatening weather.[66]

When they got back to the Twin Cities in late July, the Keystones claimed to have gone 24–1 on their southern excursion, good for an overall mark of 56–5. Mitchell's squad certainly created quite a splash away from home, but their record was not quite as good as advertised. Faribault shut the Keystones out, 7–0, on June 27, Osage, Iowa, beat them, 4–3, on July 1, Charles City edged the team 1–0 a day later, and Oelwein, Iowa, trimmed the professionals, 4–3, in ten innings three days after that. When the PV Lands of Redwood Falls topped the Minneapolis nine, 3–1, on July 9 it was not only their fifth loss of the tour, but their fifth setback in 13 days.[67]

The Gophers and the Keystones renewed their rivalry on Saturday, July 24, at the Downtown Park. Several hundred fans looked on as Johnny Davis took the hill for the Gophers against Charles Jessup for the Minneapolis squad. Kidd Mitchell's worst nightmare came true as the two former Keystones had huge games— Bobby Marshall homered and tripled in five at bats and Bill Binga stole a couple of bases. Jessup was reached for ten hits and "weakened with men on" while Davis permitted only four safeties and "his pitching in the pinches was of big league caliber." The Gophers scored once in the sixth to snap a 2–2 tie and went on to win, 5–2.[68]

Charles Jackson started for the Keystones the next day at Nicollet Park, looking to pick up another win against a Gophers club he had bedeviled the year before. The St. Paul squad scored single runs in the first and second innings, but each time the Keystones came back in the bottom of the frame to tie the game off Johnny Taylor. The Gophers tallied twice to take a 4–2 lead in the third, but Mitchell's club doggedly tied the game in the fourth with two more runs against Steel Arm Johnny. In the top of the fifth, "Slick" again relinquished the lead when the Gophers plated their fifth run and Charles Jessup came on to relieve him. Jessup set Reid's nine down without a hit until the ninth, when the Gophers hit safely four times and scored three more runs to ice their 8–4 triumph.[69]

Bobby Marshall was again a thorn in the side of his former employers, collecting two hits including a double, and playing a great game at first. Bill Binga also tormented his old mates by rapping out three more safeties, and Johnny Taylor tripled to aid his own cause. Eugene Barton recorded two of the Keystone seven hits against Taylor and Milroy McCune prevented even more damage by throwing out two runners at the plate after making great stops at third. The Minneapolis club vowed to get even when the city series resumed the following Sunday at Lexington Park, but the Gophers had even bigger fish to fry — Frank Leland's Giants were coming to town.[70]

In mid–June it was announced that the Gophers and the Leland Giants, the "greatest team of African Americans ever assembled," would play a five-game series for "the world's championship," and that Daddy Reid had "placed a large sized roll of coin on the outcome." The series, specially scheduled to coincide with the national Black Elks convention being held in St. Paul, would be contested at the Downtown Park during the last week of July.[71]

During the previous three years the Lelands had crushed every team they had played, whether they be white, black, semi-pro or from organized ball, including the Minneapolis Millers of the American Association, who dropped four out of five games to the Giants in September 1908. The eventual champs of the Chicago City League boasted an outstanding pitching staff of former Gophers Walter Ball, Bill Gatewood, and southpaw Charles "Pat" Dougherty, who had been poached from the West Baden, Indiana, Sprudels when Rube Foster hurt his ankle in mid–July. Ball would post a record of 12–1 in the city league that year, and the trio would dominate blackball for most of the next decade.[72]

Hall of Fame center fielder Preston "Pete" Hill anchored Leland's powerful lineup by hitting .311, with 15 doubles and 21 runs scored in 27 city league games that summer. Lending Hill a hand was first baseman Harry "Mike" Moore, who roughed up city league pitching by hitting .341, and Charles "Joe" Green, who stepped in when left fielder Bobby Winston fractured his ankle, and responded with a .316 average.[73]

The Gophers were also playing shorthanded. The St. Paul club was without the services of crack hitter Arthur McDougall, who had been struck by a pitch during the last game with the Keystones. Jim Taylor replaced McDougall at short, Binga returned to third, McMurray moved out to right field, and Rat Johnson came back from Long Prairie to help the Gophers out behind the plate.[74]

"A thousand or more colored fans and a good sprinkling of white ones" crammed into the tiny downtown ballpark on Monday afternoon, July 26, to watch Julius London oppose Bill Gatewood in the lid lifter. The afternoon crowd was treated to a three-hour donnybrook featuring several shifts in momentum as the hometown club pounded out 22 hits while the Giants came up with 14 safeties of their own. Jim Taylor paced the Gophers attack with four singles and a double, and McMurray, Barton, and Binga chipped in with three hits apiece. Lelands right fielder Andrew "Jap" Payne doubled once, singled twice, stole two bases and scored three times, while shortstop George Wright smashed two doubles, and Joe Green added three hits to the cause.[75]

1909 St. Paul Gophers (mid-season). Back Row (L-R): "Steel Arm" John Taylor (P), Sherman Barton (CF), Bobby Marshall (1B), Phil Reid (Owner), John Davis (P), William McMurray (C), Felix Wallace (2B). Front Row (L-R): Arthur McDougall (SS), Eugene Milliner (LF), "Candy" Jim Taylor (3B), William Binga (RF), Julius London (P). (*Minot Daily Optic*, June 2, 1910; State Historical Society of North Dakota, Bismarck)

The Gophers jumped out to a quick 1–0 lead in the first, before the Giants exploded for four runs in the fourth and added single runs in the fifth, sixth, and seventh, driving London from the hill in favor of Johnny Taylor. The Gophers, in turn, knocked out Gatewood with a three-run fourth inning, and two runs each in the sixth and seventh frames, before Walter Ball came on to stem the tide.[76]

Trailing 8–7, the Giants came up with the equalizer in the top of the ninth and pushed another run across in the 11th for a 9–8 lead. It looked like another famous Giants victory, especially when Eugene Milliner grounded out to second to start the Gophers half of the 11th. However, in lightning succession, Binga singled, Johnson doubled, and Bobby Marshall drove the first pitch Ball threw his way over the cigar sign just to the left of the center-field home run pole and into the lots across the street. The Gophers won, 10–9, and the fans, according to the *St. Paul Pioneer Press*, went wild: "Can you hear the noise? It was thick and heavy and was plentifully interspersed with cries of 'Hel-lup! Hel-lup! Hel-lup!' not by the losers but by the winners to show how badly their vanquished foes felt about it."[77]

Both clubs adjusted their lineups before the start of the second game on Tuesday. The 40-year-old Binga, not the most nimble of third basemen, switched places with McMurray in right, while the Lelands replaced catcher Pete Booker, who had gone hitless in the opener, with Sam Strothers, who collected two hits before giving way to Booker midway through the contest. In contrast to the opener, neither team scored a run during the first six innings as Johnny Davis and the Giants lefty Pat Dougherty dueled before a good-sized gathering of 1,500. Davis was aided by some fine glove work by Felix Wallace who recorded six putouts and five assists without error, and by three assists by the Gophers outfield. Dougherty was more dominant, striking out nine batters during a performance that "was as fine an exhibition of twirling as is seen, even in the big leagues."[78]

In the top of the seventh, Davis faltered and the Giants scored three times, thanks in part to errors by Davis and Bobby Marshall. The Giants pushed their advantage with three more runs in the eighth and finished their 13-hit onslaught with two more runs in the ninth. Andrew Payne was once again the catalyst for the Lelands with three hits including another double. After a relatively quiet first game, Pete Hill collected a single, double, and stole a base while scoring two runs. The Gophers broke up Dougherty's shutout in the last of the ninth, when Jim Taylor scored on the back end of a double steal, but it was too little, and much too late, to prevent the Giants 8–1 victory.[79]

The temperature prior to the start of the following afternoon's game was a steamy 85 degrees Fahrenheit, which didn't prevent 800 cranks from turning out to witness the matchup of Johnny Taylor and Walter Ball, the pitchers of record from game one. The home team staked Steel Arm Johnny to an early lead when Captain Wallace doubled to lead off the bottom of the first, stole third, and scored on Sherman Barton's two out single. Ball settled down after that and allowed only three more hits while striking out five Gopher batters over the next seven innings.[80]

Taylor was even sharper through the first eight frames, protecting his 1–0 lead by scattering four hits and striking out six batters with his unorthodox delivery. According to the *Pioneer Press*, the 29-year-old native son of Anderson, South Carolina, "would throw arms and legs about in bewildering fashion, suddenly knot up like a porcupine, and then just as suddenly his left foot would dangle and shake in the air at the astounded batter as the ball flew past him."[81]

As usual, the Gophers provided great support behind Taylor. In the fifth inning, Milliner made a running catch of a Leland fly ball up against the left-field fence and his momentum carried him into the boards "with a thud that was heard in the grandstand." As the left fielder lay stunned, an "enthusiastic youngster" raced onto the field and revived him with a glass of cold water. An inning later, Jim Taylor made a sensational back handed grab of a line drive at short, picking it off "within a foot from the ground while going at full speed."[82]

The intense heat got to Rat Johnson in the fifth inning and he was carried from the field suffering from sunstroke; he was reportedly quite ill, but was able to continue. Meanwhile, the Lelands resorted to a bit of subterfuge in the top of the eighth, when Ball was pinch-hit for by Gatewood, but illegally returned to pitch the bottom of the inning anyway.[83]

In the ninth, Taylor's toe and arm finally tired, and he gave up successive singles to Hill, second baseman Nate Harris, and Payne. The fatigued pitcher recovered to get Booker, but then third sacker Dangerfield Talbert singled and Wright slammed a two-out home run. During the onslaught, "Taylor just stood in the box and blinked his eyes as if he was waiting for the rain to blow over." Five runs crossed the plate, although according to one Gopher, if Taylor had stuck to his "toe stunt" the Giants rally would never have happened. The Lelands sent Dougherty in to pitch the bottom of the ninth and he struck out two more batters while preserving their 5–1 win.[84]

Down two games to one, the Gophers were forced to revamp their lineup once again when Rat Johnson left to fulfill his commitment with the Long Prairie team. Ironically, Johnson would leave Long Prairie in early August to finish the season with Leland's Giants. Once again McMurray replaced Johnson behind the plate while Wallace moved to shortstop and James Taylor shifted over to third. The Gophers old captain, James Smith, who was back in town for the series, was enlisted to play second base.[85]

The matchup for Thursday's crucial fourth game was a repeat of the opener, with London opposing Gatewood. Umpiring the contest, as he had throughout the series was Big Bill's old "friend," Andrew Thompson of St. Paul. Less than a year had passed since Gatewood hurled his glove into "Honest Andy's" face while protesting a call in Stillwater.[86]

There is no evidence that Thompson held a grudge, but the Gophers got off to another good start against their former teammate, collecting their only three hits of the game in the first inning. After Wallace led off the bottom of the frame with a single to left field, Gatewood retired Jim Taylor, but then McMurray launched a double to deep center and one out later Milliner smoked a drive to the same spot for a 2–0 Gopher lead. The speedy left fielder stretched his hit into a rare Downtown Park triple, but Binga couldn't bring him home. The home club scored two more in the third without the benefit of a base hit. Wallace and Taylor opened the inning by reaching on errors and both later scored on a wild pitch. Trailing 4–0, Gatewood proceeded to knuckle down and he did not permit the Gophers another base runner.[87]

Pete Hill walked in the fourth inning and scored the Lelands' first run of the game, propelled by a single by Nate Harris and a Gopher error. Hill drew another walk in the sixth and scored on a double by Harris that cut the Gopher lead in half to 4–2. London pitched into the seventh, when it appeared "that the Lelands were finding him," and Johnny Davis came on to finish the inning with no further damage done. The ever-dangerous Hill scored his third run of the game in the eighth, thanks to the third Gopher error of the afternoon, combined with *another* single by Harris and a fly ball by Payne.[88]

During the previous three games, the Giants had scored eight runs in the ninth inning, but Davis, looking to reverse the trend, got Talbert to fly out to start the final frame. Milliner couldn't hang on to Moore's long fly however, and Jim Taylor mishandled Wright's grounder, moving the tying run into scoring position and the go ahead run at first with

TWIRLER TAYLOR TWIRLS.

"Twirler Taylor Twirls." A less-than-enlightened view of "Steel Arm" Johnny Taylor's pitching delivery. (*St. Paul Pioneer Press*, July 30, 1909; Minnesota State Historical Society, St. Paul)

only one out. But Johnny Davis could pitch in the pinches. He struck out Joe Green before inducing Gatewood to ground out to Wallace at short, saving the 4–3 triumph, and pulling the Gophers even in the series.[89]

In the Friday finale, the Lelands started Pat Dougherty, while Steel Arm Johnny, true to his name, took the ball for the Gophers with only one day of rest. Although not as dominant as he had been on Wednesday, Taylor kept the Giants at bay for most of the contest, no thanks to his support. In the third inning, the usually dependable Wallace booted Joe Green's grounder, and Pete Hill doubled, which coupled with an error by Jim Taylor brought the first run of the game home. The Lelands added an insurance run in the eighth when Jap Payne singled, stole second, and scored on Moore's clutch two out single.[90]

The Gophers could do little with Dougherty, who, while striking out seven during the first seven innings, "had the local sluggers tied in all sorts of knots." Wallace walked to lead off the fourth and James Smith coaxed a free pass in the sixth, but neither runner advanced past second. When Milliner came to bat to lead off the bottom of the eighth, the Gophers were two runs down and hadn't hit safely in 14 innings, stretching all the way back to the first inning the day before.[91]

Years later Rube Foster would tell his players that they only needed to get one base hit during a ball game, but that it had to come at the right time. Perhaps he was thinking back to what now occurred at the Downtown Park. Milliner lashed a Dougherty pitch into deep center and raced around the bases for another improbable triple. Binga was up next and the reliable one delivered a base hit that cut the Giants lead to 2–1. Marshall came up with a chance to repeat his game one heroics. He lofted a fly to the outfield, but this time it stayed in the park where it was caught for the first out of the inning.[92]

Johnny Davis, said to be able to "break up any game, at any time, with his big stick," pinch-hit for Smith and promptly singled. Both he and Binga moved into scoring position after some sloppy fielding by the Lelands. Walter Ball was brought in to face John Taylor, but Steel Arm Johnny, *not* a good stick, nevertheless "hit the ball for another bingle" and Binga and Davis both scored. Wallace and Jim Taylor both flew out to end the inning, but it didn't matter. Incredibly, the Gophers had scored three runs off of two of the best pitchers of the era, with the two crucial blows being struck by pitchers.[93]

The Giants in the ninth "tried every trick known to black or white players," including switching runners, batting out of turn, and intimidating the umpire. Gatewood pinch-hit for Green, singled and stole second, but Taylor retired Dougherty, batting illegally for Ball, Pete Hill and Harris to wrap up the Gophers' championship. The Gophers had hit safely in only two innings of the last two games of the series and managed to win both of them.[94]

Leland and Foster took the loss about as well as could be expected, claiming that the five games were only "exhibition contests." Foster ungraciously wrote, "No man who ever saw the Gophers play would think of classing them world's colored champions, or would think the playing ability of the other teams was very weak." He went on to snipe that "no doubt they need the advertising." The pair also complained that the absence of Winston and Foster greatly affected the outcome of the series. James Smith countered that the Lelands had won the Chicago City League with the same lineup that faced the Gophers. Smith, who claimed that he was out of practice when he filled in for Arthur McDougall, also noted, "I fielded all right, but did not hit, which McDougall would have done; therefore the Gophers were the team that was weak, and deserve all the credit they can get for being game and having the staying qualities."[95]

It would also seem that the frequency in which the Giants relieved their starters and their shenanigans in the late stages of games three and five belies their claims that they considered the contests merely exhibitions. The Gophers had the last word on the subject when they shut out the Lelands, 2–0, on August 24 at Buxton, Iowa.[96]

Reid's club followed up their triumph over the Giants by thrashing Lindstrom, 19–1, before returning to Lexington Park on August 1 for their third game with the Keystones. Playing in front of a nice Sunday assembly of nearly 1,000 "bugs," the Minneapolis squad grabbed a quick 3–0 lead and knocked Johnny Davis out the box in the fourth inning. Third baseman Felix Wallace relieved Davis and kept the Gophers in the game by pitching two scoreless frames. When Willie McMurray was injured in the sixth, the remarkable Wallace replaced him behind the plate and Julius London came on to pitch. The indomitable Gophers fell on Charles Jessup for seven runs in the seventh inning and closed out a 8–3 city championship-clinching victory.[97]

On August 5, Irving Williams and the new world champs left on another extended tour of southern Minny, Iowa, and Wisconsin — a slightly less exotic journey than the Indianapolis, Louisville, Birmingham, Nashville, and New Orleans soiree that the Gophers brass had contemplated earlier that summer.[98]

Arthur McDougall was still absent from the lineup when the club arrived in Fennimore, Wisconsin, on August 12 to take on Jimmy Callahan's Logan Squares. Playing before immense numbers at the Grant County Fair, the Chicago leaguers spanked a banged up Gophers squad, 6–1 and 4–1. Veteran hurler Charles "Chick" Fraser, who won 175 games over 14 big league seasons, allowed only four hits while besting Johnny Taylor in the first game. Fred "Crazy" Schmidt relieved Jimmy Callahan in the fifth inning of the second contest and his "slow ball and running fire of talk held the Gophers down" to one hit and no runs. Sherman Barton had two of the Gophers hits off Fraser, including a double, and during the second game he made a couple of great catches of balls hit into the overflow crowd.[99]

The Gophers bounced back from their setback to the Squares to go 28–4 on a tour of Iowa and southern Minnesota, beating most of the teams they faced "with the greatest simplicity." Will McMurray was said to be hitting like a "demon." and "catching the game of his life." Julius London added to his string of 16 consecutive appearances without a loss during the trek and in mid–August shut out the Oelwein Olympics on back-to-back days without allowing a runner to reach third base in either game.[100]

The next weekend the Gophers traveled down to the African American burg of Buxton, Iowa, for three games with the Wonders. Johnny Taylor threw a four-hit, 5–0, shutout at the hometown squad on August 20 and London permitted only a ninth inning triple during the Gophers' 13–2 rout the next afternoon. As in most mining towns, the Sabbath was a big day in Buxton. A carnival atmosphere pervaded the town and the grandstand was invariably packed by the locals dressed in their Sunday best. Johnny Davis and Tom "Lefty" Pangburn, the Wonders' clever little ace, didn't disappoint the Buxton faithful on August 22. The pair hooked up in a tight pitcher's duel which the Gophers finally won, 4–2, after tallying twice in the 10th inning on some "heavy hitting" by Wallace and Marshall.[101]

As the Iowa tour wound down, Reid's nine veered north to make their annual appearance at the Fillmore County Fair in Preston, Minnesota. The Gophers were all set to take on the Keystones on September 2, and "never before was there a better promise of heavy gate receipts" but rain continued to wreak havoc and the game was cancelled. A day later the St. Paul club took the on Harmony nine, looking to beat them "real bad" after their defeat of the year before. Johnny Davis found himself locked up in another duel, this time with ex–Pacific Coast League hurler Melvin Blexrud, to whom "all coons looked alike." Towards the end of the tight 2–2 contest, several Gophers attempted to reach base by getting purposely hit with a pitch, before Blexrud smoked a ball into one of their ribs, ending the barnstormer's "endeavors in that direction." The Gophers prevailed 3–2 in the last of the ninth, scoring on a close play at the plate that had the fairgoers waiting "breathlessly for the umpire's decision."[102]

The washout at Preston was at least the seventh (but not final) time in 1909 that the Keystones lost a game (and revenue) to postponement. The club also had a tough go of it on the diamond during early August, being swept in a two-game series with Alexandria and splitting two games with Rat Johnson and his Long Prairie nine. To make matters worse, the team arrived in Nekoosa, Wisconsin, on August 6 for a two-game set, only to discover that the local outfit had disbanded and no one could be found to pay their guarantee.[103]

The Keystones roster was also in flux. Jesse Schaeffer left the team after the second Gophers game to catch for the Collins club in Hudson, Wisconsin. Alex Irwin was retrieved from a local team in Menomonie, Wisconsin, to replace him. The little second baseman was given a $100 a month salary and all expenses paid to captain the squad as well.[104]

51-year-old George Hopkins hit over .325 for the Keystones in 1909. Hopkins also roamed center field for Kidd Mitchell's club in 1908. (*Minneapolis Tribune*, June 13, 1909; Minnesota State Historical Society, St. Paul)

Mitchell's boys picked up a little steam by beating Merrill, Wisconsin, 8–5, on August 8, before administering a 10–0 drubbing to the locals the next day. George Hopkins was hit in the head by an errant pitch in the first game, but he recovered to drive in a run with a triple before singling during the winning rally in the 11th inning. Hopkins also came up big in the Keystones' ensuing foray to the Iron Range when his home run during the 13th inning of the club's Friday the 13th game with Hibbing proved the difference in a 2–1 win.[105]

Hibbing beat the Keystones three times in a five-game set played mostly "in a sea of mud." As the rain kept falling and the losses piled up, the Minneapolis club's behavior took a turn for the worse. The Keystones conduct during a Sunday doubleheader with the Colts almost led to a fight between the two teams and left a bad impression with the local fans. After a brief sortie to Wisconsin, Mitchell's squad invaded eastern Iowa where they lost four out of six games and their ace pitcher to boot. During the fourth inning of a 2–1 defeat to Anamosa on August 22, Charles

Jessup walked the bases full and hit the next batter to force in a run. Jackson came on in relief and Jessup had pitched his final game for the Keystones.[106]

Jessup's replacement was the suddenly available Bill Gatewood, who had been released by the Lelands shortly after their series with the Gophers. Big Bill made his presence felt immediately, closing out an August 26 win in Preston, Iowa, by putting "one or two over the plate that nobody saw." Gatewood made his first start for the Keystones two days later in Mankato, Minnesota, but a potential win was wiped out by yet another incident.[107]

The Minneapolis nine had a 9–5 lead in the top of the fifth when Keystones catcher Andrew Campbell was ejected by umpire Walter Plymat for using abusive language while coaching third base. Campbell started to leave the field when field captain Frank Davis told him to return to the box, "saying that he would show the umpire that anyone could stay on the line for all of him." Plymat, a local attorney, gave Mitchell's squad five minutes to remove Campbell and when they refused to do so he forfeited the game to the home team. The Keystones clobbered Mankato, 10–0, the next day but they were "run in" by city officials before they left town.[108]

Unrepentant and unbowed, the club made their way to Rochester and still more controversy. Plate umpire Tom O'Connor threatened to quit a game on August 30 between the Keystones and the hometown nine on account of "the beefing from the men from Senegambia." Gatewood apparently instigated much of the trouble in a 12–11 Keystones victory that was characterized by constant arguments on the field and in the grandstand.[109]

The Keystones' latest antics were reviled by pundits in Mankato and Minneapolis, with the *Winnebago City Free Press* calling the club a "dirty foul mouthed bunch." Kidd Mitchell argued in the September 5 edition of the *Minneapolis Tribune* that he had spent several hundred dollars in organizing a team composed of "gentlemanly players," and that the Keystones were "entitled to better treatment."[110]

In early September the club went 5–1 on a short trek through Michigan's Upper Peninsula before returning home for games with the Gophers and the Minneapolis All-Stars, a collection of local minor leaguers including Spike Anderson, Sally Leaguer Bill Hille and former Renville catcher Frank Kurke. Charles Jackson struck out nine and shut down the All-Stars, 6–2, on September 18, but the All-Stars bounced back the next day for a 3–2 win before 1,000 at Nicollet. Gatewood gave up only eight safe drives while striking out eight All-Stars, but the Keystones committed two errors behind him and left 11 men on base.[111]

Archie Pate took the mound at the Downtown Park on September 20 to take on his old team. The Gophers "solved" the young spitballer early, scoring three times in the first and pounding out ten hits in an easy 9–1 triumph. Johnny Taylor scattered four hits to pick up the win on a diamond that was in poor condition due to early morning rains. A second game was scheduled for the next day, but holding to form it was rained out.[112]

In late August a Keystones player told an Iowa reporter that the team had lost only 14 of the 90 games they had played. Although this accounting was slightly overgenerous, the club still finished with a great overall record. The season had been somewhat tainted, however, by the Keystones' inability to beat the Gophers. More problematic was the team's behavior, which was burning their bridges before they could cross them.[113]

The Gophers wound down their season with a series of games in the Twin Cities and western Minnesota. In a curious twist the team was opposed on two separate occasions by hurlers who later made brief appearances in the majors. On September 5 Reid's club blanked Winnebago and ringer Ray Brown, 5–0. Brown pitched a complete game victory for the

Chicago Cubs a few weeks later, in what would be his only big league contest. The Young America nine sent Minneapolis native Bert "Dutch" Brenner to the mound against Johnny Davis and the Gophers on September 25. Brenner "had tremendous speed" and struck out 11 batters, but he yielded ten hits, four to Milliner, and lost, 5–1. Brenner would also win his only decision in the majors while twirling two games for the Cleveland Naps in September 1912. Davis fanned eight Young America batters while scattering five hits to get the win but, unlike Brenner and Brown, he never got an invitation to "the show."[114]

Jim Taylor left the club in September and Jesse Schaeffer reenlisted to play second base. The Gophers made their first appearance in St. Paul in seven weeks on September 19 when they took on the H. P. Conrads at their west side park. The Conrads worked the bunting game to perfection, taking a 5–1 lead in the third and driving Johnny Taylor from the box in the process—something that hadn't happened all year. Unfortunately for Henry Martin's Conrads, their regular catcher Willie Pehle didn't show up for the ball game and Johnson, their second baseman, was pressed into duty in his place, even though he had never caught before. The Gophers ruthlessly took advantage of the neophyte backstop by stealing seven bases and scored three times on passed balls to snatch a 6–5 decision.[115]

Next on the docket for the squad was a rematch at the Redwood County Fair with the P.V. Lands, a semi-pro outfit the Gophers had beaten a couple of times back in June. This time around, St. Peter, Minnesota, ace Harry Hughes helped the PV's down the professionals twice in three attempts, 7–2 and 5–4. The Gophers took the middle game, 5–0, but the game was called after only five innings in deference to the memorial exercises for Minnesota's Governor John A. Johnson, who had died unexpectedly a few days before.[116]

The great campaign came to a close Sunday, September 26, when Reid's nine took on a local all-star team that included Phil Dellar and Bert Brenner. Johnny Taylor allowed only five hits and whiffed seven before over 1,200 at Lexington Park as the Gophers waltzed to a 5–2 win. Eugene Milliner collected four of the Gophers' eight hits off Dellar, including two doubles. The victory was Taylor's 37th of the season (his 28th with the Gophers) and it gave Reid's club a final tally of 88 wins out of 116 games played.[117]

The following Sunday, several Gophers players headed out to Norwood to help the locals settle their season long dispute with the nine in nearby Young America. Eugene Milliner and Johnny Davis suited up for Norwood along with Phil Geier, Phil Dellar, and Bert Brenner. Young America fielded a lineup that included former major leaguer Bill "Tip" O' Neill as well as Bill Binga, Bobby Marshall, Jesse Schaeffer, Artie McDougall, and Charles Jackson. Norwood edged their rivals, 8–7, thanks to two singles and a triple by Milliner, who also stole third base while Slick Jackson was left holding the ball on the mound.[118]

That same weekend another outfit calling itself the St. Paul Gophers battled to a 5–5, ten-inning tie in Chicago with the Artesians, a local semi-pro club. The faux Gophers squad featured Jimmy Smith, Eugene Barton, Haywood Rose, and George Hopkins. Tom "Lefty" Pangburn of the Buxton Wonders did the twirling and his buddy, George "Mule" Armstrong caught—both players would see action in a Gophers uniform again. The same lineup, sans Pangburn and Armstrong, took on the Elgin, Illinois, squad on October 10. Ironically enough, Walter Ball pitched but he was pummeled for 17 hits, including three home runs, in a 15–7 loss. It is unclear whether Phil Reid sanctioned these Chicago contests. The players involved had possibly gotten wind of a rumor that the portly owner was going to fold his team and were looking to exploit the Gophers' name.[119]

Bobby Marshall and Felix Wallace also made their way to Chicago in October, but it wasn't to play for the Gophers. Instead the pair each received a reported $50 a game to suit up for the Leland Giants for their epic showdown with the Chicago Cubs. During the third inning of the opener on October 18, Marshall "suddenly became affected with stage fright" and was unceremoniously benched after dropping two throws at first base that fueled a three-run Cubs rally. Wallace also committed an error during the inning, but he recovered to collect three hits during the series, including two off of Three Finger Brown, as the Cubs took three hotly contested games from the Giants.[120]

All fall and winter the supporters and owners of teams such as the Philadelphia Giants, Brooklyn Royal Giants, Cuban Stars, and Kansas City Giants also laid claim to the title of "world's colored champions" in the pages of the *Indianapolis Freeman*. In a mid–September letter to the *Freeman*, Irving Williams restated the Gophers' case and announced that the team was "ready and willing to defend this title against all comers, meeting any of our opponents half way and on terms reasonable and suggestive to both parties."[121]

The *Freeman* agreed with Williams that the Gophers had the strongest argument of all the aspirants, but their sporting editor Charles D. Marshall also stated, "There is no way the championship of 1909 can be declared won by any team unless it is played for by a correct rule and won by fair and proper decisions."[122]

Ex-Gopher Haywood "Kissing Bug" Rose joined the Keystones in 1909. The first sacker was said to be "one of the best coaches in the business" and "worth the price of admission all by himself." (*Minneapolis Tribune*, June 13, 1909; Minnesota State Historical Society, St. Paul)

The fact remained that the Gophers beat the Lelands in a series before anyone else did, and that they posted a .846 winning percentage against other black squads that year. Unfortunately for Daddy Reid, the most persuasive argument for the St. Paul club's preeminence came from Frank Leland when he signed Felix Wallace, Bobby Marshall, and the Taylor brothers away from the Gophers in November.[123]

The Gophers owner had become an unwitting victim of a Chicago baseball war. Rube Foster had taken over control of the Lelands during the summer and Frank Leland had responded by forming a club called the Chicago Giants. The defection of four of his best players to the new Windy City nine prompted Reid to dissolve his team, although his upcoming marriage and honeymoon to Europe were also mentioned as factors.[124]

A cryptic item appeared in the *Freeman* that winter urging owners of a proposed black team in Milwaukee to "steer clear of that brand of information which caused the loyal Phil Reid to quit the game at St. Paul." In little more than three months, Daddy Reid had gone from being on top of the blackball world, "with a smile on his that won't come off" to leaving the game altogether. As it transpired, the beleaguered magnate wasn't finished yet.[125]

Chapter Eight

The Boys Are Back in Town (1910)

America's biggest sports story in 1910 was unquestionably the Fourth of July showdown in Reno, Nevada, between heavyweight champion Jack Johnson and former titleholder Jim Jeffries. The country's newspapers were preoccupied with little else after the two boxers agreed to terms in late October 1909. That the heavyweight champ, the most physically powerful man in the world, was black had tremendous implications for a nation under the thrall of Jim Crow. Many white Americans wanted Jeffries to "wallop the big Smoke good and hard," while the *St. Paul Pioneer Press* observed that "to the subservient darkey who serves your coffee and rolls this morning no greater man lives than Jack Johnson."[1]

Johnson and his white paramour, Etta Duryea, spent two weeks in the Twin Cities in early March 1910 as part of a pre-fight vaudeville tour. Most of black St. Paul was said to have been at the reception on the 10th for the champ at Tschida Hall. Johnson and Duryea needed a police escort to get out of town, however, when their taxi to the train depot broke down and was surrounded by mob somewhat unsympathetic to interracial couples.[2]

The day before the fight Phil Reid reportedly received a special wire from his good friend Johnson that was encrypted in a "code" the two shared. Reid immediately began "manipulating the Johnson stock" and made an undisclosed amount of money after "Li'l Artha" knocked out Jeffries in the 15th round. The *Twin City Star* remarked, "Well, you know Phil and he won't say how far he went. But he got a 'cup of tea.'"[3]

A week after Jack Johnson escaped from St. Paul, word filtered out that the Gophers weren't finished after all. Daddy Reid's announcement that he was folding the club so he could spend the summer in Europe was greeted with such local protest that five men stepped forward and offered to keep the team going. On top of this, 148 applications had filtered in during the winter asking for games with the Gophers, so Reid and Irving Williams decided to put the band back together.[4]

Unfortunately, by the time Reid and Williams "finally gave in to public clamor," most of their championship squad had signed elsewhere. Wallace, Marshall, and the Taylor brothers were with Frank Leland's Chicago Giants; Will McMurray was named the captain of the St. Louis Giants; Eugene Milliner joined the Kansas City, Missouri, Royal Giants; and Julius London went back to the Texas League. Only Sherman Barton, Bill Binga, Johnny Davis, Artie McDougall, and Jesse Schaeffer remained from the 1909 outfit, "as they had stayed around hoping to see the old team reorganized."[5]

Bucky Barton was given the task of acquiring talent for the upcoming season. By early April a trio of Pittsburgh area players who had spent the 1909 campaign with the Buxton Wonders had been secured: catcher "Mule" Armstrong, pitcher "Lefty" Pangburn, and infielder George Bowman. Press reports also mentioned that the team had signed a pitcher named Donaldson, but the report proved to be tantalizingly inaccurate. John Donaldson later emerged as the most dominant pitcher in blackball, but when the 1910 season began the 19-year-old was pitching for the Hannaca Blues in his hometown of Glasgow, Missouri, rather than in St. Paul.[6]

Even though they missed the boat on Donaldson, the Gophers were able to make a couple of significant additions to their roster. Thomas Clarington Pangburn and George Isaac Armstrong were a top battery for several early 20th century blackball teams. Before reaching Buxton, the duo had joined forces in West Elizabeth, Pennsylvania, and with the Pittsburgh Giants. On the mound, Pangburn had a "perfect delivery," "wonderful speed," and was said to possess "a genuine spitball." The 23-year-old southpaw was also a strong hitter who batted close to .300 in 1910, and was a good glove man; long after his career had ended, Pangburn would be called the fastest outfielder the Homestead Grays ever had.[7]

Mule Armstrong was a strong, keen-eyed, heavy-hitting catcher of "considerable renown." The 24-year-old "Army" was also a fine receiver with a powerful "whip" that kept the "base runners close to the sacks," and his throws down to second were "unbeatable." In addition, the big backstop often injected "considerable ginger into his men by his coaching."[8]

George Bowman, like Pangburn and Armstrong, a native of Pennsylvania, was the brother of Brooklyn Royal Giant star Emmett Bowman and was reputedly a "hard hitting" second baseman. Filling out the right side of the infield was George Board, a longtime first baseman and captain for the Indianapolis ABC's. The "lanky first sacker" was known to be a consistent hitter who batted .304 for the ABC's between 1907 and 1908, with several base knocks coming off the great Rube Foster.[9]

Board, Pangburn, and Armstrong arrived in St. Paul on Thursday April 28 while the rest of the team had already been practicing at the Downtown Park in preparation for a Sunday opener against Phil Dellar's All Stars. A big May Day crowd of 2,500 packed into Lexington Park to watch the Gophers trim Dellar's collection of minor leaguers and semi-pros, 5–1. Johnny Davis and Lefty Pangburn shared the pitching duties for the victors, who were said to possess "a strong

"Clever" twirler Johnny Davis tossed no-hitters for the Gophers in 1907 and 1910. (*St. Paul Pioneer Press*, May 1, 1910. Courtesy of the Minnesota State Historical Society, St. Paul)

determination among the members to keep up the record that has been made in the past three years." Phil Dellar struck out 11 batters, but he was undone by his catcher, ex–Canadian Leaguer Bowers McGarry, who allowed seven stolen bases, including three by Sherman Barton.[10]

The Gophers lineup that took the field against the All Stars and a couple of Minnesota-Wisconsin League teams the following week was a work in progress. George Board at first base, George Bowman at second, Captain Bill Binga at third, Mule Armstrong behind the plate and center fielder Sherman Barton were the constants. Artie McDougall, Jesse Schaeffer and two newcomers, Dakota veteran Dave Kennedy and a player named Hill, took turns manning shortstop and the corner outfield spots.[11]

On May 3 the Eau Claire Commissioners downed the Gophers, 5–1, and followed it up with a 5–0 win the next day, as George Bowman's single was the only hit off hurler John Nicholson in the second game. In the Thursday finale, the Gophers batted around in the second inning to take a 5–2 lead, but Lefty Pangburn couldn't finish the deal. The locals scored three in the ninth, with the tying run coming across on a two-out, no-ball-and-two-strikes single by Eau Claire manager Tommy Schoonhaven. Pangburn walked the next man before giving up a single to outfielder Dan Kick, but Barton threw Schoonhaven out at the plate to save the day. In the top of the 10th, Barton walked and scored all the way from second on a wild pitch to give the Gophers a 6–5 win.[12]

The Gophers moved on to La Crosse for a weekend set with the Outcasts, marred by "inexcusable errors ... bonehead plays, and all around sluggishness." The minor leaguers handed Johnny Davis his third loss of the year on Saturday the 7th as Bill "Bots" Whittaker scattered five hits and collected three of his own in a 5–1 La Crosse victory. Davis helped the locals out by wild pitching two runs home. Pangburn also experienced a bout of wildness the next day, walking four batters and hitting two others as the Outcasts raced out to a 5–2 lead. The Gophers roared back with a five-run 7th, with the big blow being Pangburn's two-run single, and held on for a 9–5 triumph. Phil Reid was in attendance during the series and was said to be filling in fellow Kentuckian Irving Williams on the fine points of running a ball club.[13]

The Gophers management had scheduled several games in the Dakotas, where they believed the squad could make more money than in Minnesota. Prior to their initial western trip the Gophers third pitcher arrived, a "big twirler" named Ford who was said to have played with the Philadelphia Giants. Schaeffer and Hill departed the squad around this time as Kennedy took over at short while McDougall settled in left field.[14]

Ford made his debut in Norwood on May 15 and was lit up for 11 hits in the Gophers 8–5 victory. Sherman Barton continued his early season surge with a double, an outfield assist, and a "terrific home run drive." The club then ventured west to play several squads in a South Dakota independent league. The Gophers ran into a buzz saw in Aberdeen, dropping the first two games with the local team, 4–2 and 7–1, before "immense" weekday gatherings of 1,500 and 1,300 that packed "the grand stand, bleachers, and box cars" to their "uttermost." Perhaps the professionals were hoodooed by the return to the skies that week of Halley's Comet, or maybe it was Jacques and Gregory, the Aberdeen hurlers, who struck out 7 and 12 Gophers, respectively. The St. Paul club salvaged the last contest of the series, 8–0. Phil Reid left for Chicago after the game, vowing to sign four new players for his team, and return to the Hub city and "get even."[15]

Even though Dave Kennedy collected three hits in the first match against Aberdeen and seemed to be pulling off "stellar stunts as regularly as ever," he left the club after the series and was replaced at shortstop by McDougall. The Gophers proceeded to crush a pair of squads in Groton and Conde before heading east to Watertown for a four-game set with the hometown Grays. On May 21, the locals took the first contest, 7–1, behind their little southpaw Ellefson who held the Gophers to four singles while leading the Gray attack with a double and a single. A record gathering of nearly 2,500 showed up the next day to watch Ford and Watertown hurler Ed "Smiler" Pframer hook up in a tight pitcher's duel. Pframer whiffed 11 batters while Ford surrendered only five hits, and was saved several times by his outfield, which gave him "sensational support." The game was scoreless in the top of the eighth when Binga and Bowman singled to begin the frame. Armstrong was up next and as the Sunday crowd "held its breath" the big catcher doubled the runners home to secure a 2–0 Gophers triumph.[16]

Wesley, one of Daddy Reid's new recruits, arrived in time for the third contest and made a good initial impression with a single and a stolen base. Ellefson, the game one hero, came on to pitch in the fifth inning of a 1–1 tie and held down the Gophers to two scratch singles the rest of the way. Former Renville star Bert Jones collected two hits off Lefty Pangburn, and his single in the fifth drove in what proved to be the deciding run in a 5–1 Watertown win. Old Bert also made a sensational grab of a Barton line drive in the eighth inning that prevented a certain home run and "probably saved the day."[17]

Tuesday's contest was "the hardest fought" of the series, featuring another taut duel between Johnny Davis, who allowed only five lonely hits, and Ed Pframer, who struck out seven more Gophers. For awhile it looked like Armstrong's fourth-inning home run might be enough, but Davis hit Bert Jones with a pitch in the seventh and he scored all the way from first on a double by Pframer to tie it. Tom Pangburn led off the Gopher ninth by reaching second after Eikins, the Watertown first baseman, couldn't hang on to a throw from Pframer. Johnny Davis fanned, but Pangburn advanced to third on a McDougall fly to right and scored the professionals' second run when Eikins dropped a throw that would have retired George Board with the third out. Second baseman Johnny Leeds started the home ninth with a single and "Smiler" Pframer followed with a liner to left center that "had all the ear marks of a homer," until Pangburn caught the ball off his shoe tops to preserve a 2–1 Gophers victory.[18]

Reid's squad finished their initial tour with a swing through southern Minnesota and Iowa. Starting with the finale in Watertown, the Gophers reeled off 11 straight wins, but they didn't impress many people along the way. The St. Paul nine clubbed Owatonna, 12–7, on June 2, but the local newspaper complained that "they are not for a moment in the same class with the aggregation who played here some two years ago." Pangburn gave up only four hits, three of them by Paul, the Owatonna first baseman, who mashed two home runs and a double, which earned him a five-dollar bill from a grateful spectator. The Gophers committed seven errors, but that was one less than the locals made.[19]

While the Gophers were slogging their way through South Dakota, Phil Reid was in the Windy City searching for reinforcements. The big man was on hand on May 22 when Rube Foster's Leland Giants made their Chicago debut by beating the Stars of Cuba, 7–1, at Normal Park. Reid had a reserved seat and congratulated his good friend on his pitching performance and on the large crowd present. Reid also found time to book another championship series with Frank Leland's Chicago Giants, to be played in St. Paul that July.[20]

Reid's outfit wasn't the only Twin City team shaking up their roster. After two years of playing second fiddle to the Gophers, Kidd Mitchell was making some significant changes to his Keystones "with the intention of winning the championship over all teams." Big Bill

Gatewood was installed as captain and grizzled vets like George Hopkins, Willis Jones, and Alex Irwin were let go. In January, the Colonel made a big splash by inking a trio of former Indianapolis ABC's standouts who had spent the previous season with the Chicago Union Giants: James Shawler, James Lyons, and Frank Young.[21]

Jimmy Lyons was not in attendance when the Keystones gathered in Minneapolis in mid–April, but John Merida, another longtime Indianapolis ABC, was. Also along for the ride was James Coleman, a ball player from Texas, and former Gopher Clarence Lytle, who was coming off a great year with the Union Giants. From July 16 to September 3, the "Dude" won 16 straight decisions and in mid–August, he tossed a reported *three* no-hitters in 12 days including two over a club from Rockford, Illinois. Gatewood topped the list of the seven returnees from 1909, along with pitcher Charles Jackson and outfielder Eugene Barton, who were both back for a third season with the Mill City team. Shortstop Bunch Davis and third baseman Milroy McCune were the holdovers in the infield, while catchers/utilitymen Willie Green and Archie Pate had been retained as well.[22]

John "Big Boy" Merida in 1902. The Spiceland, Indiana, slugger played for the Keystones in 1910, before passing away in May 1911 at the age of 32. (Courtesy of Richard P. Ratcliff)

The ex–ABC's brought both vim and vigor to the lineup. By season's end, 25-year-old Frank Young established himself as the Keystones leadoff man and a fan favorite at second base. Kentucky-born James Shawler had played with the ABC's since their inception in 1902 and went on to captain the Union Giants during their very successful 1909 campaign. While with the Keystones, the 31-year-old outfielder "made himself famous with his great hitting," and was said to be able to knock a home run "whenever the fans ask for one." John "Big Boy" Merida was a powerful slugger from Spiceland, Indiana, who the *Indianapolis Freeman* once called "a terror of all pitchers." The 31-year-old catcher/second baseman had been the ABC's best all-around player and mashed a .515 plus slugging percentage in 1908.[23]

Unfortunately, patrons in the Twin Cities never got much of a chance to see the

Hoosier lads play. Even after the Keystones defeated the Minneapolis Millers in an exhibition that spring, the club's management had difficulty booking games in the area. During their first two seasons the team had resorted to showing up in towns a day before they were scheduled to arrive, trying to hustle another contest or two. The *Twin City Star* believed that the Mill City nine's on-the-field antics were the main cause of their problems: "A good team of good players, under good management, could secure good dates, and this can only be done if they go in to win by playing ball. That 'rough house' business can't last long and it hurts everybody." Kidd Mitchell accused the *Star* of favoring the Gophers at the expense of his squad and the Keystones never played in Minneapolis again.[24]

Instead, the Colonel focused his attention elsewhere. Thomas Waler, "one of the foremost and leading magnates in the South," urged Mitchell to move his team to Texas. "Almost since the day of emancipation," a San Antonio paper once reported, "the colored baseball championship of Texas has been a disputed question," and an informal organization of teams had existed for several years. The Keystones manager was blown away when over 3,500 people, including the Longhorn state's "most distinguished ladies and gentlemen" turned out for a Sunday game in Dallas. On April 26 Mitchell made his way to San Antonio where political boss Charley Bellinger had folded his Black Bronchos. "I am tired of' being champion," the numbers king was quoted as saying, "so thought I would give some of the others a chance." Mitchell decided to take the Black Bronchos place in the Texas Colored League and shifted his club's base of operations to Bellinger's office at 236 East Commerce Street in San Antonio.[25]

On their way to Texas the Keystones stopped off in Kansas City to play the two top black teams in the area, but most of the action ended taking place off the field. On May 14, the Kansas City, Kansas, Giants and pitcher Bill Lindsay, "the Kansas Cyclone," edged the Minneapolis club, 6–5, in the first game of a scheduled four-game series at Riverside Park. After the remaining games were rained out, Kidd Mitchell became irate when Giants owner Tobe Smith paid him only $50 out of the $200 he believed he was due.[26]

Smith pointed out that the contract between the two teams stated that the Keystones were to receive at least $50 per contest, "provided that the games should be played." The Giants owner maintained that he didn't have to pay off on the three games that were cancelled. After much haggling and consulting with attorneys Smith gave the Colonel an extra $100 "so that I might retain his friendship." Mitchell responded by hiring "two of the best young attorneys in Kansas City" and suing Smith for the other $100 he was owed. However, the Colonel soon dropped his suit after being informed that he would have to post bond for court costs because he was a non-resident of Missouri.[27]

In early June, Mitchell fired off a letter to the *Indianapolis Freeman* accusing the Kansas City magnate of hurting the game by not standing by his contracts, calling him "the most unreliable man I ever did business with." Tobe Smith refuted the Colonel's statements in a lengthy tome to the *Freeman* three weeks later. After accusing Mitchell of making "false and defamatory" statements, Smith drily remarked that he was running a business for profit, "instead of a charitable institution for the distribution of alms."[28]

The Keystones had better luck, on and off the diamond, with the Kansas City Royal Giants. The Missourians were captained by former Mitchell employee "Topeka" Jack Johnson and featured another ex–Keystone, catcher Andrew Campbell, as well as former Gopher Eugene Milliner in center field. On May 18 in Atchison, Kansas, "a small crowd composed exclusively of colored people" watched the Keystones dispose of the hometown Atchison Blues, 6–3, before downing the Giants, 10–6. The local paper noted that the Keystones were "more evenly balanced than the Giants" but that they didn't have any players as good as Johnson or Campbell.[29]

The two clubs traveled back east to Kansas City for a three-game set at Shelley Park. The Keystones "had the biggest bunch of horseshoes" and downed the Giants, 8–6, on Friday, May 20, in a "rattling good game." Jack Johnson's squad bounced back the next day and pounded 15 hits off of Archie Pate and Slick Jackson in the course of a 9–3 rout. Rain washed away a potentially good payday on Sunday and when the two teams met on Tuesday to wrap things up, the Keystones raced off to a 6–1 third-inning advantage against Royal Giant starter Lown Lee. Bill Gatewood made the lead stand until the bottom of the seventh when the Kansas City nine tallied five times to tie it up. Nonplussed, Mitchell's club scored two in the eighth and three in the ninth and held dearly on for an 11–9 victory that "was more interesting than the score would indicate." The Keystones pounded out 14 hits off Lee — Big Bill only gave up six safeties, but his defense made five errors behind him.[30]

Kidd Mitchell later indicated in the *Freeman* that the weather for the Royal Giants games had been very poor, and the gate receipts fell well below the guarantee, but unlike Tobe Smith, the Royal Giants management "paid us in full without a word." Upon leaving Kansas City, the Keystones were supposed to play two games in Albia, Iowa. Instead the team cancelled all their remaining northern dates and headed off for Bill Gatewood's hometown of San Antonio.[31]

When the Gophers returned to St. Paul for an early June set with the Conrads, they were met by a pair of familiar faces: Bobby Marshall and Jim Taylor rejoined the team after they jumped or were dropped by the Chicago Giants. While with the Giants, Marshall had smothered "the first bag greater than ever before," but neither he or Taylor hit much when the team reached Chicago and both players were noticeably missing from the starting lineup after a couple of mid–May losses to the Cuban Stars. Marshall reportedly received $40 a week plus expenses for his trouble, but he had become disillusioned with some of his teammates carrying on during a southern tour that spring. George Board, batting less than .100 at the time, was sent packing to make room for Marshall at first, while Jim Taylor was installed as the Gophers new captain.[32]

Taylor and Marshall were both in the lineup on June 5, when the Gophers tangled with the Conrads at the Downtown Park. As 900 cranks looked on, Marshall singled, stole a base, and made a brilliant spear of a line drive in his return. The professionals scored two runs in the eighth inning to snap a 3–3 tie and held on for a 5–3 victory. Johnny Davis struck out nine and allowed only five singles to pick up the win. Binga and Armstrong each had two hits, including a double apiece, while Sherman Barton connected for two sacrifice flies.[33]

At Lexington Park the next afternoon, poor weather affected both the two teams' performance and the gate receipts. Phil Reid and John Hirschfield were among the 600 Sunday faithful that watched the Gophers build up a 5–1 lead against ex–Millers hurler Joseph "Lefty" Sporer. George Bowman rapped out three of the Gophers 11 hits, and he and Mule Armstrong both tripled. Lefty Pangburn fanned seven batters and was reached for only six base knocks, but four late errors by his defense let the Conrads pull to within 5–4 in the eighth. The Gophers pushed across an insurance run in the top of the ninth , but the semi-pros tallied in the bottom of the frame to make the score 6–5 and had two men on base before "fast work by McDougall and Marshall left them there."[34]

Following the Conrad series, the Gophers departed St. Paul for a five-week trek through

St. Paul Gophers (June 1910). (L-R): Arthur McDougall (SS), George Bowman (2B), Thomas "Lefty" Pangburn (P), "Candy" Jim Taylor (3B), William Binga (RF), George "Mule" Armstrong (C), John Davis (P), Sherman Barton (CF), Wesley (Utl), Ford (P), Bobby Marshall (1B). (*Preston Times*, September 7, 1910; Minnesota State Historical Society, St. Paul)

the Dakotas and northern Minnesota. Ford left around this time, leaving Pangburn and Davis to halve the pitching duties, while Jim Taylor took over at shortstop, Wesley moved to third base, and Arthur McDougall went back to left field.[35]

On their way west, the Gophers beat Waseca and 38-year-old twirler Charles McCleary, 10–8, although the local feeling was that the St. Paul squad was "a much slower aggregation than was supposed," which "didn't have much on the local team." On May 12 the Gophers won their 17th game in a row by pounding the Watertown Grays, 8–3. The 18th straight came a day later after Binga deliberately jumped into the way of a pitch by a Watertown pitcher and Bowman tripled him home with the decisive run in a 2–1 triumph.[36]

On May 14, Reid's crew made it back to Aberdeen, where a Barton double and two hits apiece by Taylor, Armstrong, and McDougall, led to a 4–3 Gopher win. The two teams engaged in a three-hour marathon the next afternoon that see-sawed back and forth, until "the nerves of black and white were a wreck and voices frayed to a whisper." A sixth-inning homer by Aberdeen shortstop Osgood put his side up, 5–4, but Bobby Marshall doubled and scored to tie the game in the seventh. Later in the frame the Gophers had two men on and were looking to blow things wide open, but Jim Taylor lined into a triple play started by Young, the Aberdeen center fielder. Johnny Davis and his opposing number Jacques took over from there and the score was still 5–5 after 14 innings were in the books. With one down in the 15th, Bill Binga singled, Taylor doubled, and they were brought home by two-out Armstrong and Barton singles. Davis closed out the 7–5 result, much to the delight of the local black populace which, according to the *Aberdeen Daily American*, proceeded to order more pork chops and chicken for supper "than there have been for many, many days."[37]

The St. Paul outfit annexed their 23rd consecutive victory on June 18, as newcomer

Louis Johnson scattered five hits while shutting down the Minot, North Dakota, Magicians, 11–1. The Gophers latest addition was a "clever" spitball artist who would develop into one of blackball's best pitchers during the teens and early twenties.[38]

The *Twin City Star* intimated that Johnson had been a star hurler for the University of Illinois, although his name doesn't appear in any of the Illini box scores from the period. When the hurler's name *did* appear in contemporary box scores or game accounts it was almost always preceded by the nicknames "Dicta," whose origin remains a mystery, or "Spitball" which was self-explanatory.[39]

Whatever his brush with higher education might have been, Johnson joined the Indianapolis ABC's in 1908, and pitched for them until the summer of 1909 when he hooked up with Dave Wyatt's Illinois Giants. The Memphis native had a brief trial with the Leland Giants that July, and registered two one-run decisions over the Cuban Stars. Among Johnson's victories in 1910 was an 11-strikeout performance over Will McMurray's St. Louis Giants.[40]

Minot ended the Gophers' winning streak at 23 games on June 19 by upsetting the St. Paul club, 10–6. Bobby Marshall doubled twice, but he also committed three of the Gophers *ten* errors. Not all was lost however — Armstrong hit a two-run home run over the centerfield fence in the first inning, thus earning a set of cigars from the Minot Grocery company.[41]

The next day the St. Paul club encountered yet another youngster soon to appear in the big leagues: William "Nitchie" Cadreau, a 20-year-old Ojibwe fire-baller from Cloquet, Minnesota, who had once allegedly pitched a game with a broken arm. In October, under the non de plume of "Chief Chouneau," Cadreau would start the Chicago White Sox's final contest of the season and lose his sole appearance in the majors to the Tigers.[42]

Against the Gophers, Cadreau's "steam was the wonder of the evening" and he struck out seven batters while giving up but five singles. Cadreau couldn't keep Barton, Marshall, and Pangburn from stealing third base after they reached against him, however; all three runners eventually scored as the Gophers nipped the Magicians, 3–1. Pangburn allowed only four safeties and pitched out of a bases-loaded jam in the second inning to pick up the victory. Marshall committed another error and he and Pangburn got into a vocal altercation over a pop-up near home plate. The *Minot Daily Reporter* thought that the pitcher should have kept his "clam" closed, as "there was no occasion for remarks."[43]

After the Gophers captured the last three games of the series the *Reporter* lamented, "Gone is the magic of the Magicians." Johnny Davis three-hit the local nine, 7–0, on June 22 and stole home after his seventh-inning double to rub a little salt in the northern team's wounds. In the ninth, McGill, the Minot right fielder, hit a deep fly to center that "hesitated, seemed to stand still for a moment, and finally fell back into the lot," where Barton retrieved it before throwing the batter out at third. A dispirited local fan told Davis, "It's all horse luck," to which the pitcher replied, "You gimme the luck and you can have the science."[44]

The club shuffled their lineup once again after the Magicians series as Jim Taylor moved over to third, Arthur McDougall went back to shortstop, and Wesley took his spot in left field. Wesley, who was characterized as "the goat for the Gophers" who always "slides feet first" was guilty of four errors during the six Minot games, but was advised by the city daily to "cheer up" because of the great "wing" he possessed.[45]

Wesley's strong arm was not in evidence on June 24 when he filled in for Mule Armstrong in the first of a three-game weekend engagement in Valley City. The Gophers' regular backstop missed the contest with a bad hand and the strong semi-pro nine responded by stealing five bases against his replacement. Valley City starter "Big" Hank Thrall struck out nine Gophers and spaced out seven hits to garner a 5–3 win. Louis Johnson also handed out seven safeties and struck out 11 Valley City batters but he was done in by right fielder Jack Doyle who twice drove in his brother Martin from third base. The North Dakota club also got a little help from an umpire named Murphy; with the home team up by two after eight innings had been played, the local arbiter called the game on account of darkness.[46]

All three of the Gophers games in Valley City were well attended, although much to the two club's chagrin, a large number of fans in "the charity bleacher" beyond the right-field fence watched for free. The Saturday night contest was "replete with sensation after sensation," and was described as "one of those games that you read about but seldom see."[47]

Valley City scored once in the first and twice in the second to take a 3–0 lead, but the Gophers came back with four runs of their own in the third to knock Leahy, the sore-elbowed local starter, out of the game. The bases were loaded with nobody out when center fielder Martin Doyle came on in relief; the future minor leaguer got Barton to hit a grounder to shortstop "Rabbit" Melander who threw home in time to retire Jim Taylor. McDougall followed with a fly to right that Jack Doyle ran down before uncorking a "perfect peg" to the plate to nab George Bowman. Doyle only yielded a ninth-inning single to Marshall the rest of the way and he subsequently caught the Gopher slugger "between the sacks" by making a bluff throw to first after nabbing a ground ball. Johnny Davis was equally good until the bottom of the eighth when Martin Doyle "smeared" one of his pitches to right center for his second triple in two days. Jack Doyle plated his brother once again with a single to right and he came around to score moments later on a single by the first baseman Mills with the decisive run in Valley City's 5–4 win.[48]

Looking for the sweep on Sunday afternoon, the Dakota lads forged a 3–0 lead in the first against Pangburn on a hit, a couple of walks, and two errors by Lefty's favorite fielder, Marshall. In the fourth frame the Gophers combined three free passes issued by Guthrie, the Valley City starter, along with two hits and an error to score four times en route to a 7–5 victory. Jim Taylor doubled, tripled, and pilfered a base to spark the professionals while Pangburn whiffed sixteen batters, "making the heavy sluggers of the home team look like a lot of old women trying to connect with his elusive shoots."[49]

The road trip continued on to nearby Jamestown, North Dakota, where the barnstormers beat the hometown nine, 4–1 and 10–2, in two well attended twilight contests. The Gophers grabbed a 2–0 lead in the series wrap up on June 29, but the locals tied it with two runs in the fifth inning. The game was still knotted up in the eighth when another brother combination stepped to the plate. Jamestown hurler Jim Boyle was hit by a Pangburn pitch, stole second, and scored on a double by his sibling Jack to hang a 3–2 defeat on Lefty, his first loss of the year.[50]

After the loss to Jamestown, the Gophers didn't drop another game for almost three weeks— the St. Paul club swept five doubleheaders in a nine-day stretch between June 30 and July 6. Johnny Davis got the ball rolling on the last day of June by no-hitting the squad in Hope, North Dakota, 9–0, with the only Hope base runner reaching on an error. To ease the load on the pitching staff, a few of the position players took a turn in the rotation with Artie McDougall besting Fargo 4–3 on July 4th and Jim Taylor setting down Langdon, North Dakota, 3–1, two days later.[51]

The professionals experienced a few hiccups during their great run. In early July, a club in Park River, North Dakota, battled the Gophers to an eight-inning scoreless tie. Pangburn scattered five safe drives while his teammates connected for three triples against

Thomas the local twirler, but could not score before the game was called because of darkness. More trouble was waiting in Crookston, Minnesota, on July 11 when the Gophers took on the hometown nine in front of a packed grandstand. Alfred Narveson, who later pitched in the Northwestern League, held the professionals scoreless for eight innings, and his fourth-inning home run off Johnny Davis was the Cubs only run of the game. With darkness approaching in the ninth the Gophers scratched out a 1–1 tie when Barton singled, was sacrificed to second by Bowman, advanced to third on a passed ball, and scored on a single to center by Wesley. Two days later Reid's club experienced their third deadlock in a week, a 3–3 standstill with the Cass Lake, Minnesota, club, as area hurler Hermann "Pete" Schmidt fanned 12 Gophers during a seven-inning contest.[52]

The Gophers reached Hibbing in mid–July for a taut five-game series that featured two extra-inning thrillers and three games decided by one run. The series opener on Friday the 15th was played in an intense heat that didn't deter the local fans from repeatedly applauding the great deeds of each team. Hibbing starter Jensen hooked up in a duel with Lefty Pangburn, who allowed only four hits while striking out 13 of the Colts. The southpaw hurler also rapped out two of the seven Gopher safeties and was helped by his fielders who threw out several Hibbing runners at the plate. Tied at two in the ninth, the Gophers pushed the winning run across on a double, an error by Jensen, and two infield outs.[53]

During the game the next day, the St. Paul club took leads of 3–0, 4–3, and 5–4, only to have the Colts tie up the game each time. The Gophers plated two runs in the 10th inning off Hibbing reliever Dick Brookins and held on for a 7–5 win. Two thousand Iron Rangers came out on Sunday the 17th to catch the third game of the series and to watch Athos, the world's champion 145-pound wrestler take on a bull. The wrestling match didn't come off, but the ball game more than made up for it. Thanks to some reckless fielding by pitcher Jensen, the Gophers led 2–0 after three innings. As the game wore on the St. Paul club put several runners on third base with only one out, but could not get another run home. The Colts tallied once in the fourth and tied the game in the sixth when Brookins scored from third base after Johnny Davis sent a pitch sailing over Armstrong's head. The score was still knotted at two in the bottom of the ninth when Pangburn relived Davis, who had given up three consecutive hits, but no runs in the eighth. Pangburn immediately loaded the bases by walking two of the first four batters he faced and hitting a third. The port-sider struck out Jensen for the second out of the inning, but then missed on a 3–2 pitch to Brookins to walk in the winning run.[54]

Dwight Booth set down the Gophers their first two times up the following afternoon, but in the next two frames Reid's outfit fell on the Colt mainstay for five hits, including a homer by Binga, and seven runs. Brookins came on in relief, but the Gophers pounded him around as well in an 11–5 thrashing. The St. Paul nine took a 4–1 lead into the ninth inning of the series closer on July 19, only to see the Colts tie the game with four one-out singles in a row off Louis Johnson; Hibbing got the potential winning run to third base with two down before Johnson struck out Brookins looking. In the top of the 10th, Bobby Marshall rapped a base hit off Jensen and tried to stretch it into a double. Dwight Booth's throw from center appeared to nip the Gopher first baseman at second, but he was ruled safe by the umpire Lyman. After a big argument with the Colts fans and players, the frustrated arbiter threw down his indicator and left the field. Marshall later scored on the fifth Hibbing error of the day as the Gophers left town with a 5–4 win.[55]

Reid's boys were on a serious roll as they returned to St. Paul in late July, having lost only five games since May 24. Bobby Marshall, one of the fastest runners in the West, was proving to be "some elusive kid on the bases," hitting at "a .300 clip," and playing the best ball of his life. Marshall had become the idol of both black *and* white fans, with "many who attend Gopher games solely to see him." The club made another roster move near the end of their journey with Wesley, who was batting around .200 at the time, being replaced by Harry Brown, a veteran of "the leading negro clubs of the East." Brown wasn't much of a hitter, but "when it came to fast plays in the field, he was all to the good."[56]

On their way home, the travelers took on a regional all-star team in Lester Prairie on July 21. The Gophers tried to bunt repeatedly on Charles McCleary, but their old friend foiled their efforts by keeping his fastball high and tight. The crafty lefty struck out ten batters while allowing only four hits, keeping the Gophers off the board until a run-producing liner by Binga in the sixth inning. Johnny Davis parsed out six safeties and fanned eight, but he too gave up a run in the sixth after a throwing error by McDougall. With a Lester Prairie runner on second base in the eighth, McCleary made a bid to win his own game with a long fly to left, but Brown prevented a home run by spearing the ball with one hand as it passed over his head. The score remained tied at one until the ninth when two "bad" umpiring decisions followed by another Binga hit put runners on the corners. McCleary got two strikes on the next batter, but then threw wildly to third during a double steal attempt and the final run of the contest scored.[57]

The Gophers arrived back in the capitol city, ready to defend their title as "world's colored champions," in a five-game playoff at Lexington Park against Frank Leland's Chicago Giants. The series was highly publicized in both the black and mainstream press. In anticipation of a big turnout, Irving Williams put advanced tickets on sale at the Winecke and Doerr's stores as well as at Phil Reid's saloon five days before the first game.[58]

Frank Leland was so anxious for another shot at the Gophers that he paid a $100 "tax" to get out of a conflicting Chicago City League date. The Chicago magnate's new squad consisted of several members of his 1909 Leland Giants along with ex–Gophers Felix Wallace, Johnny Taylor, and "Rat" Johnson. Also on board were two promising newcomers from Texas: Left-handed slugger William Pettus, a .385 hitter for the season, and Hall of Fame flame-thrower "Cyclone" Joe Williams, who had posted a record of 115–31 (.787) during the previous five years. The Giants left fielder was Clarence "Bobby" Winston, who missed the 1909 Gophers series with a broken leg, but had returned to hit .333 in 1910.[59]

Prior to the series, ex–Keystones and longtime Chicago infielder Alex Irwin penned an in-depth article for the *Twin City Star* about the showdown. After comparing the two respective squads lineups, the "ex-professional" came to the "candid opinion" that "the Giants have just a shade (just a lighter shade) the better of it." The consensus among Gophers supporters was that "the Lelands will do the trick," but that "defeat to either team is no disgrace." A writer from the *St. Paul Dispatch* looked forward to the matchup of "two sets of the greatest colored players in the world" who he enthused were "stronger on the diamond than many of the highest salaried members of the strongest big league clubs."[60]

The Giants and Gophers would have a "great go" at each other, but Daddy Reid wasn't around to see it. Reid had turned his ball club over to his protégé Irving Williams in late July, on the eve of the portly magnate's nuptials to the famed African American singer and dancer Belle Davis. The 36-year-old Davis had rose to prominence in the late 1890's with John Isham's Octoroons, "the first great musical company of the Race," and only the second to feature black females. The fair-skinned entertainer, who sometimes had to smear on burnt cork in order to perform before white U.S. audiences, eventually went solo and emigrated to England in 1901 on a ship ironically called the *St. Paul*. Her act, a dignified cantatrice accompanied by two clowning boy dancers, became a big hit in Edwardian England as well as on the Continent, and was met with nearly universal critical acclaim.[61]

According to scribe Dave Wyatt it was Davis, the popularizer of the song "Goo Goo Eyes," who had initially "cast her gaze towards our old baseball magnate." Both parties had been betrothed before. Reid had a son, Edward, by a previous union; Davis had been wed to Henry Troy, another black expatriate entertainer. The couple was married in Chicago, where Davis' mother lived, and set sail for a European honeymoon on July 27.[62]

The Gophers didn't make the wedding, but they were given a rare day off before the playoff opener on July 24. The Giants were scheduled to arrive in St. Paul at 8 o'clock that morning, just seven hours before game time. They came in on a Northwestern line train, in two special Pullman cars that carried the ball players along with Leland, his pal Major Robert R. Jackson, and a few relatives and friends. In order to regain any edge they might have lost on their journey, the Chicago squad went through a light practice before noon.[63]

Nearly 4,500 people, including much of the Twin Cities black population, filed into Lexington Park for the Sunday lid-lifter. Felix Wallace got the ball rolling against his former teammates by smashing a Louis Johnson delivery to right field for a leadoff homer. The next man up, shortstop William Selden, reached on an error by the unnerved pitcher, and scored on a single by Bobby Winston to give the Giants a 2–0 lead. Steel Arm Johnny Taylor commemorated his return to St. Paul by walking Artie McDougall to begin the Gophers' half of the first, and failing "to show any brotherly love," hit his brother Jim with a pitch. Bill Binga bunted the runners along and George Armstrong scored McDougall with a sacrifice fly.[64]

Johnson kept the Giants scoreless for the next seven innings, striking out five while spacing out four singles. The Gophers ace helped his cause by advancing all the way to third base when Walter Ball misplayed his third inning single in right field. Johnson scored the tying run moments later on a base hit by McDougall, but the Gophers' rally fizzled when Selden threw Jim Taylor out at the plate after the latter tried to score on an Armstrong pop out to short.[65]

The score was still two-all in the top of seventh when, with runners at first and second, Ball lashed a "hot one" to first that Bobby Marshall "found a little fast," before recovering in time to retire the batter. Inexplicably, the lead runner, Mike Moore, froze at second and Marshall threw down to third baseman Jim

Irving Williams, secretary of the Gophers from 1907 through 1910. In July 1910, Phil Reid turned the team over to Williams and left for Europe on his honeymoon. (*Indianapolis Freeman*, April 16, 1910; Wisconsin Historical Society, Madison)

Taylor who tagged Moore to complete a "rather freakish" double play. George Bowman tripled with two out in the Gopher seventh and Marshall doubled him home with the go-ahead run. Steel Arm Johnny then walked Louis Johnson, but wiggled out of further trouble by inducing to McDougall pop out to second.[66]

After retiring the dangerous Pettus to begin the Giants' ninth, Johnson gave up a double to Moore before recovering to strike out Winston. Walter Ball followed with a base hit and Moore, who was running all the way this time, scored to tie the game at three. Johnson escaped without further difficulty and when the Gophers failed to tally in their half, the championship opener headed into extra innings for the second year in a row. Nate Harris singled for the Giants in the 10th, but could advance no further than second. McDougall coaxed a walk off Ball, pitching in relief of Johnny Taylor, to lead off the bottom of the frame, but he was forced out by Jim Taylor. Undaunted, Taylor stole second, motored to third after catcher Pettus' wild peg to nab him was bobbled by Mike Moore in center field, and raced home with the game-winner when Moore's throw to the hot corner went awry.[67]

Johnny Davis took to the bump the next afternoon shooting for the Gophers' fifth straight win over Leland's Giants, but the day belonged to the young guns from the Lone Star State. Joe Williams, the Giants 24-year-old "elongated heaver," struck out nine Gopher batters and was reached for only three safeties during the game's first seven frames. Davis, on the other hand, was clouted for eight base hits before being pulled after only five innings of work. Bill Pettus, playing at first base while Rat Johnson caught, collected three extra-base hits during his day's work and was only retired on a long fly to right field.[68]

The 26-year-old masher broke open a scoreless game in the fourth with a home run off Johnny Davis and drove the Gopher hurler from the hill with a homer to start the sixth. The Giants also tallied three times in the fifth inning, on a two-run home run by Rat Johnson followed by a triple by Joe Williams and a fielder's choice.[69]

With the Gophers trailing 5–0 in the eighth, Bobby Marshall led off with a single and moved to second on a pinch-hit by Lefty Pangburn. McDougall sacrificed the runners up a base right before Jim Taylor uncorked a drive off Williams. Selden saved the Giants day by catching the liner at short, before trying to double up Pangburn at second. Second baseman George Wright botched the relay, however, and Marshall trotted home; Pangburn tried to score on the play as well, but he out at the plate. There would be no ninth-inning rally for the Gophers because there was no ninth inning. Due to an error or malfeasance by "the little chap at the scoreboard" the two teams "hurried from the field" after Pangburn was retired, as the board showed nine frames had been played and "every one appeared satisfied to get home."[70]

Tom Pangburn and Walter Ball got the ball for their respective teams on July 26 for the critical third game. With two gone in the Gophers' second, Bobby Marshall slammed one of the Chicago starter's "straight ones" to right center for a home run, exactly one year to the day after the big first baseman's 11th inning drive against Ball had ignited a frenzied celebration in downtown St. Paul. On this afternoon, though, Ball's "mystifying shoots" proved too much for the Gophers to solve and he allowed only four more isolated singles.[71]

Pangburn cruised through the first two frames, but the Giants' Joe Green reached in the third on a boot by McDougall, was sacrificed to second by Ball, and scored the equalizer on a clean drive to left by Nate Harris. From that point forward, the Giants hammered the left-handed hurler's for ten more safeties and only some superlative fielding kept the Gophers in the game.[72]

Ball doubled to right field with one out in the fifth inning and promptly scored the go-ahead run on a single by Felix Wallace. The ex–Gopher captain went all the way to third on an error by Pangburn and scored on an infield out to give Chicago a 3–1 advantage. In the seventh Brown made a diving catch of a Wallace line drive and speared a drive by Harris after a long run, but he couldn't prevent the Giants from tacking on another run in the eighth as they closed out a 4–1 triumph. Nate Harris stole three bases for the victors, who were lauded for their "good judgment on the base paths," while Marshall was thrown out in the fifth trying to stretch a single into a double with his team down by two runs.[73]

The Gophers now needed to win Wednesday's game in order to keep their fading title hopes alive. In order to add a little more punch, the good-hitting Pangburn was inserted into the lineup in left field and George Bowman, who had only one hit in ten series at bats, was replaced at second base by Harry Brown. The move backfired miserably, however, as Brown erred on all five chances he accepted before Bowman reclaimed the position in the sixth inning. The Gophers committed *nine* errors in all, which combined with 11 base hits and five walks surrendered by Louis Johnson made for a very long day for the St. Paul nine.[74]

With one down in the top of the first, Nate Harris singled, swiped second, and scored the game's initial run after errors by Brown and Artie McDougall. A single, a walk, plus two fielder's choices increased the Chicago lead to 3–0 in the second inning; Leland's charges pushed their advantage to 4–0 in the fifth after singles by Harris and Winston.[75]

As the Giants pulled ahead, the Gophers' bats were being silenced by Joe Williams' fastballs. The local club finally broke through in the bottom of the fifth when a Barton walk, a Brown sacrifice, a Marshall double, and a single by Pangburn sliced the Chicago lead to 4–3. The Giants got a run back in the top of the sixth when Cyclone Joe walked and scored on a fielder's choice. Armstrong coaxed a free pass to begin the bottom of the frame and when he beat a force throw to second after a Barton grounder, both runners were safe. Bowman followed with a single and moments later the never-say-die Gophers pulled even on a two-run error by Selden.[76]

Unfortunately, the never-say-die Gophers started booting the ball around again and the Giants tallied twice off Louis Johnson in the eighth. William Selden, who had joined Leland's crew from the Illinois Giants in late June, homered off his ex-teammate Johnson in the ninth to ice it. Cyclone Joe finished a nine-strikeout day by blanking the home team during their last three at-bats, as the Giants dethroned the Gophers, 8–5.[77]

With the championship decided the Gophers had only pride to play for in the finale on Thursday. The St. Paul boys got off to a good start against John Taylor when McDougall reached on a first-inning fielding error by Joe Green and scored on a double by Sherman Barton. Wallace homered off Lefty Pangburn in the third to tie the game, however, and Moore put the Giants ahead with another dinger in the sixth. Pangburn fanned eight batters on the day, but a slew of errors and base hits enabled the Giants to score four more times in their last three at-bats. Steel Arm Johnny's fastball was too much for the Gophers and he retired the last 18 men to face him to wrap up the anticlimactic 6–1 Chicago victory.[78]

The St. Paul club had been simply overpowered by the Giants. Cyclone Joe Williams fanned 18 batters in his two starts while the Giants clouted seven home runs during the five games played. The hitting heroes were plentiful for the Chicago club: Bobby Winston, a master of hitting to the opposite field, went 10-for-21 (.476) with four stolen bases; Walter Ball wowed his former hometown fans with a 5-for-11 (.454) performance that included two doubles; and Nate Harris stole seven bases in the series while going 6-for-16 (.375).

Marshall was the lone bright spot for the Gophers, with six hits in 16 at bats (.375), leading a national scribe to declare, "At the rate Bobby Marshall is going he will be the premier first baseman next season."[79]

Looking to rebound after the Chicago series, the Gophers packed up their troubles and journeyed south to Mankato. Mule Armstrong missed the two-game weekend set, being either hurt or embarrassed; the Giants had stolen 15 bases during the playoff, including eight in the game four title clincher. The Gophers could have used him in the first contest on July 30, which Mankato won, 4–3, scoring the deciding run on an eighth-inning wild pitch by Louis Johnson. The professionals triumphed, 12–5, the next day, clobbering Charles McCleary for five runs on eight hits in only two and two-thirds innings.[80]

The Sunday win over Mankato snapped a five-game skid and sparked another long winning streak that lasted nearly three weeks and included six shutout victories. Playing before many record-breaking crowds, the St. Paul squad swept through northern Wisconsin where the only real obstacle they encountered was the train wreck that delayed their arrival in Hayward.[81]

The Gophers opponents experienced a few travel difficulties of their own. A club in New Richmond, Wisconsin, hired Minneapolis Miller Nick "Hub" Dawson to catch against the barnstormers on August 11, but the backstop missed his train had to take a cab instead. New Richmond was crushed, 16–6, and Dawson was stuck with a $25 tab (about a $550 fare today) by the cabbie. Several more ringers, including ex–Milwaukee Brewer Clarence Short, awaited the travelers in Cumberland, Wisconsin. The professionals were trying to close out an 8–5 lead in the last of the ninth when the first three Cumberland men up improbably came around to score. Two more locals reached base with only one out, but Louis Johnson got out of the jam by retiring the next two batters and the Gophers scored six times in the 10th for a 14–8 win.[82]

The Gophers revival was tempered somewhat by the departure of Bill Binga in early August. Lauded by the *Indianapolis Freeman* as the "surest hitter in the country" and "one of the veterans who still makes the youngsters hustle," the reliable one finished out the year bouncing between the barnstorming Oklahoma Giants and the Kansas City, Kansas, Giants.[83]

Upon their return from Wisconsin, the Binga-less Gophers played a few dates in southern and eastern Minnesota. The club staged "a three ring circus" while pounding Waconia, 14–6, on August 15, but it was the locals who administered a beating. Armstrong was knocked off his feet during a play at the plate; McDougall took "a bounder fair in his mouth," while Bowman and Barton were "badly shaken up" after colliding while chasing a fly ball.[84]

In late August the St. Paul club made their second trip to the Iron Range in a month, but they probably shouldn't have bothered. The Gophers lost 9 out of 12 to the Hibbing, Chisholm, and Virginia clubs in a series of games that ranged from the ridiculous to the sublime. The professionals Waterloo began in Hibbing where a revamped Colts squad won the first two meetings including a 4–0 five-hit effort by their ace Jensen on the 19th, the first time the Gophers had been blanked all year.[85]

The two teams split a Sunday doubleheader on the 21st, as the Gophers took the first quarrel, 7–1, as Louis Johnson struck out 11 batters while allowing only three singles. Johnson also cracked a homer for traveling men, who broke open a 1–1 tie in the seventh inning on a two-run single by Jim Taylor and a grand slam over the right-field fence by Bobby Marshall. The game was played under the threat of rain and both teams took turns delaying the contest "every two minutes" with a lot of "rag chewing that was totally uncalled for."[86]

The Gophers raced out to a 5–1 lead in the second game against Jensen, who had also pitched the matinee, and fortune seemed to be turning their way again. And then the Booth brothers took over. Doubles by Dwight and his little brother Carroll fueled a four-run fifth inning against Johnny Davis and the younger sibling's two-out drive over the right-field fence gave Hibbing a 7–5 walk-off win in the 10th.[87]

Irving Williams released second baseman George Bowman, who had hit poorly all season, after the doubleheader. He had apparently been "loafing around the station" during the series and "did not take any interest in the games." Bowman had sat out the first of the double dip, "after being nearly run to death on Saturday" and had occupied left field during the second contest. Williams also decided that the Gophers would only carry nine men the rest of the year, with the corner outfield spots manned by pitchers and Marshall moving to second and Harry Brown taking over at first.[88]

With the Hibbing skies darkened by forest fires raging in nearby Mesaba Junction, the two clubs engaged in another donnybrook on the 22nd. Captain Jim Taylor, pitching with "little more than a 'floater,'" kept the Gophers in the game until the sixth inning when a four-bagger by Dad Williams and a fusillade of hits gave the Colts a 7–5 lead. Louis Johnson relieved Taylor and held Hibbing scoreless the rest of the way. In the ninth Johnson homered over that right-field fence on a 3–2 count to pull the St. Paul club within a run. Jim Taylor followed with a double, stole third, and came home on a sacrifice fly to pull the Gophers even. The professionals pushed another run across in the top of the 11th off Dick Brookins and held on for an 8–7 win.[89]

The Gophers' misfortunes continued in nearby Chisholm where the local squad, well fortified by Hibbing players, blitzed the St. Paul nine, 4–1 and 9–3. Back in Hibbing on the 25th the Colts edged the Gophers, 3–2, behind Jensen, who scattered six hits for his third victory over the professionals in a week.[90]

Even worse, the Hibbing games had been poorly attended because of rain, cold weather, smoke, and a community picnic that fell on the day of the Sunday doubleheader. A Hibbing newspaper reported that

Second baseman George Bowman was one of the many Pittsburgh-area players employed by the Gophers in 1910. (*St. Paul Pioneer Press*, May 24, 1910; Minnesota State Historical Society, St. Paul)

EIGHT • *The Boys Are Back in Town (1910)* 137

the Gophers were disappointed that the gate receipts in northern Minnesota fell short of those in the Dakotas:

> The jumps from the different towns in this state are too long to play one game in each city while in the Dakotas some of the jumps are so short that two games can be played in one afternoon. A six game series is too long for a team to play in Hibbing and yet if these dates were not filled there would be no games for the Colored men on the range.[91]

The unfortunate range trek concluded with four games in Virginia. The "Hessians" scored twice off Johnny Davis in the ninth inning of the August 26 opener to knot the game at three and won 4–3 in the 10th on a squeeze play. The locals mauled the Gophers, 10–3, the next day as the professionals committed five errors and were struck out 11 times by ex–Three-I League twirler John Schmirler. The St. Paul squad pounded out 11 hits in both games of the Sunday doubleheader on the 28th, but only could manage a split. After the Gophers scored three times in the ninth inning to cop the first contest 7–4, Anthony, the Virginia catcher, went 4-for-4 with a double and a triple to lead the locals to an 8–5 win in the second game.[92]

The club stumbled south on to Spooner, Wisconsin, followed by a report stating that if they lost to the locals, the Gophers would disband to prevent "the reputation of the Champion Colored team of Minnesota to receive any serious setback." A more likely reason the Gophers were thinking of packing it in was a serious lack of cash. The team willingly agreed to play Spooner for half of the gate receipts instead of risking the usual 60–40 split.[93]

The Wisconsin outfit soon regretted paying the Gophers in advance. A ruckus arose when Mule Armstrong grabbed pitcher Clarence Short's bat as he swung at a Louis Johnson offering in the fifth inning. The local umpires awarded Short first base and the barnstormers left the field in a huff with the game tied at four. After a 30-minute argument, the black club eventually got their way after using the large gathering of nearly 1,000 fans as leverage. It didn't really matter in the end as Spooner tallied seven times in the bottom of the eighth to rout the Gophers, 11–6.[94]

The St. Paul nine didn't fold as threatened after the Spooner imbroglio and recovered to win a couple of games in western Wisconsin before heading back to Mankato. Jim Taylor evidently had enough however, leaving for Indiana in early September to join his brother C. I.'s West Baden Sprudels. Arthur McDougall went missing in action as well and George Bowman was brought back to play shortstop. The loss of Taylor was softened a bit when Eugene Milliner came back from Kansas City to man left field. Milliner was reportedly "faster than ever" and repeated blasts over the Missouri fences had won him the nickname "Home Run Gabbie."[95]

Mankato trotted out former Miller and Detroit Tiger Gene Ford to pitch the opener of a three-game series with the Gophers on September 3. Ford was touched for only six hits, but poor fielding by the hometown outfit helped the St. Paul nine prevail, 4–2. Louis Johnson whiffed seven and stranded ten Mankato base runners to pick up the win. A drizzling rain fell throughout the next day's contest which disintegrated into a "farce" after Pangburn somehow yielded ten runs on only one hit in the second inning. The southpaw passed five batters, hit one and was pulled after getting only one man out. Bobby Marshall and Harry Brown mopped up as Mankato triumphed, 10–4, in a six-inning rain-shortened game. Charles McCleary "was in grand form and had everything" for the locals, striking out eight while allowing only three measly singles to beat the Gophers for the first time in four tries that year.[96]

The Labor Day rubber match pitted Louis Johnson against Mankato's Claude Lamb, and for eight innings neither team could score. The St. Paul spitballer recorded another eight strikeouts on the day while facing only three batters over the required 27 minimum. Lamb wasn't as overpowering, but he managed to leave nine Gophers on the bases during his first eight frames. Johnson was touched for doubles in both the seventh and eighth innings, but both Mankato runners were later thrown out trying to advance on infield grounders. With Brown at third and two down in the Gophers ninth, Eugene Milliner laced a single to right to finally drive in the first run of the ball game. The locals got another man to second with only one out in the bottom of the frame, but Bobby Marshall snared a drive by longtime semi-pro first baseman Rognas and doubled off the runner to save a 1–0 Gopher victory.[97]

A Mankato paper complained that Lamb should have intentionally walked Milliner to get at Marshall who had gone hitless in the series. The big first baseman's struggles continued a few days later in Fairmont, Minnesota, when Alf Dominick struck him out *six* times during a game. Dominick, who the locals had imported at the cost of $25, fanned 11 all together, but was hit hard as the professionals administered a 14–4 defeat to the hometown team.[98]

McDougall was back in the fold when the Gophers hooked up with the North St. Paul Thoens, a rising semi-pro power, at the Downtown Park on September 10. The resulting two-hour "tug of war," played in a collegiate-like atmosphere before 950 rabid fans, was filled with "sensational fielding," "clever base running," and clutch pitching. Facing a familial lineup consisting of three McGarry's and two Gosewisch's, Johnny Davis fanned ten and held his "opponents safe at critical times." Emmet McGarry, late of the Hastings, Conrads and Minot clubs, pitched well for the department store nine, only to fall prey to the pillbox's ground rules.[99]

Down 4–1 in the sixth inning, the Gophers scored twice thanks to a couple of doubles over the short right-field porch. Armstrong came home on an error to tie the game in the eighth and another "scratch" ground rule double to right in the 10th enabled the professionals to eke out a 5–4 victory, sorely disappointing the 500 North St. Paul rooters on hand.[100]

The Thoens and nearly "800 ardent followers of independent baseball" showed up at Lexington Park the next afternoon for a Sunday rematch. Irving Williams was also on hand "to watch the money come in," but his ballclub, "owing to the threatening weather," never arrived. Because the teams had agreed to play rain or shine, the game was forfeited to the Thoens. The Gophers' no-show "put them in bad with the St. Paul fans," although several area contests were postponed and a downpour halted a preliminary game at Lexington for 20 minutes.[101]

The Gophers resurfaced later that week at the Fillmore County Fair in Preston. Irving Williams, "wearing a smile that won't come off," had secured another shot at the Chicago Giants. The rivals were to play a three-game set for the "championship of all colored ball teams," and an $800 purse ($18,000 in 21st century dollars), 65 percent of which would go to the winner.[102]

Before an enormous crowd of fair-goers, the Giants, behind Johnny Taylor, nipped Louis Johnson and the Gophers 3–2 on the 14th of September. The Chicago nine edged the St. Paul squad, 6–5, the next day, and for the third contest the Gophers started "one who they claimed was either their best or worst pitcher." The latter possibility proved to be the case as the Giants knocked the erratic hurler out of the box in the second inning of their 6–0 win.[103]

According to the Preston papers, the three games were interesting but not terribly exciting and "it was clear throughout that the Giants were somewhat superior to the Gophers." Curiously, the pre-fair wisdom held that Leland's bunch would probably take a dive, but their subsequent sweep proved "to all that the series was on the square and not fixed."[104]

The Gophers suffered an even bigger loss when Sherman Barton, their center fielder for four seasons, left around this time. The veteran's "fast work" in the field had saved many a run over the years and the *St. Paul Dispatch* pegged him as "really a great ball player" oft overlooked "because he never says anything, but in all the great points of ball he shines." Barton did not tolerate bad management. When his Quaker Giants manager failed to meet payroll before an August 1906 contest in Atlantic City, the outfielder took out a writ of attachment on the gate receipts. After the still unpaid Quakers threatened to walk off the field in the eighth inning, the team was paid their guarantee, and Barton got back the money he spent on the writ. Not surprisingly the Giants folded soon afterwards.[105]

Up next for the sagging St. Paul squad was a two-game engagement with Shakopee at the Scott County Fair. Lefty Pangburn dominated the locals in the Gophers' 7–0 victory on September 17, striking out 13 and allowing only one base runner to reach third base. The St. Paul squad hit rock bottom against the Rock Springs the next day. The less than immortal "Shooty" Niedenfuer held the Gophers to seven hits and his teammates turned five double to help him out. Johnny Davis gave up only six safeties and struck out 11 batters, but *his* fielders committed five errors. Both squads had registered twice when Bobby Marshall led off the ninth inning with a home run to put the Gophers up, 3–2. The Rock Springs, who hadn't scored since the first, were aided in the bottom of the frame by an error by Harry Brown and the Gophers failure to catch a Niedenfuer pop fly that landed in back of second base, loading the bases with two down. Larson, the Shakopee shortstop, then mashed one of Davis' deliveries to over Eugene Milliner's head in left field and the home town nine cavorted off with a 4–3 win.[106]

Pangburn, Armstrong, Bowman, Brown, and Louis Johnson all exited the squad after the second Rock Springs contest; the Shakopee games had drawn well, so perhaps the players got out while the going was good. Prior to the series the *Twin City Star* announced that Bobby Marshall, who had been practicing law out of his father's house, was retiring from sports to join a legal firm run by his former Minnesota classmate William Franklin.[107]

Marshall was still in uniform when the Gophers arrived in Springfield, Minnesota, the following weekend for a three-game series. In early August the *Pioneer Press* published a report that Springfield had defeated the Gophers, 4–1, behind a phenom named Larson who permitted only two hits and struck out 14. The only problem with account was the fact that the Gophers were in Wisconsin at the time; the fraudulent item was apparently the work of "a member of the family of practical jokers." Irving Williams was "somewhat incensed" and demanded a correction from the Springfield manager, who denied any involvement in the hoax, and felt he had "nothing to offer in the nature of a retraction." A month later, however, when the southern Minnesota town was unable to find a big attraction for their annual street carnival they were forced to reach out to the Gophers "as a last resort," and at "great expense."[108]

The Gophers lineup in Springfield consisted of Marshall, Johnny Davis, Eugene Milliner, Artie McDougall, and an outfielder named Francis who had been brought in after Barton left, augmented by a few sandlot players including former Keystones secretary Eddie

Davis. For the occasion, Springfield fielded a ringer-laden outfit made up of several players from the Minnesota-Wisconsin League, including wunderkind pitcher Harry Hughes."[109]

Hughes was opposed in the September 23 opener by Walter Stallard, a 20-year-old native of St. Paul who had been pitching for a team in Hinckley, Minnesota. Stallard's Gophers' debut was less than auspicious as he surrendered 13 hits and passed seven batters while absorbing a 14–3 loss on a very cold and rainy day. Bobby Marshall assumed the catching duties for the St. Paul nine and was victimized for ten stolen bases by the hometown Maroons. Harry Hughes pitched brilliantly for the locals, scattering five hits and striking out 16 batters; in the fifth inning the boy wonder struck out the side on nine straight pitches.[110]

The sun came out the next day and the Gophers fortunes improved with the weather. Johnny Davis fanned eight batters and scattered five hits to edge the Maroons Mike Kramer, 3–1, in a "pretty pitchers battle." Marshall allowed five more stolen bases, but he also got the Gophers off to a good start by driving home Eddie Davis in the first inning with a booming triple.[111]

Johnny Davis came back the following afternoon to take on Harry Hughes in the series decider. The very fact that Hughes was on the mound seemed to demoralize the professionals. McDougall singled to center on the first pitch of the game and Milliner beat out an infield roller in the ninth inning, but no other Gopher was able to hit safely. With "sharp curves" and "terrific speed" Hughes struck out the side in the second, fourth, and fifth frames during an 18-strikeout performance. The weary Davis gave up only eight safe drives, but the Gophers fielded in a "half hearted" manner and committed 11 errors while being routed again, 11–2. Marshall had another tough time behind the plate making six wild and unsuccessful pegs trying to head off steals. The day was also very dark which made it nearly impossible to see a fastball, only adding to the Gophers' hitting and fielding woes.[112]

Unfortunately, the weekend series was meagerly attended because of miserable weather and the local's elation over the Maroons great showing was tempered when the gate receipts fell far short of the expenses. "First class comedian" Eddie Davis managed to keep the fans who did show up "in good humor" and "kept the stands in a constant uproar by his talk and antics."[113]

While the Gophers were falling apart in Minnesota, the Keystones were having troubles of their own in Texas. Things had started promising enough when the Minneapolis club won three out of four from the Fort Worth Wonders in late May. After a four-game set with the Houston Black Buffaloes, the Keystones reached Dallas for a big series with the Black Giants. Mitchell's club took the June 11 opener, 5–1, behind Charles Jackson, before splitting a Sunday doubleheader. After Bill Gatewood dropped the first contest, 3–1, newcomer Hurley McNair edged the locals, 3–2, in the second quarrel. Jackson again downed the Black Giants, 3–2, on Monday, but Dallas salvaged the final game on the 14th by beating Gatewood, 6–3.[114]

Contrary to the opinion of a few Chicago Giants players who claimed he "couldn't pitch ball," Gatewood had reestablished himself as one of the "speediest and best spitball pitchers in the game." Big Bill had also proven to be a good manager with a sharp eye for talent. While in Houston, Gatewood lured a couple of talented youngsters away from the Black Buffaloes: 21-year-old southpaw pitcher/outfielder Hurley McNair and his batterymate James Wills.[115]

Kidd Mitchell and wife Mamie came back to the Twin Cities in late June after visiting the Knights of Pythias encampment in Waco and related that his team "was making good in the Texas League." On July 2 a note appeared in the *Indianapolis Freeman* telling a different story. Writing with remarkable candor, reserve infielder James Coleman griped that the hard to please Colonel was mistreating his squad. After extolling the virtues of his teammates, Coleman protested:

> [Mitchell] treats us as if we were a lot of dumb-brutes. He does it here because we are away from home and cannot get back, because he won't pay off on due time. All the boys are sore on him, yet they play good ball on account of Mr. Gatewood. Even he is disgusted and everyone knows that he is one of the best colored pitchers known.

Coleman closed by remarking, "Don't know who will play the manager next season, because he does not know how to treat a baseball team right."[116]

By August, Coleman was back playing for the Galveston Flyaways and Bill Gatewood was pitching for Charley Mills' St. Louis Giants. The Keystones mark when the Texas Colored League broke up in early July was a middling 6–6 and by mid–August the club was reporting "a bad season." Not surprisingly, the support in San Antonio had been less than overwhelming. Even with Cyclone Joe Williams pitching for them, the Black Bronchos had always drawn more abroad than at home. To make matters worse, Frank Davis, whose great fielding had been a drawing card for the Keystones, badly hurt his ankle in July and "the fans nearly cried."[117]

Mitchell's nine left Texas on August 15 bound for Minneapolis. On their way back the club stopped off in Kansas City for a rematch with the Royal Giants. In the August 20 opener, Topeka Jack Johnson's eighth inning two-out hit put the Giants up, 1–0, before the Keystones tied it in the ninth with a run off Charles Chiles. The Northerners pushed another run across in the top of the 10th before Johnson connected again with two out to drive the tying run home in the bottom of the frame. The Missouri squad scored again in the 12th to capture "the red-hot" game, 3–2.[118]

Riots optional. Big Bill Gatewood hurled well over 350 innings for the Gophers in 1908 and lost only four out of his first 41 appearances. He moved on to pitch for Kidd Mitchell's Keystones in 1909 and 1910. (*Osceola Sun,* September 24, 1908; Wisconsin Historical Society, Madison)

The Keystones forged a 3–1 lead against "Sunny" Jim Hamilton the next day, but the Royal Giants clubbed Charles Jackson for four runs in the seventh inning and two more in the eighth to win, 7–3. The Keystones bounced back on the 22nd when Dude Lytle set down the Kansas City aggregation, 8–2. Thus reprieved, Mitchell's squad continued east to St. Louis for a grudge match against Big Bill Gatewood and the St. Louis Giants.[119]

The two clubs were slated for a couple of games at the Mound City's Athletic Park on August 28 and 29. Kidd and Mamie Mitchell came down from Minneapolis for the series, arriving just before the first contest started in a big touring car with Giants manager Charles Mills. Pitching before a "brilliant" Sunday crowd, Gatewood whiffed five, scattered seven hits, and "held his former teammates at his mercy" as the Giants rolled, 11–2. Big Bill also cracked two hits as did St. Louis center fielder Jimmy Lyons who added a pair of stolen bases. Hurley McNair absorbed the loss for the Keystones, giving up five hits and five runs during a four-and-a-third inning stint. The Colonel and his wife were reportedly good losers, and the 22-year-old Mrs. Mitchell "attracted considerable attention with her diamonds, looking like a blaze of fire."[120]

Jimmy Lyons collected two more hits the following afternoon, but his mates could only muster three others against Dude Lytle who nailed down a 4–1 victory for the Keystones. Lyons finally appeared in a Keystones uniform later that week as the Minneapolis club battled a few area nines in St. Louis. Merten's All-Stars, a "picked aggregation" from the city's Trolley League, scored three times in the eighth inning to overtake the Keystones, 6–5, on August 30. Lytle came on to relieve Lyons the next day and his "clever work" held the All-Stars in check as Mitchell's club rebounded with a 6–3 win. The Keystones concluded their week in St. Louis by blitzing the Red Bud, Illinois, team, 6–0, on September 2. Hurley McNair struck out six and permitted but two hits, while Jimmy Lyons ruined Red Bud twirler W. Holtmann's tryout before Cardinal skipper Roger Bresnahan by beating out two safeties and swiping four more bases.[121]

Lyons rejoined the Giants following the Red Bud game, and Charley Mills "made a strike" by grabbing Clarence Lytle off the Keystones roster before they left town. The Minneapolis club's path veered south once more and they pulled into Louisville, Kentucky, in mid-September for four games with the hometown Cubs. The southern boys annexed the first two contests by punishing McNair, 9–2, on September 15 and erased a three-run deficit by scoring four runs off Charles Jackson in the eighth inning the next day to steal a 4–3 victory.[122]

It was the Keystones turn for a comeback on the 17th. Mitchell's outfit tallied twice in the first inning for an early lead, but McNair gave it back and then some by allowing five runs in the fourth. The Minneapolis squad plated single runs in the sixth and seventh and completed a 12-hit barrage with three more runs in the ninth to pull out a 7–6 win. West, the Cubs ace who had been victimized by the Keystones' rally, started his third game of the series on Sunday the 18th against Slick Jackson. West was up to the challenge and only gave up three safeties, but Jackson was even better and shut out the Cubs, 2–0, on a one-hitter.[123]

The Keystones concluded their campaign later that week in Indianapolis. Kidd Mitchell was in town to see his charges take on the ABC's in a series at Northwestern Park. On Wednesday, the 21st, the Minneapolis squad showed 500 fans, including local luminaries J.D. Howard, Archie Greathouse, and Elwood Knox, "what they knew about real-for-certain baseball" by routing the Indiana lads, 6–1. Jackson started for the Keystones, but was relieved by Hurley McNair who allowed but two hits and proved he knew how to pitch, "even if his arm was glassy." The northern nine whacked ten base knocks off the ABC's starter Harris, including two apiece by McNair and Milroy McCune.[124]

The "gala day for baseball" was a homecoming for former ABC's Frank Young, James Shawler, and John Merida, who were lauded by the *Freeman* as "great players" who "are fit for any first-class team." Mitchell returned to Minneapolis shortly thereafter; Jackson, McCune, and McNair arrived with him, planning to spend the winter in the Flour City.[125]

Controversies aside, the 1910 Keystones would prove to be Mitchell's strongest club, although many of their achievements went unrecorded. In addition to triumphs over such blackball institutions as the ABC's and St. Louis Giants, the Keystones also claimed to have downed Frank Leland's Chicago Giants sometime during the season. Even more interesting was their unsubstantiated assertion that they finally vanquished their St. Paul rivals by "not allowing the Gophers a single game in the series."[126]

Following the debacle in Springfield the Gophers were penciled in for a couple of games in western Wisconsin. On September 30, the St. Paul squad fell, 11–5, to an outfit called the Polk County All-Stars during the Polk County Fair in St. Croix Falls. The All-Stars' formidable lineup included four Minneapolis Millers who had spent significant time in the major leagues: Roy Patterson, "Long" Tom Hughes, Ollie Pickering, and Otis Clymer.[127]

The Gophers brought their tumultuous season to a close two days later with a Sunday showdown with the Thoens. A sizeable crowd of 2,200 gathered on the North St. Paul grounds to watch the clubs decide the "Twin Cities Championship." The professionals squad was a hybrid affair, combining Gophers holdovers Bobby Marshall and Eugene Milliner, with Keystones Andrew Campbell, Milroy McCune, Hurley McNair, and hurler Charles Jackson. Thoens manager Al Luger countered with one of the best pitchers in the state, professional or otherwise: local legend Adolph "Chief" Bender, a 23-year-old master of the underhand delivery.[128]

Both starters pitched great ball as Jackson allowed only one base runner through the first nine frames and Bender's unorthodox style helped him fan 16 Gophers. The submariner was bailed out of several jams by sensational plays by his teammates while Bobby Marshall brilliantly accepted 14 chances at first base "without a skip." The home team manufactured a run in the third inning when Bowers McGarry walked, was sacrificed to second by Bender, and scored on a "brilliant slide" following a wild throw trying to catch him stealing third base. The Gophers countered in the seventh when Marshall singled, McNair sacrificed him along, and a similar errant toss brought him home. The St. Paul nine proceeded to load the bases in the eighth with only one out, but some "fast fielding" by the Thoens Emmet McGarry kept them off the board. When neither side could get a base runner aboard in the ninth, the game went into extras.

Bender struck out McCune to begin the bottom of the 10th, before Milliner singled and sped home with the go-ahead run on a triple by Campbell. The big catcher tried to score on a grounder by Marshall but was tossed out at the dish. It looked like the young twirler would escape further damage, but McNair singled, plating Marshall. Jackson retired the side in order in the bottom of the inning and the "the greatest game of baseball in the history of North St. Paul," belonged to the Gophers, 3–1. Slick Jackson finished with seven strikeouts in ten innings and didn't allow a single hit in pitching the "game of his life."[129]

According to Irving Williams, the victory over the Thoens was the Gophers' 104th in 131 tries "and closed the most successful season in the history of the whirlwind twilight organization." In actuality, the Gophers lost more in the neighborhood of 37 games—still good enough for a winning percentage around .700. Although the club relinquished the blackball title, for the first time ever the Gophers had three pitchers: Lefty Pangburn, Louis Johnson, and Johnny Davis; who finished with at least 20 wins. The 30-year-old Williams, whom the *Twin City Star* feted as "yet one of the boys" and "a plain good fellow," was already looking ahead to the 1911 season "when several new players will be secured and an effort made to regain the dusky championship which now rests in the Windy City."[130]

Daddy Reid arrived in the Twin Cities in November without his new bride. The couple's wedding tour had included stops in Germany, France, and Florence, Italy where Mrs. Reid had taken leave of her husband, bound for a professional engagement in Vienna. On his way back to St. Paul, Reid made a detour to Brooklyn, New York on October 25 to witness a five-mile car race between Jack Johnson and Barney Oldfield, the "World's Champion Automobilist." The seasoned professional Oldfield easily outpaced the speed-crazy amateur Johnson in two heats, although the ever loyal Reid reported that "Jack is going to make good on the track."[131]

In fact, Johnson's extra-curricular activities and his romantic dalliances would force him to flee the country and eventually cost him his crown. In July 1910 Jack Johnson and the St. Paul Gophers were at the pinnacles of their chosen professions—things would never be so rosy again.

Chapter Nine

Not So Fast (January–June 1911)

When the Gophers took the field in 1911, they did so under new ownership and with a slightly different moniker. As the *Twin City Star* reported in mid–February, "There is no certainty that the St. Paul Colored Gopher baseball club will play this season. The booking time is on and Phil Reid has said nothing — and he knows the dope." Daddy Reid's ambivalence was not shared by Bobby Marshall. A power struggle for the club evidently broke out between the two, with the big first baseman gaining the upper hand in early April.[1]

When the dust had settled Marshall emerged as manager and captain of the team, which was now known as the Twin City Gophers, but Reid was making noises that his absence was only temporary. The *Star* mused, "Did Phil Reid and Bobby Marshall straighten out the Gopher baseball deal? What's in a name? Phil says everything — when it comes to booking in 1912." According to an article that appeared in the April 14 edition of the *Chicago Defender*:

> Manager Marshall wishes it distinctly understood that the "Twin City Gophers" are in no way connected with the famous Gophers of St. Paul, the club that was owned by "Daddy" Reid. This is an altogether different aggregation, this club being owned and controlled by Mr. Glover Shull of the city of Minneapolis, and Mr. George E. Lennon, the president and owner of the St. Paul American Association club.[2]

Eddie Davis, formerly of the Keystones front office and a late-season Gopher in 1910, was named the new secretary of the squad, replacing Irving Williams. The Gophers' longtime manager was evidently approached to work with the team in some capacity, but Williams instead moved to Chicago when the two sides could not agree on compensation.[3]

The new ownership group *seemed* promising. George Lennon was a 42-year-old clothier and amateur baseball enthusiast who had run the Saints with various degrees of success since 1902. Lennon also owned Lexington Park which ostensibly meant that the Gophers could play there for free. Lennon's involvement made the Gophers one of the first black teams ever to be operated by a member of Organized Baseball.[4]

Glover Shull, "one of the most enterprising colored business men of the Northwest," was also one of Minneapolis' "most influential and colorful characters." The 41-year-old from Chillicothe, Missouri, had recently opened his Porters and Waiter Club at 311 Hennepin Avenue, to provide a place for local black restaurant employees to "congregate for meals and recreation." Known for his correct and conservative attire, Shull promised to outfit his team "in the same uniforms that the American Association clubs use."[5]

"Bidding fair to eclipse all former efforts," Marshall moved the Gophers headquarters to his law office in the Metropolitan Life building in downtown Minneapolis, asserting that only "the best players obtainable will be signed." Pitchers Johnny Davis and Louis "Spitball" Johnson were reported to be among his early recruits, along with youngster William Selden, who had ably manned the Chicago Giants shortstop position in 1910 after George Wright was injured.[6]

Marshall spent a week in Chicago trying to find additional players for his club, which was slated to open at Lexington Park on Easter Sunday against Perry Werden's All-Stars. The new magnate wired home that he had signed none other than Rube Foster, the biggest name in blackball at the time and one of the few African American players besides Marshall well known to the Minnesota sporting public. Unfortunately, the acquisition of Foster was only a somewhat cynical publicity ploy on the part of the fledgling manager. Marshall also announced that he had inked the Barton brothers, Sherman and Eugene, but the sibling outfielders ultimately elected to play for Chicago teams, as did Louis Johnson. Other blackball luminaries such as Andrew Campbell, Mack Ramsey, and William "Bubber" Parks were said to be part of the squad as well, although none of them played an inning in the Twin Cities that summer. Dude Lytle was another familiar name that appeared on a few of the Gophers preseason rosters, but the veteran twirler was a no-show for the time being.[7]

Eventually Marshall's new charges began a couple of weeks training in Chicago "where most of the team resides," and were scheduled to reach the Twin Cities on Saturday morning the 15th. However, the evening before their scheduled arrival, the contest was called off because Marshall allegedly could not "muster his men in time for the game." Perry Werden insinuated that the Gophers cancelled because they were not anxious to face his formidable outfit, which featured such league players as "Lefty" Davis, pitcher "Pecky" Rhoades and catcher "Wild" Bill Hodgins, or cover a $100 side bet. It turned out that the real reason the game had to be postponed was that repairs to the Lexington Park grounds had made the diamond impossible to play on. The match was rescheduled for the following Sunday and Bobby Marshall was so incensed by Werden's jibes that the Gophers had ducked his club, that he offered to play the All-Stars winner-take-all for the gate receipts.[8]

Marshall claimed to have signed "four of the best colored players in the United States," during his Windy City stay, and his revamped nine was an intriguing mix of new and familiar faces. In addition to Marshall and staff ace Johnny Davis, other refugees from the 1910 Gophers squad included third baseman Harry Brown, right fielder Bill Binga, Arthur McDougall, now at second base, and novice pitcher Walter Stallard, "the big fellow" who had joined up the previous September. Jesse Schaeffer returned as well to don the catcher's gear once more, after spending his spring tutoring the La Crosse team of the Minnesota-Wisconsin League.[9]

Among the newcomers to the squad were an infielder named Williams, pitcher "Buck" Freeman, and a couple of players who had bedeviled the Gophers in the past, shortstop William Selden and first baseman/outfielder Bert Jones. Nicknamed the

Glover Shull, owner of the 1911 Twin City Gophers. (*Minneapolis Spokesman*, August 29, 1941; Minnesota State Historical Society, St. Paul)

"Yellow Kid" after the infamous comic strip character of the time that he faintly resembled, the light-skinned Jones had twirled three seasons of organized ball for the Atchison Huskers before the Kansas State League collapsed around him in August 1898. After departing the Renville All-Stars in 1905, Jones began hiring himself out to independent teams in North and South Dakota, successfully making the transition from pitcher to everyday player along the way.[10]

The 33-year-old Kansan would lead the Gophers in hitting in 1911 while splitting time between center field and first base, where he was "the greatest one handed ball player doing business," only using "both mitts occasionally," and only then because it was "customary." On the rare instances in which he now pitched, "this tricky ball tosser" operated with "a whole lot of class and a bewildering assortment that proved puzzling."[11]

William "Bee" Selden (or Seldon) was a 26-year-old product of Van Wert, Ohio, who "would rather toss or hit a ball around the diamond than eat." In May 1907 the young infielder made his professional debut with the Columbus Owls of the Ohio State Colored League, having never laid eyes on any of his teammates before the contest. For the next 18 years he would cover the middle of the diamond for many of America's top blackball teams, including the Chicago American Giants and the Indianapolis ABC's. With the Gophers, the "lightning" quick shortstop would be characterized as "a rare player and a great support to the infield," distinguishing himself by cracking several home runs while also making more than his share of errors.[12]

The signings of Jones and Selden began yielding dividends for Bobby Marshall almost immediately during the Gophers' April 23 tilt against the Werdens at Lexington. In the bottom of the first inning Jones made a sensational running catch to rob Lefty Davis of an apparent home run, and Selden later smashed a four-bagger to ice the 4–1 Gophers victory. Johnny Davis pitched seven strong innings to pick up the win while Stallard closed it out with two shutout frames. Marshall himself landed the biggest blow of the game, tripling with two runners on and two out in the fourth off "Pecky" Rhoades.[13]

Although Eddie Davis had earlier crowed in the *Chicago Defender* that the Gophers "defy the world of the Minor class and are willing to clash with the Majors if they but take a dare," the booking manager was soon advertising that the club was "open to play any independent team in the Northwest, and are not at all particular how fast these teams are." Davis quickly scheduled several exhibitions with four Minnesota-Wisconsin League outfits as well as "an extended tour of the Dakotas."[14]

The Gophers kicked off their tour of the "Minny" League camps with two weekend games in La Crosse, Wisconsin. A St. Charles, Minnesota, high-school lad named Wegmen mystified the barnstormers on April 29, scattering five hits in the Outcasts' 12–2 win. La Crosse mashed 16 safeties of their own, driving Stallard from the mound with only one out in the first inning after he walked three batters and uncorked a wild pitch. Marshall started Johnny Davis, "the grandest colored pitcher in the business" in the Sunday contest, but the Outcasts continued to "pound the ball to all corners," rapping out 13 hits in their 10–1 triumph. La Crosse starter Charlie Watson struck out eight and allowed the Gophers but two hits in eight innings of work.

Walter Stallard pitched so poorly in La Crosse, allowing five runs while only retiring three batters in two games, that he was exiled to left field. Bert Jones and Harry Brown were thrown into the rotation to pick up the slack, but the brunt of the mound duties fell on Johnny Davis, the "iron man" who ended up pitching in nearly every contest during the first half of the season. That was just fine by Davis who, according to the *Twin City Star*, "loves the game, and has the confidence of the other players who support him better than they do the other twirlers."[15]

The slender twirler could have used some of their support in Red Wing on May Day. The Manufacturers belted Davis around to the tune of 12 hits and six scores in only three innings during a 17–4 beat-down of the Twin Cities squad, the Gophers' largest margin of defeat to date. Red Wing starter Nelson Smith parsed out only three hits and whiffed seven the following afternoon but was undone by his teammates loose fielding. The Gophers manufactured two early runs off the Manufacturers on a hit, a fielder's choice, a stolen base and two Red Wing errors. Trailing 3–2 in the seventh inning, Marshall's men parlayed a walk, a hit batsman, one passed ball, and three more Red Wing miscues into another three runs. Bert Jones surrendered nine hits, but the southpaw held the leaguers to four runs in seven frames before Johnny Davis closed out the 5–4 win with two scoreless innings.[16]

Harry Brown made his first start of the season on May 3 in Eau Claire, and permitted only four singles, two of the bunt variety. Brown struck out seven, including the entire side in the second inning, but he also passed nine batters, hit another, as the Commissioners downed the Gophers, 4–1. The St. Paul aggregation suffered the ignominy as well of somehow allowing a triple steal with the bases loaded in the third inning. Johnny Davis was a one-man show the next day, pulling his team even in the series by going four-for-four at the plate with a double, while striking out six and scattering ten hits in the Gophers' 8–5 bludgeoning of Eau Claire.[17]

Brown took to the hill again on Friday the 5th, but this time the Commissioners solved him to the tune of eight hits and a 7–2 lead after the first four innings. Despite Bobby Marshall's second-inning home run that sailed over left fielder Russell Bailey's head all the way to the nearby race track, the Gophers became noticeably "disheartened and after some beefing and grumbling played loosely." Johnny Davis relieved Brown in the fifth and pitched three consecutive 1-2-3 frames while the Twin City squad pulled to within 7–5 with a three-run sixth. Davis wavered in the eighth, however, as Eau Claire first baseman Jim Callahan's two-run triple down the first-base line keyed a four-run rally that punctuated the home team's 11–5 triumph.[18]

The Gophers early season woes continued in Wausau, Wisconsin, where the hometown Lumberjacks routed them twice before large crowds. Pitching, or the lack thereof, was the culprit again. After Bert Jones absorbed a 12–7 thrashing on May 6, Harry Brown yielded five straight hits to begin the Sunday finale and was pulled in favor of Jones who muddled his way through a 8–4 beating. While the Wausau press remarked that the Gophers had several players with "considerable individual merit," it was quick to point out that the Twin City squad did not play together and were lacking "where inside work and the use of brains is necessary":

> The visitors several times in each game had opportunities to cause trouble, but just as often threw away the chance. For instance, on several occasions with three balls and no strikes the batter would pound away at the next pitched ball, either putting himself in the hole, making an easy out, or hitting into a double.[19]

The Gopher's dismal showing against the Class D teams of the Minny League was followed, not surprisingly, by a roster shakeup. Freeman and Williams who had only appeared as late-inning substitutes during the trip were released. As the Gophers readied themselves for a May 14 showdown with the H. P. Conrads, Hardiman, an infielder with the Leland Giants, was brought in to play second base and Artie McDougall headed back out to left field.[20]

Although the Conrads boasted they were in a class with the leaguers, they proved to be just the tonic the Gophers needed. A homer by the displaced McDougall highlighted a four-run rally in the third inning and Marshall's squad led 7–1 after only four and half frames had been played at Lexington. The semi-pros staged a mini-comeback, outhitting the Gophers 11–9 overall, but Johnny Davis finished with seven strikeouts and the professionals won comfortably, 8–4. An error in the right garden did feature greatly in the Gophers' four-run third, and the Conrads groused after the game that their starting outfield was in "badly crippled condition."[21]

Owing to other attractions, namely a Saints and Millers contest at Nicollet Park, the Sunday crowd at Lexington was poorer than expected, and it proved to be the Gophers' last game ever in St. Paul. Although the original plan had been for the Gophers to use Lexington when the Saints were on the road, Grover Shull signed a contract later that week for his club to play three games at Nicollet during a civic celebration in July.[22]

The dearth of Gophers games in St. Paul was an indication that Saints owner George Lennon was no longer involved in the operation, which wasn't necessarily a bad thing. Loathed by most Saints supporters, the Wisconsin native was eventually prosecuted for unpaid debts and buildings Lennon had an interest in — such as Lexington Park and St. Paul's Market Hall — had a habit of mysteriously burning down, after which he would collect a fat insurance payment.[23]

The Gophers' booking situation took a more literal hit when two members of the Minneapolis Millers assaulted Napoleon Johnson, a black St. Paul baseball fan, during a May 31 game at Lexington. A "coterie" of Saints supporters, who regularly dined at Carlings restaurant where Johnson waited tables, had bought him a box seat near the playing field so that he could heckle the Mill City team. During the second inning, Johnson's "flow of wit and humor" enraged Millers catcher Hub Dawson, he of the $25 Wisconsin cab ride, so much that he leaped into the stands and exchanged blows with the Saints rooter for two solid minutes. After Minneapolis pitcher Rube Waddell and several police officers succeeding in separating the pair, Millers manager Joe Cantillion grabbed a bat from in front of the Saints bench and cracked Johnson over the head with it. Cantillion and Dawson later pled guilty to disorderly conduct and were fined $100 each. Johnson, who was more familiarly known as William Crawdad, sued for $10,000 and eventually received a $1,400 settlement.[24]

McDougall and Schaeffer got the Gophers' six-week trek through the northwest off to a less than smooth start when they missed the train to Huron, South Dakota. Two local players were loaned to the Twin City squad for the May 16 series opener and the seven Gophers who did show up bashed out eleven hits, good enough for an 8–5 win. Bert Jones gave up three runs in the first inning, but he kept the hits well scattered after that. Bobby Marshall was the day's slugging star, mashing two triples and a single "at opportune times."[25]

Both of the absent players made the 291-mile trek west in time for the second game the following afternoon, but they weren't much help. Four hundred Huron fans took "great delight" as the hometown nine connected with everything Johnny Davis had to offer, to the tune of 21 hits and a 16–5 shellacking of the Gophers. Former Watertown twirler Ed Pframer got the win, giving up as many safeties in the five innings he worked — four — as he himself collected against Davis.[26]

Walter Stallard made his first start in nearly three weeks in Redfield, South Dakota, the next day while the Gophers took on the locals in a windstorm. A sixty-mile-per-hour gale raged throughout the contest, blowing banks of dirt directly into the grandstand, and enveloping the diamond in a dust cloud. The professionals fell behind in the fourth inning when Stallard was touched for a three-run homer by Redfield's captain George McCarl, which the Twin City club unsuccessfully argued was a foul ball. Down one in the ninth, Marshall's outfit singled three times, but couldn't get the tying run across in a 4–3 loss.[27]

Arthur McDougall was back at second base and Hardiman was stationed in the left garden by the time the Gophers posted a 6–2 decision over Aberdeen on May 20. Stallard got his first win of the season the following afternoon as the Twin Cities club downed Hankinson, North Dakota, 5–2, before a large Sunday gathering of 1,000. The Minnesota squad finished out the month with a jaunt through the southern reaches of North Dakota; they won most of their games, but there were a few potholes along the way.[28]

Johnny Davis carried a 3–0 shutout into the bottom of the ninth inning against Hankinson on the 23rd, but only a base running error kept local hurler George Rennix from tying the game with a homer. With one out and William Grawe, the hometown center fielder on first, Pearce, the local backstop, knocked a long fly to right field that Bill Binga got his mitt on but did not hold on to. Grawe, thinking the ball had been caught, retreated back to first and was tagged out after Pearce passed him on his way to second. Rennix followed with his "beautiful" home run drive over the left-field fence, but Davis fanned the next batter and the Gophers prevailed, 3–2.[29]

A day later, the Cogswell, North Dakota, nine ran up an 8–0 lead on the barnstormers after six innings and held on for an 11–7 result, mashing 14 safeties, including five of the extra-base variety off Stallard. The very next afternoon, Harry Brown gave up only two early runs and three hits to an Ellendale outfit playing their first game of the season, but the Gophers could only manage three of their own against southpaw starter Jack Heimke. Two of the professional's base knocks came in the seventh inning when Bobby Marshall doubled and Hardiman singled. As a "whooping mob" of over 600 North Dakotans looked on, Brown uncorked a high drive to right. Outfielder Billy Eiden, "the Russian Prince" raced back, caught the ball "three feet from the boards, batted his head against the planks, bruised his knuckles" and with a "quick long distance throw" just doubled Marshall off second base to preserve a 2–0 victory.[30]

More difficulty awaited the Twin City club farther north in Jamestown. On May 29, the hometown squad waxed the Gophers, 7–2, after six of their eight base hits against Harry Brown went for doubles. A two-run single by Binga and a double by Arthur McDougall put the Gophers up 3–0 in the fifth inning the next day, but they could manage only one more base hit against Jamestown starter Rhoades, who also chalked up eleven strikeouts. Pitching before a big crowd of nearly 1,000, Johnny Davis cruised into the home eighth with another three-hit shutout. Three singles, a double, a sacrifice fly, and a passed ball by Bobby Marshall later, Jamestown had four runs, good enough for a 4–3 victory. The locals grabbed a quick 5–0 lead the following afternoon, knocking Stallard from the mound after five frames, but two William Selden triples and a Marshall double helped the Gophers salvage the game, 9–6.[31]

The Gophers road show next headed 100 miles west to Bismarck, where they beat the hometown White Sox three times in early June. The Twin City outfit rallied for a 7–6 victory in the second game on the 3rd, when Marshall, Schaeffer, and Brown hit back-to-back to back home runs in a five-run sixth inning. Hurler Louis Johnson rejoined club by the time they reached Mandan on the 5th, assuming Harry Brown's place in rotation. The spitballer struck out eight in his return, but the local Grays battered him "almost at will," turning an early 5–1 deficit into an 8–5 advantage after seven innings. The Gophers scored five times in the eighth and once in the ninth to pull out an 11–8 win, as Bobby Marshall paced the professionals' ten-hit attack, with a triple and three runs scored, and Selden smacked a home run.³²

Jesse Schaeffer committed three errors against Mandan and was replaced late in the game by Bobby Marshall. By the time the club reached Dickinson, North Dakota, on June 7, the stocky backstop was gone from the club for good after five years of on again, off again service. Schaeffer eventually joined Nate Harris' Leland Giants, while Bill Binga and Marshall took turns alternating behind the plate. The Gophers could have used Schaeffer's once mighty bat in Glen Ullin on the 6th, when they fell, 3–1, after a 12-strikeout performance by the local starter Nelson, who also launched one of the longest home runs ever seen on the hometown diamond.³³

The Gophers' first game in Dickinson was a dog fight in more ways than one. William Selden put the visitors in front with a long first-inning smash that hit one of the fence supports in center field and bounded over for a two-run homer. Johnny Davis frittered away yet another 3–0 lead, however, when three scratch hits in the home half of the sixth, combined with an error by McDougall, a passed ball by Marshall, a sacrifice fly, and a two-out two run triple by the local catcher Howard, put the Gophers at the wrong end of a 4–3 score.

Davis might have been distracted by the combat between two canines that occurred in front of the grandstand during the inning. Dickinson's third baseman Robinson finally put an end to the brawl, knocking "the dogs in the head with a baseball bat to the chagrin of the[ir] owners"—Robinson's only two hits on the day. Stallard led off the top of the seventh by coaxing a walk from Dickinson's starter Davis, who then gave up a triple to center by his opposite number, Johnny Davis that tied the game at four. Binga promptly broke the tie, by dumping a Texas League single over second base, and one walk, two stolen bases and a single by Selden later, the Gophers had a 7–4 lead that they would not relinquish.³⁴

The Dickinson press was impressed by the Gophers' teamwork, suggesting that "their think tanks are working all the time" and that "their ability to get hits when needed and at opportune times, won the game for them." As Marshall's club continued their westward trek, it was their *inability* to get clutch hits that was called into question. A scribe from the *Beach Advance* complained that whenever the

Catcher Jesse Schaeffer played for the Gophers each summer from 1907–1911, and suited up for the Keystones in 1908 and 1909. At the plate he was a powerful slugger and in the field he was a "terror to base stealers." (*Minneapolis Tribune,* June 13, 1909; Minnesota State Historical Society, St. Paul)

Gophers did drop a contest to a fellow North Dakota club, it was "more often done so in the earlier games," after which the professionals would clean "up a bunch of money at the expense of local enthusiasts on the final game."[35]

There would be no accusations of sandbagging during the Gophers' two-game set in remote Wibaux, Montana. At a distance of nearly 600 miles from Minneapolis, the Montana cow town was the farthest the Gophers ever played away from home. Marshall's nine was at least familiar with the Wibaux battery, "the great Indian pitcher" William "Nitchie" Cadreau and catcher Bowers McGarry with whom the team had tangled with several times before.

Bert Jones was unexplainably missing from the lineup, so Arthur McDougall took his place in center field while ex–Keystones captain Alex Irwin appeared out of nowhere to play second base. "In a close and interesting game, full of sensational plays," the Gophers handed Wibaux their first loss of the season on June 10, as Johnson outlasted Cadreau, 7–5. The Twin Cities club also downed the hometown Tigers, 9–5, two days later, and according to the local paper, rubbed it in a little afterwards:

> Feeling that Wibaux had too many southerners or citizens who had little love for a "nigger" the Gophers were very determined to win both games from the Tigers, and before they left the city expressed themselves to the effect that they might have given us an even break ... had we not been so sarcastic.[36]

The barnstormers sandwiched a Sunday doubleheader in nearby Beach, North Dakota, between the Wibaux games. Stallard and the Gophers took the opener, 9–2, thanks to ten errors by the locals. The *Wibaux Pioneer* claimed that the Gophers made a "present" of the second game to the hometown Giants. The Gophers snapped a two-all tie in the seventh when Hardiman singled and scored on a fielder's choice, but they couldn't overcome further ninth-inning drama by Johnny Davis, who allowed singles to the first three men to face him in the Giants' 4–3 walk-off win. Beach twirler Armatrout, whose "fast ones had the dark men pricking up their ears in anticipation of battle," allowed just six hits and struck out eight batters, while Davis yielded only two safeties and fanned seven before the fateful final frame.[37]

Following the second game in Wibaux, the Gophers slogged 300 miles eastward for a contest the following afternoon in Valley City, North Dakota. The grueling back and forth travel, along with an unsettled roster, began to catch up with the squad, especially their manager. The professionals were leading 3–1 in the third inning, when Marshall pulled an unnamed Gopher hurler from the game when he forced in a run after walking three consecutive batters. The Gophers caught a break in the eventual 4–4 tie when the Valley City starter Paulson, who struck out the professionals nine times, had to retire after seven innings after being hit with a pitch.[38]

A day later the Valley City outfit annihilated the travelers, 14–1, during the first game of a doubleheader, pounding Bobby Marshall at will. The Gophers leader also passed several batters and struck out every time he was up "save once when he walked." The Twin City club managed only two hits against the local starter Leahy, and collected but three more facing former Faribault Fleck Claude Lamb in the nightcap, with their sole run coming across on a wild pitch. The professionals left the field in the seventh inning, protesting a close play at first, but they finally returned to finish a 3–1 loss marked by constant wrangling by both sides.[39]

The next labor for Marshall's road weary nine was a three-game set way up in Devils Lake, with a tough semi-pro squad featuring former New York Highlander catcher Jack

Zalusky and ex–Renville All-Star "Toot" Thompson. Bert Jones was back in center field for the first tussle on June 15, while McDougall took over at third base and Hardiman moved back to second, replacing temporary fix Alex Irwin. Harry Brown opened the festivities by knocking a second-inning pitch thrown by Lakers starter Bill Manke over the fence and then "tore around the diamond as if it was too good to be true." Devils Lake came back with a vengeance against Gophers starter Walter Stallard and reliever Louis Johnson, building a 7–4 lead after six innings. Manke delighted the big crowd on hand by fanning ten of the Twin City club, but he faltered in the top of the seventh and the Gophers tied the game on back-to-back homers by Bobby Marshall and Bert Jones. With darkness fast approaching, Johnson needed only to hold the locals down in the bottom half of the inning to gain a tie. He instead gave up a single to Zalusky, closely followed by a walk-off double to the Devils Lake left fielder Caylor, "and before the ball had been returned to the diamond the crowd was leaving."[40]

The scribes for the *Devils Lake World* singled out a couple members of the Gophers for special comment the following morning. Bill Binga, they wrote, "used to play third base until he got so fat that they put him on a soup diet — and then he ate seven plates of soup and two dishes of crackers." The *World* noted that although Binga could still hit, "he walks so slowly that by the time he gets to the bench and is fairly settled it is time for him to start back to the field." The paper also thought that Bobby Marshall "has somewhat overrated himself," leaving the "impression that fame has been too much for the cranium under his wooly locks" and "his continual kicking put him in bad with the local fans and disgusted his former friends." In Marshall's defense, accusations of biased umpiring would be a recurring theme in Devils Lake that summer, although Tucker, the local arbiter, "proved his worth" to the *World* by calmly making his decisions "without regard for the wrathy [sic] swarm of visitors."[41]

The Gophers pitching staff did little to improve Marshall's mood during a doubleheader with the Lakers on the 16th. Johnny Davis was tagged for nine hits as he dropped the afternoon game, 5–1. The twilight contest was a see-saw affair that wasn't decided until Stallard walked in the winning run with the bases loaded in the eighth and final frame to hand Devils Lake a 5–4 victory The professionals lost their sixth game in a row the next day when the Grand Forks Picketts drubbed them, 7–1, under a blinding North Dakota sun. The listless Gophers, who appeared to be "too tired to move," were handcuffed by Grand Fork's youthful southpaw Nelson who fanned seven batters and surrendered only three hits "with an arm strung with fine piano wire." Harry Brown pitched for the professionals, and although he permitted just four base hits to the Picketts, the *Grand Forks Daily Herald* reported he fielded "like a man with a monomania for looking around, as he chalked up five errors against himself by standing in the center of the turf holding the ball, while the locals romped the bases in joyful glee."[42]

The indecisive twirler's teammates chipped in with five errors of their own and things didn't improve much the following afternoon when the Gophers committed nine more miscues, including three by Brown at third base. None of this helped starter Bert Jones, who was pulled in favor of Johnny Davis after three innings, with the visitors behind, 4–0. With a little help from the locals, however, the Gophers were able to pick themselves off the mat. They cut the lead to 4–3 in the fourth when Conmy, the local center fielder, misplayed William Selden's drive into a triple. Trailing 6–4 in the seventh, the Twin City outfit loaded the bases with two outs, and Jones cleaned the sacks with a triple off the Picketts starter Thomas, who had resorted to pitching up and in after his "drop ball" injured his catcher Tim McIlraith. Davis singled in the eighth and scored on another triple, this one by Brown, to salt away a much needed 9–6 triumph.[43]

Following the Sunday finale in Grand Forks, Marshall's squad was slated to play a pair of games 300 miles due west in Washburn. Instead, the Gophers blew off their contract and headed for nearby Crookston, moving disgruntled Washburn manager J.E. Nelson to consider legal action against the club. The Twin City crew celebrated their return to Minnesota by nipping Crookston, 2–1, scoring both their runs in the first inning when a Gopher batter's long fly to the left-field fence was lost in the weeds. Stallard spaced out eight hits to pick up the win, wriggling out of several late inning jams after allowing three bases-empty doubles.[44]

Bobby Marshall "furnished considerable amusement" to the after supper crowd with his running verbal battle with local umpire Davies, but "due to his age and popularity was not thrown out for talking back." The Gophers leader was still "peevish" the next evening, but mostly with his own team. The professionals again grabbed a 2–0 first inning lead with two clean hits off Crookston's little left-hander Sisler, who then settled down and didn't allow another base runner past first base until the ninth. The locals knocked Louis Johnson out of the game with a five-run fifth, and routed the Gophers, 11–3. Marshall was hit quite "freely" in relief of Johnson and he got no help from Johnny Davis, who had gone into umpire in the third inning after the disgruntled hometown fans forced the original arbiter to retire. Davis' efforts "gave satisfaction to all save for Marshall his boss, who crabbed all the way through the contest."[45]

Marshall was no doubt frustrated by Louis Johnson's continued ineffectiveness, caused it was now revealed, by a sore arm. The young spitballer was yanked from the starting rotation and Clarence Lytle rejoined to the Gophers after a three-year absence to take his place. The "Dude" arrived just in time for a four-game set against an Alexandria club, made up of the best semi-pro players in the Upper Midwest, including soon to be major leaguer Bert Brenner.[46]

Johnny Davis was Brenner's mound opponent in the afternoon half of a twilight doubleheader on June 21. The Gophers grabbed a 1–0 lead in the first inning when Binga singled and scored on a passed ball, only to watch as Alexandria scored four times in the second on the strength of a pair of two run doubles. The professionals pulled to within one on Selden's two-run single in the third, but two more doubles netted two more tallies for the home team in the sixth and they held on for a 6–3 victory. Brenner yielded only five hits and collected three of his club's ten safeties against Davis, while Alexandria infielder Ernst drove in three runs with a couple of doubles. The evening contest immediately followed and Alex pounded Lytle for 13 hits en route to a 12–3 shellacking of the Gophers. The first three men up to bat for home club reached via walk or error, and "Big" Hank Thrall proceeded to clear the bases with a double. Three base hits later, Alexandria had a 6–0 lead after which Lytle reportedly "lost his nerve" altogether. "Dutch" Brenner pitched this second game as well, spacing out eight base knocks to pick up a remarkable doubleheader win.[47]

Over the next two days the clubs tangled twice more at a civic celebration held 30 miles south in Brooten. Alexandria won the first match-up, 8–4, behind Gophers nemesis Ed Kellar and annexed the second contest, 8–7, with former Renville twirler Pat Finnegan recording the victory. Ernst continued to be a thorn in the side of Marshall's squad, hitting a grand slam to win one of the games. The *Alexandria Post News* observed that "the Colored Gophers are not playing as classy ball as they did two or three years ago," with the decline most "noticeable in the box, [with] old timers like Lytle being substituted for men like Taylor." Even so, the Twin City nine could still pack them in; both halves of the double dip in Alexandria drew over 1,100 fans.[48]

The final setback to the Alexandria bunch was the Gophers' fifth loss in a row and their ninth in their last eleven games. The team was in disarray and even their successes were tainted. Johnny Davis pitched the club to a 6–2 win over Long Prairie on the 28th in a game that was played in a steady rain before it was halted after five innings. Things reverted to form the next day when Walter Stallard dropped a 4–1 decision to the locals and the Gophers slunk back to the Twin Cities with a losing record.[49]

Alex Irwin did not return with them. After briefly filling in for the Gophers on their western trip, the tiny infielder resurfaced in Walker, Minnesota, the home of the State Sanatorium for Consumptives. The *Walker Pilot* reported in mid–July that:

> Messrs. Irwin and Birch of Minneapolis are occupying a cottage near the school house and expect to remain here part of the summer on account of Mr. Birch's health. The gentlemen are members of the well known Colored Gopher baseball team and are also accomplished musicians.

Located 190 miles north of Minneapolis, the sanatorium administered to individuals afflicted with tuberculosis. Their records from that time have no listing of a patient named Birch, so it is unclear whether Irwin's friend was cared for there or if segregation extended to the treatment of this deadly infectious disease. While his friend convalesced, "Gopher Irwin" played a few games for the Walker town team, including a 13–6 victory over a sanatorium nine named the "Coughers."[50]

In keeping with their newly established national reputation, the Keystones were among the squads mentioned in the fledgling Southwestern Negro League of Professional Ball Clubs. According to the February 25 edition of the *Indianapolis Freeman*, the new organization was the brainchild of St. Louis Giants owner Charley Mills and was to include teams from Chicago, Kansas City, Louisville, Cincinnati, Oklahoma, and New Orleans. Ultimately, the Southwestern League, like most of the other proposed black circuits before it, never got off the ground.[51]

The 1911 edition of the Keystones was a slight rebuild of the previous year's squad, with Kidd Mitchell adding some "classy material" to a nucleus of "some of the best colored players of the country." Eugene "Cherry" Barton had left the team after three campaigns and the trio Mitchell had swiped from the ABC's—John Merida, Frank Young, and James Shawler—also jumped ship. Merida went to Missouri to toil for the Kansas City Royal Giants, but in May he tragically died of spinal meningitis. They brought "Snowball" home to Spiceland, Indiana, and laid him to rest in an unmarked Quaker grave.[52]

Mitchell's latest target du jour was the Louisville Cubs and it was reported in March that the Colonel had plucked infielders George Watson and James Wallace off their roster. Watson and Wallace never made it to Minneapolis that season, but Louisville first baseman William Embry and right fielder Bert Woods did, along with center fielder Jesse Briscoe who had captained the Fall City nine in 1909.[53]

The former Cubs joined the already existing core of pitchers Archie Pate, Charles Jackson, and Hurley McNair; catcher James Wills; third baseman Milroy McCune; and shortstop "Bunch" Davis. Also on hand were a strong-hitting left fielder named Wilson and "Card" Phillips, a second baseman "of the National league caliber," who had spent the previous season on the Pacific coast. Amazingly enough, at least seven of the Keystones batted left-handed.[54]

Allen Hurley McNair was perhaps the finest player who ever wore the Keystones colors. In 1911 the young southpaw would win over twenty games for the Minneapolis club and lead the team with a better than .350 batting average, while amassing a slugging average of over .630. The *Indianapolis Freeman* noted that McNair "showed some remarkable ability at odd times as a pitcher of cleverness" while a scribe in Charles City, Iowa, wrote that "McNair has a glove, a devout invocation, and unlimited nerve. If he didn't have he wouldn't be out there." McNair would play 26 more years in blackball, earning a reputation as a great outfielder and a deadly clutch hitter who, according to Kansas City Monarchs teammate George Giles, "could have taken two strikes on Jesus Christ and base-hit the next pitch." The speedy 5' 4", 160-pound Texan possessed keen eyesight, strong wrists, big shoulders, and loved to murder a low pitched ball.[55]

McNair's homeboy James Wills was an outstanding defensive catcher who reminded the mainstream press of Johnny Kling in that "his throwing is all that can be desired." Black sportswriters thought that the youngster from Waco, Texas, was "another [Bruce] Petway," in that he "throws like him, and the Texas players won't run on him." Everyone was in agreement that Wills was "one of the best backstops that has been here for some time."[56]

If not an upgrade, the three ex–Louisville Cubs were at least equal to the ex–ABC's they replaced: 32-year-old William "Cap" Embry had mentored Felix Wallace, among others, and would later umpire in the Negro National League. The versatile Vincennes, Indiana, ballplayer was said to be "as full of signs as a railroad yard," and was set to join a squad in Milwaukee, before Mitchell inked him to a Keystones contract. Bert Woods, Embry's one time teammate on the Danville Unions, was a pure slugger who according to the *Freeman* "would be a wonder" if only "he would use little more judgment." Although the Keystones' 1911 statistical record is rather slight, Woods would post a slugging average in the .600 range. Jesse Briscoe was a "big league" outfielder who "has a way of starting with the ball, is a good judge and makes very few errors." Briscoe's "batting and general playing" helped the Cubs lay claim to the championship of the South in 1909.[57]

The Keystones players started arriving in Minneapolis in mid–April and left for Springs Valley, Indiana, soon after to "get into playing condition for the summer." Springs Valley was the location of the West Baden and French Lick health spas, renowned for the restorative powers of their mineral springs. The two resorts were also known for the West Baden Sprudels and French Lick Plutos, a pair of dynamite black teams who squared off daily for the sporting and betting enjoyment of their hotel's wealthy patrons.[58]

Former Birmingham Giants manager C.I. Taylor had moved to West Baden in 1910, molding a powerhouse outfit that included two players Kidd Mitchell had coveted that spring, pitcher William "Dizzy" Dismukes and catcher Jack Watts. The Keystones and Sprudels faced off during a weekend series in early May with Dismukes taking to the hill on Saturday the 6th to face his former team. The young twirler had matured considerably in the two years since the Keystones had released him, and he allowed only five scattered drives, while his current teammates pounded Charles Jackson "to all corners of the lot" in the 13–1 Sprudels' rout.[59]

The aptly named West Baden hurler John Goodgame allowed only two hits the next day and fanned 17 would-be hitters. Although Hurley McNair gave up just six safeties himself, one was three-run homer to center to Sprudels first baseman Bennie Lyons and the hotel men won, 6–0. The Keystones "came out with blood in their eyes" in the Monday finale and scored twice in the top of the first inning against West Baden starter Shaw. Not to be outdone, the Sprudels loaded the bases in the bottom of the frame against Archie

Pate, and Lyons smacked another line drive over the center-field fence for a grand slam. After Lyons' smash, "the Keystones seemed to have lost hope and the Sprudels scored almost at will" during their 14–5 victory.[60]

The Keystones had little luck either with the French Lick Plutos, who also beat them three straight times, 7–4, 6–4, and 4–3, although the games were more competitive than in the Sprudels series. Kidd Mitchell had announced prior to the season that his club was once again ready, after a year's hiatus, to "book games with fast nines throughout the entire Northwest," and the Keystones left Springs Valley on a six-week journey back to Minnesota. Sometime before heading north, the Mill City aggregation reportedly played a series of games with minor league squads from the South Atlantic League and the Southern Association, tying the Mobile, Alabama, Sea Gulls of the latter circuit, 2–2.[61]

Mitchell's squad won most of their games on their way home, but as usual with the Keystones the final score was only a tiny part of the story. On May 14, Hurley McNair pitched the "extreme Northerners" over the Louisville Cubs, 8–3, and helped himself by knocking three home runs over the Spring Bank Park fences. A few days later McNair was struck out twice by Bowling Green Academy pitcher "Sea Hawk" Young and the professionals "were clearly outplayed" by the Kentucky collegians to the tune of 4–2.[62]

The Keystones arrived in Memphis, Tennessee, on May 21 for a Sunday doubleheader with the hometown Tigers. A band concert preceded the first contest and although the day was overcast, the hometown fans were "overjoyed" by one of the most exciting games ever played at Varsity Park. Things were going the Minneapolis nine's way early as they scored six times in the first three innings and knocked Tigers starter Nelson out of the box. Young, "the famous side-arm twirler" came on in relief and "as usual, kept the visitors from doing anything more." Young's machinations allowed Memphis to take an 8–6 lead into the top of the ninth, but a Tigers error and a home run by Bert Woods knotted the score. The quarrel now went into extra innings and "the way both clubs got down and played ball was something great." The game was still tied at eight when it was called on account of darkness after 15 innings, with Keystones pitcher Charles Jackson having gone the entire distance. The second half of the double bill had to be rescheduled for the following day, but nobody seemed to mind.[63]

By early June, Mitchell's charges had crossed the land of Lincoln and reached southeastern Iowa. Along the way, the Keystones took two out of three games from the DeKalb, Illinois, Bluebirds and swept a pair from the What Cheer, Iowa, Ramblers before "fair sized but exceptionally well satisfied crowds." The professionals broke up a tight game in Strawberry Point, Iowa, by scoring 15 runs in the eighth inning to crush the locals, 19–5. The first three batters up in the frame tripled and the Keystones tallied 12 times before an out was recorded.[64]

James Wills was absent from the lineup for a few games during the Iowa leg of the tour and Archie Pate filled in behind the plate. McNair blanked the tough Charles City outfit, 6–0, on June 10 as Bert Woods tripled twice and Card Phillips added a pair of doubles. Vive Lindaman, who had pitched four years with the Boston Nationals, started for the locals a day later, and, according to a Charles City paper, "had everything" and "his fast ball jumped, his curves crooked themselves with a jerk, and his spitter broke over the plate with wicked and terrific speed." Lindaman, scattered five hits, one by Jesse Briscoe on a "waste pitch" three feet over his head, and struck out eight batters. Charles Jackson also yielded only five safeties, but he got off to a miserable start on a rather cold and rainy afternoon. The Keystones vet began the home half of the first inning by hitting the lead off man with a pitch, and after fielding a subsequent sacrifice bunt, threw the ball into the crowd. "Still bewildered" Jackson wild pitched a run home before Teddy left fielder Hill mashed a screaming rocket past shortstop Bunch Davis, "that nearly tore away that gentleman's underpinning" and plated a second run. Lindaman gave up an eighth-inning score to the professionals, but he retired them in order in the ninth, as a Sunday crowd of 1,500 "wild eyed bugs" went home singing "Happy Days."[65]

The club was reinforced soon after with the arrival of Harry "Pick" Bauchman, a pitcher/infielder/boxer from Omaha, Nebraska. The "tall, lean, lanky" Bauchman was a good fielder and base stealer, who later manned second base for a couple of strong Chicago American Giants clubs. Bauchman was a light hitter on the diamond, but as a pugilist he reportedly went four rounds with heavyweight contender Fireman Jim Flynn in 1912. The 21-year-old right-hander impressed immediately by pitching his new team to a 7–2 win over the Fayette, Iowa, nine, slightly easing the sting of an earlier game where Fayette erased an 8–1 deficit by scoring six times in the eighth inning and twice in the ninth to topple the Keystones 9–8.[66]

On their way out of Iowa, the Keystones ran into Vi Lindaman once more, pitching for the Oelwein squad. The 33-year-old Charles City native had their number again, scattering seven hits while fanning five, and Oelwein rolled 7–2. The difference in the game was the local's four-run fourth against McNair that was aided greatly by a walk, a wild pitch, two poor plays at short by Bunch Davis, and a dropped third strike by Archie Pate that kept the inning alive. The Flour City bunch played their first game in Minnesota in nearly two years in Waseca on June 21, and they celebrated their return with an 11–1 win in front of a handful of fans not deterred by the "fierce heat of the day." Hometown starter Charles McCleary, that "veteran collector of baseball scalps," was pummeled for 15 hits and wasn't helped much by three Waseca catchers who surrendered seven stolen bases while also letting five passed balls get by them.[67]

The black ball player as buffoon. Newspaper advertisement for a 1911 Keystones game in DeKalb, Illinois. (*DeKalb Advertiser*, May 31, 1911, Abraham Lincoln Presidential Library, Springfield, IL)

Controversy had managed to elude the Keystones for most of the season, but that ended at Hastings the next afternoon, when the club left the Wasser Park grounds during the first inning after an unfavorable call by umpire J. P. Hoffman. The crowd was given their money back and Mitchell's outfit moved on to Blooming Prairie where they dropped a 6–4 decision to the locals. The Keystones less than triumphant return to the Twin Cities area hit another snag when their June 24 game at Lexington with the H. P. Conrads didn't come off.[68]

The two teams did hook up the following day and Conrads third baseman Shirley quickly jumpstarted things by singling to lead off the bottom of the first inning; the semi-pro's captain then swiped second base, advanced on a fielder's choice, and scored on an infield out. Mitchell's outfit tied it in the second when Jesse Briscoe doubled and crossed the plate a few moments later after an errant throw by first sacker Lefty Dehmer. The professionals forged ahead an inning later when Frank Davis scored on a wild toss by the Conrads starter Harkins, after the twirler had put him on base in the first place by plunking him with a pitch. The "local boys" peppered Hurley McNair for 15 base hits on the day, but they stilled trailed 2–1 when Harkins, Shirley, and Conrads second baseman Larson singled in succession to start the home half of the seventh. Harkins was brought home by an infield out, and Gophers football standout Lyle Pettijohn, "one of the best forward pass artists the West has ever produced," cleared the bases with a "four-bag swat to the right center field fence." Pettijohn's big blow propelled the Conrads to an eventual 5–3 win and strengthened their claim to "the independent championship of the Northwest."[69]

After the Sunday scrap with the Conrads, the Keystones took off on a six-week pilgrimage through western Minnesota and the Dakotas. Frank Davis stayed behind, ending a nearly three-year association during which the club never had to worry about the short field. The "midget shortstop" had seen it all during his tenure, but probably nothing as bizarre as an alleged incident that had taken place a couple of weeks prior in Fayette, Iowa.[70]

The Keystones had spent their downtime before a Monday afternoon tilt with the local team by going fishing on the banks of the Volga River. When a member of the Minneapolis club "captured a fish so small that it was barely visible to the naked eye," the mayor of Fayette "interposed a strenuous objection" and demanded that the offender "appear and account for this breach of law." The unnamed Keystone requested that he be allowed to change his clothes before his hearing. According to the *Fayette Reporter*, when the whole squad subsequently appeared before the authorities, "all looking more or less alike the matter took a more serious aspect, and the fisherman could not be identified with a sufficient certainty to warrant his arrest." However apocryphal, the story perfectly illustrates how African Americans were usually perceived in the early 20th century — the headline for the *Reporter* story read, "All Coons Look Alike to Him."[71]

Chapter Ten

On the Way Home (July 1911–1912)

The Gophers squad that suited up for the early July series against Perry Werden's All-Stars in Minneapolis was a dramatic improvement on the outfit that had stumbled home from the Dakotas. Frank "Bunch" Davis came over from the Keystones to cover second base for his old team while the Pennsylvania battery of Tom Pangburn and George Armstrong left the Buxton Wonders for another tour of duty with the Gophers. Armstrong's arrival gave the Twin Cities squad a legitimate catcher for the first time in nearly a month, while Pangburn brought a certain toughness that had been sorely lacking. The little left-hander had his nose broken while dropping a 5–4 decision to Cyclone Joe Williams and the Chicago Giants in June, but stayed in the game to pitch all nine innings. For the first time ever, the Gophers roster expanded to 14 players, instead of the usual ten or eleven, with Johnson, Lytle, and Hardiman being regulated to the bench.[1]

The team also got a new business manager when Henry C. Jones, a St. Paul restaurateur, replaced Eddie Davis. The revamped Gophers were set to debut with a trio of weekend games at Nicollet, and Perry Werden vowed he would "place a formidable club in the field" against them. Marshall's squad found the All-Stars pitchers slightly less than formidable on July 1 when they pounded out 15 hits and never trailed in a 10–6 win. Arthur McDougall, Bill Binga, and Lefty Pangburn had three safeties each while Mule Armstrong celebrated his return to the Twin Towns with a double and a two-run homer. Pangburn gave up 14 base knocks to the Werdens, but he whiffed nine batters and "was very effective in the pinches."[2]

The swat-fest continued the next day as the Gophers rapped out 11 singles, which combined with four walks and six All-Stars errors, paved the way to an easy 9–4 triumph. Bert Jones and Bobby Marshall chipped in with three hits apiece. Binga smoked four more base hits, in addition to pulling down a long fly ball to right in the eighth inning, and doubling a Werdens base runner off first base. Dicta Johnson started for the Gophers, but he couldn't make it past the second as Johnny Davis swooped in and pitched the rest of the way for the victory.[3]

Having evidently seen enough, Perry Werden penciled himself into the All-Stars lineup at first base for the Sunday climax. The "roly-poly" 45-year-old acquitted himself quite well by handling 18 chances "without a skip" and "got a brace of hits out of four trips up." Not even the presence of the ex-leaguer kept the Gophers, fueled by doubles by Marshall and Jones, from scoring six times in the first three frames against All-Stars starter Johnson. Walter Stallard opened the game for the Gophers by tossing six shutout innings, carrying a 7–1 advantage into the ninth before two free passes and a pair of singles netted three runs for the semi-pros. With one on, one out, and his team down by three, Perry Werden, the hero of many a Nicollet Park rally, stepped to the plate. The old Millers star mashed a drive to the left side, but Harry Brown made a sensational stop of the ball and turned a quick double play to end the game.[4]

Although they had not impressed many while on the prairie, the Gophers had wowed their big city audiences. Werdens second baseman Billy Hoke wrote in his "Texas Leaguers" column for the *Minneapolis Tribune* that "the whole outfit plays good ball all of the time and appears to know exactly what the other fellow is going to do and works accordingly." Hoke also remarked that the sweet swinging Binga "appears to be able to do what most other players fall down on — place his hits." The semi-pro infielder was equally enamored with Bobby Marshall, who while being "unusually fast on his pins for so large a man" was "plenty tall enough to grab all of the high pegs and dig the low ones out of the mire" in big league fashion.[5]

Even with his strong performance against the Werdens, Stallard was bumped once again from the pitching rotation, with the Gophers going with a veteran starting three of Pangburn, Davis, and Lytle instead. Hot off their sweep of the All-Stars, the Twin City club essayed 400 miles back to North Dakota for a Fourth of July contest in Devils Lake. Playing before a huge gathering of 1,600, the locals "were slightly off their feed," and the Gophers grabbed a quick 2–0 lead after an inning and a half. The professionals pilfered six bases and incited seven errors, but they were prevented from crossing the plate again by Lakers ace Bill Manke, who yielded only three hits, two by Binga, while striking out eight batters. Pangburn started out strong for the barnstormers, but the hometown talent "realized that there was blood on the moon" and tied the game at two in the fourth. The Gophers southpaw was touched for 12 hits on the afternoon and helped the enemy cause by walking five batters and hitting another. Devils Lake tallied three times in the seventh, twice more in the eighth and walked away with a 7–2 win.[6]

The first game "rag chewing," between the hometown fans whose oratory "would make Aristotle take the pebbles out of his mouth," and Marshall, who "talked as though his nose had caught in a door," carried over to the following afternoon. Devils Lake fell on Johnny Davis for four runs in the second inning, after which the Gophers seemed to lose their "pep" and "their laziness and soarness [sic] because they were not winning" put them at the wrong end of a 10–2 thrashing. William Selden and Marshall both tripled for the Twin City aggregation, but the Lakers clubbed Davis for 13 hits, including a home run by Jack Zalusky. According to the *Devils Lake World* the hometown cranks kept themselves entertained by razzing the Gopher bench:

> Several pertinent remarks were made during the progress of the game and were it not for this fact all excitement would have been lost. Unable to battle with the sphere, the Gophers took to flinging a word battle with the fans, the result being that the fans were not only satisfied with winning the game, but they made the Gophers look as if they were half undressed every time they opened their mouths.[7]

Perhaps it was the arrival of champion roller skater (but non-motorcycle manufacturer) Harley Davidson in town for the local Chautauqua (a lecture series/carnival hybrid that was all the rage at the time) or maybe the travelers found the betting odds more to their liking, but after five straight losses to the Devils Lake bunch, the Gophers blitzed the North Dakotans, 7–1, on the 6th to take a little cash from "the home money talkers." A subsequent *Minneapolis Journal* report offered up the opinion that "the umpire had an off day" and was thus "unable to stop the Gophers." Reversing course, Marshall's crew made a 220-mile jump back to Cass Lake, Minnesota, and slipped by the local squad, 2–1, before a large Friday night crowd. After striking out 12 Gophers the year before, local hurler "Pete" Schmidt fanned 11 more this time around and the exhausted visitors could only manage two hits off his delivery. Lefty Pangburn parsed out seven safeties while striking out seven and proved once again he could pitch out of a jam — three times a Cass Lake base runner reached third base with only one out, but couldn't score.[8]

The Twin City nine's caravan next headed east for Duluth for a pair of games with a clothing company team aptly called the Fitwells. The Gophers beat the clothiers, 6–4, at Athletic Park on July 8 and snapped a scoreless tie with a five-run sixth inning the following afternoon on their way to a 7–2 victory. William Selden and Harry Brown had keyed the victory over Devils Lake when any ball hit "in the direction of short or third base was gobbled up fast enough to elicit several double plays." The duo's "fast as lightning" work over the weekend in Duluth moved a local reporter to rave "these two players would burn up the Minny league and would soon be grabbed up by the large arena boys were it not for their shade."[9]

Marshall's club departed the Zenith City for the Iron Range, where the baseball fever had spread to such a degree that a semi-pro circuit called the Eastern Mesaba League had been formed. Many of the outfit's teams had wanted to schedule the Gophers, but were unable to because the Twin City club had no available Sunday dates, and the league's players all worked during the week. The range fans had to content themselves instead with an eight-game, seven-day showdown between the Gophers and their longtime foes, the Hibbing Colts. The professionals arrived in Hibbing on the morning of July 11, and spent a rare afternoon of practice at the local ball park in preparation for the marathon series.[10]

The rangers kicked off the series by downing the Gophers, 4–1, before a good-sized mid-week crowd. "Dad" Williams out-pitched Pangburn, striking out six batters and allowing only four hits, while his teammates got to the Gophers lefty for eight base knocks including three doubles. It could have been worse, since a high wind kept several batted balls in the ballpark. The local arbiter Cameron umpired a "nice game" save for two "raw" calls against the Gophers which didn't factor in the outcome, but his decisions the following afternoon were so one-sided in favor of the home team that even a writer for the *Hibbing News Tribune* felt "they verged on the perfectly rotten." "Odorous" decisions aside, Dwight Booth and Johnny Davis hooked up in yet another tight pitching duel reminiscent of their 1907 14-inning epic. Booth struck out five batters to Davis' two, but he also walked five and two of these came around to score in the second inning giving the Gophers an early 2–0 advantage. The visitors scored again in the eighth aided by an error by Colts right fielder Bobby Geiselman, but the locals tied the game by tallying twice in the latter half of the frame and the game soon went into extras. Johnny Davis, "with a wad of gum in his face that must have caused a muscular reaction in his jaw," drove in the go-ahead run with a base hit in the top of the 10th, before setting the home side down to close out the 4–3 win. Dwight Booth was a hard-luck loser again, and third baseman Dick Brookins was just a sore loser, intentionally spiking a sliding Gopher base runner.[11]

The Colts made nine errors the next day, including three by Brookins, "the somnambulist in up to date vaudeville," as the Gophers downed the rangers, 9–8, in a game that wasn't as close as the final score indicated. Bill Binga collected four hits, while Bunch Davis and Mule Armstrong rapped out three apiece. The local's poor pitching, lousy fielding, and "bonehead plays," continued over the weekend. The barnstormers triumphed, 8–3, in a "rather slow affair" on Saturday the 15th, powered by two Binga doubles and a home run by William Selden.[12]

The two old antagonists next tried their hands at a Sunday doubleheader. Hibbing outslugged the Gophers in both games but they were severely hindered by their second baseman Burroughs, who committed a couple of errors in each contest, moving a local scribe to moan that "a large apron tied around his waist to assist him in holding the ball would be a valuable adjunct." Clarence Lytle muscled a home run over the centerfield fence, in the opener, apparently such a rare and prodigious blast that the Dude "was forced to doff his cap to the crowd" who wildly cheered him as he circled the bases. Lytle later singled, scored another run, and ran down a deep fly ball in left field off the bat of by Hibbing catcher Red Carroll, during the Twin City club's 6–3 victory. The Dude's great day carried over to the second game when he doubled, scored a run, and scattered eight hits to pick up a 3–1 win. The veteran twirler wriggled out of a bases-loaded, nobody-out jam, and his infielders turned three fast double plays behind him. The Gophers also caught a break when, with two runners aboard, a smash by Hibbing left fielder Carroll Booth, just inside the third base bag, was called foul. Dwight Booth hit a home run for the Colts while Bert Jones homered for the professionals who also had to deal with the "constant badinage and repartee" of several home town lady fans.[13]

Frank "Bunch" Davis was the Keystones shortstop from May 1909 until he rejoined the Gophers in July 1911. Davis captained the Minneapolis squad in 1909 and hit over 300. When he hurt his ankle in 1910, the team's "fans nearly cried." (*Minneapolis Tribune*, June 13, 1909; Minnesota State Historical Society, St. Paul)

Marshall's team took Monday off while the Colts battled the Hopkins Ladies Club in an afternoon and "after dark" indoor baseball (softball) doubleheader played under electric light. According to the *News Tribune*, "the night will be turned into day by a 50,000 candle power radiant sunburst illumination," that the Des Moines–based outfit carried with them. Hibbing's largest crowd of the season turned out to witness the novelty of what later became a barnstorming staple. Night baseball wouldn't come into vogue until 1930 when the Kansas City Monarchs, owned by ex–Hopkins Ladies Club manager J.L. Wilkinson, began touring with their own portable lighting system.[14]

Louis Johnson started for the Gophers the following afternoon after a two-week hiatus, but his "bum wing" was not yet in shape. The "famous spit-ball artist" was rocked for 12 hits and he didn't use his spitter once in an 8–4 Hibbing rout. Bunch Davis, Harry Brown, and Bobby Marshall all homered off Dick Brookins, who gave up nine safeties in all to the Gophers, but still registered the win. Marshall had missed the series opener with a bad ankle, and went hitless in 17 at bats during the next five games before his drive cleared the right-field wall. The range fans gave the lanky first baseman a warm ovation as he limped around the bases.[15]

Marshall singled three times the next day and Brown homered for the second game in a row, as the Gophers crushed the locals, 9–2. The professionals roughed up former minor league twirler Jean Grady for six base hits and Dwight Booth for six more. Lefty Pangburn was also hit freely, but the Hibbing boys could not bunch their nine safeties. The Twin City club left Hibbing on route for a weekend set in Virginia, having won six out of their eight games with the Colts. The Gophers record for July stood at 13–4 and they were unquestionably playing their best ball in over a year. Unfortunately, it was at this point that the wheels started to fall off again.[16]

On July 21, Johnny Davis permitted only one base hit to the Virginia outfit through the first four innings while his teammates staked him to a 2–0 lead. The home squad banged out 13 hits in the next four frames, however, which combined with four Gophers errors resulted in an easy 10–3 win. William Selden doubled and homered, but to no avail. The Twin City club reached Virginia starter Megan for four base hits in the ninth, but "stupid base running" limited them to but one run. A day later, Virginia beat the Gophers "who seemed to be playing below their usual form," 8–5, in a "slow and uninteresting game." The visitors raked out nine hits, but they left 11 men on base and made four very costly errors. Special passenger trains were set to run along the Great Northern line from Duluth and Hibbing for the big series closer on Sunday, but it was rained out to the disappointment of many.[17]

Frank Davis, who had missed a few of the Hibbing games, left the squad soon after Virginia series. The little shortstop went back to the Windy City just in time to make a brief appearance for the Chicago American Giants. Facing Walter Ball and the Chicago Giants in a crucial playoff contest, Davis singled, scored twice and recorded ten assists for Rube Foster's men. The right side of the Gophers infield soon experienced another blow when Bobby Marshall returned to the Twin Cities to rest his sore ankle. To compensate for their loss, Hardiman took over the second base job; Harry Brown moved to first, and Arthur McDougall came in from the left garden to play third. Bert Jones went missing in action again as well, leaving Pangburn, Lytle, Stallard, and Johnson to rotate between the left and center outfield spots.[18]

Despite fielding a patchwork lineup, the Gophers more than kept their heads above water while navigating their way through the dog days of late July and early August. After trouncing clubs in Milaca and Mora, Minnesota, the professionals sloshed by the Hayward, Wisconsin, regulars, 10–4, in a rain-soaked contest on July 29. Walter Stallard started against Hayward the next afternoon, but after allowing a home run to deep right field on his second pitch, and a single to the next batter, he was pulled in favor of Clarence Lytle. The Dude put the side down with no further damage and retired the first two men up in the second before the next five locals reached base and came around to score. The game ended, seven innings and 12 more Hayward hits later, with the professionals on the wrong end of a 9–3 result. The following day the Minnesota squad ran up against a young Burleigh Grimes in Spooner. The previous summer the Gophers had roughed up the future Hall of Famer, pitching for a western Wisconsin nine, to the tune of 12–2. The 18-year-old spitballer fared better this time around, as the Gophers barely edged his squad, 3–2.[19]

In early July the Gophers had been a no-show in Superior, Wisconsin, for a series with the Turnbull–Cameron–Degler furniture team. The Twin City nine went to Devils Lake instead and hadn't informed the Superior management about their change of plans. All was forgiven a month later when the barnstormers, led by fill-in captain Bill Binga, arrived in the port city to fulfill their obligation. Only 50 customers paid to see the Gophers polish off the furniture men, 8–5, on August 5 although several other spectators lined the box cars surrounding Hislop Park to watch the game for free. The Turnballs, intimidated by the professionals or disappointed by their lousy fan support, "seemed to not take much interest in the game and at different times were seen to be napping on [the] bases." The crowd was larger the following day, but the Gophers took all the interest out of the game by scoring nine times in their first five times at bat. Dude Lytle unintentionally "endeavored to liven things up" for the Sunday crowd by giving up four runs in his five innings of work, until Johnny Davis put an end to the fun by closing out the 10–4 win with four scoreless frames.[20]

The Gophers were well on their way to salvaging their season when they returned to Alexandria on August 8 for a three-game tilt. Neither Bert Brenner nor Lefty Pangburn was scored upon during the first six innings of the Monday opener. The home team finally broke through with four runs in the bottom of the seventh, mostly because Pangburn failed to properly field two squeeze bunts. The Gophers never broke through, scratching out only five hits as Brenner shut them out, 4–0, in one hour and seven minutes. Trailing 4–0 in the top of the seventh the next day, the Twin City nine loaded the bases off a familiar foe, Al Dretchko, but then proceeded to run themselves out of the game. With his team down by four and the equalizer at the plate, Harry Brown inexplicably tried to steal second base, where he was thrown out by Port, the Alexandria backstop. Seeing Brown headed his way, Hardiman, the runner at second, set sail for third, were he was eventually tagged out when that base's occupant, Dude Lytle, refused to make a try for home. Louis Johnson singled, scoring Lytle, and Arthur McDougall plated Johnson with a base hit, but Selden flew out to left to end the inning. The locals hung on to win 4–2, in a game the Gophers would have probably tied if Brown had only stayed put.[21]

Alexandria took another early lead on the 10th, jumping on Dicta Johnson for five runs in the first five innings. The Gophers rallied against Pat Finnegan, who walked Brown with the bases loaded in the seventh to tie the game at five, but the locals tallied once in their half of the frame and twice in the eighth for an 8–5 series-sweeping victory. The Alexandria papers allowed that the Gophers had greatly improved since their visit to the city in June, with Brown being a substantial upgrade at first base over Bobby Marshall. The professionals had now dropped seven straight games to the western Minnesota outfit, mostly because of poor fundamental play.[22]

In early July, the *Twin City Star* wondered "Why can't the Keystones and Gophers get together and play a series?" The paper pointed out that, among local black fans, there was "more spirit attraction and real money" in the games of "these friendly rivals" than there was in the World Series For their part the Keystones claimed to have recently defeated both the Gophers and Perry Werden's All-Stars, but as often was the case, details were not forthcoming.[23]

The Mill City club also informed the *Star* that they "showed up to form" in a series with Alexandria, but in truth the semi-pro nine had proven to be just as inhospitable to the Keystones as they were to the Gophers. The Keystones jumped on Alexandria starter Hank Thrall for a 3–0 lead after two innings had been played on June 28, but the locals bombed Charles Jackson for four runs each in the third and fourth frames while coasting to a 9–6 win. Harry Bauchman collected three hits for the losers and scored four times while Card Phillips handled ten chances at short without an error. The two teams split a doubleheader the next day. Alexandria chased Hurley McNair from the box in the opener with four first-inning scores and cruised to an easy 10–3 triumph. The hometown squad rapped out 15 hits, while the visitors managed only six off Pat Finnegan. McNair started the second game as well, and "did a better job at pitching, "yielding but two safeties. Phillips slammed a two-run homer in the fourth inning off an ex–Minny League twirler named Lawson and McNair made it hold up for a 3–2 Keystones victory.[24]

Bunch Davis' defection to the Gophers had forced Mitchell's charges to reorder their lineup on the fly. Soon after their western swing began Keystones captain Jesse Briscoe installed himself at shortstop while Bert Woods shifted over to center field. James Wills returned to action behind the plate during the tour, regulating Archie Pate to spot duty as a backup catcher, relief pitcher, and right fielder on the occasions when Hurley McNair pitched.

The Keystones' first extended tour of North Dakota evoked many comparisons with the Gophers who had spent a considerable amount of time in the state. According to the *Grand Forks Daily Herald*: "The Keystones are a much livelier bunch of players, at least here, than were the Colored Gophers. The players all talk it up at all times, keeping their battery working smoothly and furnishing plenty of amusement to the spectators." The scribes in Hankinson, however, believed that "the Keystones played a much poorer game than the Colored Gophers."[25]

Like the Gophers before them, the Minneapolis squad soon discovered that the prairie clubs were no pushover. The Grand Fork Picketts blanked the barnstormers, 3–0, on July 2, as Thomas the local starter surrendered only three singles and whiffed ten Keystone batters. McNair allowed just four hits, but he only had himself to blame for the defeat. After giving up a leadoff single in the bottom of the third inning, the tiny southpaw botched a sacrifice bunt attempt, and after retiring the next two batters, walked "Happy" Hallett, the Grand Forks shortstop, to load the bases. Big "Spike" Spanton, a former Northern League first baseman, then lifted a short fly in back of first base, that second sacker Card Phillips made "a first class run for," only to have it fall from his glove after he reached it; two runs scored and the game was gone.[26]

The Keystones rebounded the next evening, by scoring twice in the eighth inning and three more times in the ninth to down the Picketts, 11–8. The professionals were struck out ten more times by the Grand Forks starter Leigh, but the home team made seven errors, including four consecutive miscues by their first baseman Schumacher in the second frame. A huge crowd turned out at Pickett Park on the Fourth to watch a wild and wooly affair in which the Keystones pounded out 16 hits against Thomas, the hero of game one. Hurley McNair mashed a pair of doubles and James Wills hit safely four times, including three two-baggers. The visitors

Former Louisville Cub Jesse Briscoe was the captain and center fielder for the Keystones in 1911. (*Indianapolis Freeman*, April 17, 1910; Library of Congress, Washington, D.C.)

were ahead, 5–2, in the bottom of the eighth, until a couple of errors and a two-out, two-run triple by Spike Stanton against McNair tied the score. The first four Keystones up in the ninth all reached base safely and the fifth, Will Embry, tripled to clear the bases. Wills doubled Embry home and an unassisted double play by Milroy McCune in the bottom of the frame closed out an 11–5 Keystones win. The two combatants were also scheduled to play an evening contest but it was canceled after a twenty-minute hail storm reduced the diamond to mud.[27]

Mitchell's nine arrived in Devils Lake a few days later and ran up against the kind of home cooking that the Gophers had found so distasteful. The Flour City nine was up, 4–2, in the home half of the sixth inning when a Lakers base runner whom the Keystones believed had been forced out at second, was ruled safe instead. Kidd Mitchell pulled his team off the field and when they did not return to the diamond after five minutes had elapsed, the game, along with the gate receipts, was forfeited to the home team. The *Devils Lake World* avowed that the runner "Lipps was safe easy at second, was the opinion of all," while the Keystones "showed the yellow streak when they found they were up against it." Kidd Mitchell told a Grand Forks paper later that evening that the Devils Lake bunch was "easily the worst proposition" he had ever encountered:

> According to Mitchell's story, his team played six innings and when they refused to play longer unless a different umpire was furnished, the Devils Lake team called it quits, refused to pay him any money, and to add insult to injury, refused to give the crowd back their money. Mitchell says that the man with the tickets and change took an automobile when he saw what was coming and made for the city on high speed.

Mitchell also complained that not only was arbiter "Happy" Hanlon "the rottenest umpire" he had ever dealt with, but that "the Devils Lake team was in to steal the game from the start" and that he would never go near the town again "under any consideration."[28]

The Keystones next ventured west to Bismarck where they ran into a buzzsaw named Collet on the 13th of July. The capitol city center fielder rapped out two doubles and a four-bagger against Charles Jackson, while also recording two outfield assists. The Minneapolis twirler was handed a 5–2 lead after four and a half innings, but he couldn't hold it and the professionals had to scramble to tie the game at seven in the eighth. The White Sox collected the last of their 12 hits in the last of the ninth, taking "about three minutes" to score a couple of runs and annex the game, 9–7. McNair pitched the next evening and although he was touched up for nine safeties, he also struck out ten enemy batters—twice he struck out the side after loading the bases "without exerting himself." Among the 12 Keystones hits in their 11–3 win were two solo home runs to right center field—one by Pate in the fourth, which bounced over the fence, and another by Wilson in the eighth, "which did its bouncing on the other side."[29]

Apparently the cowboys in Wibaux, Montana, had not gotten their fill of blackball as they imported the Keystones for a scrap on the 15th of July. The Flour City outfit took another 5–2 lead in the fourth, but Tigers left fielder Geist tied it in the sixth inning with a three-run homer over the left-field fence. Archie Pate bounced back from Geist's blast, the longest hit in Wibaux that season, by tossing five scoreless frames, but the Tigers plated a run with two outs in the 12th, for a 6–5 walk-off win. Jesse Briscoe had three hits, including a double for the Minnesotans, who left eight runners on base and committed five errors in the loss.[30]

James Shawler, the Keystones 1910 left fielder, had played in the opening game of the Grand Forks series, and also made a brief cameo in Wibaux, singling in his only at-bat.

Wilson didn't make the trip to Montana, and Shawler soon began manning the left garden on a regular basis, with Briscoe moving back to center, and Harry Bauchman slotting in at shortstop. The semi-pros in Beach took advantage of the barnstormer's unsettled lineup by whacking them around a couple of times. The North Dakotans gathered a dozen hits off Hurley McNair's deliveries on the 16th, scoring single runs in the seventh and eight innings to get by the Keystones, 4–2. Art Tower pitched well for the locals and outfielder "Swat" Milligan made a sensational catch in the ninth to preserve the win. Mitchell's squad tallied four times in the top of the ninth inning the following day to take a 9–5 lead, only to watch Charles Jackson allow five runs in home half as Beach stole one, 10–9.[31]

Even in 1911, there was no crying in baseball. Following their late-inning collapse in Beach, the Minneapolis club immediately packed up their troubles for a 260-mile eastward journey to Jamestown. The locals handed the tired travelers their fifth loss in six days on July 18, racking up 11 hits against Pate and then McNair in an 11–1 win. Hanson, the Jamestown mound artist, proved his mettle by scattering four safeties while striking out the free swinging professionals nine times; he also doubled, tripled, and drove in three runs. It was McNair's turn to shine the following evening. The young port-sider surrendered only three base hits and fanned seven Jamestown batters. At the plate McNair went three-for-four with a double, triple, and two runs scored in the Keystones' 4–0 victory. Mitchell's crew also beat Jamestown, 9–2, the next night in a game where ladies and gentlemen accompanying ladies were let in for free.[32]

The "fastest colored team on the road," was also one of the most resilient. Bound for a Monday game in Ortonville, Minnesota, on July 24, the Keystones stopped off in Fairmount, North Dakota, to transfer railway cars. When their train was late, and the club discovered they could not make their connection until the following day, the Keystones scrounged up a game with the local nine. Despite the last-minute nature of the contest, the streets of Fairmount soon had the appearance of a Fourth of July Celebration after "the rural telephone lines were kept warm for more than an hour advertising the game." Hanson was brought in from Jamestown to pitch, and he mystified the Minneapolis outfit again, striking out six more batters while parsing out five hits. Harry Bauchman tossed a gem for the visitors, fanning five while giving up just one safety and proving effective in the clutch; several times the hometown Colts put base runners on third base but where unable to score. The Keystones tallied twice in the first inning after two were out on a few wild throws by the Colts fielders, who "had a funny sensation in their throats which they kept swallowing to keep down" and prevailed 2–0.[33]

The Keystones finally made it back to Minnesota on July 25 and downed Graceville, 4–2, as McNair "proved a puzzle to the locals" by spacing out eight hits. Mitchell's charges outslugged Appleton, 8–6, a day later, connecting for three home runs and three triples. They also didn't connect a lot — Eldred, an Appleton player, whiffed ten of the barnstormers in the four innings he pitched, while hammering two home runs of his own.[34]

By the time the Keystones reached Long Prairie for a three-game weekend series in late July, Jesse Briscoe was holding down the first base bag and "Cap" Embry had been reduced to umpiring the odd game or two. The professionals battered the strong central Minny club, 10–2, on July 28 with Archie Pate's two-out grand slam in the second inning proving to be the most decisive blow. Fred Liese, late of the St. Paul Saints and Boston Nationals, pitched for Long Prairie the next afternoon and held the heavy hitting Keystones to only six hits while striking them out half a dozen times. Charles Jackson, who had been getting absolutely shelled for the better part of a month, gave up 15 base hits good for 28 total bases to the locals. Long Prairie rolled, 13–4, with Liese leading the way with four hits including a home run and a triple. Forrest Maynard tripled twice, hit a double, and handled 18 chances at first base without a miscue.[35]

Art Tower was imported all the way from Beach, North Dakota, to face off against McNair in the Sunday finale. Neither team scored until the sixth frame when James Shawler tripled and was brought home by a single by Bauchman. McNair hit Thiegs, the Long Prairie shortstop, with a pitch to start the bottom of the eighth, and Maynard's two-out single to center scored him from second base to tie the game. The contest was still knotted at one after the conclusion of the tenth inning when a heavy thunder storm put an end to the proceedings by driving the players and 500 fans in attendance from the field.[36]

The Colonel and his team returned to Minneapolis in early August where they spent a couple of days relaxing before heading back out on the road. Mitchell drove his car out to Carver, Minnesota, where he spent an afternoon at a Knights of Pythias picnic with his wife and their friends. The Keystones owner told the *Twin City Star* that "everybody's happy" as his squad left for a jaunt through Wisconsin.[37]

Happy or not, the Keystones' dairyland tour got off to a poor start when they missed their railway connection to Elk Mound, Wisconsin, and had to cancel their August 2 appearance. They finally showed up in nearby Colfax the next afternoon, skipping by the locals, 9–3. The Flour City bunch was still playing "snappy ball" nine days later when they defeated the optimistically named Marion Big Leaguers, 9–2, "fielding their positions splendidly and using the stick effectively when hits meant runs." The Keystones stumbled a bit on their way out of Wisconsin, as an outfit in Grand Rapids tripped up the barnstormers on August 15. A local slugger named Meister put his team up 5–0 with a "pretty" bases-clearing triple in the second inning. The visitors were held in check for most of the game by the hometown twirler Nelson until they scored twice in the seventh and eighth to pull within a run. Five of the next Keystones batters were struck out by a reliever named Foster as Grand Rapids triumphed, 5–4.[38]

The Knights of Pythias' national encampment was held in Indianapolis in 1911 and Kidd Mitchell had managed to line up his Keystones as one of the featured attractions. On August 20, the largest crowd of the season turned out at Northwestern Park for a Sunday doubleheader between the Minneapolis squad and the hometown ABC's. The locals won the first game, 12–4, which angered Mitchell's wife Mamie so much that, according to the *Freeman*, "It is said she served notice on the boys that if they didn't play ball in the second game she wouldn't take them back home, and they played." With abandonment as a motivator the Keystones battered three ABC's pitchers around the lot, and took the second game, 11–9.[39]

Another big crowd of nearly 1,000 showed up the next day as the two clubs engaged in an epic swat-fest. The Keystones blasted 10 hits off the ABC's ace Williams and five more off his replacement, Howard "Hop" Bartlett. Jesse Briscoe scored four runs and collected three of the safeties, including a double. Bert Woods also doubled for the Minneapolis squad and launched two "costly" homers for good measure. Home runs hit out of Northwestern Park were "rather expensive" because the ball was invariably lost in an adjoining canal. The Keystones fared no better on the mound. Among the ten hits Harry Bauchman allowed were *five* triples and a couple of four-baggers by third baseman Fred "Puggy" Hutchinson. The Hoosiers also stole seven bases and were poised to win the game in regulation when the Minnesotans tied the game at six with a run in the top of the ninth inning. Mitchell's club continued their revival by scoring three times in their half of the tenth and things looked dire for the ABC's when Bauchman got two quick outs in the bottom of the frame. It was the locals turn to rejoice a few minutes later when a walk, followed by an error, a single, and a triple gave the ABC's four runs and an improbable 10–9 victory. Mrs. Mitchell's response was not recorded for posterity.[40]

Milroy McCune took to the mound for the series closer on August 22, and handcuffed the home team, scattering eight hits and striking out six. The erstwhile Texan also collected three of the Keystones 15 base knocks off ABC's pitchers West and Higbee during the visitors 14–4 win. Woods contributed a double and triple while Hurley McNair chipped in with three safeties including a triple. The series split became more palatable for the Colonel when he was awarded first prize for having the best-equipped tent on the meeting's campgrounds. After the encampment ended, the Mitchell's returned to Minneapolis, while the Keystones left for Iowa.[41]

During the ABC's series, Terrell, a former Omaha Giants teammate of Harry Bauchman, played first base for the Keystones, but he didn't accompany them to the Hawkeye state. Archie Pate and James Shawler also stayed behind; when the Minneapolis club arrived in Charles City for a three-game set on September 3, their places had been taken by Eugene Barton and Nate Harris from the Leland Giants.[42]

The Teddies annexed the opener, 6–4, despite two more triples by Bert Woods. The locals landed on "the stubby Mr. McNair" for ten hits and were helped along by six Keystones errors, including three by Bauchman at short. Bauchman committed another error while pitching the following afternoon and he uncorked two wild pitches as well. This would have been all right except he also surrendered 15 base hits during Charles City's 10–2 thrashing of the Minnesota squad. With Vi Lindaman on the mound, the Iowans waxed the Mitchell's club, 16–4, in the final game on September 5 giving them four victories over the professionals in five tries. The Keystones trail goes cold after Charles City, and it is unlikely they played many (if anymore) games that summer. The team's members weren't out of work for long as Archie Pate landed first with the Louisville Cubs and then the Leland Giants, while Bert Woods and James Shawler hooked up with the ABC's.[43]

Hurley McNair took off for Chicago, playing for the Kansas City, Kansas, Giants during their visit to the Windy City. On September 16, the promising young southpaw pitched the Kansans past the mighty Chicago American Giants, 3–2, in ten innings. McNair scattered seven hits and fanned five while outdueling the great Rube Foster. Back in Kansas City in October, McNair tossed a one-hitter against the Kansas City Blues of the American Association with darkness bringing a scoreless tie to a halt after seven innings had been played.[44]

The Twin City Gophers completed their long road trip on August 13 with a one-sided victory over Lindstrom. Walter Stallard struck out 14 batters and a recently returned Bobby Marshall caught. In a strange case of being in two places at once, a club calling itself the St. Paul Gophers had been scheduled to play that same day against the Leland Giants in Chicago. The Giants were a second-tier outfit run by Nate Harris that had appropriated the name and a few players from the legendary club, without duplicating its successes. No result was published for the contest, although the Gophers later claimed to have defeated the Lelands.[45]

A few days later the *Twin City Star* reported that Bill Binga had left the Gophers, fed up with the front office, "On account of bad management they have had a disastrous season — and the players are much dissatisfied. Baseball is a business and needs good management." In the opinion of the *Star*, former manager Irving Williams "would have brought the Gophers out [a] winner, and kept all dates. Irving knows his worth, and wants pay for his services, but he could not get his price."[46]

With Binga out and Marshall reinstated at first base, the Gophers disposed of Lindstrom, 7–3, during their annual Farmers and Merchants picnic on the 16th before heading out to Osceola, Wisconsin, the next day. Playing against a junior team called the Kubs, the professionals took leads of 2–0, 5–1, and 6–3, only to fall behind 7–6 after a three-run rally by Osceola in the bottom of the seventh inning. The youngsters batted Stallard out of the box in the process and continued their hitting spree against Tom Pangburn as they connected for 17 base hits altogether. The Gophers tied it with a run in the eighth, but Osceola's second baseman Hillskottie uncorked a home run drive in the last of the ninth "that has not come back yet" for a 8–7 walk-off win. Kubs kid pitcher Staples whiffed 13 of his elders and rapped three base hits of his own.[47]

If losing to a scrub outfit wasn't bad enough, the Gophers highly anticipated Sunday matchup at Lexington with the North St. Paul Thoens was cancelled after it was discovered that the St. Paul Elks had booked the park instead. That same weekend, the *Kansas City Journal* announced that the St. Paul Gophers would be arriving in town to play a three-game series with the Kansas City, Kansas, Giants, commencing on August 19. The Minnesota nine failed to appear as scheduled, "on account of accident" it was later revealed.[48]

It really wasn't clear who was running the mess that had become the Gophers, but it certainly wasn't Glover Shull. As the Twin City team was disintegrating, their embattled owner was having problems with "undesirable persons and conditions" at his Porters and Waiters club. Looking to improve the quality of his clientele, Shull was busy "making expensive alterations for the comfort of members and visitors." Bobby Marshall, who also seemed to be pursuing a non-baseball path, was spotted playing tennis at the Minneapolis Racquet Club on August 22. In early September Marshall accepted an appointment to become a crew chief in the Minnesota State Grain Department, leaving the Gophers behind for the "hum drum paths of business."[49]

During the final days of August, a squad calling itself the St. Paul Gophers finally showed up in Kansas City. The makeup of the club was identical to the Twin City Gophers except that Bobby Marshall, Johnny Davis, and Arthur McDougall were absent. Bill Binga and Bert Jones had rejoined the team, along with a second baseman named Thompson. Two black lodges, the United Brothers of Friendship and the Sisters of the Mysterious Ten, were convening in Kansas City at the time. The Gophers and the Kansas City, Kansas, Giants were to provide the entertainment for the fraternal organizations as well as for the "stock yards fans." The Giants were led by Topeka Jack Johnson and fielded a powerful lineup featuring former Gopher Eugene Milliner in center field and emerging superstar Elwood "Bingo" DeMoss at second base.[50]

The two clubs opened their series on August 27 with a Sunday tilt at Riverside Park in Kansas City, Kansas. Louis Johnson started for the Gophers, but he soon departed in favor of Dude Lytle after giving up six hits and six runs in less than five innings. Bert Jones had three hits for the Twin City men including a double, while D. Williams, the Giants left fielder doubled, homered, and single twice in five at bats as Kansas City rolled to a 8–2 win. The Giants scored 11 runs in the first the following afternoon against Lefty Pangburn and coasted to a 13–10 triumph that really wasn't as close as score might indicate. Bert Jones had three more hits for the Twin City outfit, among them another double and triple. The cagy lefty also struck out four batters in relief of Pangburn, who walked three batters and was let down by five Gopher errors. It was Stallard's turn on the 29th, but the big youngster fared no better, giving up 17 hits as Kansas City demolished the Minnesotans, 12–0. The visitors committed six more errors, including three by Hardiman in left field before he was replaced by Bert Jones. Jones placed a couple of more hits for the Gophers while Kansas City catcher William Tenney went four-for-six with two doubles and Williams socked another home run.[51]

After an off day, the Gophers crossed bats on the 31st with the less fearsome Kansas City, Missouri, Royal Giants. Pangburn was magnificent this time around, yielding only two hits and whiffing nine Royal Giants batters. Held in check for the first five innings by Kansas City twirler Lown Lee, the northerners exploded for nine runs in their last four at bats and landed the big end of a 11–0 score. After stealing no bases against the Kansas Giants, the Gophers pilfered five from the Missourians. Mule Armstrong paced the visitors ten hit attack with a single and a double. The next afternoon, the Twin Cities nine met up again with Jack Johnson's club, this time at Kansas City's Stevens Park. Dicta Johnson was ineffective once more, as the Giants scored five times in the first inning and routed the St. Paul squad, 11–0. The dispirited Gophers were held to just four hits by Kansas City's ace hurler Harper, who doubled twice in his own cause. Williams clubbed his third home run of the series while Milliner laced a triple to go along with two singles and a pair of stolen bases. "Gabbie" had tormented his old team to the tune of 6-for-18 (.333) during the week while Williams had gone 9-for-19 (.473) with 22 total bases.[52]

Having mercifully ended their stay in Kansas City, the Gophers travelled eastward across Missouri, arriving in St. Louis on September 3 for a trio of games with Charley Mill's Giants. It was old home week again, as the star-studded Mound City squad listed five former Gophers on its roster: Rat Johnson; Felix Wallace; William McMurray; Steel Arm Johnny Taylor and his brother Jim. After falling behind early in the Sunday opener, the Gophers drove St. Louis starter Arthur "Hamp" Gilliard out of the box after four and two thirds innings by reaching him for eight hits and five runs. The third Taylor brother, Hall of Famer Ben, relieved Gilliard and his "southpaw angles" checked the Gophers to four base hits the rest of the way. Trailing 7–5 in the seventh, the Giants scored four times off Lefty Pangburn and survived a rally by the northerners in the eighth to squeak by, 9–8. Facing a fearsome lineup composed of such blackball greats as Jimmy Lyons, Joe Hewitt, and Sam Bennett, Pangburn allowed ten hits and struck out four, but also compounded his own misery by walking six batters and hitting three more, including Rat Johnson twice. William Selden had three hits for the Gophers while Dude Lytle had two including a home run. The hitting star of the day was undoubtedly Giants first baseman Tully McAdoo, who went four-for-four with a homer.[53]

The two sides met up again at Athletic Park the following afternoon for a Labor Day doubleheader. Walter Stallard started out brilliantly for the visitors in the first game, not allowing a base hit for the initial seven innings. His teammates pounded Gilliard for ten base knocks during that same time frame and piled up a seemingly insurmountable 8–1 lead. Not so. Stallard faltered in the bottom of the seventh, allowing two runs. He gave up his first hit in the eighth, and then four more, before Dude Lytle relieved him with only one out. By the time the inning was over the Giants had cut the lead to 8–6 and they plated two more runs in the ninth to tie it up. Johnny Taylor relieved Gilliard in the eighth and kept the Gophers off the board until the top of the twelfth when they tallied twice to go ahead, 10–8. Lytle couldn't make it hold up, however, as St. Louis rallied for three runs in their half of the inning, capturing the two-hour-and-twenty-six-minute epic, 11–10. The Gophers lashed out 16 hits led by Bill Binga and Bert Jones with three each. They were also the beneficiaries of two free passes and five Giants errors, but the ten runners they left on base came back to haunt them. Jimmy Lyons hit safely three times for the home team, while Felix Wallace, who uncharacteristically made three errors, singled, tripled, and swiped three of the Giants seven stolen bases.[54]

Harry Brown took Ben Taylor deep in the first inning of the second tilt, but the Giants knotted it up against Pangburn in their half of the frame. The locals added another run in the fourth and the game was called because of darkness a half-inning later with the Gophers still down, 2–1. Pangburn only allowed four base hits, while his mates collected six, but Taylor's strong work in the pinches proved to be the difference The Gophers had dropped their third consecutive one-run contest to the St. Louis nine, despite out-hitting them in every game.[55]

The same weekend his former team was swept out of the Mound City, Bobby Marshall played first base for Perry Werden's All-Stars in a pair of games in Owatonna, Minnesota. The Gophers didn't come back home after August. The club was booked for the Chisago County Fair in Rush City on September 14, but the Werden's appeared in their stead. Shortly after the St. Louis series, Tom Pangburn, George Armstrong, Walter Stallard, and Bert Jones surfaced in Springs Valley, Indiana, as part of a reorganized French Lick Plutos squad.[56]

The Minnesota quartet were immediately thrown into the fire against the Plutos archrivals, the West Baden Sprudels, who had just beaten the Pittsburgh Pirates, 2–1, in an exhibition game. In the opening match-up Pangburn dropped a 3–1 decision to the Sprudels and hurler Pleas "Hub" Miller. Bert Jones mashed a two-run homer in the first inning of the second game on September 12, and this time Pangburn made it stand up as Gophers/Plutos hybrid eked out a 2–1 win. A couple of days later Walter Stallard and Pirates-killer "Dizzy" Dismukes locked up in a duel at French Lick that went into extra innings after neither team was able to score in regulation. With two out in the bottom of the tenth and a Plutos base runner on second base, Mule Armstrong pounded a drive to left field that Miller muffed, allowing French Lick to score the only run of the game. Pangburn, Armstrong, and Louis Johnson started the next season with French Lick, although they may have found that the Indiana hamlet was not quite as enlightened as the Twin Cities. The same week the ex–Gophers arrived in 1911, the town segregated its elementary school, with the local paper rationalizing that "there is more or less unpleasantness where white and colored children attend school in the same rooms."[57]

The ensuing winter proved to be a rough one for black baseball owners in the Twin Cities. In the fall of 1911 Phil Reid opened a saloon on State Street in Chicago, along with a local named Raleigh W. Thompson. The establishment, ironically named the St. Paul Inn, was soon doing well, but "Daddy" was not. In early March 1912, Reid reportedly suffered an "attack of heart trouble," while walking the streets of St. Paul. The big man called out to a female passerby, who took him to the nearest drug store "where he received immediate relief."[58]

Kidd Mitchell wasn't feeling so hot either. Around the time of Reid's heart attack, the Colonel was struck by an automobile, resulting in numerous "painful injuries." In late April the *Twin City Star* announced that Mitchell "has decided not to bring the 'famous Keystones' out this season." Neither "Daddy" Reid nor Bobby Marshall assembled an edition of the Gophers that spring, thus lowering the curtain on big-time Minnesota blackball.[59]

Many factors had led to the two team's dissolution. For one the Gophers had been "walloping the poor country clubs out of from $40 to $50" for so long that the novelty had worn off, while apathy and resentment had set in. The national pastime was going through a rocky patch in general. The *Minneapolis Tribune* commented in August 1911 that "the present season has been one of the worst known in the history of baseball, not only from the weather standpoint, but also in the matter of attendance when fine weather prevails and baseball men are at a loss to explain the evident decrease in interest." The two black squads had also lost their local presence. Whether by design or an inability to secure bookings, the Gophers played but five games in the Twin Cities in 1911, and the Keystones only one.[60]

Rooms for rent. Kidd Mitchell's Keystone Hotel and Buffet in Minneapolis, 1911. (*St. Paul Appeal*, October 28, 1911; Minnesota State Historical Society, St. Paul)

Ultimately though, the Gophers and Keystones folded because of a lack of leadership. Daddy Reid and Kidd Mitchell had kept their teams afloat by the sheer force of their personalities. When the two black magnates wouldn't (or couldn't) participate anymore, there was no one left who was strong enough to pick up the slack.

By the autumn of 1912, Phil Reid's health was deteriorating rapidly. Suffering from heart disease, he took to his bed over his St. Paul saloon. Feeling that he would not recover, Reid told his nurse on October 15 that he had been praying for three weeks "that if it was the Lord's will to take him away, he was willing, as he knew his soul would be taken care of." He asked that the nurse pray for him and sing "It Is Well With My Soul." Reid also requested that his pastor, the Reverend E. H. McDonald, visit the next afternoon. He died, however, at 5:30 that morning of "acute gastritis," and his body was discovered by an employee.[61]

Daddy Reid's remains were taken nearby to black leader Thomas Lyles' funeral chapel where they were bestowed the Masonic rites of the 33rd or highest degree on the midnight of the 19th. The fallen magnate lay in repose the next two days during which he was viewed by several hundred people. Reid's "elegant black broadcloth casket" was surrounded by a large number of floral tributes from "friends home and abroad." Jack Johnson sent his condolences, as did many others well-wishers from all over the United States and Canada.[62]

On Monday, October 21, the funeral cortege assembled at Lyles at two o'clock in the afternoon. Reid's body was carried to the Pilgrim Baptist Church by six fellow members of the Knights Templar. A military brass band headed the procession and 25 carriages followed in line. John Hirschfield and his wife were the chief mourners. Hirschfield, who had only recently retired from the saloon he and Reid had owned together for over 13 years, was also the chief executor of his ex-partner's estate.[63]

Nearly 1,000 persons packed the church to overflowing and many more mourners were present outside. Reverend McDonald presided over a traditional Baptist service, replete with several hymns, including "Jesus Is Mine" and "Homeland." Reverend W.D. Carter of St. Louis, the previous pastor of Pilgrim and a fraternal brother of the deceased, preached the sermon, eulogizing Reid for his generosity and "other good traits of character."[64]

After the funeral Reid's corpse was carried up the hill behind the State Capitol to Oakland Cemetery, were it was placed in a vault to await

MISS BELLE DAVIS.

The Queen of the Ragtime Singers. When Gophers owner Phil Reid married famed entertainer Belle Davis in July 1910, it signaled the end of the team's great run. (*Indianapolis Freeman*, May 14, 1910; Library of Congress, Washington, D.C.)

the arrival of his wife. Belle Davis had received the news of her husband's death while in London and had headed back to the States on October 19, departing from Liverpool. The widow arrived in St. Paul ten days later and Reid was interred on the first of November.[65]

A number of friends and family had travelled from out of state for the services, including his son Eddie. Although no Gophers players were mentioned as being present, Irving Williams and Raleigh Thompson came up from Chicago to attend. In a write-up of the funeral, the *Twin City* Star remarked:

> Everybody loved "Phil" Reid. He had many friends—because it was his ambition to make them. None knew him but to love him, and he was paid the highest respect by that vast assemblage of mourners, who proved by their presence that he was a man.[66]

More than anything else, Phil Reid had advanced the cause of racial equality for his people. As the funeral ended, nearly the entire congregation paid their last respects, passing by his coffin while the Pilgrim Choir sang "When the Mists Have Rolled Away," a song of hope and redemption that lyrically declared:

> We shall know as we are known,
> Never more to walk alone,
> In the dawning of the morning
> Of that bright and happy day,
> We shall know each other better,
> When the mists have rolled away.[67]

Chapter Eleven

By Any Other Name (1913–1948)

Although the Gophers and Keystones were finished after 1911, black baseball in Minnesota was not. During the next 40 years, local and national nines traveled the state taking advantage of the good feelings raised and trails blazed by their illustrious predecessors.

In the spring of 1912, the Hennepin Clothing Company of Minneapolis organized an all-black club in an attempt to fill the void left by the Gophers and Keystones. Under the supervision of company manager Frank Buchholz, team captain Bobby Marshall assembled a squad comprised of aging professionals, like Alex Irwin and Bill Binga, and local hopefuls including 20-year-old hurler Joe Davis (no relation to John) and Marshall's younger brother Louis.[1]

Despite a couple of photo spreads in the *Minneapolis Tribune* and the big-time pedigree of a few of their players, the Hennepins were nothing more than a weekend-only, semi-pro outfit. Marshall went on record stating that he saw "no reason why the team cannot be one of the fastest in the country," but his squad did about as well that spring as the ocean liner *Titanic*, which sank in the north Atlantic. From mid–April to late July the club lost all eight games they played in the Twin Cities, including lopsided defeats to the Conrads, Camerons (the Thoens under a new name) and Perry Werden's All-Stars.[2]

The Hennepins hit fairly well, but they fielded horrendously — 35 errors in seven recorded games — and their pitchers, Davis and David "Moose" Kay, were so inconsistent that Marshall took over the twirling duties in July. Part of the team's problem was a lack of a reliable catcher; the Minneapolis Steeles stole ten bases off Binga and Marshall while clubbing the Hennepins, 14–4, in early June. A proposed late-summer tour of the Dakotas may or may not have happened, but by early August the team had disappeared from the scene and Bobby Marshall was playing for another local semi-pro club, the St. Joe-Deckerts.[3]

In June 1913 the Hennepins were reorganized by Paul Benson, who had been the team's secretary the year before. Marshall, Irwin, and Binga all returned for another go, as did Joe Davis, "a youngster with lots of smoke and a great future as a slabsman ahead of him." Johnny Davis signed on to play center field and pitch, while the catching situation was stabilized with the arrival of former Omaha Giant Lee Davis. Davis, a 23-year-old of mixed Winnebago-Sioux heritage, would become the area's premier backstop for the next quarter century. A couple of other newcomers, "Chic" Williams, an ex–Leland Giant "who has no equal as a center fielder," and Ike Bradley would also become local semi-pro stalwarts for the next several seasons.[4]

Although they advertised themselves as the Hennepin Colored Giants, the reformed club soon discovered that the Gophers' legacy was a hard one to shake. As a newspaper in Watertown, South Dakota, observed, "They are traveling under a new name, but due to [their] widespread reputation ... nearly every one still calls them the Gophers."[5]

The new name and new faces couldn't prevent the Hennepins from getting off to another slow start. On June 8, the clothiers committed 12 errors during a 17–2 loss to

Mankato that was mercifully ended after six and a half innings had been played. A couple of weeks later in St. Cloud, Johnny Davis held the hometown nine down without a run for the first five frames, and after a Bobby Marshall double gave the Mill City squad a 3–0 lead, Alex Irwin "felt in the mood to offer a libation to Africanus." Unfortunately the Pretzels ruined the party by bludgeoning Davis for eight hits good for nine runs in their next two at bats, en route to an 11–3 victory.[6]

Things improved slightly when the squad left in late June for a tour of South Dakota. The club registered its first-ever win on July 1 by scoring five runs in the ninth inning to down Webster, South Dakota, 10–5. Webster won four out five games the teams played, however. "Doc" Hildebrand bested the Hennepins three times, including a 5–0 whitewashing on the Fourth of July when he struck out 13 and allowed only three hits. Looking to capture the large end of the holiday gate receipts, the Minneapolis nine bypassed their own starters and pitched an ex–Northern Leaguer named Worthington, but the Webster lads "hit him hard and often."[7]

Starting with a 14–12 beating of Groton the next day, the Hennepins, led by the timely hitting of Bill Binga, reeled off eight straight victories in which they both scored and gave up a lot of runs. Playing before many large crowds, the Minneapolis nine wasn't above the "substitution of their strong batters for the weak, at critical places," or arguing "with the umpire, score keepers, and everyone else." The fun came to an end on July 13 when Watertown trounced the Flour City outfit, 9–2, with the only Hennepins tallies coming across on an error.[8]

Marshall was behind the plate in Watertown, but he wasn't in the lineup in Sioux Falls a week later. In 1907 the Gophers had walloped the South Dakota squad twice by an aggregate score of 13–0. The locals now more than returned the favor, scoring seven runs in the first inning off Hennepins starter Joe Williams, while cruising to a 15–0 win behind the overpowering two-hit pitching of their ace, Baker. According to the *Sioux Falls Daily Press*, "A more merciless grounding was never before given a team at Sioux Falls.... The colored gophers were absolutely at a loss. Sioux Falls had them buffaloed so that half of them could not have held on to

Former Gopher Alex Irwin organized and played for several Twin City semi-pro clubs. The original captain of the Keystones was "one of the best infielders ever seen in the Northwest independent ranks," and "the talk of every town" he played in. (*Minneapolis Tribune*, May 19, 1912; Minnesota State Historical Society, St. Paul) an ice cream cone if it had a handle to it." The disgusted Sioux Falls management canceled a scheduled Sunday rematch and sent the barnstormers packing as they did not want to "offer another exhibition like yesterday." The Hennepins' tour, slated to take them as far as eastern Montana, lost steam at this point and they once again faded quietly from the scene. Bobby Marshall joined the St. Cloud Pretzels in late July and closed the season on a tear, hitting .495 in their last four games.[9]

In the spring of 1914, Alex Irwin and Paul Benson attempted to reform the Hennepins as the Minneapolis Colored Giants. The club, with a lineup including Bobby Marshall, Johnny Davis, and Bill Binga, was scheduled to open with a May 17 contest against Perry Werden's All-Stars at Nicollet Park. The game never came off and a week later a Binga and Marshall-led outfit called the Colored Gophers was thrashed by the St. Joe-Deckerts, 15–4.[10]

With Alex Irwin seemingly out of the picture, the new squad was bankrolled by ex–St. Cloud manager Cy Olson, under the auspices of the McClellan Paper Company in Minneapolis. After the Deckerts fiasco, Marshall returned to St. Cloud to play with the Pretzels while Johnny Davis joined a telephone company team, the Tri-States, leaving Bill Binga and Lee Davis to shoulder the load. Olson mostly eschewed scheduling his new charges against Twin City semi-pro teams in favor of small town squads, but the club was still completely overmatched, losing ten out of 11 recorded contests while being outscored 116–27.[11]

The Colored Gophers reached a nadir of sorts in Owatonna on June 21, giving up 14 runs in the first inning before losing 24–0. After sending 17 men to the plate in the first, the Owatonna management pulled their starting pitcher, but the hapless Gophers still couldn't get a runner past second base against the twirling efforts of the local center fielder, first baseman, and catcher. According to a local newspaper, a large crowd turned out:

> An aggregation of hotel waiters and porters who cheekily assumed the name of the "Colored Gophers" which for so long stood for a team of big league caliber, buncoed the Owatonna management into giving them a game. From the first pitch it was evident the game was to be a joke. They could neither hit, field, nor throw the ball. They changed pitchers three times, walked 13, and hit many, often forcing in runs.[12]

The team's play improved a bit when Johnny Davis was enticed to return to the fold. The crafty veteran allowed five hits and fanned eight, while pitching the Colored Gophers to one of their few "successes" of the season, a 3–3 seven-inning tie in Little Falls on July 26. More disappointing to the Little Falls contingent was the fact that "Rat" Johnson and Rube Foster had not appeared with the Gophers as advertised, despite Cy Olson's assertion that he had sent both players money for transportation. Olson, who was apparently something of a huckster, proclaimed in September that the "Gophers have been playing great ball all season," despite the fact that there is no record of them winning a single game.[13]

Bobby Marshall re-upped with the Colored Gophers in early August after a mostly subpar season in St. Cloud. In late June Marshall had sunk archrival Melrose with a three-run ninth inning walk-off homer, but upon his departure it was noted that "his fielding has not been up to standard nor has his work with the big stick been what is expected of him." Perhaps Bobby had been distracted that summer by a newfound passion for motorcycle riding. In July the great athlete participated in the Minnesota state championship motorcycle races. The novice biker was said to possess "plenty of nerve, uses his head, and had an excellent control of his machine." Forgoing the beginner's red line at the top of the racetrack, Marshall rode the white line at the bottom instead, getting his bike up to 80 mph on his very first attempt.[14]

While Bobby Marshall was speeding around the Midway Motor dome, a new generation of blackball stars was making a name for themselves in Minnesota. In late September 1911, W. A. Brown's Tennessee Rats skirted the southern edges of the state, downing Wells, 2–1. The Holden, Missouri–based club traveled with their own minstrel show, orchestra, and vocal quartet, along with "probably the greatest strike-out pitcher the world has ever known," 20-year-old John Wesley Donaldson. With the Rats in 1911, the young flame-thrower lost only three of the 44 games he pitched and fanned 45 batters in one three-day span.[15]

The following season, Donaldson signed on with the All Nations team, based out of Des Moines, Iowa. J. Leslie Wilkinson, the former Hopkins Ladies Club manager, had assembled a touring squad composed of ball players with various heritages, including African American, Native American, Scottish, Mexican, German, Turkish, Greek, Japanese, and Chinese. With a credo of "all races can play ball together regardless of color," the All Nations gobbled up many of the Gophers and Keystones old bookings in 1912, playing about 25 games in Minnesota alone while posting an overall record of 92–22–2 (.801).[16]

During the 1912–1913 seasons, John Donaldson won 80 games against only five losses for Wilkinson's new venture, while *averaging* double-digit strikeouts per game. In 1912, the amazing port-sider struck out 21 batters against the Jackson team of Superior, Wisconsin; fanned 21 of Perry Werden's All-Stars; whiffed the first 12 men to face him in a game against Deerwood, Minnesota in early August; and the first 11 versus Marshall a few weeks later.[17]

Wilkinson employed journeyman hurlers like ex–Gopher Tommy Means to fill out his staff in 1912, but for the following season he signed future Hall of Famer Jose Mendez, giving his club one of the greatest one-two combinations ever. From 1908 to 1911 the "Black Diamond" had led the Cuban League in winning percentage four seasons in a row while posting a record of 42–8 (.840). In 1908 and 1909 the 5'9", 155-pound right-hander went 44–2 (.956) against touring North American professional squads. With Donaldson and the 28-year-old Cuban pitching on alternate days in 1913, the All Nations won 124 games, lost 17 and tied 4 (.868).[18]

Mendez and Donaldson were both on display on August 8 when the All Nations took on the Good Thunder club of southern Minnesota in one of the most remarkably pitched ball games of all time, all kidding and hyperbole aside. Opposing the barnstormers was "Cannonball" Joe Jackson, a young African American hurler from Tennessee, who had lost only two games for Good Thunder the previous season and had not been beaten in 1913. Although Jackson was "short in stature" and weighed less than 140 pounds, he mowed through the professionals' lineup, allowing only six hits over 15 innings while striking out 19 batters. Donaldson, who replaced Mendez in the eighth, was somehow even better, fanning the initial 12 men he faced, with the first three going down on a total of nine pitches. During his eight innings of relief work, "the master of the situation" was touched for only two hits while recording 21 strikeouts (out of a possible 24). The game finished in a 3–3 tie when darkness was called after 15 innings had been played. Jackson, who "certainly has the goods and delivers them with the knowledge of a born ball player," ended his pitching line with a flourish, striking out the first two batters he faced in the 15th, before intentionally walking the next, and then calmly retiring the fourth man up.[19]

The All Nations made it back to Good Thunder on August 27 and Donaldson struck out 16 more batters as the travelers downed the local nine, 8–6. Jackson fanned one more than Donaldson, but poor fielding by his teammates did him in. Wilkinson, always on the hunt for new talent, lured Jackson away from Good Thunder for the 1914 season. With Mendez pitching less due to a sore arm, the "Cannonball" was a big addition for the club fanning 14 batters in Barnesville, Minnesota, and 13 more in Hibbing in two late July starts. A month later, Jackson downed Hawarden, Iowa, 2–0, on two hits while whiffing 18. Donaldson was working at an even whiter heat, posting single-game strikeout totals of 18, 21 (twice), 22, and 26. With a fastball so rapid that it approached home plate looking like a "small bean" even on the brightest of the days, the overpowering lefty struck out 48 batters in 36 innings in one eight-day stretch.[20]

On June 27 the All Nations returned again to Good Thunder, with Jackson getting the start against his former team. Jimmy Claxton, a Canadian twirler of mixed white, black, and Native American ancestry, was on the mound for Good Thunder, and he held the All Nations nine to three hits and only two runs. The locals connected with Jackson's "smoke ball" often, but outfielders Donaldson and Mendez "were active as kangaroos and were always under the ball," limiting the home team to two hits and no scores. Two years later, Claxton managed to pitch both ends of a doubleheader for the Oakland Oaks of the Pacific Coast League, before his heritage was discovered and he was released.[21]

The only opponent that the All Nations had difficulty beating was W.S. Peters Chicago Union Giants, who seemed to have their number. Former Keystones Hurley McNair and Harry Bauchman squired the Giants into Minnesota in July 1914, splitting a pair of games with Owatonna. On September 16, Cannonball Jackson edged the Giants, 2–1, in Mason City, Iowa, on a four-hitter, but the Chicago squad bounced back the next two days, winning 3–2 at Sheffield, Iowa, and 5–4 at Fort Dodge. The following year the two clubs played a series of late-season games in southern Minnesota and Iowa that were most notable for the curious absence in the pitching box of John Donaldson and the Union's ace Dick Whitworth. Peters' outfit won at least five out of six games from Wilkinson's bunch, although the All Nations took the biggest purse of the series, shutting out the Giants, 5–0, at Lake Wilson, Minnesota, on September 3, before a throng of 5,000, "the largest gathering of people ever held in the county up to that day."[22]

While the All Nations and Union Giants were battling it out for Midwestern supremacy, the French Lick Plutos were making their own inroads in the area. The Plutos probably had greater propriety rights to the region than anybody, as they had, in a way, merged with the fading St. Paul Gophers in September 1911. The Springs Valley, Indiana, club fielded perhaps their finest team ever in 1913, going 108–33 (.765), including 25–18 versus their archrival the West Baden Sprudels and 7–0 against the Indianapolis ABC's. Led by slugging first baseman Sam Gordon, the Hoosier nine went on an extended road trip in mid–June through Wisconsin, Minnesota, North Dakota, and Iowa, "seeking contest with all the West."[23]

The Plutos arrived in St. Cloud in mid–August having laid nearly "sixty little clubs to rest." Al "Lefty" Dretchko scattered six hits as the locals downed the French Lick outfit, 4–1, on the 17th, and a week later he allowed only three as the Pretzels edged the Plutos, 3–2. The second contest was played before a huge standing room crowd of nearly 2,000 — many of whom, "gained admission in the usual and time honored fashion which often results in the necessary purchase of a new suit, or at least a lower portion thereof." Bobby Marshall scored a run, stole two bases and saved the day for St. Cloud with a running, jumping catch in right field of long drive off the bat of Plutos shortstop Johnnie Cunningham.[24]

St. Cloud had brought in second baseman Mike Gallagher from nearby Melrose for their showdown with the Red Devils and the ringer's five errors the next weekend greatly aided the French Lick club in taking the last two games of the series, 5–0 and 5–4. The Pretzels loaded the bases with no outs in the bottom of the ninth of the second contest but Pluto twirler Tom Lynch got out of the jam by striking out Sam Kinkle and inducing Dretchko and Gallagher to hit on a couple of "mush balls" in front of the plate.[25]

With second base great Elwood "Bingo" DeMoss in tow, the Plutos returned to Minnesota and St. Cloud the next summer, again encountering the stiffest competition of their tour. The French Lick nine took the first match between the teams, 4–2, on July 19, before the Pretzels trounced the Indiana lads, 11–2, a week later, pounding Red Devils pitchers McLaughlin and Bill Norman for 12 hits. Al Dretchko was again the star for the locals, striking out 11 and scattering eight hits. Bobby Marshall scored twice for St. Cloud while Bingo DeMoss went 3-for-4, with two doubles and two runs scored for the barnstormers.[26]

Minnesota fans were becoming somewhat jaded when it came to their blackball. The Plutos committed five errors and even with the easy victory, the large hometown crowd was reportedly very disappointed in the contest, having come with the expectation of seeing some "classy work" instead of the "back-lot baseball" they witnessed. Perhaps heedful of the change in patron attitudes, the Union Giants arrived in Hibbing in August 1915 with four players who doubled as a vocal group. As a feature of the contests, the quartet was scheduled to perform several selections of "their repertoire of songs which is excelled by few vaudeville troupes." The following July, the Tennessee Rats swept a series from the Winona Schellhas, but they also eased the pain somewhat by giving band concerts in town and at the park before the games.[27]

Despite the lack of success of the 1914 Colored Gophers, Cy Olson was back at it the next season, however briefly. His Colored Giants opened their season in Minneapolis on June 20 by downing the Roths club, 7–3. Dunlap, the Giants starter, struck out 12 batters and parsed out only three hits, but Olson's team vanished from view soon after.[28]

The Colored Gophers resurfaced in the spring of 1916 boasting the strongest lineup for a Twin Cities black club in several years. In addition to Bobby Marshall, Bill Binga, and Lee Davis, the new-look Gophers featured pitcher "Cannonball" Joe Jackson, the venerable Bert Jones at first base, and a couple of promising youngsters in center fielder Bob Ramsey and shortstop Harold Lewis. After dropping a 5–2 contest in mid–June to the suburban Columbia Heights nine, the Gophers reeled off several victories, including a 5–1 win over the Thirty Eighth Street Merchants, sparked by a grand slam by Chic Williams, and a 5–3 triumph over the Powers club, in which Ramsey collected four hits.[29]

Good pitching means nearly everything in baseball, and the presence of Cannonball Jackson undoubtedly was the difference between the 1916 Colored Gophers and their semi-pro predecessors. Jackson came on in relief during the Powers game and held the amateurs scoreless for the rest of the contest. Against Litchfield the following week, the diminutive hurler struck out 14 batters and scattered eight safeties as the Gophers edged the locals, 5–4. Jackson also helped himself out with a single, triple, and two runs scored. Jackson fanned 14 more batters on August 6th as the Gophers battled to a 14 inning scoreless tie with the strong M.J. Carr squad. The South St. Paul nine roughed the Cannonball up for six extra base hits and four runs when the clubs met up a couple weeks later to play off the tie — Jackson lasted only four innings in an eventual 11–8 Gophers loss. The tiny strikeout artist rejoined the All Nations club soon after and the Gophers were done for the summer.[30]

Minnesota blackball lost a link to its storied past when John Hirschfield passed away in 1916. After relinquishing his duties as the original St. Paul Gophers treasurer and selling his interest in the saloon on East Third Street, Hirschfield had managed the Ramsey County African American Club. Following a long battle with illness, the 58-year-old succumbed in his St. Paul home on May 26, and was buried near his old friend Phil Reid in the Oakland Cemetery.[31]

There would be no revival for the Keystones. Kidd Mitchell was stricken with "typhoid pneumonia" during the influenza pandemic of 1918 and died on March 29 at the age of 38. Through the intercession of his old Chicago mentor, Major Robert R. Jackson, Mitchell was interred in the full dress uniform of the Knights of Pythias and was given a military funeral at the St. Peter A.M.E. Church in Minneapolis. Numerous floral tributes filled the sanctuary and the church was completely packed as Mamie Mitchell said goodbye to her husband. The eulogy was entitled, "Christ The Great Example."[32]

The Colonel would have undoubtedly had a hard time dealing with the changing social climate of Minnesota. As Minneapolis surpassed St. Paul in both stature and number of black citizens following the First World War, the symbiotic relationship between the races began to deteriorate. During the great migration of 1910 to 1930, rural southern blacks headed en masse for northern industrial cities. Although the Twin Cities African American population of this time rose only slightly (42 percent) compared to the increases in other Midwestern communities such as Detroit (1,991 percent), Milwaukee (665 percent), and Chicago (430 percent), distrust of the new arrivals made jobs and housing increasingly difficult to secure for all black Minnesotans.[33]

Race relations in the Gopher State reached their nadir in 1920. On June 14, 19-year-old Irene Tusken and 18-year-old James Sullivan attended the James Robinson Circus in Duluth, before hanging around to watch an African American crew dismantle and load up the show. Later that night, Sullivan claimed that the couple was attacked and Tusken raped by several black workers. After receiving a call from Sullivan's father, Duluth Police Chief John Murphy rounded up about 150 circus employees and asked the teenagers to identify their assailants. The police arrested six black men in connection with the alleged incident, although Tusken's physician found no physical evidence of rape or assault when he examined her that morning.[34]

As the day wore on, an angry crowd of well over 5,000 strong gathered outside the Duluth city jail. Shortly after 9 P.M. the mob stormed the facility, and meeting no resistance from the Duluth Police, seized three of the accused, Elias Clayton, Elmer Jackson, and Isaac McGhie. After a farcical "trial," the three men were taken to a nearby street corner, and despite the pleas of two Catholic priests, lynched from a telephone pole. As Jackson calmly waited while the mob leaders secured a rope to hang him, he turned to the crowd, tossed a pair of dice to the pavement, and announced, "I won't need these anymore in this world." A young boy picked up one of the dice and "proffered it to the negro," saying: "Well, you might want to roll 'em in the next."[35]

The Minnesota National Guard was called in to secure the area and to safeguard the remaining prisoners. In the legal aftermath, two mob members were convicted of rioting and circus worker Max Mason was sentenced to 7-to-30 years in Stillwater Prison for rape, but the murderers of McGhie, Jackson, and Clayton went free. In the pages of the *Chicago Evening Post*, at least, the Duluth authorities stood "condemned in the eyes of the nation."[36]

Only three weeks before the tragedy, a Bobby Marshall–led outfit called the Minneapolis Colored Gophers had dropped a doubleheader to the Clyde Iron Works team of Duluth,

20–6 and 4–1. The following year, Marshall and pitcher Joe Davis joined a team in Estevan, Saskatchewan, Canada. The 41-year-old Marshall hit a reported .450 in 57 games, receiving "many cheers," while claiming that "he can and still will compete in baseball."[37]

Despite the growing hostility between Minnesota whites and blacks, Twin City African American nines flourished in the 1920's. Homegrown talent such as Bobby Marshall, Joe Davis, Ike Bradley, Harold Lewis, George Coleman, and George Roach formed the core of several local teams. Because most of players had day jobs, the clubs were weekend-only outfits except for a few weeks in late summer when they might pool their vacation time and barnstorm through the Dakotas. The players would often congregate at Lee Davis' house, where the veteran catcher would toss a couple of benches into the back of his truck, before driving a squad off to meet the town teams in the area.[38]

Two such semi-pro outfits helped rekindle the blackball rivalry between the Saintly and Mill cities. In the early summer of 1921, a team calling itself the Keystone Colored Giants of Minneapolis dropped a 5–4 game to the Peerless Chains team of Winona, before splitting a couple of games with a Willmar squad featuring 52-year-old Bill Binga. Like their namesakes, who turned confrontation into an art form, the 1921 Keystones riled up "the largest gathering of fans in the history" of Willmar by "hot words and a threat ... to cut short the contest if decisions weren't more to their liking."[39]

After their Fourth of July loss in Willmar, the Keystone Giants quietly exited the arena, although several of their players showed up in Lindstrom a week later playing for the Askin and Marine company team. The Minneapolis clothier club claimed to have many ex–Gophers and ex–Keystones on their roster, but after the Lindstrom squad pummeled them, 17–9, the local paper complained, "They were not in a class with the original Colored Gophers. If they had been it would have been a different game."[40]

Claiming to be "a real colored baseball organization," the Askin and Marine Colored Red Sox won 30 out of 39 games in 1922, including their last 11 in a row. Financed by white businessman W. R. McKinnon, the maroon-and-grey-clad squad was managed by right fielder/utility man Will Brooks. Bobby Marshall played third base for the Minneapolis club, Lee Davis was behind the plate and the pitching duties were handled by Joe Williams and "Lefty" Wilson.[41]

After the season "several influential men" approached Brooks and Marshall about leasing a ball park and joining the Negro National League in 1923, but nothing ever eventuated. In January 1925 the Flour City had another flirtation with the NNL, when a representative of Rube Foster arrived in Minneapolis and attempted to raise money for a team that would play at Nicollet Park when the Millers were on the road. Secure backing was not found, however, and this attempt also died on the vine.[42]

The same year the Colored Red Sox were formed, the Uptown Sanitary Shop in St. Paul also began sponsoring a sepia nine. The Uptowns were owned by Owen Howell, publisher of the black weekly newspaper, the *Northwestern Bulletin*, and featured "Steel Arm" Roach, the "young pitching speed demon." After beginning the season with several lopsided losses, including a 14–4 trouncing by a North St. Paul club, the "sanitary system boys" regrouped and in late July pounded the "Northmen" 14–9 in a rematch. Center fielder Dennis Ware went 4-for-6 with a home run, Frank Ware had five hits, and their big first baseman Mosley went 3-for-5 with a triple. In early August the Uptowns edged the J. Boureson club, 10–9, before a large Sunday crowd at Lexington, when Burton, "the sensational new recruit," bailed Roach out of a bases-loaded jam in the bottom of the ninth, by striking out the only batter he faced to end the game. The club finished their season on September 17 by thrashing

1923 Uptown Sanitary Shop Team, St. Paul, Minnesota. Bobby Marshall is standing third from right in the back row. Johnny Davis is standing second from right in the second row. (A.P. Rhodes, Minnesota State Historical Society, St. Paul)

the Woodman nine, 11–4, at Dunning Field. Roach fanned nine batters to pick up the win and slugger Bert Tucker hit his fourth home run in as many games. The Uptowns were scheduled to play the Askin Marines the following week in Minneapolis, but Will Brooks cancelled the game due to "some unforeseen obstacle."[43]

Joe Davis and Bobby Marshall joined the St. Paul team in 1923, which was now managed by Johnny Davis, who also found time to pitch an inning or two. On May 6 the Uptowns defeated the F.C. Roger squad, 15–3, in their opener with Joe Davis and George Roach allowing only one hit apiece. A few weeks later the club left for a tour of the Iron Range, billing themselves as the St. Paul Colored Gophers. Unfortunately, four Uptowns players missed the bus for Hibbing and the rest were subjected to a marathon all-night ride, arriving just before the May 28 match. Not surprisingly, the well-rested Colts thumped the tired St. Paul squad, 22–1, disappointing those in the Sunday crowd who were expecting a repeat of the Hibbing-Gophers battles of two decades prior. Carroll Booth had five hits for the rangers, including a triple and two doubles, while Bobby Marshall doubled and singled in four at-bats against his old foes. The two teams met again three days later. Although Uptowns were strengthened by the reappearance of their four missing "stars," the locals humiliated the St. Paul team, 37–1, with every member of Brady's Colts collecting at least five hits. After chasing line drives all day, the Uptown fielders "were leg weary when the contest was over," and the scorekeepers "were compelled to use page after page in their score book in keeping track of the score."[44]

The Colored Red Sox also managed to play farther afield in 1923, but they fared a little better than the Uptowns did. The Askin and Marine Company bought a Pierce Arrow car to transport the club and in early May the Red Sox took off for a month-long tour of northern Minnesota and North Dakota, with old Bert Jones manning first base.[45]

Will Brook's squad, said to be comprised of "young and active negroes who know how to play ball," won nine of 14 games on their "sizzling tour," including a 1–0 shutout of Moorhead, Minnesota. Joe Davis defected to the Minneapolis squad in mid–June, playing center field and rapping out two hits in a 9–6 defeat of Alexandria. The Uptowns and Colored Red Sox finally met up at Lexington Park on September 23. George Roach, "the speedball ace of the Sanitaries," parsed out three hits and struck out 14 batters as the St. Paul squad downed their Minneapolis rivals, 6–4. Joe Davis pitched for the Red Sox and fanned six, but "was hit freely."[46]

A few other black clubs were organized around this time, but none had the staying power of the Uptowns or Askin and Marines. The Minneapolis Buffaloes were formed in 1922 and featured Bobby Marshall and Joe Davis, fresh off their Canada excursion. On April 23 the Buffaloes downed the Uptowns, 9–7, at the Minneapolis Parade Grounds, as Davis bested George Roach on a extremely wind-blown day. The weather was much better the following week when a large crowd watched the seemingly "off color" squad drop a 9–4 decision to the Minneapolis Pantages. The Buffaloes were trounced, 12–0, by Little Falls on the Fourth of July, letting down hundreds of fans who came to the game expecting "some real baseball," and Davis and Marshall were soon playing for the Colored Red Sox.[47]

In 1923 entrepreneur Charles Gooch convinced Lee Davis, Harold Lewis and six other ex–Askin and Marine players to join his newly created Minneapolis Browns, but the former Red Sox soon drifted back to their former team. That same year the Chicago, Milwaukee, and St. Paul Railroad sponsored a black squad that went 18–12 under the management of Milton Williams, "the youngest manager in the Northwest." Another railroad team, the Pioneer Limited Giants, fielded a 1924 lineup that included Harold Lewis, Ike Bradley, "Speed" Coleman, and 24-year-old Alabaman slugger Maceo Breedlove. On June 30 in Redfield, South Dakota, George "Bullet" Roach came on in relief in the fifth inning with the Giants trailing, 7–1, and proceeded to toss eight innings of shutout ball. In the top of the ninth, Roach mashed a two-run homer to center field to tie the game at 7–7, and the Giants went on to win, 8–7, in 12 innings.[48]

The Askin and Marines faded away after the 1924 campaign and the next spring Colored Red Sox manager Will Brooks signed on to organize and run black businessman Billy Potts' Motor Company team. The new squad featured a couple of players with intriguing backgrounds. Bill Freeman, the son of ex–Gopher Bill Binga, was a 235-pound pitcher and "slugger of no mean ability." Another hurler, Lloyd "Dick" Hudson, was a "big, strapping buck with a countenance that will strike terror into most 'brush' performers." The 27-year-old Hudson had been a star fullback for the St. Mary's College of Winona's football team and played professionally in the NFL for the Minneapolis Marines in 1923. Hudson also had a brush with the law, being acquitted of the armed robbery of three Twin City taxi drivers in February 1924.[49]

With Joe Davis and Bobby Marshall also along for the ride, the Motor Company club got off to a fast start. "Billy Potts' Ethiopians" downed Princeton, Minnesota, 8–6, on May 17, the Minneapolis Great Northern team, 6–5, in ten innings on May 23, and Oxboro, Minnesota, 11–2, the following day, behind a three-hitter by Bill Freeman. The motorists ventured out to Clarkfield, Minnesota, the next weekend, but were defeated 13–

9 and 6–2 after a rash of injuries plus some shaky pitching by Hudson. Bill Freeman went on to twirl briefly for the Indianapolis ABC's that summer, and Billy Potts' team drove off into the sunset.[50]

Dick Hudson played the next two NFL seasons with the Hammond Pros, and later pitched for Dave Malarcher's Chicago Columbia Giants. The man they called "Super Six" reportedly also had a stint with the Kansas City Monarchs before beginning a rather remarkable career in sports promotion. In December 1926 Hudson took a novice black Chicago basketball team on the road for a tour of Wisconsin. The Giles Post American Legion team eventually morphed into the Savoy Big Five, which, after Hudson was eased out by a wheeler-dealer named Abe Saperstein, became the Harlem Globetrotters. Despite missing out on the brass ring with the Trotters, Hudson went on to manage a professional women's basketball squad called the Roma Girls, the Chicago Hottentots champion softball team, and Olympic track star Jesse Owens.[51]

In 1925 the Uptowns joined the Golden Valley League, becoming the only black club in a circuit made up of teams from amateur St. Paul and the adjoining area. The squad lost their first four games in league play, including an 8–7, 12-inning defeat to Lake Elmo where they committed five errors, before Johnny Davis "took command." On July 5, eight days shy of his 42nd birthday, Davis faced 34 batters, scattered five hits, and struck out 13, as the Sanitary Shop nine downed the Afton Grove outfit, 7–2.[52]

Prior to the 1927 season the Uptowns changed their name to the Colored All-Stars. Johnny Davis stayed on to manage the club, while the captain duties fell to longtime left fielder George White. After losing their opening game to Bayport, Minnesota, 3–1, on May 22, the All-Stars fell behind, 4–0, in the first inning against Oxboro a week later. Twirler George Roach steadied thereafter, and the St. Paul squad scored four times in the second, and twice in the seventh to lead, 6–4. After Oxboro pulled ahead, 8–7, Roach singled to leadoff the top of the ninth, advanced to third on a hit, and stole home to tie the game at eight. Dave Mays then relieved Roach and "held Oxboro at bay," as the All-Stars eventually won 11–9 in ten innings.[53]

During the late 1920s the first viable Minnesota black clubs outside of the Twin Cities were organized. In 1926, 40-year-old theater manager Bill Sandon formed a team called the Colored Tigers in Mankato. The Tigers featured a couple of ex–Tennessee Rats, catcher/manager Roy Wright and shortstop Charles Hilton, who would gather in "hoppers and bounders" for many Minnesota clubs for the next decade or so. The club lost their first two games, including a 17–6 thrashing at the hands of neighboring Belle Plaine, and "did not seem unduly fast" as advertised to the big crowd on hand. The Colored Tigers beat Eagle Lake, 6–5, in their next outing. Roy Wright put his squad up early, by stealing home from third in the first inning as the ball rested in the opposing pitcher's hands. Sandon's club then hit the road before dropping out of sight.[54]

Charlie Hilton showed up in southwestern Minnesota later that summer playing for the Pipestone Black Sox. In 1925, four black players, including one-time Union Giants twirler Scotty Henderson and catcher Frank Whitfield, were members of an integrated squad called the Pipestone Independents. The following May, Whitfield took over the Sioux Falls Black Sox franchise and moved the team to Pipestone. With a roster that included ex–Kansas City Monarchs pitcher Charley Lightner and former Indianapolis ABC's hurler Morris Williams, the Black Sox ran up a record of 41–15 (.732) against Iowa, Minnesota, and South Dakota nines, including an 8–3 mark against the other black outfits in the section. Although they played to some fairly large crowds along the way, the team moved to Marcus,

Iowa, in early August after Frank Whitfield sold the team to a pair of Hawkeye businessman.[55]

In 1928, Lee Davis, Bill Freeman and several other Twin City black players hooked up with an outfit called the Aberdeen Navy Cabs. The Navy Cabs had established a "fine record" and a reputation as "one of the strong traveling teams of the northwest," when they rolled into central Minnesota in mid–September to take on the strong Melrose nine. On the 16th, Bill Freeman took the mound against former University of Minnesota pitching sensation Pete Guzy, scattered six safeties, struck out a half dozen locals, and was "invincible in the pinches." In the top of the second inning, George Roach reached second base when the Melrose third baseman tossed his bunt attempt into right field. Jackson, the Navy Cabs right fielder, proceeded to lace a single to center bringing home Roach with the only run of the game. Melrose turned the tables a week later by crushing the Navy Cabs, 11–4, pounding Freeman for 15 hits including seven doubles. Pete Guzy, later a longtime football and baseball coach at Minneapolis' Edison High School, allowed only four hits and whiffed seven batters to pick up the win.[56]

Many Twin City black clubs, such as the Uptowns, were not above billing themselves as the Colored Gophers if it would help them gain a booking or two. In the spring of 1925, a full fledged revival of the team took place. Johnny Davis placed an item seeking baseball players in the March 21 edition of the *Chicago Defender*, although the squad he assembled was composed mostly of Twin Cities vets like Lee Davis and Harold Lewis. The Gophers opened the season with a Sunday game in Bertha, Minnesota, on April 26, before a "record breaking crowd." Both teams as well as the umpire were far from prime playing condition—the arbiter blew several decisions in favor of the home club, "which took a lot of fight out of the Gophers." The fact that John Donaldson pitched for the central Minnesota nine didn't help the visitor's chances either, as the legendary "master of the situation" struck out six and was reached for only three hits. One of these safeties was Bobby Marshall's ground-rule double in the fourth inning on a "gift pitch" from Donaldson that plated the Gophers only run in a 16–1 Bertha victory.[57]

Johnny Davis soon rejoined the Uptowns, but the new-look Gophers continued on without him. Traveling into Michigan's Upper Peninsula, the club edged the Hurley squad, 3–2, on June 28, before venturing over to Oshkosh, Wisconsin, a couple of weeks later to face the local Kitz & Pfeil team. On July 11 the Gophers rallied from an early five-run deficit to take a 6–5 lead in the seventh inning, only to lose the game on a two-run single off Bill Freeman in the last of the ninth. The next afternoon, the Twin City nine fell behind, 3–0, before Harry Lewis' two-run triple in the sixth frame tied the game at three. The locals pulled out again, however, thanks to a run-producing double by their pitcher Schmidt in the bottom of the eighth.[58]

In early April 1926 another advertisement was placed in th*e Defender* by one E. Faye Elliott, operating out of Phil Reid's old digs at 40 East Third Street in St. Paul:

> The St. Paul Colored Gophers
> Wants A-No. 1 ball players, pitchers, catchers, strong infield, all-around players. State lowest salary in first letter.

Led by pitcher Earl Thompson and catcher Gerhart Dunlap, the Gophers racked up a record of 6–2–2 while playing before large crowds in northwestern Minnesota and North Dakota. On August 1, the club returned to the Saintly City for a game with the strong St. Paul Police team at Lexington Park. Thompson struck out seven and collected two of the Gophers nine hits off the Police starter McGee, but he gave up 11 safeties as the lawmen won, 6–1.[59]

Outfits calling themselves the St. Paul Gophers continued to take the field in one form or another for the next four seasons. In June 1927, an ex–Detroit Star and Pipestone Black Sox pitcher named Wingfield led an undermanned Gophers club up against the Tracy, Minnesota, nine. The St. Paul squad was bashed, 10–2, as Wingfield gave up 14 hits and walked nine batters. The Gophers manager blamed their poor performance on the absence of three regulars, but as the local newspaper observed, "from the showing they made, they need nine instead of three."[60]

Earl Thompson was back with the Gophers in 1929, as they took on and defeated some of "the fastest teams of the Northwest" during the season, as well as a 5–4 victory in early August over a not-that-fast Dundas, Minnesota, nine. Less successful was a "pick-up"

Bobby Marshall and pitcher Joe Davis toiled together on many Twin Cities teams. Marshall was the first black player in NFL history and was named to the College Football Hall of Fame in 1971. (*Minneapolis Tribune*, May 26, 1912; Minnesota State Historical Society, St. Paul)

Gophers squad featuring Lee Davis and George White that showed up in Winona in September 1930 for a game against the hometown Roses and their longtime twirler Bert Jones. The locals built up an 12–2 lead after five innings, but the Gophers clawed back to within 12–8, and then loaded the bases with only one out in the top of the ninth before Jones, who drove in five runs on his own behalf, "bore down "and fanned the last two Gophers batters to end a most "pitiful exhibition of baseball."[61]

Along with the Colored Gophers revival, the 1920s also saw the emergence of the Ku Klux Klan in Minnesota. The white supremacist group was reported to have ten active chapters in Minneapolis alone, and was involved in a 1924 cross burning in Staples. In May 1926, a black aggregation wittily calling itself the Minneapolis Colored White Sox encountered a subtler form of racism in Winona. After arriving in the southern Minnesota town the night before a Sunday game, the Twin City squad was denied entry to every hotel in Winona, which forced most of the players to sleep on the team bus. The White Sox, featuring semi-pro regulars such as Ike Bradley and Harold Lewis, made nine errors the next afternoon and "several ragged plays" which were "not recorded in the scorebook." Backstop Lee Davis was victimized by nine Winona stolen bases, and Bobby Marshall was replaced at second base after several ground balls got by him. After the home team cruised to a 17–3 win, the *Winona Republican Herald* observed, "the colored boys played poorly, probably as a result of their lack of rest the night before."[62]

After a brief hiatus coinciding with the United States entry into the First World War, national black teams resumed barnstorming through the Gopher state in the early 1920s. The preeminent touring squad was the Union Giants, now under the management of one-time Gophers prospect Robert Gilkerson. From 1921 through 1935 the Spring Valley, Illinois, traveling club won well over 75 percent of their games while "distinguishing themselves with the fans both as funmakers and baseball players."[63]

Future Negro Leagues standouts such George Harney and Chet Brewer learned their craft with the Gilkersons, while pitching in tiny Minnesota burgs such as Fairmont, Windom, Lakeview, Beardsley, and Tracy. Gilkerson's outfit had quite a spirited rivalry with various aggregations in Winona. During the 1920s, the Union Giants' visit to the southeastern Minnesota town would result in record crowds, with cars circling the playing field and the grandstand and bleachers "filled to overflowing." However, in May 1932, during the dark days of the depression, only 150 people showed up to watch Winona down the Gilkersons, 6–1.[64]

The majority of the black teams that passed through Minnesota were shorter lived in nature than the Union Giants.. In May of 1921 ex–Plutos captain Sam Gordon piloted a squad called the Calgary Black Sox through Minnesota on their way to the Dakotas and Canada. The team, with future Pipestone Black Sox pitchers Wingfield and Scotty Henderson along for the ride, beat Stillwater, 12–7, in its first-ever game, before heading off for Alberta and oblivion.[65]

The Illinois Giants, the McCoy-Nolan Giants of Milwaukee, the Miami Colored Giants, the Chicago Arrow Giants, the All-Nation Clowns of Chicago, and the Boston Royal Giants were just a few of the many black clubs that followed Sam Gordon's Black Sox into Minnesota during the 1920s and 1930s. The quality of these teams was sometimes called into question, but their competitive fire was not. In July 1932 pitcher/manager O.L. Manese of the curiously named Michigan Wolverines of Nebraska angrily tried to knock the mask off the home plate umpire's head after a close call at the plate gave Winona a 10–9 walk-off win.[66]

The Roaring Twenties also witnessed the return of the black aces to the Gopher state. Just as they had done at the beginning of the 20th century, rural Minnesota communities began hiring African Americans to twirl for their teams, including four of the greatest pitchers in blackball history: John Donaldson, Dave Brown, Webster McDonald, and Chet Brewer.

After four seasons with the Kansas City Monarchs, John Donaldson revisited Minnesota in 1923 with a re-formed All Nations club. On August 28, the 32-year-old southpaw picked up where he left off, fanning 13 locals in a 6–3 All Nations victory over the Winona Chains. The next year Donaldson joined the semi-pro Bertha Fisherman of central Minnesota for hefty sum of $325 a month. The remarkable lefty posted a record of 21–3 (.875), while striking out 327 batters in 212 innings. Donaldson also hit .439 and proved to be such a drawing card that the Bertha bleachers had to be expanded to house the overflow crowds who came to see him play. After the Fisherman copped the area title with a 21–5–1 record, the local management was so pleased that they upped Donaldson's salary to $400 a month for the following year.[67]

During the next four seasons, Donaldson won 66 and lost 35 ball games for Minnesota teams in Bertha, Lismore, Melrose, and a few even smaller communities. He also posted yearly batting averages of .387, .448, .440, and .363, while continuing to strike out batters in basketfuls. With the Lismore Gophers in 1926 the "invincible John" whiffed at least 295 batters in 246 innings pitched. Donaldson also ran into his share of rough characters in the Minnesota hinterlands. In late August 1925, his Bertha club split a pair of games with a Scobey, Montana, squad featuring two of the infamous Chicago Black Sox, "Swede" Risberg and "Happy" Felsch.[68]

On the Fourth of July in 1926, Donaldson played in the outfield and relieved as his Lismore Gophers fell, 5–1, to Gilkerson's Union Giants before nearly 5,000 fans in Fairmont, Minnesota. The Union Giants twirler that day was a jug-eared southpaw called "Lefty" Wilson, who was not the Askin and Marine ace of the same name and vintage, but was in fact Dave Brown, one of the nastiest pitchers, both on and off the mound, who ever lived.[69]

Much like a batted baseball that invariably heads toward an error-prone fielder, trouble always seemed to find Dave Brown. After beginning a promising pitching career with the Dallas Black Giants, the 23-year-old Texan was signed by Rube Foster for his Chicago American Giants club in 1919. After pitching only two games for the Chicago nine, Brown was convicted of highway robbery, but acting on a promise he had made to the delinquent pitcher's mother, Big Rube posted a $20,000 bond for his release. The young curve-baller racked up a 29–8 record while leading the American Giants to the first three National Negro League titles, but in early 1923, he raised Foster's ire by jumping to the Lincoln Giants of the Eastern Colored League.[70]

Brown would also wear out his welcome in New York. During the early-morning hours of April 28, 1925, a man named Benjamin Adair was shot to death during an altercation in the streets of Harlem. Four men involved in the scuffle, including ballplayers Oliver Marcelle, Frank Wickware, and Brown, quickly hailed a taxi and left the scene. Later that day, law enforcement officers came looking for the players only to find that Brown, the alleged triggerman, had skipped town. The enigmatic left-hander fled to the Midwest and by spring 1926 was pitching for the Union Giants. The 2,000-plus fans who witnessed his eight-inning relief stint in Winona on July 12 had no idea they were watching a wanted-killer pitch. The local paper lauded him the next day for his "perfect control" and "great exhibition of twirling." Soon after, Brown joined the Pipestone Black Sox, winning three games for the southwestern Minnesota club. On July 18, Brown tossed a one-hitter and fanned 14 batters as the Black Sox blanked Granite Falls, 10–0. During the contest, his Pipestone teammates asked the southpaw to cut loose "just for fun," and Brown struck out the side with the minimum nine pitches required.[71]

Apparently finding western Minnesota to his liking, Brown subsequently pitched three games for the tiny town of Ivanhoe, before leading the Wanda club to the 1926 Tri-County League title, fanning 18 Comfrey batters in a playoff game. Although they were eliminated in the first round of the State Amateur Tournament in St. Paul, Wanda brought Brown back for the following season and he again pitched them to a Tri-County championship, striking out 23 more Comfrey lads in a two-game playoff sweep. In 1928, the fugitive southpaw replaced John Donaldson as the ace of the Bertha Fisherman, winning 14 times while losing on eight occasions. The season was not a big success on or off the field, however, and Brown, rumored to be involved in illegal bootlegging, was not brought back.[72]

One of Brown's Bertha defeats was to the Little Falls club, and their submarine twirler Webster McDonald. When the central Minnesota town decided to form a semi-pro outfit in 1928, they tried to ink John Donaldson, but the great lefty passed and recommended the 28-year-old Chicago American Giant ace instead. McDonald, who would go 14–4 against white major league competition in his career, later claimed that the committee that traveled to the Windy City to sign him believed Donaldson and he were related. Lured by a salary of $350 a month plus expenses, Little Falls' "perfect gentleman" proceeded to win 98 games against only 8 losses over the next four seasons. Former Colored Gopher John Van was the Little Falls catcher in 1928, but the Kansas backstop "wasn't the man they should have chosen," according to McDonald, and after reportedly winking at a white female fan, he was replaced by ex–Kansas City Monarch and Bertha Fisherman Sylvester "Hooks" Foreman.[73]

On August 29, 1930, the Minneapolis Millers traveled to Charles Lindbergh's hometown to play an exhibition game. Before a "howling mob" of 3,800, McDonald "bewildered" a heavy hitting Millers lineup that included 13 past or future major leaguers, scattering nine hits and striking out six batters. The submariner gave up a solo blast in the sixth inning to Mill City slugger Nick Cullop, the American Association leader that year with 54 home runs and 152 runs batted in, but he "tightened up in the pinches" to secure a 4–3 Little Falls win. Halsey Hall, the dean of Twin City sportswriters, later gave most of the credit for the "glorious" victory to McDonald and Foreman. Former semi-pro standout Al "Lefty" Dretchko broadcast the game via radio and told "the world about Little Falls, its natural resources and industrial features."[74]

McDonald got a chance to compete against the man who landed him his Minnesota gig, when John Donaldson joined the St. Cloud Saints in 1930. Working with only a game-to-game contract, the 38-year-old southpaw whiffed 109 batters in 157 innings, while compiling a 12–6 record for the Granite City nine. Little Falls won four out of six games from the Saints that summer, with McDonald outdueling Donaldson on at least two instances. On August 31, Donaldson's St. Cloud club was edged, 5–2, by a visiting Little Falls squad and their starter "Lefty" Wilson, a.k.a. Dave Brown. After spending the 1929 campaign in Sioux City, Iowa, the troubled left-hander joined Little Falls when McDonald went down with an injury. Although John Donaldson, Webster McDonald, and "Hooks" Foreman undoubtedly knew his real identity, the scofflaw from Texas pitched the rest of the summer in relative anonymity.[75]

Dave Brown apparently departed central Minnesota after the season. He later resurfaced in Greensboro, North Carolina, in 1938 when he was arrested for robbing a man and fracturing his skull with a sandbag. Although he was earning $750 a month by the end of his tenure, Webster McDonald left Little Falls after the 1931 campaign to be nearer to his ailing wife.[76]

John Donaldson re-upped with the Kansas City Monarchs in 1931, accompanying J.L. Wilkinson's team into Minnesota in July. On the 15th in Winona, the Monarchs, trying "to give the fans their money's worth," clubbed the hometown Roses, 16–0. Three days later, the Missouri squad took on the Crookston Red Sox and former Monarch Chet Brewer. The 24-year-old finesse pitcher had been recruited by the northwestern Minnesota squad, after spending the previous six seasons in Kansas City. The local populace rolled out the red carpet for the Leavenworth, Kansas, native and his catcher John Van, as well as their families; Brewer later recalled that the hospitality he received in Crookston made it "one of the most beautiful summers I lived."[77]

The Monarchs were less hospitable to Crookston as they blanked the Red Sox, 6–0. Brewer allowed only six hits to a powerful Kansas City lineup that included Newt Allen, Tom Young, and Carroll "Dink" Mothell, but his fielders committed nine errors behind him. Before he left town Donaldson apparently also tried to steal his former teammate's job, because as Brewer drily noted, "there wasn't any brotherly love in my profession."[78]

Desperate times call for desperate measures. Prior to his St. Cloud and Monarchs gigs, Donaldson had reverted to his barnstorming roots, throwing in his lot in the spring of 1929 with the Cuban House of David team. The improbably titled squad, which included many Minnesota blackballers like Bill Freeman and Charlie Hilton, but no Cubans, was operated out of Minneapolis and Muscatine, Iowa, by one Ray L. Doan. Doan also booked games for the Benton Harbor, Michigan, religious sect whose name the team appropriated. The club featured the Hancock brothers, Art and Charlie, a pair of ex–Negro Leaguers who later found a home with many Dakota semi-pro outfits, and like their namesakes, the players reportedly wore beards.[79]

In 1930 the team, now known as the Colored House of David, tore through the Midwest, racking up a reported record of 143–31 (.803), while claiming to have played before more people than any "traveling semi-pro club in baseball." Donaldson came back to helm the squad during the first half of the 1931 season, and Dave Brown *might* have been the Wilson who pitched and played right field for the club in 1930 and 1931.[80]

Sadly, one Colored House of David player's journey ended far too soon. After a Sunday game in June 1929, a 22-year-old pitcher named Raymond "Jack" Potts drowned in a reservoir near Moorhead, Minnesota, while swimming with some of his teammates. They recovered Potts' body the next day, 930 miles and forever away from his home in Chickasha, Oklahoma.[81]

Prior to the 1932 season, John Donaldson bought a baseball park near Fairmont, Minnesota, and organized a black team to play in it. The John Donaldson All-Stars included Colored House of David mainstays Bill Freeman and Charlie Hilton, as well as "Hooks" Foreman and ex–Kansas City Monarchs backstop Roosevelt "Chappie" Gray. Charlie Hancock, once touted as the "black Babe Ruth," was signed to play first base, and the pride of the Minneapolis Keystones, Hurley McNair, returned to Minnesota after several years to man left field.[82]

The All-Stars made their Fairmont debut on May 22, trouncing the Corwith, Iowa, team, 8–1, as Donaldson fanned 11 batters and Charlie Hilton collected four hits in five tries, including three doubles. After an early homestand, the All-Stars headed out on a circuit through northern Minnesota, South Dakota, and Iowa, spurred by the hot hitting of 44-year-old Hurley McNair, who was usually good for at least two base knocks a game. By owning their own park, the All-Stars were able to garner the lion's share of the gate receipts from their home games. Unfortunately, the southern Minnesota town was too small to support a ball club, and Donaldson's squad left Fairmont for good in early July.[83]

The 1930s witnessed the arrival of a new breed of Minnesota blackballers when players like Tom English, Ernest "Chinx" Worley, Wellington Coleman, and Jake Footes provided the backbone for many Twin City clubs. New teams emerged as well. In 1931 the St. Paul Monarchs were formed out of the ashes of the St. Paul Gophers by local go-getter Frank Boyce. The squad, which played mostly out-of-town games, featured veterans such as George Roach, Earl Thompson, and "the grand old man," Bobby Marshall. In late July 1932, the Monarchs rode a ten-game winning streak into Lexington Park to battle the St. Paul Milk nine, the best amateur team in the city. The Milk Men battered Thompson for 17 hits and routed the Monarchs, 9–3, in front of a Sunday crowd of 2,000. Maceo Breedlove rapped out three base knocks for the losers, and the 52-year-old Marshall connected for a pinch-hit single in the eighth inning.[84]

The Stillman brothers, George and Arthur, two young Minneapolis grocery store owners, began sponsoring a club called Twin Cities Colored Giants in 1934. The Giants played their first game in early May, blitzing a club from Arkansas, Wisconsin, 23–4. Big Bill Freeman allowed only one hit in six innings of work, while Wellington Coleman laced five hits,

The Twin City Colored Giants circa 1935. Ball caps bearing their insignia are now sold online for more money than the team earned per game. (*Twin City Herald*, August 15, 1936; Minnesota State Historical Society, St. Paul)

Tom English pilfered three bases, and the Giants third baseman Vick homered twice and tripled. A couple of weeks later, the Giants headed out to North Dakota to take on an integrated Jamestown Red Sox team that featured four Negro League stars including Ted "Double Duty" Radcliffe. The powerful Red Sox pounded out 23 hits off Bill Freeman and a reliever while running up a lead of 19–3 before the game was ended after the top of the seventh "at the request of the Colored Giants." Double Duty struck out ten Giants batters and singled five times in his own behalf.[85]

In August 1935 the Giants perhaps unwisely returned to North Dakota to take on a fantastic Bismarck semi-pro squad that listed on its roster Hall of Fame pitchers Satchel Paige and Hilton Smith, plus multiple East-West All-Star Game participants Barney Morris and Quincy Trouppe. The Giants, with the exception of 35-year-old slugger Maceo Breedlove, were simply overmatched, losing 8–5, 9–5, and 21–6. The 6'2", 200-pound Breedlove singled twice against Morris in the first contest and singled and homered off Smith in the second. Breedlove, who later gained notoriety selling beer while wearing an a umbrella hat at Bloomington's Metropolitan Stadium, saved his best for the Sunday finale, bashing a two-run homer off Paige in the top of the first, before doubling his next two times up. In the ninth inning, Paige took to the field with only a catcher and first baseman, and struck out the first two Giants before Breedlove once more approached the plate. After fouling off several blazing Paige fastballs, the Giants right fielder drove a curveball into left field and circled the bases, having demonstrated to blackball's greatest pitcher "who the baddest man with a bat around these parts was."[86]

Back in St. Paul, the Monarchs morphed into another edition of the Colored Gophers after the 1932 season. Jake Footes managed and caught for a series of mid–30s squads that boasted, "when the Saints are away, the Gophers will play — at Lexington Park." Mostly though, the Gophers played in such exotic Minnesota locales as Ironton, Lake Elmo, and Nerstrand. The club welcomed the Northern League's Winnipeg Maroons to St. Paul's Como Park in early May 1936, but the Canadians "trimmed them to badly they lost count of the score."[87]

The Twin Cities community of the 1920s and 1930s developed few players who actually played in the organized Negro Leagues, but this was due more to location and lack of opportunity than ability. Bill Freeman had stints with the Indianapolis ABC's and Cuban Stars, while pitcher Johnny Walton (like future major league stars Paul Molitor and Joe Mauer, a graduate of Cretin High School) briefly appeared with the Chicago American Giants in 1939.[88]

The hometown product with the most significant tenure in the Negro Leagues was undoubtedly Marcenia "Toni" Stone, one of the greatest female athletes in Minnesota history. Born in West Virginia in 1921, Stone spent most of her early life in St. Paul, where the self-professed tomboy and baseball fanatic made her reputation by starring for the Girls Highlex Softball Club. In 1936, she joined the Twin City Giants, impressing one teammate who later remembered that the 15-year-old Stone "could throw just like a man." The following year, the 5'7", 146-pounder pitched George White's Giants to a 5–3 record through July, and it was predicted that she would one day be as famous as Olympic hero "Babe" Didrikson.[89]

After spending several years with Oakland, California, area semi-pro teams, Stone joined the New Orleans Creoles as a second baseman in 1949, and was named to the Negro Southern League All-Star Game the next season. In 1953 Stone was signed by the Indianapolis Clowns and became the first woman to play in the Negro American League. Although her hiring was thought by many to be a publicity stunt, Stone hit .243 in 50 games, winning the respect of the Clowns Hall of Fame manager Oscar Charleston, who let her "get up there and hit." Stone was batting only .217 in mid–June, raising the ire of *Pittsburgh Courier* columnist Wendell Smith, who allowed that her average was "not bad for a dame," and was higher than 22 male players, who in Smith's opinion, "shouldn't be permitted to play in the Little League" if they couldn't "out-hit a frauline." In July Stone broke up a no-hit bid by Kansas City Monarchs pitcher Berto Nunez, and made "several sensational plays" including a fine stop to start a twin-killing, during the Clowns 5–4 win over the Birmingham Black Barons before 11,000 Washington, D.C., fans.[90]

As the Great Depression worsened during the 1930's, only the strongest black teams were able to survive. Blackball's premier franchise, the Kansas City Monarchs, dropped out of the Negro National League after 1930 and became a barnstorming outfit. In July 1932 the Monarchs clobbered the Winona Roses, 16–2, in a game notable for the brilliant fielding of second baseman Newt Allen and Shortstop Willie Wells. The attendance for the twilight contest was "disappointingly small," however, and when the Monarchs revisited Winona in September 1934 they brought the House of David team along with them. This time, a big crowd was on hand to see Kansas City top the "Bearded Boys," 4–1, in ten innings. The ageless John Donaldson scattered six hits to pick up the win, hit safely three times, and scored the go ahead run in the top of the tenth, after doubling to right center off fading Hall of Famer Grover Cleveland Alexander.[91]

In July 1938 the Monarchs trounced the Chicago American Giants, 18–3, in a Negro American League contest at Lexington Park. After the game the Twin Cities leading black newspaper, the *Minneapolis Spokesman* bitterly complained, "At least 2,000 colored fans who would have attended were not there because Abe Saperstein, promoter of the game, did not inform the Negro population of the Twin Cities through the Negro press." By the late 1930s, Saperstein, the owner of professional basketball's Harlem Globetrotters, had established himself as the main booking agent of black baseball for the Northwest. He got his start in 1927 when Walter Ball, reasoning that a white face would be more successful in securing rural Midwestern dates than a black one, hired the then 25-year-old Chicagoan to schedule games for his touring team. In late May 1932, Saperstein dispatched his Cleveland Black Friars with a "galaxy of stars," including former American Giants catcher and manager Jim Brown to Minnesota, where they were beaten, 10–6, by Winona.[92]

Having gotten the *Spokesman*'s hint, Saperstein adroitly publicized a July 1939 engagement between Kansas City and Chicago in the black *Twin City Herald*, with the result that between "four and five thousand fans" were on hand at Lexington as the Monarchs vanquished their old rivals, 14–1. The following year Saperstein began sending the Miami Ethiopian Clowns, and their garishly white grease-painted faces, pseudo–African names ("Selessie," "Aussa," "Tarzan") and shadow-ball comedy routines northward. The Clowns, who could also play a little baseball, thumped the Cincinnati Buckeyes, 15–3, in front of 3,000 at Lexington in July 1940. Back at the St. Paul park a month later, the comedians tripped up the NAL defending champion Monarchs, 6–2, before "one of the largest crowds to ever witness a professional Negro baseball game in the Twin Cities."[93]

After the 1941 season, both the Negro National and Negro American Leagues issued edicts prohibiting their clubs from playing any more games with the "Ethiopians," explaining that "the painting of faces by the Clowns players, their antics on the diamond and their style of play was a detriment to Negro league baseball." The mostly black owners were perhaps more upset with the five percent fee that Saperstein was collecting for publicizing the lucrative East-West All-Star Game, and were looking to cut into his piece of the action. Not being able to join them, Saperstein instead decided to beat them, and in March 1942 the wily entrepreneur surreptitiously formed the Negro Major Baseball League of America.[94]

Ostensibly created to heed President Franklin D. Roosevelt's wartime call for "more baseball as a morale builder," the new circuit reportedly consisted of six "outstanding" independent clubs: Syd Pollack's newly transplanted Cincinnati Clowns, plus the Chicago Brown Bombers, Boston Royal Giants, Detroit Black Sox, Baltimore Black Orioles, and the Minnesota–St. Paul Gophers. The Gophers were said to be owned by an entity called the Twin Cities Booster Syndicate and Jim Brown was announced as the fledgling team's manager.[95]

Despite the reported involvement of such notables as recently deposed NAL commissioner Major Robert R. Jackson and former football star Fritz Pollard, Saperstein's Negro Major Baseball League turned out to be a shadow operation consisting of only three teams, the Chicago Brown Bombers, the Clowns, and whoever the Clowns were playing at the time. In St. Paul, Lexington Park officials allotted the new organization ten Sunday and night dates. Because the Twin City franchise still hadn't surfaced by late spring, the Brown Bombers and the House of David nine played a Sunday doubleheader at Lexington on May 31.[96]

In April, the Clowns, the Brown Bombers, and Black Sox began training in the Miami area. While down south, the Detroit squad, made up of Birmingham Black Barons retreads and youngsters like 23-year-old infielder Johnny Britton, lost several contests to their league rivals, and the Florida Hoboes. Returning to Detroit in late May, the Sox were convincingly swept by the Black Barons in a double-dip, and on June 7 the struggling Michigan squad was clobbered, 13–9, by the semi-pro East Chicago, Indiana, Giants. Two weeks later, a retooled Black Sox club appeared at Lexington Park as the Minneapolis–St. Paul Gophers.[97]

Jim Brown claimed he had "spent weeks" assembling a team of which the Twin Cities would be proud, but his Gophers were really just the Detroit outfit with a few key additions, namely pitcher Vic Galloway and Black Barons reject Reece "Goose" Tatum. Fittingly, the neo–Gophers were slated to premier with a Sunday twin bill against the Chicago American Giants, managed by one-time St. Paul favorite "Candy" Jim Taylor. The Minnesota African American community was anxious for the new team to succeed. Noting that "whisky guzzling" and unruly behavior by black fans had marred recent Negro League games at Lexington, the *Spokesman* implored their readers to behave responsibly so as to avoid driving white spectators away.[98]

"Goose" Tatum helped the home team make a favorable impression against the American Giants by collecting two of their seven hits, including a triple, in the June 21 lid-lifter. Vic Galloway scattered five safeties and the Gophers tallied twice in the bottom of the eighth inning to take a 4–2 lead. In the top of the ninth, Galloway was hit on the wrist by a drive and had to retire. Candy Jim's squad got to his replacement, Boering, and loaded the bases with two outs before eleven-time all-star Alex Radcliffe singled to drive in the third Chicago run. The Giants runner on second also tried to score on the play, but Tatum's perfect peg from left field to catcher Rufus Hatten cut him down at the plate, preserving a 4–3 win.[99]

Tatum hit safely twice more in the second game, drove in a couple of runs, and made two sensational catches which drew "prolonged applause" from the nearly 1,100 fans present. Outfielder Sam Seagraves and first baseman Prim Hall provided the rest of the lumber, as the Twin City club coasted to a 5–1 victory. In its game report the following morning, the *St. Paul Pioneer Press* sang the praises of Tatum, calling the 24-year-old from Arkansas:

> ... one of those rare specimens in baseball, a natural clown who can back up his antics up in actual play. Reese Tatum, amiable, flat-footed, high stepping outfielder who runs bases like Stephen Fetchit but wallops the ball like Babe Ruth, won both games and the crowd's heart.[100]

During the following week, the Gophers played four games with the Cincinnati Clowns in Wisconsin and St. Paul. On June 23 at Milwaukee's Borchert Field, the funnymen scored twice in the top in the top of the sixth inning, and Jack Matchett blanked the Gophers the rest of the way to nail down a 6–5 Cincinnati victory. Back at Lexington the following night, first baseman Len Lindsey's ("Yahodi") base running and two-run fourth inning single paced the Clowns' 12–3 triumph, assisted in no small part by seven Gophers errors. The clubs returned to Lexington for a Sunday doubleheader on the 28th, but a steady rain brought an end to the proceedings after only five innings of the first contest had been played. Vic Galloway gave up only two hits, but consecutive errors in the second inning due to a wet ball and infield gave the Cincinnati squad the only run of the game. "The diminutive" Leo "Preacher" Henry allowed only one hit and struck out six of the Twin City club "with a fireball that blazed," to pick up the win The Clowns completed their four-game sweep the next night as Peanuts Nyasses, a.k.a. Eddie Davis, pitched and clowned his way to a 7–0 four-hit decision before 1,500 fans in La Crosse. The "Ethiopians" 14-hit onslaught was paced a home run by center fielder Ralph Coles ("Askari") and three base hits, including two straight triples by their third baseman Ray Owens ("Kankol").[101]

Rufus Hatten was the Minneapolis-St. Paul Gophers catcher in 1942. (*Minneapolis Spokesman*, July 10, 1942; Minnesota State Historical Society, St. Paul)

Next up for the Gophers was a four-game set with the third "league" member, the Chicago Brown Bombers, managed by blackball legend "Bingo" DeMoss. On July 1, the Minnesotans downed the Bombers, 5–2, before 1,300 paid customers in Waterloo, Iowa. The Iowans were mightily amused by "Goose" Tatum's oversized first baseman's mitt, but were less impressed by the quality of play, which the *Waterloo Daily Courier* rated Class D at best. Vic Galloway parsed out five hits and struck out six Bombers to register the win.[102]

The two squads then headed north across the border to Winnipeg, Manitoba. More than 2,200 fans turned out at Osborne Stadium on July 6 to watch the Chicago squad jump out to a 5–2 lead after five innings. Vic Galloway was not sharp this time around, allowing seven hits in a little over eight innings of work, while fanning only two. He also allowed a second-inning, run-scoring triple to his opposite number, "Beans" Williams. The Gophers pulled closer in the top of the seventh, when "Goose" Tatum cracked a two-run homer onto the nearby Amphitheatre rink, but the Bombers tacked on another run in their half to go up 6–4. After Williams retired the first Gophers batter of the ninth, Art Wilbert, "Goose" Tatum, and Prim Hall singled to load the bases and Sam Seagraves blasted a double to clear them. "Bish" Tyson then singled and Rufus Hatten followed with the Gophers 17th hit of the night, a triple to the center-field fence, before Galloway and two relievers closed out the Gophers 10–6 victory in the bottom of the frame.[103]

The next night nearly 1,800 Canadians witnessed perhaps "the poorest exhibition of Negro baseball" in Winnipeg for several years. Loose work by the Gophers infield gave the Windy City lads a 3–0 lead after only two and a half innings had been played. The Gophers rallied again to tie the score in the sixth, but an eighth-inning double by Bomber second baseman Bernie Longest brought the deciding run home in a 4–3 Chicago victory. Roosevelt Davis struck out eight batters, scattered seven singles, and survived *seven* errors by his fielders for a hard earned victory. The Gophers "Lefty" Buwn allowed nine hits to the Illinois squad, but three of them were doubles, including the game-winner.[104]

Because Abe Saperstein was part owner of the Black Barons, he was able to import Birmingham pitcher Gread "Lefty" McKinnis and catcher Ted "Double Duty" Radcliffe for the Gophers' July 12 doubleheader at Lexington. McKinnis mowed down the Brown Bombers in the first contest, giving up just two base hits, while striking out 12 batters to notch a 3–0 triumph. The Black Barons southpaw also doubled, and gave himself a 1–0 lead with a home run blast off Roosevelt Davis onto the neighboring Coliseum Ballroom roof. Tatum drove in the other two runs with a single and a triple. The Cincinnati Clowns bounced the Gophers 12–5 in the second game, as the more than 1,500 fans present watched Eddie Davis stifle the Gophers again.[105]

Two errors led to an early 4–0 Cincinnati advantage, and the *Minneapolis Spokesman* later commented that the Gophers "entered the game looking like a beaten team." Which might have been the point — either the Clowns really had their number, or like the Globetrotters perennial patsies, the Washington Generals, the Minnesota squad wasn't allowed to win. The beat-down continued on July 21 at Columbus, Ohio's, Red Bird Stadium when a local "race game record" 5,000 fans braved the rain to see the Ethiopians double-up the Gophers, 8–4.[106]

The next night in Cincinnati, the Clowns scored two runs in the bottom of the first inning after two were out and Eddie "Peanuts" Davis made it stand up for a 3–1 victory. The knuckleballer allowed only three hits and whiffed seven for the win, while the comedians got to Gophers starter Ulysses "Cowboy" Evans for ten base knocks. The two teams met for the last time on July 27 at Sulphur Dell in Nashville, Tennessee, when the Clowns decimated the Gophers, 21–8, for their eighth straight win in the season series. The Cincinnati attacked was fueled by right fielder Lamb Barbee's three-run home run over the center-field fence, and by 11 Gophers errors.[107]

The Gophers came back to Ohio a couple of nights later to battle the Fort Wayne Shamrocks at Halloran Park in Lima. Yankees prospect John Howard started for the semipro champs of Indiana and fanned 14 Gophers while doling out nine singles. The Hoosiers tallied five times in the third inning, sparked by a triple steal that so unnerved Twin City starter Barney Higdon that had to be relieved by Ulysses Evans. The Gophers tied the game at five with a run in the eighth, and they loaded the bases with one out in the ninth on a walk, error, and base hit. The next batter hit into a fielder's choice, and the go-ahead run came across when the Indiana lads failed to convert it into an inning-ending double play. Rufus Hatten's third hit drove another tally across and a double steal accounted for the eighth Gophers run. The Shamrocks put two men aboard with only one out in their half, but Tyson and Tatum made two running catches to end the contest, and snap the amateur's 18-game winning streak.

The Gophers were scheduled to appear in to St. Paul on August 14 for a twilight doubleheader at Lexington with the House of David boys. Instead the club was "reorganized" and played the rest of the summer as the New York Lincoln Giants, beginning with a 5–0 triumph on August 9 over an all-star team in Muskegon, Michigan.[108]

After his brief time with the Gophers, Johnny Britton embarked on a storied career that led him to such disparate place as Winnipeg, Manitoba, and Japan's Osaka Province. In 1952 Abe Saperstein negotiated the third baseman's transfer from the St. Louis Browns organization to the Hankyu Braves, making Britton one of the first African Americans to play in the Japanese Leagues. Fellow Gopher Reece Tatum rapped out two hits the 1947 East-West All-Star Game as a member of the Clowns, before achieving basketball immortality with the Harlem Globetrotters. The 6'3" outfielder evidently left a few broken hearts behind in the Twin Cities, including one "St. Paul Lassie," renowned for her "silly, loud screaming" and binoculars, who didn't care "if he does belong to anyone else."[109]

Because of the Clowns' overwhelming popularity and box-office appeal, the NAL was forced to capitulate and add the club to the circuit in January 1943. Having won this battle for supremacy, Saperstein disbanded the Black Sox/Gophers/Giants unit, but he continued to book games in St. Paul. Because of gas rationing due to the Second World War, the only big-time "race baseball" at Lexington in 1943 was on August 8, when the Clowns, featuring ex–Gophers Tatum, Ulysses Evans, and Johnny Britton, met the Black Barons in a Sunday doubleheader on "Goose Tatum Day." Presumably the "St. Paul Lassie" was also on hand.[110]

The next year was also a light one for blackball at Lexington. The only game came in early July, when the Harlem Globetrotters baseball team took on the House of David. In a cynical if not typical ploy, Saperstein had bought the NAL's St. Louis Stars, outfitted it with a few youngsters including ex–Gophers infielders Collins Jones and Leaman Johnson, and renamed it after his basketball squad. The confrontation between the Trotters and the "whiskered aggregation" was apparently so popular that Saperstein brought them back in 1945.[111]

With travel restrictions being eased near the end of the war, 1945 proved to be a boon for Negro League fans in Minnesota. In early June, a new St. Louis Stars club was booked to take on the New Orleans Black Pelicans in a series of games at Lexington, Nicollet Park, and the All-Sports Stadium in Duluth. A couple of weeks later the Birmingham Black Barons and "Candy" Jim Taylor's Chicago American Giants were also sent to play in all three venues. In July the Philadelphia Hilldales and the Detroit Motor City Giants of the fledgling United States League were slated to play four contests in the three cities. As a perhaps much needed extra attraction, track star Jesse Owens was scheduled to race a horse at the games, as well as "sprint, hurdle and base-circling handicap tests against the fastest players of the two teams."[112]

The local black nines also soldiered on through the war. George White was the manager of a 1944 Twin City Colored Giants squad that listed old vets "Chinx" Worley and Maceo Breedlove on its roster. In late May the Giants visited Osceola, a place where the original Gophers had experienced very little success. The Giants also fared poorly against the Wisconsin club, gifting them three runs on errors, in an eventual 13–8 loss. White and a 48-year-old Breedlove were still at it as late as July 1949, when their Twin City Colored Gophers were edged, 5–2, by a squad from Lewiston, Minnesota.[113]

Of course everything changed on October 23, 1945, when Jackie Robinson was signed by Branch Rickey and the Brooklyn Dodgers organization. The ex–UCLA and Kansas City Monarchs star's successful ascension to the major leagues in 1947 smashed Organized Baseball's color line once and for all. Considering Minnesota's long tradition of integrated baseball, it was perhaps no coincidence that the Dodgers and New York Giants, the two biggest advocates of black players, bought control of the St. Paul and Minneapolis minor league franchises around this time. Six of the first 19 African Americans to follow Robinson into the majors played with either the Saints or Millers: Dan Bankhead, Artie Wilson, Hank Thompson, Monte Irvin, Willie Mays, and Roy Campanella.[114]

Although manager Leo Durocher kept the 26-year-old Campanella with the Dodgers at the start of the 1948 season, Rickey shipped him to St. Paul on May 18 to integrate the American Association. After a miserable 1-for-20 start at the plate, the former Baltimore Elite Giants backstop began ripping up the A.A. By the time he was recalled to the Dodgers on June 30, Campanella was batting .325 (40-for-123) with 13 home runs. During one torrid week in June, the "terror of St. Paul," homered in six consecutive games and drove in 20 runs.[115]

Campanella made his Twin Cities debut during a Memorial Day weekend series with the Millers. On May 30 at Nicollet, the St. Paul catcher launched two long home runs to left, but the Saints lost, 17–9, anyway. The next morning at Lexington, Campanella tripled to the right-field scoreboard to give the his

A player employed in the early 1940s by Abe Saperstein, variously identified in contemporary newspapers as Prim Hall, Clarence McMullen, and Bruce Wright. (*Minneapolis Spokesman*, May 25, 1942; Minnesota State Historical Society, St. Paul)

club an early 2–0 lead, and hit a round-tripper over the left-field fence his next time up, as the Saints won their home opener, 11–6. Over 7,500 fans watched the Sunday contest in Minneapolis and nearly 10,500 took in the Monday matinee in St. Paul. *Minneapolis Spokesman* writer Carl T. Rowan, who observed that the games drew more black patrons to Nicollet and Lexington than perhaps at any other time in their history, noted, "One gent, his speech obviously aided by the beer he had consumed, delighted in telling the fans standing in the aisles that 'There was a colored man out here yesterday who hit two home runs.'" Rowan, soon to be one of the country's most preeminent journalists and later an U.S. ambassador to Finland, also related, "Nobody seemed bothered that the first negro was playing Triple A ball on their fields. Few, indeed seemed to wonder why it had taken so long."[116]

Chapter Twelve

After Many a Summer

Many of the Gophers and Keystones, as well as their contemporaries, stayed in baseball well into the Roaring Twenties and beyond. Their longevity is not surprising given the lack of good job opportunities available to African Americans at the time. A few of their careers, however, ended prematurely.

Following his stint in Renville, George Wilson led an outfit in Sheboygan, Wisconsin, to the 1906 Lake Shore League championship. The big southpaw racked up an 18–3–1 record for the southeastern Wisconsin nine while whiffing 218 batters in 202 innings. Wilson pitched Sheboygan to four consecutive victories to start the season, striking out 47 of the opposition with his bewildering submarine delivery. Upon the recommendation of his old catcher, "Rat" Johnson, Wilson twirled for the famed Club Havana in the Cuban League that winter, but he was ineffective, losing six while winning only three and allowing nearly seven runs a game. The opposition batted only .236 against him, but the Lions' shaky defense committed 142 errors in 31 games. Wilson did lead the league in hit batsmen with 11.[1]

After an ownership dispute in Sheboygan, Wilson signed on with a rival squad in Manitowoc for 1907. Ironically, the veteran lefty debuted for his new team in Sheboygan on May 5, losing 1–0, despite striking out eight of his former teammates. By early September Wilson had won seven of 11 games he pitched in the Lake Shore League and was leading the association's pitchers in fielding. Manitowoc went on to capture the league title and Wilson received a silver loving cup for winning the batting crown with a .338 average. In September, the veteran hurler turned down a $500 a month offer from Club Havana, claiming that his arm could no longer take the strain of pitching winter ball.[2]

Wilson re-upped with Manitowoc in 1908, but he left in mid–August when the team's management failed to adequately compensate him for pitching in a game against Sheboygan. Following a great uproar by the local fans, Wilson was enticed to rejoin the squad as a left fielder and the club rolled to another Lake Shore championship. After pitching in Cuba during the fall of 1908, Wilson returned to Michigan to care for his ailing father, promising to return to play for Manitowoc in 1909.[3]

But he never did. Instead Wilson retired to Palmyra to work on the family farm, although he still found time to pitch Sunday games for county teams, where he was still an "all around star" and "a clever and effective twirler." Wilson began acting erratically, however, either from the effects of syphilis or from being hit in the head with a pitch (or both), and he had to be institutionalized in the Kalamazoo State Hospital for the insane.[4]

During his career it had been pointed out how the outstanding lefty had kept in good condition by refraining from all tobacco and drink. Other vices were harder to shake. Big George Wilson succumbed from the effects of general paresis on November 26, 1915, at the age of forty. Once after watching him pitch, White Sox owner Charles Comiskey said he would give a fortune for Wilson if he were white and eligible to play in the major leagues—empty promises like Comiskey's were the only things Wilson ever got from organized baseball.[5]

The summer before Wilson's death, another former Minnesota southpaw, Howard Petway, won 12 straight games for the Nashville Athletics. Petway, who also briefly played for the Hennepins in 1912, returned to the Twin Cities for good around 1916 and married a local girl. Sadly, in late October 1918 the 34-year-old Tennessean died in St. Paul, leaving behind a two-year-old son and an infant daughter.[6]

Many players drifted back to Chicago after their baseball careers had ended. Eugene Milliner became a Pullman porter while George Taylor, with baseball still "oozing from his knob," took a job in the Spalding sporting goods store. Spitballer Clarence Lytle waited tables in a railroad dining car. Willis Jones was the head porter at the Congress Club, before attempting a comeback with Gilkerson's Union Giants after the First World War. Will Horn rose to prominence as an "expert osteopath," while Fred Roberts found work as a butcher. After Roberts' oldest son Norman was killed in action overseas, Roberts' mother Julia, who had raised Norman "from babyhood," became so grief stricken that she was interred in a sanitarium.[7]

Former Gophers infielder James Smith, a sergeant in the Philippines during the Spanish American War, reenlisted during the Great War, from which he emerged a captain. Smith, "one of the most honored men of the American Army," received the Croix de Guerre from the French government for leading the Allied capture of a German town. After the conflict, Smith came back to Chicago and wrote for the *Defender* before joining the postal service.[8]

The Barton brothers also returned to the City of Broad Shoulders. Sherman Barton manned center field for Frank Leland's Chicago Giants until 1912. Irving Williams described Barton's play during the Leland's 1911 showdown with the Chicago American Giants as "phenomenal," and that his batting and pitching were the features of the games, a boast somewhat belied by his .153 batting average in the series. Barton settled in the Windy City with his dressmaker wife, Lilly, and found employment as a repair man in a furniture factory. The great outfielder's heart finally gave out in July 1947, when he was 72. His younger brother Eugene, who became a Pullman

The whole show: George Wilson in 1902 with the Waseca EACO's. The most perfect pitching machine that ever lived died in a Michigan asylum at the age of forty. (*St. Paul Pioneer Press*, June 22, 1902; Minnesota State Historical Society, St. Paul)

porter when he hung up his cleats, was but 42 years of age when he passed away in Chicago in July 1922.[9]

Other ex–Gophers went back home after their time in the Minnesota sun. Julius London could be found pitching in the Negro Texas League as late as 1915, before he started driving a truck for a living in Houston. William Selden covered the middle of the infield for such top-flight black nines as the Indianapolis ABC's and Chicago American Giants, until he returned to western Ohio in 1915. "The lightning shortstop from Van Wert" continued to play "sensational" ball for segregated and integrated squads alike in Ohio and Indiana for the next 25 years while working as a porter during the off season. In 1940 a Van Wert newspaper marveled, "Although 55 years old, Seldon still plays heads up ball and can circle the bases faster than most youngsters."[10]

After kicking around with the French Lick Plutos and Chicago Giants, the inseparable battery of Lefty Pangburn and Mule Armstrong headed back east around 1913. The pair, along with ace twirler Sell Hall, made up the core of the Pittsburgh Colored Collegians, who did their best to educate the independent nines in the Pennsylvania and Ohio area. Prior to the U.S. entry into the First World War, the Colored Collegians battled a young black club called the Homestead Grays for local supremacy. During their game at Olympic Park in McKeesport, Pennsylvania, the Grays knocked Sell Hall out of the box (considered an almost impossible feat at the time) to win what blackball legend Cum Posey later regarded as his most important victory.[11]

By 1938, Armstrong and Pangburn were still working together in a trucking business in Elizabeth, Pennsylvania. In August of that year Pangburn attended an old-timer's game at Forbes Field in Pittsburgh between a bevy of former Grays stars, including Cyclone Joe Williams, and a club of former white semi-pro standouts. Wendell Smith wrote in the *Pittsburg Courier*:

> [Pangburn] was in and out of the dugout all through the game. He couldn't play Sunday because he tips the scales at 250 pounds and they couldn't find a uniform to fit him. In his heyday, Honey weighed 168. And they always had a uniform ready for "Honey" in those days. He was plenty good!

George Armstrong made a fortune from a coal mine he owned with his brother Pete in Lewiston, Pennsylvania. The pair also operated the Corner Tavern in the Hill district in Pittsburgh, as well as the Montooth Hotel in the Beltzhoover area. Until Mule Armstrong's death in April 1954, the brothers financed several Steel Town baseball teams including the powerful 18th Ward club, and in 1946 they backed the Brooklyn Brown Bombers in Branch Rickey's United States League.[12]

Not surprisingly, many of the ex–Keystones traveled a less sophisticated path than their Gopher counterparts: William Dewberry was a junk dealer in Chicago, William Embry a laborer in Vincennes, Indiana, and Charles Jessup, a factory worker in Joliet, Illinois. Topeka Jack Johnson became a police officer in Topeka, Kansas, although he continued to dabble in baseball and boxing throughout the 1920s. On Thanksgiving Day in 1920, Topeka Jack battled Jack Johnson at Leavenworth Federal Penitentiary, where the ex-heavyweight champ had been incarcerated for violating the Mann Act. With 2,000 inmates looking on, the "clever" Kansas fighter "set a fast pace," but he was ultimately out-boxed and out-punched by his former sparring partner during a four-round exhibition.[13]

Harry Bauchman, another former Keystone and pugilist, had the dubious distinction of being one of the first high-profile African American athletes to be arrested after a domestic dispute. In April 1919 the one-time American Giants second baseman was picked up by the

Chicago police after a complaint by his wife Mae, but he was later released when his bride failed to make an appearance in court. The couple's marriage disintegrated in 1923 and Bauchman had a warrant sworn out on him for adultery. The libidinous infielder remarried the following year and died in Chicago in 1931 at the early age of 41, after a brief bout with heart disease.[14]

Perhaps more significant than their on-the-field accomplishments were the baseball achievements of the St. Paul Gophers *after* their playing careers were over. Ten members of the 1909 championship squad alone went on to pilot professional teams, while two of their number, George Johnson Jr. and Jim Taylor, are counted among the greatest managers ever.

William McMurray was named captain of the St. Louis Giants in 1910, and under his tutelage, the Missouri squad became one of the leading black teams in the country. The up-and-coming St. Louis nine arrived in Chicago in late September for a big series with Frank Leland's Giants. The "Show-Me's" dropped the first contest, 6–3, but scored three runs off Walter Ball in the ninth inning the next day to cop the second game, 4–3. McMurray wasn't around for the finish, as he had to leave the field after breaking a leg sliding into second base. McMurray recovered sufficiently to play one more year with his hometown team before spending three seasons with the West Baden Sprudels.[15]

Felix Wallace succeeded McMurray as the captain of the St. Louis Giants in 1911. The ex–Gophers leader would continue to run the Mound City club for most of the next 15 years, although he spent a few seasons out east with the Lincoln Giants and a couple of other squads. It was Wallace who first realized the value of Jimmy Lyons as an everyday player and converted the novice pitcher into an outfielder. While on a 1924 spring training trip in Texas, Wallace spotted an 18-year-old shortstop with the Houston Black Buffaloes named Willie Wells, and brought the future Hall of Famer back north to St. Louis. Bill "Plunk" Drake, who pitched five seasons for Wallace, remembered him as "one of the greatest shortstops" ever, and favorably compared his manager to St. Louis Browns Hall of Famer Bobby Wallace. Felix Wallace died prematurely in 1925 and in 1952 was named to the *Pittsburgh Courier*'s all-time blackball team as a utility man. The *Indianapolis Freeman* once censured the fiery infielder from Kentucky for his run-ins with umpires, commenting that "fighting does not constitute ball playing in this section of the country."[16]

After his sore arm woes with the Gophers in 1911, Louis "Dicta" Johnson rebounded the next season by pitching brilliantly first for the French Lick Plutos and then for Rube Foster's American Giants. The *Freeman* seemed to think that the twirler's turnaround was due in part to his recent marriage: "Since Louis Johnson became a 'newly-wed' he seems to take on more 'steam' as a pitcher." In June of 1913, Johnson threw a no-hitter in Chicago against Coogan's Smart Set club, striking out seven, as the Giants ended the New York team's 21-game winning streak with a 9–0 victory. Johnson almost ruined everything in the second inning by walking the bases full, but he got out of the jam by striking out Smart Sets left fielder Smith.[17]

Perhaps miffed by the theft of his winter overcoat from his Chicago home, Johnson jumped C. I. Taylor's Indianapolis ABC's in 1914, where he became the second most successful twirler in team history, racking up records of 20–4 in 1915 and 15–10 during their championship 1916 season. Johnson was drafted into the U.S. Army in early 1918, and played service ball along with James Smith on the 183rd Brigade team. Following his return from Europe, Johnson went 13–10 for the 1921 ABC's, before flirting with management by piloting the Pittsburgh Keystones during the second half of the 1922 NNL season and the Toledo Tigers in early 1923. The old spitballer, once considered "one of the best pitchers that ever graced the diamond," could be found throwing wet ones with Joe Green's Chicago Giants as late as 1925.[18]

Way back in 1910, Walter Ball declared that he would go into vaudeville when his arm gave out. Fourteen years later, however, he was still chucking the pill in the Windy City. In 1912 the twirler won 23 straight decisions for the St. Louis Giants until the American Giants clobbered him, 10–4, in July. The following year, Ball headed eastward to pitch for the Brooklyn Royal Giants, striking out 15 batters while downing a Trenton, New Jersey, club, 2–0, in a mere 53 minutes. Ball returned to Chicago in 1917 and toiled the next eight years with his old teammate Joe Green's Giants. After his playing days were over, the great pitcher managed a couple of Chicago-area teams, including the aptly named the Walter Ball's. He made it back to Minnesota in 1930 while on a Canadian tour with one of his clubs. Ball stopped off in his old St. Cloud stomping grounds, walking into former manager Frank Thielman's hardware store and asking, "Is the paymaster here?"[19]

One of the old St. Paul hurler's final brushes with glory came in August 1936 on Rube Foster Day at the American Giants Park, when he pitched for a squad of old-time Giants against a team of former local white stars. Ironically, 70-year-old Fred "Crazy" Schmidt, who had bested Ball in the Gophers' first-ever game 29 years before, edged him by an identical 6–4 score. Ball died in December 1946 in the Cook County Hospital at the age of 69, and was buried in an unmarked grave in Lincoln Cemetery. He spent the last years of his life as a coach for the Chicago Sports Association, teaching the game he loved to young children.[20]

After leaving the Gophers, Jim Taylor became black baseball's premier third baseman, making such a strong impression on Dizzy Dismukes that he was later named to that twirler's all-time team. He batted cleanup on the powerhouse Chicago American Giants clubs of 1912–1913 and hit .315 for his brother C. I.'s 1916 Indianapolis ABC's squad. Taylor joined the Dayton Marcos in 1919, and became their player-manager the following season. For the next 28 years the "Napoleon of the National League" was the lead man for one outfit after another, eventually winning more games than any other blackball skipper. Along the way Taylor became a proprietor of a sweet shop in Chicago's Brookmont Hotel, and acquired the non de plume "Candy Jim."[21]

Taylor led the St. Louis Stars to the Negro National League title in 1928, although he was fined $25 and suspended nine days by President William Hueston for "actions unbecoming to a ballplayer and a manager," after a July confrontation with the Detroit Stars. Three years later, Taylor was managing the ABC's when an Indianapolis fan was attacked in the stands by members of his old St. Louis squad. Taylor groused that rowdyism was rampant among black players and that the Stars where the worst offenders: "Discipline, the keynote to the success of the big leagues, seems to be grossly lacking in the organization of the Negro National League."[22]

The consummate professional, Candy Jim had no patience for weak owners, incompetent umpires, or out-of-condition players who were only interested in a paycheck. As a result he ended up managing over 15 different clubs during his tenure. Known to "raise more cain than a peeved plantation owner when players refuse to follow orders," Taylor boasted he would leave his own mother behind if she wasn't on the team bus on time. "This is a business," he would exclaim, "so take it seriously." The very superstitious Taylor once went several years refusing to replace his baseball shoes, until they were "too far gone to wear for even one more day," because he had never been on a losing team while wearing them. Taylor also wouldn't allow his charges to eat peanuts during a game, much to the delight of opposing players who would get his goat by tossing peanut shells into his dugout.[23]

Candy Jim's M.O. was to build his squads through youngsters and players other clubs had discarded. His philosophy was simple yet sound: "Try to understand your men. Know their abilities, and know when to change pitchers." As a manager Taylor was responsible for the development of many great players including Ed Rile, Wade Johnston, Walter "Rev" Cannady, as well as Hall of Famers Willie Wells and George "Mule" Suttles. James "Cool Papa" Bell, who served under Taylor in the 1920s with the St. Louis Stars, and then again in the early 1940s with the American Giants and Homestead Grays, remembered that his manager "kept his ballplayers loose, and you loved to play for him."[24]

While overseeing the Detroit Stars in 1933, Candy Jim bribed Ray Dandridge's father $25 to get the young Richmond, Virginia, infielder to go north with his team. One day in practice Taylor took the future Hall of Famer's bat away from him, gave him a heavier 37-ounce model, and announced, "I'm gonna show you how to hit." Taylor proceeded to demonstrate to his protégé the art of pulling an inside pitch, hitting a ball thrown down the center of the plate up the middle, and how to take an outside pitch to the opposite field. Dandridge was suitably impressed:

> I think to myself, "I'm up there swinging, and he's showing me the moves, how to step into the ball, how to step forward." I stopped swinging for the fences. That man taught me a lot about hitting. It's a good thing I listened. I tried it. If he can hit line drives like that — beautiful — I could hit line drives from one side to another too.

Taylor was less prescient about a young backstop he picked up for a 1930 game in Scranton, Pennsylvania, reportedly stating that the Hall of Fame–bound Josh Gibson would never make it as a catcher.[25]

Candy Jim got a second chance to manage Gibson with the Negro League All-Star team that captured the 1936 Denver Post Tournament. Taylor also directed the Gibson-powered Homestead Grays to two consecutive Negro World Series titles in 1943 and 1944, but his inability to get along with the enigmatic superstar, however, led to his dismissal after the second championship. Taylor managed in four East West All-Star Games, later claiming that his biggest thrill ever in baseball was being selected as the West's skipper in the inaugural 1933 contest. As "funds were low" at the time, Candy Jim had to borrow the necessary $60 train fare to Chicago from an opposing manager in Bogalusa, Mississippi, in order to make the contest. Fired by the American Giants in a cost cutting move after the 1947 season, the 64-year-old master strategist was slated to pilot the Baltimore Elite Giants the following spring. He fell seriously ill, however, and died in the People's Hospital in Chicago in early April 1948.[26]

Dr. J. B. Martin, the American Giants owner who had just canned Taylor, eulogized the lifelong bachelor in the pages of the *Chicago Defender* as "a great baseball manager" who "was at all times a perfect gentleman" and always "tried hard to win." At Candy Jim's funeral, though, not one message of condolence was read or any word uttered from any representative of the 12 current Negro League clubs about the man who had devoted his life to their game. Taylor was buried in Chicago's Burr Oak Cemetery in a grave that lay unmarked until 2004 when Jeremy Krock, a Peoria, Illinois doctor, raised enough funds to erect a headstone.[27]

Although Candy Jim's sibling John Taylor was never again as dominant as he was with the Gophers in 1909, when he might have been the best pitcher on the planet, he remained

See that my grave is kept clean. "Candy" Jim Taylor's headstone in Burr Oak Cemetery near Chicago.

an outstanding blackball pitcher for several years. After spending a season each with the Chicago and St. Louis Giants, Steel Arm Johnny went to West Baden in 1912 to pitch for another family member, C. I. In late June 1913, the Sprudels came to Chicago for a Sunday game with the American Giants. Over 6,000 fans, the largest crowd "in the history of semi-pro ball," were on hand to celebrate the unfurling of the American Giants championship pennant from the California Winter League. Big Bill Gatewood started for Foster's men and put a damper on the festivities by hitting the first two West Baden batters. Four hits and a sacrifice fly later, the Sprudels had staked Steel Arm Johnny to a 5–0 lead. In the bottom of the second inning, the crowd rose as Jim Taylor stepped into the batter's box to face his big brother:

> It was Greek against Greek, and the excitement was intense. Taylor's bat was on his shoulder, and he brought it off twice before the ball was pitched, showing Steel-arm where he wanted it. Steel-arm nodded, wound up and put it there. The batter hit a terrific drive. But the other Greek was there, too. He struck his gloved hand up and in it the sphere stuck, while the crowd went wild.[28]

John Taylor fanned only three batters on the day, but he scattered nine hits to pick up a 7–5 victory over the powerful Chicago squad. That August, with the American Giants facing elimination in their bitter championship series with the Lincoln Giants, Foster imported the clutch twirler to pitch against a murderous lineup that included Spottswood Poles, Home Run Johnson, and John Henry Lloyd. Squaring off against his old rival Cyclone Joe Williams, Taylor fanned six and allowed only four safeties while whitewashing the New Yorkers, 3–0.[29]

Before he "retired" in 1917 to go into business, John Taylor put in time with C. I.'s Indianapolis ABC's, as well as running and pitching for the Louisville White Sox. Earlier in his career, the legendary hurler had coached at his alma mater, Biddle University in Charlotte, North Carolina, and at M & I College in Holly Springs, Mississippi. After his playing days were over Taylor became the manager for a number of Illinois teams including the Peoria Black Devils; in 1924 he became the first pitching coach in Negro Leagues history when his sibling Ben put him in charge of the Washington Potomacs staff. He was still in the game as late as 1930 when he could be found managing the "Our" club of Springfield, Illinois. The last of the four famous Taylor brothers also operated a Turkish bathhouse for several years in Peoria, where he passed away at the age of 75 in March 1956. In 2007, Jeremy Krock and the Pekin, Illinois, YWCA installed a headstone for Steel Arm Johnny in Peoria's Springdale Cemetery.[30]

George "Rat" Johnson was on the downside of his playing career when he left the Gophers, but the *Indianapolis Freeman* noted in 1910 that the veteran backstop, now known as "Chappie," was leading all Chicago-area players in drawing extra bonuses. Although his "old batting eye [had] not forsaken him," Johnson's legs began to give out and after tours with the St. Louis Giants and the Schenectady, New York, Mohawk Giants, he moved into a player/manager/ownership role in 1916 with the Dayton, Ohio, Chappies.[31]

Following a stint in a Dayton airplane factory during the First World War, Chappie hit .214 in a backup role for the Atlantic City Bacharach Giants in 1919. The 44-year-old Johnson landed in Virginia the next year, convincing his old pals Frank Wickware, Bill Gatewood and Harry Bauchman to play for his Norfolk All-Stars. After a couple of seasons down south, Johnson moved his base of operations to the Northeast. Beginning with the Philadelphia Royal Stars in 1922, the old catcher led a succession of barnstorming teams that acted as a proving ground for some of the finest talent in blackball, including Jesse "Nip" Winters, Holsey "Scrip" Lee, Dick Seay, and Webster McDonald.[32]

Obtaining players "anywhere he could get them from," Johnson routinely ransacked the rosters of the Lincoln Giants, Brooklyn Royal Giants, and Hilldale, making the "arch raider" as popular among the owners of the Eastern Colored League "as a cloudburst at an A.O.H. picnic." Chappie was considered such an exceptional leader and mentor that Cum Posey named him to his all-time squad as a coach. Johnson's talents did not go unnoticed by Organized Baseball — at various times the old catcher was a spring training instructor for the Cincinnati Reds and Washington Senators.[33]

Standout Negro Leagues outfielder and baserunner Ted Page credited Johnson with turning him into a top-flight professional and for teaching him the art of the drag bunt. Page liked Chappie "better than any manager I played under," and remembered that he "could look at a ballplayer, watch him play, be around him a little while, and discover if he had ability." According to "Terrible" Ted:

> Chappie was a good con man. He could look in your pocket, and if you had a dollar, before you knew it, you were handing it to him. And you know, Chappie conned me. He conned me into realizing that I was very fast, Chappie would say, "If I was your age"—this is where he got to me, see?—"if I was your age and could run like you can, nobody would ever stop me from getting on base."[34]

Not all of Johnson's players were as appreciative. In the latter part of the 1926 season, Chappie had a run-in with his chief gate attraction, William "Buck" Ewing. Ewing, whom Johnson had once lauded as "the greatest catcher in baseball," left the squad and also caused a mutiny in the All-Stars ranks by forming his own club with several of his teammates. "Run out of central New York" by his ex-protégé's team, Johnson relocated a new All-Stars outfit to Quebec. The crafty campaigner landed on his feet once more and it was reported that Chappie had "such a strange hold on the town that the Negro, French, and Eskimo citizens are going to run him for Lord Mayor or something at the next elections."[35]

In 1933 Johnson moved his All-Stars back to Syracuse, New York, where they played in the otherwise all-white Journal-American semi-pro league. Circuit president and former New York Giants pitcher George "Hooks" Wiltse announced, "I do not see how the color of a man's skin can have anything to do with his ball playing or ability." The All-Stars proved to be a great drawing card for the league, attracting over 4,000 people to a June game in nearby Liverpool. Chappie even got into the act during the contest, sparking a winning rally in the eighth inning on a squeeze play. Johnson tried to schedule Connie Mack's Philadelphia Athletics that season, but the major leaguers declined, citing "organized baseball's rules regarding games between negro and white clubs." The All-Stars did take on the Rochester Red Wings, but the International Leaguer's clipped them, 9–3.[36]

The All-Stars run in Syracuse came to a crashing halt, literally. In April 1934 Chappie was behind the wheel of a vehicle which struck another car injuring an 84-year-old man. Thirteen months later, a local woman named Edith Wells was killed in a head-on collision with an auto driven by All-Stars catcher Boston "Babe" Hopson. The 45-year-old Wells was driving in Herkimer, New York, when she pulled out of traffic in an attempt to pass other automobiles and hit Hopson's car, which was trying to do the same thing. Johnson was hospitalized with a fractured hip, and three of his players, including Hopson, suffered cuts and bruises. Ultimately no charges were filed, although both drivers were found to be negligent, and Hopson was fined $5 for driving without a license. Less than 48 hours before the fatal accident, a sedan transporting six of the All-Stars from New York to Syracuse late at night slammed into the back of an unlighted trailer, overturning the touring car and injuring two of the players.[37]

Johnson was also beset by legal troubles involving his club, including a $164 judgment levied against him by a local magistrate for non-payment to a contractor for infield dirt. But as the old receiver was fond of saying, "A man may be down, but he is never out." By the summer of 1936 he was back barnstorming through the Northeast with an outfit called the Brooklyn Cuban Stars. He also found time to manage the Brooklyn Rens basketball squad, help train New York middleweight Ralph De John, and serve as a hunting guide for former Boston Braves manager George Stallings.[38]

In 1940 Johnson became the first black trainer in the history of the Southern Conference when he was hired by Clemson University. The venerable backstop soon became the favorite of the South Carolina school's 3,500 cadets:

> Chappie, bearing the scars of a catcher, a right hand with knarled [sic] and crooked fingers, loves to sit back and talk baseball. In fact, some of the football players say that Chappie's idea of Heaven is a baseball diamond where all the old stars gather and swap stories of the good old days.[39]

Chappie remained in his capacity as Clemson's head trainer until August 1949 when he died at his home after a long illness at the age of 73. Regarded by many to be one of the finest signal-callers ever, Johnson was immortalized in Canadian author John Craig's 1979 fictionalized memoir, *Chappie And Me*. The novel tells the semi-comic, possibly true story of how a white semi-pro first baseman was enlisted by Johnson to impersonate one of his injured players, and used black shoe polish to conceal his heritage.[40]

Chappie and Me is ostensibly set in the summer of 1939 just prior to the outbreak of the Second World War, although the author notes in the dedication that it is "the novelist's license to shape time and place to his purpose." The book recounts how Craig (rechristened Joe Giffen for dramatic purposes) and Chappie's All-Stars barnstorm through the Upper Midwest, including two memorable stops in Hibbing, Minnesota, which is called Hobblin to protect the not-so-innocent. Especially informative is a passage where the old master instructs the young Canadian on the finer points of the initial sack. Johnson, described by Craig as being as black as a "ton of coal," impressed upon the ex-semi-pro that a first baseman should never look for the bag when taking a throw. "You gotta *feel* where it's at," he explained. As a means of demonstration, Chappie had Craig toss him a few balls:

> I threw wide right, wide left, into the dirt, over his head. Each time he'd catch the ball in my well worn mitt, and then one foot would dart back like a snake's tongue and just brush some part of the bag. He wasn't young, and he didn't seem to move real quick; but he got throws I couldn't have reached, not and touch that sack. It was as if there was elastic in those old legs, or some kind of extension, so that he could stretch them out a foot or more when he had to.[41]

William Gatewood never had a book written about him, but he should have. In the spring of 1919, the *Chicago Defender* ruminated on the career of Johnson's former batterymate, then beginning his 21st season in blackball: "A word concerning 'Gatewood.' It is said that whiskey gets better as it ages and so does 'Big Bill.'" The tall Texan spent the 20th century's second decade pitching one huge game after another for a succession of outstanding teams. In 1911 Gatewood was employed by Frank Leland's Chicago Giants for their showdown series with the Foster's American Giants. On July 3, he struck out eight and scattered six hits to pick up a 7–3 decision over Rube's squad. The next afternoon, Big Bill relieved Cyclone Joe Williams in the bottom of the first after the Fosters had tallied three times, and retired the side without further damage. He kept the "Rubens" in check until the sixth inning when Pete Hill whacked one of his "heat balls" for a double. At this point Gatewood's famous temper resurfaced and his next pitch hit Bill Monroe on the head. After Rube Foster ran for the stricken Monroe(!), Bruce Petway singled home both runners as the American Giants rolled to a 7–5 win. The always strong hitting Gatewood powered the Lelands' attack by walloping three safeties including a double and triple.[42]

George "Rat" Johnson with the Gophers mascot in 1908. (*Renville Star Farmer*, June 4, 1909; Minnesota State Historical Society, St. Paul)

Big William was yet

toeing the rubber in 1926 for the Albany, Georgia, Giants of the Negro Southern League. In late June the 44-year-old threw a no-hit, no-run game against the powerful Birmingham Black Barons with only one ball being hit out of the infield. Two years later the aging twirler joined the St. Louis Giants on an East Coast tour, posting wins over East Orange and Jersey City, the two top semi-pro teams in the area. Gatewood started a game against John Henry Lloyd's Lincoln Giants in the Bronx and was leading the Eastern Colored League club, 5–3, when he was relieved in the eighth inning. Although St. Louis went on to lose the game, Gatewood's performance greatly impressed former Cuban X-Giants manager Ed Lamar, who judged him to be squarely in Lloyd's class.[43]

But it was as a leader of men that Bill Gatewood gained his greatest notoriety. In 1922 he was named player-manager of the St. Louis Stars of the Negro National League. That spring the squad picked up a 19-year-old knuckleballer named James Bell from the semi-pro East St. Louis Cubs. Gatewood made the youngster ride the bench for a month, telling him, "I might pitch you and I might not." In early May Gatewood finally inserted Bell into a game in Indianapolis against the ABC's. Moping up during an 11–5 loss, the novice southpaw struck out three batters with his wicked curveball, reportedly including Hall of Famers Ben Taylor and Oscar Charleston. Six days later Bell took the hill against the American Giants in Chicago and allowed only six hits while downing the NNL champs, 6–2. Bell fell asleep on the train prior to his next start in Detroit, prompting his teammates to nickname the unflappable rookie "Cool." "We've got to add something to it," Gatewood insisted, "We'll call him Cool Papa." That winter while the Stars were playing in California, Gatewood supposedly moved the future Hall of Famer to center field and converted him into a switch-hitter to take advantage of his blazing speed.[44]

Bill Drake later recalled how Gatewood improved his control by having the St. Louis twirler throw at stationary objects before games, telling him pitching was like a shooting gallery — "you got to aim, you got to pick a target." Not all young pitchers were as willing as Drake to follow Big Bill's advice. Gatewood was the on-the-field boss when Leroy "Satchel" Paige joined the Birmingham Black Barons in 1927. When Big Bill demonstrated the proper way to grip a curveball, the 21-year-old prodigy told his manager, "I don't do it that way." Paige also announced that because his command was so good, "There ain't no need for signs." Evidence showed otherwise. After the rookie hurler ignited a bench-clearing brawl by beaning three St. Louis Stars batters to begin a game in late June, Gatewood regulated him to relief duty.[45]

After a bit of fine tuning, Gatewood reinserted Paige into the Birmingham rotation in August and the Black Barons rode his arm to the second-half NNL pennant. The Alabamans were swept in a four-game playoff by the Chicago American Giants, however, and Gatewood was relieved of his post, allegedly because he didn't start Paige in the final contest. The big man returned to his home in northern Missouri, where he was appointed player-manager of the Moberly Eagles. Despite his banishment to the bushes, Gatewood's ability to cultivate talent had not diminished — two of his Eagles players, outfielder Jimmy Crutchfield and pitcher Leroy Matlock, were soon starring in the Negro Leagues.[46]

Gatewood had less success mentoring his own son. In 1933, 15-year-old William Gatewood, Jr. was arrested for burglary, and four years later the troubled youth was sent to the state penitentiary on the same charge. After his prison stretch was up, "Buddy" Gatewood, who was also a ballplayer, joined his father's Gatewood Browns in time for the 1939 season opener. With his club trailing by one run late in the game, Big Bill came on to pinch-hit with Bill Jr. on third base. The elder Gatewood hit a slow roller to short and his boy came home to knot the contest. Former Kansas City Monarch Alfred "Army" Cooper struck out 19 batters for the Moberly squad, but he received a no-decision when the game ended in a 4–4 tie.[47]

Despite having the Moberly ball park named in his honor, Big Bill's team reformed without him after the 1939 season. He later became estranged from family, and died in December 1962 at the advanced age of 81 in Columbia, Missouri. In 1955 Gatewood was named to sportswriter Fay Young's all-time team, but perhaps his finest testimonial came from the lanky young fire-baller he once taught the hesitation pitch to. When he was inducted into the Hall of Fame in 1971, Leroy "Satchel" Paige was asked if any other Negro Leaguers should be inducted in Cooperstown. Paige noted that "there were a lot of Satchels around when I pitched," including "a couple of great managers in Bill Gatewood and Rube Foster. Someday, I hope they will be joining me here."[48]

Some of the ballplayers who came to Minnesota never left. Alex Irwin was still kicking around the Twin Cities in 1922, trying to organize a ball club called the Gray Devils. Following his involvement with the Uptowns, Johnny Davis became an umpire in St. Paul, eventually receiving an outstanding service award for his contributions to amateur baseball. He stopped working games in 1941 and died five years later at the age of 63. Davis married a white woman named Elisabeth Ebert in 1918; although they never had any children of their own, they raised Lizzy's nephew John when his mother died two days after his birth. When Davis passed away, his two granddaughters threw away much of his memorabilia, save for a team picture of the 1907 Gophers, who had brought him north in the first place. One of the last games the wily hurler ever pitched came in 1934, when at the age of 51, Davis and 54-year-old Bobby Marshall made up the battery for Minneapolis White Sox at a Twin Cities Elks convention. The "grand old timers" teamed up one final time to blank the Leslie Lawrence post team, 15–0.[49]

In January 1917, Dave Wyatt wrote in the *Indianapolis Freeman* that Michigan native William Binga, "formerly a player, manager, and A1 handler of youngsters," would be placed in charge of the Detroit club in a proposed Negro League. The circuit never materialized, however, and two years later the old hitting machine teamed up with his pal Johnny Davis on the International Harvester's squad in the St. Paul Amateur Association. Shortly thereafter, Binga moved to the western Minnesota town of Willmar where he resided for over 20 years, playing on the local ball team and taking "part in skating events." The 51-year-old Binga batted around .320 for Willmar in 1921, although he did commit 10 errors in the 17 games he played in the field. He died in Minneapolis General Hospital in October 1950 at the age of 81 and was mourned by his son Bill Freeman, his daughter-in-law, three grandchildren and "many friends."[50]

Bobby Marshall was playing competitive baseball as late as 1940 and his football career lasted nearly as long. As the first professional black quarterback in U.S. history he piloted the Minneapolis-based Deans to three consecutive Minnesota state football championships from 1907 to 1909, while throwing passes "for greater distances and with better precision than any man." On a cold, wet Thanksgiving Day in 1908, Marshall's 35-yard field goal enabled the Deans to tie the powerful Chicago Eckersalls, 4–4.[51]

By 1911 Marshall was playing left end with the Minneapolis Marines, wrapping his ribs with a padded metal washboard because the modern passing game had "brought the need of extra armour." The Marines copped the Minnesota title in 1913 and by 1915 they were playing out-of-state games. Marshall powered the squad to the Twin City championship that season, beating the St. Paul Laurels with a 40-yard drop kick with three minutes to go, "while the crowd held its breath." Earlier in the contest Marshall had twice destroyed St. Paul scoring chances, first forcing a fumble by sacking the quarterback sack deep in Minneapolis territory and then returning an interception of a sure touchdown pass 27 yards. In 1916 and 1917 the Marines were considered one of the top ten professional clubs in the country, going 15–0–1 against major competition while outscoring their opponents 455 to 48. The only blemish on their record was a 1916 Thanksgiving Day scoreless tie with the Minnesota All Stars before an overflow throng of 8,000 at Nicollet Park. The All-Stars were essentially the 1916 Minnesota Gophers team that Walter Camp, the dean of American football writers, had dubbed the "most perfect of history."[52]

The Marines didn't field a squad in 1918 because of the influenza epidemic and several of their top players, including Marshall, defected to the Rock Island, Illinois, Independents. Marshall was named to the All American Professional team in 1919, and on October 3, 1920, he became the first African American to play in the National Football League, booting two extra points during Rock Island's 45–0 thrashing of the Muncie Flyers. Unlike the acclaim that has been bestowed upon Jackie Robinson and the other black players who integrated Major League Baseball, the NFL has yet to properly commemorate Marshall's achievement. The battle-scarred end spent the 1920 season playing on the Iron Range and later toiled for the semi-pro Minneapolis Liberties, before returning to the NFL in 1925 with the Duluth Kelleys. As he neared his 50th birthday, Marshall shifted to the less-mobile position of tackle and played for a succession of lesser Midwestern outfits until 1936, allowing that "I can't run as fast as I could, but I know where I am going better."[53]

During the first half of the 20th century, Bobby Marshall was, as Harry Davis, son of longtime catcher Lee Davis and a Twin Cities Civil Rights activist aptly noted, the "image, the mentor, and the star," of the Minnesota black community. He began coaching football in 1907 at Minneapolis Central High School, and was also an assistant at the University of Minnesota, before becoming the head man at Parker College in Winnebago during the fall of 1909. Marshall later coached football and boxing at the Phyllis Wheatley settlement house in Minneapolis, tutored Golden Gloves fighters, refereed youth football, and was honored by the Big Brothers program in 1936.[54]

Although he never really could "throw off" his love of sports, Marshall worked 39 years in the State Grain Inspection Department, where he was said to have put to good use the "aggressive methods which won renown upon the athletic fields." Minnesota Governor Luther Youngdahl was the keynote speaker at his testimonial dinner in 1950, which was attended by 600 people including U of M coaching legend Bernie Bierman. In recognition of his many achievements, the Minneapolis Millers granted him a lifetime pass to their games, which he loved attending, despite years of being shunned by Organized Baseball.[55]

Bobby Marshall loved games of all kinds, once commenting that the drive to win was "what I live on." Sometimes, however, life got in the way. Prior to Minnesota's big game with Chicago in 1906, Marshall had to pass two exams for "unremoved conditions," before he was allowed to play. In 1918 Bobby married Irene Knott, an attractive young woman from Montana, 20 years his junior, but their union was to be filled with sadness. In June 1939 Marshall was granted a divorce from his wife on the "grounds of cruel and inhuman treatment and infidelity." The couple, who had three children "approaching maturity," at the time, eventually reconciled.[56]

During the 1950s Marshall was stricken with Alzheimer's disease, probably due to absorbing over forty years of bone-crunching hits on the athletic field. After several instances of forgetting his car at Millers games and riding a bus home instead, wealthy U of M alumni hired a limousine to transport the old first baseman to the contests. In July 1958 Marshall's 35-year-old son Billy, a former Gold Glove champion, dropped dead from heart failure on Keller Golf Course in St. Paul, while playing a round with his friends. Bobby Marshall, who had been in failing health for at least three years, entered a state hospital a few weeks later and died there on August 27, at the age of 78.[57]

Once called "one of America's greatest all-around athletes," by Minneapolis sportswriter George Barton, Marshall's demise was greeted by little fanfare in the Twin City or national press. His spectacular gridiron achievements were finally acknowledged in 1971, when he was posthumously named to the College Football Hall of Fame. Twenty years later, Marshall was among the inaugural class inducted into the University of Minnesota's Athletic Hall of Fame. In December 1999 the *Minneapolis Star-Tribune* placed Marshall at number 51 in their ranking of the Top 100 Minnesota Sports figures of the 20th Century, a considerable undervaluation when one considers the wealth of his accomplishments. In a life full of defining moments, Marshall's was framed early on by the 1906 Minnesota-Chicago contest where he ran the great Walter Eckersall down from behind to prevent a game-winning touchdown. The *Chicago Tribune* led off its game story by remarking "without disparagement to the other twenty men in the game, it was Marshall against Eckersall, and the colored lad won."[58]

Billy Williams, who preceded Marshall as Minnesota's preeminent black slugger, is now primarily remembered for something he *didn't* do. In April 1902 Williams was at first base when a semi-pro squad called the Prairie Leaguers upset the Minneapolis Millers, 4–3, at Lexington Park. After twice flying out to deep right field Williams singled to ignite the busher's three-run eighth inning rally and later came around to score the tying run. After the game a scout offered the "light complexioned" first baseman a contract to play for Ned Hanlon, then manager of the National League Brooklyn Superbas, but he turned it down. Just one year earlier, Hanlon's protégé John McGraw also tried to circumvent the color line when he signed the Columbia Giants Charlie Grant to his American League Baltimore Orioles squad, but he was ultimately unsuccessful in his attempt to pass the second baseman off as a Cherokee Indian. In 1904 McGraw reportedly asked the "aquiline nosed, straight haired" Williams to attempt a similar subterfuge, but he again refused, saying, "I am a Negro. I am proud of my race and wouldn't masquerade as an Indian for all the money in the world."[59]

Minnesota Governor-elect John Johnson was so taken by Williams that he hired him in 1905 to be his personal clerk for the then respectable sum of $900 a year. Williams, who previously served in a similar role with "Happy John" Lind, greatly impressed his new boss by designing a number of intricate book cases to store the governor's documents. Williams and the sports enthusiast Johnson were known to hold "many conferences over the prospects in the leagues." State officials would also go to the former Mechanic Arts star "for consul" before a big football game, as he had correctly predicted the outcome of the Minnesota-Wisconsin showdown five years in a row.[60]

Billy Williams was known for "making friends wherever he goes," and was dubbed the "prince of personality." He once so wowed a visiting party from Japan's Waseda University during a tour of the state capitol, that they asked him to coach their baseball team. Williams politely declined the offer, holding on to his position in the governor's office even after Johnson's premature death in 1909. Democrat and Republican executives alike "became so used to him, that they never thought of reappointing him." Whenever an issue arose concerning the Minnesota black community, Williams was "consulted before any actual procedure takes place." By using his vacation time during the summer, the "governor's messenger" kept his baseball career going for 22 years. In 1910 "hitting as well as ever," Williams occupied first base for the Sauk Rapids nine and toured the Dakotas with the Twin City All-Stars.[61]

The *Minneapolis Spokesman* feted Williams in 1945, after he had served in his post for 40 years. At the same time the paper equated his position to that of a mere receptionist and pointed out that "had he been white, we believe he would have long ago have been elected to important posts in the state government." Williams retired in 1957 after 52 years on the job. He had been the executive aide to 14 successive governors, and personally met with Presidents Taft, Wilson, Harding, Coolidge, Roosevelt (Franklin), and Truman. After an illness of almost 18 months, he passed away in November 1963 at the age of 86. The flags on all Minnesota government buildings were ordered to be flown at half mast in his honor, and seven of the state's governors attended his funeral.[62]

In 1902 Billy Williams was offered a contract by Brooklyn manager Ned Hanlon to play in the National League, but he turned it down. (*St. Paul Appeal*, May 17, 1902; Minnesota State Historical Society, St. Paul)

Billy Williams wasn't the only blackballer to make his mark on Minnesota politics. Even though he was a Gopher for only a short period of time, Sam Ransom became a major player in the local civil rights movement. The old Hyde Park star liked St. Paul so much that made it his home after his stint with Daddy Reid's squad, taking a job as a doorman at a local men's club. During the autumn he coached football, mentoring Nashville's Meharry College to black southern championships in 1910 and 1911, before moving on to oversee the "crack Lane College eleven" in Jackson, Mississippi. Ever the optimist, Ransom reported that there was great progress being made in the "advancement for negro people" below the Mason-Dixon Line.[63]

When the United States entered the First World War in 1917, Ransom attempted to qualify for the officer training program at St. Paul's Fort Snelling, but was turned down. He instead went back to Chicago, enlisting as a private in the Illinois Eighth Infantry where his "keen mentality, resourcefulness, and ability to lead men" soon advanced him to the rank of sergeant. Ransom's regiment was one of the first African American units to see action in France, and he was cited for bravery after leading a successful raid on a heavily defended German position. In November 1918, Ransom, who had risen through the ranks "from the trenches up" all the way to first lieutenant, was wounded in action in a battle outside of Leon, and was awarded the Purple Heart.[64]

After the war, Ransom went back to St. Paul looking for "a job with a future," and landed a position as a post office clerk. He became an organizer for the local branch of the NAACP, and in March 1942 he was named by Minnesota's "Boy Wonder" Governor Harold Stassen to serve as a major on the state's Defense Force. It was initially hoped that Ransom's appointment was the "opening wedge" in a movement to desegregate the United States home militia units, but Stassen insisted "it has no effect on that matter," and he angrily terminated an interview when a black reporter told him, "That's what I was afraid of." When asked if his new position was for a "Jim Crow outfit," Ransom replied that he was working "for all the citizens, and not for any particular race group."[65]

Not all of Minnesota's citizens were pleased with Ransom's efforts on their behalf. In May 1944, Ransom's wife Queenie, while out selling poppies for the American Legion, was refused service by the St. Paul café she had been standing in front of for three hours. Ransom went back to the establishment three days later, shortly after two white members of the NAACP's Legal Committee had been waited on at the café's counter. Ransom also sat down at the counter and after several minutes was informed by a man who emerged from the kitchen that "we do not serve colored people here." When Ransom asked him if he knew that there was a federal law against discrimination, the man replied that he did. Ransom then asked a waitress who had turned on her heels back to the kitchen upon his arrival, who or where the owner was. She told him that she did not know, but it didn't matter because "you are not going to be served." The major then left the restaurant and when asked, the woman informed the two undercover NAACP investigators that she never waited on blacks "And we don't serve them beer, either, because white people don't want to drink out of the same glasses or eat out of the same plates, and we can not afford to throw them away."[66]

A warrant was then issued by the Ramsey County Attorney for the arrest of the man who had refused to serve Ransom, the café's owner and fellow World War One vet, Anton Switek. During his court appearance Switek avowed that "he liked colored people," but that Ransom and his wife were turned away because the white customers had complained of their presence. The presiding judge asked the major what he thought Switek's punishment should be; after stating, "I have no animosity toward this man," Ransom suggested a six-month suspended sentence in the county work house and a $100 fine. Ransom also refuted Switek's claim about his customer's disapproval by noting, "There were no complaints, because you testified you had not served any colored people."[67]

Ransom retired from the United States Postal Service in 1953 after 32 years of service. When the *St. Paul Pioneer Press* interviewed him at the time, the "always civic minded" mailman humbly admitted that he had also been a member of Minnesota's first Interracial Commission, a Masonic grand master, a commander of an American Legion Post, as well as an active leader in the Pilgrim Baptist Church. He died in St. Paul in February 1970 at the age of 86, and was interred in Fort Snelling National Cemetery, alongside many of the soldiers the Army prevented him from leading.[68]

The physical landscape of the Twin Cities had dramatically changed since Sammy Ransom first arrived there to play in 1907. The saloon and city block where Daddy Reid once poured drinks had been razed long ago. The Downtown Park was abandoned after the 1910 season, with a large bakery built on the site. Nicollet Park was torn down after the Millers final game in 1955 to be replaced by a Northwestern National Bank building. Lexington Park gave way to a Red Owl Grocery Store after the Saints moved into newer digs in 1957. Three years after Ransom's death, 87-year-old Thomas "Lefty" Pangburn breathed his last

Samuel Ransom came to St. Paul to play for the Gophers in 1907, and liked the city so much that he stayed for the next 63 years. (Chicago Historical Museum, SDN-001508)

in Elizabeth, Pennsylvania, and like the places they had played in, the St. Paul Gophers were gone.[69]

In July 1942 Commissioner of Baseball Kennesaw Mountain Landis made the ridiculous and blatantly untrue assertion that there was no rule, "formal or informal, or any understanding, unwritten, subterranean or sub-anything," preventing blacks from playing in the majors. *Minneapolis Tribune* sportswriter George Barton wrote a lengthy follow-up column that, while questioning the sincerity of Landis' remarks, also quoted an unnamed local black minister who contended that African Americans "had no desire" to play big league ball if they were not wanted:

> Billy Williams and Bob Marshall played with white teams in the northwest. But I believe both will agree with me that they would not have accepted offers from teams in organized baseball because they are too intelligent and have too much pride to court humiliation from white players in major and minor leagues.[70]

Barton's article was roundly denounced by the Twin Cities black community. Calling his opinions "poppycock," the *Minneapolis Spokesman* noted that Barton had used a photograph of Bobby Marshall in his piece, but didn't bother to interview him. The *Spokesman* also observed that both Williams and Marshall had been "robbed of thousands of dollars" because of organized baseball's prejudiced attitudes, and that "barring one-tenth of the country's population from full democratic participation in it is something of which we should all be ashamed." Barton wrote back to the paper asking for forgiveness, although still insisting that he was only echoing the thoughts of "prominent Negroes," and that he counted Williams, Marshall, and Sam Ransom among his "dearest friends."[71]

On April 11, 1961, nearly 20 years after George Barton's column appeared, center fielder Lenny Green stepped into the batter's box at Yankee Stadium to face Whitey Ford. In doing so the 27-year-old from Detroit became the first African American to play for a major league team representing Minnesota. The Twins experienced great success on the field during their first ten years in the Twin Cities—a 887–730 (.548) record, two division titles, and an American League pennant, primarily because of black players like Green, Earl Battey, Zoilo Versalles, Vic Power, Tony Oliva, Jim Grant, Cesar Tovar, and Rod Carew.[72]

The Twins also drew well on the prairie — the club averaged more than 1.3 million fans annually during their first decade in Minnesota, and twice led the American League in attendance during that span. Their owner seemed to believe that this was due to the racial makeup of the area rather than the team's good play. During a Waseca Lions Club function in September 1978, Calvin Griffith made several ill-advised and controversial remarks about his players and the Minnesota community in general. Speaking in the town that George Wilson and Billy Holland had helped put on the map, Griffith admitted that the real reason that he relocated his team from Washington, D.C., to Minnesota was "when I found you only had 15,000 blacks here. Black people don't go to ball games, but they'll fill up a rassling ring and put up a chant that will scare you to death. We came here because you've good, hard working white people here."[73]

Unfortunately for the 66-year-old Griffith, *Minneapolis Tribune* reporter Nick Coleman was in attendance at the event with his father-in-law, and managed to write down many of the owner's bon mots. Calvin's charges were understandably upset when Coleman's article on the event appeared in the *Tribune* a few days later, with outfielder "Disco" Danny Ford stating that it was going to be "a burden" for black players to put on the Twins uniform. Seven-time American League batting champ Rod Carew, whom Griffith had called a "damn fool" for accepting less money to stay with the club, angrily retorted, "I'm not going to be a nigger on his plantation," which forced an off-season trade to the California Angels. Griffith responded to the ensuing critical firestorm by positing that he was just trying to be funny and added, "Racism is a thing of the past. Why do we have colored ballplayers on our club? If you don't have them, you're not going to have a club."[74]

Fittingly enough, when the Twins won their World Series titles in 1987 and 1991, they were powered by Kirby Puckett, a black centerfielder from the south side of Chicago. During the 1997 season and again in 2005, the Minnesota squad paid homage to the Negro Leagues by donning the Gophers navy-blue and white uniforms. The Twins 24-year-old black hurler LaTroy Hawkins thought his July 1997 start "was kind of neat. It was of ironic that I got to pitch today." Less ironic was Hawkins' pitching line, as he gave up six runs in less than five innings while the Cleveland Indians pummeled the Twins/Gophers, 12–5, at the Metrodome in Minneapolis.[75]

Although they were only in existence for five years, the St. Paul Gophers won nearly four hundred and fifty ball games, while spreading the gospel of blackball to places it had never been before. Through their generative spirit the Gophers were also able to pass along the knowledge and experience they had gathered to a new wave of black ballplayers. The *Indianapolis Freeman* wrote in their 1910 pre-season profile that the St. Paul nine had "established for themselves, their race, and city a reputation and record never before equaled."

St. Paul Gophers (May 22, 1909). Back Row (L-R): Eugene Milliner (LF), Julius London (P), George "Rat" Johnson (C), Phil Reid (Owner), Felix Wallace (2B), William Binga (RF), Bobby Marshall (1B). Front Row (L-R): Sherman Barton (CF), Arthur McDougall (SS), Archie Pate (P), William McMurray (3B), Dick Garrison (P). (Courtesy of the National Baseball Hall of Fame Library, Cooperstown, NY)

The *Freeman* also postulated that the Gophers were the most "sensational" team that the great Northwest had ever seen:

> ... for with their superb play, marvelous fielding and clever base running, along with some of the brainiest tricks known to baseball, they have startled the entire fandom throughout the Western States and further evidenced the fact that the Negro race stands for clean sport and is equal, if not superior, to his white brother in athletics.[76]

There should be little dispute that the Gophers and the Keystones were ball teams of major league quality. Since 1986, approximately 30 percent of the men who have played major league baseball have been black. Using this percentage, and keeping in mind that baseball, rather than basketball or football, was once the sport de jour for African Americans, it is logical to assume that *at least* 110 black ball players (about ten blackball clubs) would have annually populated the early 20th century big leagues if they had been allowed to. Both Minnesota teams easily ranked among the top ten black squads during each year of their existences.[77]

The St. Paul Gophers legacy is undeniable. A century after they last played, faded postcards of the team sell for several hundreds of dollars in online auctions. In 2007 the Nike footwear company, "continuing their tribute to the Negro leagues of Baseball," introduced a line of brown leather sneakers bearing the team's insignia. The amount of money that the multinational conglomerate charged for a pair of the St. Paul Colored Gophers Nike Air Max 90's would have undoubtedly paid the monthly salary for at least one of Daddy Reid's players.[78]

Although none of the Gophers are enshrined in the National Baseball Hall of Fame, a 1909 photograph of the team is part of the permanent collection at Cooperstown. The image was taken in May of that year after they had just trounced the Hibbing Colts, 17–2, and reveals a weary bunch of barnstormers along with a justifiably proud Phil Reid. Although most of the St. Paul Gophers' accomplishments have been forgotten, every pitch they threw and every run they scored brought clarity to America's social landscape, one game at a time.[79]

Appendix I

Game Chronologies and Team Statistics

Game Chronologies: Both the Gophers and Keystones chronologies are based on data retrieved from the *St. Paul Pioneer Press, St. Paul Dispatch, St. Paul Daily News, St. Paul Appeal, Minneapolis Tribune, Minneapolis Journal, Twin City Star, Indianapolis Freeman, New York Age,* and newspapers from all over the Upper Midwest. The use of *italics* indicates a home game. If more than one pitcher was used, the winner, if known, is indicated in **bold type**. The symbol "[ml]" denotes a minor league opponent. When more than one result was given, the score from the local paper is given and the second tally is shown in {brackets}. All the opposing teams are from Minnesota unless otherwise noted.

Team Statistics: Due to the lack of published schedules, minimal media coverage, and the loss over time of contemporary reporting, the Gophers and Keystones statistical record remains incomplete. However, many of the games they played have been accounted for, and box or line scores have survived for many of these. While the statistical record, especially the batting statistics, appears somewhat underwhelming, it must be remembered that the box scores for almost all of the Gophers and Keystones losses have survived, while many of their wins went underreported. Add to this the fact that both teams played during the height of the deadball era and that it was bad for business to run up the score on an inferior opponent. There are many recorded instances of the Gophers and Keystones putting on the brakes late in games they had salted away.

Key for batting and fielding statistics: The player's dominant position is in **bold type**. Runs and stolen bases were not always included in box scores. A small percentage of at-bat totals were estimated, based on known at-bat totals for that player. (G=Games; AB=At-Bats; H=Hits; D=Doubles; T=Triples; HR=Home Runs; BA=Batting Average; R=Runs; SB=Stolen Bases; SF=Sacrifices; PO=Putouts; A=Assists; E=Errors; FA=Fielding Average)

Key for pitching statistics: (G=Games; GS=Games Started; CG=Complete Games; IP=Innings Pitched; W=Wins; L=Losses; H=Hits; R=Runs; RPG=Runs Per Game Average; SO=Strikeouts; BB=Bases on Balls; HBP=Hit By Pitch; SH=Shutouts)

St. Paul Gophers/Twin City Gophers 1907–1911

Aggregate record in games accounted for: 376–154–11 (.705)

1907 St. Paul Gophers: Given record: 90 wins out of 106 games. Record in games accounted for: 86–17–2 (828). Captains: Walter Ball, James Smith, George Taylor.

April 7	Logan Squares at Chicago (IL)		Postponed
13	South Bend (IN) [ml]		Postponed
14	South Bend (IN) [ml]		Postponed
21	Riverviews at Chicago (IL)		L 4–6 (Ball)
27	Green Bay (WI) [ml]		Postponed
28	Green Bay (WI) [ml]		Postponed
30	Eau Claire (WI) [ml]		Postponed

Appendix I

Date	Opponent	Result
May 1	Eau Claire (WI) [ml]	W 4–2 (Horn/ **Means**)
2	Eau Claire (WI) [ml]	W 6–1 (**Ball**/ Lytle)
5	*Lund Lands at the Downtown Park, St. Paul*	Postponed
6	Calumet (MI) [ml]	L 4–5, 7 innings (Ball)
18	Lund Lands at Nicollet Park, Minneapolis	W 10–9
19	Austin-Westerns at Lexington Park, St. Paul	W 3–1 (Lytle)
20	Grand Rapids (WI)	W 6–4, 10 innings (Means)
22	Houston	W 6–2
23	Plainview	W 8–6 (Horn/ **Smith**)
24	Plainview	W 17–1 (Smith)
25	Chatfield	W 16–3, 7 innings (Means)
26	Winona	W 18–4
27	Tomah (WI)	Scheduled; no result found
28	Ontario (WI) at Wilton (WI)	W 17–1
30	Cashton (WI)	W 7–1
–	Galesville (WI)	W
31	La Crosse (WI) Athletes	Scheduled; no result found
June 1	*Lund Lands at the Downtown Park, St. Paul*	W 10–0
2	Austin-Westerns at Lexington Park, St. Paul	L 2–3 (Davis)
5	Pine Island	W 12–2
6	Kenyon	W 7–3
8	*Lund Lands at the Downtown Park, St. Paul*	W 11–7 (Lytle)
9	Winona	W 9–0
15	Minneapolis All-Stars at St. Paul	W 4–3, 12 innings (Davis)
16	Premos at St. Paul	W 8–6 (Lytle)
17	Staples	W
18	Fergus Falls	W 10–0
19	Crookston	W 13–1 (Smith)
20	Fargo (ND)	W 8–1 (Horn)
21	Fargo (ND)	W 4–2
22	Grand Forks (ND)	Scheduled; not played
23	Hibbing	W 4–0, 14 innings (Davis)
24	Hibbing	Postponed after 4 innings (T 2–2)
25	Hibbing	W 7–3 (Lytle)
26	Hibbing	L 1–5 (**Horn**/ Davis)
28	Kellogg	Cancelled
29	Minneapolis Toozes at Nicollet Park, Minneapolis	W 8–1 (Lytle)
30	Minneapolis Toozes at Minnehaha Driving Park, Minneapolis	W 6–2 (Davis)
July 1	Houston	W 12–0
2	La Crosse (WI) [ml]	W 1–0 (Davis)
4	Caledonia	W 1–0 (Horn)
5	Rushford	W 14–1 (Lytle)
10	Granite Falls	W 7–1
11	Flandreau (SD)	W 2–1
12	Flandreau (SD)	W 7–0
13	Edgerton	W 3–1 (Davis)
14	Lennox (SD)	W 5–3 (Means/ Davis)
15	Parker (SD)	W 7–0
16	Madison (SD)	W 10–0
17	Wessington Springs (SD)	W 7–0 (Means)
18	Wessington Springs (SD)	W 5–4, 10 innings (Davis)
19	Wessington Springs (SD) at Woonsocket (SD)	W 2–0
20	Webster (SD)	Postponed
21	Webster (SD) at Holmquist (SD)	W 8–6, 10 innings
22	Langford (SD)	W 4–2
23	Britton (SD)	W 23–7 (Means/ Davis)
24	Aberdeen (SD)	W 17–3 (Means)
25	Aberdeen (SD)	W 32–10 (Ransom/ Lytle)
26	Granite Falls	W 4–1
27	Sioux Falls (SD) at Luverne	W 8–0 (Lytle)
28	Sioux Falls (SD)	W 5–0 (Davis)
29	Edgerton	W 3–1 (Lytle)
30	Edgerton at Sherburn	W 6–0 (Davis)

	31	Winnebago	W 5–1
August	1	Wells	W 6–1
	2	Plainview	W 9–1 (Davis)
	3	Mazeppa	W 28–0
	4	Stillwater	T 2–2, 7 innings (Lytle)
	6	Chaska at Lester Prairie	W 8–3 (Davis)
	7	Rochester	W 12–0 (Lytle)
	8	Rochester	W 3–2 (Davis)
	10	Hibbing	W 4–3 (Lytle)
	11	Hibbing	L 2–4 (Davis)
	12	Hibbing	W 8–4 (Lytle)
	13	Hibbing	L 1–4 (Davis)
	14	Chisholm	W 9–3
	15	Eveleth	W 10–8 (Lytle)
	16	Eveleth	W 10–3
	17	Virginia	W 15–2
	18	Virginia	W 2–0 (Lytle)
	21	Watertown	W 6–5, 10 innings (**Means**/ Davis)
	22	Jordan	W 4–2 (Lytle)
	23	Alexandria	L 14–22 (Davis)
	24	Alexandria	W 13–3 (Lytle)
	25	South St. Paul	W 7–2 (Means)
	27	Hastings	W 9–2 (Means)
	28	Shakopee	W 5–0
	29	St. James	W 11–1 (Means)
	31	*Hibbing at the Downtown Park, St. Paul*	L 3–4 (Lytle)
September	1	*Hibbing at Lexington Park, St. Paul*	W 8–3 (Davis)
	2	*Hibbing at St. Paul*	L 0–6 (Lytle)
	3	*Hibbing at the Downtown Park, St. Paul*	L 0–4 (Davis)
	6	Hudson (WI)	Withdrew in first inning
	7	Osceola (WI)	L 3–4 (Means/ **Lytle**)
	8	Chaska	W 5–4 (Davis)
	12	Osage (IA)	W 10-?
		Osage (IA)	W 6–0 (Means)
	13	Leroy	W 19–3 {15–4} (Means)
	14	Decorah (IA)	W 5–4 (Lytle)
	16	Caledonia	W 5–1 (Davis)
	17	Rochester	W 5–2 (Means)
	18	Rochester	W 7–0 (Lytle)
	19	Red Wing at Zumbrota	W 5–0 (Davis)
	20	Harmony at Preston	W 5–3 (**Means**/ Davis)
	21	St. Paul Saints [ml] at the Downtown Park, St. Paul	W 1–0 (Lytle)
	22	St. Paul Saints [ml] at South St. Paul	L 3–6 (Davis)
	23	St. Paul Saints [ml] at the Downtown Park, St. Paul	W 5–3 (Foster)
	24	St. Paul Saints [ml] at the Downtown Park, St. Paul	T 4–4, 8 innings (Lytle/Davis)
	25	Osceola (WI)	L 0–5 (Lytle)
	28	Faribault at Nicollet Park, Minneapolis	L 3–10 (Davis)
	29	Faribault at Minnehaha Driving Park, Minneapolis	L 2–4 (Lytle)
October	6	Chicago Union Giants	L 4–10 (Lytle)
	13	Felix Colts at Chicago (IL)	L 0–2 (Lytle)
		Riverviews at Chicago (IL)	Scheduled; no result found

1907 St. Paul Gophers Pitching Statistics

Pitcher	G	GS	CG	IP	W	L	H	R	RPG	SO	BB	HBP	SH
Clarence Lytle	29	26	22	235	19	7	137	82	3.14	60	20	2	5
John Davis	28	22	22	221	15	7	158	79	3.21	120	14	0	5
Thomas Means	17	16	10	119	14	0	71	35	2.64	32	5	0	2
Will Horn	5	5	1	23	2	1	5	3	1.17	11	5	1	1
Walter Ball	3	3	2	23	1	2	23	12	4.69	16	8	0	0

Pitcher	G	GS	CG	IP	W	L	H	R	RPG	SO	BB	HBP	SH
James Smith	3	2	2	18	3	0	10	2	1.00	9	4	0	0
Rube Foster	1	1	1	9	1	0	5	3	3.00	10	4	0	0
Sam Ransom	1	1	0	-	-	-	-	-	-	-	-	-	-

The hit, strikeout, and bases on balls totals are based on 212 innings pitched by Davis; 181 innings pitched by Lytle; 101 innings pitched by Means; and 14 innings pitched by Horn. Wild pitches: Lytle 1; Johnny Davis 1; Foster 1; Horn 1.

1907 St. Paul Gophers Batting and Fielding Statistics

Player/Position	G	AB	H	D	T	HR	BA	R	SB	SF	PO	A	E	FA
Fred Roberts 3B/2B/SS	43	165	39	5	1	1	.236	25	5	4	48	55	20	.837
George Taylor 1B/2B/C	42	164	32	4	0	1	.195	27	6	1	387	21	9	.978
Sherman Barton CF	44	163	38	7	0	1	.233	21	5	1	64	6	4	.946
Jesse Schaeffer C/RF	39	163	48	12	2	6	.294	26	5	0	199	42	10	.920
Frank Davis SS/C	38	155	33	10	0	3	.213	25	3	0	59	103	21	.885
Clarence Lytle P/RF/LF	38	143	28	3	1	0	.195	17	5	2	35	34	5	.932
Willis Jones LF	35	134	31	6	0	0	.231	28	7	3	56	3	0	1.000
John Davis P/RF/2B	27	100	24	0	0	1	.240	10	4	1	31	39	6	.921
Sam Ransom 2B/P/RF	21	85	17	3	1	0	.200	14	3	0	36	45	8	.910
Thomas Means P/RF/LF	13	43	5	1	0	0	.116	3	0	0	7	10	0	1.000
James Smith 3B/P	11	42	9	1	0	0	.214	8	5	1	19	30	8	.860
Will Horn P/RF/1B	7	25	5	0	0	1	.200	3	2	0	11	5	1	.941
Will McMurray 2B/3B/SS/C	6	18	4	0	0	0	.222	1	0	1	16	12	1	.965
Rube Foster P/RF	2	9	1	1	0	0	.111	0	0	0	1	4	0	1.000
Dell Matthews LF	2	8	1	0	0	0	.125	1	0	0	2	0	1	.666
Dick Wallace C	2	8	2	0	0	0	.250	1	0	0	4	6	1	.909
Walter Ball P	2	7	0	0	0	0	.000	0	0	0	5	4	0	1.000
William Binga 3B	1	4	0	0	0	0	.000	0	0	0	2	1	0	1.000
Andrew Campbell C	1	4	1	0	0	0	.250	0	0	0	11	2	0	1.000
Haynes RF	1	4	0	0	0	0	.000	0	0	0	1	1	0	1.000
Harry Hyde 2B/RF	1	4	0	0	0	0	.000	0	0	0	2	2	1	.800
Albert Toney SS	1	4	1	0	0	0	.250	0	0	0	4	2	0	1.000
Bill Harkins 2B	1	3	0	0	0	0	.000	0	0	0	4	3	1	.875
Bob Marshall C	1	3	1	0	0	0	.333	0	1	0	3	0	1	.750
Johnson C	1	-	-	-	-	-	-	-	-	-	-	-	-	-

Passed Balls: Schaeffer 6; Marshall 1.

1908 St. Paul Gophers: Given record: 97–26–1. Record in games accounted for: 87–28–1 (.754) Captain: George "Rat" Johnson.

April 26	Alamos at Chicago (IL)	Postponed
29	Duluth [ml] at Aurora (IL)	W 9–3 (Petway)
30	Rockford (IL) [ml]	L 1–7 (Gatewood)
May 1	Madison (WI) [ml]	Postponed
2	Madison (WI) [ml]	T 5–5, 14 innings (Lytle/Gatewood)
3	Madison (WI) [ml]	W 8–7 (Petway/**Gatewood**)
4	Oshkosh (WI) [ml]	L 6–8 (Gatewood)
5	Oshkosh (WI) [ml]	Postponed
6	Oshkosh (WI) [ml]	L 1–6, 7 innings (Petway)
11	Grand Rapids (WI)	W 10–0, 5 innings (Lytle)
12	Arcadia (WI)	W 10–0 (Petway)
13	Galesville (WI)	W 6–0 {5–0} (Gatewood)
15	Spring Grove	W 8–2
16	Harmony	W 9–4
17	Viroqua (WI)	W 4–3 (Lytle/ Petway)
18	Viroqua (WI)	Postponed
19	Houston	W 9–2 {6–2} (Lytle)
20	Dodge Center	W 9–4 (Gatewood)
21	Rochester	Postponed
22	Pine Island	W 10–0
23	Lund Lands at Nicollet Park, Minneapolis	W 6–0 (Gatewood)
24	Lund Lands at Minnehaha Driving Park, Minneapolis	Postponed
26	Lake Crystal	W 8–1 (Petway)
27	Winnebago	W 3–0 (Lytle)
29	Owatonna	W 4–0
30	*Austin-Westerns at the Downtown Park, St. Paul*	L 4–5 (Gatewood)
31	*Austin-Westerns at Lexington Park, St. Paul*	W 2–1 (Petway)
June 3	Hastings	W 8–6 (Lytle)
4	New Richland	W 5–0, 10 innings (Gatewood)
5	Le Seuer at Mankato	W 9–8
6	Lake Crystal at Mankato	W 9–0
7	Stillwater	W 11–0 (Gatewood)
9	Cumberland (WI)	W 5–0 (Lytle)
10	Hayward (WI)	W 7–1 (**Petway**/ Wallace)
11	Rice Lake (WI)	W 14–0
13	Belle Plaine	W 9–3 (Lytle)
14	Lund Lands at Minnehaha Driving Park, Minneapolis	L 0–1 (Gatewood)
16	*Lund Lands at the Downtown Park, St. Paul*	L 5–7 (Lytle)
17	*Lund Lands at the Downtown Park, St. Paul*	W 3–0 (Gatewood)
18	Long Prairie	W 3–1 (Lytle)
19	Long Prairie	W 3–1, 7 innings (Petway/ F. **Davis**)
20	Staples	W 4–1 (Lytle)
21	Staples	W 10–7 (Gatewood)
22	Island Park (Breckenridge-Wahpeton, ND)	W 6–1 (F. Davis)
23	Island Park (Breckenridge-Wahpeton, ND)	Postponed
24	Island Park (Breckenridge-Wahpeton, ND) at Graceville	W 8–5 (Lytle)
25	Redwood Falls	W 6–2
26	Redwood Falls	W 6–1
27	Arlington	Postponed
28	Red Wing	W 5–0 (Lytle)
30	Cloquet	W 6–0 (Lytle)
July 1	Hibbing at Duluth	L 2–4 (Gatewood)
2	Hibbing at Duluth	L 6–7 (Lytle)
3	Hibbing	W 4–1 (Gatewood)
4	Hibbing	L 6–7 (Lytle/ **Gatewood**)
5	Hibbing	L 4–7 (Lytle)
6	Hibbing	L 4–6 (Gatewood)

Appendix I

	7	Eveleth	W 15–3 (Lytle)
	8	Eveleth	L 6–9 (Gatewood)
	9	Hibbing	W 7–5 (**Lytle**/ Gatewood)
	10	Virginia	W 4–0 (Gatewood)
	11	Virginia	W 4–1 (Lytle)
	12	Virginia	L 0–4 (Gatewood)
	14	*Austin-Westerns at the Downtown Park, St. Paul*	L 5–6 (Lytle/ **Gatewood**)
	15	Hastings	L 4–7 (Lytle/ F. Davis)
	16	*Austin-Westerns at the Downtown Park, St. Paul*	W 7–4 (Gatewood)
	19	Faribault	W 7–5 (Gatewood)
	20	Renville	W 4–3 (Lytle)
	21	Cottonwood	W 8–0
	22	Luverne	W 6–3
	23	Flandreau (SD)	W
	24	Flandreau (SD)	W 5–4
	27	Jasper	W 3–0 (Lytle)
	29	Pipestone	W 10–6, 7 innings
	30	Madison (SD)	L 3–4, 12 innings (Gatewood)
August 1	Parker (SD)	W 6–1
	2	Lennox (SD)	W 3–2 (Gatewood)
	3	Sheldon (IA)	W 20–12
	4	Rock Rapids (IA)	W 4–2
	5	Slayton	W 3–2 (Gatewood/ Lytle)
	6	Jackson	W 2–1 (Gatewood)
	7	Winnebago	W 12–3 (Knight)
	8	Austin	W 7–2
	9	Albert Lea	W 2–0 (Gatewood)
	10	Northwood (IA)	W 9–3
	11	Osage (IA)	Postponed
	12	Cresco (IA)	L 1–3 (Lytle)
	13	Calmar (IA)	W 15–3
	14	*National Indians at Fennimore (WI)*	W 6–1
	16	Caledonia	W 11–2 (Lytle)
	17	Spring Grove	L 1–4 (F. Davis)
	18	Wycoff	W 22–6
	19	Rochester	W 8–6 (Lytle)
	20	Rochester	W 9–1 (Gatewood)
	21	Waseca	W 3–2 (Lytle)
	22	Lindstrom	W 8–3 (Gatewood)
	23	Stillwater	W 22–2 (Gatewood/ **Lytle**)
	24	River Falls (WI)	Scheduled; did not appear
	26	*Hibbing at Lexington Park, St. Paul*	L 3–6 (Gatewood)
	27	*Minneapolis Keystones at the Downtown Park, St. Paul*	W 6–2 (Gatewood)
	28	*Hibbing at St. Paul*	W 5–0 (Foster)
	29	*Hibbing at the Downtown Park, St. Paul*	W 8–2 (Lytle)
	30	Minneapolis Keystones at Minnehaha Driving Park, Minneapolis	L 2–9 (Gatewood)
	31	*Hibbing at St. Paul*	Scheduled; no result found but it was reported that the Gophers lost
September 1	*Hibbing at St. Paul*	W 3–2
	4	Watertown	W 14–7
	5	*Prairie Island Indians at the Downtown Park, St. Paul*	W 13–5 (Johnson)
	6	Faribault	W 10–2 (Gatewood)
	7	Janesville	W 6–1 (Wallace)
	8	Albert Lea at Fairmont	W 8–6
	10	Austin-Westerns at Garden City	W 9–6
	11	Austin-Westerns at Garden City	W 5–4
	13	Red Wing	L 3–5 (Horn)
	15	St. Paul Saints [ml] at Winnebago	L 7–8, 10 innings (Gatewood)
	16	St. Paul Saints [ml] at Winnebago	L 2–5 (Gatewood)
	17	Harmony at Preston	L 7–8, 10 innings (Lytle/**Gatewood**)

	18	Black River Falls (WI) at Preston	W 17–2
	19	St. Paul Saints [ml] at the Downtown Park, St. Paul	L 2–9 (Gatewood)
	20	Minneapolis Keystones at Minnehaha Driving Park, Minneapolis	L 3–4 (Lytle)
	21	*Minneapolis Keystones at the Downtown Park, St. Paul*	W 6–3 (Horn/ **Gatewood**)
	22	Minneapolis Keystones at Nicollet Park, Minneapolis	W 6–0 (Lytle)
	23	Wright County All-Stars at Howard Lake	W 6–1
	24	Shakopee	W 10–1
	26	Osceola (WI) at Amery (WI)	W 5–0, 5 innings (Lytle)
	27	Osceola (WI) at St. Croix Falls (WI)	L 2–4 (Gatewood)
	30	Minneapolis Keystones at Rochester	Cancelled
October	1	Minneapolis Keystones at Winona	Cancelled
	2	Minneapolis Keystones at La Crosse (WI)	Cancelled
	3	La Crosse (WI)	W 7–6 (Gatewood)
	4	La Crosse (WI)	L 1–4 (Jones)

1908 St. Paul Gophers Pitching Statistics

Pitcher	G	GS	CG	IP	W	L	H	R	RPG	SO	BB	HBP	SH
Bill Gatewood	43	37	36	333	21	17	137	136	3.67	114	55	12	7
Clarence Lytle	39	37	30	312	28	6	142	85	2.45	71	40	5	12
Howard Petway	7	7	4	51	5	1	23	12	2.11	16	11	1	1
Frank Davis	3	2	2	26	2	1	14	6	2.08	8	1	0	0
Will Horn	2	2	1	10	0	1	8	7	6.30	8	0	0	0
Rube Foster	1	9	1	9	1	0	0	0	0.00	–	2	1	1
Nathan Knight	1	1	1	9	1	0	–	3	3.00	–	–	–	0
Felix Wallace	1	1	1	9	1	0	4	1	1.00	–	–	–	0
George Johnson	1	1	1	8	1	0	3	5	4.44	8	8	0	0
Willis Jones	1	1	0	8	0	1	–	4	4.50	–	–	–	0

The hit, strikeout, and bases on balls totals are based on 246 innings pitched by Gatewood; 208 innings pitched by Lytle; and 17 innings pitched by Davis. Wild pitches: Lytle 3; Gatewood 2; Frank Davis 1.

1908 St. Paul Gophers Batting and Fielding Statistics

Player/Position	G	AB	H	D	T	HR	BA	R	SB	SF	PO	A	E	FA
Frank Davis SS/P	40	170	38	6	1	0	.223	24	11	4	57	73	18	.880
George Johnson C/1B/P	40	155	37	6	0	3	.238	20	3	12	235	39	10	.964
Felix Wallace 2B/3B/P	39	152	49	10	1	0	.322	24	10	0	84	80	17	.906
Sherman Barton CF/2B	38	137	36	7	2	0	.262	12	14	1	50	7	3	.950
Willis Jones LF/2B/P	39	129	38	7	1	0	.294	13	11	2	55	4	2	.967
Clarence Lytle P/RF/CF	37	127	29	1	0	2	.228	13	8	2	33	43	4	.950
Bill Gatewood P/RF/1B/2B/3B	36	123	21	2	2	4	.170	19	4	0	58	47	11	.905
Haywood Rose 1B/C	33	114	29	6	0	0	.254	13	5	2	258	9	21	.967
Will McMurray 3B/2B/RF	33	104	25	7	1	2	.240	12	8	1	38	44	20	.803
Harry Boone RF/2B	7	26	3	0	1	0	.115	0	0	0	12	0	1	.923
Howard Petway P/RF	7	23	2	0	0	0	.086	0	1	0	1	5	1	.857

Player/Position	G	AB	H	D	T	HR	BA	R	SB	SF	PO	A	E	FA
Will Horn P/LF/1B	2	8	1	0	0	0	.125	1	0	0	11	0	0	1.000
Jesse Schaeffer RF/SS/C	2	8	1	0	0	0	.125	2	1	0	4	3	4	.636
Williams 3B/RF	2	8	1	0	0	0	.125	0	0	0	2	4	3	.666
Tom Means RF/CF	2	6	0	0	0	0	.000	1	0	0	0	0	1	.000
Willie Green RF	1	6	1	0	0	0	.166	0	0	0	0	0	0	.000
William Binga 3B	1	5	3	0	0	0	.600	1	0	0	4	2	1	.857
Eugene Barton LF	1	4	1	1	0	0	.250	0	0	0	0	0	1	.000
Botts RF	1	4	1	0	0	0	.250	0	0	0	0	0	0	.000
Rube Foster P	1	4	1	0	0	0	.250	0	0	0	0	0	0	.000
Sam Ransom 1B	1	4	0	0	0	0	.000	0	0	0	10	0	0	1.000
Ralph Nelson RF	1	3	0	0	0	0	.000	0	0	0	0	0	0	.000
Nathan Knight P	1	-	-	-	-	-	-	-	-	-	-	-	-	-

Passed Balls: Johnson 3.

1909 St. Paul Gophers: Reported record: 86 wins out of 106 games played. Record in games accounted for: 75–27–3(.728). Captain: Felix Wallace.

May 8	La Crosse (WI) [ml]		L 3–8 (Garrison)
9	La Crosse (WI) [ml]		L 2–4 (London)
10	La Crosse (WI) [ml]		L 9–10 (Pate)
17	Kenyon		W 6–0 (London)
18	Kenyon		W reported; no result found
19	Kenyon		W reported; no result found
20	Hibbing		L 2–11 (**Pate**/ London)
21	Hibbing		W 5–4, 10 innings (Garrison)
22	Hibbing		W 17–2 (Pate)
23	Hibbing		L 6–16 (London)
24	Hibbing		W 8–2 (Garrison)
25	Moose Lake		W 12–10
27	*H.P.Conrads at the Downtown Park, St. Paul*		W 11–0 (London)
28	*H.P.Conrads at the Downtown Park, St. Paul*		W
30	Faribault		L 8–9 (Pate)
31	Faribault		T 3–3, 8 innings (London) Faribault claimed forfeit win
June 3	New Richland		W 1–0 (London)
7	*H.P.Conrads at the Downtown Park, St. Paul*		L 2–4 (Pate)
8	H.P.Conrads at Premo Park, St. Paul		W 11–8 (London)
8	Waterville		W 9–2
10	Sherburn		W 9–0
11	*Hibbing at the Downtown Park, St. Paul*		W 9–8
12	*Hibbing at the Downtown Park, St. Paul*		W 5–4, 11 innings (Garrison)
13	Renville		W 8–1 (London)
14	Renville		W 9–1 (Taylor)
15	Redwood Falls		W 5–4 (Garrison)
16	Redwood Falls		W 13–0 (London)
18	Hankinson (ND)		L 2–4 (Garrison)
19	Groton (SD) at Cogswell (ND)		W 4–2
20	Fargo (ND)		W 3–0 (London)
21	Hope (ND)		W 11–1 (Garrison)
	Hope (ND)		W 6–3 (Taylor)

	22	Alexandria	T 1–1, 9 innings (London)
		Alexandria	L 1–2 (Garrison)
	23	Alexandria	W 7–2 (Taylor)
	24	Sauk Center	W 8–1
	25	Long Prairie	L 0–4 (**Garrison**/ Taylor)
	26	Long Prairie	W 7–0 (London)
	27	Bemidji	W 16–1 (Taylor)
	28	Bemidji	W 10–5 (Garrison)
	29	Grand Rapids	W 6–3 (London)
	30	Grand Rapids	W 6–3, 6 innings (Garrison)
July	1	Hibbing	W 5–3 (Taylor)
	2	Hibbing	L 2–3 (London)
	3	Hibbing	L 4–8 (Garrison)
	4	Hibbing	W 5–1 (Taylor)
	5	Hibbing	L 2–3
		Hibbing	L 0–8
	6	Hibbing at Eveleth	W 8–1 (Wallace)
	7	Eveleth	W 17–10, 11 innings (Garrison/**Taylor**)
	9	Hayward (WI)	W 11–8 (London)
	10	Ashland (WI)	W 8–4 (Garrison)
	11	Ashland (WI)	W 9–0, 5 innings (Taylor)
	13	Bessemer (MI)	W 11–3
		Bessemer (MI)	W 3–2, 10 innings (**Garrison**/ London)
	14	Rhinelander (WI)	W 5–2, 5 innings (McMurray)
	15	Barron (WI)	W 14–5
	16	Cumberland (WI)	W 10–0
	17	Mankato	W 7–1 (Davis)
	18	Mankato	L 1–3
	20	Alexandria	W 6–5 (**London**/ Davis)
	21	Alexandria	W 10–2 (Taylor)
	22	Alexandria	L 0–1 (Davis)
	24	*Minneapolis Keystones at the Downtown Park, St. Paul*	W 5–2 (Davis)
	25	Minneapolis Keystones at Nicollet Park, Minneapolis	W 8–4 (Taylor)
	26	*Leland Giants at the Downtown Park, St. Paul*	W 10–9, 11 innings (London/ **Taylor**)
	27	*Leland Giants at the Downtown Park, St. Paul*	L 1–8 (Davis)
	28	*Leland Giants at the Downtown Park, St. Paul*	L 1–5 (Taylor)
	29	*Leland Giants at the Downtown Park, St. Paul*	W 4–3 (**London**/ Davis)
	30	*Leland Giants at the Downtown Park, St. Paul*	W 3–2 (Taylor)
	31	Lindstrom	W 18–1 (London)
August	1	*Minneapolis Keystones at Lexington Park, St. Paul*	W 8–3 (Davis/ Wallace/ **London**)
	8	Hartland	W 11–2 (Davis)
	9	Houston	W 8–4
	10	New Albin (IA)	L 2–3
	12	Logan Squares at Fennimore (WI)	L 1–6 (Taylor)
	13	Logan Squares at Fennimore (WI)	L 1–4 (Davis)
	14	Oelwein (IA)	W 14–0 (London)
	15	Oelwein (IA)	W 3–0 (London)
	16	Manchester (IA)	W 8–3 (Davis)
	17	Grundy Center (IA)	W 8–0
	19	Eldora (IA)	L 1–2
	20	Buxton (IA) Wonders	W 5–0 (Taylor)
	21	Buxton (IA) Wonders	W 13–2 (London)
	22	Buxton (IA) Wonders	W 4–2, 10 innings (Davis)
	23	Hiteman (IA)	L
	24	Leland Giants at Buxton (IA)	W 2–0
	29	Dysart (IA)	W 9–1 (London)
	30	Charles City (IA)	L 5–6 (Davis)
	31	Clear Lake (IA) at Mason City (IA)	W 9–0 (Taylor)
September	2	Minneapolis Keystones at Preston	Postponed

3	Harmony at Preston	W 3–2 (Davis/ **London**)
4	Charles City (IA)	W 3–0 (Taylor)
5	Charles City (IA) at Lawler (IA)	W 6–1 (London)
6	Austin	Scheduled; no result found
10	Winnebago	W 5–0
11	Sherburn	W 3–2 (London)
12	Sherburn	W 3–0, 10 innings (Davis)
13	Sherburn at Jackson	W
14	Sherburn at Fairmont	Postponed
18	Shakopee	W 14–0
19	H.P.Conrads at West Side Park, St. Paul	W 6–5 (Taylor/ **Davis**)
20	*Minneapolis Keystones at the Downtown Park, St. Paul*	W 9–1 (Taylor)
21	*Minneapolis Keystones at the Downtown Park, St. Paul*	Postponed
22	Redwood Falls	L 2–7
23	Redwood Falls	W 8–0, 5 innings
24	Redwood Falls	L 4–5
25	Young America	W 5–1 (Davis)
26	*All-Stars at Lexington Park, St. Paul*	W 5–2 (Taylor)
October 3	Artesians at Chicago (IL)	T 6–6, 10 innings (Pangburn)
10	Elgin (IL)	L 7–15 (Ball)

1909 St. Paul Gophers Pitching Statistics

Pitcher	G	GS	CG	IP	W	L	H	R	RPG	SO	BB	HBP	SH
Julius London	29	25	21	213	21	3	108	61	2.57	49	18	0	8
John Taylor	22	19	18	177	18	2	97	36	1.83	93	23	3	5
John Davis	18	15	13	141	10	4	70	37	2.36	56	10	0	2
Dick Garrison	15	15	11	121	9	5	98	62	4.61	37	16	4	0
Archie Pate	5	5	4	35	1	4	43	25	6.43	7	10	0	0
Felix Wallace	2	1	1	11	1	0	5	1	0.82	–	–	–	0
Tom Pangburn	1	1	1	10	0	0	8	5	4.50	7	0	–	0
Walter Ball	1	1	0	7	0	1	17	15	19.22	1	3	–	0
Will McMurray	1	1	0	5	1	0	–	2	3.60	–	–	–	0

The hit, strikeout, and bases on balls totals are based on 177 innings pitched by London; 150 innings pitched by Taylor; 115 innings pitched by Davis; and 112 innings pitched by Garrison. Wild pitches: Davis 2; Garrison 1.

1909 St. Paul Gophers Batting and Fielding Statistics

Player/Position	G	AB	H	D	T	HR	BA	R	SB	SF	PO	A	E	FA
Felix Wallace 2B/C/SS/3B/P	37	165	45	6	2	1	.272	20	4	2	89	84	10	.945
Sherman Barton CF	38	159	44	15	2	2	.276	18	1	5	67	8	2	.974
William Binga RF/3B	38	156	45	3	2	0	.288	19	5	2	41	32	11	.869
Eugene Milliner LF/RF	37	156	51	7	6	2	.326	21	2	2	44	10	6	.900
Will McMurray C/LF/3B/P	37	148	32	5	0	3	.216	21	0	3	132	32	10	.942
Bobby Marshall 1B	37	143	37	7	2	2	.258	18	6	5	389	16	12	.971
Artie McDougall SS	26	104	35	8	0	1	.336	13	1	2	28	65	16	.853
Jim Taylor 3B/SS	23	103	25	3	4	0	.242	8	1	3	33	45	12	.866
Julius London P/RF	18	56	10	1	0	0	.178	5	2	0	5	28	3	.916

Player/Position	G	AB	H	D	T	HR	BA	R	SB	SF	PO	A	E	FA
George Johnson C	11	45	11	2	0	1	.244	9	1	1	43	14	2	.964
John Taylor P/RF	11	34	7	1	1	0	.206	3	0	1	25	5	2	.934
John Davis P/RF/2B/LF	11	31	5	1	0	0	.161	3	2	1	12	26	2	.950
Dick Garrison P/RF	10	26	5	0	0	0	.192	2	1	1	3	18	1	.954
Archie Pate P/RF	6	24	5	1	1	0	.208	2	2	0	7	7	1	.933
James Smith 2B/SS	4	14	3	1	1	0	.214	1	0	0	4	8	2	.857
Eugene Barton LF	2	9	1	0	0	0	.111	0	-	-	6	0	0	1.000
George Hopkins RF	2	9	1	0	0	0	.111	1	-	-	0	0	0	.000
Jackson 3B	2	9	1	0	0	1	.111	1	-	-	3	8	0	1.000
Haywood Rose 1B	2	9	1	0	0	0	.111	1	-	-	22	0	1	.956
Sloan CF	2	9	1	0	0	0	.111	1	-	-	2	0	0	1.000
Dave Wyatt 2B	2	9	4	1	1	0	.444	3	-	-	1	4	3	.625
Jesse Schaeffer 2B/SS	2	7	1	0	0	0	.142	1	2	0	0	8	3	.727
C. Smith C	2	6	1	0	0	0	.166	1	-	-	8	0	1	.888
Tom Pangburn P	1	5	1	0	0	0	.200	1	-	-	3	2	0	1.000
Walter Ball P	1	4	1	1	0	0	.250	1	-	-	0	0	0	.000
George Armstrong C	1	3	1	0	0	0	.333	1	-	-	4	2	0	1.000

Passed Balls: McMurray 2; Johnson 2.

1910 St. Paul Gophers: Given record: 104 wins out of 131 games. Record in games accounted for: 81–37–3 (.681) Captains: William Binga, Jim Taylor.

May 1		Phil Dellar's All-Stars at Lexington Park, St. Paul	W 5–1 (Davis/ Pangburn)
	3	Eau Claire (WI) [ml]	L 1–5 (**Davis**/ Pangburn)
	4	Eau Claire (WI) [ml]	L 0–5 (Davis)
	5	Eau Claire (WI) [ml]	W 6–5, 10 innings (Pangburn)
	7	La Crosse (WI) [ml]	L 1–5 (Davis)
	8	La Crosse (WI) [ml]	W 9–5 (Pangburn)
	15	Norwood	W 8–5 (**Ford**/ Pangburn)
	16	Aberdeen (SD)	Postponed
	17	Aberdeen (SD)	L 2–4 (Pangburn)
	18	Aberdeen (SD)	L 1–7 (Davis) W 8–0
	19	Groton (SD)	W 14–5 {15–5} (Ford)
	20	Conde (SD)	W 22–9
	21	Watertown (SD)	L 1–7 (Davis)
	22	Watertown (SD)	W 2–0 (Ford)
	23	Watertown (SD)	L 1–5 (Pangburn)
	24	Watertown (SD)	W 2–1 (Davis)
	25	Groton (SD)	W 13–4
	27	Renville	W 20–0
	29	Shakopee	W 6–5 (**Davis**/ Pangburn)
	30	Shakopee	W 8–3 (Pangburn)
	31	Blooming Prairie	W 15–5

June 1	Caledonia at Decorah (IA)	W 12–5
2	Owatonna	W 12–7 (Pangburn)
3	Ellendale	W 7–2
4	*H.P.Conrads at the Downtown Park, St. Paul*	W 5–3 (Davis)
5	H.P.Conrads at Lexington Park, St. Paul	W 6–5 (Pangburn)
8	Waseca	W 10–8, 8 innings (Davis)
12	Watertown (SD)	W 8–3 (Davis)
13	Watertown (SD)	W 2–1 (Pangburn)
14	Aberdeen (SD)	W 4–3 (Davis/ **Pangburn**)
15	Aberdeen (SD)	W 7–5, 18 innings (Pangburn/ **Davis**)
17	Fessenden (ND)	W 6–2
18	Minot (ND)	W 11–1 (Johnson)
19	Minot (ND)	L 6–10 (**Davis**/ Johnson)
20	Minot (ND)	W 3–1 (Pangburn)
21	Minot (ND)	W 5–3 (Johnson)
22	Minot (ND)	W 7–0 (Davis)
23	Minot (ND)	W 4–3 (Pangburn)
24	Valley City (ND)	L 3–5, 5 innings (Johnson)
25	Valley City (ND)	L 4–5 (Davis)
26	Valley City (ND)	W 7–5 (Pangburn)
27	Jamestown (ND)	W 4–1 (Johnson)
28	Jamestown (ND)	W 10–2 (Davis)
29	Jamestown (ND)	L 2–3, 8 innings (Pangburn)
30	Hope (ND)	W 3–2 (Johnson)
		W 9–0 (Davis)
July 1	Devils Lake (ND)	W 7–0 (Pangburn)
		W 4–2 (Johnson)
3	Fargo (ND)	W 16–6 (Davis)
4	Fargo (ND)	W 4–3 (McDougall)
		W 6–3 (Pangburn)
6	Langdon (ND)	W 3–1 (Taylor)
		W 8–3 (Davis)
7	Park River (ND)	T 0–0, 8 innings (Pangburn)
8	Grafton (ND)	W 6–3 (Barton/Binga)
		W 6–1, (Johnson)
10	Grand Forks (ND) at East Grand Forks	W 12–5 (Johnson)
11	Crookston	T 1–1, 9 innings (Davis)
12	Crookston	W 10–2
13	Cass Lake	T 3–3, 7 innings
14	Grand Rapids	W 10–2
15	Hibbing	W 3–2 (Pangburn)
16	Hibbing	W 7–5, 10 innings
17	Hibbing	L 2–3 (Davis/ **Pangburn**)
18	Hibbing	W 11–5 (Pangburn)
19	Hibbing	W 5–4, 10 innings (Johnson)
21	Lester Prairie	W 2–1 (Davis)
22	Hinckley	W 12–5 (Pangburn)
23	Lindstrom	Scheduled: no result found
24	*Chicago Giants at Lexington Park, St. Paul*	W 4–3, 10 innings (Johnson)
25	*Chicago Giants at Lexington Park, St. Paul*	L 1–5, 8 innings (**Davis**/ Taylor)
26	*Chicago Giants at Lexington Park, St. Paul*	L 1–4 (Pangburn)
27	*Chicago Giants at Lexington Park, St. Paul*	L 5–8 (Johnson)
28	*Chicago Giants at Lexington Park, St. Paul*	L 1–6 (Pangburn)
30	Mankato	L 3–4 (Johnson)
31	Mankato	W 12–3 (Pangburn)
August 3	Osceola (WI)	W 10–1 {7–1}
4	Barron (WI)	W 10–2 {7–1} (Davis)
5	Ladysmith (WI)	W 15–6 (Davis)
6	Springfield	L 1–4 (Davis) Result was revealed to be a hoax
7	Hayward (WI)	W 3–0 (Pangburn)
		W 3–0, 5 innings (Johnson)
8	Cumberland (WI)	W 14–8, 10 innings (Johnson)
9	Rice Lake (WI)	W 15–1

10	Amery (WI)	Scheduled: no result found
11	New Richmond (WI)	W 16–6 (Pangburn)
12	Spooner (WI)	W 2–0 (Johnson)
13	Lindstrom	W 2–0 (Pangburn)
14	Lindstrom	W 7–1 (Johnson)
15	Waconia	W 14–6 (Davis)
17	Hinckley	W 7–0 (Johnson)
18	Moose Lake	W 7–0
19	Hibbing	L 0–4 (Davis)
20	Hibbing	L 5–10
21	Hibbing	W 7–1 (Johnson)
		L 5–7, 10 innings (Davis)
22	Hibbing	W 8–7, 11 innings (Taylor/**Johnson**)
23	Chisholm	L 1–4 {1–3} (Davis)
24	Chisholm	L 3–9 (2–6) (Pangburn)
25	Hibbing	L 2–3 (Johnson)
26	Virginia	L 3–4, 10 innings (Davis)
27	Virginia	L 3–10 (**Taylor**/ Brown)
28	Virginia	W 7–4 (Johnson)
		L 5–8 (Johnson)
30	Spooner (WI)	L 6–11 (Johnson)
September 1	Cadott (WI)	W 6–2
2	Owen (WI)	W 3–1 (Pangburn)
3	Mankato	W 4–2 (Johnson)
4	Mankato	L 4–10, 7 innings (**Pangburn**/Marshall/Brown)
5	Mankato	W 1–0 (Johnson)
7	Winnebago	W 10–3
8	Fairmont	W 14–4 (Johnson)
9	Montgomery	W 12–3
10	North St. Paul Thoens at the Downtown Park, St. Paul	W 5–4 (Davis)
11	North St. Paul Thoens at Lexington Park, St. Paul	Game not played; Thoens claim forfeit win
14	Chicago Giants at Preston	L 2–3 (Johnson)
15	Chicago Giants at Preston	L 5–6
16	Chicago Giants at Preston	L 0–6
17	Shakopee	W 7–0 (Pangburn)
18	Shakopee	L 3–4 (Davis)
23	Springfield	L 3–14 (Stallard)
24	Springfield	W 3–1 (Davis)
25	Springfield	L 2–11 (Davis)
30	Polk County (WI) All-Stars at St. Croix Falls (WI)	L 5–11
October 1	Minneapolis All Stars at St. Croix Falls (WI)	Scheduled; no result found
2	North St. Paul Thoens	W 3–1, 10 innings (Jackson)

1910 St. Paul Gophers Pitching Statistics

Pitcher	G	GS	CG	IP	W	L	H	R	RPG	SO	BB	HBP	SH
John Davis	38	37	24	299	21	14	200	145	4.36	130	42	3	2
Tom Pangburn	37	30	25	256	21	8	133	96	3.37	143	62	15	4
Louis Johnson	26	25	24	224	19	7	125	82	3.29	129	38	8	3
Ford	3	3	2	25	3	0	5	10	3.60	12	2	0	1
Jim Taylor	4	3	1	18	1	1	2	9	4.50	6	12	0	0
Charles Jackson	1	1	1	10	1	0	0	1	0.90	7	1	0	0
Artie McDougall	2	1	1	10	1	0	5	3	2.70	2	0	0	0
Walter Stallard	1	1	1	8	0	1	13	14	15.75	7	7	0	0
Bobby Marshall	1	–	0	4.3	0	0	2	–	–	3	4	1	0
Harry Brown	2	0	0	0.3	0	0	0	0	0.00	0	0	0	0
Sherman Barton	1	1	0	–	–	0	–	–	–	–	–	–	0
William Binga	1	0	0	–	–	0	–	–	–	–	–	–	0

The hit, strikeout, and bases on balls totals are based on 202 innings pitched by Davis; 192 innings pitched by Pangburn; 178 innings pitched by Johnson; and 8 innings pitched by Stallard. Ford's strikeout and walk totals are based on 16 innings pitched and his hit totals based on 9 innings pitched. McDougall's strikeout and walk totals are based on 11 innings pitched and his hit totals based on 10 innings pitched. Taylor's strikeout and walk totals are based on 17 innings pitched and his hit totals based on 3 innings pitched. Wild pitches: Davis 4; Johnson 4; Pangburn 2.

1910 St. Paul Gophers Batting and Fielding Statistics

Player/Position	G	AB	H	D	T	HR	BA	R	SB	SF	PO	A	E	FA
Artie McDougall SS/LF/3B/P/C	58	229	51	6	0	0	.222	26	10	7	90	89	23	.886
Sherman Barton CF/P	55	215	44	12	0	1	.204	25	12	10	84	8	6	.938
George Armstrong C	57	209	60	15	3	5	.287	33	5	3	346	64	14	.966
George Bowman 2B/SS/CF/LF	52	193	38	1	4	0	.196	21	14	7	95	117	16	.929
William Binga RF/3B/SS/P	48	178	54	6	1	2	.303	32	5	5	60	30	11	.891
Bobby Marshall 1B/2B/C/3B/P	48	174	46	9	5	4	.263	29	22	1	404	38	34	.929
Jim Taylor 3B/SS/P	43	169	46	6	3	0	.272	16	13	7	58	93	16	.904
John Davis P/LF/2B/RF/1B	44	153	27	6	0	0	.176	10	8	4	49	101	7	.955
Tom Pangburn P/RF/LF/CF/2B	47	146	43	5	5	3	.294	23	9	1	48	48	15	.864
Wesley 3B/LF/SS/C	22	83	17	2	0	0	.204	15	3	1	35	21	13	.811
Harry Brown LF/1B/3B/P/C/2B/SS	22	71	15	3	0	0	.211	7	1	3	112	11	9	.931
Louis Johnson P/RF/LF	21	71	14	0	0	2	.197	14	6	1	12	50	6	.912
George Board 1B	15	56	4	0	0	0	.071	1	4	0	150	8	9	.946
Eugene Milliner LF	6	27	7	2	0	0	.260	4	4	0	7	0	0	1.000
Jesse Schaeffer RF/LF	6	23	3	0	0	0	.130	1	2	1	6	2	3	.727
Dave Kennedy SS/RF	6	22	6	1	0	0	.273	3	3	0	3	10	2	.866
Francis 2B/RF	4	13	1	0	0	0	.077	0	1	0	-	-	-	-
Ford P/RF/1B	4	12	3	2	0	0	.250	1	0	0	9	3	3	.800
C. Davis	3	11	0	0	0	0	.000	1	0	0	-	-	-	-
Eddie Davis 1B	3	11	2	1	0	0	.181	1	0	0	-	-	-	-
Williams	3	11	0	0	0	0	.000	1	0	0	-	-	-	-
Walter Stallard P	3	10	2	0	0	0	.200	1	1	0	-	-	-	-
Hill RF/SS	3	9	0	0	0	0	.000	0	0	0	4	1	0	1.000
Willis Jones LF	1	4	1	0	0	0	.250	0	0	0	1	0	0	1.000
Lee	1	4	0	0	0	0	.000	0	0	0	-	-	-	-
Andrew Campbell	1	-	1	-	1	-	-	-	-	-	-	-	-	-
Charles Jackson P	1	-	-	-	-	-	-	-	-	-	-	-	-	-
Milroy McCune	1	-	-	-	-	-	-	-	-	-	-	-	-	-
Hurley McNair	1	-	1	-	-	-	-	-	-	1	-	-	-	-

Passed Balls: Armstrong 12.

1911 Twin City Gophers: No given record. Record in games accounted for: 47–45–2 (.510) Captains: Bobby Marshall, William Binga.

April 23	Perry Werden All-Stars at Lexington Park, St. Paul	W 4–1 {5–1} (Davis)
29	La Crosse (WI) [ml]	L 2–12 (**Stallard**/ Jones/Marshall)
30	La Crosse (WI) [ml]	L 1–10 (**Davis**/ Stallard/Marshall)
May 1	Red Wing [ml]	L 4–17 (Davis)
2	Red Wing [ml]	W 5–4 (Jones/ Davis)
3	Eau Claire (WI) [ml]	L 1–4 (Brown)
4	Eau Claire (WI) [ml]	W 8–5 (Davis)
5	Eau Claire (WI) [ml]	L 5–11 (**Brown**/ Davis)
6	Wausau (WI) [ml]	L 7–12 (Jones)
7	Wausau (WI) [ml]	L 4–8 (Brown/ Jones)
14	H.P.Conrads at Lexington Park, St. Paul	W 8–4 (Davis)
16	Huron (SD)	W 8–5 (Jones)
17	Huron (SD)	L 5–16 (Davis)
18	Redfield (SD)	L 3–4 (Stallard)
19	Redfield (SD)	W 12–8 (Jones)
20	Aberdeen (SD)	W 6–2 (Davis)
21	Hankinson (ND)	W 5–2 (Stallard)
23	Hankinson (ND)	W 3–2 (Davis)
24	Cogswell (ND)	L 7–11 (Stallard)
25	Ellendale (ND)	L 0–2 (Brown)
26	Wyndmere (ND)	T 0–0, 4 innings
27	Elliott (ND)	W 8–5
28	Great Bend (ND)	W 11–2
29	Jamestown (ND)	L 2–7 (Brown)
30	Jamestown (ND)	L 3–4 (Davis)
31	Jamestown (ND)	W 9–6 (Stallard/**Jones**)
June 1	Jamestown (ND)	Postponed
2	Bismarck (ND)	W 5–1, 7 innings (Davis)
3	Bismarck (ND)	W 7–6
4	Bismarck (ND)	W 6–0, 7 innings (Brown)
5	Mandan (ND)	W 11–8 (Johnson)
6	Glen Ullin (ND)	L 3–4
7	Dickinson (ND)	W 7–4 (Davis)
8	Dickinson (ND)	W 8–5 (Stallard)
9	Beach (ND)	Postponed
10	Wibaux (MT)	W 7–5 (Johnson)
11	Beach (ND)	W 9–2 (Stallard)
		L 3–4 (Davis)
12	Wibaux (MT)	W 9–5
13	Valley City (ND)	T 4–4
14	Valley City (ND)	L 1–14 (Marshall)
		L 1–3
15	Devils Lake (ND)	L 7–8, 7 innings (Stallard/**Johnson**)
16	Devils Lake (ND)	L 1–5 (Davis)
		L 4–5, 8 innings (Stallard)
17	Grand Forks (ND)	L 1–7 (Brown)
18	Grand Forks (ND)	W 9–6 (Jones/ **Davis**)
19	Crookston	W 2–1 (Stallard)
20	Crookston	L 3–11 (**Johnson**/ Marshall))
21	Alexandria	L 3–6 (Davis)
		L 3–12 (Lytle)
22	Alexandria at Brooten	L 4–8
23	Alexandria at Brooten	L 7–8
28	Long Prairie	W 6–2, 5 innings (Davis)
29	Long Prairie	L 1–4 (Stallard)
July 1	Perry Werden All-Stars at Nicollet Park, Minneapolis	W 10–6 (Pangburn)
2	Perry Werden All-Stars at Nicollet Park, Minneapolis	W 9–4 (Johnson/**Davis**)
3	Perry Werden All-Stars at Nicollet Park, Minneapolis	W 7–4 (Stallard)

	4 Devils Lake (ND)	L 2–7 (Pangburn)
	5 Devils Lake (ND)	L 2–10 (Davis)
	6 Devils Lake (ND)	W 7–1 (Lytle)
	7 Cass Lake	W 2–1 (Pangburn)
	8 Duluth Fitwells	W 6–4 (Lytle)
	9 Duluth Fitwells	W 7–2 (Lytle/ Hudson)
	11 Hibbing	No game was played
	12 Hibbing	L 1–4 (Pangburn)
	13 Hibbing	W 4–3, 10 innings (Davis)
	14 Hibbing	W 9–8 (**Lytle**/ Davis)
	15 Hibbing	W 8–3 (Pangburn)
	16 Hibbing	W 6–3 (Davis)
		W 3–1 (Lytle)
	18 Hibbing	L 4–8 (Johnson)
	19 Hibbing	W 9–2 (Pangburn)
	21 Virginia	L 3–10 (Davis)
	22 Virginia	L 5–8 (Pangburn)
	23 Virginia	Postponed
	27 Milaca	W 18–3
	28 Mora	W 11–6
	29 Hayward (WI)	W 10–4 (Davis)
	30 Hayward (WI)	L 3–9 (Stallard/ **Lytle**)
	31 Spooner (WI)	W 3–2
August	5 Turnball-Cameron-Degler (Superior, WI)	W 8–5 (Stallard)
	6 Turnball-Cameron-Degler (Superior, WI)	W 9–5 (**Lytle**/ Davis)
	8 Alexandria	L 0–4 (Pangburn)
	9 Alexandria	L 2–4 (Lytle)
	10 Alexandria	L 5–8 (Johnson)
	13 Lindstrom	W (Stallard)
	Leland Giants at Chicago	Scheduled; no result found but the Gophers claimed victory
	16 Lindstrom	W 7–3
	17 Osceola (WI)	L 7–8 (Stallard/ **Pangburn**)
	19 Kansas City (KS) Giants	Cancelled; games on the 20th and 21st are also cancelled
	20 North St. Paul Thoens at Lexington Park, St. Paul	Cancelled
	27 Kansas City (KS) Giants	L 2–8 (**Johnson**/ Lytle)
	28 Kansas City (KS) Giants	L 10–13 (**Pangburn**/ Jones)
	29 Kansas City (KS) Giants	L 0–12 (Stallard)
	31 Kansas City (MO) Royal Giants	W 11–0 (Pangburn)
September	1 Kansas City (KS) Giants	L 0–11 (**Johnson**/Lytle/ Brown)
	2 Kansas City (KS) Giants	Scheduled; no result found
	3 St. Louis (MO) Giants	L 8–9 (Pangburn)
	4 St. Louis (MO) Giants	L 10–11, 12 innings (Stallard/ **Lytle**)
		L 1–2, 5 innings (Pangburn)
	5 St. Louis (MO) Giants	Scheduled; no result found

1911 TWIN CITY GOPHERS PITCHING STATISTICS

Pitcher	G	GS	CG	IP	W	L	H	R	RPG	SO	BB	HBP	SH
John Davis	26	20	19	188	14	9	172	105	5.02	80	22	2	0
Walter Stallard	20	18	13	127	8	6	82	76	5.38	45	22	2	0
Tom Pangburn	13	12	10	89	5	8	88	46	4.65	55	37	5	1
Clarence Lytle	10	8	5	57	5	3	58	41	6.47	12	8	1	0
Bert Jones	9	5	3	53	3	1	35	38	6.45	9	2	0	0
Louis Johnson	10	8	4	45	2	6	36	40	8.00	17	16	2	0
Harry Brown	8	7	4	44	1	5	27	27	5.65	28	21	4	1
Bobby Marshall	4	1	1	14	0	1	27	26	16.71	1	2	0	0
Hudson	1	-	-	-	-	-	-	-	-	-	-	-	-

The hit, strikeout, and bases on balls totals are based on 154 innings pitched by Davis; 89 innings pitched by Pangburn; 32 innings pitched by Jones; 37 innings pitched by Brown;

and 29 innings pitched by Johnson. Stallard's strikeout and walk totals are based on 73 innings pitched and his hit totals based on 81 innings pitched. Lytle's strikeout and walk totals are based on 30 innings pitched and his hit totals based on 46 innings pitched. Marshall's strikeout and walk totals are based on 3 innings pitched and his hit totals based on 11 innings pitched. Wild pitches: Stallard 2; Davis 1; Johnson 1.

1911 St. Paul Gophers Batting and Fielding Statistics

Player/Position	G	AB	H	D	T	HR	BA	R	SB	SF	PO	A	E	FA
William Binga RF/C/3B/LF	48	196	53	7	0	0	.267	27	4	0	64	21	5	.944
William Selden SS/CF	54	186	53	5	7	7	.285	35	5	4	93	81	26	.870
Bert Jones CF/1B/P/2B	41	164	50	9	3	2	.305	20	4	0	153	25	6	.970
Artie McDougall 2B/LF/3B/CF/SS	41	151	35	6	1	1	.231	30	9	3	55	50	14	.882
Harry Brown 3B/P/1B	50	145	30	3	1	5	.207	19	8	3	121	86	27	.884
Bobby Marshall 1B/C/P/3B/2B	42	145	40	6	6	5	.275	24	5	1	290	23	8	.972
John Davis P/LF/CF/1B/RF	30	104	28	7	0	0	.269	9	1	2	27	53	9	.900
George Armstrong C	26	96	24	8	0	1	.250	11	3	2	99	23	1	.968
Hardiman LF/2B/RF	28	94	15	2	0	0	.160	14	3	0	37	21	10	.853
Clarence Lytle CF/P/LF	21	66	12	1	0	2	.185	9	0	1	35	9	3	.935
Walter Stallard P/LF/CF/RF	21	62	10	0	0	2	.161	12	2	0	19	18	5	.839
Tom Pangburn P/LF/RF/CF	14	52	13	1	0	0	.250	2	0	0	4	12	6	.730
Louis Johnson P/RF/LF/CF	15	41	3	0	0	0	.073	5	1	0	15	9	2	.923
Frank Davis 2B	12	40	11	2	0	1	.273	7	3	1	18	24	1	.976
Jesse Schaeffer C/CF	14	38	14	2	1	2	.368	7	0	1	60	14	3	.961
Thompson 2B/SS/3B	8	31	7	1	0	0	.226	0	1	0	5	18	5	.821
Alex Irwin 2B/SS	3	12	3	0	0	0	.250	0	0	0	0	7	0	1.000
Loft RF	1	4	0	0	0	0	.000	1	0	0	0	0	0	.000
Terrell LF	1	4	0	0	0	0	.000	0	0	0	4	1	0	1.000
Buck Freeman LF	1	1	1	0	0	0	1.000	0	0	0	0	0	0	.000
Williams LF/1B	2	–	0	0	0	0	.000	0	0	0	0	0	0	.000
Hudson P	1	–	–	–	–	–	–	–	–	–	–	–	–	–

Passed Balls: Armstrong 3; Marshall 2; Schaeffer 1.

Selected St. Paul Gophers Pitching Statistics 1907–1911

Pitcher/YRS	G	GS	CG	IP	W	L	H	R	RPG	SO	BB	HBP	SH
John Davis **1907, 09–11**	110	94	78	849	60	34	598	365	3.88	386	88	5	9

Pitcher/YRS	G	GS	CG	IP	W	L	H	R	RPG	SO	BB	HBP	SH
Clarence Lytle 1907–08, 11	78	71	60	604	52	16	337	208	3.09	143	68	3	17
Tom Pangburn 1909–10, 11	51	43	36	355	26	16	229	147	3.72	205	99	20	5
Bill Gatewood 1908	43	37	36	333	21	17	137	136	3.67	114	55	12	7
Louis Johnson 1910, 11	36	33	28	269	21	13	161	122	4.08	146	54	10	3
Julius London 1909	29	25	21	213	21	3	108	61	2.57	49	18	0	8
John Taylor 1909	22	19	18	177	18	2	97	36	1.83	93	23	3	5
Walter Stallard 1910–11	21	19	14	135	8	7	95	90	6.00	52	29	2	0
Dick Garrison 1909	15	15	11	121	9	5	98	62	4.61	37	16	4	0
Tommy Means 1907, 08	17	16	10	119	14	0	71	35	2.64	32	5	4	2

The hit, strikeout, and bases on balls totals are based on 683 innings pitched by Davis; 435 innings pitched by Lytle; 290 innings pitched by Pangburn; 246 innings pitched by Gatewood; 207 innings pitched by Johnson; 177 innings pitched by London; 150 innings pitched by Taylor; 112 innings pitched by Garrison; and 101 innings pitched by Means. Stallard's strikeout and walk totals are based on 81 innings pitched and his hit totals based on 89 innings pitched. Wild Pitches: Davis 8; Johnson 5; Lytle 4; Gatewood 2; Pangburn 2; Stallard 2; Garrison 1.

SELECTED ST. PAUL GOPHERS BATTING AND FIELDING STATISTICS 1907–1911

Player/Position	G	AB	H	D	T	HR	BA	R	SB	SF	PO	A	E	FA
Sherman Barton CF 1907–10	176	674	162	41	4	4	.240	76	32	17	265	29	15	.951
William Binga RF/3B 1907–11	136	540	155	16	3	2	.287	79	14	7	171	86	28	.901
Artie McDougall SS/LF 1909–11	125	484	121	19	3	3	.250	69	20	12	163	204	53	.873
Bobby Marshall 1B 1907, 09–11	128	465	124	22	13	11	.266	71	34	7	1086	77	55	.954
Johnny Davis P 1907, 09–11	112	388	84	14	0	1	.216	32	15	8	109	219	24	.931
Frank Davis SS 1907–08, 11	90	365	82	18	1	4	.224	56	17	5	134	200	40	.893
Clarence Lytle P 1907–08, 11	93	336	69	5	1	4	.205	39	13	5	103	86	12	.940
Felix Wallace 2B 1908–11	76	317	94	16	3	1	.296	44	14	2	173	164	27	.925
George Armstrong C 1909–10, 11	84	308	85	23	3	6	.275	45	8	5	449	89	15	.972
Jim Taylor 3B 1909–11	66	272	71	9	7	0	.261	24	21	11	91	138	28	.891
Will McMurray C/3B 1907–09	76	270	61	12	1	5	.225	34	8	6	182	91	31	.898
Willis Jones LF 1907–08, 10	75	267	70	13	1	0	.262	39	18	5	113	7	2	.983
Jesse Schaeffer C/2B 1907–11	63	239	74	14	3	8	.309	37	10	3	269	69	23	.936
Harry Brown 3B/1B 1910–11	72	216	45	6	1	5	.208	26	9	6	233	97	36	.901
Tom Pangburn P 1909–10, 11	52	203	57	6	5	3	.280	26	9	1	52	60	21	.842

Player/Position	G	AB	H	D	T	HR	BA	R	SB	SF	PO	A	E	FA
George Johnson C/1B 1908–09	51	200	48	8	0	4	.240	29	4	12	278	53	12	.965
George Bowman 2B 1910	52	193	38	1	4	0	.197	21	14	7	95	117	16	.929
William Selden SS **1911**	54	186	53	5	7	7	.285	35	5	4	93	81	26	.870
Eugene Milliner LF 1909, 10	43	183	58	9	6	2	.316	25	6	2	51	10	6	.910
Fred Roberts 3B/2B 1907	43	165	39	5	1	1	.236	25	5	4	48	55	20	.837
George Taylor 1B 1907	42	164	32	4	0	1	.195	27	6	1	387	21	9	.978
Bill Gatewood P 1908	36	123	21	2	2	4	.171	19	4	0	58	47	11	.905
Haywood Rose 1B/C 1908, 09	35	123	30	6	0	0	.243	14	5	2	280	9	22	.928
Louis Johnson P 1910, 11	36	112	17	0	0	2	.151	19	7	1	27	59	8	.914

Passed Balls: Armstrong 15; Schaeffer 7; Johnson 5; Marshall 3; McMurray 2.

Minneapolis Keystones 1908–1911

Aggregate record in games accounted for: 161–88–5 (.643) Note: Because the 1907 Minneapolis Keystones were a semi-pro club consisting of local players, their lineup can be found in Appendix III.

1908 Minneapolis Keystones: Given record: 88–19–2. Record in games accounted for (66–21–1, .755) Captains: Alex Irwin; "Topeka" Jack Johnson.

April 12		Interurbans at Minneapolis	Scheduled; no result found
	19	Lund Lands at Minnehaha Driving Park, Minneapolis	L 1–2, 11 innings (Graham)
	26	Lund Lands at Minnehaha Driving Park, Minneapolis	W 5–0 (Ball)
May 3		Stillwater	W 5–0 (Jessup)
	17	Kenyon	W 4–3 (Graham)
	19	St. Charles	W 10–7
	20	St. Charles	W
	21	Chatfield	W 2–0, 7 innings
	22	Houston	W 11–6 (Graham)
	24	Caledonia	W 9–1{7–1 (Jessup)
	25	Galesville (WI)	T 2–2, 12 innings (Ball)
	27	Superior (WI)	Postponed
	28	Superior (WI)	Postponed
	29	Superior (WI)	Postponed
	30	Hibbing	Postponed
	31	Hibbing	L 2–5 (Jessup)
June 1		Hibbing	W 7–3 (Ball)
	2	Chisholm	W 5–1 (Graham/ **Jessup**)
	3	Eveleth	W 17–3 (**Ball**/ Graham))
	4	Eveleth	L 2–7 (**Graham**/ Jessup)
	5	Superior (WI)	W 8–5 (Graham/ **Ball**)
	6	Lund Lands at Nicollet Park, Minneapolis	L 7–8 (Jessup)
	7	Lund Lands at Minnehaha Driving Park, Minneapolis	W 12–10 (**Graham**/Jessup) Second game not played
	8	Plainview	W 8–0
	9	Plainview	W 8–3
	10	Rochester	W 9–2 (Jessup)
	11	Rochester	W 16–4
	14	South St. Paul	W 7–2 (Jessup)

20	Ramsey (SD) at Montrose (SD)	W 4–3
21	Lennox (SD) W 3–1 (Jessup)	
22	Flandreau (SD)	W 4–2 (Graham)
23	Jasper	W 8–3 (Marshall)
24	Lamberton	W 5–0 (Jessup)
27	New Prague	Postponed
28	Tonka Bay	W 7–2 (Jessup)
30	Hastings	L 1–3, 7 innings (Graham)
July 1	Austin	W 3–2 (Marshall)
2	Austin	W 9–2 (Graham)
4	Calmar (IA) at Mabel	W 4–3
5	Harmony	W 9–3
6	Osage (IA)	L 2–5 (**Marshall**/ Jessup)
7	Osage (IA)	W 4–0 (Jessup)
9	Calmar (IA)	W 2–1
10	Manchester (IA)	W 7–1 (Graham)
11	Oelwein (IA)	W 6–3 (Freeman)
12	Oelwein (IA)	W 5–3, 17 innings (Jessup)
13	West Union (IA)	L 0–2, 8 innings (Freeman)
14	Waukon (IA)	W 11–8
16	Decorah (IA)	W 11–4 (Freeman/ **Jessup**)
17	Cresco (IA)	W 4–0 (Jessup)
18	Tripoli (IA)	Scheduled; no result found
19	Winona	W 3–0 (Freeman)
23	Janesville	W 8–3, 8 innings (Freeman)
24	Wells	Scheduled; no result found
25	Tracy	Scheduled; no result found
26	Albert Lea	L 5–6, 10 innings (Freeman/**Jessup**)
27	Redwood Falls	L 3–6
28	Redwood Falls	Scheduled; no result found
29	Granite Falls	W 11–1
30	Island Park (Breckenridge-Wahpeton, ND)	W 13–11 (Jessup)
31	Island Park (Breckenridge-Wahpeton, ND)	L 3–8 (Freeman)
August 1	Island Park (Breckenridge-Wahpeton, ND)	Cancelled
2	Lund Lands at Minnehaha Driving Park, Minneapolis	W 12–4 (Jessup)
3	Lund Lands at the Downtown Park, St. Paul	L 1–9 (Dewberry)
4	Lund Lands at Lexington Park, St. Paul	W 6–4 (Jackson)
5	Ellsworth (WI)	W 6–3 (Marshall)
6	Menomonie (WI)	W 6–4
7	Eau Claire (WI)	W 8–2 (Dewberry)
8	Merrill (WI)	L 5–11 (Jackson)
9	Merrill (WI)	L 0–2 (Jessup)
10	Stevens Point (WI)	W 18–2
11	Medford (WI)	W 1–0, 10 innings
12	Chippewa Falls (WI)	W 11–2 (Jessup)
13	Chippewa Falls (WI)	W 6–2 (Marshall)
14	Cumberland (WI)	L 5–7 (Dewberry)
15	New Prague	W 10–2 (Jackson)
16	Faribault	L 0–2 (Jessup)
18	Monticello	W 6–0
19	Shakopee	W 13–3 {12–2} (Jackson)
20	Elk River	W 7–3
22	Buffalo	W 8–0
23	Red Wing	W 1–0 (Jackson)
24	Arlington	W 9–0 (Jessup)
26	Jordan	W 10–0, 6 innings
27	St. Paul Gophers at the Downtown Park, St. Paul	L 2–6 (Jessup)
30	*St. Paul Gophers at Minnehaha Driving Park, Minneapolis*	W 9–2 (Jackson)
September 1	Cresco (IA)	W 2–0 {3–0} (Jessup)
4	Des Moines (IA) Invincibles	W 15–3
5	Des Moines (IA) Invincibles; Vim team; or Hopkins Brothers at Des Moines (IA)	Doubleheader scheduled; no result found

	6	Buxton (IA) Wonders	Scheduled; no result found
	7	Buxton (IA) Wonders	Scheduled; no result found
	8	Hiteman (IA)	W
	12	St. Peter	L 4–10 (**Dewberry**/ Jessup)
	13	Medford (WI)	L 1–3
	14	Medford (WI)	W 8–1 (13–3) (Jessup)
	16	Menomonie (WI)	W 11–3 {11–2} (Dewberry)
	17	Menomonie (WI)	W 17–0 {12–2}
	18	Rochester at Zumbrota	W 7–3 {11–3}
	20	*St. Paul Gophers at Minnehaha Driving Park, Minneapolis*	W 4–3 (Jackson)
	21	St. Paul Gophers at the Downtown Park, St. Paul	L 3–6 (**Dewberry**/ Jessup)
	22	*St. Paul Gophers at Nicollet Park, Minneapolis*	L 0–6 (Jackson)
	27	Minneapolis All-Stars at Minnehaha Driving Park, Minneapolis	Postponed
	30	St. Paul Gophers at Rochester	Cancelled
October	1	St. Paul Gophers at Winona	Cancelled
	2	St. Paul Gophers at La Crosse (WI)	Cancelled
	4	*Minneapolis All-Stars at Minnehaha Driving Park, Minneapolis*	L 0–11 (Jackson)

1908 MINNEAPOLIS KEYSTONES PITCHING STATISTICS

Pitcher	G	GS	CG	IP	W	L	H	R	RPG	SO	BB	HBP	SH
Charles Jessup	29	21	21	214	18	6	92	60	2.58	122	20	3	6
Charles Jackson	9	9	9	80	6	3	58	43	4.83	31	10	6	0
Graham	12	12	7	72	6	3	58	33	4.12	26	22	6	0
W.J. Freeman	7	7	4	52	3	2	25	23	3.93	6	0	0	1
William Dewberry	6	6	4	43	2	4	37	28	5.86	15	5	1	0
Bob Marshall	5	5	4	41	4	1	21	15	3.29	5	1	0	0
Walter Ball	5	3	3	34	4	1	18	5	1.32	33	15	2	1
Nelson	1	1	0	.3	0	0	1	1	27.27	0	3	0	0

The hit, strikeout, and bases on balls totals are based on 57 innings pitched by Graham and 34 innings pitched by Ball. Dewberry's hit totals are based on 40 innings pitched and his strikeout and walk totals on 17 innings pitched. Freeman's hit totals are based on 34 innings pitched and his strikeout and walk totals on 25 innings pitched. Jackson's hit totals are based on 71 innings pitched and his strikeout and walk totals are based on 62 innings pitched. Marshall's hit totals are based on 27 innings pitched and his strikeout and walk totals on 23 innings pitched. Jessup's run totals are based on 209 innings pitched; his strikeout totals on 152 innings pitched; his hit totals on 133 innings pitched, and his walk totals on 105 innings pitched. Wild pitches: Graham 8; Ball 2; Jackson 2; Duberry 1; Jessup 1.

1908 MINNEAPOLIS KEYSTONES BATTING AND FIELDING STATISTICS

Player/Position	G	AB	H	D	T	HR	BA	R	SB	SF	PO	A	E	FA
William Binga 3B/1B	32	144	40	1	1	0	.277	26	4	0	44	64	18	.857
Eugene Barton LF/CF	32	139	42	6	0	2	.302	21	9	1	43	2	9	.833
Alex Irwin SS/3B/LF	33	134	23	2	1	0	.171	12	6	4	40	83	22	.848
George Hopkins CF	31	133	36	3	1	1	.270	25	4	2	35	1	2	.947
Jack Johnson 1B/RF/2B/3B/SS	32	130	35	3	3	3	.269	25	5	0	227	22	10	.961

Player/Position	G	AB	H	D	T	HR	BA	R	SB	SF	PO	A	E	FA
Bob Marshall RF/1B/P	31	107	21	2	1	0	.196	14	4	6	128	4	3	.977
Fred Roberts 2B/RF	23	98	16	1	0	0	.163	11	6	2	54	52	9	.921
Dick Wallace C/RF	19	75	16	1	1	0	.213	6	3	1	105	13	5	.959
Andrew Campbell C	15	58	14	5	2	0	.241	8	5	1	99	12	5	.956
Charles Jessup P/RF	16	55	11	2	1	1	.200	7	1	2	13	29	3	.933
Charles Jackson P	7	26	4	0	0	0	.153	5	2	0	3	15	2	.900
Walter Ball P/RF	6	22	3	1	0	0	.136	2	0	1	5	8	1	.928
Graham P	6	21	2	0	0	0	.095	0	0	0	1	6	1	.875
William Dewberry P/2B	6	25	6	0	0	1	.240	2	0	0	11	11	1	.956
W. J. Freeman P	4	12	1	0	0	0	.083	1	1	1	2	6	1	.888
Francis LF	1	3	0	0	0	0	.000	0	0	0	0	0	0	.000
Taylor RF	1	3	0	0	0	0	.000	0	0	0	1	0	0	1.000
Nelson P	1	-	-	-	-	-	-	-	-	-	-	-	-	-

Passed Balls: Wallace 2; Campbell 1.

1909 Minneapolis Keystones: Last given record: 14 losses out of 90 games by August 31. (The club went 12–8 in 20 verified games thereafter). Record in games accounted for (46–28–1, .620) Captains: Willis Jones, Frank Davis, Alex Irwin.

April 20	South High School at Minneapolis	L 4–10 (Graves)
May 16	Merrill (WI)	W 3–1, 8 innings (Jessup)
		Merrill claimed forfeit win
17	Merrill (WI)	L 1–2, 10 innings (Jackson)
20	Ellsworth (WI)	L 4–6 (**Sandford**/ Jessup)
22	Faribault at Nicollet Park, Minneapolis	W 1–0 (Jessup)
23	Faribault at Nicollet Park, Minneapolis	W 1–0, 11 innings (Jackson)
28	Biwabik	W
29	Hibbing	W 8–3 (Jessup)
30	Hibbing	W 7–5 (Jackson)
31	Hibbing	L 5–7 (Jessup)
June 1	Hibbing	Postponed
2	Hibbing	Postponed
3	Rice Lake (WI)	W 6–3 (Sandford)
4	Barron (WI)	W 21–3
5	Hibbing at Nicollet Park, Minneapolis	W 2–1 (Jessup)
6	Hibbing at Nicollet Park, Minneapolis	L 2–3 (Jackson/ **Jessup**)
12	Merrill (WI) at Nicollet Park, Minneapolis	Postponed
13	Merrill (WI) at Nicollet Park, Minneapolis	W 3–1 (**Jessup**/ Jackson)
16	Janesville	W 5–2
18	Lanesboro	W 7–0 (Green)
19	Harmony	W 8–5, 10 innings (Jackson)
20	Harmony	W 2–1 (Dismukes/ **Jessup**)
22	Waterville	W 8–4 (Jackson)
27	Faribault	L 0–7 (Dismukes/ Jessup)
28	Cresco (IA)	W 3–2 (Pate)
29	Cresco (IA)	W 6–3 (Jackson)
30	Osage (IA)	W 11–4
July 1	Osage (IA)	L 3–4 (? / Jackson)

Game Chronologies and Team Statistics 245

	2	Charles City (IA)	L 0–1 (Jackson)
	4	Oelwein (IA)	T 0–0, 7 innings (Jackson)
	5	Oelwein (IA)	L 3–4, 10 innings (Jessup)
	8	Redwood Falls	W 6–5
	9	Redwood Falls	L 1–3
	11	Red Wing	W 5–2 (Jackson)
	16	Waukon (IA)	W 4–2 (Pate)
	17	Northwood (IA)	W 10–4 (**Pate**/ Jessup)
	18	Luverne	W 2–0, 10 innings
	19	Adrian	Scheduled; no result found
	20	Dell Rapids (SD)	W 2–1 (Jessup)
	21	Flandreau (SD)	W 2–1
	24	St. Paul Gophers at the Downtown Park, St. Paul	L 2–5 (Jessup)
	25	*St. Paul Gophers at Nicollet Park, Minneapolis*	L 4–8 (**Jackson**/ Jessup)
	27	Cumberland (WI)	W 7–5
August	1	St. Paul Gophers at Lexington Park, St. Paul	L 3–8 (**Jessup**/ Jackson)
	2	Alexandria	L 5–9 (Jackson)
	3	Alexandria	L 1–3 (Jessup)
	4	Long Prairie	L 2–7 (Pate)
	5	Long Prairie	W 4–1 (Jackson)
	6	Nekoosa (WI)	Cancelled
	7	Nekoosa (WI)	Cancelled
	8	Merrill (WI)	W 8–5, 11 innings (Pate/ **Jackson**)
	9	Merrill (WI)	W 10–0 (Jessup)
	12	Hibbing	L 1–5 (Jessup)
	13	Hibbing	W 2–1, 13 innings (Jackson)
	14	Hibbing	L 3–5 (Pate)
	15	Hibbing	L 3–4, 11 innings (Jessup)
			W 8–2 (Jackson)
	16	Chisholm	W 11–1
	18	Rice Lake (WI)	W 3–0
	19	Ladysmith (WI)	W 11–0
	21	Strawberry Point (IA)	L 2–4
	22	Anamosa (IA)	L 1–2 (Jessup/ **Jackson**)
	23	Monticello (IA)	W 5–2
	24	Maquoketa (IA)	L 2–3
	25	Maquoketa (IA)	Postponed
	26	Preston (IA)	W 6–3 (**Pate**/ Gatewood)
	27	Maquoketa (IA)	L 2–4 (Jackson)
	28	Mankato	W 9–5, 6 innings (Gatewood) Mankato claimed forfeit win
	29	Mankato	W 10–0 (Jackson)
	30	Rochester	W 12–11
	31	Rochester	L 1–2 (Jackson)
September	1	New Richmond (WI)	L 3–4 (Pate/ Davis)
	2	St. Paul Gophers at Preston	Postponed
	4	Escanaba (MI)	W 7–4 (Gatewood)
	5	Escanaba (MI)	W 11–7 (Pate)
	6	Escanaba (MI)	W 1–0, 10 innings (Jackson)
	7	Rapid River (MI)	W 2–0 (Pate)
	8	Rapid River (MI)	W 3–1 (Jackson)
	9	Gladstone (MI)	Postponed
	10	Gladstone (MI)	L 2–3 (Jackson)
	12	Soo (MI)	Postponed
	17	Zumbrota	W 7–0 (**Pate**/ Jackson)
	18	*Minneapolis All-Stars at Nicollet Park, Minneapolis*	W 6–2 (Jackson)
	19	Minneapolis All-Stars at Nicollet Park, Minneapolis	L 2–3 (Gatewood)
	20	St. Paul Gophers at the Downtown Park, St. Paul	L 1–9 (Pate)
	21	St. Paul Gophers at the Downtown Park, St. Paul	Postponed

25	Minneapolis All-Stars at Nicollet Park, Minneapolis	Cancelled
26	Minneapolis All-Stars at Nicollet Park, Minneapolis	Cancelled

1909 Minneapolis Keystones Pitching Statistics

Pitcher	G	GS	CG	IP	W	L	H	R	RPG	SO	BB	HBP	SH
Charles Jackson	28	22	19	209	13	8	129	59	2.54	141	36	14	3
Charles Jessup	21	15	12	137	7	9	98	42	2.75	84	25	9	2
Archie Pate	12	12	8	89	7	3	63	42	4.55	34	11	0	1
Bill Gatewood	4	3	2	23	1	1	26	12	4.69	13	3	3	0
Robert Sandford	2	2	1	14	1	1	14	9	5.78	3	2	0	0
William Dismukes	2	2	0	10	1	0	-	4	3.60	3	-	-	0
Willie Green	1	1	1	9	1	0	4	0	0.00	-	-	-	1
Graves	1	1	1	9	0	1	-	10	10.00	-	-	-	-
Frank Davis	1	0	0	2	0	0	-	-	-	-	-	-	-

Dismukes' strikeout totals are based on 5 innings pitched. Gatewood's hit totals are based on 23 innings pitched; and his strikeout and walk totals on 22 innings pitched. Jackson's hit totals are based on 188 innings pitched; his strikeout totals on 185 innings pitched and walk totals on 175 innings pitched. Jessup's hit totals are based on 126 innings pitched; his strikeout totals on 114 innings pitched; and his walk totals on 91 innings pitched. Pate's run totals are based on 83 innings pitched; his hit totals on 70 innings pitched; and his strikeout and walk totals on 60 innings pitched. Wild pitches: Gatewood 2; Jessup 2: Pate 1

1909 Minneapolis Keystones Batting and Fielding Statistics

Player/Position	G	AB	H	D	T	HR	BA	R	SB	SF	PO	A	E	FA
Eugene Barton LF/2B/CF	40	148	40	4	1	2	.270	18	4	2	41	7	3	.941
Frank Davis SS/3B/P	42	144	45	8	1	1	.312	20	6	4	52	87	8	.945
Willis Jones RF/CF/LF/2B	40	136	33	5	2	0	.242	16	10	2	31	3	1	.971
Haywood Rose 1B/RF/C	40	135	25	5	0	0	.185	10	3	2	350	7	10	.972
George Hopkins CF	33	119	39	5	1	1	.327	8	2	1	40	1	3	.931
Milroy McCune 3B/SS	34	108	20	0	0	0	.185	4	1	2	41	65	10	.913
Andrew Campbell C	29	87	25	7	0	0	.287	9	4	0	184	23	4	.981
Jesse Schaeffer 2B	22	74	18	4	0	1	.243	8	3	3	34	38	10	.878
Willie Green C/3B/2B/P	22	67	10	2	0	1	.149	8	0	1	78	16	3	.969
Charles Jackson P/RF	20	60	16	0	0	1	.266	6	1	0	17	42	3	.951
Alex Irwin 2B/SS/C	16	50	11	0	0	0	.220	2	1	1	22	26	4	.923
Archie Pate P/OF	12	38	9	0	0	1	.236	5	1	0	4	22	1	.962
Charles Jessup P	12	37	5	1	0	0	.135	3	1	0	4	36	5	.911
Bill Gatewood P/RF/1B/2B	5	10	2	0	0	0	.200	2	0	0	0	2	0	1.000
Robert Sandford P	2	1	0	0	0	0	.000	1	0	0	1	0	1	.500

Player/Position	G	AB	H	D	T	HR	BA	R	SB	SF	PO	A	E	FA
Dizzy Dismukes P	2	-	-	-	-	-	-	-	-	-	-	-	-	-
Graves P	1	-	-	-	-	-	-	-	-	-	-	-	-	-

Passed Balls: Campbell 6; Green 3.

1910 Minneapolis Keystones: No given record. Record in games accounted for (18–11, .620) Captain: Bill Gatewood

Spring	Minneapolis Millers [ml]	W
May 14	Kansas City (KS) Giants at Kansas City, MO	L 5–6
15	Kansas City (KS) Giants at Kansas City, MO	Postponed
16	Kansas City (KS) Giants at Kansas City, MO	Postponed
17	Kansas City (KS) Giants at Kansas City, MO	Doubleheader postponed
18	Atchison (KS)	W 6–3
	Kansas City (MO) Royal Giants at Atchison, KS	W 10–6 {11–7 (Lytle)}
19	Kansas City (MO) Royal Giants at Atchison, KS	Postponed
20	Kansas City (MO) Royal Giants	W 8–6 {8–2 (Jackson)}
21	Kansas City (MO) Royal Giants	L 3–9 {2–7, 5 innings} (**Pate**/Jackson)
22	Kansas City (MO) Royal Giants	Postponed
24	Kansas City (MO) Royal Giants	W 11–9 {11–4}(Gatewood)
26	Albia (IA)	Cancelled
27	Albia (IA)	Cancelled
28	Fort Worth (TX) Wonders	Won three games of a four-game series with Fort Worth
29	Fort Worth (TX) Wonders	
30	Fort Worth (TX) Wonders	
31	Fort Worth (TX) Wonders	
June 4	Houston (TX) Black Buffaloes	Scheduled; no result found
5	Houston (TX) Black Buffaloes	Scheduled; no result found
6	Houston (TX) Black Buffaloes	Scheduled; no result found
7	Houston (TX) Black Buffaloes	Scheduled; no result found
11	Dallas (TX) Black Giants	W 5–1 (Jackson)
12	Dallas (TX) Black Giants	L 1–3 (Gatewood) W 3–2 (McNair)
13	Dallas (TX) Black Giants	W 3–2 (Jackson)
14	Dallas (TX) Black Giants	L 3–6 (Gatewood)
July 2	New Orleans Colored Baseball Club	Scheduled at San Antonio (TX); no result found
August 20	Kansas City (MO) Royal Giants	L 2–3, 12 innings (Bonny)
21	Kansas City (MO) Royal Giants	L 2–7 (Jackson)
22	Kansas City (MO) Royal Giants	W 8–2 {5–3} (Lytle)
28	St. Louis (MO) Giants	L 2–11 (**McNair**/ Jackson)
29	St. Louis (MO) Giants	W 4–1 (Lytle)
30	Merten's All-Stars at St. Louis	L 5–6, 8 innings (Johnson)
31	Merten's All-Stars at St. Louis	W 6–3 (Lyons/ Lytle)
September 2	Red Bud (IL) at St. Louis	W 6–0, 7 innings (McNair)
4	Paducah (KY) Cubs	Scheduled; no result found
5	Paducah (KY) Cubs	Scheduled; no result found
15	Louisville (KY) Cubs	L 5–7 {2–9}(McNair)
16	Louisville (KY) Cubs	L 3–4 (Jackson)
17	Louisville (KY) Cubs	W 7–6 (McNair)
18	Louisville (KY) Cubs	W 2–0 (Jackson)
21	Indianapolis ABC's	W 6–1 (**Jackson**/ McNair)
22	Indianapolis ABC's	Scheduled; no result found
23	Indianapolis ABC's	Scheduled; no result found

Appendix I

1910 Minneapolis Keystones Pitching Statistics

Pitcher	G	GS	CG	IP	W	L	H	R	RPG	SO	BB	HBP	SH
Charles Jackson	8	7	6	57	4	2	22	22	3.51	3	1	1	1
Hurley McNair	6	5	4	38	3	2	29	22	5.16	13	8	2	1
Clarence Lytle	3	3	3	27	3	0	5	9	3.00	1	3	0	0
Bill Gatewood	3	3	3	25	1	2	6	18	6.48	-	-	-	0
Bonny	1	1	1	9	0	1	-	3	3.00	-	-	-	0
Archie Pate	1	1	-	-	0	1	-	-	-	-	-	-	0
James Lyons	1	1	0	-	-	0	-	-	-	-	-	-	0

Gatewood's hit totals are based on 9 innings pitched. Jackson's hit totals are based on 33 innings pitched and his strikeout and walk totals on 7 innings pitched. Lytle's hit, strikeout, and bases on balls totals are based on 9 innings pitched. McNair's hit totals are based on 23 innings pitched and his strikeout and walk totals on 15 innings pitched. Wild pitches: McNair 2.

1910 Minneapolis Keystones Batting and Fielding Statistics

Player/Position	G	AB	H	D	T	HR	BA	R	SB	SF	PO	A	E	FA
Frank Young 2B/1B	5	21	2	0	0	0	.094	3	1	1	16	9	3	.892
Frank Davis SS	5	19	5	0	0	0	.267	2	2	0	4	17	2	.913
Eugene Barton CF	5	19	5	0	0	0	.267	0	0	0	6	0	0	1.000
James Shawler LF	5	17	7	0	0	0	.400	2	5	1	10	0	1	.961
Milroy McCune 3B	5	15	2	1	0	0	.133	0	1	1	7	6	2	.866
Hurley McNair P/RF	4	13	5	1	0	0	.375	0	1	0	2	6	2	.800
John Merida C/1B	4	12	2	0	0	0	.166	1	0	1	31	1	1	.969
James Wills C	4	11	4	1	0	0	.377	2	3	0	17	6	0	1.000
Clarence Lytle P/1B/RF	2	8	1	0	0	0	.125	0	0	0	11	1	0	1.000
Willie Green C/2B	2	6	0	0	0	0	.000	0	0	0	7	0	0	.000
Archie Pate P/RF	1	5	1	0	0	0	.200	0	0	0	1	5	0	1.000
James Lyons RF/P	2	3	2	0	0	0	.666	0	4	0	0	1	0	1.000
Bill Gatewood P	3	-	-	-	-	-	-	-	-	-	-	-	-	-
Bonny P	1	-	-	-	-	-	-	-	-	-	-	-	-	-
James Coleman	-	-	-	-	-	-	-	-	-	-	-	-	-	-

Passed Balls: Wills 1.

1911 Minneapolis Keystones: No given record. Record in games accounted for (31–28–3, .524) Captain: Jesse Briscoe.

Spring	Mobile (AL) [ml]	T 2–2
May 6	West Baden (IN) Sprudels	L 1–13 (Jackson)
7	West Baden (IN) Sprudels	L 0–6 (McNair)
8	West Baden (IN) Sprudels	L 5–14 (Pate)
–	French Lick (IN) Plutos	L 4–7
–	French Lick (IN) Plutos	L 4–6

Game Chronologies and Team Statistics 249

–	French Lick (IN) Plutos	L 3–4
14	Louisville (KY) Cubs	W 8–3 (McNair)
16	Louisville (KY) Cubs	Scheduled; no result found
–	Bowling Green (KY) Academy	L 2–4 (Pate)
21	Memphis (TN) Tigers	T 8–8, 15 innings {15–15} (Jackson)
22	Memphis (TN) Tigers	Doubleheader scheduled; no result found
23	Memphis (TN) Tigers	Scheduled; no result found
31	DeKalb (IL) at Rochelle (IL)	W 5–4 {4–3 (Jackson)}
June 1	DeKalb (IL)	L 4–6
2	DeKalb (IL)	Postponed
–	DeKalb (IL)	W 5–2 (McNair)
6	What Cheer (IA)	W 4–2 (McNair)
7	What Cheer (IA)	W 7–6
–	Strawberry Point (IA)	W 19–5
10	Charles City (IA)	W 6–0 (McNair)
11	Charles City (IA)	L 1–2 (Jackson)
12	Fayette (IA)	L 8–9
–	Fayette (IA)	W 7–2 (Bauchman)
15	Mason City (IA)	W 8–2 (Jackson)
–	All-Stars	W 5–2 (Pate)
18	Oelwein (IA)	L 2–7 (**McNair**/ Bauchman)
21	Waseca	W 11–1 (McNair)
22	Hastings	Withdrew in the first inning
23	Blooming Prairie	L 4–6 (Jackson)
24	H.P.Conrads at Lexington Park, St. Paul	Postponed
25	H.P.Conrads at Lexington Park, St. Paul	L 3–5 (McNair)
28	Alexandria	Postponed
29	Alexandria	L 6–9 (Jackson)
30	Alexandria	L 3–10 (**McNair**/ Pate)
		W 3–2 (McNair)
July 2	Grand Forks (ND)	L 0–3 (McNair)
3	Grand Forks (ND)	W 11–8 (Jackson)
4	Grand Forks (ND)	W 11–5 (McNair)
	Second game of doubleheader	postponed
6	Langdon (ND)	W
		W
9	Fargo (ND)	W 14–4
10	Devils Lake (ND)	W 4–2, 6 innings
		Devils Lake claimed forfeit win
13	Bismarck (ND)	L 7–9 (Jackson)
14	Bismarck (ND)	W 11–3, 8 innings (McNair)
15	Wibaux (MT)	L 5–6, 12 innings (Pate)
16	Beach (ND)	L 2–4 (McNair)
17	Beach (ND)	L 9–10 (Jackson)
18	Jamestown (ND)	L 1–11 (**Pate**/ McNair)
19	Jamestown (ND)	W 4–0, 7 innings (McNair)
20	Jamestown (ND)	W 9–2
23	Hankinson (ND)	W 13–4
24	Fairmount (ND)	W 2–0 (Bauchman)
	Ortonville	Cancelled
25	Graceville	W 4–2 (McNair)
26	Appleton	W 8–6
28	Long Prairie	W 10–2 (McNair)
29	Long Prairie	L 4–13 (**Jackson**/ Pate)
30	Long Prairie	T 1–1, 10 innings (McNair)
August 2	Elk Mound (WI)	Cancelled
3	Colfax (WI)	W 9–3
12	Marion (WI)	W 9–2
15	Grand Rapids (WI)	L 4–5
20	Indianapolis ABC's	L 4–12 {2–10}
		W 11–9 {8–6} (McNair)
21	Indianapolis ABC's	L 9–10, 10 innings (Bauchman)
22	Indianapolis ABC's	W 14–4 (McCune)

September 3	Charles City (IA)	L 4–6 (McNair)
4	Charles City (IA)	L 2–10 (Bauchman)
5	Charles City (IA)	L 4–16

1911 Minneapolis Keystones Pitching Statistics

Pitcher	G	GS	CG	IP	W	L	H	R	RPG	SO	BB	HBP	SH
Hurley McNair	21	20	18	162	12	7	107	66	3.66	58	18	6	2
Charles Jackson	11	11	10	95	3	7	72	75	7.10	14	5	2	0
Archie Pate	7	5	4	49	1	4	23	40	7.34	5	7	1	0
Harry Bauchman	5	4	4	39	2	2	61	34	7.84	9	4	1	1
Milroy McCune	1	1	1	9	1	0	8	4	4.00	6	2	1	0

Bauchman's strikeout and walk totals are based on 30 innings pitched. Jackson's hit totals are based on 67 innings pitched; his walk totals on 38 innings pitched and his strikeout totals on 30 innings pitched. McNair's hit totals are based on 136 innings pitched and strikeout and walk totals on 90 innings pitched. Pate's hit totals based on 27 innings pitched and his strikeout and walk totals on 17 innings pitched. Wild pitches: Bauchman 3; Jackson 1; McNair 1.

1911 Minneapolis Keystones Batting and Fielding Statistics

Player/Position	G	AB	H	D	T	HR	BA	R	SB	SF	PO	A	E	FA
Milroy McCune 3B/P	21	93	22	4	2	0	.236	10	1	3	33	35	12	.850
Card Phillips 2B/SS/3B	22	92	22	4	3	1	.239	11	6	3	41	50	9	.910
Jesse Briscoe CF/SS/1B/LF	21	91	26	4	4	0	.285	14	1	3	73	11	9	.903
Bert Woods RF/CF/LF	21	77	21	3	5	4	.272	16	4	3	16	4	2	.909
Hurley McNair P/RF/CF/LF/2B	18	76	27	6	3	3	.355	12	7	0	17	24	5	.891
William Embry 1B/SS	15	61	8	1	0	0	.131	8	3	0	149	10	6	.963
Archie Pate C/P/RF	15	59	8	1	0	2	.135	5	6	1	46	20	3	.956
James Wills C	13	51	13	1	0	0	.254	5	2	0	56	10	3	.956
Harry Bauchman SS/P/2B/1B/3B	11	46	15	0	0	0	.326	10	2	2	24	18	9	.823
Wilson LF	11	40	12	2	0	1	.300	10	0	3	25	2	2	.931
James Shawler LF	7	25	8	0	1	0	.320	4	1	2	9	0	0	1.000
Frank Davis SS	6	22	8	2	0	0	.363	6	2	0	11	17	4	.875
Terrell 1B	2	9	3	0	0	0	.333	0	0	1	26	1	1	.964
Eugene Barton LF	2	6	2	0	0	0	.333	0	0	0	2	2	1	.800
Harris RF/2B	2	6	1	0	0	0	.166	0	0	0	2	2	0	1.000

Passed Balls: Wills 5; Pate 3.

Selected Minneapolis Keystones Pitching Statistics 1908–1911

Pitcher/YRS	G	GS	CG	IP	W	L	H	R	RPG	SO	BB	HBP	SH
Charles Jackson 1908–11	56	49	44	441	26	20	281	199	4.06	189	52	23	4

Pitcher/YRS	G	GS	CG	IP	W	L	H	R	RPG	SO	BB	HBP	SH
Charles Jessup													
1908–09	50	36	33	351	25	15	190	102	2.65	202	45	12	8
Hurley McNair													
1910–11	27	25	22	200	15	9	136	88	3.96	71	26	8	3
Archie Pate													
1909–10, 11	20	18	12	138	8	8	86	82	5.59	39	18	1	1
Graham													
1908	12	12	7	72	6	3	58	33	4.12	26	22	6	0
W.J. Freeman													
1908	7	7	4	52	3	2	25	23	3.93	6	0	0	1
Bill Gatewood													
1909–10	7	6	5	48	2	3	32	30	5.62	13	3	3	0

Freeman's hit totals are based on 34 innings pitched and his strikeout and walk totals on 25 innings pitched. Gatewood's hit totals are based on 32 innings pitched and his strikeout and walk totals on 22 innings pitched. Graham's hit, strikeout, and bases on balls totals are based on 57 innings pitched. Jackson's hit totals are based on 359 innings pitched; his strikeout totals on 284 innings pitched and his walk totals on 282 innings pitched. Jessup's run totals are based on 346 innings pitched; his hit totals on 259 innings pitched; his strikeout totals on 266 innings pitched and his walk totals on 196 innings pitched. McNair's hit totals are based on 159 innings pitched and his strikeout and walk totals on 105 innings pitched. Pate's run totals are based on 132 innings pitched; his hit totals on 97 innings pitched and his strikeout and walk totals on 77 innings pitched. Wild Pitches: Graham 8; Jackson 3; Jessup 3; McNair 3; Gatewood 2; Pate 1.

Selected Minneapolis Keystones Batting and Fielding Statistics 1908–1911

Player/Position	G	AB	H	D	T	HR	BA	R	SB	SF	PO	A	E	FA
Eugene Barton														
LF 1908–10, 11	79	312	89	10	1	4	.285	39	13	3	92	11	13	.887
George Hopkins														
CF 1908–09	64	252	75	8	2	2	.297	33	6	3	75	2	5	.939
Milroy McCune														
3B 1909–11	60	216	44	5	2	0	.203	14	3	6	81	106	24	.886
Frank Davis														
SS 1909–11	53	185	58	10	1	1	.313	28	10	4	67	121	13	.935
Alex Irwin														
SS 1908, 09	49	184	34	2	1	0	.184	14	7	5	62	109	26	.868
Andrew Campbell														
C 1908–09	44	145	39	12	2	0	.268	17	9	1	283	35	9	.972
William Binga														
3B 1908	32	144	40	1	1	0	.277	26	4	0	44	64	18	.857
Willis Jones														
RF 1909	40	136	33	5	2	0	.242	16	10	2	31	3	1	.971
Haywood Rose														
1B 1909	40	135	25	5	0	0	.185	10	3	2	350	7	10	.972
Jack Johnson														
1B/RF 1908	32	130	35	3	3	3	.269	25	5	0	227	22	10	.961
Jesse Schaeffer														
2B/C 1908–09	35	128	25	5	1	1	.195	15	4	3	65	53	15	.887
Charles Jackson														
P 1908–11	37	119	32	0	0	1	.268	12	4	0	33	84	9	.928
Bob Marshall														
RF/1B 1908	31	107	21	2	1	0	.196	14	4	6	128	4	3	.977
Archie Pate														
P/C 1909–10, 11	28	102	18	1	0	3	.176	10	7	1	51	47	4	.960
Fred Roberts														
2B 1908	23	98	16	1	0	0	.163	10	7	2	54	52	9	.921

Player/Position	G	AB	H	D	T	HR	BA	R	SB	SF	PO	A	E	FA
Charles Jessup P 1908–09	28	92	16	3	1	1	.173	10	2	2	17	65	8	.911
Card Phillips 2B/SS 1911	22	92	22	4	3	1	.239	11	6	3	41	50	9	.910
Jesse Briscoe CF/SS 1911	21	91	26	4	4	0	.285	14	1	3	73	11	9	.903
Hurley McNair P/RF 1910–11	22	89	32	7	3	3	.359	12	8	0	19	30	7	.875
Bert Woods RF 1911	21	77	21	3	5	4	.271	16	4	3	16	4	2	.909
Dick Wallace C 1908	19	75	16	1	1	0	.213	6	3	1	105	13	5	.959
Willie Green C/3B 1909–10	24	73	10	2	0	1	.136	8	0	1	85	16	3	.971
James Wills C 1910–11	17	62	17	2	0	0	.274	7	5	0	73	16	3	.967
William Embry 1B 1911	15	61	8	1	0	0	.131	8	3	0	149	10	6	.963
Harry Bauchman SS/P 1911	12	46	15	0	0	0	.326	10	2	2	24	18	9	.823
James Shawler LF	12	43	15	0	1	0	.348	6	6	3	19	0	1	.950

Passed Balls: Campbell 7; Wills 6; Pate 3; Green 3; Wallace 1.

Appendix II

Player Register

This register covers the careers of those black professional ball players who spent significant amounts of time with Minnesota teams prior to 1920. The sources in compiling this index include James A. Riley's *The Biographical Encyclopedia of the Negro Baseball Leagues*; *The Negro Leagues Book* edited by Dick Clark and Larry Lester; Sol White's *History of Colored Base Ball, with Other Documents on the Early Black Game 1886–1936,* compiled by Jerry Malloy; Frank Leland's *Frank Leland's Baseball Club*; John Holway's *The Complete Book of Baseball's Negro Leagues*; Phil Dixon and Patrick J. Hannigan's *The Negro Baseball Leagues: A Photographic History*; *Swinging for the Fences* edited by Steven R. Hoffbeck; Paul Debono's *The Indianapolis ABC's* and *The Chicago American Giants*; *Black Baseball and Chicago* edited by Leslie A. Heaphy; James E. Brunson's *The Early Image of Black Baseball*, as well as United States Census records and the Minnesota and Illinois State Death Indexes. Many newspapers also provided a wealth of information including the *Chicago Tribune*; *Chicago Defender*; *Indianapolis Freeman*; *New York Age*; *Minneapolis Tribune*; *Minneapolis Journal*; *St. Paul Appeal*; *St. Paul Pioneer Press*; *St. Paul Dispatch*; *St. Paul Daily News*; *Twin City Star* and dozens of small town papers throughout the Midwest. The players' predominant positions are listed as well as any other vital information that is known about them. In the case of conflicting information, the least likely is listed in brackets.

Black Professionals in Minnesota 1884–1906

Robert Footes (also Foote) C
From Cincinnati, OH.

1894–1900	Chicago Unions
1900–1901	Waseca (MN) EACO's
1901	Chicago Unions (late in season)
1902	Chicago Columbia Giants
1902	Chicago Colored Stars (late in season)
1902–1903	Chicago Union Giants
1903–1904	Philadelphia Giants
1906	Brooklyn Royal Giants

"Bud" Fowler (born John W. Jackson) 2B/P/MGR

Born March 16, 1858, in Fort Plain, NY; died February 26, 1913, in Frankfort, NY. BR, TR. 5'7" 155 lbs.

–	New Castle (PA)
1878	Chelsea (MA)
1878	Lynn (MA) Live Oaks (International Association)
1878	Worcester (MA) (International Association)
1879	Malden (MA) (Eastern Massachusetts League)
–	Pittsfield (MA)
–	South Adams (MA)
1881	Guelph (Ontario, Canada) Maple Leafs
1881	Petrolia (Ontario, Canada) Imperials
–	Bradford (PA)
–	Painesville (OH)
–	Niles (OH)
–	East Liberty (PA)
1882	New Orleans Pickwicks
1883	Richmond (VA) Swans
1884	Stillwater (MN) (Northwestern League)
1885	Keokuk (IA) (Western League)
1885	Pueblo (CO) (Colorado League)
1885	Portland (ME) (Eastern New England League)
1886	Topeka (KS) (Western League)
1887	Binghamton (NY) (International Association)

1887	Montpelier (NH) (Vermont League)	1907	Philadelphia Giants (Cuban fall league)
1887	Laconia (NH)	1907–1908	Pop Watkins All Stars
1887	New York Gorhams	1908	Brooklyn Royal Giants
1888	Lafayette (IN) (Released before season)		Umpire NNL
1888	Crawfordsville (IN) (Central Interstate League)		
1888	Terre Haute (IN) (Central Interstate League)		
1888	Santa Fe (NM) (New Mexico League)		
1889	Greenville (MI) (Michigan State League)		
1890	Sterling (IL)—Galesburg (IL) (Illinois-Iowa League)		
1890	Burlington (IA) (Illinois-Iowa League)		
1891	Findlay (OH)		
1891	Lincoln (NE) Giants		
1892	Lincoln (NE)—Kearney (NE) (Nebraska State League)		

Harry Hyde 3B

Born August 1869 in Nashville, TN.

–	London Giants
1896–1901	Chicago Unions
1901	Waseca (MN) EACO's
1901	Algona (IA)
1902–1907	Chicago Union Giants
1907	St. Paul Gophers (late in season)
1908	Fuqua Giants (IL)
1908	Davenport (IA) Giants
1909	Chicago Union Giants

1893–1894	Findlay (OH)
1895	Page Fence Giants (Adrian, MI)
1895	Adrian (MI) (Michigan Sate League)
1895	Lansing (MI) (Michigan Sate League)
1896–1899	Findlay (OH)
1897	Galveston (TX) (winter league)
1898	Cuban Giants
1899–1900	All American Black Tourists (Findlay, OH)
1900	Barnes American Giants
1900	Monrovia (IN)
1901	Smoky City Giants
1902	Colored All Americans
1903	All American Black Tourists (Columbus, OH)
1904	Kansas City (MO) Stars
1909	All American Black Tourists (Frankfort, NY)
–	Los Angeles (CA)
–	San Bernardino (CA)
–	Lima (OH)
–	Watertown (WI)
–	Mobile (AL) (winter league)
–	El Paso (TX) (winter league)
–	Houston (TX) (winter league)
–	Oxford (MS) (winter league)

William Joyner SS/UTL

Born in 1868; from Memphis, TN; died January 16, 1933, in Chicago, IL.

1893–1900	Chicago Unions
1900	Waseca (MN) EACO's
1901	Chicago Unions
1901–1903	Chicago Union Giants

George Richardson 2B

Born in Topeka, Kansas, 1874; died of tuberculosis prior to February 1917.

1900–1901	Chicago Unions
1901–1902	Chicago Union Giants
1902–1903	Algona (IA) Brownies
1904	Renville (MN) All Stars

Bert Wakefield 1B

Born May 1872 in Troy, Kansas.

1895–1896	Emporia (KS) (Kansas State League)
1896	Atchison (KS) (Kansas State League)
1898	Salina (KS) (Kansas State League)
1899–1901	Chicago Unions
1901	Chicago Union Giants
1902	Algona (IA) Brownies
1904	Renville (MN) All Stars
1908	Kansas City (KS) Giants

William Holland ("Billy") P/OF

Born February 1874 in Alabama. TL.

1894	Chicago Unions
1895–1896	Page Fence Giants
1897–1899	Chicago Unions
1900	Chicago Columbia Giants
1900–1902	Waseca (MN) EACO's
1903	Algona (IA) Brownies
1904	Chicago Union Giants (early in season)
1904	Renville (MN) All Stars
1904	Chicago Unions (late in season)
1905	Leland Giants
1906–1907	Brooklyn Royal Giants

William Frank Williams ("Billy") 1B

Born October 24, 1877, in St. Paul, MN; died November 13, 1963, in St. Paul, MN. 182 lbs.

c.1894–1897	St. Paul (MN) Spaldings
c.1898–1900	Hamm's Exports (St. Paul, MN)
1898	St. Paul (MN) Capitols
1898	New Brighton (MN) Packers
1898	Shakopee (MN) Browns
1900	Red Wing (MN)
1901	Litchfield (MN)
1902	Prairie Leaguers (St. Paul, MN)
1902	West Publishing (St. Paul, MN)

1902	Royalton (MN)	–	Philadelphia Giants
1902	Lennon and Gibbons (St. Paul, MN)	1906	West Elizabeth (PA)
1902	St. Cloud (MN)	1908	Pittsburgh Giants
1903	Chippewa Falls (WI)	1909	Buxton (IA) Wonders
1907	Chaska (MN)	1909–1910	St. Paul Gophers (late in season, 1909)
1908	Lund Lands (Minneapolis, MN)	1911	Buxton (IA) Wonders
1908	Austin Westerns (St. Paul, MN)	1911	Twin City Gophers
1909	Young America (MN)	1911–1912	French Lick (IN) Plutos
1909–1910	Phil Dellar All-Stars (Minneapolis, MN)	1912	Chicago Union Giants
1910	Sauk Rapids (MN)	1913	Chicago Giants
1910	Twin City All-Stars (MN)	1913–1916	Pittsburgh Colored Collegians
		-	Homestead Grays

George H. Wilson P

Born July 1875 in Michigan; died November 26, 1915, in Kalamazoo, MI. TL.

Walter Ball P

Born 1881 in Detroit, MI; died December 15, 1946, in Chicago, IL. BR, TR.

1894	Adrian (MI) Light Guard	1896–1899	St. Paul amateur and semi-pro teams including the Nationals; Funk Exports; Young Cyclones; Bostons; L.G. Hoffman Caterpillars, The Dreies; Pioneer Press club; St. Anthony Park Manufacturing Company.
1895	Page Fence Giants		
1895	Adrian (MI) (Michigan State League)		
1896–1898	Page Fence Giants		
1899–1900	Chicago Columbia Giants		
1900–1902	Waseca (MN) EACO's		
1901	Chicago Columbia Giants (late in season)		
1903	Chicago Union Giants (preseason)	1900	Devils Lake (ND)
1903	St. Cloud (MN)	1900	Grand Forks (ND)
1903	Algona (IA) Brownies (late in season)	1901	University of North Dakota
1903	Cuban X-Giants (Cuban fall league)	1901	Cass Lake (MN)
1904–1905	Chippewa Falls (WI)	1901	Lakota (ND)
1905	Renville (MN) All Stars	1901	York (ND)
1905	Chicago Union Giants (late in season)	1902	St. Cloud (MN)
1906	Sheboygan (WI)	1902	Royalton (MN)
1907	Havana (Cuban winter league)	1903	York (ND)
1907–1908	Manitowoc (WI)	1903	Chicago Union Giants
1908	Cuban fall league	1904	Cuban X-Giants
		1904	Chicago Union Giants

Ed Woods ("Doggie") P

1891	Ansonia Cuban Giants (Connecticut State League)	1905	Cuban X-Giants
		1905	Brooklyn Royal Giants
1895–1898	Chicago Unions	1905	Leland Giants
1897	Page Fence Giants	1906	Quaker Giants (NY)
1897	Waupon (WI)	1906	Leland Giants
1899	Winona (MN)	1907	St. Paul Gophers
1899	La Crosse (WI)	1907	Chicago Union Giants
1900	Waseca (MN) EACO's	1907	Leland Giants
1901–1902	Algona (IA) Brownies	1908	Fe (Cuban winter league)
1903	Renville (MN)	1908	Minneapolis Keystones
1903	Appleton (MN)	1908–1909	Leland Giants
1903	Glencoe (MN)	1909	St. Paul Gophers (late in season)
1904	Renville (MN) All Stars	1910	Fe (Cuban winter league)
1904	Grey Eagle (MN)	1910	Chicago Giants
		1910/1911	Leland Giants (California winter league)

The St. Paul Gophers 1907–1911

George Isaac Armstrong ("Mule"; "Army") C

Born July 28, 1885, in Elizabeth, PA; died April 27, 1954, in Pittsburgh, PA.

1911	Chicago Giants
1911	Cuban winter league
1912	Royal Poinciana Hotel (Palm Beach, FL) (winter league)
1912	St. Louis Giants
1912	Chicago Giants
1913	Royal Poinciana Hotel (Palm Beach, FL) (winter league)

1913	Brooklyn Royal Giants		1914	Colored Gophers (Minneapolis, MN)
1913	Mohawk (Schenectady, NY) Giants		1916	Colored Gophers (St. Paul, MN)
1914	Lincoln Giants (NY)		1919	International Harvesters (St. Paul, MN)
1914	Lincoln Stars (NY)		1921	Willmar (MN)
1915	Chicago American Giants		1923	Willmar (MN)
1917–1924	Chicago Giants		1926	Willmar (MN)
1926	Walter Ball's (Chicago, IL) (MGR)			
1938	Chicago Columbia Giants (MGR)			

George L. Board 1B

Born October 8, 1880, in Kentucky.

1902–1909	Indianapolis ABC's
1910	St. Paul Gophers
1910–1913	Indianapolis ABC's

Sherman Barton ("Bucky") CF

Born February 2, 1875, in Illinois; died July 11, 1947, in Chicago, IL. BR, TR.

1896	Chicago Unions
1897	Cuban X-Giants
1898	Page Fence Giants
1899–1901	Chicago Columbia Giants
1900	Chicago Unions
1902	Chicago Union Giants
1902–1903	Algona (IA) Brownies
1904–1905	Chicago Union Giants
1906	Quaker Giants (NY)
1906	Cuban X-Giants
1906	Fuqua Giants (IL)
1906	Chicago Union Giants
1907–1910	St. Paul Gophers
1909/1910	Royal Poinciana Hotel (Palm Beach, FL) (listed on pre-season roster)
1911–1912	Chicago Giants

George Bowman 2B

From Coraopolis, PA.

1907	Frankford (PA) Giants
1907	Pittsburgh Giants
1908	Cleveland Giants
1909	Buxton (IA) Wonders
1910	St. Paul Gophers
1911	Omaha Giants

Harry Brown 3B/UTL

Played for many of the "leading clubs of the East" before the Gophers.

1910	St. Paul Gophers
1911	Twin City Gophers

William Henry Binga 3B/RF

Born February 26, 1869, in Michigan; died October 14, 1950, in Minneapolis, MN.

1895–1898	Page Fence Giants
1895	Adrian (MI) (Michigan State League)
1899–1901	Chicago Columbia Giants
1902	Chicago Union Giants
1902	Chicago Columbia Giants (late in season)
1903	Philadelphia Giants
1904	Chicago Union Giants
1905	Leland Giants
1906	Quaker Giants (NY)
1906–1907	Philadelphia Giants
1907	Royal Poinciana Hotel–Breaker's Hotel (Palm Beach, FL) (winter league)
1907	St. Paul Gophers (late in season)
1907	Chicago Union Giants (late in season)
1908	Minneapolis Keystones
1908–1910	St. Paul Gophers (late in season 1908)
1909	Norwood (MN) (one game)
1910	Oklahoma Giants (late in season)
1910	Kansas City (KS) Giants (late in season)
1911	Twin City Gophers
1912–1913	Hennepin Clothing Co. (Minneapolis, MN)
1913	French Lick (IN) Plutos (listed on pre-season roster)

Frank Davis ("Bunch") SS

BR, TR.

1906–1907	Chicago Union Giants
1907–1908	St. Paul Gophers
1909–1911	Minneapolis Keystones
1911	Twin City Gophers
1911	Chicago American Giants
1911	Leland Giants

John Barton Davis P

Born July 13, 1883, in Kentucky; died October 7, 1946, in St. Paul, MN. BR, TR.

1902	Chicago Columbia Giants
1903	Chicago Union Giants
1903	Algona (IA) Brownies
1904	Chicago Union Giants
1904	Chicago Unions
1905–1906	Leland Giants
1906–1907	Chicago Union Giants
1907	St. Paul Gophers
1907	Philadelphia Giants (Cuban fall league)
1908	Fe (Cuban winter league)
1908	Galesville (WI)
1908	Harmony (MN) (one game)
1909–1910	St. Paul Gophers
1909	Young America (MN) (one game)
1911	Twin City Gophers
1913	Hennepin Clothing Co. (Minneapolis, MN)

1914	Colored Gophers (Minneapolis, MN)	1920	Norfolk All-Stars
1914	Tri-States (Minneapolis, MN)	1920–1921	Detroit Stars
1919	International Harvesters (St. Paul, MN)	1922	St. Louis Stars (MGR)
1923–1925	Uptown Sanitary Team (St. Paul, MN) (MGR)	1923	Toledo Tigers
1927	St. Paul Colored All-Stars (MGR)	1923	Milwaukee Bears
1934	Minneapolis White Sox	1925	Memphis Red Sox
		1926	Albany (GA) Giants (MGR)
		1927	St. Louis Stars
		1927	Birmingham Black Barons (MGR)
		1928	St. Louis Giants
		1929–1931	Moberly (MO) Eagles (MGR)
		1934–1939	Gatewood Browns (Moberly, MO) (MGR)

Richard William Garrison ("Dick"; "Buster") P

Born May 28, 1886; from Pittsburgh, PA.

1904	Smoky City Giants
1907	Pittsburgh Giants
1908	Cleveland Giants
1908	Leland Giants
1909	St. Paul Gophers
1911	Pittsburgh Unions
1911	Pittsburgh Giants

William Miller Gatewood ("Big Bill") P

Born August 22, 1881, in San Antonio, TX; died December 8, 1962, in Columbia, MO. BR, TR. 6'7" 240 lb [6' 195 lb].

1899	San Antonio Rosebuds
1901	Austin (TX) Reds
1905	Paducah (KY) Nationals
1906	Leland Giants
1906	Illinois Giants
1906	Cuban X-Giants
1907	Royal Poinciana Hotel-Breaker's Hotel (Palm Beach, FL) (winter league)
1907	Leland Giants
1907	Philadelphia Giants (Cuban fall league)
1908	Leland Giants
1908	St. Paul Gophers
1909	Leland Giants
1909	Philadelphia Giants
1909–1910	Minneapolis Keystones
1909/1910	Royal Poinciana Hotel (Palm Beach, FL) (winter league)
1910	St. Louis Giants
1910/11	Leland Giants (California winter league)
1911–1912	Chicago Giants
1912/1913	Chicago American Giants (California winter league)
1912–1913	Chicago American Giants
1913	Chicago Giants
1914	Palm Beach (FL) (winter league)
1914	Lincoln Giants (NY)
1915	Chicago American Giants
1915–1916	St. Louis Giants
1917	Indianapolis ABC's
1917–1919	St. Louis Giants

Hardiman 2B

1911	Leland Giants
1911	Twin City Gophers

William Horn P

BR, TR.

1896–1900	Chicago Unions
1901	Chicago Columbia Giants
1902–1903	Algona (IA) Brownies
1904	St. Joseph (MO)
1904	Philadelphia Giants
1905	Leland Giants
1906	Quaker Giants (NY)
1906	Leland Giants
1906	Illinois Giants
1906	Chicago Union Giants
1907	St. Paul Gophers
1907–1908	Chicago Union Giants
1908	Leland Giants
1908	St. Paul Gophers (late in season)
1909	Chicago Union Giants
1910	Illinois Giants

George Johnson Jr. ("Rat"; "Chappie") C/1B

Born May 10, 1876, in Bellaire, OH, died August 17, 1949, in Clemson, SC. BR, TR. 5'9" 160 lbs.

1896–1898	Page Fence Giants
1899–1902	Chicago Columbia Giants
1901–1903	Chicago Union Giants
1903	Algona (IA) Brownies
1904–1905	Philadelphia Giants
1905	Renville (MN) All-Stars
1905	Chicago Union Giants (late in season)
1906	Quaker Giants (NY)
1906	Philadelphia Giants
1906	Cuban X-Giants (Cuban fall league)
1906–07	Havana (Cuban winter league)
1907	Brooklyn Royal Giants
1908	Breaker's Bulldogs (Palm Beach, FL) (winter league)
1908–1909	St. Paul Gophers

1909	Hastings (MN)
1909	Long Prairie (MN)
1909	Leland Giants
1910	Chicago Giants
1910/1911	Leland Giants (California winter league)
1911–1912	St. Louis Giants
1912	Breaker's Bulldogs (Palm Beach, FL) (winter league)
1913	Royal Poinciana Hotel (Palm Beach, FL) (winter league)
1913–1914	Mohawk (Schenectady, NY) Giants
1914	St. Louis Giants
1914	Louisville White Sox
1914	Chicago American Giants
1915	West Baden Sprudels
1916–1917	Dayton Chappies (MGR)
1917	Pennsylvania Red Caps of New York
1918	Custer's Baseball Club of Columbus (OH) (MGR)
1919	Bacharach (Atlantic City, NJ) Giants
1920–1921	Norfolk All-Stars (MGR)
1922–1923	Philadelphia Royal Stars (MGR)
1924–1927	Chappie Johnson's All-Stars (MGR)
1929–1930	Chappie Johnson's All-Stars of Canada (MGR)
1931	Chappie Johnson's Royal Giants (MGR)
1932–1935	Chappie Johnson's All-Stars (MGR)
1936	Chappie Johnson's Brooklyn Cuban Stars (MGR)

Louis Johnson ("Dicta"; "Spitball") P

Born June 20, 1887, in Elizabethtown, IL. BR, TR.

1908–1909	Indianapolis ABC's
1909	Danville (IL) Giants
1909–1910	Illinois Giants
1909	Leland Giants
1910	St. Paul Gophers
1911	Leland Giants
1911	Twin City Gophers
1912	French Lick (IN) Plutos
1912–1914	Chicago American Giants
1914	Louisville White Sox
1914–1917	Indianapolis ABC's
1915	Breaker's Bulldogs (Palm Beach, FL) (winter league)
1916	Royal Poinciana Hotel (Palm Beach, FL) (winter league)
1917	183rd Brigade team (Rockford, IL)
1919–1920	Detroit Stars
1920–1922	Indianapolis ABC's
1922	Pittsburgh Keystones (MGR)
1923	Toledo Tigers (MGR)
1923	Milwaukee Bears
1923	Chicago American Giants
1924–1925	Chicago Giants

Bert Jones P/OF

Born January 1878 in Kansas. TL.

1896–1898	Atchison (KS) (Kansas State League)
1898–1901	Chicago Unions
1901	Algona (IA)
1901	Chicago Union Giants
1902–1903	Algona (IA) Brownies
1902	Chicago Colored Stars (late in season)
1904–1905	Renville (MN) All Stars
1906	Brookings(SD)
1907	Bottineau (ND)
1908	Bryant(SD)
1908	Renville (MN)
1909	Groton (SD)
1909	Renville (MN)
1910	Watertown (SD)
1911	Twin City Gophers
1911	French Lick (IN) Plutos
1914	New Ulm (MN)
1916	Colored Gophers (St. Paul, MN)
1923	Askin & Marine Colored Red Sox (Minneapolis, MN)

Willis Jones LF

From Cincinnati, OH. BR, TR.

1895–1901	Chicago Unions
1901–1902	Chicago Union Giants
1902	Chicago Columbia Giants
1903	Algona (IA) Brownies
1904	Chicago Unions
1905–1906	Chicago Union Giants
1907–1908	St. Paul Gophers
1909	Minneapolis Keystones
1909–1912	Chicago Union Giants (late in season, 1909)
1910	St. Paul Gophers (one game)
1916	Cuban X-Giants
1920–1921	Gilkerson's Union Giants

Julius L. London P

Born November 7, 1882, in Texas; died March 25, 1958, in Harris County, TX.

1908	Memphis Union Giants
1909	Houston Black Buffaloes
1909	St. Paul Gophers
1910	Dallas Black Giants
1911	Chicago American Giants
1915	Galveston Black Pirates

Clarence Lester Lytle ("Dude") P

Born Dec. 22, 1879, in Illinois; died March 4, 1937, in Chicago, IL. BR, TR.

1901	Chicago Columbia Giants
1901	Chicago Colored Giants
1901–1903	Chicago Union Giants (late in season in 1903)

1904	Chicago Unions		1908	New Orleans Black Pelicans
1905–1906	Chicago Union Giants		1908	Memphis Union Giants
1906	Leland Giants		1908	San Antonio Black Bronchos
1907–1908	St. Paul Gophers		1909–1910	St. Paul Gophers
1909–1910	Chicago Union Giants		1909	Hudson (WI) (one game)
1910	Minneapolis Keystones		1909	Norwood (MN) (one game)
1910	St. Louis Giants		1911	Twin City Gophers
1911	Twin City Gophers			
1912	Chicago Union Giants			
1917	Fuqua Colored Giants (IL)			

William Joseph McMurray C/3B

Born February 26, 1882, in St. Louis, MO.

1905	Lloyd's Giants (St. Louis, MO)
1906	St. Louis Giants
1907	Chicago Union Giants
1907–1909	St. Paul Gophers
1910–1911	St. Louis Giants
1912–1914	West Baden (IN) Sprudels

Robert Wells Marshall ("Bobby") 1B

Born March 12, 1880, in Milwaukee, WI; died August 27, 1958, in Minneapolis, MN. 6'1" 180 lbs.

1906–1907	University of Minnesota
1906	Lund Lands (Minneapolis, MN)
1907	St. Paul Gophers
1907	Lamoure (ND)
1908	Minneapolis Keystones
1909	St. Paul Gophers
1909	Norwood (MN) (one game)
1909	Leland Giants
1909/1910	Royal Poinciana Hotel (Palm Beach, FL) (listed on pre-season roster)
1910	Chicago Giants
1910	St. Paul Gophers
1911	Twin City Gophers
1911	Perry Werden All-Stars (Minneapolis, MN)
1912–1913	Hennepin Clothing Co. (Minneapolis, MN)
1912	St. Joe Saints (Minneapolis, MN)
1913–1914	St. Cloud (MN) Pretzels
1914	Sauk Rapids (MN)
1914	Colored Gophers (Minneapolis, MN)
1915	Cokato (MN)
1916	Colored Gophers (St. Paul, MN)
1919	Mott (ND)
1919	Regent (ND)
1920	Minneapolis Colored Gophers
1921	Estevan (Saskatchewan, Canada)
1922	Minneapolis Buffalos (Minneapolis, MN)
1922	Askin & Marine Colored Red Sox (Minneapolis, MN)
1923	Uptown Sanitary Team (St. Paul, MN)
1925	St. Paul Colored Gophers
1925	Potts Motor Company (Minneapolis, MN)
1926	Minneapolis Colored White Sox
1927–1928	Johnny Baker Post team (St. Paul, MN)
1932	St. Paul Monarchs
1934	Minneapolis White Sox

Thomas Means P

BR, TR.

1899	Louisville Brotherhood
1900–1901	Chicago Unions
1901	Chicago Union Giants
1902	Chicago Columbia Giants (Big Rapids, MI)
1902	Chicago Colored Stars (late in season)
1903	Algona (IA) Brownies (late in season)
1904	Chicago Union Giants
1904	Chicago Unions
1907	Leland Giants
1907	St. Paul Gophers
1908	Fuqua Giants (IL)
1908	Davenport (IA) Giants
1908	Chicago Union Giants
1908	St. Paul Gophers (late in season)
1909	Louisville Cubs (early in season)
1912	All Nations

Eugene J. Milliner ("Gene"; "Gabbie") LF

Born November 27, 1878, in Hot Springs, Arkansas; died January 15, 1921, in Denver, CO.

–	Arlingtons (Hot Springs, AR)
1902–1903	Chicago Union Giants
1906–1907	Brooklyn Royal Giants
1909	St. Paul Gophers
1909	Young America (MN) (one game)
1910	Kansas City (MO) Royal Giants
1910	St. Paul Gophers
1911	Kansas City (KS) Giants
1911	Kansas City (MO) Royal Giants (one game)

Arthur McDougall SS

1905	Paducah (KY) Nationals
1906	St. Louis Giants
1908	Paducah (KY) Nationals

Thomas Clarington ("Lefty") Pangburn P

Born July 20, 1886, in Pennsylvania; died January 1973 in Elizabeth, PA. 5'7" 168 lbs. TL.

1906	West Elizabeth (PA)
1908	Pittsburgh Giants

1909	Buxton (IA) Wonders
1909–1910	St. Paul Gophers (late season in 1909)
1911	Buxton (IA) Wonders
1911	Twin City Gophers
1911–1912	French Lick (IN) Plutos
1914–1916	Pittsburgh Colored Collegians
–	Homestead Grays

Howard Petway P

Born 1884 in Tennessee; died October 27, 1918, in Ramsey County, MN. TL.

1905	Paducah (KY) Nationals
1906	Leland Giants
1908	St. Paul Gophers
1912	Hennepin Clothing Co. (Minneapolis, MN)
1915	Nashville Athletics

Samuel L. Ransom 2B

Born July 4, 1883, in Chicago, IL; died February 16, 1970, in Minneapolis, MN. 5'9" 154 lbs. BR, TR.

1905–1907	Beloit College (WI)
1907–1908	St. Paul Gophers (one game in 1908)

Fred Douglas Roberts ("Pop") 2B

Born January 28, 1873, in Danville, Illinois. BR, TR.

–	Danville (IL) Unions
1902	Chicago Unions
1902–1903	Chicago Union Giants
1902	Chicago Columbia Giants (Big Rapids, MI) (late in season)
1904	Chicago Unions
1905	Chicago Union Giants
1905	Chicago Columbia Giants
1906	Chicago Union Giants
1906	Leland Giants
1907	St. Paul Gophers
1907	Chicago Union Giants (late in season)
1908	Minneapolis Keystones
1909	Fuqua Giants (IL)
1909–1910	Illinois Giants

Haywood Rose ("Kissing Bug") 1B/C

Born 1870 (1873) in Nashville, TN; died January 7, 1947 in Chicago, IL.

1899	Louisville Brotherhood
1901	Chicago Unions
1901	Algona (IA) Brownies
1902	Chicago Columbia Giants
1902	Chicago Colored Stars (late in season)
1903	Chicago Union Giants
1904	Chicago Unions
1904–1906	Chicago Union Giants
1905	Chicago Columbia Giants
1907–1908	Leland Giants
1908	St. Paul Gophers

1909	Fuqua Giants (IL)
1909	Minneapolis Keystones
1909	St. Paul Gophers (late in season)
1910	Louisville Cubs
1911	Leland Giants
1911	Chicago Union Giants

Jesse Schaeffer ("Babe") C/UTL

Born 1882 in Illinois. BR, TR.

1904	Chicago Unions
1904	Chicago Union Giants
1906	Chicago Union Giants
1907	St. Paul Gophers
1908	Galesville (WI)
1908	St. Paul Gophers
1908–1909	Minneapolis Keystones
1909	Hudson (WI)
1909–1910	St. Paul Gophers
1909	Norwood (MN) (one game)
1911	Twin City Gophers
1911	Chicago Giants
1911	Leland Giants
1914	East St. Louis (IL) Giants

William Henry Selden (also Seldon) ("Bee"; "Seldom") SS

Born February 4, 1885, in Ohio.

1907	Columbus (OH) Owls
1907	Rockford (OH)
1907	Monroeville (IN)
1908	Columbus (OH) Giants
1908	Dayton Giants
1909	Lima (OH) Giants
1910	Illinois Giants
1910	Chicago Giants
1911	Twin City Gophers
1911–1912	Indianapolis ABC's (late in season 1911)
1912	French Lick (IN) Plutos
1912	Chicago American Giants
1913–1914	Indianapolis ABC's
1914	Mohawk (Schenectady, NY) Giants
1914	Chicago Giants
–	Dayton Marcos
1915	Lima (OH) Colonials
1916	Cascade (OH)
1917	Fort Wayne (IN) Giants
1919	Fort Wayne (IN) Giants
1919	Selden's Van Wert (OH) All-Stars
1919	Chicago Keystones
1920–21	Fort Wayne (IN) Giants (MGR)
1921	Fort Wayne (IN) Pyramids
1922	Riddle's All-Stars (Fort Wayne, IN)
1931	Paulding County (OH) Giants (MGR)
1932	Van Wert (OH) Merchants
1933	Bellefontaine (OH) Grays
1933	Paulding County (OH) Giants

James H. Smith SS/3B

Born in Illinois in 1876.

–	Chicago Uniques (Juniors)
1897	Chicago Clippers
–	9th United States Cavalry team
–	48th United States Volunteers team
1901–1902	Chicago Unions
1902	Chicago Columbia Giants
1902–1903	Chicago Union Giants
1902	Chicago Colored Stars (late in season)
1903	Algona (IA) Brownies
1904	Chicago Unions
1904	Cuban X-Giants
1905–1906	Leland Giants
1906	Illinois Giants
1907	St. Paul Gophers
1907–1908	Chicago Union Giants
1908	Leland Giants
1909	Fuqua Giants (IL)
1909	Illinois Giants
1909	St. Paul Gophers
1910	Chicago Union Giants
1910	Chicago Giants
1911	Leland Giants
1918	183rd Brigade team (Rockford, IL) (MGR)

Walter Stallard P

Born September 6, 1888 [1890], in Minnesota.

1910	Hinckley (MN)
1910	St. Paul Gophers
1911	Twin City Gophers
1911	French Lick (IN) Plutos (late in season 1911)
1912–1913	Louisville Cubs
1913–1914	Indianapolis ABC's

George H. Taylor 1B

From Three Rivers, MI. BR, TR.

1889	Aspen (CO) (Colorado State League)
1890	Denver Athletic Club (Denver, CO)
1890	George F. Higgins Club (Denver, CO)
1890	Mays Club (Denver, CO)
1890–1891	Lincoln (NE) Giants
1892	Beatrice (NE) (Nebraska State League)
1893	Denver (CO)
1893	Scott team (Denver, CO)
1894	Council Bluffs (IA) Maroons
1895	Page Fence Giants
1896	Denver (CO) (Colorado State League)
1896–1898	Page Fence Giants
–	Cuban Giants
–	Philadelphia Giants
1902–1904	Chicago Union Giants (late in season 1902)
1905–1906	Leland Giants
1907	St. Paul Gophers
1908	Chicago Union Giants
1909	Illinois Giants

James Taylor ("Candy Jim") 3B

Born February 1, 1884, in Anderson, SC; died April 3, 1948, in Chicago, IL. 5'9" 185 lbs. BR, TR.

1901–1903	Amateur South Carolina clubs
1904–1909	Birmingham Giants
1909	St. Paul Gophers
1910	Chicago Giants
1910	St. Paul Gophers
1910	West Baden Sprudels
1911	St. Louis Giants
1912	West Baden Sprudels
1912–1913	Chicago American Giants
1913	West Baden Sprudels
1914	Indianapolis ABC's
1915	Louisville White Sox
1915	Chicago Black Sox
1915	West Baden Sprudels
1915–1918	Indianapolis ABC's
1919–1921	Dayton Marcos (MGR)
1922–1923	Cleveland Tate Stars (MGR)
1923	Toledo Tigers (MGR)
1923–1925	St. Louis Stars (MGR)
1926	Cleveland Elites (MGR)
1926	Detroit Stars (MGR)
1927–1929	St. Louis Stars (MGR)
1930	Memphis Red Sox (MGR)
1931–1933	Indianapolis ABC's (MGR)
1933	Detroit Stars (MGR)
1933–1934	Nashville Elite Giants (MGR)
1934–1935	Wilson's Elite Giants (California winter league) (MGR)
1935	Columbus Elite Giants (MGR)
1935–1936	Royal Giants (California winter league) (MGR)
1936	Washington Elite Giants (MGR)
1936	Negro League All-Stars (MGR)
1937–1939	Chicago American Giants (MGR)
1940	Birmingham Black Barons (MGR)
1941–1942	Chicago American Giants (MGR)
1943–1944	Homestead Grays (MGR)
1945–1947	Chicago American Giants (MGR)
1948	Baltimore Elite Giants (MGR)

John Boyce Taylor ("Steel-Arm Johnny") P

Born August 8, 1880, in Anderson, SC; died March 25, 1956, Peoria, IL. BR, TR. 5'10" 170 lbs.

1898	Biddle University (Charlotte, NC)
1898	Greenwood (SC) Red Stockings
1898	Greenville (SC)
1899	Biddle University (Charlotte, NC) (Coach)
1899–1900	Anderson (SC)
1903–1909	Birmingham Giants

1905	Biddle University (Charlotte, NC) (Coach)		1906	Leland Giants
1908	M & I College (Holly Springs, MS) (Coach)		1906	Illinois Giants
			1908–1911	Minneapolis Keystones (late in season 1911)
1909	St. Paul Gophers		1908	St. Paul Gophers (late in season)
1909–1910	Royal Poinciana Hotel (Palm Beach, FL) (winter league)		1909	St. Paul Gophers (late in season)
			1911	Leland Giants
1910	Chicago Giants			
1910	West Baden (IN) Sprudels			
1911	St. Louis Giants			
1912–1913	West Baden (IN) Sprudels			
1912	Cuban winter league			
1913	Chicago American Giants			
1914–1916	Indianapolis ABC's			
1915	Louisville White Sox (MGR)			
1915	Chicago Black Sox			
1918	Farmington (IL) (MGR)			
1920	Peoria Black Devils (MGR)			
1920	Indianapolis ABC's			
1924	Washington Potomacs (Coach)			
1929–1930	Springfield (IL) Giants (MGR)			

Harry Bauchman (also Bockmann) ("Pick") 2B/SS/3B

Born June 6, 1890, in Nebraska; died June 20, 1931, in Chicago, IL. BR, TR.

1911	Omaha Giants
1911	Minneapolis Keystones
1911–1914	Chicago Giants
1913–1914	Chicago Union Giants
1915–1921	Chicago American Giants
1915/1916	Cuban winter league
1917	Chicago Union Giants
1919	Chicago Giants
1920	Norfolk All-Stars
1922–1923	Chicago Giants

Felix Wallace ("Dick") 2B/SS

Born July 22, 1882 [1884], in Owensboro, Kentucky; died July 19, 1925, in Owensboro, KY. BR, TR.

1903–1905	Paducah (KY) Nationals
1906–1907	Cuban Giants
1907	Philadelphia Giants (Cuban fall league)
1908	Fe (Cuban winter league)
1908–1909	St. Paul Gophers
1909	Leland Giants
1910	Chicago Giants
1911–1914	St. Louis Giants
1912	Cuban winter league
1913	Breakers Bulldogs (Palm Beach, FL) (winter league)
1914	Lincoln Giants (NY)
1915–1916	St. Louis Giants
1916	Breakers Bulldogs (Palm Beach, FL) (winter league)
1916–1917	Bacharach Giants (Atlantic City, NJ)
1917	Breakers Bulldogs (Palm Beach, FL) (winter league)
1917–1918	Lincoln Giants (NY)
1918	Brooklyn Royal Giants
1919	Hilldale (late in season)
1918–1921	St. Louis Giants (MGR 1920–21)
1924	St. Louis Giants (MGR)

Wesley 2B/LF

1910	St. Paul Gophers

The Minneapolis Keystones 1908–1911

Eugene Barton ("Cherry") LF

Born in Illinois, April 27, 1880; died July 3, 1922, in Chicago, IL.

Jesse Briscoe CF

1909–1910	Louisville Cubs (listed on pre-season roster 1910)
1910	West Baden (IN) Sprudels
1910	New York Giants
1911	Minneapolis Keystones
1912	Louisville Cubs
1913	Louisville White Sox
1913	Indianapolis ABC's (late in season)
1914	Louisville White Sox

Andrew Campbell C

Born in Texas in 1875.

1893–1898	Galveston (TX) Flyaways
–	Arlingtons (Hot Springs, AR)
1901–1902	Fort Worth (TX) Colts
1901	Cuban Giants
1902	Chicago Unions
1902–1903	Chicago Union Giants
1905	Texas Steers
1905–1906	Leland Giants
1907	St. Paul Gophers
1908	Minneapolis Keystones
1908	Long Prairie, MN
1908–1909	Minneapolis Keystones
1909	Chicago Union Giants (early in season)
1910	Kansas City (MO) Royal Giants
1910	St. Paul Gophers (late in the season)

William James Dewberry (also Duberry) P/2B

Born September 5, 1874, in Chicago, IL; died September 1, 1946, in Chicago, IL.

1903–1904	Chicago Union Giants		1910	Buxton (IA) Wonders
1908	Leland Giants		1911	Twin City Gophers
1908	Minneapolis Keystones		1911	Walker (MN)
			1912–1913	Hennepin Clothing Co. (Minneapolis, MN)
			1914	Minneapolis Colored Giants (MGR)

William Ross Embry ("Cap") 1B/CF

Born August 28, 1878, in Knox, IN; died January 10, 1956, in Fayette, KY.

1905	Danville (IL) Unions
1908	Louisville Unions
1909	Idaho Stars (Vincennes, IN)
1909–1910	Louisville Cubs
1910	Chicago Union Giants
1911	Minneapolis Keystones

Umpire NNL, 1923

Graham P

TR

1907	Chicago Union Giants
1908	Minneapolis Keystones

Willie Green ("The Eat") C

1905	Lloyd's Giants (St. Louis, MO)
1906	St. Louis Giants
1906	Chicago Union Giants
1908	St. Paul Gophers
1909–1910	Minneapolis Keystones
1910–1911	St. Louis Giants
1912	Leland Giants

George Hopkins P/2B/CF

Born in Missouri in 1858.

1888–1889	New Orleans Pinchbacks
1890	Pensacola (FL) Grants
1890–1895	Chicago Unions
1895	Page Fence Giants
1896–1899	Chicago Unions
1901–1902	Algona (IA) Brownies
1902	Chicago Colored Stars (late in season)
1904	Chicago Unions
1905–1907	Chicago Union Giants
1908–1909	Minneapolis Keystones
1909	St. Paul Gophers (late in season)

Alexander Charles Irwin (also Irvin) ("Happy"; "Bud") SS/2B

Born April 4, 1881 [1882], in South Carolina; lived in Evanston, IL.

1904	Chicago Unions
1905	Chicago Union Giants
1906	Leland Giants
1906	Illinois Giants
1906	Fuqua Giants (IL)
1908	Minneapolis Keystones
1909	Menomonie (WI) White Sox
1909	Elk Mound (WI)
1909	Cadott (WI)
1909	Minneapolis Keystones

Charles Jackson ("Slick"; "Baby") P

1906	Fuqua Giants (IL)
1908–1911	Minneapolis Keystones
1909	Norwood (MN) (one game)
1910	St. Paul Gophers (late in season)

Charles Jessup P

Born April 18, 1881, in Kentucky.

1907	Chicago Union Giants
1908	Minneapolis Keystones
1909	Chicago Union Giants
1909	Minneapolis Keystones
1909–1912	Chicago Union Giants

Jack Johnson ("Topeka Jack") 1B/2B

Born in 1883. 6'1" 180 lbs. BR.

1904	Chicago Unions
1905	Chicago Union Giants
1906	Topeka Giants
1907	Chicago Union Giants
1908	Minneapolis Keystones
1909	Kansas City (KS) Giants
1910	Kansas City (MO) Royal Giants
1911	Kansas City (KS) Giants
1911	Kansas City (MO) Royal Giants (one game)
1912	Kansas City Giants
1917	Topeka Giants (MGR)

Milroy McCune 3B

Born July 4, 1883, in Texas.

1909–1911	Minneapolis Keystones
1913	Chicago Giants

Hurley McNair P/OF

Born October 28, 1888, in Marshall, TX; died December 2, 1948, in Kansas City, MO. BB, TL. 5'6" 150 lbs.

1910	Houston Black Buffaloes
1910–1911	Minneapolis Keystones
1910	St. Paul Gophers (late in season)
1911	Kansas City (KS) Giants
1911	Chicago Giants
1912	Kansas City (MO) Royal Giants
1912	Brooklyn Royal Giants
1912–1913	Chicago Giants
1913	Kansas City (KS) Giants
1913–1914	Chicago Union Giants
1914	Kansas City (MO) Royal Giants

1915–1916	Chicago American Giants		1915	Chicago Giants
1916	Chicago Union Giants		1916	Bowser's Indianapolis ABC's
1917	Lost Island (IA) Giants		1917	Chicago Giants
1917	All Nations		1920	Winnipeg Giants

"Card" Phillips 2B/SS

1911   Minneapolis Keystones

1918–1919	25th Infantry Regiment
1919	Chicago Union Giants
1919	Detroit Stars
1920–1927	Kansas City Monarchs
1920/21	Los Angeles White Sox (California winter league)
1921/22	Colored All Stars (California winter league)
1922/23	Los Angeles White Sox (California winter league)
1924/25	Los Angeles White Sox (California winter league)
1924/25	St. Louis Giants (California winter league)
1928	Detroit Stars
1930–1931	Gilkerson's Union Giants
1932	John Donaldson's All Stars (Fairmont, MN)
1934	Kansas City Monarchs
1937	Cincinnati Tigers
Umpire NNL	

James Shawler LF

Born 1879 in Kentucky.

1902–1909	Indianapolis ABC's
1908–1909	Chicago Union Giants
1909	Leland Giants (late in season)
1910–1911	Minneapolis Keystones
1911–1913	Indianapolis ABC's (late in season 1911)
1912	Abram's Indianapolis ABC's

Dick Wallace ("Noisy") C

1904	Chicago Unions
1906	Fuqua Giants (IL)
1907	St. Paul Gophers (late in season)
1907	Chicago Union Giants (late in season)
1908	Minneapolis Keystones
1909	Fuqua Giants (IL)
1909–1910	Illinois Giants
1909	St. Paul Gophers (late in season)
1910	Chicago Giants (late in season)
1911	Havana Stars of Chicago

John H. Merida ("Snowball"; "Big Boy") 2B/C

Born May 1879 in Spiceland, IN; died May 13, 1911, in Kansas City, MO.

1895–1903	Spiceland Academy (IN)
c. 1905	Krell-French Piano Company (New Castle, IN)
1907–1909	Indianapolis ABC's
1910	Minneapolis Keystones
1911	Kansas City (MO) Royal Giants

James A. Wills (also Wells) C

From Waco, TX.

1910	Houston Black Buffaloes
1910–1911	Minneapolis Keystones

Wilson LF

1911   Minneapolis Keystones

Archie Pate P/OF

Born July 15, 1886 [1883], in Wisconsin; died April 16, 1936, in Chicago, IL.

1908	Fuqua Giants (IL)
1908	Davenport (IA) Giants
1908–1909	Chicago Union Giants
1909	Fuqua Giants (IL)
1909	St. Paul Gophers
1909	Hudson (WI) (one game)
1909	Janesville (MN)
1909–1911	Minneapolis Keystones
1911	Louisville Cubs
1911	Leland Giants
1911	Chicago Giants
1912	St. Louis Giants
1912–1914	Chicago Giants
1914	New York Stars
1915	Chicago Union Giants
1915	Chicago Black Sox
1915	New York Black Sox

Bert Woods OF

1905	Danville (IL) Unions
1907	Danville (IL) Unions
1908	Louisville Cubs
1909	Danville (IL) Unions
1909	West Baden (IN) Sprudels
1910	French Lick (IN) Plutos
1910	Louisville Cubs
1911	Minneapolis Keystones
1911	Indianapolis ABC's (late in season)

Frank Young 2B/P

Born 1885 in Indiana.

1907	Indianapolis ABC's
1908–1909	Chicago Union Giants
1910	Minneapolis Keystones

Appendix III

Rosters of Minnesota Black Teams 1876–1945

Taking a cue from the accounts in Steve Hoffbeck's *Swinging for the Fences*, I have listed only the most significant all-black Minnesota clubs prior to integration. For the most part the rosters were taken from actual box scores and the players are listed in order of number of appearances, with owners and managers listed first. Teams and players who were mentioned in preseason or pre-game lineups but for whom there is no evidence they actually appeared in a game are shown in *italics*. The player's dominant position is shown in **bold** type. As the players' names were reported inconsistently, the spelling that appeared most frequently has been used. Because first names were rarely printed in box scores and the players on the same team often shared the same surname, it was not always possible to make definitive identifications. The Gophers and Keystones rosters can be found in Appendix I.

1876

Minneapolis Unions

Dick Jackson
Lewis Mason
D. Williams
James Cunningham
Abe Myrick
G. Williams
Gardner
Cheatum
Johnson
T. Williams
Geo. Todd
E.H. Hamilton
Wm. Berry

St. Paul Blue Stars

W. M. Johnson
C. Allen
F. Gill
W. Gill
Wm. B. Perkins
T. Combs
Edwards
Murray
Bally
W. F. Johnson
W. Barnes
J. Combs

1887

St. Paul Quicksteps

Wm. D. Carter .... Mgr
Charles A. Lett Cpt/2B
James M. Duke .... P
Andrew Leboo .... RF/CF
Wm. H. Spigner ...... LF/RF/CF
Wm. N. Brown 1B
T. H. Young C
Harry W. Fairfax .... SS
C. Wilkins 3B
Alan F. Newton 3B/LF
A. Hester .... CF
Williams .... LF
Andrew A. Cotton .... Sub

1897

Douglass Base Ball Club

C.M. Tibbs .... Mgr
Howard .... P
Hall C
A.M. Lee .... P
C.H. Miller C
Willie Williams 1B
Geo. Bailey 2B
Harrp Franklin 3B
Andrew Combs .... SS
R. Farr .... LF
John Kelley .... CF
Willie Greene .... RF

1905

St. Paul Giants

D. Saunders .... Mgr
Charley Myrick 3B
Fisher .... P
Yeiser C
George Wilson .... P
Billy Williams Cpt/1B

1907

Colored Independent Club (Minneapolis)

Norman F. Williams .... Mgr
Robert Carson C
Zeak Harper .... P
Harry Lee .... SS
"Spike" Wheaton 1B
Ted Williams 2B
Claud O' Brien 3B
Westley Slemmens .... RF
Joe Williams .... LF
Eddie Williams .... CF

Minneapolis Keystones

Oliver 3B
Johnson 1B
J. Williams .... CF
Reese 2B
Charley Myrick C
Smith .... LF
Winse .... RF
Taylor .... P
Williams .... P
Powell C

1912

Hennepin Clothing Company (Minneapolis)

Frank H. Buchholz ..... Mgr
Paul Benson .... Secretary
Bobby Marshall .. Cpt/P/C/1B
"Skoogs" Davis ..... CF/P/LF
William Binga C/3B/1B
L. Marshall .... RF
Alex Irwin 2B
David "Moose"
  Kay P/3B/1B/C
Nelson 1B/LF/CF
Starks .... SS
Jones LF/2B
Perry 3B/LF
Williams 3B/LF
Bannister .... SS
Howard Petway .... CF
Dick Settles .... LF
Hughes 1B
Wergen .... LF/P
Hickman 3B
"Buck" Freeman .... P
Joe Davis .... P
Eddie Davis 1B
Sam Ransom 2B
"Big Chief" Baker .... SS
Sandford 3B
Roy Jones .... OF
John Davis .... P
Arthur McDougall .... SS

1913

Hennepin Clothing Company (Minneapolis)

Paul R. Benson .... Mgr
Bobby Marshall C/3B
William Binga 3B/RF/CF
Ike Bradley .... LF/RF
Lee Davis C
Alex Irwin 2B
"Chic" Williams CF/2B

"Smiles" Iverson
  (Ivester) .... SS
Joe Williams .... P/LF
Joe Davis .... P/OF
John Davis .... P/OF
Clark 1B
"Moose" Kay .... P/RF
"Slim" Nelson 1B
Starks .... SS
Dick Settles 2B
P. Davis .... P
Worthington .... P
Earl Hamilton .... P
"Bud" Johnson .... SS
Redmond .... LF
Clarkson 1B

1914

Minneapolis Colored Giants

Benson .... Mgr
Alex Irwin .... Cpt/ 2B
L. Marshall .... RF
Binga 3B
Clark .... CF
"Moose" Kay .... P
"Smokey Joe" Williams ..... P
Lee Davis C
Wilson .... LF
Simpson .... P
Ivester C
"Slim" Nelson 1B
Porter .... Utl
Stark .... Utl
Giddington .... Utl
Bobby Marshall
"Chick" Williams
Joe Davis
Johnny Davis

Colored Gophers (Minneapolis)

Cy Olson .... Mgr
Lee Davis C
Clarke 1B
William Binga 3B/C/P
Nelson P/2B/CF
"Chick" Jones CF/2B
K. Jones .... LF/SS
Iverson (Ivester) SS/2B
John Davis P/2B
"Moose" Kay ... RF/CF/3B/P
Simpson .... P/OF
Kenneson 2B/RF/SS/3B
Williams .... CF/RF
Bobby Marshall ..... RF/SS/P
Lewis (Touis) .... SS

A. Jones 2B
Carl Jones .... LF
L. Jones .... CF
Bliss .... RF
Grant

1915

Colored Giants

Cy Olson .... Mgr
Dunlap .... P
Joe Davis .... P
Bob Marshall

1916

St. Paul Colored Giants

"Cannonball" Jackson ..... P
Davis C

Minneapolis Colored Gophers

L. Davis C
Chick Williams .... LF
"Cannonball" Joe Jackson .. P
Ramsey .... CF
Bob Marshall 3B
"Lefty" Simpson .... P
Bert Jones 1B
J. Davis .... P
William Binga .... RF
Hicks 2B
Lewis .... SS

1917

Duluth Steel Plant Colored Team

L. Reed
J. Simmons
T. Durand
J. Mark
L. Rayford
T. Ramsey
B. Canty
J. Fish
W. Ferguson
R. Morris
R. Murphy

1920

Minneapolis Colored Gophers

"Bud" Davis C
Williams .... P

Schumacker .... P
Bob Marshall 3B
"Smokeball" Davis .... P
Pringle 1B
Stride 2B
Lewis .... SS
"Duke" Williams .... OF
Kay .... OF
John Williams .... OF

1921

Colored Askin & Marines (Minneapolis)

Will Brooks .... Mgr/RF
Lewis 2B
Bradley 1B
Henderson .... SS
Arnold .... P
Smith .... LF
Sidney C
Dayton .... CF
Eddie .... CF
Carl 3B

Keystone Colored Giants (Minneapolis)

Ramsey .... CF/P
Carey 2B
Bradley LF/2B
Kay RF/1B
Williams 3B
Allen .... P/OF
Jones 1B/P
Davis .... P
Lewis .... SS
Blackman .... RF
Jackson C
Crawford .... P

1922

Askin & Marine Colored Red Sox (Minneapolis)

Will Brooks ...... Mgr/Cpt/RF
Harry Lewis LF/2B
Harold Lewis .... SS/LF
Bob Ramsey .... CF
Lee Davis C
Bobby Marshall 3B
Riebe 1B/2B/SS
Hempel 2B/1B
Blackman .... RF
Wilson .... P/RF
Joe Williams .... P
Ike Bradley 1B
Joe Davis .... P

Speed Coleman 3B/2B
Hutchinson .... RF
Harry Davis 2B
E. Jackson .... RF

Minneapolis Colored Buffaloes

Joe Davis .... P
Lee Davis C
Bobby Marshall

Uptown Sanitary Shop Team (St. Paul)

"Steel Arm" Roach .... P
Harry Davis P/2B/OF
Carter Coleman 3B/LF
Du Love .... CF/C
J. West
Tim Howard C
Tucker
Mosley 1B
Dwyer C
Dennis Ware
Frank Ware
Burton .... P
Rudolph .... LF
White .... RF
Dyer .... SS
Wicks .... RF
Goldie
Chink .... SS
Clariborne 1B
McNeal 2B

1923

Askin & Marine Colored Red Sox (Minneapolis)

Wn. R. McKinnon ... Owner
Will Brooks ..... Mgr/RF/Utl
Harold Lewis SS/1B
Roy Jackson .... LF
Lee Davis .... Cpt/C
Bert Jones 1B
George C. Howard 3B
"Coop"
  Longley 2B/P/OF/SS
Eddie Blackman .... CF
Blackburn .... CF/RF/LF/P
"Lefty" Wilson ..... P/LF/RF
Joe Davis .... P/CF
Geo. Coleman 2B
H. Jones 2B
Burnett .... CF
Tanner 2B
Bert Tucker
Bobby Marshall 1B
Edgar Jackson .... RF

Sonny Lucas .... Utl
Tommy Young .... Utl

Minneapolis Browns

Charles L. Gooch .. President
W. A. Smith .... Mgr
Isaac Bradley
Eddie Blackman
Lefty Williams
Joe Davis
Bob Ramsey
Lee Davis
Harold Lewis
Joe Williams
Gilbert Rice
John Craig
Otto Mitchell
M. Richards
Art Jones
Jesse Reed

Uptown Sanitary Shop Team (St. Paul)/St. Paul Colored Gophers

Owen Howell .... Owner
John Davis Mgr/P/RF/2B
Bobby Marshall 3B/2B/C
E. Roach .... P
Dennis Ware .... SS
George White 2B/LF
Mosley 1B
Du Love .... Cpt/CF/P
James West ...... LF/CF/RF
L'p'mb .... RF/P/LF
Howard C
Luck C
Lee Davis C
Joe Davis .... P
Hogan
Tucker
H. Davis .... P
Williams .... P
Coleman 2B

1924

Askin & Marine Colored Red Sox (Minneapolis)

Will Brooks .... Mgr
Coleman 3B
Bradley 1B
Hogan .... CF
Davis .... P
Moseley .... LF
King 2B
Luck C
Roach .... RF
Lewis .... SS

Chicago, Milwaukee, & St. Paul Railroad Team

George Connelly ..... Owner
G. A. Van Dyke ...... Owner
Milton Williams .... Mgr
Macey Breedlove
Bert Lewis
Dayton Blackburn
Fred Breedlove
Steve Banner
Richardson
Jesse Reed
Joe Carter
Ray Lewis
Edgar Jackson
Joe Scott

Pioneer Limited Giants

Bob Ramay .... P
"Bullet" Roach .... P
Lucke
Coleman
Lewis
Bradley

Uptown Sanitary Shop Team (St. Paul)

Johnny Davis .... Mgr

1925

Potts Motor Company (Minneapolis)

Billy Potts .... Owner
Bill Brooks .... Mgr
Eddie Boyd .... P/SS
Bobby Marshall 1B
E. Jackson .... OF/C
H. Rice 2B
B. Suggs 3B
Luck C
Bill Freeman .... P
D. Blackman .... OF
Robinson .... P
D. Freeman
Hudson .... P
Joe Davis .... P
Cooper C
A. Freeman .... OF
Roberts .... P

St. Paul Colored Gophers

Coleman 2B
Lewis .... SS
Mosley .... CF/P
Teeters 1B
L. Davis C
Ewing .... P/CF
Bob Marshall 3B
Bradley .... LF
Du Love .... RF
Barber .... P
Freeman .... P
Boyd 3B
G. Davis .... RF
Ramsay .... LF

Uptown Sanitary Shop Team (St. Paul)

Owen Howell .... Owner
John Davis .... Mgr/P
Harold Roach .... P
Jones .... P
Brown C
Dennis Ware C
Lionel West 1B
Eugene Jackson .... LF
James West .... RF
Timothy Howard C
Ottis Woodward .... CF
George White .... LF
Savannah Fields .... SS
Johnnie Williams .... Utl
Lawrence Tucker 3B
L. Lloyd Hoggatt 2B

1926

Minneapolis Colored White Sox

Harold Lewis .... SS
Bobby Marshall 2B
D. Blackman .... RF
Ike Bradley .... CF
Lee Davis C
Bert Lewis 1B
Stonney 3B
Eddie Blackman .... LF/P
Lee Johnson .... P
B. Smith .... C/P
M. Johnson 2B

Pipestone (MN) Black Sox

Frank Whitfield ...... Mgr/C
Ewing .... P
Grayson 2B
Morris "Stringbean"
   Williams .... P
Joseph 3B
Charles Lightner .... P
Hilton .... SS
Wingfield P/2B/SS/OF
Wright .... CF
Blackwax .... P
Licks 1B
Palmer .... C/RF
Green .... LF
Scotty Henderson ...... P/RF
Smith C/2B
"Lefty Wilson"
   (Dave Brown) .... P

St. Paul Colored Gophers

E. Faye Elliott ..... Organizer
Thompson .... P
Dunlap C
Coleman .... SS
Napier (Napul) .... P/LF
Hughes .... P/RF
Van 1B
Hagn .... CF
Howard 2B
Henton 3B
Goodwin .... P

Sandon's Colored Tigers (Mankato, MN)

Bill Sandon Owner/1B
Roy Wright .... Mgr/C
"Chick" Williams ... P/CF/LF
Charles Hilton .... SS
Ousley (Ausley) ...... LF/RF
Burke 1B/CF
English 3B
Lewis 2B/P
Parks RF/2B
Jackson .... P
Sandon

1927

Colored All Stars (St. Paul)

John Davis .... Mgr
George "Butter" Roach .... P
Jimmy Lee 3B
Foster .... OF
Singleton .... SS
Jones .... RF
Coleman 2B
Winnie C
"Scotty" .... P
Davie Mays 1B/P
George White .... Cpt/LF
Savannah Fields 2B
Robinson .... Inf
Du Love .... OF

St. Paul Colored Gophers

Singleton .... SS

P. Jones . . . . LF
A. Jones 2B
Scottie 1B
West . . . . RF
Bowen . . . . CF
Saleman 3B
Wingfield . . . . P
Davis C

1928

Aberdeen Navy-Cabs

Steamen 2B
Matters . . . . SS
Coleman 3B
Roach . . . . CF/LF
Jackson . . . . RF
Davis C
Freeman . . . . P
Biddick 1B
Benford . . . . LF
Van 1B
Crowley . . . . CF

Twin City Colored Giants

Harris 1B
Blackman . . . . CF/RF
Jenkins 2B
Johnson C
Hickey . . . . SS
Roach . . . . RF/P
Lewis 3B
Woodard . . . . LF
Mays . . . . P
Coles . . . . P
Benson 1B

1929

St. Paul Colored Gophers

Thompson . . . . P
Davis C

Cuban House of David/
Colored House of David

John Donaldson . . . Mgr/P/CF
Art Hancock . . . . SS
Charlie Hancock 1B/C
"Gabby" Streets CF/2B
Nick Jones . . . . RF/LF/CF
Manville "Buzz"
   Boldridge 3B
Charlie Hilton 2B
Blake . . . . P
Louis Williams C
Ernest Worley . . . . LF/RF
Maurice "Doolittle"
   Young P/1B/LF/RF

Bill Freeman . . . . P
Collins . . . . P
Raymond "Jack"
   Potts . . . . P
Fox . . . . P

1930

Colored House of David

Ray Doan . . . . Mgr
Charlie Hancock C/1B
Hilton 2B/SS
Boldridge 3B/P
Broadway . . . . LF
Campbell . . . . P
Wilson . . . . P
Van . . . . P
Dramar 2B
Everett . . . . SS
Hamilton 1B
Jones . . . . RF
Streets . . . . CF
Neil C
Walton 3B
Worley . . . . LF

St. Paul Colored Gophers

Robertson . . . . SS
Jackson . . . . LF/P
White . . . . CF
Lee 1B
Farell 2B
Davis C
Gyden . . . . RF
Roosevelt 3B
King . . . . P/LF

1931

Colored House Of David

Boldridge 3B
Everett . . . . SS/C
Streets CF/2B/SS
Hilton 2B
Jones . . . . RF/LF/CF
Wright . . . . LF/C
Williams C
Gill 1B
Bill Freeman . . . . P
Barker . . . . CF/LF
Worley . . . . LF
Hancock 1B
Truesdale . . . . P
Young P/1B
Porter . . . . P/RF
Wilson . . . . RF
John Donaldson . . . . P

1932

John Donaldson All-Stars
(Fairmont, MN)

John
   Donaldson . . Mgr/P/CF/LF
Hurley
   McNair LF/RF/CF/3B
Starks 2B/3B/1B/SS/OF
Joe "Jelly Roll"
   Barker CF/3B/2B
Charlie Hilton 2B/SS
Roosevelt "Chappie"
   Gray 1B/C
George Jones . . . . P/RF/CF
Robert "Piggy"
   Hawkins 3B/SS
F. Slyvester "Hooks"
   Foreman C
Bill Freeman . . . . P/CF
Charlie Hancock SS/1B
N. Jones . . . . RF/LF
McDonald P/1B/RF
J. Moore Allen . . . . . . P/LF/RF
Cunningham 1B/C
Smith 3B/SS
Worley 3B/SS
Street 2B
Ham'lon . . . . SS
Graves 1B
Buzz Boldridge *3B*
Anderson

St. Paul Monarchs

Frank Boyce . . . . Owner
Gerhart Dunlap C
Earl Thompson . . . . P
George Earl Roach . . . . PH
Bobby Marshall 1B
Bill Coleman 3B
Jimmy Lee 2B/1B
Bill Johnson . . . . SS
Thomas English . . . . CF
Victor McGowan . . . . OF
"Rubber Arm"
   Johnson . . . . OF/C
Vick . . . . LF
Bedeau . . . . SS
Louis 2B
Breedlove . . . . RF
Engles . . . . CF
Burke . . . . PR

1934

Twin Cities/Minneapolis
Colored Giants

Vicks 3B

Oler (Ollie) 1B
Harris .... CF
Bill Freeman .... P
Coleman .... SS
Lee Davis C
Foot 2B
K. Jackson .... P
Maceo Breedlove .... RF
English
Jackson .... LF

1935

Minneapolis Colored Giants

Hall .... P
Howell .... P
Bennard C
James C

Minneapolis Keystone Tigers

Bill Brooks .... Mgr
Gene Harris .... Asst

Minnesota Colored Gophers/Twin Cities Colored Giants

Jake Foote
  (Footes) Mgr/C/1B
Wellington Coleman .. 2B/3B
Maceo Breedlove .... RF
Hopwood .... CF
Chinx Worley 1B/LF
Hamilton .... SS
"Lefty" Porter .... P/LF
Carter 3B
Victor McGowan ... LF/Ump
Thorpe .... P
Thompson .... P
Tom English .... *SS*
Charles Hilton *2B*
John Van .... *C*
Ollie Pettiford *1B*
Jean Thomas
Bill Freeman *1B*
Dennis Ware .... *C*
Gean Tucker
E.N. Smith
Robert Wethers

1936

St. Paul Colored Giants

Jackson .... P
Davies C

St. Paul Gophers

White .... CF
Worley 2B
Oler 1B
Foots C
Flash .... SS
Roach .... LF
Taylor 3B
Johnson .... RF
Thompson .... P
Wakeoff .... P

1937

Phyllis Wheatley House Team (Minneapolis)

Sylvester Carter ...... Coach
Minzie Davis .... P/OF
Donald Strawder .... P/OF
Bill Freeman .... P
Billy Roach .... P
Ed Jackson C
Burton Lewis C
Stafford Lott .... Inf
Red Martin .... Inf
Leroy Reese .... Inf
Everett Vaughn .... Inf
Donald Sessions .... Inf
Barnell Breedlove .... Inf
Charles Miller .... Inf
Ward Bell .... OF
Cozwell Breedlove .... OF
Lawrence Brown .... OF

Twin Cities/St. Paul Colored Giants

George White .... Mgr/CF
Tom English .... Cpt
Worley 3B
T. Porter 1B/P
J. Feets C
J. Johnson .... RF
Jimmy Lee 2B
F. Johnson .... SS
G. Roach .... P
Wakoff .... P
Guyden .... Utl
Martin .... Utl
Marcenia "Toni" Stone .... P

1942

Minneapolis-St. Paul Gophers

Jim Brown .... Mgr

Rufus Hatten C
Reese "Goose" Tatum .. LF/1B
Oscar "Bish" Tyson ...... CF
Vic Galloway .... P
Prim "Babe" Hall 1B/P
Samuel Seagraves ... RF/LF/C
Johnny Britton 3B
Collins Jones .... SS
Joe "Barney" Higdon ... P/RF
Ted "Double Duty"
  Radcliffe .... C/P
"Lefty" Buwn .... P
Art Wilbert .... LF
Ulysses "Cowboy" Evans ... P
Thomas 3B/2B
F. Burns .... P/LF
"Copperknee"
  Thompson 2B/SS
Gready "Lefty"
  McKinnis .... P
Davis P/2B
J. Burns 1B/LF
Boering .... P
Cook .... RF
Mack 2B
Simpson 2B
George Perisee .... LF
Matthews .... P
Leamon Johnson 3B
"Big" Jim Johnson .... P

1944

Twin Cities Colored Giants (St. Paul)

George White .... Mgr/LF
Reddick SS/3B
Maceo Breedlove .... P
James C
L. Smith 2B/1B
P. Archer .... P
E. Tinsley .... RF/Utl
Louis (Pud) White 3B/P
C. Worley 2B
G. Haskins .... CF
A. Guiden .... RF
J. Jones C
A. Jones .... LF
Warberg 2B
Preston .... SS
Jones .... CF
Johnson .... SS
Foots C

Chapter Notes

Chapter One

1. Harold Seymour, *Baseball Volume III: The People's Game* (New York: Oxford University Press, 1990), 532–533, 541.
2. Jules Tygiel, "Black Ball," in *Total Baseball*, ed. John Thorn and Pete Palmer (New York: Warner, 1989), 548.
3. Steven R. Hoffbeck, "Prince Honeycutt and the Fergus Falls Musculars," in *Swinging for the Fences*, ed. Steven R. Hoffbeck (St. Paul: Minnesota Historical Society Press, 2005), 11–12.
4. Hoffbeck, "Prince Honeycutt," 12; *Minneapolis Tribune* August 31 and September 21, 1876.
5. William D. Green, "They Didn't Want to Play with Fisher," in *Swinging for the Fences*, 7–10; *Winona Weekly Republican*, September 29 and October 27, 1875.
6. Tygiel, "Black Ball," 548.
7. *New York Age* (New York), February 25, 1909; Bob Tholkes, "Bud Fowler and the Stillwaters," in *Before the Dome: Baseball in Minnesota When the Grass Was Real*, ed. David Anderson (Minneapolis: Nodin Press, 1993), 79; James A. Riley, *The Biographical Encyclopedia of the Negro Baseball Leagues* (New York: Carroll & Graf, 2002), 294–295; *Boston Globe* (Massachusetts), April 25, 1878; Phil Dixon with Patrick J. Hannigan, *The Negro Baseball Leagues: A Photographic History* (Mattituck, N.Y.: Amereon House, 1992), 43.
8. Riley, *Biographical Encyclopedia of the Negro Baseball Leagues*, 294–295; *New York Age* (New York), February 25, 1909; Robert Peterson, *Only the Ball Was White* (New York: Oxford University Press, 1992), 19–20; *Oshkosh Daily Northwestern* (Wisconsin), July 15, 1898.
9. Tholkes, "Bud Fowler," 79–80.
10. Tholkes, "Bud Fowler," 79–80; *Quincy Whig* (Illinois), May 8, 1884 reprinted in the *Stillwater Daily Sun* May 10, 1884; *Stillwater Daily Sun*, May 10, 1884.
11. Dan Cagley, "Bud Fowler and the Stillwater Nine, 1884," in *Swinging for the Fences*, 18; Tholkes, "Bud Fowler," 80.
12. Tholkes, "Bud Fowler," 81–82; Cagley, "Bud Fowler," 24.
13. Tholkes, "Bud Fowler," 82; John Holway, *The Complete Book of Baseball's Negro Leagues: The Other Half of Baseball History*, ed. Lloyd Johnson and Rachel Borst (Fern Park, Fla.: Hastings House, 2001), 18.
14. Dixon and Hannigan, *The Negro Baseball Leagues*, 52; Peterson, *Only the Ball Was White*, 28–29; Mark Ribowsky, *A Complete History of the Negro Leagues 1884 to 1955* (Secaucus, N.J.: Carol, 1997), 27.
15. *Minneapolis and St. Paul Western Appeal*, August 13, 20, 1887; *St. Paul City Directory* 1886–1887, 1889–1890, 1891–1892; James E. Brunson III, *The Early Image of Black Baseball*, (Jefferson, N.C.: McFarland, 2009), 84.
16. *Minneapolis and St. Paul Western Appeal*, August 20, 1887; *Shakopee Scott County Argus*, August 31, 1887.
17. *St. Paul Dispatch*, August 29, 1887.
18. David Vassar Taylor, "The Blacks," in *They Chose Minnesota: A Survey of the State's Ethnic Groups*, ed. June Drenning Holmquist (St. Paul: Minnesota Historical Society Press, 1981), 74; *Minneapolis and St. Paul Western Appeal*, June 9, 1888.
19. Dixon and Hannigan, *The Negro Baseball Leagues*, 57.
20. Michael E. Lomax, *Black Baseball Entrepreneurs* (Syracuse: Syracuse University Press, 2003), 124, 128.
21. Ibid., 124, 131.
22. Sol White, *History of Colored Base Ball, With Other Documents on the Early Black Game 1886–1936*, ed. Jerry Malloy (Lincoln: University of Nebraska Press, 1996), xxxii, 24; Peterson, *Only the Ball Was White*, 146; Lomax, *Black Baseball Entrepreneurs*, 135; *Oshkosh Daily Northwestern* (Wisconsin), July 15, 1898.
23. White, *History of Colored Base Ball*, xxxii–xxxiii; Lomax, *Black Baseball Entrepreneurs*, 136–139.
24. *Minneapolis Tribune*, April 17, 1895.
25. *Minneapolis Tribune*, April 17, 21, 22, 23, 25, 27, 1895; *St. Paul Daily Globe*, April 24, 26, 1895.
26. *Minneapolis Tribune*, April 21, 22, 23, 25, 1895; Stew Thornley, *On to Nicollet* (Minneapolis: Nodin Press, 1988), 15–16; Stew Thornley, *Baseball in Minnesota: The Definitive History* (St. Paul: Minnesota Historical Society Press, 2006), 34; Dixon and Hannigan, *The Negro Baseball Leagues*, 75.
27. *St. Paul Pioneer Press*, April 25, 1895.
28. White, *History of Colored Base Ball*, xxxiii–xxxv; *Adrian Daily Times and Expositor* (Michigan), June 10, 1895.
29. White, *History of Colored Base Ball*, xxxv; Riley, *Biographical Encyclopedia of the Negro Baseball Leagues*, 596; *Winona Daily Herald*, May 1, 3, 1896.
30. *Winona Daily Republican*, July 6, 1897; Lomax, *Black Baseball Entrepreneurs*, 159–160; *Iowa State Reporter* (Waterloo, Iowa), August 16, 1903.
31. White, *History of Colored Base Ball*, 28; *Chicago Tribune* (Illinois), April 8, 1899.
32. Lomax, *Black Baseball Entrepreneurs*, 158; White, *History of Colored Base Ball*, 38.
33. Ribowsky, *Complete History of the Negro Leagues*, 47–49.
34. *Twin City Star*, July 22, 1911; *National Advocate*, December 12, 1918; United States Government World War I Registration Card, roll 1682638, serial number 232, September 12, 1918.
35. *National Advocate*, December 12, 1918; *St. Paul Pioneer Press*, April 14, June 27, July 11, August 12, 15, 1898; *Shakopee Scott Country Argus*, September 1, 1898.
36. *Red Wing Republican*, September 8, 1900; *Goodhue County News*, September 13, 1900; *Twin City Star*, July 22, 1911.
37. *Royalton Banner*, July 26, 1902; Jim Karn, "Drawing the Color Line on Walter Ball," in *Swinging for the Fences*, 33–34; 1910 United States Census, Cook County, Illinois.
38. Karn, "Drawing the Color Line," 34–35; *St. Paul Dispatch*, August 11, 1897.
39. Karn, "Drawing the Color Line," 35.

40. Karn, "Drawing the Color Line," 36; *St. Paul Pioneer Press*, April 25, May 30, 1898.
41. Karn, "Drawing the Color Line," 36–37; *St. Paul Pioneer Press*, August 7, 19, 1899; Ribowsky, *Complete History of the Negro Leagues*, 187.
42. Dixon and Hannigan, *The Negro Baseball Leagues*, 75; Riley, *Biographical Encyclopedia of the Negro Baseball Leagues*, 294–295; White, *History of Colored Base Ball*, 161; Peterson, *Only the Ball Was White*, 40; *Oshkosh Daily Northwestern* (Wisconsin), July 15, 1898.
43. Karn, "Drawing the Color Line," 37–40.

Chapter Two

1. Dixon and Hannigan, *The Negro Baseball Leagues*, 75–76.
2. Ibid., 80.
3. Riley, *Biographical Encyclopedia of the Negro Baseball Leagues*, 878; *Waseca Radical*, June 21, 1899.
4. *Waseca Radical*, May 23, 1900.
5. *Waseca Journal*, October 16, 1900.
6. *Waseca Journal*, October 16, 1900; Lomax, *Black Baseball Entrepreneurs*, 130.
7. *Waseca Journal*, October 16, 1900; 1930 United States Census, Cook County, Illinois.
8. *Waseca Journal*, October 16, 1900; Lomax, *Black Baseball Entrepreneurs*, 138; Riley, *Biographical Encyclopedia of the Negro Baseball Leagues*, 387; Ribowsky, *Complete History of the Negro Leagues*, 49; 1900 United States Census, Cook County, Illinois; E.L. Thorndike, *Thorndike Barnhart Advanced Dictionary* (Glenview, Ill.: Scott, Foresman, 1974), 335.
9. Dixon and Hannigan, *The Negro Baseball Leagues*, 75; *Waseca Journal*, October 16, 1900; Riley, *Biographical Encyclopedia of the Negro Baseball Leagues*, 873.
10. Dixon and Hannigan, *The Negro Baseball Leagues*, 75; *Adrian Daily Times and Expositor* (Michigan), June 4, 1895; Denny Moyer, *110 Years of Baseball in Sheboygan, Wisconsin*, January 19, 2008.
11. Vassar Taylor, "The Blacks," 74.
12. *Waseca Journal*, October 16, 1900 ; *Waseca Radical*, September 4, 1901; Mark Okkonen, *1900–1910 Minor League Rosters*, http://www.sabr.org/sabr.cfm?a=cms,c, 1638, April 25, 2006; *Freeborn County Standard*, September 5, 1900.
13. *St. Paul Pioneer Press*, May 13, 1901, quoted in the *Waseca Radical*, May 15, 1901; *Waseca Radical*, May 8, June 5, 12, July 3, 1901.
14. *Waseca Radical*, June 26, 1901.
15. Ibid., June 12, 1901.
16. *Waseca Radical*, July 3, 1901, July 24, 1901; *Waterloo Courier* (Iowa), August 21, 1903.
17. *Waseca Radical*, August 21, 1901.
18. David Kemp and Roger Wildin, "The Algona Brownies, Champs of the West," in *The Baseball Research Journal* (Kansas City: Society for American Baseball Research, 1987), 76.
19. *Chicago Tribune*, (Illinois), July 26, 1901; Kemp and Wildin, "The Algona Brownies," 76–77; Joel Zoss and John Bowman, *Diamonds in the Rough: The Untold Story of Baseball* (Lincoln: University of Nebraska Press, 2004), 136; *Waterloo Courier* (Iowa), August 21, 1903; *Benson Times*, August 18, 1903.
20. *Litchfield News Ledger*, June 20, 1901; *Waseca Radical*, October 2, 1901.
21. *St. Paul Pioneer Press*, August 12, 1901; Sheila Morris, Co-Director, Waseca County Historical Society, correspondence with author, October 11, 2007; *Aberdeen Daily News* (South Dakota), August 21, 1901.
22. *St. Paul Pioneer Press*, August 12, 1901.
23. *Waseca Radical*, August 21, 1901.
24. *Waseca Radical*, October 2, 1901; Moyer, *110 Years of Baseball*, January 19, 2008; *The Baseball Encyclopedia*, ed. Joseph L. Reichler (New York: Macmillan, 1979), 2003; "The Pitcher Register," in *Total Baseball*, 1998; SABR Minor League Database, http://www.baseball-reference.com/minors/.
25. Dick Clark and Larry Lester, ed., *The Negro Leagues Book* (Cleveland: Society for American Baseball Research, 1994), 56; *Waseca Journal Radical*, May 15, 29, 1902.
26. *Waseca Journal Radical*, June 19, July 3, 1902; *St. Paul Pioneer Press* June 23, 1902.
27. *Waseca Journal Radical*, July 10, 24, 1902.
28. Karn, "Drawing the Color Line," 37–40; *St. Cloud Daily Journal Press*, May 26, June 16, 30, 1902.
29. Karn, "Drawing the Color Line," 48; *St. Cloud Daily Journal Press*, September 2, 1902.
30. Karn, "Drawing the Color Line," 44; *St. Cloud Daily Times*, July 14, 1902.
31. *St. Cloud Daily Times*, July 14, 1902, June 10, 1930; Okkonen, *1900–1910 Minor League Rosters*.
32. *St. Cloud Daily Times*, August 9, 1902.
33. Karn, "Drawing the Color Line," 48; *St. Cloud Daily Journal Press*, August 4, 1902.
34. *St. Cloud Daily Times*, August 15, 1902; *Twin City Star* July 22, 1911; *Minneapolis Spokesman*, November 21, 1963.
35. Karn, "Drawing the Color Line," 49–51.
36. *Brainerd Dispatch*, July 25, 1902; *Waseca Journal Radical*, September 4, 1902; *Waseca Journal Radical*, April 9, 1903.
37. Kemp and Wildin, "The Algona Brownies," 77–78.
38. Ibid., 78
39. Kemp and Wildin, "The Algona Brownies," 78–79; *Manitoba Free Press* (Manitoba, Canada), September 18, 21, 1903; Okkonen, *1900–1910 Minor League Rosters*.
40. *Manitoba Free Press* (Manitoba, Canada), September 18, 1903; *St. Paul Pioneer Press*, September 21, 1903; Okkonen, *1900–1910 Minor League Rosters*.
41. *Manitoba Free Press* (Manitoba, Canada), September 22, 1903; *St. Paul Pioneer Press*, September 21, 1903.
41. *Manitoba Free Press* (Manitoba, Canada), September 22, 1903; *St. Paul Pioneer Press*, September 21, 1903.
42. Kemp and Wildin, "The Algona Brownies," 79.
43. Karn, "Drawing the Color Line," 49.
44. *St. Cloud Daily Times*, May 16, 1903.
45. *St. Cloud Daily Times*, May 18, June 15, 1903; Karn, "Drawing the Color Line," 50.
46. *La Crosse Press* (Wisconsin), June 22, 1903; *St. Cloud Daily Journal Press*, June 24, 1903.
47. *St. Cloud Daily Times*, July 15, September 21, 1903.
48. *St. Cloud Daily Times*, September 21, 1903; *St. Cloud Daily Journal Press*, August 13, 1903.
49. *St. Cloud Daily Times*, August 11, 1903.
50. *St. Cloud Daily Times*, September 8, 15, 21, 1903; *St. Cloud Daily Journal Press*, September 21, 1903; *Stillwater Gazette*, September 21, 1903; Okkonen, *1900–1910 Minor League Rosters*.
51. Kemp and Wildin, "The Algona Brownies," 79; *Renville Star Farmer*, April 8, 1904, April 7, 1905.
52. *Minneapolis Tribune*, April 3, 1904; *Renville Star Farmer*, July 10, 1903, July 31, 1905.
53. Riley, *Biographical Encyclopedia of the Negro Baseball Leagues*, 447, 661, 806; Bob Davids, "Chronological Registry of 19th Century Black Players in Organized Baseball," in *History of Colored Base Ball*, 167–168; Zoss and Bowman, *Diamonds in the Rough*, 144; *Renville Record*, April 27, 1904; 1900 United States Census, Cook County, Illinois.
54. *Renville Record*, May 4, 11, 1904; *Renville Star Farmer*, May 13, 1904.

55. *Renville Record*, May 18, 1904.
56. *Renville Record*, May 4, 11, 25, 1904; *Renville Star Farmer* May 6, 1904; *Redwood Falls Gazette*, June 1, 1904; *Melrose Beacon*, June 17, 1904; *Sauk Center Herald*, June 23, 1904.
57. *Renville Record*, July 6, 13, August 10, 1904.
58. *Renville Star Farmer*, July 15, 1904.
59. *St. Paul Pioneer Press*, August 15, 1904; *Renville Star Farmer*, August 26, 1904.
60. *Renville Record*, August 31, 1904; *Renville Star Farmer*, May 6, August 5, 1904.
61. *Renville Record*, May 4, 25, August 3, 31, 1904; *Renville Star Farmer*, July 22, 1904.
62. *Renville Record*, May 4, August 31, 1904.
63. *Renville Star Farmer*, September 12, 1904, April 7, May 5, 1905; Riley, *Biographical Encyclopedia of the Negro Baseball Leagues*, 388.
64. *Renville Star Farmer*, May 19, 1905; *Long Prairie Leader*, July 16, 1909; Riley, *Biographical Encyclopedia of the Negro Baseball Leagues*, 432–433; Holway, Johnson and Borst, *The Complete Book of Baseball's Negro Leagues*, 47; Robert Charles Cottrell, *The Best Pitcher In Baseball* (New York: New York University Press, 2001), 21.
65. *Renville Star Farmer*, May 26, June 2, 1905.
66. *Renville Star Farmer*, June 30, 1905; Joe Niese, "George Wilson," in *Wisconsin West Magazine*, 24; *Eau Claire Leader* (Wisconsin), July 6, 1905.
67. *Renville Star Farmer*, July 7, 21, 28, August 4, 1905.
68. Ibid., May 12, September 8, 1905.
69. White, *History of Colored Base Ball*, 46; Riley, *Biographical Encyclopedia of the Negro Baseball Leagues*, 433.
70. *Minneapolis Tribune*, August 12, 1906; Moyer, "110 Years of Baseball"; Dixon and Hannigan, *The Negro Baseball Leagues*, 27.

Chapter Three

1. Cottrell, *The Best Pitcher in Baseball*, 32; *Chicago Defender* (Illinois), February 21, 1915.
2. Frank Leland, *Frank Leland's Baseball Club* (Chicago: Fraternal, 1910), 4, 6; Cottrell, *The Best Pitcher in Baseball*, 42; Holway, *Blackball Stars*, 11–13.
3. Riley, *Biographical Encyclopedia of the Negro Baseball Leagues*, 48; *Chicago Tribune* (Illinois), September 17, 1906.
4. *Twin City Star*, October 19, 26, 1912; *St. Paul Appeal*, October 26, 1912; *St. Paul City Directory* 1888–1889, 1889–1890, 1894; 1880 United States Census, Hennepin County, Minnesota.
5. *St. Paul Appeal*, June 3, 1916; *Twin City Star*, October 26, 1912; *St. Paul City Directory* 1901; *Indianapolis Freeman*, April 16, 1910.
6. *St. Paul Dispatch*, June 10, 1905; *St. Paul Daily News*, June 10, 1905.
7. *St. Paul Pioneer Press*, June 12, 1905; *St. Paul Daily News*, June 12, 1905.
8. *St. Paul Pioneer Press*, June 12, 1905.
9. *Duluth News Tribune*, February 23, 1907; Leland, *Frank Leland's Baseball Club*, 9; Karn, "Drawing the Color Line," 38; *La Crosse Tribune* (Wisconsin), February 20, 1907.
10. *Chicago Tribune* (Illinois), July 16, September 17, October 22, 1906.
11. *St. Paul Dispatch*, May 18, 1907.
12. *Chicago Inter Ocean* (Illinois), April 7, 8, 1907; Peterson, *Only the Ball Was White*, 64; *South Bend Tribune* (Indiana), April 13, 15, 1907.
13. *Chicago Inter Ocean* (Illinois), April 21, 22, 1907; Leland, *Frank Leland's Baseball Club*, 5.
14. *Chicago Inter Ocean* (Illinois), April 22, 1907; Reichler, *The Baseball Encyclopedia*, 2003; *Chicago American* (Illinois), April 22, 1907.
15. *Chicago Tribune* (Illinois), April 15, 1907; *Green Bay Daily Gazette* (Wisconsin), April 27, 1907; *Eau Claire Daily Telegram* (Wisconsin), May 2, 1907.
16. *St. Paul Appeal*, August 31, 1907.
17. *St. Paul Dispatch*, May 3, 1907, May 30, August 23, 1908; *St. Paul Appeal*, August 31, 1907; Riley, *Biographical Encyclopedia of the Negro Baseball Leagues*, 764; *Iowa State Reporter* (Waterloo, Iowa), August 16, 1903; *Chicago Tribune* (Illinois), May 4, 1902; Paul Debono, *The Indianapolis ABC's* (Jefferson, N.C.: McFarland, 1997), 77–78.
18. 1880 United States Census, McLean County, Illinois; *Indianapolis Freeman* (Indiana), July 30, 1910; Paul Debono, *The Chicago American Giants* (Jefferson, N.C.: McFarland, 2007), 20; "Philadelphia Giants Win Black Championship," in *Middle Innings: A Documentary History of Baseball 1900–1948*, ed. Dean A. Sullivan (Lincoln: University of Nebraska Press, 1998), 23–24; *Mesaba Ore and the Hibbing News*, June 29, 1907; *Olmstead County Democrat*, August 9, 1907; Peterson, *Only the Ball Was White*, 150; *Chicago Tribune* (Illinois), September 24, 1897.
19. *St. Paul Appeal*, August 31, 1907; *Eau Claire Leader* (Wisconsin), May 2, 1907; White, *History of Colored Base Ball*, 62; *St. Paul Daily News*, July 20, 1907; *St. Paul Dispatch*, June 20, 1908; *Indianapolis Freeman* (Indiana), October 19, 1907, January 8, 1910.
20. *Caledonia Journal*, July 10, 1907; *Decorah Journal* (Iowa), September 17, 1907.
21. *Green Bay Daily Gazette* (Wisconsin), April 24, 26, 27, 29, 1907; *Chicago Tribune* (Illinois), April 29, 1907.
22. *Eau Claire Daily Telegram* (Wisconsin), May 2, 1907; Okkonen, *1900–1910 Minor League Rosters*.
23. *Eau Claire Daily Telegram* (Wisconsin), May 3, 1907.
24. *St. Paul Pioneer Press*, May 6, 7, 1907; *Minneapolis Tribune*, May 7, 1907.
25. *St. Paul Pioneer Press*, May 7, 1907.
26. *Minneapolis Tribune*, February 2, 1908; *Mankato Weekly Review*, June 4, 1907.
27. *Minneapolis Tribune*, February 2, 1908; *St. Paul City Directory* 1908; *St. Paul Dispatch*, June 26, 1907; Leland, *Frank Leland's Baseball Club*, 9; *Indianapolis Freeman* (Indiana), September 25, 1909.
28. *Minneapolis Journal*, May 19, 1907; *St. Paul Pioneer Press*, May 20, 1907.
29. Steven R. Hoffbeck, "Bobby Marshall, the Legendary First Baseman," in *Swinging For The Fences*, 60–61; Richard Rainbolt, *Gold Glory* (Wayzata, Minn: Ralph Turtinen, 1972), 35–36; Chuck Frederick, *Leatherheads of the North; The True Story of Ernie Nevers and the Duluth Eskimos* (Duluth: X-Communications, 2007), 36; Leland, *Frank Leland's Baseball Club*, 17; *Chicago Tribune* (Illinois), November 11, 1906.
30. *St. Paul Pioneer Press*, May 20, 1907; *St. Paul Dispatch*, May 20, 1907.
31. Ibid.
32. Ibid.
33. Ibid.
34. *St. Paul Pioneer Press*, May 20, 1907; Hoffbeck, "Bobby Marshall," 61; Leland, *Frank Leland's Baseball Club*, 16; *Minneapolis Journal*, June 16, 1907.
35. *Mesaba Ore and the Hibbing News*, June 29, 1907; *St. Paul Pioneer Press*, June 3, 1907; 1910 United States Census, Ramsey County, Minnesota; *St. Paul Dispatch*, June 6, 7, 1907; *Young America Eagle*, September 24, 1909; Sevro Nieto, *Early U.S. Blackball Teams In Cuba* (Jefferson, N.C.: McFarland, 2008), 59.
36. *St. Paul Pioneer Press*, June 2, 3, 1907; SABR Minor League Database.
37. William Watts Folwell, *A History of Minnesota; Vol-*

ume IV (St. Paul: Minnesota Historical Society, 1929, reprinted 1969), 50–53; Hibbing Chamber of Commerce, www.hibbing.org/visitor_info.html, January 1, 1906; United States Bureau of the Census, Thirteenth Census of the United States Taken in the Year 1910 (Washington, D.C.: Government Printing Office, 1913); *St. Paul Daily News*, June 29, 1907; *St. Paul Dispatch*, August 27, 1907.

38. *Mesaba Ore and the Hibbing News*, June 29, 1907.

39. *Mesaba Ore and the Hibbing News*, June 29, 1907; *Duluth News Tribune*, June 25, 1907.

40. *Minneapolis Tribune*, June 29, 30, July 1, 1907; *Iowa State Reporter* (Waterloo, Iowa), August 16, 1903 *Chicago Tribune* (Illinois), June 24, 1907, January 5, 1940.

41. *Minneapolis Tribune*, June 27, 1907; *Chicago Tribune* (Illinois), November 30, 1902, April 29, 1903, January 5, 1940; *Anaconda Standard* (Montana), July 21, 1918; *St. Paul Pioneer Press*, May 10, 1953.

42. *La Crosse Daily Chronicle* (Wisconsin), July 3, 1907; Reichler, *The Baseball Encyclopedia* 1763; *La Crosse Tribune* (Wisconsin), July 8, 1907.

43. *Chicago Tribune* (Illinois), September 3, 1907; *Indianapolis Freeman* (Indiana), September 21, 1907; *Aberdeen Daily Republican* (South Dakota), July 24, 25, 26, 1907; *Jerauld County Review* (South Dakota), July 25, 1907; *Webster World* (South Dakota), July25, 1907.

44. *St. Paul Dispatch*, August 31, 1907; *Wessington Springs True Republican* (South Dakota), July 25, 1907.

45. *Stillwater Daily Gazette*, August 5, 1907; *St. Paul Pioneer Press*, August 4, 1907; *Mazeppa Tribune*, August 7, 1907; *St. Paul Daily News*, August 1, 1907.

46. *St. Paul Dispatch*, August 7, 1907; *Chaska Weekly Valley Herald*, August 8, 1907; *Lester Prairie News*, August 8, 1907.

47. *St. Paul Dispatch*, August 8, 9, 1907; *Mesaba Ore and the Hibbing News*, August 17, 1907; Reichler, *The Baseball Encyclopedia*, 1731; SABR Minor League Database.

48. *St. Paul Dispatch*, August 16, 19, 21, 1907; *Minneapolis Tribune*, August 25, 1907.

49. *Alexandria Post News*, August 29, 1907; *Alexandria Citizen*, August 29, 1907; SABR Minor League Database.

50. *St. Paul Dispatch*, August 24, 1907; *Alexandria Post News*, August 29, 1907; *Alexandria Citizen*, August 29, 1907.

51. *St. Paul Dispatch*, August 31, 1907; *Olmstead County Democrat*, September 20, 1907; Measuring Worth, "Six Ways to Compute the Relative Value of a U.S. Dollar Amount, 1974 to Present," http://www.measuringworth.com/uscompare/, November 11, 2008.

52. *Mesaba Ore and the Hibbing News*, September 7, 1907.

53. *Mesaba Ore and the Hibbing News*, September 7, 1907; *St. Paul Daily News*, September 4, 1907.

54. *St. Paul Dispatch*, September 7, 1907.

55. *St. Paul Pioneer Press*, September 8, 1907; *Osceola Sun* (Wisconsin), August 4, 1910.

56. *Young America Eagle*, September 13, 1907; *Chaska Weekly Valley Herald*, September 12, 1907.

57. *Chicago Tribune* (Illinois), July 8, 1907; United States Government World War I Registration Card, roll number 1653177, serial number 1388, September 11, 1918; *Bemidji Daily Pioneer*, June 28, 1909; *New York Age* (New York), July 13, 1911; *Indianapolis Freeman* (Indiana), October 16, 1910.

58. *Minneapolis Tribune*, September 18, 1907; *Red Wing Daily Republican*, September 20, 1907; Reichler, 2030; *Preston Times*, August 21, 1907; *Harmony News*, September 26, 1907.

59. *St. Paul Pioneer Press*, September 16, 20, 21, 1907; Reichler, *The Baseball Encyclopedia*, 867; Stew Thornley, *Baseball in Minnesota*, 156; Eliot Asinof, *Eight Men Out* (New York: Henry Holt, 1987), 162, 262; *New York Times* (New York), October 13, 1951.

60. *St. Paul Pioneer Press*, September 22, 1907; Anderson, *Before the Dome*, 23.

61. *St. Paul Pioneer Press*, September 22, 1907.

62. *St. Paul Pioneer Press*, September 23, 1907; 1910 United States Census, Dakota County, Minnesota.

63. Cottrell, *The Best Pitcher in Baseball*, 35–38; *St. Paul Dispatch*, September 21, 1907; *Chicago Tribune* (Illinois), September 16, 1907.

64. *St. Paul Pioneer Press*, September 24, 1907; *St. Paul Daily News*, September 24, 1907.

65. *St. Paul Pioneer Press*, September 24, 1907.

66. Anderson, *Before the Dome*, 23; Larry Millett, *Lost Twin Cities* (St. Paul: Minnesota Historical Society Press, 1992), 220–221; Thornley, *Baseball in Minnesota*, 36; *Indianapolis Star* (Indiana), April 3, 1910.

67. *St. Paul Pioneer Press*, September 24, 1907.

68. Andrew Foster, "How To Pitch," in *History of Colored Base Ball*, 99; *St. Paul Pioneer Press*, September 24, 1907.

69. *St. Paul Pioneer Press*, September 25, 1907; *St. Paul Daily News*, September 25, 1907; *St. Paul Dispatch*, September 25, 1907.

70. *St. Paul Dispatch*, September 26, 1907; *Osceola Sun* (Wisconsin), September 26, 1907; Reichler, *The Baseball Encyclopedia*, 1922; SABR Minor League Database.

71. *Minneapolis Tribune*, September 29, 1907: *St. Paul Pioneer Press*, September 29, 1907.

72. *Minneapolis Tribune*, September 30, 1907: *St. Paul Pioneer Press*, September 30, 1907.

73. *St. Paul Pioneer Press*, September 30, 1907; *Minneapolis Tribune*, September 28, 1907

74. *Indianapolis Freeman* (Indiana), September 14, October 12, 1907; *Chicago Tribune* (Illinois), October 7, 14, 1907.

75. *St. Paul Appeal*, August 31, 1907; *St. Paul Dispatch*, September 16, 1907; *Minneapolis Tribune*, September 26, 1907.

76. *St. Paul Appeal*, August 31, 1907; *Minneapolis Tribune*, July 26, 1908.

77. Sol White, "History of Colored Baseball During 1907," in *History of Colored Base Ball*, 119; *Mesaba Ore and the Hibbing News*, August 17, 1907; *St. Paul Dispatch*, August 10, 1907.

78. *Indianapolis Freeman* (Indiana), October 19, 1907.

Chapter Four

1. Peterson, *Only the Ball Was White*, 77.

2. White, *History of Colored Base Ball*, 65–67; The National Association for Music Education, "Facts from 1907," http://www.menc.org/centennial/factsfrom1907.html, August 29, 1907; Newsvine.Com, "The U.S. in 1907," http://ok.newsvine.com/_news/2007/12/28/1190742-the-us-in-1907-the-difference-a-century-makes, February 4, 2008; Peterson, *Only the Ball Was White*, 148; Measuring Worth.

3. *St. Paul Dispatch*, August 10, 1907; *Indianapolis Freeman* (Indiana), March 20, 1909; ESPN.com, "Alex Rodriguez," http://sports.espn.go.com/mlb/players/profile?statsId=5275, March 4, 2008; Measuring Worth.

4. White, *History of Colored Base Ball*, 65–67; *Edgerton Enterprise*, July 11, 1907; *Granite Falls Tribune*, June 30, 1907; *Cumberland Advocate* (Wisconsin), June 4, 1908; *Waconia Patriot*, August 12, 1910; *Kanabec County Times*, June 21, 1911; David W. Anderson, *More Than Merkl,* (Lincoln: University of Nebraska Press, 2000), 12.

5. *Bemidji Daily Pioneer*, June 27, 1907; June 28, 29, 1909.

6. *Preston Times*, September 8, 1909.

7. *Red Wing Republican*, June 29, 1908; *Cogswell Enterprise* (North Dakota), June 24, 1909.

8. *Pine Island Record*, May 28, 1908; *Lake Crystal Union*, June 3, 1908.
9. *Long Prairie Leader*, June 22, 1909.
10. Norman K. Risjord, *A Popular History of Minnesota* (St. Paul: Minnesota Historical Society Press, 2005), 80, 148, 151, 160–161, 164–167, 192–194; Minnesota Revenue, "A brief history of Minnesota taxes," http://www.taxes.state.mn.us/other_supporting_content/history_mn_tax.shtml, March 6, 2008.
11. Dee Brown, *Bury My Heart At Wounded Knee* (New York: Washington Square Press, 1981), 58–60.
12. D.H. Rule, "The Northfield, Minnesota Robbery," http://www.civilwarstlouis.com/History/jamesnorthfield.htm, February 29, 2008.
13. Love To Know: Classic Encyclopedia, "Minnesota," http://www.1911encyclopedia.org/Minnesota#Population, February 29, 2008; US Census Bureau, Population Division, "Minnesota — Race and Hispanic Origin for Selected Large Cities and Other Places: Earliest Census to 1990," http://www.census.gov/population/www/documentation/twps0076.html, February 22, 2008
14. Vassar Taylor, "The Blacks," 75, 80; Steven R. Hoffbeck, "Opposing the Color Line in Minnesota, 1899," in *Swinging for the Fences*, 55.
15. Vassar Taylor, "The Blacks," 77–78.
16. Ibid.
17. *St. Paul Appeal*, May 30, 1908; Vassar Taylor, "The Blacks," 79.
18. Hoffbeck, "Opposing the Color Line," 55; *Minneapolis Tribune*, August 25, 1908; *St. Paul Daily News*, May 21, 1909.
19. Vassar Taylor, "The Blacks," 79–80; *St. Paul Appeal*, May 30, 1908.
20. *St. Paul Pioneer Press*, August 5, 1907; *Stillwater Daily Gazette*, June 8, August 24, 1908; *Duluth News Tribune*, July 5, 1908; *Mesaba Ore and the Hibbing News*, July 10, 1909; *Fargo Forum and Daily Republican* (North Dakota), June 21, 1909, July 4, 1910.
21. *St. Paul Pioneer Press*, April 26, 1908; *Minneapolis Tribune*, April 26, 1908; *La Crosse Tribune* (Wisconsin), April 1, 1909.
22. *Edgerton Enterprise*, July 18, 1907.
23. *Minneapolis Tribune*, August 30, 1908; Peterson, *Only the Ball Was White*, 155; Anderson, *More Than Merkle*, 30.
24. *Lake Crystal Union*, September 16, 1908.
25. Anderson, *More Than Merkle*, 31; *Hayward Sawyer County Record* (Wisconsin), August 11, 1910; *Long Prairie Leader*, June 23, 1908; *Jamestown Daily Capitol* (North Dakota), June 28, 1910.
26. Anderson, *More Than Merkle*, 31; *Austin Herald*, September 21, 1907.
27. *Indianapolis Freeman* (Indiana), August 7, 1909; Jeffrey Powers Beck, *The American Indian Integration of Baseball* (Lincoln: University of Nebraska Press, 2004), 58; Janet Bruce, *The Kansas City Monarchs* (Lawrence: University Press of Kansas, 1985), 15; Thornley, *Baseball in Minnesota*, 170; *Waterloo Daily Courier* (Iowa), February 16, April 5, 1907; *Waterloo Evening Reporter* (Iowa), August 2, 1907, April 20, 1909.
28. White, *History of Colored Base Ball*, 74 ; *Worth County Index* (Iowa), August 13, 1908; *Moody County Enterprise* (South Dakota), July 18, 1907; *La Crosse Tribune* (Wisconsin), May 23, 1907; *Beach Advance* (North Dakota), June 16, 1911.
29. *Aberdeen News* (South Dakota), July 25, 1907; *Lake Crystal Union*, June 2, 1908; *Lindstrom Chisago County Press*, August 27, 1908; *La Crosse Chronicle* (Wisconsin), July 3, 1907.
30. *Olmstead County Democrat*, August 9, 1907; *Bemidji Pioneer*, July 28, 1909; *Fairmont Daily Sentinel*, September 9, 1910.
31. Anderson, *More Than Merkle*, 20–23; John B. Holway and Bob Carroll, "Lives Of The Players," in *Total Baseball*, 356.
32. *New Richland Star*, June 3, 1909; *Duluth Evening Herald*, July 7, 1908.
33. *Crookston Daily Times*, July 11, 1910; *Devils Lake World* (North Dakota), June 15, 1911.
34. *Moose Lake Star Gazette*, August 18, 1910; *Houston Signal*, May 30, 1907; *Ashland Daily Press* (Wisconsin), July 12, 1909.
35. *Minneapolis Tribune*, June 30,, 1907; *St. Paul Pioneer Press*, July 30, 1909; July 31, 1910; *Pine Island Record*, June 6, 1907; *Decorah Journal* (Iowa), September 17, 1907; *Eldora Semi-Weekly Herald* (Iowa), August 21, 1909; *Caledonia Argus*, August 21, 1908; *Barron County Shield* (Wisconsin), August 5, 1910; *Redwood Falls Gazette*, June 16,1909; *Calmar Courier* (Iowa), August 14, 1908.
36. *Alexandria Post News*, August 29, 1907; *Chisholm Tribune Herald*, August 26, 1910; *Chisago County Free Press*, August 5, 1909.
37. *Vernon County Censor* (Wisconsin), May 20, 1908; *Viroqua Republican* (Wisconsin), May 21, 1908.
38. *Hankinson News* (North Dakota), June 24, 1909; *Minot Daily Reporter* (North Dakota), June 20, 23, 1910.
39. *Minot Daily Reporter* (North Dakota), June 21, 22, 23, 24, 1910.
40. *Young America Eagle*, October 1, 1909; *Zumbrota News*, September 28, 1907; *St. Paul Pioneer Press*, August 12, 1910; Steven R. Hoffbeck, "The Championship Year of the St. Paul Colored Gophers: 1909," unpublished manuscript, 9.
41. *Minneapolis Tribune*, August 29, 1909; *Mesaba Ore and the Hibbing News*, May 22, 1909, July 22, 1911; *Hibbing News Tribune*, July 14, 1911.
42. *Alexandria Citizen*, August 23, 1907; *Rock Rapids Review* (Iowa), August 6, 1908; *Minneapolis Tribune*, June 1, 1907; *Valley City Evening Times Record* (North Dakota), June 15, 1911.
43. *Red Wing Daily Republican*, September 20, 1907; *Sioux Falls Daily Press* (South Dakota), July 30, 1907.
44. *Lake Crystal Union*, June 10, 1908; *Sherburn Advanced Standard*, September 16, 1909.
45. Thornley, *Baseball in Minnesota*, 36–37; David Trombley, "Saint Paul Saints History 1902–1919," http://www.usfamily.net/web/trombleyd/SaintsHistory02-19.htm, February 16, 2009.
46. Kristin M. Anderson and Christopher W. Kimball, "Twin Cities Baseball Parks: Designing the National Pastime," in *Minnesota History* (St. Paul: Minnesota Historical Society Press, Fall 2003), 344–345; *St. Paul Daily News*, June 3, 1909.
47. Thornley, *Baseball in Minnesota*, 33–34, 99–100.
48. Hoffbeck, "Bobby Marshall," 172; *Minneapolis Tribune*, June 3, July 1, 1907, July 26, 1909; 1905 Minnesota State Census, Hennepin County, Minnesota; 1910 United States Census, Hennepin County, Minnesota.
49. Hoffbeck, "Bobby Marshall," 172; *Twin City Star*, June 2, July 21, 1910, July 8, 1911.
50. *Springfield Advance*, September 29, 1910; *Mankato Daily Free Press*, August 1, 1910; *Redwood Reveille*, June 18, 1909.
51. *Lester Prairie News*, July 25, 1907, July 14, 1910; *Red Wing Daily Republican*, June 26, 1908; *Preston Republican*, August 20, 1909, September 7, 1910; *Breckenridge Telegram*, August 22, 1907; Powers Beck, *American Indian Integration of Baseball*, 54–55, 64.
52. *Hibbing Tribune*, June 30, 1908; *Red Wing Daily Republican*, September 12, 1908; *Redwood Falls Gazette*, September 15, 1909; *Waconia Patriot*, August 12, 1910; *St. Paul Pioneer Press*, May 1, 24, 1910.
53. Minnesota State Legislature, "Minnesota State

Symbols—Unofficial, Proposed, or Facetious," http://www.leg.state.mn.us/leg/Unsym.asp#animal, March 13, 2008; *St. Paul Pioneer Press,* May 2, June 1, August 4, September 23, 1907; *St. Paul Appeal,* August 31, 1907.

54. Thornley, *Baseball in Minnesota,* 131, 134, 141; *Hibbing Daily Tribune,* July 3, 1908; *Charles City Daily Intelligencer* (Iowa), September 17, 1908; *Devils Lake World* (North Dakota), July 22, 1911; *St. Paul Dispatch,* September 7, 1907; *St. Paul Pioneer Press,* September 20, 1909.

55. *Mazeppa Tribune,* August 7, 1907; *Wycoff Messenger,* August 20, 1908; *Blue Earth Faribault County Register,* September 16, 1909.

56. *Waseca Journal Radic*al, August 26, 1908, June 10, 1910; *Mankato Daily Free Press,* July 19, 1909, August 2, 1910; *Lester Prairie News,* July 14, 1910; *Osceola Sun* (Wisconsin), October 1, 1908, October 6, 1910; *Minneapolis Tribune,* May 14, 1911; Measuring Worth.

57. *Crookston Times,* June 21, 1907; *Caledonia Argus,* June 3, 1910; *Bemidji Daily Pioneer,* June 28, 1909; *Waconia Patriot,* August 12, 1910; *Lindstrom Chisago County Press,* August 18, 1910.

58. *Austin Weekly,* May 17, 1911; *Marshall Lyon County Reporter,* August 16, 1911; *Charles City Daily Intelligencer* (Iowa), September 17, 1908.

59. *Marshall Lyon County Reporter,* August 16, 1911; *Charles City Daily Intelligencer* (Iowa), September 17, 1908; *Minneapolis Tribune,* October 11, 1908; *Duluth News Tribune,* July 18, 1910.

60. *Caledonia Journal,* July 10, 1907; *Edgerton Enterprise,* July 18, 1907; *Jerauld County Review* (South Dakota), July 25, 1907; *Mesaba Ore and the Hibbing News,* August 17, 1907; *Olmstead County Democrat,* August 16, 1907; *Harmony News,* September, 16, 1907.

61. John Craig, *Chappie and Me* (New York: Dodd, Mead, 1979), 178–179; *Fairmont Sentinel Daily,* September 9, 1908.

62. *Aberdeen Daily News* (South Dakota), July 25, 1907; *Aberdeen Daily American* (South Dakota), July 25, 1907; *Cumberland Advocate* (Wisconsin), June 11, 1908; *Bemidji Daily Pioneer,* June 28, 1910; *Grand Forks Daily Herald* (North Dakota), July 12, 1910; *Martin County Sentinel,* September 16, 1910.

63. *Red Wing Daily Republican,* September 20, 1907; *Mesaba Ore and the Hibbing News,* July 22, 1911.

64. Seymour, *Baseball Volume III: The People's Game,* 189–191.

65. *Renville Star Farmer,* July 17, 1908; *La Crosse Tribune* (Wisconsin), July 6, 1907.

66. *Plainview News,* May 17, 1907; *Luverne Rock County Herald,* July 17, 1908; *New Richmond News* (Wisconsin), August 10, 1910; *Chisholm Herald,* August 16, 1907; *Langford Bugle* (South Dakota), July 26, 1907.

67. *Cottonwood Current,* July 24, 1908; *Owatonna Journal Chronicle,* June 5, 1908; *Rice Lake Chronotype* (Wisconsin), June 12, 1908.

Chapter Five

1. *Indianapolis Freeman* (Indiana), November 9, 23, December 27, 1907, February 15, June 20, 1908; Debono, *The Indianapolis ABC's,* 22–23.

2. *Minneapolis Tribune,* February 2, March 1, 1908.

3. *St. Paul Appeal,* May 30, 1908.

4. *St. Paul Pioneer Press,* April 5, 1909; *St. Paul Dispatch,* May 3, 1907; *Long Prairie Leader,* September 7, 1911; *St. Paul Appeal* 5/30/1908; Dixon and Hannigan, *The Negro Baseball Leagues,* 67; *Indianapolis Freeman* (Indiana), July 1, 1911; Phil Dixon, *Phil Dixon's American Baseball Chronicles: Great teams: The 1905 Philadelphia Giants Volume Three* (Charleston, S.C.: Booksurge, 2006), 151.

5. Riley, *Biographical Encyclopedia of the Negro Baseball League,* 433; Leland, *Frank Leland's Baseball Club,* 12; *Pittsburgh Courier* (Pennsylvania), March 8, 1941.

6. Riley, *Biographical Encyclopedia of the Negro Baseball Leagues,* 309, 936; William F. McNeil, *Black Baseball Out of Season* (Jefferson, N.C.: McFarland, 2007), 9–11; Shawn Selby, "William 'Big Bill' Gatewood," in *Black Baseball and Chicago,* ed. Leslie A. Heaphy (Jefferson, N.C.: McFarland, 2007), 79; *San Antonio Daily Light* (Texas), August 12, 1899.

7. *Indianapolis Freeman* (Indiana), January 11, 1908; Dixon and Hannigan, *The Negro Baseball Leagues,* 71.

8. *Chicago .Defender* (Illinois), August 29, 1942; Holway, Johnson and Borst, *Complete Book of Baseball's Negro Leagues,* 154.

9. Gary Ashwill, "Philadelphia Giants in Cuba, 1907," http://agatetype. "Ptypepad.com/agate_type/2006/07/index.html, June 10, 2006; *Aurora Beacon* (Illinois), April 20, 1908.

10. *Duluth Herald,* July 2, 1908; *St. Paul Dispatch,* July 17, 1908; *Preston Times* (Iowa), August 27, 1909.

11. 1900 and 1910 United States Census, Daviess County, Kentucky; United States Government World War I Registration Card, roll 1683848, serial number 1411, September 9, 1918; Riley, *Biographical Encyclopedia of the Negro Baseball League,* 812; Leland, *Frank Leland's Baseball Club,* 18. *St. Paul Dispatch,* May 30, 1908; Nieto, 59.

12. *St. Paul Dispatch,* May 30, 1908; *St. Paul Appeal,* May 30, 1908; Wikipedia, http://en.wikipedia.org/wiki/Triatominae, September 11, 2007.

13. *Preston Times* (Iowa), August 27, 1909; Kemp and Wildin, "The Algona Brownies," 77; Riley, *Biographical Encyclopedia of the Negro Baseball League,* 682.

14. Riley, *Biographical Encyclopedia of the Negro Baseball League,* 624: 1880 United States Census, Davidson County, Tennessee; 1900 United States Census, Davidson County, Tennessee; *Wilkin County Gazette,* June 19, 1908.

15. Ashwill, "Philadelphia Giants in Cuba"; Mark Rucker and Peter C. Bjarkman, *Smoke: The Romance and Lore of Cuban Baseball* (Kingston, N.Y.: Total Sports, 1999), 259; List or Manifest of Alien Passengers for the U.S. Immigration Officer at New Orleans, January 4, 1908; *Galesville Republican* (Wisconsin), April 23, 1908.

16. *Galesville Republican* (Wisconsin), April 30, May 21, 28, June 4, 11, 18, 25, July 2, 9, 16, 23, 30, August 6, 13, 20, 1908.

17. *Minneapolis Tribune,* March 1, April 26, 1908; *Aurora Beacon* (Illinois), April 30, 1908.

18. *Rockford Daily Register Gazette* (Illinois), May 1, 1908.

19. *St. Louis Star* (Missouri), August 27, 1910; *Minneapolis Tribune,* March 1, 1908; *Madison Daily Democrat* (Wisconsin), May 3, 1908; *Wisconsin State Journal* (Madison, Wisconsin), May 4, 1908.

20. Holway and Carroll, "Lives Of The Players," 344; Reichler, *The Baseball Encyclopedia,* 985–986; *Oshkosh Daily Northwestern* (Wisconsin), May 5, 6, 1908: SABR Minor League Database.

21. *Wisconsin Valley Leader* (Wisconsin), May 14, 1908; *St. Paul Dispatch,* May 13, 1908; *Dodge County Star,* May 21, 1908.

22. Mary Lethert Wingerd, "Separated at Birth: The Sibling Rivalry of Minneapolis and St. Paul," http://www.oah.org/pubs/nl/2007feb/wingerd.html, May 10, 2008; Risjord, *A Popular History of Minnesota,* 230.

23. *Twin City Star,* April 6, 1918; *Davison's Minneapolis City Directory 1906*; *St. Paul Appeal,* May 11, 1912.

24. *Twin City Star,* April 6, 1918; *Escanaba Morning Press* (Michigan), September 14, 1909; *Indianapolis Freeman* (Indiana), September 24, 1910.

25. *Dodge Center Record,* April 16, 1908; *Merrill Daily*

Herald (Wisconsin), August 7, 1909; *Indianapolis Freeman* (Indiana), September 24, 1910; *Waterville Advance*, June 30, 1909; *Duluth News Tribune*, June 6, 1908.

26. *Escanaba Morning Press* (Michigan), September 14, 1909; *Indianapolis Freeman* (Indiana), September 24, 1910; *Breckenridge Telegram*, August 6, 1908.

27. 1900 United States Census, Hennepin County, Minnesota; *St. Paul Daily News*, June 12, 1905; *Minneapolis Tribune*, June 3, 1907; *St. Paul Pioneer Press*, August 16, 1907; *Monticello Times*, August 22, 1907.

28. *Minneapolis Journal*, April 6, 19, 1908; *Minneapolis Tribune*, April 12, 1908.

29. *Minneapolis Journal*, April 5, 6 1908; Hoffbeck, "Bobby Marshall," 164, 168; *Twin City Star*, July 21, 1910.

30. *Minneapolis Journal*, April 6, 26, 1908; White, *History of Colored Base Ball*, 26, 63; Riley, *Biographical Encyclopedia of the Negro Baseball Leagues*, 392; 1880 United States Census, Saint Louis, Missouri; *Chicago Tribune* (Illinois), August 19, 1888, August 30, 1889.

31. 1900 United States Census, Cook County, Illinois; *Minneapolis Tribune*, July 26, 28, 1908; *Dunn County News* (Wisconsin), July 29, 1909; Reichler, *The Baseball Encyclopedia*, 1274; *Indianapolis Freeman* (Indiana), April 15, 1911; *Walker Pilot*, July 14, 1911; *Twin City Star*, June 23, 1910.

32. *Minneapolis Tribune*, June 28, 1908; Geoffrey C. Ward, *Unforgivable Blackness* (New York: Alfred A. Knopf, 2004), 413; *Duluth News Tribune*, October 25, 1908; *Topeka Daily Capitol* (Kansas), April 19, 1906; *Atchison Daily Globe* (Kansas), May 19, 1910.

33. *Lincoln State Journal* (Nebraska), June 6, 1928; Clay Moyle, *Sam Langford, Boxing's Greatest Uncrowned Champion* (Seattle: Bennett and Hastings, 2008), 321; *Oakland Tribune* (California), December 22, 1911; *Duluth News Tribune*, October 25, 1908; *Topeka Daily Capitol* (Kansas), April 19, 1906; *Topeka Plain Dealer* (Kansas), April 20, 1906; Ward, 413.

34. *Minneapolis Journal*, April 6, 1908; 1900 United States Census, McLean County, Illinois; *St. Paul Pioneer Press*, April 9, 1911; *Redwood Falls Gazette*, July 14, 1909; *Indianapolis Freeman* (Indiana), July 23, 1910.

35. *Minneapolis Journal*, April 6, 1908; *Minneapolis Tribune*, April 20, July 12, 1908; July 29, 1913; *Twin City Star*, July 21, 1910.

36. *Minneapolis Journal*, April 19, 1908; Roberto Gonzalez Echevarria, *The Pride Of Havana* (New York: Oxford University Press, 1999), 128; Leland, *Frank Leland's Baseball Club*, 10; *Chicago Tribune* (Illinois), September 8, 1907; Dixon and Hannigan, *The Negro Baseball Leagues*, 98; *Minneapolis Tribune*, June 7, 1908; *Eveleth News*, June 6, 1908;

37. United States Government World War I Registration Card, roll 1613510, serial number 3149, September 12, 1918; 1910 United States Census, Will County, Illinois; *Minneapolis Tribune*, May 23, June 5, 14, 1909; *Rhinelander The New North* (Wisconsin), August 18, 1910.

38. *Minneapolis Tribune*, April 20, July 3, 1908; SABR Minor League Database.

39. *Minneapolis Tribune*, April 27, 1908; *Stillwater Daily Gazette*, May 4, 1908.

40. *Minneapolis Tribune*, May 3, June 7 1908.

41. *Galesville Republican* (Wisconsin), May 28, 1908.

42. *Duluth News Tribune*, June 6, 1908; *Superior Telegram* (Wisconsin), June 6, 1908.

43. Leland, *Frank Leland's Baseball Club*, 10; *Minneapolis Tribune*, June 14, 1908; *Indianapolis Freeman* (Indiana), April 16, 1910.

44. *Mankato Weekly Review*, August 31, 1909; *Rochester Post and Daily Record*, August 31, 1909; *Manchester Press* (Iowa), July 16, 1908.

45. *Redwood Falls Gazette*, July 14, 1909; *Long Prairie News*, August 6, 1909.

46. *Delaware County News* (Iowa), July 15, 1908; *Manchester Press* (Iowa), July 16, 1908; *West Union Gazette* (Iowa), July 17, 1908.

47. *Stillwater Daily Gazette*, May 4, 1908; *Dell Rapids Times* (South Dakota), July 22, 1909; *Galesville Republican* (Wisconsin), May 28, 1908.

48. *Taylor County Star News* (Wisconsin), September 18, 1908; *West Union Argo* (Iowa), July 15, 1908.

49. *Chippewa Falls Weekly Herald* (Wisconsin), August 21, 1908; *Rochester Post and Daily Record*, August 31, 1909.

50. *Redwood Falls Gazette*, July 14, 1909; *Long Prairie Leader*, August 6, 1909; United States Government World War I Registration Card, roll 1452473, September 12, 1918.

51. *Moody County Enterprise* (South Dakota), July 22, 1909; *Minneapolis Tribune*, September 13, 1908; *Hibbing Tribune Daily*, August 17, 1909; *Barron County Shield* (Wisconsin), June 11, 1909.

52. *Minneapolis Tribune*, May 24, 1908; SABR Minor League Database.

53. *Minneapolis Tribune*, May 24, 31, 1908

54. *St. Paul Pioneer Press*, May 31, 1908; SABR Minor League Database.

55. *St. Paul Pioneer Press*, May 31, 1908.

56. Ibid.

57. Ibid.

58. Ibid.

59. *St. Paul Pioneer Press*, June 1, 1908.

60. Ibid.

61. Ibid.

62. *St. Paul Pioneer Press*, June 4, 1908; *New Richland Star*, June 11, 1908.

63. *St. Paul Pioneer Press*, June 8, 1908; *Stillwater Daily Gazette*, June 8, 1908.

64. *St. Paul Dispatch*, June 15, 1908; *Minneapolis Tribune*, June 15, 1908; SABR Minor League Database.

65. Ibid.

66. *St. Paul Dispatch*, June 15, 1908; *Minneapolis Tribune*, June 15, 1908

67. *Minneapolis Tribune*, June 15, 1908.

68. *Minneapolis Tribune*, June 14, 1908; *St. Paul Pioneer Press*, June 17, 1908; *St. Paul Dispatch*, June 17, 1908.

69. *St. Paul Pioneer Press*, June 18, 1908.

70. *Long Prairie Leader*, June 19, 23, 1908.

71. *Long Prairie Leader*, June 23, 1908; *Sawyer County Record* (Wisconsin), June 11, 1908; *Minneapolis Tribune*, July 19, 1908.

72. *Long Prairie News*, June 23, 1908; *St. Paul Dispatch*, June 22, 1908.

73. *St. Paul Pioneer Press*, June 29, 1908; *Red Wing Daily Republican*, June 29, 1908.

74. *St. Paul Pioneer Press*, June 29, 1908; *Red Wing Daily Republican*, June 29, 1908; *St. Paul Dispatch*, June 20, 1908.

Chapter Six

1. *Minneapolis Tribune*, July 19, 26, 1908.
2. *Minneapolis Tribune*, August 2, 1908.
3. *Minneapolis Tribune*, July 26, August 2, 16, 1908.
4. *Minneapolis Tribune*, June 7, 1908; SABR Minor League Database.
5. *Minneapolis Tribune*, June 7, 1908.
6. *Minneapolis Tribune*, June 8, 1908; SABR Minor League Database.
7. *Minneapolis Tribune*, July 3, 19, 1908; *Minneapolis Journal*, June 28, 1908; *Hastings Daily Gazette*, June 30, July 2, 1908.
8. *Minneapolis Tribune*, June 7, July 1, 12, August 16, 23, 1908.
9. *Minneapolis Tribune*, July 26, 1908; *Osage News* (Iowa), July 9, 1908.

10. *Oelwein Register* (Iowa), July 15, 1908; SABR Minor League Database.
11. *Oelwein Register* (Iowa), July 15, 1908; SABR Minor League Database.
12. *Oelwein Register* (Iowa), July 15, 1908.
13. *Oelwein Register* (Iowa), July 15, 1908.
14. *West Union Argo* (Iowa), July 15, *Decorah Journal* (Iowa), July 21, 1908; *Decorah Republican* (Iowa) as reported in the *Merrill Daily Herald* (Wisconsin), August 7, 1908.
15. *Duluth Evening Herald*, July 2, 3, 1908.
16. *Duluth Evening Herald*, July 2, 1908; *Duluth News Tribune*, July 2, 1908, July 26, 1909; SABR Minor League Database.
17. *Duluth Evening Herald*, July 3, 1908; *Duluth News Tribune*, July 3, 1908; SABR Minor League Database.
18. *Duluth Evening Herald*, July 4, 1908.
19. *Duluth News Tribune*, July 5, 1908; *Hibbing Daily Tribune*, July 7, 1908.
20. *Duluth News Tribune*, July 5, 1908; *Hibbing Daily Tribune*, July 7, 1908, July 18, 1910.
21. *Duluth News Tribune*, July 6, 1908; *Hibbing Daily Tribune*, July 7, 1908.
22. *Duluth Evening Herald*, July 7, 1908; *Hibbing Daily Tribune*, July 10, 1908.
23. *Duluth Evening Herald*, July 8, 1908; *Duluth News Tribune*, July 9, 1908.
24. *Duluth Evening Herald*, July 10, 1908; *Hibbing Daily Tribune*, July 10, 1908.
25. *Hibbing Daily Tribune*, July 3, October 13, 1908.
26. *Duluth Evening Herald*, July 13, 1908; *Duluth News Tribune*, July 11, 1908; *The Virginian*, July 14, 1908.
27. *Duluth News Tribune*, July 13, 1908; *The Virginian*, July 14, 1908.
28. Ibid.
29. *Duluth News Tribune*, July 13, 1908; *Minneapolis Tribune*, July 19, 1908.
30. *St. Paul Pioneer Press*, July 14, 15, 1908.
31. *St. Paul Pioneer Press*, July 16, 1908.
32. *St. Paul Dispatch*, July 17, 1908; *St. Paul Pioneer Press*, July 17, 1908; *Minneapolis Journal*, July 19, 1908.
33. *St. Paul Dispatch*, July 17, 1908; *St. Paul Pioneer Press*, July 17, 1908.
34. *Minneapolis Journal*, July 19, 1908.
35. *St. Paul Dispatch*, July 17, 1908; *Minneapolis Journal*, July 19, 1908.
36. *Minneapolis Tribune*, July 19, 26, 1908; *St. Paul Dispatch*, July 30, 1908.
37. *Faribault Journal*, July 22 1908; *Minneapolis Tribune*, July 26, 1908; *Jasper Journal*, July 31, 1908; *St. Paul Dispatch*, July 30, 1908.
38. *Renville Star Farmer*, July 24, 1908; *St. Paul Dispatch*, August 22, 1908; *Madison Daily Sentinel* (South Dakota), July 31, 1908; *Howard County Times* (Iowa), August 13, 1908; *Spring Grove Herald*, August 20, 1908; SABR Minor League Database.
39. *Eau Claire Leader* (Wisconsin), August 20, 1908; *Fennimore Times* (Wisconsin), August 19, 1908; Hoffbeck, "Barnstorming Teams," in *Swinging For The Fences*, 83; *Rochester Post and Record*, August 20, 1908; *Waseca Journal Radical*, August 26, 1908.
40. *St. Paul Dispatch*, August 10, 1908; *Winnebago City Free Press*, August 8, 1908; *St. Paul Pioneer Press*, August 8, 1908.
41. *Minneapolis Tribune*, June 28, July 19, 26, August 2, 1908; *Decorah Journal* (Iowa), July 21, 1908.
42. *Albert Lea Evening Tribune*, July 27, 1908; *Albert Lea Times Enterprise*, July 29, 1908; *Wahpeton Globe Gazette* (North Dakota), August 6, 1908.
43. Leland, *Frank Leland's Baseball Club*, 6; *Minneapolis Tribune*, July 26, August 30, September 25, 1908, May 2, 1909; *Red Wing Daily Republican*, August 24, 1908.
44. *Minneapolis Tribune*, August 1, 2, 3, 4, 1908; *St. Paul Dispatch*, August 3, 1908; *St. Paul Pioneer Press*, August 4, 5, 1908; 1920 United States Census, Cook County, Illinois; Okkonen, *1900–1910 Minor League Rosters*.
45. *Merrill Daily Herald* (Wisconsin), August 5, 8, 1908; SABR Minor League Database.
46. *Minneapolis Tribune*, August 15, 1908, June 27, 1909; *New Prague Times*, August 20, 1908; *Faribault Journal*, August 19, 1908.
47. *Minneapolis Tribune*, August 2, 23, 1908; *Monticello Times*, August 20, 1908.
48. *Lindstrom Chisago County Press*, August 27, 1908; *Stillwater Daily Gazette*, August 24, 1908; *St. Paul Pioneer Press*, August 24, 1908; *St. Paul Dispatch*, August 24, 1908; SABR Minor League Database.
49. *Stillwater Daily Gazette*, August 24, 1908; *St. Paul Pioneer Press*, August 24, 1908; *St. Paul Dispatch*, August 24, 1908.
50. Wikipedia, "Springfield Race Riot of 1908," http://en.wikipedia.org/wiki/Springfield_Race_Riot_of_1908, June 6, 2008; Time Line of African American History, 1901–1925, http://memory.loc.gov/ammem/aap/timelin3.html, May 18, 2008.
51. *Stillwater Daily Gazette*, August 24, 1908; *St. Paul Pioneer Press*, August 24, 1908; 1910 United States Census, Washington County, Minnesota; *Jordan Independent*, August 27, 1908.
52. *Stillwater Daily Gazette*, August 24, 1908; *St. Paul Pioneer Press*, August 24, 1908; *Jordan Independent*, August 27, 1908.
53. *Stillwater Daily Gazette*, August 24, 1908.
54. *Stillwater Daily Gazette*, August 24, 1908; *Jordan Independent*, August 27, 1908; *River Falls Journal* (Wisconsin), August 27, 1908.
55. *San Antonio Light* (Texas), August 22, 1908; *Minneapolis Tribune*, August 30, 1908.
56. *Minneapolis Journal*, August 25, 1908; *St. Paul Dispatch*, August 26, 1908.
57. *St. Paul Pioneer Press*, August 26, 1908; Okkonen, *1900–1910 Minor League Rosters*; SABR Minor League Database; Holway, Johnson and Borst, *Complete Book of Baseball's Negro Leagues*, 53; *Moberly Weekly Monitor* (Missouri), September 23, 1906; January 10, 1908; *Duluth News Tribune*, September 1, 1907.
58. *St. Paul Pioneer Press*, August 27, 1908; *Minneapolis Tribune*, August 30, 1908.
59. *Minneapolis Journal*, August 25, 1908; Kemp and Wildin, "The Algona Brownies," 78.
60. *St. Paul Pioneer Press*, August 28, 1908; *Shakopee Times*, August 21, 1908.
61. *St. Paul Pioneer Press*, August 28, 1908.
62. *St. Paul Pioneer Press*, August 28, 1908; *St. Paul Dispatch*, August 28, 1908.
63. Cottrell, *The Best Pitcher in Baseball* 44; *Chicago Tribune* (Illinois), August 7, 1908.
64. *St. Paul Pioneer Press*, August 29, 1908; *St. Paul Daily News*, August 29, 1908.
65. *St. Paul Daily News*, August 30, 1908; *St. Paul Pioneer Press*, August 31, 1908.
66. *Minneapolis Tribune*, August 29, 31, 1908; *St. Paul Dispatch*, August 30, 1908.
67. *St. Paul Pioneer Press*, August 31, 1908; *Minneapolis Tribune*, August 31, 1908; *Minneapolis Journal*, August 31, 1908.
68. *St. Paul Pioneer Press*, August 31, 1908; *Minneapolis Tribune*, August 31, 1908.
69. *Cresco Howard County Times* (Iowa), September 3, 1908; *Des Moines Daily News* (Iowa), September 5, 1908; BlackPast.org, "Buxton, Iowa (1895–1927)," http://www.blackpast.org/?q=aah/buxton-iowa-1895–1927, June 20, 2008; Seymour, *Baseball Volume III: The People's Game*, 585.

70. *St. Peter Herald*, September 18, 1908; Rainbolt, *Gold Glory*, 36; SABR Minor League Database.
71. *Taylor County News* (Wisconsin), September 18, 1908; *Minneapolis Tribune*, October 4, 1908; *Menomonie Times* (Wisconsin), September 18, 1908.
72. *Hibbing Daily Tribune*, September 4, 1908; *Mesaba Ore and the Hibbing News*, September 5, 1908; *Waconia Patriot*, August 28, 1908.
73. *St. Paul Pioneer Press*, September 4, 1908; *Minneapolis Journal*, September 4, 1908.
74. *St. Paul Dispatch*, September 6, 1908
75. *Faribault Journal*, September 9, 1908; *Fairmont Daily Sentinel*, September 9, 1908.
76. *Mankato Daily Free Press*, September 11, 1908; *Lake Crystal Union*, September 16, 1908; *Mapleton Blue Earth County Enterprise*, September 4, 1908; *Minneapolis Tribune*, September 13, 1908
77. *Red Wing Republican*, September 8, 1900, September 19, 1908; *St. Paul Pioneer Press*, September 14, 1908.
78. *St. Paul Pioneer Press*, September 13, 1908; Reichler, 1207, 1751.
79. *St. Paul Pioneer Press*, September 16, 1908; *Winnebago City Free Press*, September 19, 1908; *St. Paul Dispatch*, August 10, 1910.
80. *Minneapolis Journal*, September 17, 1908; *Winnebago City Free Press*, September 19, 1908.
81. *Harmony News*, May 21, September 24, 1908; SABR Minor League Database.
82. *Harmony News*, September 10, 24, 1908.
83. *St. Paul Pioneer Press*, September 20, 1908; *St. Paul Dispatch*, September 20, 1908.
84. *Minneapolis Journal*, September 17, 1908; *Minneapolis Tribune*, September 13, 20, 1908.
85. *Minneapolis Tribune*, September 21, 1908.
86. Ibid.
87. Ibid.
88. Ibid.
89. *St. Paul Pioneer Press*, September 22, 1908; *Minneapolis Journal*, July 19, 1908.
90. *St. Paul Pioneer Press*, September 22, 1908.
91. *St. Paul Pioneer Press*, September 23, 1908; *Minneapolis Tribune*, August 2, 1908
92. *Howard Lake Herald*, September 17, 24, 1908.
93. *Shakopee Scott County Argus*, September 25, 1908; *Osceola Sun* (Wisconsin), September 24, October 1, 1908.
94. SABR Minor League Database. Thornley, *On to Nicollet*, 78; *Minneapolis Tribune*, September 29, 1908.
95. *Minneapolis Tribune*, September 29, October 4, 1908.
96. *Minneapolis Tribune*, September 28, 30, 1908; *Rochester Daily Post and Record*, September 25, 1908; *Winona Republican Herald*, September 28, 1908; *La Crosse Tribune* (Wisconsin), September 28, 1908.
97. *Minneapolis Tribune*, October 4, 5, 1908; Powers-Beck, 187.
98. *Minneapolis Tribune*, October 4, 5, 1908; *Eau Claire Daily Telegram* (Wisconsin), August 8, 1908.
98. *Minneapolis Tribune*, October 4, 5, 1908; *Eau Claire Daily Telegram* (Wisconsin), August 8, 1908; *Duluth News Tribune*, September 26, October 4, 13, 29, 30, 1908.
99. *La Crosse Sunday Chronicle* (Wisconsin), October 4, 1908.
100. *La Crosse Sunday Chronicle* (Wisconsin), October 4, 1908; *La Crosse Tribune* (Wisconsin), October 5, 1908; SABR Minor League Database.
101. *Minneapolis Tribune*, July 19, September 13, 1908.

Chapter Seven

1. *St. Paul City Directory 1912*.
2. *Minneapolis Tribune*, April 4, May 2, 1909.
3. *Chicago Tribune* (Illinois), April 10, May 1, 1909; *Indianapolis Freeman* (Indiana), May 15, 1909.
4. *New York Age* (New York), April 22, 1909; *St. Paul Daily News*, May 3, 1909; *Indianapolis Freeman* (Indiana), May 15, 1909.
5. *Chicago Tribune*, August, 24, October 1, 1905; *Twin City Star*, July 21, 1910; *Cedar Rapids Daily Republican* (Iowa), April 24, 1906; *San Antonio Light* (Texas), June 15, July 27, August 22, 1908.
6. United States Government World War I Registration Card, roll 1907639, serial number 3475, September 12, 1918; *Polk's Houston City Directory 1917*, R.L. Polk and Company, Houston, Texas, 1917; 1910 United States Census, Harris County, Texas; *San Antonio Light* (Texas), July 27, 1908; *Galveston Daily News* (Texas), April 3, 1909; *St. Paul Pioneer Press*, August 16, 1909: *Fargo Forum* ((North Dakota), June 21, 1909.
7. *St. Paul Dispatch*, May 15, 1909; *Zumbrota News*, September 24, 1909; *Waukon Standard* (Iowa), July 22, 1909; *Indianapolis Freeman* (Indiana) July 24, August 14, 1909, July 15, 1911; *Hayward Sawyer County Record* (Wisconsin), July 15, 1909; *St. Paul Pioneer Press*, June 13, 1909.
8. *St. Paul Daily News*, May 3, 1909; *St. Paul Dispatch*, May 15, 1909.
9. *Hayward Sawyer County Record* (Wisconsin), July 15, 1909; Denis J. Gullickson and Carl Hanson, *Before They Were Packers* (Blue Earth, Wisconsin: Trails Books, 2004), 165.
10. *La Crosse Daily Chronicle* (Wisconsin), May 9, 1909.
11. *La Crosse Tribune* (Wisconsin), May 10, 1909; *La Crosse Chronicle* (Wisconsin), May 11, 1909; SABR Minor League Database.
12. *La Crosse Daily Chronicle* (Wisconsin), May 11, 1909; Okkonen, *1900–1910 Minor League Rosters*.
13. Riley, *Biographical Encyclopedia of the Negro Baseball Leagues*, 552; *Fitchburg Daily Sentinel* (Massachusetts), August 13, 1906; *Indianapolis Freeman* (Indiana), February 5, August 6, 20, 1910; *Young America Eagle*, October 1, 1909; 1900 U.S. Census, Garland County, AR; United States Government World War I Registration Card, roll 1452460, September 7, 1918.
14. *Kenyon News*, May 19, 1909; *Hibbing Daily Tribune*, May 21, 1908.
15. *Duluth News Tribune*, May 21, 1909; *Hibbing Daily Tribune*, May 21, 1909; *Mesaba Ore and the Hibbing News*, May 22, 1909.
16. *Duluth News Tribune*, May 22, 1909; *Hibbing Daily Tribune*, May 25, 1909, July 18, 1910.
17. *Duluth News Tribune*, May 23, 24, 1909; *Hibbing Daily Tribune*, May 25, 1909.
18. *Duluth News Tribune*, May 25, 1909; *Hibbing Daily Tribune*, May 25, 1909.
19. *Moose Lake Star Gazette*, May 27, 1909; *St. Paul Pioneer Press*, May 28, 31, 1909, *St. Paul Daily News*, June 3, 1909; *St. Paul Dispatch*, June 4, 1909; Okkonen, *1900–1910 Minor League Rosters*.
20. *Long Prairie Leader*, May 11, June 4, 1909; *La Crosse Daily Chronicle* (Wisconsin), May 8, 1909; *Minneapolis Tribune*, May 31, 1909.
21. *Stillwater Gazette*, May 19, 1909; *Minneapolis Tribune*, May 31, 1909; *St. Paul Pioneer Press*, April 22, 1911.
22. *Faribault Journal*, June 2, 1909; *Minneapolis Tribune*, May 31, 1909.
23. *Minneapolis Tribune*, June 1, 1909.
24. *Faribault Journal*, June 2, 1909; *Minneapolis Tribune*, June 1, 1909; *Minneapolis Journal*, June 1, 1909.
25. *New Richland Star*, June 3, 1909.
26. *St. Paul Pioneer Press*, June 6, 7, 1909.
27. *St. Paul Dispatch*, June 11, 1909; *St. Paul Pioneer Press*, June 9, 1909; Leland, *Frank Leland's Baseball Club*, 13.

28. Leland, *Frank Leland's Baseball Club*, 14–15; Riley, *Biographical Encyclopedia of the Negro Baseball Leagues*, 768; *San Antonio Light* (Texas), July 20, 22, 1908; *Indianapolis Freeman* (Indiana), October 30, 1909.
29. Leland, *Frank Leland's Baseball Club*, 13; *Minot Daily Reporter* (North Dakota), June 21, 1910; Cottrell, *The Best Pitcher in Baseball*, 175–176.
30. *St. Paul Daily News*, June 10, 1909; *St. Paul Pioneer Press*, June 13, 1909.
31. *St. Paul Daily News*, June 13, 1909; *St. Paul Pioneer Press*, June 13, 1909.
32. *St. Paul Pioneer Press*, July 17, 1909.*Minneapolis Tribune*, July 18, 1909.
33. *Renville Star Farmer*, June 18, 1909; *Hankinson News* (North Dakota), June 24, 1909; *Cogswell Enterprise* (North Dakota), June 17, 24, 1909.
34. *Alexandria Citizen*, June 24, 1909; Okkonen, *1900–1910 Minor League Rosters*.
35. *Long Prairie Leader*, June 29, 1909; *Alexandria Post News*, July 29, 1909.
36. Ibid.
37. *Bemidji Daily Pioneer*, June 28, 29, 1909; *Itasca County Independent*, July 1, 1909.
38. *Hibbing Daily Tribune*, July 2, 1909; *Duluth News Tribune*, July 2, 3, 1909.
39. *Duluth News Tribune*, July 4, 5, 1909; *Hankinson News* (North Dakota), June 24, 1909.
40. *Mesaba Ore and the Hibbing News*, July 10, 1909; *Hibbing Daily Tribune*, July 6, 1909.
41. *Hibbing Daily Tribune*, July 6, 1909; *Duluth Evening Herald*, July 6, 1909.
42. *Duluth News Tribune*, July 7, 1909; *Duluth Evening Herald*, July 7, 1909.
43. *Duluth News Tribune*, July 8, 1909.
44. *Ashland Daily Press* (Wisconsin), July 12, 1909.
45. *Bessemer Herald and the New Free Press* (Michigan), July 17, 1909.
46. *St. Paul Pioneer Press*, July 17, 1909; *St. Paul Daily News*, July 18, 1909.
47. *Mankato Daily Free Press*, July 19, 1909; *Mankato Weekly Review*, July 20, 1909.
48. *St. Paul Daily News*, July 18, 1909; *Alexandria Post News*, July 22, 1909; *Alexandria Citizen*, July 22, 1909.
49. *St. Paul Daily News*, May 1, 1909; *Alexandria Post News*, July 29, 1909.
50. *Indianapolis Freeman*, (Indiana) June 26, 1909; *St. Paul Daily News*, July 22, 1909; *Minneapolis Tribune*, July 24, 1909.
51. *Minneapolis Tribune*, May 2, 23, 1909.
52. *Minneapolis Tribune*, April 4, May 2, 16, 22, 1909; *Indianapolis Freeman* (Indiana), March 11, 1911; United States Government World War I Registration Card, roll 1953276, September 12, 1918.
53. *Minneapolis Tribune*, April 21, May 16, 1909.
54. *Merrill Daily Herald* (Wisconsin), May 17, 1909.
55. *Merrill Daily Herald* (Wisconsin), May 17, 1909; *Pierce County Herald* (Wisconsin), May 27, 1909.
56. *Minneapolis Tribune*, April 18, May 23, 1909.
57. *Minneapolis Tribune*, May 31, 1909; *Pierce County Herald* (Wisconsin), May 27, 1909.
58. *Mesaba Ore and the Hibbing News*, June 1, 1909.
59. *Rice Lake Chronotype* (Wisconsin), June 11, 1909; *Barron County Shield* (Wisconsin), June 11, 1909; *Minneapolis Tribune*, June 6, 1909.
60. *Minneapolis Tribune*, June 7, 1909; SABR Minor League Database.
61. *Merrill Daily Herald* (Wisconsin), June 14, August 7, 1909; *Minneapolis Tribune*, June 14, 1909; SABR Minor League Database.
62. *Minneapolis Tribune*, June 11, 1909; Debono, *The Indianapolis ABC's*, 138–139.
63. *Janesville Argus*, June 23, 1909; United States Government World War I Registration Card, roll 1452467.
64. *Waterville Advance*, June 23, 30, 1909; 1900 United States Census, Hennepin County, Minnesota; 1910 United States Census, Le Sueur County, Minnesota; *Waukon Standard* (Iowa), July 22, 1909.
65. *Cresco Howard County Times* (Iowa), July 1, 1909.
66. *Oelwein Daily Register* (Iowa), July 7, 1909; *Hibbing Daily Tribune*, August 17, 1909; *Minneapolis Tribune*, July 12, 1909.
67. *Minneapolis Tribune*, June 28, July 24, 1909; *Osage Mitchell County Press* (Iowa), July 7, 1909; *Charles City Daily Intelligencer* (Iowa), July 3, 1909; *Oelwein Register* (Iowa), July 7, 1909; *Redwood Falls Gazette*, July 14, 1909.
68. *St. Paul Pioneer Press*, July 25, 1909.
69. *St. Paul Pioneer Press*, July 26, 1909; *Minneapolis Tribune*, July 26, 1909.
70. *Minneapolis Tribune*, July 26, August 1, 1909.
71. *St. Paul Pioneer Press*, June 13, 1909; *St. Paul Daily News*, June 14, July 25, 1909; *St. Paul Appeal*, June 19, 1909; *Indianapolis Freeman* (Indiana), July 24, 1909.
72. *St. Paul Appeal*, June 19, 1909; *St. Paul Daily News*, July 25, 1909; *Minneapolis Tribune*, September 26, 1908; *Chicago Tribune* (Illinois), July 13, 26, 1909; Riley, 48.
73. Gary Ashwill, "Mike Moore," http://agatetype.typepad.com/agate_type/2006/07/index.html, June 6, 2006; *Chicago Defender* (Illinois), September 15, 1917; Leland, *Frank Leland's Baseball Club*, 9, 17–18, 20.
74. *Minneapolis Tribune*, July 26, 1909; *Indianapolis Freeman* (Indiana), December 11, 1909; *Long Prairie Leader*, July 30, 1909.
75. *St. Paul Pioneer Press*, July 27, 1909.
76. Ibid.
77. *St. Paul Pioneer Press*, July 27, 1909; *Minneapolis Tribune*, July 27, 1909.
78. *St. Paul Pioneer Press*, July 27, 28, 1909.
79. *St. Paul Pioneer Press*, July 28, 1909.
80. *St. Paul Daily News*, July 29, 1909; *St. Paul Pioneer Press*, July 29, 1909.
81. Leland, *Frank Leland's Baseball Club*, 14; *St. Paul Pioneer Press*, July 29, 1909.
82. *St. Paul Pioneer Press*, July 29, 1909.
83. *Long Prairie Leader*, July 30, 1909; *St. Paul Pioneer Press*, July 29, 1909.
84. *St. Paul Pioneer Press*, July 29, 1909.
85. *Long Prairie Leader*, July 30, August 10, 1909; *Indianapolis Freeman* (Indiana), December 11, 1909.
86. *St. Paul Pioneer Press*, July 30, 1909; *Stillwater Daily Gazette*, August 24, 1909.
87. *St. Paul Pioneer Press*, July 30, 1909.
88. Ibid.
89. Ibid.
90. *St. Paul Pioneer Press*, July 31, 1909.
91. Ibid.
92. Peterson, 111; *St. Paul Pioneer Press*, July 31, 1909.
93. *Twin City Star*, July 21, 1910; *St. Paul Pioneer Press*, July 31, 1909.
94. *St. Paul Pioneer Press*, July 31, 1909.
95. *Indianapolis Freeman* (Indiana), September 25, November 13, December 11, 1909.
96. *St. Paul Appeal*, September 18, 1909.
97. *St. Paul Pioneer Press*, August 2, 1909; *Indianapolis Freeman* (Indiana), August 7, 14, 1909.
98. *Minneapolis Tribune*, July 18, 1909; *St. Paul Pioneer Press*, August 5, 1909.
99. *La Crosse Tribune* (Wisconsin), August 11, 1909; *Chicago Tribune* (Illinois), August 13, 14, 1909; *Fennimore Times* (Wisconsin), August 18, 1909; Reichler, 1715.
100. *St. Paul Pioneer Press*, August 16, September 15, 1909; *St. Paul Daily News*, September 26, 1909; *Indianapolis Freeman* (Indiana), August 28, 1909.

101. *Indianapolis Freeman* (Indiana), August 28, 1909; Janice A. Beran, "Diamonds In Iowa: Blacks, Buxton, and Baseball," in *Journal of African American History* (Washington, D.C.: Association for the Study of African American Life and History, Volume 87, January 2002), 64–65.
102. *Preston Republican*, September 3, 1909; *Harmony News*, September 9, 1909; Okkonen, *1900–1910 Minor League Rosters*.
103. *Alexandria Citizen*, August 5, 1909; *Long Prairie Leader*, August 6, 1909; *Merrill Daily Herald*, (Wisconsin), August 7, 1909.
104. *Dunn County News* (Wisconsin), July 29, 1909; *Minneapolis Tribune*, August 1, 2, 1909.
105. *Merrill Daily Herald* (Wisconsin), August 9, 10, 1909; *Duluth News Tribune*, August 14, 1909.
106. *Hibbing Daily Tribune*, August 17, 1909; *Anamosa Journal* (Iowa), August 26, 1909.
107. *Preston Times* (Iowa), August 27, 1909; *Mankato Daily Free Press*, August 30, 1909.
108. *Mankato Daily Free Press*, August 30, 1909; *Winnebago City Free Press*, September 4, 1909; 1910 United States Census, Blue Earth County, Minnesota.
109. *Olmstead County Democrat*, September 3, 1909.
110. *Winnebago City Free Press*, September 4, 1909; *Minneapolis Tribune*, September 5, 1909.
111. *Minneapolis Tribune*, September 19, 20, 1909.
112. *St. Paul Pioneer Press*, September 21, 1909.
113. *Strawberry Point Mail Press* (Iowa), August 26, 1909.
114. *Blue Earth Faribault County Register*, September 16, 1909; *Young America Eagle*, October 1, 1909; Reichler, *The Baseball Encyclopedia*, 1599, 1607; "The Pitcher Register," in *Total Baseball*, 1611.
115. *St. Paul Pioneer Press*, September 20, 1909.
116. *Redwood Falls Gazette*, June 16, 23, September 29, 1909; *Redwood Reveille*, June 18, 1909.
117. *St. Paul Daily News*, September 26, 1909; *St. Paul Pioneer Press*, September 27, 1909.
118. *Young America Eagle*, October 8, 1909; SABR Minor League Database.
119. *Chicago Inter Ocean* (Illinois), October 4, 11, 1909.
120. *Indianapolis Freeman* (Indiana), October 23, 1909; *Chicago Tribune* (Illinois), October 19, 1909; Hoffbeck, "Bobby Marshall," 69.
121. *Indianapolis Freeman* (Indiana), September 11, 18, October 2, 9, 16, November, 20, 1909.
122. *Indianapolis Freeman* (Indiana), September 11, October 16, 1909.
123. *Indianapolis Freeman* (Indiana), November 20, 1909; *Chicago Defender* (Illinois), January 22, 1910.
124. *Chicago Tribune* (Illinois), September 24, 1909; *Indianapolis Freeman* (Indiana), October 2, 1909; *St. Paul Pioneer Press*, April 10, 1910.
125. *Indianapolis Freeman* (Indiana), August 7, 1909; January 8, 1910.

Chapter Eight

1. Ward, *Unforgivable Blackness*, 166–67, 173; *St. Paul Pioneer Press*, March 11, 1910.
2. *St. Paul Pioneer Press*, March 11, 1910; Ward 180.
3. Ward, *Unforgivable Blackness*, 210–211; *Twin City Star*, July 7, 1910.
4. *Indianapolis Freeman* (Indiana), March 26, 1910; *St. Paul Dispatch*, April 8, 1910; *St. Paul Pioneer Press*, April 10, 1910.
5. *Indianapolis Freeman* (Indiana), April 2, 9, 16, 1910; *St. Paul Dispatch*, April 8, 27, 1910.
6. *St. Paul Pioneer Press*, April 10, 1910; Holway, *Blackball Stars*, 352; *Indianapolis Freeman* (Indiana), May 2, July 4, 1908, August 7, 1909, May 28, 1910; United States Government World War I Registration Card, June 5, 1917; *Glasgow Missourian* (Missouri), May 12, 1910.
7. Holway, *Blackball Stars*, 352; *Pittsburgh Post* (Pennsylvania), July 1, 1906; United States Government World War II Registration Card, Roll Number WW2_2139316, Serial Number, 475, April 26, 1942; United States Government World War I Registration Card, Roll Number 1852335; *Owatonna Daily Journal Chronicle*, June 3, 1910; *Shakopee Scott County Argus*, September 23, 1910; *Minneapolis Tribune*, July 2, 1911; *Twin City Star*, July 8, 1911; *Pittsburgh Courier* (Pennsylvania), Aug 13, 1938.
8. Holway, *Blackball Stars*, 352; United States Government World War I Registration Card, Roll Number 1852335; 1920 United States Census, Allegheny County, Pennsylvania; *Watertown Daily Public Opinion* (South Dakota), May 23, 1910; *Valley City Evening Times* (North Dakota), June 25, 27, 1910; *Twin City Star*, July 21, 1910, July 8, 1911.
9. Riley, *Biographical Encyclopedia of the Negro Baseball Leagues*, 97; *Indianapolis Freeman* (Indiana), May 2, 1908; *St. Paul Pioneer Press*, May 24, 1910; *Watertown Daily Public Opinion*, (South Dakota), May 25, 1910; Debono, *The Indianapolis ABC's*, 127.
10. *St. Paul Pioneer Press*, April 29, May 2, September 11, 1910.
11. *St. Paul Pioneer Press*, May 2, 1910; *Eau Claire Daly Telegram* (Wisconsin), May 4, 5, 6, 1910; *La Crosse Daily Chronicle* (Wisconsin), May 8, 10, 1910; *Grand Forks Daily Herald* (North Dakota), April 1, 1914.
12. *Eau Claire Daly Telegram* (Wisconsin), May 4, 5, 6, 1910; SABR Minor League Database.
13. *La Crosse Daily Chronicle* (Wisconsin), May 8, 10, 1910; SABR Minor League Database; 1910 United States Census, Ramsey County, Minnesota.
14. *Hibbing Daily Tribune*, August 26, 1910; *St. Paul Pioneer Press*, May 24, 1910.
15. *Young American Eagle*, May 20, 1910; *Aberdeen Daily American* (South Dakota), May 18, 19, 1910; *Aberdeen Daily News* (South Dakota), May 19, 1910.
16. *Aberdeen Daily American* (South Dakota), August 3, 1909, May 18, 1910; *Aberdeen Daily News* (South Dakota), September 3, 1910; *Groton Independent* (South Dakota), May 26, 1910; *Watertown Daily Public Opinion* (South Dakota), May 23, 1910; *St. Paul Pioneer Press*, May 24, 1910.
17. *Watertown Daily Public Opinion* (South Dakota), May 24, 1910.
18. *Watertown Daily Public Opinion* (South Dakota), May 25, 1910; *Aberdeen Daily News* (South Dakota), September 9, 1910.
19. *Owatonna Daily Journal Chronicle*, June 3, 1910.
20. *Chicago Tribune* (Illinois), May 23, 1910; *St. Paul Pioneer Press*, May 24, 1910; *Indianapolis Freeman* (Indiana), May 28, 1910.
21. *Indianapolis Freeman* (Indiana), January 8, April 16, 1910.
22. 1910 United States Census, Hennepin County, Minnesota; *Indianapolis Freeman* (Indiana), September 25, 1909, April 16, 1910.
23. *Indianapolis Freeman* (Indiana), July 16, 23, September 24, 1910; Debono, *The Indianapolis ABC's*, 41, 147, 153, 163; Certificate of Death, Bureau of Vital Statistics, Missouri State Board of Health, Registered Number, 1748, May 15, 1911.
24. *St. Louis Republic* (Missouri), September 2, 1910; *Harmony News*, June 24, 1909; *Cresco Howard County Times* (Iowa), July 1, 1909; *Merrill Daily Herald* (Wisconsin), August 7, 1909; *Twin City Star*, June 23, 30, 1910.
25. *Indianapolis Freeman* (Indiana), May 14, June 4, 18, 1910; *San Antonio Daily Light* (Texas), August 12, 1899;

San Antonio Light and Gazette (Texas), April 10, 1910; *San Antonio Light* (Texas), June 14, 1937.

26. *Kansas City Journal* (Missouri); May 15, 1910; *Indianapolis Freeman* (Indiana), June 4, 25, 1910; Riley, 484.
27. *Indianapolis Freeman* (Indiana), June 25, 1910.
28. *Indianapolis Freeman* (Indiana), June 4, 25, 1910.
29. *Atchison Daily Globe* (Kansas), May 19, 1910; *Kansas City Journal* (Missouri), May 22, 1910.
30. *Kansas City Journal* (Missouri), May 21, 22, 24, 25 1910; Riley, 474.
31. *Indianapolis Freeman* (Indiana), June 4, 1910; *Monroe County News* (Iowa), May 26, June 2, 1910; Selby, "William 'Big Bill' Gatewood," 79.
32. *Indianapolis Freeman* (Indiana), April 23, August 6, 1910; *Chicago Defender* (Illinois), April 9, 1910; *Chicago Tribune* (Illinois), May 2, 12, 13, 16, 1910; Hoffbeck, "Bobby Marshall," 71; *Twin City Star*, July 14, 1910.
33. *St. Paul Pioneer Press*, June 5, 1910.
34. *St. Paul Pioneer Press*, June 6, 1910; *Twin City Star*, June 9, 1910; SABR Minor League Database.
35. *St. Paul Pioneer Press*, June 6, 1910; *Aberdeen Daily American* (South Dakota), June 15, 1910.
36. *Waseca Journal Radical*, June 15, 1910; *Watertown Daily Public Opinion* (South Dakota), June 13, 14, 1910.
37. *Aberdeen Daily American* (South Dakota), June 15, 16, 1910.
38. *Minot Daily Reporter* (North Dakota), June 20, 1910; *Twin City Star*, June 21, 1910; *Indianapolis Freeman* (Indiana), April 22, 1911; Debono, *The Indianapolis ABC's*, 144.
39. *Twin City Star*, June 21, July 14, 21, 1910; *Chicago Tribune* (Illinois), April 29, May 27, 1906, May 10, 17, 19, 1907; Debono, *The Indianapolis ABC's*, 144; *St. Paul Pioneer Press*, April 2, 1911.
40. *Indianapolis Freeman* (Indiana) June 20, 1908, April 16, June 11, 1910; *Chicago Tribune* (Illinois), July 4, 15, August 8, 1909, May 16, 23, 1910.
41. *Minot Daily Reporter* (North Dakota), June 20, 1910.
42. *Minot Daily Reporter* (North Dakota), June 21, 1910; Thornley, *Baseball in Minnesota*, 153; Reichler, *The Baseball Encyclopedia*, 1633.
43. *Minot Daily Reporter* (North Dakota), June 21, 1910.
44. *Minot Daily Reporter* (North Dakota), June 22, 23, 24, 1910.
45. *Minot Daily Reporter* (North Dakota), June 20, 21, 22, 23, 24, 1910.
46. *Valley City Evening Times* (North Dakota), June 25, 1910.
47. *Valley City Evening Times* (North Dakota), June 25, 27, 1910.
48. *Valley City Evening Times* (North Dakota), June 25, 27, 1910; SABR Minor League Database.
49. *Valley City Evening Times* (North Dakota), June 27, 1910.
50. *Jamestown Daily Alert* (North Dakota), June 26, 27, 28, 1910; *St. Paul Pioneer Press*, June 5, 1910.
51. *Minneapolis Tribune*, July 1, 1910; *Hope Pioneer* (North Dakota), July 7, 1910; *Devils Lake Inter Ocean* (North Dakota), July 8, 1910; *Fargo Forum* (North Dakota), July 4, 5, 1910; *Cavalier County Republican* (North Dakota), July 7, 1910; *St. Paul Pioneer Press*, July 8, 1910; *Grafton News and Times* (North Dakota), July 15, 1910.
52. *Park Gazette News* (North Dakota), July 15, 1910; *St. Paul Dispatch*, July 12, 1910; *Cass Lake Times*, July 16, 1910, July 8, 1911; *Duluth Evening Herald*, July 15, 1910; SABR Minor League Database.
53. *Duluth News Tribune*, July 16, 1910; *Hibbing Daily Tribune*, July 16, 1910.
54. *Hibbing Daily Tribune*, July 15, 18, 1910; *Duluth News Tribune*, July 18, 1910.
55. *Hibbing Daily Tribune*, July 19, 20, 1910; *Duluth News Tribune*, July 20, 1910
56. *Valley City Evening Times* (North Dakota), June 27, 1910; *St. Paul Dispatch*, July 13, 1910; *Minneapolis Tribune*, July 2, 1911; *Hibbing Daily News*, July 17, 1911.
57. *Lester Prairie News*, July 14, 21, 1910.
58. *Twin City Star*, July 14, 21, 1910; *St. Paul Pioneer Press*, July 17, 24, 1910; *St. Paul Dispatch*, July 12, 19, 1910.
59. *St. Paul Pioneer Press*, July 17, 1910; Riley, *Biographical Encyclopedia of the Negro Baseball Leagues*, 623, 854–55, 877.
60. *Twin City Star*, July 21, 1910; *St. Paul Dispatch*, July 12, 1910.
61. *Chicago Defender* (Illinois), May 5, 1934; Bernard L. Peterson, Jr., *The African American Theatre Directory, 1816–1960: A Comprehensive Guide to Early Black Theatre Organizations, Companies, Theatres, and Performing Groups* (Westport, Conn.: Greenwood Press, 1997), 157; Jeffrey Green, *Black Edwardians: Black People in Britain 1901–1914* (New York: Routledge, 1998), 81–82; Rainer E. Lotz, "From Minstrelsy to Jazz: Cross-cultural links between Germans and Afro-Americans," http://www2.hu-berlin.de/fpm/popscrip/themen/pst08/Lotz.htm, September 3, 2008.
62. *Indianapolis Freeman* (Indiana), January 29, July 30, 1910; *Twin City Star*, October 26, November 4, 1910, November 2, 1912; *Chicago Defender* (Illinois), July 2, 1910.
63. *Twin City Star*, July 14, 1910; *St. Paul Pioneer Press*, July 17, 24, 1910.
64. *St. Paul Pioneer Press*, July 25, 1910.
65. Ibid.
66. Ibid.
67. Ibid.
68. *St. Paul Pioneer Press*, July 26, 1910; Riley, *Biographical Encyclopedia of the Negro Baseball Leagues*, 854.
69. *St. Paul Pioneer Press*, July 26, 1910; Riley, *Biographical Encyclopedia of the Negro Baseball Leagues*, 623; *Indianapolis Freeman* (Indiana), August 6, 1910.
70. *St. Paul Pioneer Press*, July 26, 1910.
71. *St. Paul Pioneer Press*, July 27, 1910.
72. Ibid.
73. Ibid.
74. *St. Paul Pioneer Press*, July 28, 1910.
75. Ibid.
76. Ibid.
77. *St. Paul Pioneer Press*, July 28, 1910; *Indianapolis Freeman* (Indiana), June 11, 1910; Riley, 707, 883.
78. *St. Paul Pioneer Press*, July 29, 1910.
79. *St. Paul Pioneer Press*, July 25, 26, 27, 28, 29, 1910; *Twin City Star*, July 21, 1910; *Indianapolis Freeman* (Indiana), August 13, 1910.
80. *Mankato Daily Free Press*, August 1, 1910.
81. *Osceola Sun* (Wisconsin), August 11, 1910; *Hayward Sawyer County Record* (Wisconsin), August 4, 1910; *New Richmond News* (Wisconsin), August 13, 1910; *Spooner Advocate* (Wisconsin), August 19, 1910.
82. *New Richmond News* (Wisconsin), August 13, 1910; *Cumberland Advocate*, August 4, 11, 1910; *St. Paul Pioneer Press*, August 9, 1910; Okkonen, *1900–1910 Minor League Rosters*.
83. *Indianapolis Freeman* (Indiana), May 28, August 6, 1910; *Chicago Tribune* (Illinois), August 29, September 4, 1910; *Kansas City Journal* (Missouri), October 23, 1910.
84. *Waconia Patriot*, August 12, 1910.
85. *Duluth News Tribune*, August 20, 1910; *Hibbing News Tribune*, August 22, 1910.
86. *Duluth News Tribune*, August 22, 1910; *Hibbing Daily Tribune*, August 22, 1910.
87. *Duluth News Tribune*, August 20, 1908, August 22, 1910; *Hibbing Daily Tribune*, August 22, 1910.
88. *Hibbing Daily Tribune*, August 26, 1910.

89. *Duluth Herald,* August 22, 1910; *St. Paul Pioneer Press,* July 26, 1910; *Duluth News Tribune,* August 23, 1910.
90. *Hibbing Daily Tribune,* August 26, 1910; *Chisholm Tribune Herald,* August 26, 1910.
91. *Hibbing Daily Tribune,* August 26, 1910.
92. *Duluth News Tribune,* August 27, 28, 29, 1910; *Hibbing Daily Tribune,* August 26, 1910; SABR Minor League Database.
93. *Hibbing Daily Tribune,* August 26, 1910; *Spooner Advocate* (Wisconsin), September 2, 1910.
94. *Spooner Advocate* (Wisconsin), September 2, 1910.
95. *St. Paul Dispatch,* September 2, 1910; *St. Paul Pioneer Press,* September 3, 1910; *Indianapolis Freeman* (Indiana), August 6, 20, September 17, 1910.
96. SABR Minor League Database. *Mankato Daily Free Press,* September 5, 1910.
97. *Mankato Daily Free Press,* September 6, 1910.
98. *Fairmont Daily Sentinel,* September 9, 1910; *Fairmont Martin County Independent,* September 10, 1910.
99. *St. Paul Pioneer Press,* June 5, September 11, 1910; *Alexandria Post News,* June 11, 1908; *Minot Daily Reporter* (North Dakota), June 19, 1910; *North St. Paul Sentinel,* September 16, 1910.
100. *St. Paul Pioneer Press,* September 11, 1910.
101. Ibid.
102. *Twin City Star,* September 1, 1910; *Preston Times,* September 7, 1910;
103. *St. Paul Pioneer Press,* September 15, 1910; *Preston Times,* September 21, 1910.
104. *Preston Times,* September 21, 1910; *Preston Republican,* September 23, 1910.
105. *Valley City Evening Times,* (North Dakota), June 27, 1910; *St. Paul Dispatch,* June 20, 1908; *Philadelphia Inquirer,* (Pennsylvania), August 10, 1906.
106. *St. Paul Dispatch,* September 19, 1910; *Minneapolis Tribune,* September 21, 1910; *Shakopee Scott County Argus,* September 9, 23, 1910; *Shakopee Tribune,* September 23, 1910.
107. Hoffbeck, "Bobby Marshall," 168; *Twin City Star,* September 16, 1910.
108. *St. Paul Pioneer Press,* August 7, 1910; *Springfield Advance,* August 11, September 29, 1910.
109. *Springfield Advance,* September 22, 29, 1910.
110. United States Government World War I Registration Card, roll 1504017, June 5, 1917; 1905 Minnesota State Census, Goodhue County; *Mille Lacs County Times,* September 7, 1910; *Springfield Advance,* September 29, 1910.
111. *Springfield Advance,* September 22, 29, 1910.
112. *Springfield Advance,* September 29, 1910.
113. Ibid.
114. *Indianapolis Freeman* (Indiana), June 18, 25, 1910.
115. *Indianapolis Freeman* (Indiana), April 30, July 2, 23, 1910; Riley, *Biographical Encyclopedia of the Negro Baseball Leagues,* 540.
116. 1910 United States Census, Hennepin County, Minnesota; *Twin City Star,* June 23, 1910; *Indianapolis Freeman* (Indiana), July 2, 1910.
117. *Indianapolis Freeman* (Indiana), July 16, 23, August 6, 1910; *San Antonio Light and Gazette* (Texas), April 10, 1910; *Galveston Daily News* (Texas), July 3, 1910.
118. *Indianapolis Freeman* (Indiana), July 23, 1910; *Kansas City Post* (Missouri), August 21, 1910.
119. *Kansas City Journal* (Missouri), August 22, 23, 1910; *Indianapolis Freeman* (Indiana), September 17, 1910.
120. *St. Louis Republic* (Missouri), August 27, 29, 1910; *Indianapolis Freeman* (Indiana), September 3, 1910; 1910 United States Census, Hennepin County, Minnesota.
121. *St. Louis Globe Democrat* (Missouri), August 30, 1910; *St. Louis Republic* (Missouri), August 31, September 1, 2, 3, 1910.
122. *St. Louis Republic* (Missouri), September 4, 1910; *Indianapolis Freeman* (Indiana), September 17, 24, 1910.
123. *Indianapolis Freeman* (Indiana), September 24, 1910.
124. *Indianapolis Star* (Indiana), September 21, 22, 1910; *Indianapolis Freeman* (Indiana), September 24, 1910; Debono, *The Indianapolis ABC's,* 49, 70.
125. *Indianapolis Freeman* (Indiana), September 24, 1910; *Twin City Star,* September 30, 1910.
126. *Grand Forks Daily Herald* (North Dakota), July 1, 1911.
127. *St. Croix Falls Standard Press* (Wisconsin), September 23, October 14, 1910; *Osceola Sun* (Wisconsin), October 6, 1910; SABR Minor League Database.
128. *St. Paul Dispatch,* September 6, 1910; *St. Paul Pioneer Press,* October 3, 1910; James Ericson, "Hail to the Chief: A Research Paper Chronicling the Life and Baseball Exploits of John Adolph 'Chief' Bender," http://www.isd.net/~jime/chief.htm, August 9, 2004.
129. *St. Paul Pioneer Press,* October 3, 1910.
130. *St. Paul Pioneer Press,* October 3, 1910; *Twin City Star,* September 30, 1910; 1910 United States Census, Ramsey County, Minnesota.
131. Ward, *Unforgivable Blackness,* 239, 242–243; *Twin City Star,* November 4, 1910.

Chapter Nine

1. *Twin City Star,* February 18, 1911.
2. *Twin City Star,* April 8, 1911; *Chicago Defender* (Illinois), April 15, 1911.
3. *Twin City Star,* April 15, July 8, August 19, 1911.
4. David Trombley, "Saint Paul Saints History 1902–1919," http://www.usfamily.net/web/trombleyd/Saints History02-19.htm, February 16, 2009; 1900 United States Census, Ramsey County, Minnesota.
5. *Chicago Defender* (Illinois), April 15, 1911; *Minneapolis Spokesman,* August 29, 1941.
6. *Indianapolis Freeman* (Indiana), July 30, August 6, 1910, April 22, 1911; *St. Paul Pioneer Press,* April 2, 16, 1911; Hoffbeck, "Bobby Marshall," 72.
7. *Minneapolis Tribune,* April 13, 1911; *Twin City Star,* April 15, 1911; *St. Paul Pioneer Press,* April 22, 1911; Clark and Lester, *The Negro Leagues Book,* 216; Riley, *Biographical Encyclopedia of the Negro Baseball Leagues,* 367, 604.
8. *St. Paul Pioneer Press,* April 13, 22, 1911; *Minneapolis Tribune,* April 14, 15, 19, 1911.
9. *Chicago Defender* (Illinois), April 15, 1911; *St. Paul Pioneer Press,* April 22, 1911; *Minneapolis Tribune,* April 24, August 14, 1911.
10. *St. Paul Pioneer Press,* April 22, 1911; *Minneapolis Tribune,* April 2, 1908, April 7, 1912; Zoss and Bowman, 144; *Kansas Semi-Weekly Capital* (Topeka, Kansas), August 9, 1898; SABR Minor League Database.
11. 1900 United States Census, Cook County, Illinois; *Minneapolis Tribune,* August 12, 1906, April 12, 1908, July 2, 1911; *Wausau Daily Record Herald* (Wisconsin), May 9, 1911.
12. United States Government World War I Registration Card, roll 1851249, serial number 807, September 12, 1918; *Van Wert Daily Times-Bulletin* (Ohio), May 14, 1940; *Fort Wayne News and Sentinel* (Indiana), June 15, 1920; *Twin City Star,* July 8, 1911.
13. *St. Paul Pioneer Press,* April 24 1911; *Minneapolis Tribune,* April 24, 1911; *Twin City Star,* April 29, 1911.
14. *Chicago Defender* (Illinois), April 15, 1911; *St. Paul Pioneer Press,* April 13, 29, 1911.
15. *La Crosse Daily Chronicle* (Wisconsin), April 30, 1911; *La Crosse Tribune* (Wisconsin), May 1, 1911; *La Crosse Leader Press* (Wisconsin), May 1, 1911; *Twin City Star,* July 8, 1911.

16. *Red Wing Daily Republican*, May 2, 3, 1911.
17. *Eau Claire Daily Telegram* (Wisconsin), May 4, 5, 1911; *Eau Claire Leader* (Wisconsin), May 4, 5, 1911.
18. *Eau Claire Daily Telegram* (Wisconsin), May 6, 1911; *Eau Claire Leader* (Wisconsin), May 6, 1911; SABR Minor League Database.
19. *Wausau Daily Record Herald*, (Wisconsin), May 9, 1911.
20. *Chicago Tribune* (Illinois), April 17, 1911; *St. Paul Pioneer Press*, May 14, 1911.
21. *St. Paul Dispatch*, June 22, 1911; *St. Paul Pioneer Press*, May 14, 15, 1911.
22. *Twin City Star*, May 20, 1911; *Indianapolis Freeman* (Indiana), April 22, 1911.
23. Anderson and Kimball, 345–347; 1900 United States Census, Ramsey County, Minnesota; Trombley, "Saint Paul Saints History 1902–1919."
24. Thornley, *Baseball in Minnesota*, 53; *Twin City Star*, June 3, 1911; *Mankato Daily Free Press*, June 26, 1911.
25. *Daily Huronite* (South Dakota), May 17, 1911.
26. *Daily Huronite* (South Dakota), May 18, 1911.
27. *Redfield Journal* (South Dakota), May 19, 1911; *Aberdeen American* (South Dakota), May 19, 1911; *Aberdeen Daily News* (South Dakota), September 14, 1910; 1900 United States Census, Scott County, Iowa.
28. *Aberdeen Daily American* (South Dakota), May 21, 1911; *Hankinson News* (North Dakota), May 25, 1911.
29. *Hankinson News* (North Dakota), May 25, 1911; 1910 United States Census, Richland County, North Dakota.
30. *Fargo Forum* (North Dakota), May 25, 1911; *Aberdeen American* (South Dakota), May 26, 1911; *Dickey County Leader* (North Dakota), June 1, 1911; *North Dakota Record* (Ellendale, North Dakota), June 1, 1911.
31. *Jamestown Daily Alert*, (North Dakota), May 31, June 1, 1911.
32. *Bismarck Daily Tribune* (North Dakota), June 3, 5, 1911; *Mandan News* (North Dakota), June 9, 1911.
33. *Chicago Tribune* (Illinois), September 11, 1911; *Mandan News* (North Dakota), June 9, 1911; *Glen Ullin News* (North Dakota), June 9, 1911.
34. *Dickinson Recorder Post* (North Dakota), June 8, 1911.
35. *Dickinson Recorder Post* (North Dakota), June 8, 1911; *Beach Advance* (North Dakota), June 16, 1911.
36. *St. Paul Pioneer Press*, June 12, 1911; *Wibaux Pioneer* (Montana), June 16, 1911; *Golden Valley Chronicle* (Beach, North Dakota), June 16, 1911.
37. *Wibaux Pioneer* (Montana), June 16, 1911; *Beach Advance* (North Dakota), June 16, 1911; *Golden Valley Chronicle* (Beach, North Dakota), June 16, 1911.
38. *Valley City Evening Times Record* (North Dakota), June 14, 1911.
39. *Valley City Evening Times Record* (North Dakota), June 15, 1911.
40. *Devils Lake World* (North Dakota), June 15, 16, July 22, 1911; Reichler, 1533.
41. *Devils Lake World* (North Dakota), June 16, 1911.
42. *Devils Lake World* (North Dakota), June 17, 1911; *St. Paul Pioneer Press*, June 18, 1911; *Grand Forks Daily Herald* (North Dakota), June 18, 1911.
43. *Grand Forks Daily Herald* (North Dakota), June 20, 1911.
44. *Bismarck Daily Tribune* (North Dakota), June 20, 1911; *Crookston Daily Times*, June 20, 1911.
45. *Crookston Daily Times*, June 20, 21, 1911; *Minneapolis Journal*, June 21, 1911; *Minneapolis Tribune*, June 25, 1911.
46. *Crookston Daily*, Times June 21, 1911; *Alexandria Post News*, June 29, 1911.
47. *Alexandria Post News*, June 29, 1911.
48. Ibid.
49. *Long Prairie Leader*, June 8, 1911; *Long Prairie-Todd County Argus*, July 6, 1911.
50. *Walker Pilot*, July 14, 21, 1911.
51. *Indianapolis Freeman* (Indiana), February 25, 1911.
52. *Indianapolis Freeman* (Indiana), May 27, 1911; *Twin City Star*, April 1, 1911; Debono, *The Indianapolis ABC's*, 147; Certificate of Death, Bureau of Vital Statistics, Missouri State Board of Health, Registered Number, 1748, May 15, 1911.
53. *Indianapolis Freeman* (Indiana), March 11, 1911; *Minneapolis Tribune*, April 16, 1911.
54. *Minneapolis Tribune*, April 16, 1911; *Grand Forks Daily Herald* (North Dakota), July 1, 1911; *Long Prairie Leader*, August 3, 1911.
55. *Indianapolis Freeman* (Indiana), September 24, 1910; *Floyd County Advocate Herald* (Iowa), September 5, 1911; Dixon and Hannigan, *The Negro Baseball Leagues*, 74, 87; Larry Lester, *Baseball's First Colored World Series* (Jefferson, N.C.: McFarland, 2006), 77–78.
56. *Minneapolis Tribune*, April 11, 1911; *Grand Forks Herald* (North Dakota), July 4, 1911; *Indianapolis Freeman*, July 23, 1910.
57. Riley, *Biographical Encyclopedia of the Negro Baseball Leagues*, 267; 1910 United States Federal Census, Knox County, Indiana; *Indianapolis Freeman* (Indiana), August 7, October 9, 1909, March 12, September 17, 1910, March 4, 1911; *Logansport Daily Pharos* (Indiana), September 25, 1905.
58. *Minneapolis Tribune*, April 16, 1911; Debono, *The Indianapolis ABC's*, 30–31.
59. Debono, *The Indianapolis ABC's*, 32–33; *Indianapolis Freeman* (Indiana), March 11, May 20, 1911.
60. Debono, *The Indianapolis ABC's*, 34; *Indianapolis Freeman*, (Indiana) May 20, 1911; Riley, 326.
61. *Indianapolis Freeman* (Indiana), June 3, 1911; *Minneapolis Tribune*, April 16, 1911; *St. Paul Pioneer Press*, June 24, 1911.
62. *Indianapolis Freeman*, (Indiana), May 27, July 8, 1911; *Louisville Courier Journal* (Kentucky), May 15, 1911; Lester, *Baseball's First Colored World Series*, 78.
63. *Memphis Commercial Appeal* (Tennessee), May 21, 22, 1911; *Indianapolis Freeman* (Indiana), June 3, 1911.
64. *DeKalb Advertiser* (Illinois), June 1, 2 1911; *Indianapolis Freeman* (Indiana), July 8, 1911; *What Cheer Patriot* (Iowa), June 8, 1911; *Strawberry Point Mail Press* (Iowa), June 15, 1911.
65. *Indianapolis Freeman* (Indiana), July 8, 1911; *Floyd County Advocate Herald* (Iowa), June 13, 1911; *Oelwein Register* (Iowa), June 16, 1911; Reichler, 1849.
66. *Oelwein Register* (Iowa), June 19, 1911; Riley 66–67; *Indianapolis Freeman* (Indiana), July 8, 1911; *Chicago Defender* (Illinois), August 11, 1923, June 27, 1931; *Fayette Reporter* (Iowa), June 15, 1911.
67. *Oelwein Register* (Iowa), June 19, 1911; *Waseca Herald*, June 23, 1911; *Waseca Journal Radical*, June 28, 1911.
68. *Hastings Gazette*, June 24, 1911; *Minneapolis Tribune*, June 25, 1911; *St. Paul Dispatch*, June 22, 1911.
69. *St. Paul Pioneer Press*, June 26, 1911; *Waseca Herald*, June 23, 1911.
70. *Oelwein Register* (Iowa), June 19, 1911; *Minneapolis Tribune*, April 16, 1911.
71. *Fayette Reporter* (Iowa), June 15, 1911.

Chapter Ten

1. *Indianapolis Freeman* (Indiana), June 24, 1911; *Kansas City Journal* (Missouri), April 24, 1911; *Twin City Star*, July 8, 1911.

2. *Twin City Star*, July 8, 1911, October 26, 1912; *Minneapolis Journal*, June 29, 1911; *Minneapolis Tribune*, July 2, 1911.
3. *Minneapolis Tribune*, July 3, 1911.
4. Reichler, *The Baseball Encyclopedia*, 1497; *Minneapolis Tribune*, July 4, 1911.
5. *Minneapolis Tribune*, July 9, 1911.
6. *Devils Lake World* (North Dakota), July 5, 1911.
7. *Devils Lake World* (North Dakota), July 5, 6, 1911.
8. *Devils Lake World* (North Dakota), July 5, 6, 7, 1911; *Minneapolis Journal*, July 8, 1911; *Cass Lake Times*, July 8, 1911.
9. *Devils Lake World* (North Dakota), July 7, 1911; *Duluth News Tribune*, July 10, 11 1911.
10. *Duluth News Tribune*, July 11, 17, 1911.
11. *Hibbing Daily Tribune*, July 13, 14, 1911.
12. *Hibbing Daily Tribune*, July 15, 17, 1911; *Mesaba Ore and the Hibbing Times*, July 15, 22, 1911.
13. *Hibbing Daily Tribune*, July 17, 1911; *Mesaba Ore and the Hibbing Times*, July 22, 1911.
14. *Hibbing Daily Tribune*, July 17, 18, 1911; Bruce, *The Kansas City Monarchs*, 15, 70; *Des Moines Daily News* (Iowa), May 6, 1911.
15. *Hibbing Daily Tribune*, July 17, 19, 1911.
16. *Hibbing Daily Tribune*, July 20, 1911; Baseball Reference.com, Minor League Player Encyclopedia, http://www.baseball-reference.com/minors/player:cgi?id+grady-00lj-, April 21, 2009.
17. *Virginian*, July 28, 1911; *Duluth News Tribune*, July 17, 21, 1911; *Virginia Enterprise*, July 28, 1911.
18. *Chicago Tribune* (Illinois), August 21, 1911; *Twin City Star*, August 12, 1911; *Hayward Sawyer County Record* (Wisconsin), August 3, 1911.
19. *Kanabec County News*, August 4, 1911; *Hayward Sawyer County Record* (Wisconsin), August 3, 1911; *Montreal Gazette* (Quebec, Canada), April 19, 1939; Reichler, *The Baseball Encyclopedia*, 1743.
20. *Superior Telegram* (Wisconsin) July 6, August 6, 1911; *Duluth News Tribune*, August 6, 7, 1911.
21. *Alexandria Post News*, August 10, 1911; *Alexandria Citizen*, August 10, 1911; *Minneapolis Journal*, August 9, 1911.
22. *Alexandria Post News*, August 10, 1911; *Alexandria Citizen*, August 10, 1911; *Minneapolis Journal*, August 10, 1911.
23. *Twin City Star*, July 8, 1911; *Grand Forks Daily Herald* (North Dakota), July 1, 1911; *Long Prairie Leader*, July 20, 1911.
24. *Twin City Star*, July 8, 1911; *Alexandria Post News*, July 6, 1911; *Alexandria Citizen*, July 6, 1911.
25. *Grand Forks Daily Herald* (North Dakota), July 4, 1911; *Hankinson News* (North Dakota), July 27, 1911.
26. *Grand Forks Daily Herald* (North Dakota), May 13, July 4, 1911.
27. *Grand Forks Daily Herald* (North Dakota), July 4, 5, 1911.
28. *Devils Lake World* (North Dakota), July 11, 1911; *Grand Forks Daily Herald* (North Dakota), July 11, 1911.
29. *Bismarck Daily Tribune* (North Dakota), July 14, 15, 1911.
30. *Wibaux Pioneer* (Montana), July 21, 1911.
31. *Grand Forks Daily Herald* (North Dakota), July 4, 1911; *Wibaux Pioneer* (Montana), July 21, 1911; *Golden Valley Chronicle* (Beach, North Dakota), July 21, 1911; *Beach Advance* (North Dakota), July 21, 1911.
32. *Jamestown Daily Alert* (North Dakota), July 19, 20, 1911; *St. Paul Dispatch*, September 8, 1911.
33. *Hankinson News* (North Dakota), July 27, 1911; *Fairmount News* (North Dakota), July 28, 1911.
34. *Graceville Enterprise*, July 28, 1911; *Appleton Press*, July 27, 1911.
35. *Long Prairie Leader*, August 3, 1911; Trombley, "Saint Paul Saints History 1902–1919."
36. *Long Prairie Leader*, August 3, 1911.
37. *Twin City Star*, August 5, 1911.
38. *Eau Claire Leader* (Wisconsin), August 4, 1911; *Colfax Messenger* (Wisconsin), August 4, 1911; *Marion Advertiser* (Wisconsin), August 18, 1911; *Grand Rapids Tribune* (Wisconsin), August 16, 1911.
39. *Indianapolis Freeman* (Indiana), August 26, 1911; *Indianapolis Star* (Indiana), August 21, 1911.
40. *Indianapolis Freeman* (Indiana), August 26, 1911; *Indianapolis Star* (Indiana), August 22, 1911; Debono, *The Indianapolis ABC's*, 164.
41. *Indianapolis Star* (Indiana), August 23, 1911; *Twin City Star*, September 2, 1911.
42. *Indianapolis Freeman* (Indiana), January 21, 1911; *Indianapolis Star* (Indiana), August 22, 23, 1911.
43. *Floyd County Advocate Herald* (Iowa), September 5, 8, 1911; *Charles City Daily Intelligencer* (Iowa), September 4, 5, 6, 1911; *Chicago Tribune* (Illinois), September 3, 24, 1911; *Indianapolis Star* (Indiana), September 11, 25, 1911.
44. *Chicago Tribune* (Illinois), September 11, 17, 1911; *Kansas City Times* (Missouri), October 9, 1911.
45. *Minneapolis Tribune*, August 14, 1911; *Chicago Defender* (Illinois), August 5, 1911; *Chicago Tribune* (Illinois), August 8, 1911; *Chicago Daily Journal* (Illinois), August 12, 1911; *Kansas City Journal* (Missouri), August 19, 1911.
46. *Twin City Star*, August 19, 1911.
47. *Lindstrom Chisago County Press*, August 3, 1911; *Osceola Sun* (Wisconsin), August 24, 1911; *St. Paul Pioneer Press*, August 19, 1911.
48. *Minneapolis Tribune*, August 14, 1911; *North St. Paul Sentinel*, August 18, 1911; *Kansas City Journal*, (Missouri), August 18, 25, 1911.
49. *Twin City Star*, September 23, 1911; *St. Paul Appeal*, September 2, 1911, October 25, 1913.
50. *Kansas City Post* (Missouri), August 31, 1911; Joe W. Trotter, "African American Fraternal Associations in American History: An Introduction," http://ssh.duke journals.org/cgi/reprint/28/3/355.pdfhttp://ssh.duke journals.org/cgi/reprint/28/3/355.pdf, May 14, 2009.
51. *Kansas City Journal* (Missouri), August 28, 29, 30, 1911; *Kansas City Times* (Missouri), August 24, 1910; Riley, *Biographical Encyclopedia of the Negro Baseball Leagues*, 771.
52. *Kansas City Journal* (Missouri), August, 28, 29, 30, 1911, September 1, 2, 1911.
53. *St. Louis Republic* (Missouri), September 4, 1911; Riley, *Biographical Encyclopedia of the Negro Baseball Leagues*, 77, 318, 379; *Indianapolis Freeman* (Indiana), October 30, 1909.
54. *St. Louis Republic* (Missouri), September 5, 1911.
55. *St. Louis Republic* (Missouri), September 5, 1911.
56. *St. Paul Pioneer Press*, September 4, 1911; *Rush City Post*, September 8, 22, 1911; *Springs Valley Herald* (Indiana), September 14, 1911; *Indianapolis Freeman* (Indiana), September 23, 1911.
57. *Springs Valley Herald* (Indiana), September 7, 14, 21, 1911; *Indianapolis Freeman* (Indiana), September 23, 1911, July 13, September 7, 1912; Riley, *Biographical Encyclopedia of the Negro Baseball Leagues*, 552.
58. *Twin City Star*, November 4, 1911, March 9, May 4, 1912, *Chicago Defender* (Illinois), October 7, 1911.
59. *Twin City Star*, March 30, April 20, 1912.
60. *Alexandria Post News*, June 22, 1911; *Lake Crystal Union*, September 16, 1908; *Minneapolis Tribune*, August 4, 1911.
61. *Twin City Star*, October 19, 26, 1912; *St. Paul Appeal*, October 26, 1912.
62. *Twin City Star*, October 19, 26, 1912; *St. Paul Appeal*, October 26, 1912;.Vassar Taylor, "The Blacks," 79.

63. *Twin City Star*, October 19, 26, 1912; *St. Paul Appeal*, October 19, 26, 1912.
64. *Twin City Star*, October 26, 1912; *St. Paul Appeal*, October 26, 1912.
65. *St. Paul Appeal*, October 19, 1912; *Twin City Star*, October 26, November 2, 1912.
66. *Twin City Star*, October 26, 1912; *St. Paul Appeal*, October 26, 1912.
67. *Twin City Star*, October 26, 1912; Annie H. Barker, "When The Mists Have Rolled Away," http://www.hymntime.com/tch/htm/w/h/e/whenmist.htm, February 12, 2009.

Chapter Eleven

1. *Minneapolis Tribune*, April 7, June 3, 1912; 1900, 1920 United States Census, Hennepin County, Minnesota; United States Government World War I Registration Card, roll 1675522, June 5, 1917.
2. *Minneapolis Tribune*, April 21, May 19, 26, June 10, 1912; *St. Paul Pioneer Press*, May 19, June 1, 1912.
3. *Minneapolis Tribune*, May 1, June 3, August 5, 1912; *St. Paul Pioneer Press*, July 1, 15, 1912; *Winona Republican Herald*, May 8, 1935; *Watertown Daily Public Opinion* (South Dakota), July 12, 1913.
4. *Minneapolis Tribune*, June 4, 21, 1913; Kyle McNary, "Maceo Breedlove: Big Fish in a Small Pond," in *Swinging for the Fences*, 113–114; 1910 United States Census, Douglas County, Nebraska; United States Government World War I Registration Card, roll 1675522, June 5, 1917.
5. *Watertown Daily Public Opinion* (South Dakota), July 12, 1913.
6. *Mankato Daily Free Press*, June 7, 1913; *St. Cloud Daily Times*, June 23, 1913.
7. *Webster World* (South Dakota), July 3, 10, 1913; *Webster Reporter and Farmer* (South Dakota), July 3, 10, 1913.
8. *Groton Independent* (South Dakota) July 8, 1913; *Aberdeen Daily American* (South Dakota), July 10, 1913; *Grant County Review* (Milbank, South Dakota), July 10, 1913; *Redfield Press* (South Dakota), July 17, 1913; *Watertown Daily Public Opinion* (South Dakota), July 14, 1913; *Minneapolis Tribune*, July 20, 1913.
9. *Sioux Falls Daily Press* (South Dakota), July 20, 1913; *St. Cloud Daily Times*, August 18, 1913; *Minneapolis Tribune*, June 21, 1913; Hoffbeck, "Bobby Marshall," 73.
10. *Chicago Defender* (Illinois), February 28, 1914; *Minneapolis Journal*, May 17, 1914; *Minneapolis Tribune*, May 25, 1914
11. *Minneapolis Tribune*, June 21, 1913, June 7, 1914; .*St. Paul Pioneer Press*, June 7, 22, 1914.
12. *Owatonna Daily Chronicle*, June 26, 1914.
13. *Little Falls Daily Transcript*, July 27, 1914; *Minneapolis Tribune*, September 13, 1914
14. *St. Paul Pioneer Press*, June 22, 1914; *St. Cloud Daily Times*, July 31, 1914; *Twin City Star*, July 4, 1914.
15. *Wells Forum Advocate*, October 6, 1911; *Chicago Defender* (Illinois), October 7, 1916; *Humboldt Independent* (Iowa), September 14, 1911; United States Government World War I Registration Card, roll 1683219, June 5, 1917; Pete Gorton, "1911 to 1917: The Making of the World's Greatest Negro Pitcher," unpublished manuscript, 2; Pete Gorton, "John Wesley Donaldson, a Great Mound Artist," in *Swinging for the Fences*, 87.
16. *Chicago Defender* (Illinois), October 7, 1916; Gorton, "John Wesley Donaldson," 87–88.
17. *Duluth News Tribune*, June 17, 1912; *Minneapolis Tribune*, June 4, 1913; Gorton, "John Wesley Donaldson," 87–88.
18. Gorton, "John Wesley Donaldson," 88; *Little Falls Daily Transcript*, July 26, 1914; Rucker and Bjarkman, *Smoke: The Romance and Lore of Cuban Baseball*,.72, 74, 250; Ashwill, "Jose del Valle Mendez, Part II."
19. *Lake Wilson Pilot*, June 19, 1914; *Good Thunder Herald*, August 14, 1913; *Minneapolis Tribune*, August 9, 1913; *Indianapolis Freeman* (Indiana), October 7, 1916; Gorton, "1911 to 1917," 4–5.
20. Gorton, "1911 to 1917," 5–6; *Good Thunder Herald*, August 28, 1913; Peter C. Bjarkman, *A History of Cuban Baseball 1864–2006* (Jefferson, N.C.: McFarland, 2007), 141; *Marshall News Messenger*, August 28, 1914; *Barnesville Headlight*, July 24, 1914; *Hibbing Daily Tribune*, July 23, 1914; *St. Paul Pioneer Press*, August 27, 1914.
21. *Good Thunder Herald*, July 2, 1914; Powers Beck, *American Indian Integration of Baseball*, 162; Tom Hawthorn, "The Rocky Saga of Vagabond 'Tribesman' Jimmy Claxton," in *Rain Check: Baseball in the Pacific Northwest* (Cleveland: Society for American Baseball Research, 2006), 44, 126.
22. *Owatonna Journal Chronicle*, July 10, 1914; Pete Gorton, "All Nation's vs. Chicago Union Giants 1914–1916," unpublished manuscript, 1–7; Phil S. Dixon, *The Monarchs 1920–1938 Featuring Wilbur "Bullet" Rogan* (Sioux Falls, S.D.: Mariah Press, 2002), 23.
23. Debono, *The Indianapolis ABC's*, 35–36.
24. Debono, The Indianapolis ABC's, 35; *St. Cloud Daily Times*, August 18, 25, 1913; *Duluth News Tribune*, August 13, 1913; *Chicago Defender* (Illinois), April 9, 1921.
25. *St. Cloud Daily Times*, September 2, 1913; Riley 499.
26. *St. Cloud Daily Times*, September 2, 1913, July 20, 27, 1914.
27. *St. Cloud Daily Times*, July 27, 1914; *Duluth News Tribune*, August 29, 1915; *Winona Republican Herald*, July 3, 1916.
28. *Minneapolis Tribune*, June 21, 1915.
29. *Minneapolis Tribune*, June 12, July 2, 11, 17 1916; *Minnesota Messenger*, September 30, 1922.
30. *Minneapolis Tribune*, July 17, 1916; *Litchfield Independent*, July 26, 1916; *Duluth News Tribune*, July 31, 1916; *St. Paul Pioneer Press*, August 7, 21, 1916; *Fort Dodge Messenger* (Iowa), September 19, 1916.
31. *St. Paul Appeal*, June 3, 1916; *Twin City Star*, June 3, 1916.
32. *St. Paul Appeal*, April 6, 1918; *Twin City Star*, April 6, 1918.
33. Hoffbeck, "Bobby Marshall," 74; Vassar Taylor," The Blacks," 82; University of Missouri-Kansas City, "The Races in Detroit: The Black Migration to Detroit," http://www.law.umkc.edu/faculty/projects/ftrials/sweet/racesindetroit.html, October 28, 2008; Milwaukee Public Television, "The Making of Milwaukee," http://www.themakingofmilwaukee.com/people/stories.cfm., October 28, 2008.
34. Wikipedia, "The Duluth Lynchings."
35. Wikipedia, "The Duluth Lynchings"; *Duluth News Tribune*, June 16, 1920.
36. Wikipedia, "The Duluth Lynchings"; Vassar Taylor, *African Americans in Minnesota*, 61.
37. *Duluth News Tribune*, May 22, 24, 1920; *Minnesota Messenger*, July 16, October 1, 1921.
38. McNary, 114.
39. *Winona Republican Herald*, June 25, 27, 1921; *Willmar Tribune*, July 6, 1921.
40. *Chisago County Free Press*, July 14, 1921.
41. *National Advocate*, September 3, 1921; *Willmar Republican Gazette*, August 3, 1922; *Minnesota Messenger*, March 10. 1923; *Northwestern Bulletin*, April 28, June 16, 1923.
42. *Minnesota Messenger*, September 30, 1922; *Northwestern Bulletin*, January 17, 1925.
43. *North St. Paul Courier*, May 17, July 26, 1922; *North-

western Bulletin, May 6, July 29, August 12, September 30, 1922, June 16, September 15, 22, 1923.

44. *Northwestern Bulletin*, May 12, May 26, 28, 29, 31, 1923; *Hibbing Daily Tribune*, May 26, 1923.

45. *Minnesota Messenger*, March 10, 1923; *Northwestern Bulletin*, May 12, June 16, 1923.

46. *Northwestern Bulletin*, June 23, September 29, 1923; *Cass Lake Times*, June 14, 1923; *Alexandria Citizen News*, June 14, 1923.

47. *Northwestern Bulletin*, April 29, May 6, 1922; *Little Falls Daily Transcript*, July 5, 1922; Hoffbeck, "Bobby Marshall," 75.

48. *Minnesota Messenger*, February 24, 1923; *Northwestern Bulletin*, February 16, July 5, 1924; McNary, 112.

49. *Ironwood Daily Globe* (Michigan), July 18, 1930; *Minneapolis Spokesman*, October 20, 1950; *Clarkfield Advocate*, June 4, 1925; *Winona Republican Herald*, June 25, 1938; *Northwestern Bulletin*, February 16, 1924; DatabaseFootball.com, "Dick Hudson," http://www.databasefootball.com/players/playerpage.htm?ilkid=HUDSODIC01, August 22, 2009.

50. *Northwestern Bulletin*, May 23, 30, June 6, 1925; *Clarkfield Advocate*, May 28, June 4, 1925; Debono, *The Indianapolis ABC's*, 174.

51. databaseFootball.com, "Dick Hudson"; Ben Green, *Spinning The Globe* (New York: Amistad, 2005), 36–42, 48; *Chicago Defender* (Illinois), July 4, 1931, August 30, 1941, March 28, 1942; *Winona Republican Herald*, June 25, 1938; Bob Carroll, "Doc Young and the Hammond Pros," http://www.profootballresearchers.org/Coffin_Corner/17-01-596.pdf, August 27, 2009.

52. *Northwestern Bulletin*, May 16, 30, June 6, July 11, 1925; United States Government World War I Registration Card, 1675895, serial number 2357, April 12, 1918.

53. *St. Paul Echo*, May 28, June 4, 1927.

54. 1920 United States Census, Blue Earth County, Minnesota; 1930 United States Census, Blue Earth County, Minnesota; *Mankato Daily Record Press*, May 28, 31, June 4, 1926; *Belle Plaine Herald*, June 3, 1926.

55. Alan Muchlinski and David Muchlinski, "The Pipestone Black Sox," http://instructional1.calstatela.edu/amuchli/Pipestone.htm, December 8, 2004; Gary Ashwill, "Forgotten Negro Leaguers #3 & #4: Lightner & Linder," http://agatetype.typepad.com/agate)_type/2007/10/forgotten-neg-1.html, October 9, 2007; Clark and Lester, *The Negro Leagues Book*, 233; *Chicago Tribune* (Illinois), June 9, 1919.

56. *Melrose Beacon*, September 6, 20, 27, 1928; Stew Thornley, "Nicollet Park," http://stewthornley.net/nicollet_park.html, August 27, 2009.

57. *Chicago Defender* (Illinois), March 21, 1925; *Long Prairie Leader*, April 30th, 1925.

58. *Northwestern Bulletin*, June 6, 1925; *Ironwood Daily Globe* (Michigan), June 29, 1925; *Oshkosh Daily Northwestern* (Wisconsin), July 13, 1925.

59. *Chicago Defender* (Illinois), April 3, 1926; *St. Paul Echo*, July 31, 1926; *Crookston Daily Times*, July 23, 1926; *St. Paul Pioneer Press*, August 2, 1926; *Twin City Herald*, July 23, 1932.

60. *Tracy Headlight Herald*, June 10, 1927; Alan Muchlinski and David Muchlinski, "The Pipestone Black Sox," http://instructional1.calstatela.edu/amuchli/Pipestone.htm, December 8, 2004.

61. *Northfield News*, August 9, 16, 1929; *Winona Republican Herald*, September 20, 22, 1930.

62. Gorton, "John Wesley Donaldson," 94; *Winona Republican Herald*, May 17, 1926.

63. *Winona Republican Herald*, August 15, 1921, June 17, 1935; Scott Simkus, "Gilkerson's Union Giants," http://scottsimkus.wordpress.com/2009/03/09/gilkersons-union-giants/, August 31, 2009.

64. *Chicago Defender* (Illinois), August 2, 1924, July 21, 1928; Riley, 105, 357; *Winona Republican Herald*, June 12, 1922, May 31, 1932.

65. *Minnesota Messenger*, May 21, 1921; *Chicago Defender* (Illinois), April 9, 1921; *Aberdeen Daily American* (South Dakota), June 24, 1921.

66. *Winona Republican Herald*, August 15, 1921, September 27, 1926, August 20, 1929, August 3, 1931, June 27, July 15, 1932, July 16, 1936.

67. *Winona Republican Herald*, August 27, 1923; Gorton, "John Wesley Donaldson," 91–96; Alan Muchlinski, "John Donaldson and His Association With Minnesota Baseball," http://instructional1.calstatela.edu/amuchli/Donaldson1.htm, August 9, 2004.

68. Gorton, "John Wesley Donaldson," 98–103; Muchlinski, "John Donaldson And His Association With Minnesota Baseball."

69. Pete Gorton, "The Mystery of Lefty Wilson," in *Swinging for the Fences*, 108.

70. Gorton, "The Mystery of Lefty Wilson," 108. Cottrell, *The Best Pitcher in Baseball*, 156, 160, 163, 165; Riley, *Biographical Encyclopedia of the Negro Baseball Leagues*, 117–118; *Chicago Defender* (Illinois), March 17, 1923.

71. *Winona Republican Herald*, July 12, 1926; *Davenport Democrat and Leader* (Iowa), June 21, 1926; Muchlinski and Muchlinski, "The Pipestone Black Sox"; Ashwill, "The Mysterious Fate of Dave Brown."

72. Gorton, "The Mystery of Lefty Wilson," 109–110; Pete Gorton, electronic correspondence with author, July 29, 2009.

73. Gorton, "The Mystery of Lefty Wilson," 110; Gorton, "John Wesley Donaldson," 103; John B. Holway, *Voices From the Great Black Baseball Leagues* (New York: Da Capo Press, 1992), 72, 74, 79–80; *St. Paul Pioneer Press*, August 2, 1926; Riley, *Biographical Encyclopedia of the Negro Baseball Leagues*, 533–534.

74. *Little Falls Daily Transcript*, August 30, 1930; Stew Thornley, "Minneapolis Millers Individual Statistics 1921–1930," http://stewthornley.net/millers_1921_1930.html, September 8, 2009; SABR Minor League Database.

75. Muchlinski, "John Donaldson and His Association With Minnesota Baseball"; Gorton, "The Mystery of Lefty Wilson," 111; *St. Cloud Daily Times*, May 31, September 1, 1930; *Little Falls Daily Transcript*, August 18, 1930.

76. Gary Ashwill, "Dave Brown and the Case of the Glossy Green Shirt," http://agatetype.typepad.com/agate_type/dave-brown/, March 4, 2009, March 04, 2009; Holway, *Voices From the Great Black Baseball Leagues*, 81.

77. *Winona Republican Herald*, July 16, 1931; John Holway, *Black Diamonds*, 24, 28–29, 37; Gorton, "John Wesley Donaldson," 104.

78. *Crookston Daily Times*, July 20, 1931; Holway, *Black Diamonds*, 29.

79. Muchlinski, "John Donaldson and His Association With Minnesota Baseball"; *Ironwood Daily Globe* (Michigan), August 12, 1930; *Bismarck Daily Tribune* (North Dakota), June 20, 1929; Riley, *Biographical Encyclopedia of the Negro Baseball Leagues*, 352; Dixon and Hannigan, *The Negro Baseball Leagues*, 133, 142.

80. *Winona Republican Herald*, August 29, 1931; *Bismarck Daily Tribune* (North Dakota), July 7, 1930; July 15, 1931.

81. *Red River Valley News* (Glyndon, MN) June 20 1929; 1920 United States Census, Grady County, Oklahoma.

82. Gorton, "John Wesley Donaldson," 105–106; Riley, *Biographical Encyclopedia of the Negro Baseball Leagues*, 333, *Fairmont Daily Sentinel*, August 29, 1932; *Winona Republican Herald*, August 29, 1931; *Sioux Falls Daily Argus* (South Dakota), June 10, 1932.

83. Gorton, "John Wesley Donaldson," 106–107;

Crookston Daily Times, May 31, 1932; *Sioux Falls Daily Argus* (South Dakota) June 10, 1932; *Sioux City Journal* (Iowa), June 27, 1932.

84. *Twin City Herald*, July 23, 1932; *Bismarck Daily Tribune* (North Dakota), June 20, 1929; *Minneapolis Spokesman*, March 29, 1935; *St. Paul Pioneer Press*, August 1, 1932.

85. McNary, 113, 115, 117; 1930 United States Census, Hennepin County, Minnesota; *Twin City Herald*, May 19, 1934.

86. McNary, 112, 116, 118–119; Larry Lester, *Black Baseball's National Showcase: The East-West All-Star Game 1933–1953* (Lincoln: University of Nebraska Press, 2001), 435, 445.

87. *Minneapolis Spokesman*, March 29, 1935; *Albert Lea Evening Tribune*, August 14, 1933; *Twin City Herald*, August 15, 29, 1936; *Winnipeg Free Press* (Manitoba, Canada), May 5, 1936.

88. Riley, *Biographical Encyclopedia of the Negro Baseball Leagues*, 297; *Minneapolis Spokesman*, June 14, 1939, April 18, 1944.

89. McNary, 114; Terri Ann Finneman, "Toni Stone: A Tomboy to Remember," in *Swinging for the Fences*, 149–151; *Minneapolis Spokesman*, July 30, 1937.

90. Finneman, "Toni Stone," 150–154; *Pittsburgh Courier* (Pennsylvania), July 8, 1950; June 20, July 11, August 1, 1953; Bruce, *The Kansas City Monarchs*, 143.

91. Bruce, *The Kansas City Monarchs*, 67; *Winona Republican Herald*, July 20, 1932, September 20, 1934.

92. *Minneapolis Spokesman*, July 15, 1938; Green, *Spinning the Globe*, 14, 33–34; *Winona Republican Herald*, May 28, October 15, 1932.

93. *Twin City Herald*, July 8, 15, 1939, July 13, 1940; *Minneapolis Spokesman*, July 14, 1939, July 19, 1940; *Twin City Leader*, August 24, 1940.

94. *Chicago Defender* (Illinois), January 3, March 28, 1942; *Pittsburgh Courier* (Pennsylvania), March 28, 1942; Neil Lanctot, *Negro League Baseball: The Rise and Ruin of a Black Institution*, (Philadelphia: University of Pennsylvania Press, 2004), 114.

95. *Chicago Defender* (Illinois), March 28, 1942.

96. *Chicago Defender* (Illinois), March 28, May 23, June 6, 1942; *Atlanta Daily World* (Georgia), April 29, 1942.

97. *Chicago Defender* (Illinois), April 18, 25, May 30, June 6, 20, 1942; *Pittsburg Courier* (Pennsylvania), April 18, 1942;

98. *Chicago Defender* (Illinois), June 20, 1942.

99. *St. Paul Pioneer Press*, June 22, 1942; *Chicago Defender* (Illinois), June 27, 1942; Lester, *Black Baseball's National Showcase*, 430–431.

100. *St. Paul Pioneer Press*, June 22, 1942; Green, *Spinning the Globe*, 153–154.

101. *Chicago Defender* (Illinois), April 25, June 20, August 1, 1942; *Milwaukee Journal* (Wisconsin), June 24, 1942; *St. Paul Pioneer Press*, June 25, 29, 1942; *La Crosse Tribune* (Wisconsin), June 29, 1942; Riley, *Biographical Encyclopedia of the Negro Baseball Leagues*, 377, 592.

102. *Waterloo Daily Courier* (Iowa), July 1, 2, 1942.

103. *Winnipeg Free Press* (Manitoba, Canada), July 7, 1942.

104. *Winnipeg Free Press* (Manitoba, Canada), July 8, 1942.

105. Larry Powell, *Black Barons of Birmingham: The South's Greatest Negro League Team and its Players* (Jefferson, N.C.: McFarland, 2009), 40; *St. Paul Pioneer Press*, July 13, 1942; *Chicago Defender* (Illinois), July 18, 1942.

106. *Minneapolis Spokesman*, July 17, 1942; *Columbus Evening Dispatch* (Ohio), July 22, 1942; *Chicago Defender*, September 5, 1942.

107. *Chicago Defender* (Illinois), July 25, August 1, 1942; *Nashville Banner* (Tennessee), July 28, 1942.

108. *Lima Daily News* (Ohio), July 29, 30, 1942; *Chicago Defender* (Illinois), August 8, 1942; *Atlanta Daily World* (Georgia), August 11, 1942; *Benton Harbor News Palladium* (Michigan), August 19, 1942.

109. Barry Swanton, *The ManDak League: Haven for Former Negro League Ballplayers, 1950–1957* (Jefferson, N.C.: McFarland, 2006), 46; SABR Asian Baseball Committee, "Japanese Baseball Timeline," http://asianbb.sabr.org/japanesebaseballtimeline.html, September 15, 2009; Riley, *Biographical Encyclopedia of the Negro Baseball Leagues*, 110–111, 760; *Pittsburgh Courier* (Pennsylvania), July 25, 1942.

110. *Pittsburgh Courier* (Pennsylvania), January 9, 1943; *Minneapolis Spokesman*, August 6, 1943.

111. *Minneapolis Spokesman*, July 7, 1944, July 13, 1945.

112. *Minneapolis Spokesman*, May 25, June 8, July 6, 1945.

113. *Minneapolis Spokesman*, April 21, June 2, 1944; *Winona Republican Herald*, August 1, 1949.

114. Peterson, *Only the Ball Was White*, 190; Ted Genoways, "Roy Campanella and the Breaking of the Color Barrier," in *Swinging for the Fences*, 131.

115. Genoways, "Roy Campanella," 125; Riley, *Biographical Encyclopedia of the Negro Baseball Leagues*, 146; *St. Paul Pioneer Press*, May 18, July 1, 1948; *Minneapolis Spokesman*, June 18, 1948; SABR Minor League Database.

116. *St. Paul Pioneer Press*, May 31, June 1, 1948; *Minneapolis Spokesman*, June 4, 1948; Wikipedia, "Carl Rowan."

Chapter Twelve

1. Niese, "George Wilson," 24; Moyer, "110 Years of Baseball." Ashwill, "George H. Wilson."

2. Niese, "George Wilson," 24–25; Moyer, "110 Years of Baseball." *Racine Daily Journal* (Wisconsin), September 9, 1907.

3. *Chicago Tribune* (Illinois), May 6, 1907, September 21, 1908; *Racine Daily Journal* (Wisconsin), September 9, 1907; Niese, "George Wilson," 24–25; *Sheboygan Daily Press* (Wisconsin), August 18, September 1, 1908, May 20, 1909.

4. *Racine Daily Journal* (Wisconsin), September 9, 1907; 1910 United States Census, Lenawee County, Michigan; *Adrian Daily Telegraph* (Michigan), November 27, 1915; Ed King, personal correspondence from the Lenawee Historical Society Museum, Lenawee County, Michigan.

5. *Racine Daily Journal* (Wisconsin), September 9, 1907; State of Michigan, 1915 Record of Deaths, Kalamazoo County; *Adrian Daily Telegraph* (Michigan), November 27, 1915.

6. Riley, *Biographical Encyclopedia of the Negro Baseball Leagues*, 624; *Minneapolis Tribune*, June 10, 1912; Minnesota Death Index 1908–2002, Certificate Number 030473, Record Number 255155; 1920 United States Census, Ramsey County, Minnesota.

7. *Chicago Defender* (Illinois), April 7, 1917, October 19, November 2, 1918, May 1, 1920; 1930 United States Census, Cook County, Illinois; United States Government World War I Registration Card, Roll 1452460, Number 6058, September 7, 1918; *Winona Republican Herald*, July 18, August 15, 1921; United States Government World War I Registration Card, roll 1613932, serial number 125, September 17, 1918.

8. 1900 United States Federal Census; *Chicago Defender* (Illinois), April 12, June 28, September 20, 1919; 1920 United States Census, Cook County, Illinois.

9. *Twin City Star*, July 8, 1911; *Chicago Tribune* (Illinois), July 3, 6, 30, 31, August 14, 21, September 18, 1911, May 26, 1912; 1930 United States Census, Cook County,

Illinois; State of Illinois Certificate of Death, Number 21515, July 11, 1947; United States Government World War I Registration Card, roll 1452473, September 12, 1918; State of Illinois Certificate of Death, Number 6016958, July 3, 1922.

10. *Galveston Daily News* (Texas), May 10, 1915; *Polk's Houston City Directory 1917*; *Indianapolis Freeman* (Indiana), August 24, 1912; *Lima Daily News* (Ohio), April 28, 1915; *Fort Wayne News and Sentinel* (Indiana), July 10, 1919; June 15, 1920; *Fort Wayne Journal Gazette* (Indiana), May 10, 1921; *Van Wert Daily Times-Bulletin*, (Ohio), May 14, 1940.

11. *Indianapolis Freeman* (Indiana), July 13, 1912; *Chicago Defender* (Illinois), July 9, 1913, January 23, 1915, June 24, 1916; *Pittsburgh Courier* (Pennsylvania), February 11, 1933; *Pittsburgh Daily Dispatch*, (Pennsylvania), September 28, 1913; *Pittsburgh Post*, (Pennsylvania), July 25, 1915, July 2, 1916.

12. *Pittsburgh Courier* (Pennsylvania), April 23, Aug 6, 13, 1938, May 1, 8, 1954; Rob Ruck, *Sandlot Seasons* (Urbana: University of Illinois Press, 1993), 70.

13. United States Government World War I Registration Card, roll 1613932, serial number,1181, September 19, 1918; United States Government World War I Registration Card, roll 1613146, serial number,199, September 12, 1918; United States Government World War I Registration Card, roll 1613510, serial number, 3149, September 12, 1918; Phil S. Dixon, *The Monarchs 1920–1938 Featuring Wilbur "Bullet" Rogan*, 24; *Lincoln State Journal* (Nebraska), June 6, 1928; *Chicago Tribune* (Illinois), November 26, 1920.

14. *Chicago Defender* (Illinois), April 19, 1919, August 11, 1923; June 27, 1931.

15. *Indianapolis Freeman* (Indiana), April 16, 1910, May 23, 1914; *Chicago Tribune* (Illinois), September 25, 26, 1910; September 16, 1912; *Chicago Defender* (Illinois), July 5, 1913.

16. Clark and Lester, *The Negro Leagues Book*, 96; Riley, *Biographical Encyclopedia of the Negro Baseball Leagues*, 812; Holway, *Voices From the Great Black Baseball Leagues*, 29, 356; *Chicago Defender* (Illinois), August 9, 1924; *Indianapolis Freeman* (Indiana), July 27, 1912; *Pittsburgh Courier* (Pennsylvania), March 8, 1930, March 5, 1932, April 19, 1952; Larry Lester, electronic correspondence with author, March 2010.

17. *Indianapolis Freeman*, (Indiana), July 27, 1912, May 31, 1913; *Chicago Defender* (Illinois), June 14, 1913.

18. Debono, *The Indianapolis ABC's*, 144; Riley, *Biographical Encyclopedia of the Negro Baseball Leagues*, 439–440; *Chicago Defender* (Illinois), June 14, 1913, February 28, 1914, March 23, 1918, March 24, April 28, 1923, May 9, 1925.

19. *Indianapolis Freeman* (Indiana), August 6, 1910; *Chicago Defender* (Illinois), July 20, 1912, July 19, 1913, July 5, 1924, May 22, 1926, December 21, 1946; *Chicago Tribune* (Illinois), July 18, 1912; Riley, 47–48; *St. Cloud Daily Times*, June 10, 1930; Karn, 53.

20. *Chicago Defender* (Illinois), August 8, 1936, December 21, 1946; "George Walter Ball," in *Black Baseball and Chicago*, 43.

21. Riley, *Biographical Encyclopedia of the Negro Baseball Leagues*, 764–766; Gary Ashwill, "Negro League Managers," http://agatetype.typepad.com/agate_type/2006/07/index.html, July 28, 2006; Larry Lester, Sammy J. Miller, and Dick Clark, *Black Baseball in Chicago* (Chicago: Arcadia, 2000), 59; *Chicago Defender* (Illinois), May 8, 1926; December 23, 1929; *Pittsburgh Courier* (Pennsylvania), January 5, 1929.

22. *Chicago Defender* (Illinois), July 29, 1928, July 4, 1931.

23. Michael Harkness-Roberto, "Candy Jim Taylor," in *Black Baseball and Chicago*, 161–163; *Chicago Defender* (Illinois), February 10, 1934; *Pittsburgh Courier* (Pennsylvania), July 25, 1936; Dixon and Hannigan, *The Negro Baseball Leagues*, 170.

24. Harkness-Roberto, "Candy Jim Taylor," 161–163; *Chicago Defender* (Illinois), December 21, 1929, January 13, 1945; Dixon and Hannigan, *The Negro Baseball Leagues*, 127.

25. Holway, *Blackball Stars*, 355–356; Riley, 776.

26. Riley, *Biographical Encyclopedia of the Negro Baseball Leagues*, 776; Mark Ribowsky, *The Power And The Darkness* (New York: Simon & Schuster, 1996), 278; *Pittsburgh Courier* (Pennsylvania), July 25, 1936; Dixon and Hannigan, 303; *Chicago Defender* (Illinois), April 10, 17, 1948; Debono. *The Chicago American Giants*, 216.

27. *Chicago Defender* (Illinois), April 17, July 31, 1948; Harkness-Roberto, 163.

28. *Chicago Defender* (Illinois), July 5, 1913; Riley 767–768; Debono, *The Chicago American Giants*, 46.

29. *Chicago Defender* (Illinois), July 5, 1913; *Chicago Tribune* (Illinois), August 13, 1913.

30. Riley, *Biographical Encyclopedia of the Negro Baseball Leagues*, 767–768; *Chicago Defender* (Illinois), June 12, 1915, June 8, 1918; June 21, 1930, August 7, 1936; *Pittsburgh Courier* (Pennsylvania), April 12, 1924; Debono, *The Indianapolis ABC's*, 159–160; Lester, "Steel Arm Gets a Headstone."

31. *Long Prairie Leader*, September 7, 1911; *Chicago Defender* (Illinois), June 9, 1917; *Pittsburgh Courier* (Pennsylvania), April 11, 1925, March 8, 1941; *Indianapolis Freeman* (Indiana), August 6, 1910; Riley, *Biographical Encyclopedia of the Negro Baseball Leagues*, 432–434.

32. *Pittsburgh Courier* (Pennsylvania), March 8, 1941; Riley, *Biographical Encyclopedia of the Negro Baseball Leagues*, 433–34, 474, 533, 876–877; *Chicago Defender* (Illinois), May 1, 15, 1920, June 18, 1921; Holway, *Voices From the Great Black Baseball Leagues*, 149.

33. Holway, *Voices from the Great Black Baseball Leagues*, 149; *Pittsburgh Courier* (Pennsylvania), April 11, 1925, December 18, 1937, March 8, 1941; *Florence Morning News* (South Carolina), August 18, 1949.

34. Holway, *Voices From The Great Black Baseball Leagues*, 149.

35. *Kingston Daily Freeman* (New York), June 4, 1927; *Pittsburgh Courier* (Pennsylvania), April 11, 1925, May 24, 1928; Riley, *Biographical Encyclopedia of the Negro Baseball Leagues*, 272.

36. *Chicago Defender* (Illinois), May 13, June 10, 1933; *Syracuse Herald* (New York), August 15, September 26, 1933.

37. *Syracuse Herald* (New York), April 23, 1934, May 4, 8, 1935.

38. *Syracuse Herald* (New York), December 17, 1933; September 22, 1934, July 22, 1936, June 19, 1938; *Pittsburgh Courier* (Pennsylvania), April 11, 1925; *Monessen Daily Independent* (Pennsylvania), November 5, 1941.

39. *Pittsburgh Courier* (Pennsylvania), March 8, 1941.

40. *Florence Morning News* (South Carolina), August 18, 1949; *New York Amsterdam News* (New York), March 6, 1929; Craig, *Chappie and Me*, 33–36.

41. Craig, *Chappie and Me*, 7–11.

42. *Chicago Defender* (Illinois), July 8, 1911, May 10, 1919; *Chicago Tribune* (Illinois), July 4, 1911.

43. *Chicago Defender* (Illinois), May 15, July 10, 1926; *Pittsburgh Courier* (Pennsylvania), July 21, August 18, 1928.

44. *Chicago Defender* (Illinois), April 15, 1922; Holway, *Voices From the Great Black Baseball Leagues*, 112–118; Ashwill, "How Cool Papa Got His Name."

45. Holway, *Voices From The Great Black Baseball Leagues*, 29; Powell, *Black Barons of Birmingham*, 19–20.

46. Holway, Johnson and Borst, *Complete Book of Baseball's Negro Leagues*, 225; *Moberly Monitor-Index and Democrat* (Missouri), April 10, May 25, August 19, 1929, August 3, 1934; Dixon and Hannigan, *The Negro Baseball Leagues*, 186.
47. *Moberly Monitor-Index and Democrat* (Missouri), August 8, 1933, October 25, 1937, May 15, 1939.
48. *Moberly Monitor-Index and Democrat* (Missouri), August 3, 1934, April 24, 1940; Jeremy Krock, electronic correspondence with author, November 13, 2007; *Chicago Defender* (Illinois), August 20, 1955; Riley, *Biographical Encyclopedia of the Negro Baseball Leagues*, 310, 936; *Washington Post* (District of Columbia), August 10, 1971.
49. *Northwestern Bulletin*, May 6, 1922; *St. Paul Pioneer Press*, October 9, 1946; Kathleen Ebert, electronic correspondence with author, October 14, 17, 18, 21, 2007; *Minneapolis Spokesman*, September 7, 1934.
50. *Indianapolis Freeman* (Indiana), January 27, 1917; *St. Paul Pioneer Press*, May 11, June 29, July 22, 1919; *Minnesota Messenger*, March 4, 1922; *Minneapolis Spokesman*, October 20, 1950.
51. Hoffbeck, "Bobby Marshall," 167–168, 170; *Chicago Tribune* (Illinois), November 27, 1908.
52. Hoffbeck, "Bobby Marshall," 169; Keith McClellan, *The Sunday Game* (Akron: University of Akron Press, 1998), 24, 275, 277, 280–282, 438–439; *Chicago Defender* (Illinois), November 6, 1915; Rainbolt, *Gold Glory*, 31.
53. Hickoksports.com, "The Minneapolis Marines," http://www.hickoksports.com/history/minnmarines.shtml; Bob Braunwart and Bob Carroll, "The First NFL Game(s)," http://www.profootballresearchers.org/Coffin_Corner/03-02-059.pdf, November 12, 2008; Hoffbeck, "Bobby Marshall," 169–170.
54. Hoffbeck, "Bobby Marshall," 164, 171.
55. *St. Paul Appeal*, October 25, 1913; Hoffbeck, "Bobby Marshall," 171; Steven R. Hoffbeck, "Bobby Marshall, the Legendary First Baseman," in *Swinging for the Fences*, 78.
56. Hoffbeck, "Bobby Marshall," 168–169, 171; *Duluth News Tribune*, October 24, 1906; *Minneapolis Spokesman*, June 30, 1939.
57. Hoffbeck, "Bobby Marshall, the Legendary First Baseman," 78–79; *Minneapolis Spokesman*, July 25, August 29, 1958.
58. Hoffbeck, "Bobby Marshall, the Legendary First Baseman," 79; Rainbolt, *Gold Glory*, 35–36; *Chicago Tribune* (Illinois), November 11, 1906.
59. *St. Paul Pioneer Press*, April 21, 1902; *National Advocate*, December 12, 1918; Riley, *Biographical Encyclopedia of the Negro Baseball Leagues*, 330; *Minneapolis Tribune*, August 5, 1942.
60. *Minnesota Messenger*, June 16, 1923; *St. Paul Appeal*, December 30, 1905.
61. *Minneapolis Tribune*, July 31, August 7, 1910; *National Advocate*, December 12, 1918; *Northwestern Bulletin*, April 28, 1923; *Minnesota Messenger*, June 16, 1923.
62. *Minneapolis Spokesman*, January 12, 1945, November 21, 1963; *Minneapolis Star-Tribune*, February 23, 2000.
63. *Chicago Defender* (Illinois), July 7, 1917; *Anaconda Standard* (Montana), July 21, 1918; *Duluth News Tribune*, July 21, 1918; *Twin City Star*, December 2, 1910.
64. *Duluth News Tribune*, July 21, 1918; *Chicago Defender* (Illinois), July 17, August 11, 1917, January 26, July 13, 1918; *Minneapolis Spokesman*, March 20, 1942.
65. *St. Paul Pioneer Press*, May 10, 1953; *Minneapolis Spokesman*, March 20, 1942; *Chicago Defender* (Illinois), April 11, 1942.
66. *Minneapolis Spokesman*, June 2, 1944.
67. Ibid.
68. *St. Paul Pioneer Press*, May 10, 1953; *Minneapolis Spokesman*, February 19, 1970.
69. Trombley, "Saint Paul Saints History 1902–1919"; Thornley, *Baseball in Minnesota*, 107, 109–110; United States Social Security Death Index, "Thomas Pangburn," 187-01-8249, January 1973.
70. *Winnipeg Free Press* (Manitoba, Canada), July 18, 1942; *Minneapolis Tribune*, August 5, 1942.
71. *Minneapolis Spokesman*, August 7, 14, 1942.
72. Retrosheet.org, "Minnesota Twins 6, New York Yankees 0," http://www.retrosheet.org, September 15, 2007; Reichler, *The Baseball Encyclopedia*, 505–549, 980.
73. Baseball-Reference.com, "Minnesota Twins Attendance, Stadiums, and Park Factors," http://www.baseball-reference.com/teams/MIN/attend.shtml, November 12, 2009; Thornley, *Baseball in Minnesota*, 200–201; *Chicago Tribune* (Illinois), October 1, 1978.
74. Thornley, *Baseball in Minnesota*, 200–201; *Hartford Courant* (Connecticut), October 2, 1978.
75. *Minneapolis Star-Tribune*, July 12, 1997, July 11, 2005.
76. *Indianapolis Freeman* (Indiana), April 16, 1910.
77. Mark Armour, "The Effects of Integration, 1947–1986," in *The Baseball Research Journal* (Cleveland: Society for American Baseball Research, 2007), 54.
78. KixandtheCity.com, "A look at the Untold Truth St. Paul Colored Gophers Air Max 90," http://www.kixandthecity.com/index.php?tag=nike-air-max, December 21, 2007.
79. Kevin Mulroy, ed., *Baseball as America: Seeing Ourselves Through Our National Game* (Washington: National Geographic Society, 2002), 76–77.

Bibliography

Newspapers
(All are from Minnesota unless otherwise noted)
Aberdeen Daily American (South Dakota)
Aberdeen Daily News (South Dakota)
Aberdeen Daily Republican (South Dakota)
Adrian Daily Telegraph (Michigan)
Adrian Daily Times and Expositor (Michigan)
Albert Lea Times Enterprise
Albert Lea Evening Tribune
Alexandria Citizen
Alexandria Citizen News
Alexandria Post News
Anaconda Standard (Montana)
Anamosa Journal (Iowa)
Appleton Press
Ashland Daily Press (Wisconsin)
Atchison Daily Globe (Kansas)
Atlanta Daily World (Georgia)
Aurora Beacon (Illinois)
Austin Weekly
Barnesville Headlight
Barron County Shield (Wisconsin)
Beach Advance (North Dakota)
Belle Plaine Herald
Bemidji Daily Pioneer
Benson Times
Benton Harbor News Palladium (Michigan)
Bessemer Herald and the New Free Press (Michigan)
Bismarck Daily Tribune (North Dakota)
Blue Earth Faribault County Register
Boston Globe (Massachusetts)
Brainerd Dispatch
Breckenridge Telegram
Breckenridge Wilkin County Gazette
Caledonia Argus
Caledonia Journal
Calmar Courier (Iowa)
Cass Lake Times
Cavalier County Republican (North Dakota)
Cedar Rapids Daily Republican (Iowa)
Charles City Daily Intelligencer (Iowa)
Chaska Weekly Valley Herald
Chicago American (Illinois)
Chicago Daily Journal (Illinois)
Chicago Defender (Illinois)
Chicago Inter Ocean (Illinois)
Chicago Tribune (Illinois)
Chippewa Falls Weekly Herald (Wisconsin)
Chisago County Free Press
Chisholm Herald
Chisholm Tribune Herald
Clarkfield Advocate
Cogswell Enterprise (North Dakota)
Colfax Messenger (Wisconsin)
Columbus Evening Dispatch (Ohio)
Cottonwood Current
Cresco Howard County Times (Iowa)
Crookston Daily Times
Cumberland Advocate (Wisconsin)
Daily Huronite (South Dakota)
Davenport Democrat and Leader (Iowa)
Decorah Journal (Iowa)
DeKalb Advertiser (Illinois)
Delaware County News (Iowa)
Dell Rapids Times (South Dakota)
Des Moines Daily News (Iowa)
Devils Lake Inter Ocean (North Dakota)
Devils Lake World (North Dakota)
Dickey County Leader (North Dakota)
Dickinson Recorder Post (North Dakota)
Dodge Center Record
Dodge County Star
Duluth Evening Herald
Duluth News Tribune
Dunn County News (Wisconsin)
Eau Claire Daily Telegram (Wisconsin)
Eau Claire Leader (Wisconsin)
Edgerton Enterprise
Eldora Semi-Weekly Herald (Iowa)
Escanaba Morning Press (Michigan)
Eveleth News
Fairmont Daily Sentinel
Fairmont Martin County Independent
Fargo Forum (North Dakota)
Fargo Forum and Daily Republican (North Dakota)
Faribault Journal
Fennimore Times (Wisconsin)
Fitchburg Daily Sentinel (Massachusetts)
Florence Morning News (South Carolina)
Floyd County Advocate Herald (Iowa)
Fort Dodge Messenger (Iowa)
Fort Wayne Journal Gazette (Indiana)
Fort Wayne News and Sentinel (Indiana)
Freeborn County Standard

Galesville Republican (Wisconsin)
Galveston Daily News (Texas)
Glasgow Missourian (Missouri)
Glen Ullin News (North Dakota)
Golden Valley Chronicle (Beach, North Dakota)
Goodhue County News
Graceville Enterprise
Grafton News and Times (North Dakota)
Grand Forks Daily Herald (North Dakota)
Grand Rapids Tribune (Wisconsin)
Granite Falls Tribune
Grant County Review (Milbank, South Dakota)
Green Bay Daily Gazette (Wisconsin)
Groton Independent (South Dakota)
Hankinson News (North Dakota)
Harmony News
Hartford Courant (Connecticut)
Hastings Daily Gazette
Hayward Sawyer County Record (Wisconsin)
Hibbing Daily Tribune
Hibbing News Tribune
Hope Pioneer (North Dakota)
Houston Signal
Howard County Times (Iowa)
Howard Lake Herald
Humboldt Independent (Iowa)
Indianapolis Freeman (Indiana)
Indianapolis Star (Indiana)
Iowa State Reporter (Waterloo, Iowa)
Ironwood Daily Globe (Michigan)
Itasca County Independent
Jamestown Daily Alert (North Dakota)
Jamestown Daily Capitol (North Dakota)
Janesville Argus
Jasper Journal
Jerauld County Review (South Dakota)
Jordan Independent
Kanabec County News
Kansas City Journal (Missouri)
Kansas City Post (Missouri)
Kansas Semi-Weekly Capital (Topeka, Kansas)
Kenyon News
Kingston Daily Freeman (New York)
La Crosse Daily Chronicle (Wisconsin)
La Crosse Leader Press (Wisconsin)
La Crosse Press (Wisconsin)
La Crosse Tribune (Wisconsin)
Lake Crystal Union
Lake Wilson Pilot
Langford Bugle (South Dakota)
Lester Prairie News
Lima Daily News (Ohio)
Lincoln State Journal (Nebraska)
Lindstrom Chisago County Press
Litchfield Independent
Litchfield News Ledger
Little Falls Daily Transcript
Logansport Daily Pharos (Indiana)

Long Prairie Leader
Long Prairie-Todd County Argus
Louisville Courier Journal (Kentucky)
Luverne Rock County Herald
Madison Daily Democrat (Wisconsin)
Madison Daily Sentinel (South Dakota)
Manchester Press (Iowa)
Mandan News (North Dakota)
Manitoba Free Press (Manitoba, Canada)
Mankato Daily Free Press
Mankato Daily Record Press
Mankato Weekly Review
Mapleton Blue Earth County Enterprise
Marion Advertiser (Wisconsin)
Marshall Lyon County Reporter
Marshall News Messenger
Martin County Sentinel
Mazeppa Tribune
Melrose Beacon
Memphis Commercial Appeal (Tennessee)
Menomonie Times (Wisconsin)
Merrill Daily Herald (Wisconsin)
Mesaba Ore and the Hibbing News
Mille Lacs County Times
Milwaukee Journal (Wisconsin)
Minneapolis and St. Paul Western Appeal
Minneapolis Journal
Minneapolis Spokesman
Minneapolis Star-Tribune
Minneapolis Tribune
Minnesota Messenger
Minot Daily Reporter (North Dakota)
Moberly Monitor-Index and Democrat (Missouri)
Moberly Weekly Monitor (Missouri)
Monessen Daily Independent (Pennsylvania)
Monroe County News (Iowa)
Monticello Times
Montreal Gazette (Quebec, Canada)
Moody County Enterprise (South Dakota)
Moose Lake Star Gazette
Nashville Banner (Tennessee)
National Advocate
New Prague Times
New Richland Star
New Richmond News (Wisconsin)
New York Age (New York)
New York Amsterdam News (New York)
New York Times (New York)
North Dakota Record (Ellendale, North Dakota)
North St. Paul Courier
North St. Paul Sentinel
Northfield News
Northwestern Bulletin
Oakland Tribune (California)
Oelwein Daily Register (Iowa)
Oelwein Register (Iowa)
Olmstead County Democrat
Osage Mitchell County Press (Iowa)

Bibliography

Osceola Sun (Wisconsin)
Oshkosh Daily Northwestern (Wisconsin) Owatonna Daily Journal Chronicle
Park Gazette News (North Dakota)
Philadelphia Inquirer (Pennsylvania)
Pierce County Herald (Wisconsin)
Pine Island Record
Pittsburgh Courier (Pennsylvania)
Pittsburgh Daily Dispatch (Pennsylvania)
Pittsburgh Post (Pennsylvania)
Plainview News
Preston Republican
Preston Times
Preston Times (Iowa)
Racine Daily Journal (Wisconsin)
Red River Valley News (Glyndon, Minnesota)
Red Wing Daily Republican
Redfield Journal (South Dakota)
Redfield Press (South Dakota)
Redwood Falls Gazette
Redwood Reveille
Renville Record
Renville Star Farmer
Rhinelander The New North (Wisconsin)
Rice Lake Chronotype (Wisconsin)
River Falls Journal (Wisconsin)
Rochester Post and Daily Record
Rock Rapids Review (Iowa)
Rockford Daily Register Gazette (Illinois)
Royalton Banner
Rush City Post
St. Cloud Daily Journal Press
St. Cloud Daily Times
St. Croix Falls Standard Press (Wisconsin)
St. Louis Globe Democrat (Missouri)
St. Louis Republic (Missouri)
St. Louis Star (Missouri)
St. Paul Appeal
St. Paul Daily Globe
St. Paul Daily News
St. Paul Dispatch
St. Paul Echo
St. Paul Pioneer Press
St. Peter Herald
San Antonio Daily Light (Texas)
San Antonio Light and Gazette (Texas)
Sauk Center Herald
Sawyer County Record (Wisconsin)
Shakopee Scott County Argus
Shakopee Times
Shakopee Tribune
Sheboygan Daily Press (Wisconsin)
Sherburn Advanced Standard
Sioux City Journal (Iowa)
Sioux Falls Daily Argus (South Dakota)
Sioux Falls Daily Press (South Dakota)
South Bend Tribune (Indiana)
Spooner Advocate (Wisconsin)
Spring Grove Herald
Springfield Advance
Springs Valley Herald (Indiana)
Stillwater Daily Gazette
Stillwater Daily Sun
Strawberry Point Mail Press (Iowa)
Superior Telegram (Wisconsin)
Syracuse Herald (New York)
Taylor County Star News (Wisconsin)
Topeka Daily Capitol (Kansas)
Topeka Plain Dealer (Kansas)
Tracy Headlight Herald
Twin City Herald
Twin City Leader
Twin City Star
Valley City Evening Times Record (North Dakota)
Van Wert Daily Times-Bulletin (Ohio)
Vernon County Censor (Wisconsin)
Virginia Enterprise
Virginian
Viroqua Republican (Wisconsin)
Waconia Patriot
Wahpeton Globe Gazette (North Dakota)
Walker Pilot
Waseca Herald
Waseca Journal
Waseca Journal Radical
Waseca Radical
Washington Post (District of Columbia)
Waterloo Daily Courier (Iowa)
Waterloo Evening Reporter (Iowa)
Watertown Daily Public Opinion (South Dakota)
Waterville Advance
Waukon Standard (Iowa)
Wausau Daily Record Herald (Wisconsin)
Webster Reporter and Farmer (South Dakota)
Webster World (South Dakota)
Wells Forum Advocate
Wessington Springs True Republican (South Dakota)
West Union Argo (Iowa)
West Union Gazette (Iowa)
What Cheer Patriot (Iowa)
Wibaux Pioneer (Montana)
Wilkin County Gazette
Willmar Republican Gazette
Willmar Tribune
Winnebago City Free Press
Winnipeg Free Press (Manitoba, Canada)
Winona Daily Herald
Winona Daily Republican
Winona Republican Herald
Winona Weekly Republican
Wisconsin State Journal (Madison, Wisconsin)
Wisconsin Valley Leader (Wisconsin)
Worth County Index (Iowa)
Wycoff Messenger
Young America Eagle
Zumbrota News

Books, Journals, Periodicals

Anderson, David, ed. *Before the Dome: Baseball in Minnesota When the Grass Was Real*. Minneapolis: Nodin Press, 1993.

Anderson, David W. *More Than Merkle*. Lincoln: University of Nebraska Press, 2000.

Anderson, Kristin M., and Christopher W. Kimball. "Twin Cities Baseball Parks: Designing the National Pastime." In *Minnesota History*. St. Paul: Minnesota Historical Society Press, Fall 2003.

Armour, Mark. "The Effects of Integration, 1947–1986." In *The Baseball Research Journal*. Cleveland: Society for American Baseball Research, 2007.

Asinof, Eliot. *Eight Men Out*. New York: Henry Holt, 1987.

Beran, Janice A. "Diamonds in Iowa: Blacks, Buxton, and Baseball." In *Journal of African American History*. Washington: Association for the Study of African American Life and History, January 2002.

Bjarkman, Peter C. *A History of Cuban Baseball 1864–2006*. Jefferson, N.C.: McFarland, 2007.

Brown, Dee. *Bury My Heart at Wounded Knee*. New York: Washington Square Press, 1981.

Bruce, Janet. *The Kansas City Monarchs*. Lawrence: University Press of Kansas, 1985.

Brunson, James, III. *The Early Image of Black Baseball*. Jefferson, N.C.: McFarland, 2009.

Clark, Dick, and Larry Lester, ed. *The Negro Leagues Book*. Cleveland: Society for American Baseball Research, 1994.

Cottrell, Robert Charles. *The Best Pitcher in Baseball*. New York: New York University Press, 2001.

Craig, John. *Chappie and Me*. New York: Dodd, Mead, 1979.

Debono, Paul. *The Chicago American Giants*. Jefferson, N.C.: McFarland, 2007.

_____. *The Indianapolis ABC's*. Jefferson, N.C.: McFarland, 1997.

Dixon, Phil. *American Baseball Chronicles: Great Teams: The 1905 Philadelphia Giants Volume Three*. Charleston, S.C.: Booksurge, 2006.

_____. *The Monarchs 1920–1938 Featuring Wilbur "Bullet" Rogan*. Sioux Falls, S.D.: Mariah Press, 2002.

Dixon, Phil, with Patrick J. Hannigan. *The Negro Baseball Leagues: A Photographic History*. Mattituck, N.Y.: Amereon House, 1992.

Echevarria, Roberto Gonzalez. *The Pride of Havana*. New York: Oxford University Press, 1999.

Folwell, William Watts. *A History of Minnesota; Volume IV*. 1929. Reprint, St. Paul: Minnesota Historical Society, 1969.

Frederick, Chuck. *Leatherheads of the North: The True Story of Ernie Nevers and the Duluth Eskimos*. Duluth: X-Communications, 2007.

Gorton, Pete. "All Nation's vs. Chicago Union Giants 1914–1916." Unpublished article.

_____. "1911 to 1917: The Making of the World's Greatest Negro Pitcher." Unpublished manuscript.

Green, Ben. *Spinning the Globe*. New York: Amistad, 2005.

Green, Jeffrey. *Black Edwardians: Black People in Britain 1901–1914*. New York: Routledge, 1998.

Gullickson, Denis J., and Carl Hanson. *Before They Were Packers*. Blue Earth, Wisc.: Trails Books, 2004.

Hawthorn, Tom. "The Rocky Saga of Vagabond 'Tribesman' Jimmy Claxton." In *Rain Check: Baseball in the Pacific Northwest*. Cleveland: Society for American Baseball Research, 2006.

Heaphy, Leslie A., ed. *Black Baseball and Chicago*. Jefferson, N.C.: McFarland, 2007.

Hoffbeck, Steven R. "Bobby Marshall: Pioneering African American Athlete." In *Minnesota History*. St. Paul: Minnesota Historical Society Press, Winter 2004–05.

_____. "The Championship Year of the St. Paul Colored Gophers: 1909." Unpublished manuscript.

_____, ed. *Swinging for the Fences*. St. Paul: Minnesota Historical Society Press, 2005.

Holmquist, June Drenning, ed. *They Chose Minnesota: A Survey of the State's Ethnic Groups*. St. Paul: Minnesota Historical Society Press, 1981.

Holway, John. *Black Diamonds*. New York: Stadium Books, 1991.

_____. *Blackball Stars*. New York: Carroll & Graf, 1992.

_____. *Voices from the Great Black Baseball Leagues*. New York: Da Capo, 1992.

Holway, John, with Lloyd Johnson and Rachel Borst, ed. *The Complete Book of Baseball's Negro Leagues: The Other Half of Baseball History*. Fern Park, Fla.: Hastings House, 2001.

Kafka, Franz. *The Basic Kafka*. New York: Pocket Books, 1979.

Kemp, David, and Roger Wildin. "The Algona Brownies, Champs of the West." In *The Baseball Research Journal*. Kansas City, Mo.: Society for American Baseball Research, 1987.

Lanctot, Neil. *Negro League Baseball: The Rise and Ruin of a Black Institution*. Philadelphia: University of Pennsylvania Press, 2004.

Leland, Frank. *Frank Leland's Baseball Club*. Chicago: Fraternal Printing, 1910.

Lester, Larry. *Baseball's First Colored World Series*. Jefferson, N.C.: McFarland, 2006.

_____. *Black Baseball's National Showcase: The East-West All-Star Game: 1933–1953*. Lincoln: University of Nebraska Press, 2001.

Lester, Larry, Sammy J. Miller and Dick Clark. *Black Baseball in Chicago*. Chicago: Arcadia, 2000.

Lomax, Michael E. *Black Baseball Entrepreneurs*. Syracuse: Syracuse University Press, 2003.

McClellan, Keith. *The Sunday Game*. Akron: University of Akron Press, 1998.

McNeil, William F. *Black Baseball Out of Season*. Jefferson, N.C.: McFarland, 2007.

Millett, Larry. *Lost Twin Cities*. St. Paul: Minnesota Historical Society Press, 1992.

Morris, Peter. "Bud Fowler's Lost Years." In *Black Ball*. Jefferson, N.C.: McFarland, 2009.

Moyle, Clay. *Sam Langford, Boxing's Greatest Uncrowned Champion*. Seattle: Bennett and Hastings, 2008.

Mulroy, Kevin, ed. *Baseball as America: Seeing Ourselves Through Our National Game*. Washington: National Geographic Society, 2002.

Niese, Joe. "George Wilson." In *Wisconsin West Magazine*. Eau Claire, Wisc.: Modern Marketing & Graphics, June 2008.

Nieto, Sevro. *Early U.S. Blackball Teams in Cuba*. Jefferson, N.C.: McFarland, 2008.

Peterson, Bernard L., Jr. *The African American Theatre Directory, 1816–1960: A Comprehensive Guide to Early Black Theatre Organizations, Companies, Theatres, and Performing Groups*. Westport, Conn.: Greenwood, 1997.

Peterson, Robert. *Only the Ball Was White*. New York: Oxford University Press, 1992.

Powell, Larry. *Black Barons of Birmingham: The South's Greatest Negro League Team and its Players*. Jefferson, N.C.: McFarland, 2009.

Powers Beck, Jeffrey. *The American Indian Integration of Baseball*. Lincoln: University of Nebraska Press, 2004.

Rainbolt, Richard. *Gold Glory*. Wayzata, Minn: Ralph Turtinen, 1972.

Reichler, Joseph L., ed. *The Baseball Encyclopedia*. New York: Macmillan, 1979.

Ribowsky, Mark. *A Complete History of the Negro Leagues 1884 to 1955*. Secaucus, N.J.: Carol, 1997.

_____. *The Power and the Darkness*. New York: Simon & Schuster, 1996.

Riley, James A. *The Biographical Encyclopedia of the Negro Baseball Leagues*. New York: Carroll & Graf, 2002.

Risjord, Norman K. *A Popular History of Minnesota*. St. Paul: Minnesota Historical Society Press, 2005.

Ruck, Rob. *Sandlot Seasons*. Urbana: University of Illinois Press, 1993.

Rucker, Mark, and Peter C. Bjarkman. *Smoke: The Romance and Lore of Cuban Baseball*. Kingston, N.Y.: Total Sports, 1999.

Seymour, Harold. *Baseball. Volume III: The People's Game*. New York: Oxford University Press, 1990.

Sullivan, Dean, ed. *Middle Innings: A Documentary History of Baseball 1900–1948*. Lincoln: University of Nebraska Press, 1998.

Swanton, Barry. *The ManDak League: Haven for Former Negro League Ballplayers, 1950–1957*. Jefferson, N.C.: McFarland, 2006.

Thorn, John, and Pete Palmer, eds. *Total Baseball*. New York: Warner, 1989.

Thornley, Stew. *Baseball in Minnesota: The Definitive History*. St. Paul: Minnesota Historical Society Press, 2006.

_____. *On to Nicollet*. Minneapolis: Nodin Press, 1988.

Vassar Taylor, David. *African Americans in Minnesota*. St. Paul: Minnesota Historical Society Press, 2002.

Ward, Geoffrey C. *Unforgivable Blackness*. New York: Alfred A. Knopf, 2004.

White, Sol. *History of Colored Base Ball, With Other Documents on the Early Black Game 1886–1936*. Edited by Jerry Malloy. Lincoln: University of Nebraska Press, 1996.

Zoss, Joel, and John Bowman. *Diamonds in the Rough: The Untold Story of Baseball*. Lincoln: University of Nebraska Press, 2004.

Electronic Websites and Articles

Ancestry.com
Baseball Reference.com
BlackPast.org
Classic Encyclopedia.org
DatabaseFootball.com
ESPN.com
GenealogyBank.com
Hibbing.org
Hickoksports.com
Hymntime.com
KixandtheCity.com
Library of Congress (www.loc.gov)
Mapquest.com
Measuringworth.com
Mid-Continent Public Library (www.mcpl.lib.mo.us)
Minnesota State Department of Revenue (www.taxes.state.mn.us)
Minnesota State Legislature (www.leg.state.mn.us)
National Association for Music Education (www.menc.org)
Newsvine.com
NewspaperArchive.com
Profootballresearchers.org
Retrosheet.org
Society for American Baseball Research (www.sabr.org)
United States Census Bureau (www.census.gov)
Wikipedia.org
Winona Newspaper Project (www.winona.edu/library)
Ashwill, Gary. "Dave Brown and the Case of the Glossy Green Shirt." http://agatetype.typepad.com/agate_type/dave-brown/

_____. "Forgotten Negro Leaguers #3 & #4: Lightner & Linder." http://agatetype.typepad.com/

agate)_type/2007/10/forgotten-neg-1.html
⸻. "George H. Wilson." http://agatetype.typepad.com/agate_type/george-h-wilson/
⸻. "How Cool Papa Got His Name." http://agatetype.typepad.com/agate_type/cool-papa-bell/
⸻. "Jose del Valle Mendez, Part II." http://agatetype.typepad.com/agate_type/2009/06/ive-obtained-a-much-better-copy-of-the-world-war-i-draft-card-for-jos%C3%A9-m%C3%A9ndez-in-chicago-which-confirms-that-he-was-emp.html
⸻. "Mike Moore." http://agatetype.typepad.com/agate_type/2006/07/index.html
⸻. "The Mysterious Fate of Dave Brown." http://agatetype.typepad.com/agate_type/2008/10/the-mysterious-fate-of-dave-brown.html
⸻. "Negro League Managers." http://agatetype.typepad.com/agate_type/2006/07/index.html
⸻. "Philadelphia Giants in Cuba, 1907." http://agatetype.typepad.com/agate_type/2006/07/index.html
Braunwart, Bob, and Bob Carroll. "The First NFL Game(s)." http://www.profootballresearchers.org/Coffin_Corner/03-02-059.pdf
Carroll, Bob. "Doc Young and the Hammond Pros." http://www.profootballresearchers.org/Coffin_Corner/17-01-596.pdf
Ericson, James. "Hail to the Chief: A Research Paper Chronicling the Life and Baseball Exploits of John Adolph 'Chief' Bender." http://www.isd.net/~jime/chief.htm
Henehan, Brendan. "Minnesota Black Newspaper Index." http://collections.mnhs.org/duluthlynchings/html/blacknewspaperindex.pdf
Illinois State Archives. "Database of Illinois Death Certificates, 1916–1950." http://www.cyberdriveillinois.com/departments/archives/idphdeathindex.html
Lotz, Rainer E. "From Minstrelsy to Jazz: Cross-Cultural Links between Germans and Afro-Americans." http://www2.hu-berlin.de/fpm/popscrip/themen/pst08/Lotz.htm
Milwaukee Public Television. "The Making of Milwaukee." http://www.themakingofmilwaukee.com/people/stories.cfm.
Minnesota Historical Society. "Minnesota Death Certificates Index." http://people.mnhs.org/dci/Search.cfm
Moyer, Denny. "110 Years of Baseball in Sheboygan, Wisconsin." http://www.sheboyganbaseball.org/history/HistoryDetails.php?id=3
Muchlinski, Alan. "John Donaldson and His Association With Minnesota Baseball." http://instructional1.calstatela.edu/amuchli/Donaldson1.htm
Muchlinski, Alan, and David Muchlinski. "The Pipestone Black Sox." http://instructional1.calstatela.edu/amuchli/Pipestone.htm
Okkonen, Mark. "1900–1910 Minor League Rosters." http://www.sabr.org/sabr.cfm?a=cms,c,1638

Rule, D.H. "The Northfield, Minnesota Robbery." http://www.civilwarstlouis.com/History/jamesnorthfield.htm
SABR Asian Baseball Committee. "Japanese Baseball Timeline." http://asianbb.sabr.org/japanese-baseballtimeline.html
SABR Minor League Database. http://www.baseball-reference.com/minors/
Simkus, Scott. "Gilkerson's Union Giants." http://scottsimkus.wordpress.com/2009/03/09/gilkersons-union-giants/
Thornley, Stew. "Minneapolis Millers Individual Statistics 1921–1930." http://stewthornley.net/millers_1921_1930.html
⸻. "Nicollet Park." http://stewthornley.net/nicollet_park.html
Trombley, David. "Saint Paul Saints History 1902–1919." http://www.usfamily.net/web/trombleyd/SaintsHistory02-19.htm
Trotter, Joe W. "African American Fraternal Associations in American History: An Introduction." http://ssh.dukejournals.org/cgi/reprint/28/3/355.pdfhttp://ssh.dukejournals.org/cgi/reprint/28/3/355.pdf
University of Missouri-Kansas City. "The Races in Detroit: The Black Migration to Detroit." http://www.law.umkc.edu/faculty/projects/ftrials/sweet/racesindetroit.html.
Wingerd, Mary Lethert. "Separated at Birth: The Sibling Rivalry of Minneapolis and St. Paul." http://www.oah.org/pubs/nl/2007feb/wingerd.html

Interviews and Correspondence

Ebert, Kathleen. Electronic correspondence with author, October 2007.
Gorton, Pete. Electronic correspondence with author, July 2009.
King, Ed. Personal correspondence from the Lenawee Historical Society Museum, Lenawee County, Michigan.
Krock, Jeremy. Electronic correspondence with author, November 2007.
Lester, Larry. Electronic correspondence with author, March 2010.
Morris, Sheila, Co-Director, Waseca County Historical Society. Electronic correspondence with author, October 2007.

Public Records

Davison's Minneapolis City Directory: 1906. Minneapolis: Minneapolis Directory Co.
St. Paul City Directories: 1886–1912. St. Paul: R.L. Polk and Company.
State of Michigan: 1915 Record of Deaths, Kalamazoo County.

Index

Numbers in ***bold italics*** indicate pages with photographs.

Aberdeen, South Dakota 40, 62, 122, 127, 150
Aberdeen Daily American 127
Aberdeen Navy-Cabs 188
Adams, John Q. 52, 59
Adrian, Michigan 8, 9, 16
Adrian Daily Times and Expositor 16
African Americans: Antebellum South 5; early 20th century 14, 217; great migration 183; lynchings of 88; Minnesota 8, 9, 16, 51–52, 183, 215, 217, 219–220; *see also* racial attitudes; racial incidents
Afton Grove, Minnesota 187
Aitkin, Minnesota 20
Alamos baseball club (Chicago) 67
Albany Giants (Georgia) 213
Albert Lea, Minnesota 15, 16, 17, 20, 60, 61, 86, 93
Albia, Iowa 126
Alexander, Grover Cleveland "Pete" 30, 196
Alexandria, Minnesota 42, 55, 57, 104, 106, 116, 154, 155, 165, 186
Alexandria Post News 55, 154
Algona Brownies (Iowa) 17, 19, 20, 22–23, 25, 28, 67, 71, 90
All-Nation Clowns of Chicago 190
All Nations baseball club (Des Moines) 180–181, 182, 191
Allen (La Crosse player) 100
Allen, Newt 193, 196
American Association (major league) 6
American Association (minor league) 44, 45, 47, 59, 74, 80, 90, 94, 110, 145, 170, 192, 201
American League 11, 47, 96, 216, 220
Amery, Wisconsin 96
Anamosa, Iowa 116
Anderson, "Spike" 72, 76, 117
Anderson, Tommy 80
Annis, William 22
Anoka High School 20
Anson, Adrian "Cap" 17
Anthony (Virginia, Minnesota player) 137
Appleton, Minnesota 168
Arkansas, Wisconsin 194
Armatrout (Beach player) 152
Armstrong, George "Mule" 59, 118, 120, 121, 122, 123, 126, ***127***, 128, 130, 132, 134, 135, 137, 138, 139, 160, 162, 172, 173, 205
Armstrong, William 14
Artesians baseball club (Chicago) 36, 118
Ashland, Wisconsin 55, 106
Ashland Daily Press 55, 106
Askin and Marine Colored Red Sox (Minneapolis) 184, 185, 186, 191
Atchison, Kansas 125
Atchison Huskers 147
Athletic Park (Duluth) 81, 162
Athletic Park (Minneapolis) 9
Athletic Park (St. Louis) 142, 172
Austin-Westerns baseball club (Minneapolis) 36–39, 60, 74–76, 83–84, ***85***, 93

Baasen (Hastings player) 84
Bacharach Giants (New Jersey) 210
Bailey, Russell 148
Ball, Walter 11–***12***, 13, ***20***–21, 22, 31, ***33***, 34, 35, 36, 50, 71–72, 73, 79, 99, 110, 112, 114, 118, 132, 133–134, 164, 196, 206, 207
Baltimore, Maryland 31
Baltimore Black Orioles 197
Baltimore Elite Giants 201, 208
Baltimore Orioles (American League) 216
Baltimore Orioles (Eastern League) 93
Baltimore Orioles (National League) 55
Bankhead, Dan 201
Barbee, Lamb 199
Barnesville, Minnesota 181
Barron, Wisconsin 108
Bartlett, Howard "Hop" 169
Barton, Eugene "Cherry" 71, 73, 74, 91, 97, 98, 107, 109, 110, 118, 124, 155, 170, 204–205
Barton, George 216, 219–220
Barton, Sherman "Bucky" ***1***, 9, 19, ***33***, 34, 35, 36, ***37***, 38, 40, ***41***, 42, ***43***, 46, 47, ***62***, 64, ***65***, 67, 71, 75, 76, 77, 78, 83, ***88***, 90, 96, 99, 101, 103, 105, 110, ***111***, 112, 115, 120, 122, 123, 126, ***127***, 128, 129, 130, 134, 135, 139, 146, 204, ***221***
Bartos, John 102
Battey, Earl 220
Bauchman, Harry (Harry Bockmann) 158, 165, 168, 169–170, 181, 205–206, 210
Bauchman, Mae 206
Bayport, Minnesota 187
Beach, North Dakota 152, 168, 169
Beach Advance 151–152
Beardsley, Minnesota 190
Bell, James "Cool Papa" 208, 213
Belle Plaine, Minnesota 187
Bellinger, Charles 125
Beloit College 40
Bemidji, Minnesota 50, 105
Bemidji Daily Pioneer 50
Bender, Adolph "Chief" 143
Benevolent and Protective Order of Elks fraternal order 32, 52, 60, 69, 89, 110, 214
Bennett, Sam 172
Benson, Paul 177, 179
Bernstein (Austin-Westerns player) 84
Bertha, Minnesota 188, 191, 192
Bessemer, Michigan 106
Biddle University 209
Biersdorfer, Charles 74
Bies (Merrill player) 87
Binga, William "Bill" ***1***, 9, 47, 71, 72, 73, 74, 81, 87, 95, 97, 98, 99, 103, 104, 105, 106, 109 110, ***111***, 113, 114, 118, 120, 122, 123, 126, ***127***, 130, 131, 132, 135, 146, 150, 151, 153, 154, 160, 161, 162, 164, 170, 171, 172, 177, 178, 179, 182, 184, 186, 214, ***221***
Binghamton, New York 7, 8
Birmingham, Alabama 31, 99, 109
Birmingham Black Barons 196, 197, 199, 200, 213
Birmingham Giants 79, 89, 91, 99, 103–104, 156
Bismarck, North Dakota 25, 150, 167, 195
Black River Falls, Wisconsin 94
Blanchard, Fred 41, 87
Blexrud, Melvin 116
Blooming Prairie, Minnesota 159
Board, George 121, 122, 123, 126
Boering (Minneapolis-St. Paul Gophers player) 197
Bond, Tommy 6
Booker, James "Pete" 111, 112
Boone, Harry 81
Booth, Carroll 136, 163, 185
Booth, Dwight 39, 41, 82, 83, 91, 101, 105, 130, 136, 162, 163

297

Index

Boston Braves 211
Boston Nationals 64, 157, 168
Boston Red Stockings (National League) 6
Boston Royal Giants 190, 197
Bostons baseball club (Minneapolis) 12
Botts (La Crosse groundskeeper) 98
Bowling Green Academy baseball club (Kentucky) 157
Bowman, Emmett 121
Bowman, George 120, 121, 122, 123, 126, **127**, 129, 130, 133, 134, **136**, 137, 139
Boyce, Frank 194
Boyle, Jack 129
Boyle, Jim 129
Bradley, Ike 177, 184, 186, 190
Brady (Lund Lands player) 77
Brady, Judge Thomas 39, 61, 82, 101, 104
Brainerd, Minnesota 20
Breaker's Hotel baseball club (Palm Springs, Florida) 65
Breckinridge, Minnesota 69–70, 86
Breedlove, Maceo 186, 194, 195, 201
Brennan (Merrill player) 107
Brenner, Bert "Dutch" 118, 154, 165
Bresnahan, Roger 142
Brewer, Chet 190, 191, 193
Briscoe, Jesse 155, 156, 157, 159, **166**, 167, 168, 169
Britt, Iowa 17
Britton, Johnny 197, 200
Britton, South Dakota 40
Brookings, South Dakota 29, 42
Brookins, Dick 89, 105, 108, 130, 136, 162, 163
Brooklyn Brown Bombers 205
Brooklyn Cuban Stars 211
Brooklyn Dodgers 108, 201
Brooklyn Royal Giants 22, 35, 64, 101, 119, 121, 207, 210
Brooklyn Superbas 216
Brooks, Will 184, 185, 186
Brooten, Minnesota 154
Brown, Dave (aka Lefty Wilson) 191–192, 193
Brown, Harry 131, 134, 136, 137, 138, 139, 146, 147, 148, 150, 153, 154, 160, 162, 163, 164, 165, 173
Brown, Jim 196, 197
Brown, Mordecai "Three Finger" 100, 119
Brown, Ray 117–118
Brown, W.A. 180
Bryn Mawr Park (Minneapolis) 26
Buchholz, Frank 177
Bungo (Long Prairie player) 78
Burke (Cresco player) 109
Burroughs (Hibbing player) 162–163
Burton (Uptown player) 184
Buwn, "Lefty" 199

Buxton, Iowa 92, 115
Buxton Wonders 92, 115, 118, 120, 121, 160

Cadreau, William Nitchie" 128, 152
Cadwallader, Ralph 87
Caledonia, Minnesota 44, 61, 63
Calgary Black Sox (Alberta) 190
California Angels 220
California Winter League 209, 213
Callahan, Jim (Eau Claire player) 148
Callahan, Jimmy (Chicago White Sox manager) 34, 115
Calligan, Charlie 43, 82, 83
Calumet, Michigan 36
Cameron (Hibbing umpire) 162
Camp, Walter 215
Campanella, Roy 201–202
Campbell, Andrew **33**, 34, 70, 79, 80, 87, 90, 107, 117, 125, 126, 143, 146
Campeau (Chippewa Falls player) 74
Canadian League 14, 122
Cannady, Walter "Rev" 208
Cantillion, Joe 149
Carew, Rod 220
Carrington, North Dakota 28
Carroll (Austin-Westerns player) 38
Carroll, Red 101, 108, 163
Carter, Rev. W.D. 175
Carter, William 7
Cass Lake, Minnesota 130, 161–162
Caylor (Devils Lake player) 153
Chamberlain, South Dakota 67
Chance, Frank 64
Chappie and Me (Novel) see Craig, John (author)
Chappie Johnson All-Stars 210–211
Charles City, Iowa 60, 61, 109, 156, 157, 158, 170
Charleston, Oscar 196, 213
Charlotte Observer 103
Chaska, Minnesota 41, 44
Chelsea, Massachusetts 6
Chicago, Illinois 10, 31, 34, 47, 64, 67, 99, 118, 122, 146, 155, 173, 183, 208, 220
Chicago American 34
Chicago American Giants 147, 158, 164, 170, 191, 192, 195, 196, 197, 200, 204, 205, 206, 207, 208, 209, 212, 213
Chicago Arrow Giants 190
Chicago Brown Bombers 197, 198, 199
Chicago City League 34, 45, 91, 110, 114, 131
Chicago Colored Gophers see St. Paul Gophers (1907)
Chicago Columbia Giants (1899–1903) 10, 14, 15, 16, 28, 216
Chicago Columbia Giants (1938) 187

Chicago Cubs 64, 66, 67, 100, 118, 119
Chicago Defender 145, 147, 188, 204, 208, 212
Chicago Evening Post 183
Chicago Giants 119, 120, 123, 126, 131, 132–135, 138–139, 140, 143, 145, 160, 204, 205, 207, 212
Chicago Hyde Park High School 39, 217
Chicago, Milwaukee, and St. Paul Railroad baseball club (St. Paul) 186
Chicago Spaldings 31, 66
Chicago Tribune 10, 37, 216
Chicago Union Giants 10, 19, 22, **29**, 31, 33, 34, 35, 36, 39, 40, 47, 54, 66, 70–71, 90, 100, 124
Chicago Unions 8, 10, 11, 14, 15, 16, 17, 25, 66, 71, 93
Chicago White Sox (American League) 34, 46, 60, 80, 96, 128, 203
Chicago White Stockings (National League) 17
Chiles, Charles 141
Chippewa Falls, Wisconsin 21, 25, 27, 28, 54, 74
Chisago County Free Press 55
Chisholm, Minnesota 39, 42, 55, 135, 136
Cincinnati, Ohio 64, 155, 199
Cincinnati Buckeyes 196
Cincinnati Clowns 197, 198, 199
Cincinnati Reds 44, 210
Clarkfield, Minnesota 186–187
Claxton, Jimmy 181
Clemson University 211
Cleveland, Ohio 64
Cleveland Black Friars 196
Cleveland Indians 220
Cleveland Naps 18
Clyde Iron Works baseball club (Duluth) 183–184
Clymer, Otis 143
Cogswell, North Dakota 51, 104, 150
Coleman, George 184
Coleman, James 124, 141
Coleman, Nick 220
Coleman "Speed" 186
Coleman, Wellington 194
Coles, Ralph (aka Askari) 198
Colfax, Wisconsin 169
College Football Hall of Fame 216
Color line: Minnesota 14, 20, 52, 89, 191, 201–202; organized baseball 6, 7, 17, 89, 201, 211, 219–220; see also racial attitudes
Colored All-Stars see Uptown Sanitary baseball club
Colored Gophers (1914–1916) 179, 182
Colored House of David baseball club (Iowa) 193
Columbia Heights, Minnesota 182
Columbus, Ohio 199
Columbus Owls 147

Comfrey, Minnesota 192
Comiskey, Charley 10, 203
Como Park (St. Paul) 195
Conde, South Dakota 123
Conmy (Grand Forks player) 153
Coogan's Smart Set baseball club (New York) 206
Cook, Fred 94–95
Cooper, Alfred "Army" 214
Corbett, Ted 45
Corwith, Iowa 193
Coughlin, Sam 60, 77, 80, 84, *85*
Couture (Hibbing player) 81
Craig, John (author) 61, 211–212
Cresco, Iowa 86, 92, 109
Criss, Dode 43
Crookston, Minnesota 39, 61, 130, 154, 193
Crutchfield, Jimmy 213
Cuban Giants 8, 66, 86
Cuban House of David baseball club (Iowa) 193
Cuban League 64, 67, 71, 180, 203
Cuban Stars 66, 77, 119, 126, 128, 195
Cuban X-Giants 9, 22, 25, 28, 35, 213
Cullop, Nick 192
Cumberland, Wisconsin 87, 135
Cunningham, John H. 32
Cunningham, Johnnie 181

Dallas Black Giants (Texas) 140, 191
Dandridge, Ray 208
Danville Unions (Illinois) 156
Davies (Crookston umpire) 154
Davis (Dickinson player) 151
Davis, Alphonso "Lefty" 44, 46, 94, 146, 147
Davis, Belle 131–132, 144, *175*, 176
Davis, Eddie (aka Peanuts Nyasses) 198, 199
Davis, Eddie (Minneapolis Keystones secretary) 70, 71, 72, 139–140, 145, 147, 160
Davis, Frank "Bunch" 34, 35, *37*, 38, 39, *41*, 42, *43*, 44, 46, 47, 64, *65*, 74, *75*, 76, 77, 78, 83, 84, *88*, 91, 94, 95, 107, 108, 117, 124, 141, 155, 158, 159, 160, 162, *163*, 164, 166
Davis, Harry 215
Davis, Joe 177, 179, 184, 185, 186, *189*
Davis, John Barton "Johnny" 22, 38, 39, 40, *41*, 42, *43*, 44, 45, 47, 66, 67, 68, 72, 83, 94, 106, 109, *111*, 112, 113–114, 115, 116, 118, 120, *121*, 122, 123, 126, *127*, 128, 129, 130, 131, 133, 136, 137, 138, 139, 140, 144, 145, 146, 147–148, 149, 150, 151, 152, 153, 154, 155, 160, 161, 162, 164, 165, 171, 177, 178, 179, *185*, 187, 188, 214
Davis, Leland "Lee" 177, 182, 184, 186, 188, 190, 215
Davis, Roosevelt 199
Dawson, Nick "Hub" 135, 149

Dayton Chappies (Ohio) 210
Dayton Marcos (Ohio) 207
Decorah, Iowa 36, 81
Decorah Journal 81
Decorah Republican 81
Deerwood, Minnesota 180
Dehmer, "Lefty" 103, 159
DeKalb, Illinois 157, **158**
Delano, Minnesota 27
Dell (Austin-Westerns player) 75–76
Dellar, Phil 102, 118, 122; Phil Dellar All-Stars 121–122
DeMoss, Elwood "Bingo" 171, 182, 198
Des Moines Invincibles (Iowa) 92
Detroit, Michigan 8, 11, 64, 183, 213, 214, 220
Detroit Black Sox 197
Detroit Motor City Giants 200
Detroit Stars 66, 189, 207, 208
Detroit Tigers 137
Devils Lake, North Dakota 60, 152–153, 161, 162, 164, 167
Devils Lake World 153, 161, 167
Dewberry, William 86, 87, 92, 96, 205
Dickinson, Edward 89, 90, 95
Dickinson, North Dakota 151
Diggins (St. Cloud player) 21
DiMaggio, Joe 44
Dismukes, William "Dizzy" 104, 108–109, 156, 173, 207
Doan, Ray.L. 193
Dodge Center, Minnesota 68
Dominick, John "Alf" 21, 42, 138
Donaldson, John 2, 120–121, 180–181, 188, 191, 192, 193, 196; John Donaldson All-Stars 193–194
Donlin, Mike 34; Mike Donlin All-Stars 45, 72
Dougherty, Charles "Pat" 1, 110, 112, 114
Downend, Garfield 43–44
Downtown Park (St. Paul) 36, 42, 44, 45, **58**, 59, 74, 77, 83, 84, 87, 90, 91, 92, 94, 95, 96, 102, 103, 104, 109, 110, 113, 114, 117, 121, 126, 138, 218; characteristics 46, 58, 91
Doyle, Jack 129
Doyle, Martin 129
Drake, Bill "Plunk" 206, 213
Dretchko, Al "Lefty" 42, 104, 106, 165, 181, 182, 192
Drill, Lew 44, 45
Duke, James 7
Duluth, Minnesota 67, 81, 98, 183–184, 200
Duluth Fashions 23
Duluth Fitwells 162
Duluth Kelleys 215
Duluth News Tribune 89
Duncan, Frank 99
Dunlap (Minneapolis Colored Giants player) 182
Dunlap, Gerhart 188
Dunleavy, Jack "Skeeter" 45, 46, 95

Durocher, Leo 201
Duryea, Etta 120

Eagle Lake, Minnesota 187
East Chicago Giants (Indiana) 197
East St. Louis Cubs (Illinois) 213
East-West All-Star Game 195, 197, 200, 208
Eastern Colored League 191, 210, 213
Eastern Mesaba League 162
Eau Claire, Wisconsin 36, 98, 122, 148
Eau Claire Leader 28
Ebert, Elizabeth 214
Eckersall, Walter 39, 216; Chicago Eckersalls 214
Edgerton, Minnesota 53, 61
Eiden, Billy "the Russian Prince" 150
18th Ward baseball club (Pittsburgh) 205
Eiken, Adolph 44
Eikens (Watertown player) 123
Eldred (Appleton player) 168
Elgin, Illinois 118
Elk Mound, Wisconsin 169
Elks fraternal order *see* Benevolent and Protective Order of Elks
Ellefson (Watertown, South Dakota player) 123
Ellendale, North Dakota 150
Elliott, E. Faye 188
Ellsworth, Wisconsin 107
Elysian, Minnesota 14
Embry, William "Cap" 155, 156, 167, 168, 205
English, Tom 194, 195
Ernst (Alexandria player) 154
Essick, Bill "Vinegar" 44, 45, 46
Estevan, Saskatchewan 184
Evans, Ulysses "Cowboy" 199, 200
Eveleth, Minnesota 39, 42, 83, 105
Ewing, William "Buck" 210

Fagan, Jimmy 42
Fairmont, Minnesota 55, 62, 93, 138, 190, 191, 193–194
Fairmount, North Dakota 168
Fargo, North Dakota 26–27, 39, 53, 129
Fargo Forum 25
Faribault, Minnesota 47, 60, 84, 87, 91, 93, 102–103, 108, 109, 152
Farris, Frank "Rube" 44–45
Fayette, Iowa 158, 159
Fayette Reporter 159
F.C. Roger baseball club (St. Paul) 185
Fe baseball club (Havana, Cuba) 67, 71
Felix Colts (Chicago) 47
Felsch, Oscar "Happy" 191
Fennimore, Wisconsin 86, 115
Fergus Falls, Minnesota 5, 39
Findlay, Ohio 12

Finnegan, Pat *26*, 28, 154, 165
Fisher, W.W. 5–6
Flandreau, South Dakota 17, 19
Florida Hoboes 197
Flynn, Jim "Fireman" 158
Fogel, Gus 100
Footes, Jake 194, 195
Footes, Robert "Bob" *15*–16, 17, *18*, 19
Force, Frank 59
Foreman, Sylvester "Hooks" 192, 193
Ford (St. Paul Gophers player) 122, 123, *127*
Ford, Charles "Whitey" 220
Ford, Dan "Disco" 220
Ford, Gene 45–46, 137
Fort Dodge, Iowa 17, 19, 22, 181
Fort Snelling (St. Paul) 51, 217, 218
Fort Snelling baseball club 7, 26
Fort Wayne Shamrocks (Indiana) 199–200
Fort Worth Wonders (Texas) 140
Fortune magazine 69
Foster (Grand Rapids, Wisconsin player) 169
Foster, Andrew "Rube" 31, 32, 35, 45–46, 47, 91, 94, 99, 110, 114, 119, 121, 123, 146, 164, 170, 179, 184, 191, 206, 207, 209, 212, 214
Foster, Sam 16, 21, 23, *24*, 27
Foster, Will 16
Fowler, "Bud" (aka John W. Jackson) 6–7, 8, 9, 12–13
Francis (St. Paul Gophers player) 139
Francis, William T. 52, 53
Franklin, William 139
Fraser, Charles "Chick" 115
Freeman, Bill 186, 187, 188, 193, 194, 195, 214
Freeman, "Buck" 146, 148
Freeman, George "Slow Ball" 81
Freeman, W.J. 80, 86
Freemasons order 32, 175, 218
French Lick Plutos (Indiana) 156, 157, 173, 181–182, 190, 205, 206
Fuelling, "Peanuts" 109
Funk's Exports baseball club (St. Paul) 11

Galesville, Wisconsin 67, 68, 72, 73, 83
Gallagher, Mike 182
Galloway, Bill 14
Galloway, Vic 197, 198, 199
Galveston Flyaways (Texas) 141
Garden City, Minnesota 54, 93
Garner, Iowa 17
Garrett, Alvin 10
Garrison, Richard "Dick" *1*, 100, 101, 104, 105, 106, *221*
Gatewood, William "Big Bill" 64, *65*, 66, 67, 68, 74, 76, 77, 81, 82, 83, 84, 86, 87, *88*, 89, 90, 91, 94, 95, 96, 98, 99, 100, 110, 111, 112, 113, 114, 117, 123–124, 126, 140, *141*, 142, 209, 210, 212–214

Gatewood, William, Jr. "Buddy" 213–214
Gehring, Hank 94, 95, 97
Geier, Phil "Red" 45, 94, 95, 118
Geiselman, Bobby 42, 101, 105, 108, 162
Geist (Wibaux player) 167
Gibson, Josh 208
Gilchrist, William 81, 82, 91
Giles, George 156
Gilkerson, Robert 99, 190
Gilkerson's Union Giants (Iowa) 187, 190, 191, 204
Gilliard, Arthur "Hamp" 172
Gilligan, Jack 42, 43, 82, 83, 91
Glaze, John 39, 41
Glen Ullin, North Dakota 151
Glencoe, Minnesota 24–25, 26
Glockner, Roy 80
Golden Valley League 187
Gomez Vernon "Lefty" 44
Gooch, Charles 186
Good Thunder, Minnesota 180, 181
Goodgame, John 156
Gordon, Sam 181, 190
Gosewisch brothers (North St. Paul players) 138
Graceville, Minnesota 168
Grady, Jean 163
Graggion, Joe 68
Graham (Minneapolis Keystones player) 71, 72, 73, 80
Graham, George "Peaches" 44, 45, 47
Graham, Oscar 80
Grand Forks, North Dakota 13, 20, 62, 153, 154, 166, 167
Grand Forks Daily Herald 153, 166
Grand Forks Daily Plain Dealer 13
Grand Rapids, Minnesota 105
Grand Rapids, Wisconsin (Wisconsin Rapids) 68, 169
Granite Falls, Minnesota 192
Grant, Charlie 216
Grant, Jim 220
Grawe, William 150
Gray, Roosevelt "Chappie" 193
Great Northern baseball club (Minneapolis) 186
Greathouse, Archie 142
Greaves (Austin-Westerns player) 75
Green, Charles "Joe" 110, 114, 133, 134, 207
Green, Lenny 220
Green, Willie 68, 107, 124
Green Bay, Wisconsin 34, 36
Gregory (Aberdeen player) 122
Gregory, Charles 6
Grey Eagle, Minnesota 27
Griffin (Lund Lands player) 76
Griffith, Calvin 220
Grimes, Burleigh 164
Groh, Henry "Heinie" 68
Groton, South Dakota 104, 123, 178
Guthrie (Valley City player) 129
Guzy, Pete 188

Hale, Phil 59
Hall, Charley "Sea Lion" 94, 95
Hall, Halsey 192
Hall, Prim 197, 199, *201*
Hall, Sell 205
Hallett, "Happy" 166
Hamilton, Jim "Sunny" 142
Hammond Pros (Indiana) 187
Hamm's Exports baseball club (St. Paul) 11
Hancock, Art 193
Hancock, Charlie 193
Hankinson, North Dakota 57, 104, 150, 166
Hankyu Braves (Japan) 200
Hanlon, "Happy" 167
Hanlon, Ned 216
Hannaca Blues (Missouri) 121
Hanson (Jamestown player) 168
Hardiman (St. Paul Gophers player) 148, 150, 152, 153, 160, 164, 165, 172
Hardy Arthur (aka William Norman) 49, 182
Harkins (H.P. Conrads player) 159
Harlem Globetrotters 187, 196, 199, 200
Harlem Globetrotters baseball club 200
Harmony, Minnesota 44, 61, 94, 115–116
Harper (Kansas City Giants player) 172
Harney, George 190
Harris (Indianapolis ABCs player) 143
Harris, Nate 112, 113, 114, 133, 134, 151, 170
Hastings, Dennis 94
Hastings, Minnesota 76, 80, 83, 84, 138, 159
Hatten, Rufus 197, *198*, 199, 200
Havana, Cuba 66
Havana Lions 64, 203
Hawarden, Iowa 28, 29, 181
Hawkins, LaTroy 220
Hawley, Emerson "Pink"
Hayward, Wisconsin 40, 54
Heimke, Jack 150
Heimkes, Ed 45
Henderson, Scotty 187–190
Hennepin Clothing Company baseball club (Minneapolis) 177–179, 204
Henry, Leo "Preacher" 198
Hentschell, I. John 59
Hewitt, Joe 172
Hibbing, Minnesota 39, 53, 57, 62, 98, 101, 136, 137, 163, 164, 181, 182, 211–212
Hibbing Colts 39, 41–42, 43, 47, 55, 61, 81–82, 83, 89, 91, 92, 101, 104, 105, 106, 108, 116, 130, 135–136, 162–163, 164, 185, 222
Hibbing News Tribune 102, 162, 163
Higbee (Indianapolis ABCs player) 170

Index

Higdon, Barney 200
Hildebrand, "Doc" 178
Hill (Charles City player) 158
Hill (St. Paul Gophers player) 122
Hill, Preston "Pete" 110, 112, 113, 114, 212
Hilldale baseball club (Philadelphia) 210
Hille, Bill 117
Hillebrand, Homer 27, 45
Hillskottie (Osceola player) 171
Hilton, Charlie 187, 193
Hinckley, Minnesota 140
Hirschfield, John J. 32, 33, 34–35, *43*, 64, *65*, 99, 126, 175, 183
Hoch, Len 8
Hodgins, Bill "Wild" 146
Hoffman, J.P. 159
Hoke, Billy 26, 161
Holland, William "Billy" 9, 15–16, 17, *18*, 19, 21, 22, 23, 25, *26*, 27, 28, 35, 220
Holtmann, W. 142
Homestead Grays (Pittsburgh) 121, 205, 208
Honeycutt, Prince 5
Hope, North Dakota 129
Hopkins, Minnesota 70
Hopkins, George *29*, *70*, 71, 73, 74, 81, 96, 107, 108, *116*, 118, 124
Hopkins Brothers baseball club (Des Moines) 54
Hopkins Brothers Ladies baseball club (Des Moines) 163, 180
Hopson, Boston "Babe" 211
Horeja Brothers baseball club (St. Paul) 12
Horn, William 8, 11, 19, 22, 34, 35, *37*, 39, 40, 93, 96, 98, 204
Houghton, Michigan 89
House of David baseball club (Michigan) 196, 197, 200
Houston Black Buffaloes 100, 140, 206
Hovlick, Joe 80–81
Howard (Dickinson player) 151
Howard, J.D. 142
Howard, John 199
Howard Lake, Minnesota 96
Howell, Owen 184
H.P. Conrads baseball club (St. Paul) 60, 102, 103, 109, 118, 126, 138, 148–149, 159, 177
Hudson, Wisconsin 43, 102, 116
Hudson, Lloyd "Dick," "Super Six" 186, 187
Hueston, William 207
Huggins, Miller 66
Hughes, Harry 92, 118, 140
Hughes, Tom "Long" 143
Hurley, Michigan 188
Huron, South Dakota 149
Hutchinson, Fred "Puggy" 169
Hyde, Harry 17, 18, 19, *29*, 47

Illinois Giants 128, 134, 190
Indianapolis, Indiana 31, 207
Indianapolis ABCs 108, 121, 124, 128, 142–143, 147, 155, 156, 169–170, 181, 187, 195, 205, 206, 207, 209, 213
Indianapolis Clowns 195–196
Indianapolis Freeman 35, 48, 62, 69, 99, 100, 119, 124, 125, 126, 135, 141, 143, 155, 156, 169, 206, 210, 214, 220, 220–221
Indianapolis Indians 89
International Association 6
International Harvesters baseball club (St. Paul) 214
International League 7, 211
Iola, Kansas 71
Iron Range (Minnesota) 39, 41, 53, 72, 78, 81, 101, 105, 108, 116, 135, 136, 162, 185, 215
Ironton, Minnesota 195
Irvin, Monte 201
Irwin, Alex *29*, 71, 80, 91, 95, 116, 124, 131, 152, 153, 155, 177, *178*, 179, 214
Ivanhoe, Minnesota 192

J. Boureson baseball club (St. Paul) 184
Jackson (Aberdeen Navy-Cabs player) 188
Jackson, Charles "Slick" 86, 87, 91, 95, 96, 97, 107, 108, 109, 117, 118, 124, 126, 140, 142, 143, 155, 156, 157, 158, 165, 167, 168–169
Jackson, Dick 5
Jackson, Joe "Cannonball" 180, 181, 182
Jackson, Major Robert R. 69, 132, 183, 197
Jacobson (Medford player) 92
Jacques (Aberdeen player) 122, 127
Jamestown, North Dakota 129, 150, 168, 195
Janesville, Minnesota 109
Jeannette, Joe 71
Jeffries, Jim 120
Jenkins Brothers baseball club (Kansas City) 71
Jensen (Hibbing player) 130, 135, 136
Jessup, Charles 47, 71, 72, 73, 79, 80, 81, 86, 87, 90, 92, 96, 107, 108, 109, 110, 115, 116–117, 205
John Donaldson All-Stars 193–194
Johnson (H.P. Conrads player) 118
Johnson (Perry Werden All-Stars player) 160
Johnson (St. Paul Gophers player) 36, 37
Johnson, Ban 11
Johnson, "Bat" 42, 46
Johnson, George Jr. "Rat," "Chappie" *1*, 9, 22, 28, 29, 49, *50*, 61–62, 64–*65*, 75, 76, 77, 78, 81, 82, 83, *88*, 90, 91–92, *93*, 94, 96, 99, 100, 101, 102, 104–105, 110, 111, 112, 113, 116, 131, 133, 172, 179, 203, 206, 210–*212*, *221*; Chappie Johnson All-Stars 210–211

Johnson, Grant "Home Run" 8, 35, 209
Johnson, Jack (Heavyweight champion) 32, 120, 144, 175, 205
Johnson, Jack "Topeka Jack" *29*, 47, 71, 73, 95, *97*, 98, 125, 126, 141, 171, 205
Johnson, Gov. John A. 51, 118, 216
Johnson, Leaman 200
Johnson, Louis "Dicta" 127–128, 129, 130, 132, 133, 134, 135, 136, 137, 138, 139, 144, 145, 146, 150, 152, 153, 154, 160, 163, 164, 165, 171, 172, 173, 206–207
Johnson, Napoleon (aka William Crawdad) 149
Johnson, Walter 30
Johnston, Wade 208
Jones, Bert 10, 19, 25, *26*, 27–28, 29, 104, 123, 146–147, 148, 149, 152, 153, 160, 163, 164, 171, 172, 173, 182
Jones, Bert (Winona player) 190
Jones, Collins 200
Jones, Henry C. 160
Jones, Ross 98
Jones, Willis 8, 22, 23, *29*, *33*, 35, 36, *37*, 40, *41*, 42, *43*, 45–46, 48, 55, 59, *60*, 64, *65*, 74, 75, 76, 82, 83, 84, 86, *88*, 98, *107*, 108, 124, 204
Joyner, William "Bill" *15*
Jude, Frank 92

Kansas City, Missouri 36, 64, 125, 137, 155, 171
Kansas City Blues (Missouri) 19, 170
Kansas City Giants (Kansas) 69, 119, 125, 135, 170, 171–172
Kansas City Journal 171
Kansas City Monarchs (Missouri) 156, 163, 187, 191, 192, 193, 196, 201, 214
Kansas City Royal Giants (Missouri) 120, 125–126, 141–142, 155, 172
Kansas State League 25, 71, 147
Kay, David "Moose" 177
Keeler, Willie "Wee" 55
Kehoe, Eddie 102, 103
Kellar, Ed 76, 7, 78, 154
Kelley, Mike 22
Kelley, William 22, 23
Kennedy, Dave 122–123
Kenyon, Minnesota 101
Keystone Colored Giants (Minneapolis) 184
Keystone Hotel and Buffet (Minneapolis) 69, *174*
Kick, Dan 122
Kinkle, Sam 76, 182
Kleffman, Frank 82
Kletschka, Emil, Jr. 109
Kletschka, Emil, Sr. 109
Kline, Ed 100
Kling, Johnny 67, 156
Knight, Nathan 86

Knights of Pythias fraternal order 32, 69, 141, 169, 183
Knox, Elwood 142
Kolbe (Red Wing umpire) 57
Koons, Percy 87
Koukalik, Joe 21
Kramer, Mike 140
Krock, Dr. Jeremy 208, 210
Ku Klux Klan 190
Kurke, Frank 28, 117

La Crosse, Wisconsin 23–24, 40, 54, 94, 97, 98, 100–101, 122, 146, 147, 198
La Crosse Press 23
Lake Benton, Iowa 19
Lake Crystal, Minnesota 58
Lake Crystal Union 51, 54
Lake Elmo, Minnesota 187, 195
Lake Shore League 34, 203
Lake View House baseball club (Cleveland) 7
Lake Wilson, Minnesota 181
Lakeview, Minnesota 190
Lamar, Ed 213
Lamb, Claude 87, 102, 108, 137–138, 152
Lamoure, North Dakota 38
Landis, Judge Kennesaw Mountain 219
Lane College 217
Langdon, North Dakota 129
Langford, Fred 64
Langford, Sam 71
Langford, South Dakota 63
Larson (H.P. Conrads player) 159
Larson (Shakopee player) 139
Larson (Springfield player) 139
Laughlin, Joe 74–76
Laurels baseball club (St. Paul) 11
Lawson (Alexandria player) 166
Lazzeri, Tony 44
Leach, Helon 42, 104
Leahy (Valley City player) 152
Le Claire, Bill 46
Lee, Holsey "Scrip" 210
Lee, Lown 126, 172
Leeds, Johnny 123
Leigh (Grand Forks player) 166
Leland, Frank 8, 10, 16, 22, 31, 73, 114, 119, 131, 132
Leland Giants (Chicago) 1, 28, 29, 31, 33, 34, 36, 45, 47, 49, 65, 66, 67, 71, 79, 86, 91, 99, 107, 110–115, 117, 119, 123, 128, 131, 148, 151, 170, 177
Lennon, George 145, 149
Lennon and Gibbons baseball club (St. Paul) 16, 21
Lester Prairie, Minnesota 41, 131
Lett, Alvin 100
Lett, Charles 7
Lewis, Harold 182, 184, 186, 188, 190
Lewiston, Minnesota 201
Lexington Park (St. Paul) 11, 12, 17, 18, 19, 22, 27, 32, 37, 38, 42, 75, 87, 89, 110, 115, 118, 121, 126, 131, 132, 138, 145, 146, 147, 149, 159, 171, 184, 186, 188, 194, 195, 196, 197, 198, 199, 200, 201, 202, 216, 218; characteristics 58
L.G. Hoffman Caterpillars (St. Paul) 12
Liese, Fred 168, 169
Lightner, Charley 187
Lima, Ohio 199
Lincoln Giants (New York) 191, 200, 206, 209, 210, 213
Lind, Gov. John 51, 52, 216
Lindaman, Viv 157–158, 170
Lindsay, Bill 125
Lindsey, Len (aka Yahodi) 198
Lindstrom, Minnesota 54, 55, 87, 115, 170, 171, 184
Lismore, Minnesota 191
Litchfield, Minnesota 17, 19, 182
Little Diamond baseball club (Minneapolis) 8
Little Falls, Minnesota 179, 186, 192–193
Liverpool, Louis 5, 44
Lloyd, John Henry "Pop" 49, 66, 107, 209
Logan Squares (Chicago) 34, 66, 115
London, Julius *1*, 99–100, 101, 102, 103, 104, 105, 106, 110, *111*, 113, 115, 120, 205, **221**
Long Prairie, Minnesota 51, 73, 74, 76, 80, 87, 102, 104–105, 110, 113, 116, 155, 168–169
Longest, Bernie 199
Louisville, Kentucky 64, 155
Louisville Cubs 142, 155, 156, 157, 170
Louisville White Sox 209
Luger, Al 143
Lund Lands baseball club (Minneapolis) 28, 36, 37, 72, 74, 76–77, 78, 79–80, 86, 87
Lyman (Hibbing umpire) 101, 130
Lyman, Art 88
Lynch (Dodge Center player) 68
Lynch, Tom 182
Lyndale baseball club (Minneapolis) 7
Lynn Live Oaks (Massachusetts) 6
Lyons, Benny 156–157
Lyons, Jimmy 124, 142, 172, 173, 206
Lytle, Clarence "Dude" 8, **29**, **33**, 35, **37**, 38, 39, 40, **41**, 42, **43**, 44–45, 47, 64, **65**, 77, 78, 81–**82**, 83–84, 86, **88**, 89, 90, 91, 94, 95, 96, 98, 100, 124, 142, 146, 154, 160, 161, 163, 164, 165, 171, 172, 204

M & I College 210
Madison, South Dakota 86
Madison, Wisconsin 68
Mahling (Faribault player) 103
Malloy (Faribault player) 103
Maloney, Joe 57
Manchester, Iowa 73
Mandan, North Dakota 150, 151
Manese, O.L. 190
Manitoba Free Press 23
Manitowoc, Wisconsin 203
Mankato, Minnesota 16, 58, 106, 117, 135, 137–138, 177–178, 187
Manke, Bill 153, 161
Marcelle, Oliver 191
Marcus, Iowa 187–188
Marion, Wisconsin 169
Marsh, "Lefty" 108
Marshall, Bill 216
Marshall, Charles D. 119
Marshall, Irene Knott 215
Marshall, Louis 177
Marshall, Robert Wells "Bobby" *1*, 37, 38, 70, 72, 74, 80, 91, 100, 105, 106, 109, 110, ***111***, 112, 114, 115, 118, 119, 120, 126, **127**, 128, 129, 130, 131, 132–133, 134–135, 136, 137, 138, 139, 140, 143, 145, 146, 147, 148, 149, 150, 151, 152, 153, 154, 160, 161, 163, 164, 165, 170, 171, 173, 177, 178, 179–180, 181, 182, 183–184, **185**, 186, 188, **189**, 190, 194, 214–216, 219–220, **221**
Marshall, Minnesota 20, 180
Martin, Henry 25, 44, 60, 97, 118
Martin, Dr. J.B. 208
Mason City, Iowa 20, 23, 25, 181
Matchett, Jack 198
Matlock, Leroy 213
Mauer, Joe 195
Maynard Forrest 169
Mays, Dave 187
Mays, Willie 201
Mazeppa, Minnesota 60
McAdoo, Tully 172
McCarl, George 150
McCarthy (umpire) 18, 163
McCleary, Charles 16, **18**, 19, 47, 60, 76, 84, 86, 87, 93, 103, 106, 127, 131, 135, 137, 158
McCormick, Jim 71
McCoy-Nolan Giants of Milwaukee 190
McCune, Milroy 107, 110, 124, 143, 155, 167, 170
McDonald, Rev. E.H. 175
McDonald, Webster 191, 192–193, 210
McDougall, Arthur *1*, 59, 99, 100, 101, 103, 110, ***111***, 114, 115, 118, 120, 122, 123, 126, **127**, 128, 129, 131, 132, 133, 134, 135, 137, 138, 139, 140, 146, 148, 149, 150, 151, 152, 153, 160, 164, 165, 171, **221**
McGarry, Bowers 122, 143, 152
McGarry, Emmet 138, 143
McGee (St. Paul Police player) 188
McGhee, Fredrick L. 52
McGill (Minot player) 128
McGraw, John 216
McIlraith, Tim 154
McKinnis, Gread "Lefty" 199
McKinnon, Wm.R. 184
McLaughlin (French Lick Plutos player) 182
McMullen, Bruce **201**

Index

McMurray, William *1*, 44, 45–46, 55, 64, *65*, 74, 75, 77, 81, 83, 86, **88**, **90**, 91, 94, 96, 99, 101, 102, 104, 105, 106, 110, *111*, 113, 115, 120, 128, 172, 206, ***221***
McNair, Allen "Hurley" 140, 142–143, 155, 156, 157, 158, 159, 165, 166, 167, 168, 169, 170, 181, 193, 194
McNamara (Austin-Westerns player) 75
Means, Thomas 8, 34, 35, *37*, *41*, 42, *43*, 44, 47, 96, 98, 180
Medford, Wisconsin 92
Megan (Virginia, Minnesota player) 164
Meharry College 217
Meister (Grand Rapids, Wisconsin player) 169
Melander, "Rabbit" 129
Mellang, Teddy 86, 92
Melrose, Minnesota 179, 182, 188, 191
Mendez, Jose 180, 181
Menomonie, Wisconsin 27, 92, 116
Memphis, Tennessee 99
Memphis Tigers 157
Memphis Union Giants 99, 100
Merida, John "Big Boy" 124, 143, 155
Merriam Park Crescents 12
Merrill, Wisconsin 87, 107, 108, 116
Merten's All-Stars 142
Meyers, Benny 74, 75
Meyers, John Tortes "Chief" 94, 95
Miami Colored Giants (Florida) 190
Miami Ethiopian Clowns (Florida) 196
Michigan State League 8, 16
Michigan Wolverines of Nebraska 190
Mike Donlin All-Stars 45, 72
Milaca, Minnesota 164
Miller, Fred "Lefty" 38
Miller, Pleas "Hub" 173
Milligan, "Swat" 168
Milliner, Eugene "Gabbie" *1*, 101, 102, 103, 104, 105, 106, *111*, 112, 113, 114, 118, 120, 125, 137, 138, 139, 140, 143, 171, 172, 204, ***221***
Mills (Valley City player) 129
Mills, Charley 141, 142, 155
Milwaukee, Wisconsin 37, 119, 156, 183, 198
Milwaukee Brewers (American Association) 44, 80, 82, 135
Minneapolis, Minnesota 5, 6, 8, 9, 31, 36, 37, 51–52, 59, 68–69, 70, 89, 124–125, 142, 145, 149, 155, 156, 169, 170, 171, 183, 190, 193, 194; rivalry with St. Paul 68–69, 184
Minneapolis All-Stars 117
Minneapolis Brown Stockings 7
Minneapolis Browns 186

Minneapolis Buffaloes 186
Minneapolis Central High School 37, 70, 215
Minneapolis Colored Giants 182
Minneapolis Colored Gophers 183–184
Minneapolis Deans 70, 214
Minneapolis Edison High School 188
Minneapolis Javas 26
Minneapolis Journal 59, 84, 161
Minneapolis Keystones 2, 16, 177, 180, 183, 184, 193, 203, 205; behavior 73–74, 117; demise 173–175; formation 70–71; on the field incidents 69, 72–73, 107, 109, 117, 159, 167; pitching problems 86, 108; quality 74, 221; style of play 90, 166; umpiring and 73–74, 117, 159, 167; weather woes 108, 109, 116, 117; (1907) 70; (1908) 72–73, 79–81, 86–87, 89, 90–92, 95–96, 97–98 (1909) 107–110, 115, 116–117; (1910) 125–126, 140–143; (1911) 156–159, 165–170
Minneapolis Liberties 215
Minneapolis Marines 186, 214, 215
Minneapolis Millers 6–7, 9, 16–17, 27, 35, 44, 59, 60, 71, 74, 83, 87, 95, 96, 108, 110, 125, 126, 135, 137, 143, 149, 160, 184, 192, 201, 215, 216, 218
Minneapolis Pillsbury baseball club 23
Minneapolis-St. Paul Gophers 197–200
Minneapolis South High School 107
Minneapolis Spokesman 196, 197, 199, 202, 217, 219
Minneapolis Star-Tribune 216
Minneapolis Steeles 177
Minneapolis Toozes (ZZ's) 19, 39, 42, 47, **56**
Minneapolis Tribune 25, 53, 59, 79, 97, 117, 161, 173–174, 177, 219, 220
Minneapolis Unions 5, 70
Minneapolis White Sox 190, 214
Minnehaha Driving Park (Minneapolis) 47, 59, 72, 76, 79, 87, 89, 91, 92, 95, 97
Minnesota 44, 90, 91, 171, 179, 180, 182, 216, 217, 218; history and characteristics 51, 60, 183
Minnesota All-Stars 215
Minnesota Twins 35, 220
Minnesota-Wisconsin League 100, 122, 140, 146, 147
Minor, Bill 23
Minot, North Dakota 57, 128, 138
Minot Daily Reporter 128
Mitchell, Edward Franklin "Kidd," "Colonel" *69*–70, 71, 73, 79, 81, 86, 87, 95, 97, 106–107, 108, 109, 117, 123–124, 125, 126, 140–141, 142–143, 155, 156, 157, 167, 169, 170, 173, 175, 183

Mitchell, Mamie 140, 142, 169–170, 183
M.J. Carr baseball club (St. Paul) 182
Moberly, Missouri 213, 214
Mobile Sea Gulls (Alabama) 157
Molitor, Paul 195
Monahl (Oelwein player) 80
Monroe, Bill 212
Monticello, Minnesota 70, 87
Montreal, Quebec 48, 210
Moon (Bessemer player) 106
Moore, Harry "Mike" 25, 110, 113, 114, 132–133, 134
Moorhead, Minnesota 186, 193
Moose Lake, Minnesota 102
Mora, Minnesota 164
Morris, Barney 195
Mothell, Carroll "Dink" 193
Mueller (Red Wing player) 93
Munoz, Jose 67
Murtagh, Edward 17, 25
Muscatine, Iowa 193
Muskegon, Michigan 200
Myrick, Abe 70
Myrick, Charles 70

Narveson, Alfred 130
Nashville, Tennessee 199, 217
Nashville Athletics 204
National Association for the Advancement of Colored People (NAACP) 52–53, 218
National Association of Baseball Players 5
National Baseball Hall of Fame 214, 222
National Football League 215
National Indians (Kansas) 86
National League 6, 17, 94, 216
Nebraska Indians 17
Negro American League (NAL) 195, 196, 197, 200
Negro Major Baseball League of America 197
Negro National League (NNL) 156, 184, 190, 191, 1996, 207, 213
Negro Southern League 195, 213
Nekoosa, Wisconsin 116
Nelson (Glen Ullin player) 151
Nelson (Grand Forks player) 153
Nelson (Grand Rapids, Wisconsin player) 169
Nelson (Memphis Tigers player) 157
Nelson, Andy "Peaches" 46
Nelson, J.B. 154
Nelson, Ralph 89
Nerstrand, Minnesota 195
New Brighton Packers (Minneapolis) 11
New Homes baseball club (St. Paul) 11
New Orleans, Louisiana 155
New Orleans Black Pelicans 99, 200
New Orleans Creoles 196
New Orleans Pinchbacks 71
New Prague, Minnesota 87

New Richland, Minnesota 55, 76, 103, 109
New Richmond, Wisconsin 135
New York, New York 41, 144, 191, 220
New York Giants 34, 201, 211
New York Highlanders 152
New York Yankees 44, 49, 199, 220
Niagara Movement 52
Nicholson, John 122
Nicollet Park (Minneapolis) 36, 47, 74, 79, 95, 96, 107, 108, 109, 117, 149, 160, 179, 184, 200, 202, 215, 218; characteristics 59
Niedenfuer, "Shooty" 139
Nike footwear company 221–222
Norfolk All-Stars (Virginia) 210
Norman, William *see* Hardy, Arthur
North St. Paul, Minnesota 138, 143, 184
North St. Paul Thoens 138, 143, 171, 177
Northern Copper County League 89
Northern League 20, 22, 23, 26, 36, 45, 67, 76, 108, 166, 178, 195
Northern Pacific baseball club (St. Paul) 28
Northfield, Minnesota 51
Northwestern Bulletin 184
Northwestern League (1884) 6
Northwestern League (20th Century) 38, 130
Northwestern Park (Indianapolis) 142, 169
Norton, Fred 86
Norwood, Minnesota 118, 122
Nunez, Berto 196
Nyasses, Peanuts *see* Davis, Eddie

O'Brien, Pete 95
O'Connor, Tom 117
Oelwein, Iowa 80–81, 109, 115, 158
Oelwein Register 80
Official Baseball Guide 46, 54
Ohio State Colored League 147
Oklahoma Giants 135
Oldfield, Barney 44
O'Leary, George 36
Oliva, Tony 220
Olson, Cy 179, 182
Omaha Giants (Nebraska) 170, 177
O'Malley, Jimmy 45, 46
183rd Brigade baseball club (Illinois) 206
O'Neil, Tom 74–75
O'Neill, Bill "Tip" 118
Ortonville, Minnesota 27, 168
Osage, Iowa 80, 109
Osceola, Wisconsin 43–44, 46, 96, 171, 201
Osceola Sun 46
Osgood (Aberdeen player) 127
Oshkosh, Wisconsin 68, 188
Our baseball club of Springfield, Illinois 210

Owatonna, Minnesota 19, 123, 173, 179, 181
Owens, Jesse 187, 200
Owens, Ray (aka Kankol) 198
Oxboro, Minnesota 186, 187
Oyler, Andy 71

Pacific Coast League 38, 92, 102, 116, 181
Padron, Luis 67
Paducah, Kentucky 31
Paducah Nationals 66, 99
Page, Ted 210
Page Fence Giants (Michigan) 8–10, 16, 28, 35, 71
Paige, Leroy "Satchel" 195, 213, 214
Palomino, Emilio 67
Pangburn, Thomas "Lefty" 115, 118, 120, 121, 122, 123, 126, **127**, 128, 129, 130, 133, 134, 137, 139, 144, 160, 161–162, 163, 164, 165, 171, 172, 173, 205, 218–219
Park River, North Dakota 129–130
Parker College 215
Parks, William "Bubber" 146
Pate, Archie **1**, 100, 101, 102, 103, 109, 117, 124, 126, 155, 156–157, 158, 166, 167, 168, 170, **221**
Patterson, John "Pat" 8, 10, 12
Patterson, Roy 60, 96, 143
Pattison, John 25
Paul (Owatonna player) 123
Paulson (Valley City player) 152
Payne, Andrew "Jap" 35, 110, 112, 113, 114
Pearce (Hankinson player) 150
Pehle, Willie 118
Peoria Black Devils (Illinois) 210
Perham, Minnesota 5
Perry Werden All-Stars 146, 147, 160, 161, 165, 173, 177, 179, 180
Peters, William 8, 10
Peters Union Giants (Illinois) 181, 182
Pettijohn, Lyle 92, 159
Pettus, William 131, 133
Petway, Bruce 67, 99, 156, 212
Petway, Howard **65**, 67, 75, 76, **77**, 78, 81, 204
Pframer, Ed "Smiler" 123, 149
Phil Dellar All-Stars 121–122
Philadelphia Athletics 211
Philadelphia Giants 28, 29, 31, 35, 47, 64, 67, 71, 107, 119, 122
Philadelphia Hilldales baseball club 200
Philadelphia Royal Stars 210
Phillips, "Card" 155, 157, 165–166
Pickering, Ollie 143
Pietz, Cy 84, **85**
Pioneer Limited Giants (Minneapolis) 168
Pipestone, Minnesota 92, 187
Pipestone Black Sox 187, 189, 190, 191–192
Pittsburgh, Pennsylvania 64, 121, 205

Pittsburgh Colored Collegians 205
Pittsburgh Courier 196, 205, 206
Pittsburgh Giants 121
Pittsburgh Keystones 207
Pittsburgh Pirates 27, 40, 173
Plymat, Walter 117
Poles, Spottswood 209
Polk County All-Stars (Wisconsin) 143
Pollard, Fritz 197
Port (Alexandria player) 165
Posey, Cum 205, 210
Potts, Bill 186–187
Potts, Raymond "Jack" 193
Potts Motor Company baseball club (Minneapolis) 186–187
Power, Vic 220
Powers baseball club (Minneapolis) 182
Prairie Island Indians (Minnesota) 92–93
Prairie Leaguers baseball club (St. Paul) 216
Premo Park (St. Paul) 58, 103
Preston, Iowa 117
Preston, Minnesota 44, 94, 115, 116, 138, 139
Preston Times (Minnesota) 50
Princeton, Minnesota 186
Puckett, Kirby 35, 220
P.V. Lands baseball club *see* Redwood Falls, Minnesota

Quaker Giants (New York) 31, 139
Quillen, Lee 95
Quincy Whig 6

racial attitudes: Indiana 173; Iowa 159; Minnesota 7–8, 20, 14, 51–52, 54, 183, 184, 190, 193, 197, 201–202, 218, 219–220; newspaper cartoons **56**, **85**, **113**, **158**; newspapers 7–8, 11–12, 55, 69–70; organized baseball 7, 13, 17, 211, 219–220; United States 14, 20, 120, 217; *see also* color line
racial incidents: Duluth, Minnesota 183; Hankinson, North Dakota 57; Minneapolis, Minnesota 149; Minot, North Dakota 57; St. Paul, Minnesota 51, 52, 218; Staples, Minnesota 190; Springfield, Illinois 88; Viroqua, Wisconsin 57; Wibaux, Montana 152; Winona, Minnesota 190
Radcliffe, Alex 197
Radcliffe, Ted "Double Duty" 195, 199
Raiter, Chrissie 104, 106
Ramsey, Bob 182
Ramsey, Mack 146
Ransom, Queenie 218
Ransom, Samuel 39–40, **41**, 42, **43**, 44, 70, 74, 217–218, **219**, 220
Red Bud, Illinois 142
Red Wing, Minnesota 11, 44, 50, 57, 61, 62, 78, 86–87, 92, 93, 109, 148

Redfield, South Dakota 149–150, 186
Redwood Falls, Minnesota 59, 73, 74, 109, 118
Redwood Falls Gazette 27
Redwood Reveille 59
Reid, Edward 131, 176
Reid, Philip Edward "Daddy" *1*, 31–*32*, 33, 34, 36, 39, 40, *41*, *43*, 44, 45, 47, 53, 57, 59, 60, 61, 64, *65*, 69, 77, 79, *88*, 91, 92, 95, 98, 99–100, 103, 106, 110, *111*, 118–119, 120, 122, 123, 126, 131–132, 144, 145, 173, 175–176, 183, 188, 218, *221*, 222
Rennix, George 104, 150
Renville, Minnesota 25, 32, 63, 86, 104
Renville All-Stars 25–30, *26*, 32–33, 64, 117, 123, 147, 153, 154, 203
Renville Record 27
Rhoades (Jamestown player) 150
Rhoades, "Pecky" 146, 147
Rice Lake, Wisconsin 108
Richardson, George 25, *26*, 28
Rickey, Branch 201, 205
Rile, Ed 208
ringers: concept 60; St. Cloud and 182; St. Paul Gophers and 47, 60–61, 94, 117, 135, 140; Waseca EACO's and 17, 18–19
Risberg, Charles "Swede" 191
River Falls, Wisconsin 89
Riverside Park (Kansas City) 125, 171
Riverviews baseball club (Chicago) 35
Roach, George "Bullet" 184–185, 186, 187, 188, 194
Roberts, Fred "Pop" *29*, *33*, 34, 35, 36, *37*, 38, 39, *41*, *43*, 44, 45, 46, 47, 64, 70, 71, 80, 87, 204
Roberts, Julia 204
Roberts, Norman 204
Robinson (Dickinson player) 151
Robinson, Jackie 201, 215
Rochester, Minnesota 41, 54, 61, 74, 86, 97, 117
Rochester Red Wings (New York) 211
Rock Island Independents (Illinois) 215
Rockford, Illinois 67–68, 124
Rockford Daily Register Gazette 68
Rodebaugh, Ed J. 45, 46
Rodriguez, Alex 49
Roe, Rob 43
Rogers, Ed 27
Rognas (Mankato player) 138
Ronesch, Jerry 80
Rose, Haywood "Kissing Bug" 17, *29*, 59, *65*, 66–*67*, 68, 74, 75, 81, *88*, 90, 91, 95, 96, 107, 118, *119*
Roths baseball club (Minneapolis) 182
Rowan, Carl T. 202
Royal Poinciana Hotel baseball club (Palm Beach, Florida) 65

Ruelbach, Ed 66
Rushford, Minnesota 40
Russell (Oelwein player) 81

Sage, George 101, 104, 108
Sage, Leo 82, 89, 101, 105, 108
St. Cloud, Minnesota 19, 22, 193, 207
St. Cloud, Minnesota baseball club 20, 21, 23–25, *24*, 32, 178, 179, 181–182, 192
St. Croix Falls, Wisconsin 96, 143
St. Joe-Deckerts (Minneapolis) 177, 179
St. John's University (Minnesota) 20
St. Louis, Missouri 31, 32, 42, 44, 64, 68, 142, 172, 175
St. Louis Browns (American Association) 10
St. Louis Browns (American League) 42, 43, 44, 200, 206
St. Louis Cardinals 142
St. Louis Giants 86, 99, 120, 128, 141, 142, 143, 155, 172–173, 206, 207, 209, 210, 213
St. Louis Stars 200, 207, 208, 213
St. Louis Terriers 100
St. Mary's College (Minnesota) 186
St. Paul, Minnesota 1, 5, 6, 8, 9, 11, 12, 32, 40, 46, 48, 51, 52, 53, 58, 64, 87, 88, 99, 120, 121, 132, 133, 138, 149, 173, 183, 192, 197, 200, 201, 214, 216, 218; rivalry with Minneapolis 68–69, 184
St. Paul Appeal 34, 52, 59
St. Paul Blue Stars 5
St. Paul Camerons 177
St. Paul Capitols 11
St. Paul Cretin High School 195
St. Paul Daily News 32, 59, 104
St. Paul Dispatch 11–12, 40, 47, 59, 66, 84, 90–91, 93, 131, 139
St. Paul Giants 32–33, 70
St. Paul Gophers (1907–1911) 2, 8, 16, 19, 22, *85*, 177, 180, 181, 183, 184, 190, 201, 203, 204, 205, 206, 207, 208, 214, 219, 220; behavior 55, 161; clowning 54–55; contracts 49; demise 173–175; fans 52, 62; finances 49–51, 137; formation 33; legacy 177, 220–222; lodging 50, 54; makeup of team 34; management 34–35, 36, 99, 120, 122, 131, 145, 160, 170–171; naming 60–61; newspaper coverage 55, *56*, 59; on the field incidents 43, 57, 75, 83, 87–89, 103, 128, 135, 137; opponents level of play 60; photographs and publicity 59; playing conditions 58; quality 47, 63, 221; salaries 49; sandbagging 61–62, 151–152; scheduling 36, 50, 53, 122; small towns and 61–62; style of play 35–36, 38, 55, 90, 106, 122, 148, 164–165, 166; travel 53–54; umpiring 57;

(1907) *33*, 34, 36–39, *37*, 40–47, *41*, *43*; (1908) *65*, 67–68, 74–78, 79, 81–84, 86, 87–92, *88*, 93–97, 98; (1909) *1*, 100–103, 104–106, 109–116, *111*, 117–119, *221*; (1910) 121–123, 126–131, *127*, 132–140, 143–144; (1911) 147–149, 150–155, 160–165, 170–173
St. Paul Gophers (1925–1930) 188–190, 194
St. Paul Gophers (1933–1936) 195
St. Paul Laurels 215
St. Paul Mechanic Arts High School 10, 216
St. Paul Milk baseball club 194
St. Paul Monarchs 194–195
St. Paul Pioneer Press 11–12, 16, 17–18, 19, 23, 33, 38, 45, 53, 59, 75, 111, 112, 120, 139, 198, 218
St. Paul Police baseball club 188
St. Paul Quicksteps 7–8
St. Paul Red Caps 5
St. Paul Saints 6, 9, 11, 17, 19, 22, 23, 35, 43, 44–46, 64, 72, 74, 86, 93–95, 102, 106, 145, 149, 168, 195, 201–202, 215
St. Paul Spaldings 11
St. Peter, Minnesota 92
Sally League *see* South Atlantic League
San Antonio, Texas 31, 103, 125, 126, 141
San Antonio Black Bronchos 88, 99, 103–104
Sandford, Robert 107, 108
Sandon, Bill 187; Sandon's Colored Tigers 187
Saperstein, Abe 187, 196, 197, 199, 200
Sauk Center, Minnesota 24, 27
Saunders, D. 32
Schaeffer, Jesse *33*, 34, 35, 36, *37*, 38, 40, *41*, 42, *43*, 44, 45, 46, 47, 67, 68, 72, 83, 84, 86, 87, 97, 98, 107, 108, 116, 118, 120, 122, 146, 149, 150, *151*
Schenectady Mohawk Giants (New York) 210
Schlichter, Walter "Slick" 31
Schmidt (Oshkosh player) 188
Schmidt, Fred "Crazy" 34, 115, 207
Schmidt, Hermann "Pete" 130, 161
Schmirler, John 137
Schoonhaven, Tommy 122
Schroeder, Len 36, 72, 96
Schumacher (Grand Forks player) 166
Scobey, Montana 191
Seagraves, Sam 197, 199
Seay, Dick 210
segregation in baseball *see* color line
Selden, William 132, 133, 134, 145, 146, 147, 150, 151, 153, 154, 161, 162, 164, 165, 172, 205
Sessions, Perry 23

Shakopee, Minnesota 7, 11, 96, 139
Shakopee Scott County Argus 7
Shaw (West Baden Sprudels player) 157
Shaw, Frank "Demon" 22
Shaw University 103
Shawler, James 124, 143, 155, 167–168, 169, 170
Sheboygan, Wisconsin 16, 29, 203
Sheffield, Iowa 181
Sheldon, Iowa 57
Shelley Park (Kansas City) 126
Sherburn, Minnesota 58, 103
Shirley (H.P. Conrads player) 159
Short, Clarence 135, 137
Shull, Glover 145, *146*, 149, 171
Sioux City, Iowa 192
Sioux Falls, South Dakota 57, 178–179
Sioux Falls Black Sox 187
Sioux Falls Daily Press 178
Sisler (Crookston player) 154
Sisters of the Mysterious Ten maternal order 171
Smith (Coogan's Smart Set player) 206
Smith, Charles 59
Smith, Hilton 195
Smith, James H. 34, 35, 36, *37*, 38, 39, 49, 113, 114, 118, 204, 207
Smith, Nelson 148
Smith, Ted 108
Smith, Tobe 69, 125, 126
Smith, Wendell 196, 205
South Atlantic League (Sally League) 117, 157
South Bend, Indiana 34
Southern Association 157
Southwestern Negro League 155
Spanton, "Spike" 166
Speiser, Frank 79
Spencer, Fred "Hack" 44, 47, 78, 83
Spillane, "Doc" 57
Spooner, Wisconsin 54, 137, 164
Sporer, Joseph "Lefty" 126
Sporting Life 6
Spring Grove, Minnesota 63, 86
Springfield, Illinois 88, 210
Springfield, Minnesota 139–140, 143
Springs Valley, Indiana 156, 157, 173
Stabeck, Henry 25, *26*, 28
Stallard, Walter 140, 146, 147, 149, 150, 151, 152, 153, 154, 155, 160, 161, 164, 170, 171–172, 173
Stallings, George 211
Staples (Osceola player) 171
Staples, Minnesota 78, 190
Stars of Cuba 123
Stassen, Gov. Harold 218
Stephenson, Andrew 72
Sterling, Lewis 14
Stewart, Joe "Ace" 25
Stillman, Arthur 194
Stillman, George 194
Stillwater, Minnesota 6–7, 21, 25, 40, 41, 51, 53, 72, 76, 87–89, 97, 113, 183, 190
Stillwater Daily Gazette 89
Stillwater Daily Sun 6
Stone, Marcenia "Toni" 195–196
Strawberry Point, Iowa 157
Strothers, Sam 111
Sullivan (Austin-Westerns player) 38
Summerville, William 107
Sunday League 36, 44, 47
Superior, Wisconsin 69, 72–73, 81, 164–165, 180
Syracuse, New York 211

Talbert, Dangerfield *33*, 34, 112, 113
Tatum, Reece "Goose" 197, 198, 199, 200
Taylor, Ben 99, 172, 173, 213
Taylor, Charles Isham (C.I.) 89, 99, 137, 156, 206, 209
Taylor, George 10, *29*, *33*, 34, 35, 36, *37*, 38, 39, *41*, *43*, 46, 47, 48, 64, 66, 204
Taylor, James "Candy Jim" 99, 103, 104, 106, 110, *111*, 112, 113, 114, 118, 119, 120, 126, *127*, 128, 129, 132–133, 135, 136, 137, 172, 197, 200, 206, 207–208, *209*
Taylor, John "Steel Arm" 99, 103–104, 105, 106, 110, *111*, 112, *113*, 114, 115, 118, 119, 120, 131, 132, 133, 134, 138, 172, 208–210
Taylor, Rolla 8
Tennessee Rats (Missouri) 180, 182, 187
Tenney, William 172
Terrell (Minneapolis Keystones player) 170
Texas Colored League 65, 99, 120, 125, 141, 205
Thiegs (Long Prairie player) 169
Thielman, Frank 207
Thirty Eighth Street Merchants baseball club (Minneapolis) 182
Thomas (Grand Forks player) 153–154, 166
Thomas (Park River player) 129–130
Thompson (St. Paul Gophers player) 171
Thompson, Andrew "Honest Andy" 40, 76, 88–89, 113
Thompson, Earl 188, 189, 194
Thompson, George 57
Thompson, Hank 201
Thompson, Raleigh W. 173, 176
Thompson, "Toot" 153
Thrall, Hank "Big" 129, 154, 165
Toledo Blue Stockings (Ohio) 6
Toledo Tigers (Ohio) 207
Toney, Albert *33*, 34
Topeka, Kansas 31
Topeka Giants 49, 71
Tousignant (Faribault player) 47
Tovar, Cesar 220
Tower, Art 168, 169
Tracy, Minnesota 189, 190
Tretter, Louis 104, 106
Tri-States baseball club (Minneapolis) 179
Trouppe, Quincy 195
Tucker (Devils Lake umpire) 153
Tucker, Bert 185
Turnball-Cameron-Degler baseball club (Wisconsin) 164–165
Turosky, Vic 100
Twin City All-Stars 217
Twin City Colored Giants (1935–1937) *194*–195
Twin City Colored Giants (1944) 200–201
Twin City Colored Gophers (1949) 201
Twin City Gophers *see* St. Paul Gophers 1911
Twin City Herald 196
Twin City Star 59, 120, 125, 128, 131, 139, 144, 145, 147–148, 165, 169, 170, 173, 176
Tyson, Oscar "Bish" 199, 200

United Brothers of Friendship fraternal order 171
United States League 200, 205
University of Chicago 37, 216
University of Illinois 128
University of Minnesota 21, 37, 38, 42, 60, 92, 106, 159, 188, 215, 216
University of St. Thomas (Minneapolis) 38, 76
Upper Peninsula (Michigan) 106, 117, 188
Uptown Sanitary baseball club (St. Paul) 184–*185*, 186, 188, 214; become Colored All-Stars 187; travel as St. Paul Gophers 185

Valley City, North Dakota 128–129, 152
Van, John 192, 193
Van Wert, Ohio 147, 205
Versalles, Zoilo 220
Vick (Twin Cities Colored Giants player) 195
Virginia, Minnesota 39, 42, 60, 83, 135, 137, 164
Viroqua, Wisconsin 57

Waconia, Minnesota 61, 135
Waconia Patriot 59
Waddell, Rube 35, 64, 149
Wakefield, Bert 25, *26*, 28
Waldren, Roy 86
Waler, Thomas 125
Walker, Moses Fleetwood 6, 17
Walker, Weldy 6
Walker, Minnesota 155
Walker Pilot 155
Wallace (Austin-Westerns player) 37–38
Wallace, Bobby 206
Wallace, Dick "Noisy" 47, 70, 72, 79, 80, 81, 87

Index

Wallace, Felix *1*, 64, **65**, 66, 67, 75–76, 78, 81, 83, 84, **88**, 90, 93, 94–95, 98, 99, **102**, 105, 106, **111**, 112, 113, 114, 115, 118, 119, 120, 131, 132, 134, 156, 172, 173, 206, *221*
Wallace, James 155
Walton, Johnny 195
Wanda, Minnesota 192
Ward, Roscoe 14
Ware, Dennis 184
Ware, Frank 184
Waseca, Minnesota 14, 25, 32, 86, 127, 158, 220
Waseca EACO's 14–22, **15**, **18**, 24, 47, 86
Waseca Journal 15
Waseca Journal Radical 19, 22
Waseca Radical 14
Waseda University 216
Washburn, North Dakota 154
Washington, Tom **29**
Washington, D.C. 196, 220
Washington Generals 199
Washington Potomacs 210
Washington Senators 80, 210
Waterloo, Iowa 198
Waterloo Daily Courier 198
Watertown, Minnesota 42, 92
Watertown, South Dakota 123, 127, 149, 177, 178
Waterville, Minnesota 69, 109
Watson, Charles "Doc" 100, 147
Watson, George 155
Watts, Jack 156
Waukon, Iowa 109
Wausau, Wisconsin 148
Webster, South Dakota 27, 40, 178
Webster City, Iowa 20
Wegmen (La Crosse player) 147
Wells, Willie 196, 206, 208
Wells, Minnesota 180
Werden, Perry "Moose" 9, 27, 46, 146, 160; Perry Werden All-Stars 146, 147, 160, 161, 165, 173, 177, 179, 180
Wesley (St. Paul Gophers player) 123, **127**, 128, 130, 131
Wessington Springs, South Dakota 40, 61
Wessington Springs True Republican 40
West (Louisville Cubs; Indianapolis ABCs player) 142, 170
West (Lund Lands player) 76
West Baden Sprudels (Indiana) 110, 137, 156–157, 173, 181, 206, 209
West Union, Iowa 73, 81
Western Canada League 42

Western League 9, 11, 16, 17, 19
What Cheer, Iowa 157
Wheaton, Minnesota 24
Wheeler, Eddie 108
When the Mists Have Rolled Away (composed by Annie H. Barker) 176
White, George 187, 190, 195, 200–201
White, Sol 47, 49, 71; *Official Baseball Guide* 46, 54
White Bear Lake, Minnesota 25
Whitehead, Walter 98
Whitfield, Frank 187–188
Whittaker, Bill "Bots" 122
Whitworth, Dick 181
Wibaux, Montana 152, 167
Wibaux Pioneer 152
Wickware, Frank 107, 191, 210
Wilbert, Art 199
Wilkinson, J. Leslie 163, 180, 181, 193
Williams (Indianapolis ABCs player) 169
Williams (St. Paul Gophers player, 1908) 84, 86
Williams (St. Paul Gophers player, 1911) 146, 148
Williams, "Beans" 199
Williams, "Chic" 177, 182
Williams, D. (Kansas City Giants player) 171–172
Williams, "Dad" 101, 136, 162
Williams, Irving 36, 41, **43**, 53, 59, 64, **65**, 86, 99, 115, 119, 120, 122, 131, **132**, 136, 138, 139, 143, 144, 145, 170–171, 176, 204
Williams, Joe (Askin and Marine player) 184
Williams, Joe "Cyclone" 99, 104, 131, 133, 134, 141, 160, 205, 209, 212
Williams, Joe (Hennepin Clothing Company player) 178
Williams, Milton 186
Williams, Morris 187
Williams, William Frank "Billy" 10–**11**, 17, 18, 19, 21, 32, 41, 44, 74, 84, 216–**217**, 219, 220
Willmar, Minnesota 19, 184, 214
Wills, James 141, 155, 156, 166, 167
Wilson (Minneapolis Keystones player) 155, 167, 168
Wilson, Artie 201
Wilson, Cal 104
Wilson, Carter 35
Wilson, George H. 2, 9–10, 16, 17, **18**, 19, 21, 22, 23–**24**, 25, 27, 28, 29–30, 32, 203–**204**, 220
Wilson, Lefty (Askin and Marine player) 184

Wilson, Lefty (Bertha player) *see* Brown, Dave
Wiltse, George "Hooks" 211
Windom, Minnesota 190
Wingfield (Pipestone Black Sox player) 189, 190
Winnebago, Minnesota 60, 86, 93–94, 117, 215
Winnebago City Free Press 117
Winnipeg, Manitoba 199, 200
Winnipeg Maroons 22–23, 195
Winona, Minnesota 5, 9–10, 14, 97, 182, 184, 186, 190, 191, 193, 196
Winona Republican Herald 190
Winston, Clarence "Bobby" 110, 114, 131, 132, 133, 134
Winters, Jesse "Nip" 210
Wisconsin-Illinois League 67, 94
Wisconsin Rapids, Wisconsin *see* Grand Rapids, Wisconsin
Wisconsin State League 33, 34, 40, 77
Wolf, Bill 16, 19
Wolfe, Wilbert 19
Wolfe, William 19
Wolford, John "Jack" 86, 98, 100
Woods, Bert 155, 156, 157, 166, 169, 170
Woods, Robert "Doggie" 14, **15**, 17, 24–25, **26**, 27
Woodstock, Ontario 14
Worley, Ernest "Chinx" 194, 201
Worman, Robert 92
Worthington (Hennepin Clothing Company player) 178
Wright, Bruce **201**
Wright, George 110, 112, 113, 133, 145
Wright, Roy 187
Wright County All-Stars (Minnesota) 96
Wyatt, Dave 29–30, 47, 101, 128, 132, 214
Wycoff, Minnesota 60

Young (Aberdeen player) 127
Young (Memphis Tigers player) 157
Young, Fay 214
Young, Frank 124, 143, 155
Young, "Sea Hawk" 157
Young, Tom 193
Young America, Minnesota 118
Young Cyclones baseball club (St. Paul) 11, 12

Zalusky, Jack 152–153, 161
Zumbrota, Minnesota 44
Zumbrota News 57

www.ingramcontent.com/pod-product-compliance
Lightning Source LLC
Chambersburg PA
CBHW081158230426
43666CB00016B/2848